Regulating Artificial Intelligence

Thomas Wischmeyer • Timo Rademacher
Editors

Regulating Artificial Intelligence

Editors
Thomas Wischmeyer
Faculty of Law
University of Bielefeld
Bielefeld, Germany

Timo Rademacher
Faculty of Law
University of Hannover
Hannover, Germany

ISBN 978-3-030-32363-9   ISBN 978-3-030-32361-5 (eBook)
https://doi.org/10.1007/978-3-030-32361-5

© Springer Nature Switzerland AG 2020
This work is subject to copyright. All rights are reserved by the Publisher, whether the whole or part of the material is concerned, specifically the rights of translation, reprinting, reuse of illustrations, recitation, broadcasting, reproduction on microfilms or in any other physical way, and transmission or information storage and retrieval, electronic adaptation, computer software, or by similar or dissimilar methodology now known or hereafter developed.
The use of general descriptive names, registered names, trademarks, service marks, etc. in this publication does not imply, even in the absence of a specific statement, that such names are exempt from the relevant protective laws and regulations and therefore free for general use.
The publisher, the authors, and the editors are safe to assume that the advice and information in this book are believed to be true and accurate at the date of publication. Neither the publisher nor the authors or the editors give a warranty, expressed or implied, with respect to the material contained herein or for any errors or omissions that may have been made. The publisher remains neutral with regard to jurisdictional claims in published maps and institutional affiliations.

This Springer imprint is published by the registered company Springer Nature Switzerland AG.
The registered company address is: Gewerbestrasse 11, 6330 Cham, Switzerland

Preface: Good Artificial Intelligence

Mission and Methodology

Policy and business decisions with broad social impact are increasingly based on machine learning-based technology, today commonly referred to as artificial intelligence (AI). At the same time, AI technology is becoming more and more complex and difficult to understand, making it harder to control whether it is used in accordance with existing laws. Given these circumstances, even tech enthusiasts call for a stricter regulation of AI. Regulators, too, are stepping in and have begun to pass respective laws, including the right not to be subject to a decision based solely on automated processing in Article 22 of the EU's General Data Protection Regulation (GDPR), Section 140(d)(6) and (s) of the 2018 California Consumer Privacy Act on safeguards and restrictions concerning commercial and non-commercial 'research with personal information', or the 2017 amendments to the German Cartels Act and the German Administrative Procedure Act.

While the belief that *something* needs to be done about AI is widely shared, there is far less clarity about *what exactly* can or should be done and how effective regulation might look like. Moreover, the discussion on AI regulation sometimes only focuses on worst case scenarios based on specific instances of technical malfunction or human misuses of AI-based systems. Regulations premised on well-thought-out strategies and striving to balance opportunities and risks of AI technologies (cf. Hoffmann-Riem) are still largely missing.

Against this backdrop, this book analyses the factual and legal challenges the deployment of AI poses for individuals and the society. The contributions develop regulatory recommendations that do not curb technology's potential while preserving the accountability, legitimacy, and transparency of its use. In order to achieve this aim, the authors all follow an approach that might be described as 'threefold contextualization': Firstly, the analyses and propositions are norm-based, i.e. consider and build on statutory and constitutional regimes shaping or restricting the design and use of AI. Secondly, it is important to bear in mind that AI technologies, to put it briefly, provide instruments addressing real-life problems which so far humans had to solve: officers, doctors, drivers, etc. Hence, it does not suffice to ask whether or not AI 'works well' or 'is dangerous'. Instead, it is necessary to compare the characteristics of the new technology with the corresponding human actions it replaces or complements on a case-by-case basis. Therefore, the question asked in the following chapters is whether AI actually 'works *better*' or is '*more* dangerous' than the human counterpart from the point of view of the respective legal framework. Thirdly, this book and the selection of its authors reflect the necessity of not only having an *inter*disciplinary understanding, but also taking a decidedly *intra*disciplinary approach in developing a legal perspective on AI regulation. This presupposes that private and public law scholars, legal theoreticians, and scholars of economic law approach the subject in the spirit of mutual cooperation.

4   The debate on AI regulation is global. The influence of EU law has been growing since the coming into force of the GDPR in 2018. Nonetheless, the scholarly discourse, pursuant to the technological leadership in this field, mostly focuses on the United States. Intentionally or not, scholars frequently adapt a normative and conceptual framework tailored to US constitutional and administrative tradition, e.g. focusing on AI 'accountability'. This book's authors all have German or Swiss legal backgrounds and are thus well acquainted with EU law, bringing a different legal tradition to the global discourse. This tradition is shaped by many decades of comparatively strict and comprehensive data protection legislation and is, therefore, correspondingly diverse and 'rich'. Therefore, the following chapters will, when it comes to describing *existing* AI laws and regulations, predominantly refer to German and EU law. Nevertheless, these references merely serve to illustrate which challenges AI poses for regulators across the globe.

Artificial Intelligence

5   From a technological point of view, there is no such thing as 'the' AI. While most attention is currently paid to techniques extracting information from data through 'machine learning', AI research actually encompasses many different sub-fields and methodologies.[1] Similarly, machine learning is not a monolithic concept, but comprises a variety of techniques.[2] These range from traditional linear regression over support vector machines and decision tree algorithms to various types of neural networks.[3] Moreover, most machine learning-based systems are a 'constellation' of

---

[1] Russell and Norvig (2010); Kaplan (2016); Wischmeyer (2018), pp. 9 et seq.
[2] The terms machine learning and AI are used synonymously in this volume.
[3] Cf. EU High Level Expert Group (2018), pp. 4–5.

processes and technologies rather than one well-defined entity, which makes it even more difficult to determine the scope of the meaning of AI.[4] As such, AI is a field of research originating from the mid-1950s—the Dartmouth Summer Research Project is often mentioned in this context. Today, its scholars mostly focus on a set of technologies with the ability to 'process potentially very large and heterogeneous data sets using complex methods modelled on human intelligence to arrive at a result which may be used in automated applications'.[5]

Against this backdrop, some scholars advocate abandoning the concept of AI and propose, instead, to address either all 'algorithmically controlled, automated decision-making or decision support systems'[6] or to focus specifically on machine learning-based systems.[7] Now, for some regulatory challenges such as the societal impact of a decision-making or decision support system or its discriminatory potential, the specific design of the system or the algorithms it uses are indeed only of secondary interest. In this case, the contributions in this volume consider the regulatory implications of 'traditional' programs as well (cf., e.g. Krönke, paras 1 et seq.; Wischmeyer, para 11). Nevertheless, the most interesting challenges arise where advanced machine learning-based algorithms are deployed which, at least from the perspective of the external observer, share important characteristics with human decision-making processes. This raises important issues with regard to the potential liability and culpability of the systems (see Schirmer). At the same time, from the perspective of those affected by such decision-making or decision support systems, the increased opacity, the new capacities, or, simply, the level of uncertainty injected into society through the use of such systems, lead to various new challenges for law and regulation.

Structure and Content

This handbook starts with an extensive introduction into the topic by *Wolfgang Hoffmann-Riem*. The introduction takes on a—at first glance—seemingly trivial point which turns out to be most relevant and challenging: you can only *regulate* what you *can* regulate! In this spirit, *Hoffmann-Riem* offers an in-depth analysis of why establishing a legitimate and effective governance of AI challenges the

---

[4]Kaye (2018), para 3. Cf. also Ananny and Crawford (2018), p. 983: 'An algorithmic system is not just code and data but an *assemblage* of human and non-human actors—of "institutionally situated code, practices, and norms with the power to create, sustain, and signify relationships among people and data through minimally observable, semiautonomous action" [...]. This requires going beyond "algorithms as fetishized objects" to take better account of the human scenes where algorithms, code, and platforms intersect [...].'
[5]Datenethikkommission (2018).
[6]Algorithm Watch and Bertelsmann Stiftung (2018), p. 9.
[7]Wischmeyer (2018), p. 3.

regulatory capacities of the law and its institutional architecture as we know it. He goes on to offer a taxonomy of innovative regulatory approaches to meet the challenges.

8 The following chapters address the *Foundations of AI Regulation* and focus on features most AI systems have in common. They ask how these features relate to the legal frameworks for data-driven technologies, which already exist in national and supra-national law. Among the features shared by most, if not all AI technologies, our contributors speak the following:

9 Firstly, the dependency on processing vast amounts of personal data 'activates' EU data protection laws and consequently reduces the operational leeway of public and private developers and users of AI technologies significantly. In his contribution, *Nikolaus Marsch* identifies options for an interpretation of the European fundamental right to data protection that would offer, for national and EU legislators alike, more leeway to balance out chances and risks associated with AI systems. The threats AI systems pose to human autonomy and the corresponding right to individual self-determination are then described by *Christian Ernst*, using the examples of health insurances, creditworthiness scores, and the Chinese Social Credit System. *Thomas Wischmeyer* critically examines the often-cited lack of transparency of AI-based decisions and predictions ('black box' phenomenon), which seem to frustrate our expectation to anticipate, review, and understand decision-making procedures. He advises policy makers to redirect their focus, at least to some extent, from the individuals affected by the specific use of an AI-based system in favour of creating institutional bodies and frameworks, which can provide an effective control of the system. *Alexander Tischbirek* analyses most AI technologies' heavy reliance on statistical methods that reveal correlations, patterns, and probabilities instead of causation and reason and thus are prone to perpetuate discriminatory practices. He—perhaps counterintuitively—highlights that, in order to reveal such biases and distortions, it might be necessary to gather and store more personal data, rather than less. Finally, *Jan-Erik Schirmer* asks the 'million-dollar question', i.e. whether or not AI systems should be treated as legal persons, or as mere objects, answering that question with a straightforward 'a little bit of each'.

10 While the design and use of AI-based systems thus raise a number of general questions, the success of AI regulation is highly dependent on the specific field of application. Therefore, regulatory proposals for the *Governance of AI* must consider the concrete factual and legal setting in which the technology is to be deployed. To this end, the chapters in Part II examine in detail several industry and practice sectors in which AI is, in our view, shaping decision-making processes to an ever-growing extent: social media (by *Christoph Krönke*), legal tech (by *Gabriele Buchholtz*), financial markets (by *Jakob Schemmel*), health care (by *Sarah Jabri* and *Fruzsina Molnár-Gabor*), and competition law (by *Moritz Hennemann*). The analyses reveal that in most of these settings AI does not only present itself as the *object* of regulation, but, often simultaneously, as a potential *instrument* to apply and/or enforce regulation. Therefore, most chapters in Part II also include considerations regarding *Governance through AI*. Other articles, namely the chapters on administrative decision-making under uncertainty (by *Yoan Hermstrüwer*), law enforcement

(by *Timo Rademacher*), public administration (by *Christian Djeffal*), and AI and taxation (by *Nadja Braun Binder*), actually focus on AI technologies that are supposed to apply and/or support the application of the law.

University of Hannover, Hannover Timo Rademacher
Germany
University of Bielefeld, Bielefeld Thomas Wischmeyer
Germany

References

AlgorithmWatch (2018) Automating society – taking stock of automated decision-making in the EU. www.bertelsmann-stiftung.de/de/publikationen/publikation/did/automating-society. Accessed 6 Mar 2019

Ananny M, Crawford K (2018) Seeing without knowing: limitations of the transparency ideal and its application to algorithmic accountability. New Media Soc 20(3):973–989

Datenethikkommission (2018) Empfehlungen der Datenethikkommission für die Strategie Künstliche Intelligenz der Bundesregierung. www.bmi.bund.de/SharedDocs/downloads/DE/veroeffentlichungen/2018/empfehlungen-datenethikkommission.pdf?__blob=publicationFile&v=1. Accessed 6 Mar 2019

EU High Level Expert Group on Artificial Intelligence (2018) A definition of AI: main capabilities and scientific disciplines. EU Commission. https://ec.europa.eu/digital-single-market/en/news/definition-artificial-intelligence-main-capabilities-and-scientific-disciplines. Accessed 6 Mar 2019

Kaplan J (2016) Artificial intelligence. Oxford University Press, Oxford

Kaye D (2018) Report of the Special Rapporteur on the promotion and protection of the right to freedom of opinion and expression. 29 August 2018. United Nations A/73/348

Russell S, Norvig P (2010) Artificial intelligence, 3rd edn. Addison Wesley, Boston

Wischmeyer (2018) Regulierung intelligenter Systeme. Archiv des öffentlichen Rechts 143:1–66

Contents

Artificial Intelligence as a Challenge for Law and Regulation 1
Wolfgang Hoffmann-Riem

Part I Foundations of Artificial Intelligence Regulation

Artificial Intelligence and the Fundamental Right to Data Protection:
Opening the Door for Technological Innovation and Innovative
Protection 33
Nikolaus Marsch

Artificial Intelligence and Autonomy: Self-Determination in the Age of
Automated Systems 53
Christian Ernst

Artificial Intelligence and Transparency: Opening the Black Box 75
Thomas Wischmeyer

Artificial Intelligence and Discrimination: Discriminating Against
Discriminatory Systems 103
Alexander Tischbirek

Artificial Intelligence and Legal Personality: Introducing
"Teilrechtsfähigkeit": A Partial Legal Status Made in Germany 123
Jan-Erik Schirmer

Part II Governance of and Through Artificial Intelligence

Artificial Intelligence and Social Media 145
Christoph Krönke

Artificial Intelligence and Legal Tech: Challenges to the Rule
of Law 175
Gabriele Buchholtz

**Artificial Intelligence and Administrative Decisions
Under Uncertainty** 199
Yoan Hermstrüwer

Artificial Intelligence and Law Enforcement 225
Timo Rademacher

Artificial Intelligence and the Financial Markets: Business as Usual? ... 255
Jakob Schemmel

**Artificial Intelligence and Public Governance: Normative Guidelines
for Artificial Intelligence in Government and Public Administration** ... 277
Christian Djeffal

**Artificial Intelligence and Taxation: Risk Management in Fully
Automated Taxation Procedures** 295
Nadja Braun Binder

Artificial Intelligence and Healthcare: Products and Procedures 307
Sarah Jabri

Artificial Intelligence in Healthcare: Doctors, Patients and Liabilities ... 337
Fruzsina Molnár-Gábor

Artificial Intelligence and Competition Law 361
Moritz Hennemann

Contributors

Nadja Braun Binder Faculty of Law, University of Basel, Basel, Switzerland

Gabriele Buchholtz Bucerius Law School, Hamburg, Germany

Christian Djeffal Munich Center for Technology in Society, Technical University of Munich, Munich, Germany

Christian Ernst Helmut-Schmidt-Universität/Universität der Bundeswehr Hamburg, Hamburg, Germany

Moritz Hennemann Institute for Media and Information Law, Department I: Private Law, Albert-Ludwigs-Universität Freiburg, Freiburg, Germany

Yoan Hermstrüwer Max Planck Institute for Research on Collective Goods, Bonn, Germany
Transatlantic Technology Law Forum, Stanford Law School, Stanford, CA, USA

Wolfgang Hoffmann-Riem Bucerius Law School, Hamburg, Germany

Sarah Jabri Department of Law, University of Constance, Constance, Germany

Christoph Krönke Institute for Public Policy and Law, Ludwig Maximilian University of Munich, Munich, Germany

Nikolaus Marsch Rechtswissenschaftliche Fakultät, Saarland University, Saarbrücken, Germany

Fruzsina Molnár-Gábor Heidelberg Academy of Sciences and Humanities, BioQuant Centre, Heidelberg, Germany

Timo Rademacher Faculty of Law, University of Hannover, Hannover, Germany

Jakob Schemmel Institute for Staatswissenschaft and Philosophy of Law, Albert-Ludwigs-University Freiburg, Freiburg, Germany

Jan-Erik Schirmer Faculty of Law, Humboldt-Universität zu Berlin, Berlin, Germany

Alexander Tischbirek Faculty of Law, Humboldt-Universität zu Berlin, Berlin, Germany

Thomas Wischmeyer Faculty of Law, University of Bielefeld, Bielefeld, Germany

Artificial Intelligence as a Challenge for Law and Regulation

Wolfgang Hoffmann-Riem

Contents

1 Fields of Application for Artificial Intelligence 2
2 Levels of Impact 3
3 Legal Aspects 5
4 Modes of Governance 6
5 Exercising the State's Enabling Responsibility Through Measures for Good Digital Governance 7
    5.1 Displacements in the Responsibility of Public and Private Actors 7
    5.2 Innovative Case-law as an Example 9
    5.3 System Protection 10
    5.4 Systemic Protection 11
    5.5 Regulatory Guidelines 11
    5.6 Regarding Regulatory Possibilities 12
6 Obstacles to the Effective Application of Law 14
    6.1 Openness to Development 14
    6.2 Insignificance of Borders 15
    6.3 Lack of Transparency 17
    6.4 Concentration of Power 17
    6.5 Escaping Legal Constraints 18
7 Types of Rules and Regulations 18
    7.1 Self-structuring 19
    7.2 Self-imposed Rules 19
    7.3 Company Self-regulation 20
    7.4 Regulated Self-regulation 20
    7.5 Hybrid Regulation 22
    7.6 Regulation by Public Authorities 22
    7.7 Techno-regulation 23
8 Replacement or Supplementation of Legal Measures with Extra-Legal, Particularly Ethical Standards 23
9 On the Necessity of Transnational Law 24
References 25

W. Hoffmann-Riem (✉)
Bucerius Law School, Hamburg, Germany

© Springer Nature Switzerland AG 2020
T. Wischmeyer, T. Rademacher (eds.), *Regulating Artificial Intelligence*,
https://doi.org/10.1007/978-3-030-32361-5_1

Abstract The Introduction begins by providing examples of the fields in which AI is used, along with the varying impact that this has on society. It focuses on the challenges that AI poses when it comes to setting and applying law, particularly in relation to legal rules that seek to preserve the opportunities associated with AI while avoiding or at least minimising the potential risks. The law must aim to ensure good digital governance, both with respect to the development of algorithmic systems generally but also with respect to the use of AI specifically. Particularly formidable are the challenges associated with regulating the use of learning algorithms, such as in the case of machine learning. A great difficulty in this regard is ensuring transparency, accountability, responsibility, and the ability to make revisions, as well as preventing hidden discrimination. The Chapter explores the types of rules and regulations that are available. At the same time, it emphasises that it is not enough to trust that companies that use AI will adhere to ethical principles. Rather, supplementary legal rules are indispensable, including in the areas examined in the Chapter, which are mainly characterised by company self-regulation. The Chapter concludes by stressing the need for transnational agreements and institutions.

1 Fields of Application for Artificial Intelligence

The ongoing process of digital transformation[1] is being accomplished in part with the use of artificial intelligence (AI), an interdisciplinary technology that aims to use large data sets (Big Data), suitable computing power, and specific analytical and decision-making procedures in order to enable computers to accomplish tasks that approximate human abilities and even exceed them in certain respects.[2]

AI is used, for example, in search engines, in communication platforms and robots (see Krönke), in intelligent traffic-control systems, for automated administrative or judicial decision-making (see Buchholtz, Djeffal, Hermstrüwer), in automated vehicle-assistance systems, in medical diagnostics and therapy (see Jabri, Molnár-Gábor), in smart homes, and in cyberphysical production systems (Industry 4.0), as well as in the military field. The expansion of algorithm-based analytical and decision-making systems that work with AI also facilitates new forms of surveillance

---

[1] The literature on digital transformation is highly diverse. See, inter alia, Cole (2017), Pfliegl and Seibt (2017), Rolf (2018), Kolany-Raiser et al. (2018) and Precht (2018). For an illustration of the diversity of the issues this raises, see the articles in No. 10 (2017) of Elektrotechnik & Informationstechnik, pp. 323–88.

[2] For an introduction to AI: Russell and Norvig (2012), Kaplan (2016), Lenzen (2018) and Misselhorn (2018).

and for controlling behaviour (see Rademacher),[3] but also new kinds of criminal activity.[4]

AI is—currently—dominated by techniques of machine learning. The term refers to computer programs that are able to learn from records of past conduct.[5] Machine learning is used for such purposes as identifying patterns, evaluating and classifying images, translating language in texts, and automatically generating rough audio and video cuts (e.g. 'robot journalism'). Also possible are even more advanced applications of AI, sometimes referred to as 'Deep Learning'.[6] This has to do with IT systems that, by using neural networks, are capable of learning on their own how to enhance digital programs created by humans and thus of evolving independently of human programming.

The expansion of AI's capabilities and the tasks for which it can be used is associated with both risks and opportunities. The following will look at the challenges that AI poses for law and regulation.[7]

2 Levels of Impact

Given the pervasiveness of digitalisation in many areas of society, it would be too narrow to limit remarks about the role of law and about regulatory options to individual aspects, such as only to the direct treatment of AI in and of itself. AI is one of many elements associated with the use of intelligent IT systems. Its significance can vary with regard to the type of processing and the impact on actions. Accordingly, each area of the legal system faces different challenges, which call not only for overarching rules but also in many cases for area-specific responses.

The legal treatment of AI must overcome the still dominant view that associates AI primarily with surveillance. The same applies to the law of data protection, which has long focused on the regulation of digital interactions. It has prioritised the treatment of personal information and, in particular, the protection of privacy.[8] Admittedly, data protection remains significant also with respect to the use of AI, insofar as personal information is processed with it. However, a variety of other data are also exploited, including information that is stripped of its personal connection through anonymisation and data that lack any past or present personal connection,

---

[3]Hoffmann-Riem (2017).
[4]On the latter: Bishop (2008) and Müller and Guido (2017).
[5]Surden (2014), p. 89.
[6]See e.g. Goodfellow et al. (2016).
[7]For insight into the variety of challenges and proposed approaches for solving them, see Jakobs (2016), Pieper (2018), Bundesnetzagentur (2017), Eidenmüller (2017), Castilla and Elman (2017), BITKOM (2017), Schneider (2018), Djeffal (2018), Bafin (2018) and Bundesregierung (2018).
[8]See, inter alia, Roßnagel (2003, 2017) and Simitis et al. (2019).

such as machine-generated data in the area of Industry 4.0.[9] In addition to data protection law, many other legal areas may be relevant in dealing with AI and the manifold ways in which it can be used, such as telecommunications law, competition law (see Hennemann), the law of the protection of intellectual property, and liability law (see Schirmer), particularly product liability law. Also important is law that is specific to the relevant field of application, such as medical law (see Jabri), financial markets law (see Schemmel), and road traffic law.

7   Particularly important for the realisation of individual and public interests are the effects associated with abilities to use complex IT systems in various areas of society. Therefore, the risks and opportunities associated with AI and its applications require a broad-based analysis. In the process, the view should not be confined to services provided directly with digital technologies using AI (i.e. the output). Also important is the impact that the use of complex IT system has on those to whom decisions are addressed or on affected third parties (i.e. impact as micro-effects). Moreover, it may be appropriate to identify the farther-reaching, longer-term impact on the relevant areas of society or on society as a whole and to determine the extent to which such impact is significant for law and regulation (i.e. outcome as macro-effects).

8   This point is illustrated by the fact that a number of new digitally based services have an impact not only on those to whom such services are addressed but also on third parties, as well as on the viability of social sub-systems. For instance, digitalisation and the use of AI provide substantial abilities to influence lifestyles, experiences, cultural orientations, attentions, and civic values, with potential effects on private life, the educational system, the development of public opinion, and political decision-making processes (see Krönke).[10]

9   In addition, specific (remote) effects can be observed in various sub-areas of society. For example, robotics, which is being used to increase efficiency and save costs in production processes, can massively alter the labour market, including working conditions. The same can be expected from the growing use of Legal Technology in the field of legal services (see Buchholtz). New sales channels for goods, which can be purchased on platforms like Amazon, also alter markets, such as retail markets, and this may have an impact on the urban availability of businesses and service providers and thus on the nature of social interaction (see Hennemann). The brokering of lodging through Airbnb has an impact on the availability of long-term residential housing, as well as on the hotel industry. The algorithmic control of dealings on financial markets can lead to unpredictable developments, such as collapsing or skyrocketing prices, etc. (see Schemmel).

10   When information technology systems that employ state-of-the-art infrastructures and the latest technologies, including highly developed AI, are used for purposes of wide-ranging social engineering or to control the economic and state order and individual and social behaviour, this has particularly far-reaching significance for

---

[9]See Sattler (2017).
[10]See e.g. Latzer et al. (2016), p. 395.

all three levels of effect mentioned (output, outcome, and impact). This is the direction in which trends are currently headed in China. Commercially oriented companies—primarily, but not limited to, such market-dominant IT companies as the Alibaba Group (inter alia, various trading platforms and the widespread online payment system Alipay) or Tencent Holdings (inter alia, social networks, news services, online games)—are working closely with state institutions and the Communist Party in order to extensively collect data and link them for a variety of analyses. The aim is to optimise market processes, align the social behaviour of people with specific values (such as honesty, reliability, integrity, cleanliness, obeying the law, responsibility in the family, etc.), and ensure state and social stability. China is in the process of developing a comprehensive social scoring system/social credit system (currently being pilot tested, but soon to be applied in wide areas of China).[11] It would be short-sighted to analyse the development of this system primarily from the aspect of the surveillance and suppression of people. Its objectives are much more extensive.[12]

The aim of this Introduction cannot and should not be to examine and evaluate the Chinese social credit system. I mention it only to illustrate the potentials that can be unleashed with the new opportunities for using information technology. This Chapter is limited to discussing the challenges facing law and regulation under the conditions currently prevailing in Germany and the EU.

3 Legal Aspects

Digital technologies, including AI, can have desired or undesired effects from an ethical, social, or economic perspective. Depending on the result of such an assessment, one important issue is whether the creation and/or use of AI requires a legal framework and, in particular, regulatory boundaries in order to promote individual and public interests and to protect against negative effects.

It goes without saying that when digital technologies are used, all relevant norms in the areas affected are generally applicable, such as those of national law—in Germany, civil, criminal and public law, as well as their related areas—and of transnational and international law, including EU law. Such laws remain applicable without requiring any express nexus to digitalisation. But it needs to be asked whether and to what extent these laws, which largely relate to the conditions of the 'analog world', meet the requirements associated with digitalisation and, in particular, with AI or instead need to be modified and supplemented.

Another question is where such new or newly created laws that relate or are relatable to digitalisation should be located within the overall context of the legal system. It is well known that individual legal norms are linked in systematic terms

---
[11]See Chen and Cheung (2017), Creemers (2018) and Dai (2018).
[12]Creemers (2018) and Dai (2018).

with other parts of the legal system. In addition, in many cases they are embedded in complex regulatory structures—in Germany often called 'Regelungsstrukturen'.[13] This term comprises the relevant norms and specialised personnel used for problem-solving and the formal and informal procedures of interaction that can be utilised for specifying the law and applying it. Also relevant are the resources (such as time, money, and expertise) and forms of action available in organisations, as well as, where necessary, the opportunities and measures for collaboration and networking between various actors, both public and private. Such regulatory structures can exhibit significant complexity in multilevel systems, such as those in the EU.

4 Modes of Governance

15   The creation of law and, in particular, of measures for regulation by public authorities must be tailored to the modes selected to solve the problem in a given case (the 'modes of governance': market, competition, negotiation, networking, contract, and digital control).[14] How do these modes and their specific configuration help to achieve socially desirable goals and avoid undesired effects? Appropriate standards are needed in order to determine what is desired. They include, in particular, fundamental constitutional values (including democracy, rule of law, and social justice; see Article 20 of the German Basic Law (*Grundgesetz*, GG)), protection of the freedom to develop economically, culturally, politically, and the like, prevention of manipulation and discrimination, and much more. Also particularly important are the principles, objectives, and values enshrined in the Treaty on European Union and in the Charter of Fundamental Rights of the European Union, as well as in other EU legal acts.

16   One challenge consists of ensuring good governance in connection with the development of algorithmic systems—'governance of algorithms'[15]—and their application—'governance by algorithms'.[16] Luciano Floridi describes 'governance of the digital' as follows:

> Digital Governance is the practice of establishing and implementing policies, procedures and standards for the proper development, use and management of the infosphere. It is also a matter of convention and good coordination, sometimes neither moral nor immoral, neither legal nor illegal. For example, through digital governance, a government agency or a company may (i) determine and control processes and methods used by data stewards and data custodians in order to improve the data quality, reliability, access, security and availability of its services; and (ii) devise effective procedures for decision-making and for the identification of accountabilities with respect to data-related processes.[17]

---

[13] See Hoffmann-Riem (2016), pp. 9–12.
[14] On governance generally, see Benz and Dose (2010) and Schuppert (2011).
[15] Saurwein (2015).
[16] Just and Latzer (2016) and Latzer et al. (2016).
[17] See Floridi (2018).

The area of good governance also includes observing ethical requirements and ensuring compliance.[18]

One of several examples of important standards for configuring AI is a list created by the European Group on Ethics in Science and New Technologies, an entity organised by the European Commission, in its Statement on Ethics of Artificial Intelligence, Robotics and 'Autonomous' Systems: (a) human dignity; (b) autonomy; (c) responsibility; (d) justice, equity, and solidarity; (e) democracy; (f) rule of law and accountability; (g) security, safety, bodily and mental integrity; (h) data protection and privacy; and (i) sustainability.[19] Even though the group placed such standards within the field of ethics, this does not alter the fact that they also have substantial legal relevance. This highlights the interaction frequently seen between law and ethics. Law also has ethical foundations, and ethical principles are shaped in part through law (see Sect. 8).

There are many ways to ensure good governance. In this regard, the measures do not need to take the form of written rules. Also important are, for example, technical approaches, such as the chosen technical design (see Sect. 5.4).

5 Exercising the State's Enabling Responsibility Through Measures for Good Digital Governance

However, good governance does not come about on its own. Where the focus is primarily on law, as in this Chapter, the key aspects are the legal and, moreover, extra-legal (e.g. ethical or moral) requirements, as well as the response by those to whom the requirements are addressed, such as their willingness to comply with them. The tasks of the state include creating or modifying law that facilitates and stimulates good digital governance.

5.1 *Displacements in the Responsibility of Public and Private Actors*

In this regard, the digital transformation is confronted by a realignment of the relationship between private and public law that began much earlier, namely as a result of, in particular, measures of deregulation and privatisation. In recent decades, there has been a significant shift in responsibility to private actors, especially in the fields of telecommunications and information technology and related services. This includes the business fields of the large IT firms, particularly the global Big Five: Alphabet/Google, Facebook, Amazon, Microsoft, and Apple. They mainly act

---
[18]Floridi (2018), pp. 4 et seq.
[19]European Group on Ethics in Science and New Technologies (2018), pp. 16 et seq.

according to self-created guidelines that are set and enforced unilaterally in most cases, including where third parties are concerned, such as the users of their services.[20]

22 The heavy weight of private self-structuring and self-regulation (see Sect. 7) does not however alter the fact that state authorities are responsible for protecting individual and public interests. Nonetheless, the displacements have changed the basic conditions under which state authorities exercise influence and the instruments available to them, as well as the prospects for success.

23 Although because of the protection they enjoy through fundamental rights, private entities are generally unconstrained in the specification and pursuit of their interests, they are not fully relieved of the obligation to pay regard to the interests of others and to matters of public interest. It is the state's role to concentrate on stimulating and encouraging private individuals to pursue the common good, thereby enabling them to provide public services that previously were managed by the state—without the latter completely abdicating its responsibility for overseeing the process.[21] Public-private partnerships have been introduced for standard setting and oversight in several areas, all of which demand sophisticated and previously untried legal frameworks.[22] As the role of public authorities has changed, many authors in Germany have taken to referring to the state as the 'Gewährleistungsstaat', which Gunnar Folke Schuppert (2003) calls in English the 'ensuring state' and others the 'enabling state'. They stress the state's 'Gewährleistungsverantwortung', i.e. its responsibility to ensure sufficient legal and non-legal guarantees to protect the common good.[23] In the following, I will refer to 'Gewährleistungsverantwortung' as the state's 'enabling responsibility'.

24 Where necessary, the state is under a positive obligation to create a framework for safeguarding, above all, the exercise of political, economic, social, cultural, and other fundamental rights. Positive obligations of the state are recognised not only in the German legal system but also, increasingly, with regard to the Charter of Fundamental Rights of the European Union and to the European Convention on Human Rights, as well as in a number of international agreements.[24] Norm-based requirements for meeting positive obligations can be found not only in fundamental rights but also in the provisions concerning constitutional principles (e. g. Article 20 GG) and fundamental values (e. g. Article 2 of the Treaty on European Union).

25 To the extent that digital transformation is shaped by private entities, the enabling state is tasked with protecting individual and public interests, including through law. The state has the ability, as well as the obligation, to create suitable structures, provide normative orientation for conduct, and, if necessary, set boundaries.

---

[20]Nemitz (2018), pp. 2 et seq.
[21]See Voßkuhle and Wischmeyer (2017), p. 90.
[22]See Voßkuhle and Wischmeyer (2017), p. 90.
[23]See Ruge (2004); Franzius (2009); Schulze-Fielitz (2012), pp. 896 et seq.
[24]Fischer-Lescano (2014); Schliesky et al. (2014); Marauhn (2015); Harris et al. (2018), pp. 24–27; Marsch (2018), chapter 4.

Because change is happening so quickly, developments must furthermore be continuously monitored, and action must be taken when they go awry.

The specification of these requirements through interpretation or amendment of existing law or through creation of new law also consists of responding to change, in our case, to technological and social changes associated with digitalisation.

5.2 Innovative Case-law as an Example

Examples of how the law is capable of responding to non-legal changes can also be found in case-law, such as several IT-related innovations by the German Federal Constitutional Court in the area of fundamental rights. As early as 1983, the Court elaborated a 'fundamental right to informational self-determination' in response to the risks to the protection of the right of privacy that were associated with emerging digitalisation.[25] In 2008 the Court took the innovative step of extending the reach of fundamental rights protection to the 'fundamental right to the guarantee of the confidentiality and integrity of information technology systems'.[26] Although owing to the subject matter of the dispute, this decision was directed at online searches of an individual's personal computer, the Court later held in 2016 that the protection afforded to information technology systems covers more than simply the computers used by individuals but also includes the networking of those computers with other computers, such as in connection with storage of data in the cloud.[27] At the same time, it emphasised that data that are stored on external servers with a legitimate expectation of confidentiality are also deserving protection. Protection is also granted where a user's movements on the internet are tracked. As a result, the use of AI associated with such networks also may fall within the protective scope of this fundamental right.

As is the case with the fundamental right to informational self-determination, the Court has understood this right—often referred to in literature as the 'IT fundamental right'—as giving greater specificity to the constitutional guarantee of human dignity and the protection of free development of personality (Articles 1 (1) and 2 (1) GG). Norms like Articles 1 and 2 of the German Basic Law, but also other fundamental rights, do more than simply obligate the state to refrain from placing restrictions on the rights of individuals; they also require the state to guarantee that individuals are protected against acts by others and to take positive action to safeguard human rights. This latter mandate is referred to as the 'third-party' or 'horizontal' effect of

---

[25] Bundesverfassungsgericht 1 BvR 209, 269, 362, 420, 440, 484/83 'Volkszählung' (15 October 1983), BVerfGE 89, p. 1; see also, inter alia, Britz (2007).

[26] Bundesverfassungsgericht 1 BvR 370, 595/07 'Online-Durchsuchungen' (27 February 2008), BVerfGE 124, p. 313; Luch (2011); Wehage (2013); Hauser (2015).

[27] Bundesverfassungsgericht 1 BvR 966, 1140/09 'BKA-Gesetz' (20 April 2016), BVerfGE 141, pp. 264-265, 268 et seq., 303 et seq.

fundamental rights.[28] However, in order to be able to implement this guarantee, targeted legal norms are necessary. Examples include the law of data protection and the law of IT security. Legal measures concerning the treatment of AI and the ensuring of the innovation responsibility associated with it should likewise be bound by this concept.

5.3 System Protection

29 The above-mentioned IT fundamental right relates to the protection of information technology systems, i.e. to system protection. The right mandates that public authorities must protect the integrity of IT systems not only against unjustified interference by the state but also, in addition, against that by third parties. Constitutional requirements that measures be taken to protect the viability of information technology systems, or at least that there be possibilities for doing so, can also be derived from other fundamental rights (such as, inter alia, Articles 3, 5, 6, 10, 13, and 14 GG), as well as in addition from provisions concerning constitutional principles and fundamental values (see Sect. 5.1): The state's responsibility for guaranteeing the realisation of such objectives becomes all the more pressing as individual and public interests become increasingly affected by digital technologies, as well as by the business models, modes of conduct, and infrastructures tailored to those technologies. This responsibility ultimately means ensuring a viable democracy, enforcing compliance with the requirements of the rule of law, implementing protection founded on social justice, taking measures to prevent risks that are foreseeable and not yet foreseen (here, such as the further development and use of AI), as well as safeguarding the capabilities of important institutions, such as the market. Of particular significance is ensuring the quality of technical IT systems, including taking measures to protect cybersecurity.[29]

30 System protection is particularly important in the IT sector, because individuals as users are virtually unable to influence how the system is configured and are no longer capable of recognising threats, i.e. where they have no ability whatsoever to protect themselves individually. Moreover, the protection of important social areas is certain to fail if the employment of protective measures depends exclusively on the initiation and outcome of individual and thus gradual actions. The task here is an important one for society as a whole, which also must manage it as a whole with the aid of law. System protection is an important starting point for this.

---

[28]Dolderer (2000); Calliess (2006), margin nos. pp. 5 et seq.; Schliesky et al. (2014); Knebel (2018).
[29]Wischmeyer (2017) and Leisterer (2018).

5.4 Systemic Protection

System protection should not be confused with systemic protection. The latter uses the relevant technology for building into the technical system itself measures that independently safeguard protected interests, especially those of third parties.[30] The objective here, in particular, is protection through technology design,[31] including through default settings intended to increase protection.[32] Such systemic protection has long been utilised as a means of data protection. A current example can be found in Article 25 of the EU General Data Protection Regulation (GDPR): Data protection by design and by default. Article 32 GDPR contains additional requirements. However, the field to which data protection through design can be applied is considerably broader and also covers the use of AI. Discussions are also focusing on the extent to which the effectiveness not only of basic legal principles but also, to supplement them, basic ethical principles can be ensured (or at least facilitated) through technology design.[33]

5.5 Regulatory Guidelines

Exercise of the state's enabling responsibility (particularly through the legislature, the government, and the public administration), ideally supported by private actors involved in the development and utilisation of intelligent IT systems, requires clarification not only of objectives but also of strategies and concepts for implementing them. This can be accomplished by formulating guidelines directed at them. In this regard, I will borrow from Thomas Wischmeyer's list of such guidelines[34] but also augment it:

– Exposure of the regulatory effect of intelligent systems;
– Appropriate quality level for intelligent systems;
– No discrimination by intelligent systems;
– Data protection and information security in connection with the use of intelligent systems;
– Use of intelligent systems that is commensurate with the problem;
– Guarantee of transparency in connection with the use of intelligent systems;
– Clarity about liability and responsibility in connection with the use of intelligent systems;

---

[30] Spiecker gen. Döhmann (2016), pp. 698 et seq.
[31] Yeung (2008, 2017).
[32] Hildebrandt (2017) and Baumgartner and Gausling (2017).
[33] Winfield and Jirotka (2018); European Group on Ethics in Science and New Technologies (2018); Data Ethics Commission (2019).
[34] Wischmeyer (2018), Part III 1-6, IV.

- Enabling of democratic and constitutional control of intelligent systems;
- Protection against sustained impairment of the living standards of future generations by intelligent systems;
- Sensitivity to errors and openness to revision of intelligent systems.

Although this list could be expanded, it serves here to illustrate the multifaceted aspects of the regulatory tasks.

5.6 *Regarding Regulatory Possibilities*

33   In view of the diverse number of fields in which AI is used, this Chapter obviously cannot describe all possible instruments for achieving a legal impact on the development and use of AI. Instead, I will give several examples along with general remarks. Area-specific suggestions for legal approaches are also presented in the subsequent Chapters in this volume (particularly in Part II).

34   The proposition has been put forward above (Sect. 2) that in many cases it is not enough to develop rules for AI that are detached from the contextual conditions of the areas in which they are applied and, above all, from the specific ways in which they are applied.[35] Also conceivable are rules that are applicable across a number of areas. In this regard, a starting point is offered by the types of norms that are applied in the law of data protection (see Marsch). These norms are applicable to AI where personal data are processed.[36] Moreover, they can to some extent be used as a template for rules designed to safeguard legally protected interests other than privacy.

35   One instrument that can be used in nearly every field in which AI is used are prospective impact assessments (see Article 35 GDPR). Certification by publicly accredited or government bodies, such as for particularly high-risk developments and/or possible uses of AI, can also be provided for (see Articles 42 and 43 GDPR). To the extent that, as is customarily the case, certification is voluntary (see Article 42 (3) GDPR), it makes sense to create incentives for its enforcement, such as by exempting or limiting liability, e.g. for robotics under product liability law. In sensitive areas, however, certification can also be made obligatory by law.

36   Because further developments and the pace of software changes are often unpredictable, particularly in learning algorithmic systems, continual monitoring is also called for, as are retrospective impact assessments carried out through self-monitoring and/or outside monitoring. Such monitoring can be facilitated by duties to document software and software changes and, in the case of learning systems, the training programs (see Wischmeyer, paras 15, 48). It may also make sense to impose

---

[35] See also Pagallo (2016), pp. 209 et seq.; Scherer (2016); Tutt (2017); Martini and Nink (2017). See also Veale et al. (2018).
[36] One area of growing importance is the use of facial-recognition technologies, which employ AI extensively.

duties to label the utilised data and to keep logs about the application and use of training programmes, as well as reporting and information duties.[37]

Particularly in intelligent information technology systems, it is especially difficult to create measures that ensure appropriate transparency, accountability, responsibility, and, where appropriate, the ability to make revisions (see Sect. 6.3).[38] Steps also have to be taken to ensure the continuous development of standards for evaluating trends, such as adapting ethical requirements in the face of newly emerging fields of application and risks, particularly with respect to the limits associated with recognising and controlling consequences.

Moreover, imperative (command and control) law may be indispensable, such as for preventing discrimination (see Tischbirek) and for ensuring the safeguarding of cybersecurity, which is particularly important for the future.[39] Also conceivable are prohibitions or restrictions for special applications. German law already provides for these in some cases, such as for automated decisions by public authorities.[40] However, it can be expected that the fields of application will expand considerably, particularly as e-government becomes more commonplace, and, above all, that new experiences will engender restrictions on applications.

In view of the risks and opportunities associated with AI, which extend far beyond the processing of personal data, it needs to be clarified whether it makes sense to assign monitoring responsibilities to current data protection authorities. If so, their powers would have to be expanded, and they would need to have larger staffs with corresponding expertise. Ideally, however, an institution should be created at the German federal level or at the EU level that specialises particularly (but not only) in the monitoring of AI, such as a digital agency. For the U.S., Andrew Tutt (2017) has proposed the establishment of an authority with powers similar to those of the Food and Drug Administration. In addition to monitoring,[41] such an institution should also be entrusted with developing standards (performance

---

[37]On these possibilities, see e.g. (although specifically in relation to the protection of privacy) Leopoldina et al. (2018).

[38]For more about these problem areas, please see the multifaceted considerations by Wischmeyer (2018) in his article on 'Regulation of Intelligent Systems'. Requiring further exploration are, in particular, his suggestions relating to the establishment of a 'collaborative architecture for reason-giving and control': Wischmeyer (2018), pp. 32 et seq. See also Wischmeyer, in this volume.

[39]Wischmeyer (2017) and Beucher and Utzerath (2013).

[40]Cf. sections 3a; 24 (1); 35a; 37 (2), (3), and (4); and 41 (2) sentence 2 of the German Administrative Procedure Act (*Verwaltungsverfahrensgesetz*, VwVfG); section 32a (2), No. 2 of the German Fiscal Code (*Abgabenordnung*, AO); section 31a of Book X of the German Social Code (*Sozialgesetzbuch* [SGB] X).

[41]One way to do this is by certifying AI systems. Corresponding information is necessary for this purpose. See e.g. Scherer (2016), p. 397: 'Companies seeking certification of an AI system would have to disclose all technical information regarding the product, including (1) the complete source code; (2) a description of all hardware/software environments in which the AI has been tested; (3) how the AI performed in the testing environments; and (4) any other information pertinent to the safety of the AI.'

standards, design standards, liability standards) or at least be involved in their development.

40　The possibilities for exercise of the state's enabling responsibility that have been discussed here primarily describe only approaches, but not the standards that can be used to test whether the use of AI leads to unacceptable risks in a certain field of application. These standards must be in line with constitutional as well as transnational legal requirements, but they also should satisfy ethical principles (see Sects. 4 and 8).

41　The technical difficulties associated with implementing legal instruments must be left aside here. However, insofar there is a need for new instruments that require further innovations, consideration should also be given to legally driven 'innovation forcing'.[42] This means using law to establish targets or standards that in accordance with the current standard of development are not yet able to be met but the meeting of which is plausible. Such law then specifies an implementation period. If that period expires without implementation, and if it is not extended, the development and use of the relevant type of AI must be stopped.

6 Obstacles to the Effective Application of Law

42　A number of aspects specific to the field of information technology, as well as to the business models used to exploit it, can be expected to pose difficulties for effective regulation. Only a few of them will be discussed here.

6.1 Openness to Development

43　In view of the relentless speed of technological change, the development of new fields of activity and business models, and the changes to society associated with each of them, the application of law will in many cases have to take place with a significant amount of uncertainty.[43] Because of lack of knowledge and, often, unpredictability, there is a risk that legal measures may be ineffective or have dysfunctional consequences. On the one hand, a legal rule must be amenable to new innovations in order to avoid obstructing the opportunities associated with digitalisation, but not be so flexible as to be ill-suited to averting or minimising risks. On the other, the legal system must make it possible to shift direction where the legal objective is not met and/or unforeseen negative consequences occur (measures for reversibility). In this regard, self-learning information technology systems lead to

---

[42]See Hoffmann-Riem (2016), pp. 430 et seq., with further references.

[43]On dealing with uncertainty and lack of knowledge generally, see Hoffmann-Riem (2018), Part 5, with further references.

significant risks, particularly where, without being noticed, learning processes set out in directions that cause undesired or even irreversible consequences.

It is presumably no coincidence today that warnings are increasingly being raised about the risks associated with the use of AI and that regulatory protection is being called for, including by individuals who have devoted their careers to the development of artificial intelligence and have used it extensively in their businesses, such as PayPal co-founder and Tesla owner Elon Musk, Microsoft co-founder Bill Gates, and Apple co-founder Steve Wozniak.[44] The brilliant researcher Stephen Hawking shared this concern. While acknowledging the tremendous potential of AI, he called for increased focus on the issue of AI security.[45] Very often warnings about the consequences of AI relate not just to specific applications but also to the fundamental risk that AI could defy human control and develop destructive potentials for humanity as a whole.

One of many examples of risks involves how we should deal with brain transplants and other neural devices that use AI.[46] The discussion of future risks focuses not just on the primarily ethical consequences for human development and the concept of human intelligence and the way it functions. There are also fears about new forms of cybercrime, such as the hacking of pacemakers and other AI-controlled implants. For instance, Gasson and Koops state:

> The consequences of attacks on human implants can be far greater to human life and health than is the case with classic cybercrime. Moreover, as implant technology develops further, it becomes difficult to draw an exact border between body and technology, and attacks not only affect the confidentiality, integrity and availability of computers and computer data, but also affect the integrity of the human body itself. The combination of network technologies with human bodies may well constitute a new step change in the evolution of cybercrime, thus making attacks on humans through implants a new generation of cybercrime.[47]

6.2 *Insignificance of Borders*

Difficulties involving the legal treatment of complex information technology systems also result from the fact that in many respects, technologies dissolve borders or demand action in borderless areas.[48] For instance, the digital technologies employed,

---

[44]For references, see Scherer (2016), p. 355. On risks (also in relation to other consequences of IT), see the—sometimes alarmist—works by Bostrom (2014) and Tegmark (2017). See also Precht (2018) and Kulwin (2018). It is telling that Brad Smith (2017), President and Chief Legal Officer of Microsoft, has called for the creation of an international 'Digital Geneva Convention', which focuses mainly on cyberattacks and thus cybersecurity, but makes no mention of issue of AI. See https://blogs.microsoft.com/on-the-issues/2017/02/14/need-digital-geneva-convention/.

[45]Hawking (2018), p. 209 et seq., 213 et seq.

[46]See e.g. Wu and Goodman (2013).

[47]See Gasson and Koops (2013), p. 276.

[48]Cornils (2017), pp. 391 et seq.; Vesting (2017); Hoffmann-Riem (2018), pp. 36–37.

the infrastructures, and the business models utilised are not confined by any borders or, in exceptional cases, have only limited regional borders, such as national borders. They are often available on a transnational and, in particular, global basis. The same applies to the services provided with digitalised technology, as well as their effects. To the same extent, the use of AI also takes place mostly in unbordered spaces. Large, globally positioned IT companies in particular are interested in operating as far as possible with uniform structures that have a global or transnational reach. For these companies, regulations that are set down in various national legal systems and accordingly differ from one another constitute an impediment to the use of their business models. As a result, they look for and exploit opportunities to thwart or avoid such regulations.[49]

47 However, this does not mean that it is impossible to subject transnationally operating companies to legal regulations with territorially limited applicability, insofar as they operate on that territory. A recent example is Article 3(1) GDPR, which specifies that the GDPR 'applies to the processing of personal data in the context of the activities of an establishment of a controller or a processor in the Union, regardless of whether the processing takes place in the Union or not.' Complementary regulations are contained in section 1 of the German Federal Data Protection Act (*Bundesdatenschutzgesetz*, BDSG) (new version).

48 The relative insignificance of borders also relates to other dimensions discussed here. For instance, in the IT sector, the borders are blurring between hardware and software, and certain problems can be solved both in the hardware area and with software. Also, private and public communication are becoming blended to an ever-greater extent.[50] Offline and online communication are increasingly interwoven—as on the Internet of Things—meaning that a new type of world, which some call the 'online world', is becoming the norm.[51]

49 The impact that the insignificance of borders has on legal regulation is also evident in the fact that digitalisation affects nearly all areas of life, meaning that requirements can be, or even may have to be, imposed on the use of AI both across the board and, if necessary, for each area specifically.

50 To the extent that use is made of self-learning algorithmic systems that enhance their software independently, tackle new problems, and develop solutions to them, these systems transcend the limits of the field of application or the abilities for problem-solving that were placed on them by their initial programming.

---

[49]Nemitz (2018).

[50]See, inter alia, Schmidt (2017), focusing on social media.

[51]Floridi (2015); Hildebrandt (2015), pp. 41 et seq., pp. 77 et seq.

6.3 Lack of Transparency

Although digital transformation has created new spaces for generating, capturing, and exploiting information that previously were essentially inaccessible, technology design and other measures of secrecy block access to the approaches employed and to the results.[52] Lack of transparency can also result from the collaboration involved in developing various program components and creating hardware. This is all the more so the case where there is insufficient knowledge about the 'building blocks' originating from the other actors involved and about how these components function. Where learning algorithms are used, not even the programmers involved in the creation of the algorithms know the programs that are being modified by automatic learning. Even though it is possible to overcome the black-box character of information technology systems,[53] such as through reverse engineering, this normally presupposes a high level of expertise and the use of complex procedures. The barriers are significant (see Wischmeyer).

Examples of legal obstacles to transparency include where algorithms are recognised as business secrets[54] or as official secrets (section 32a (2), No. 2 Fiscal Code—*Abgabenordnung*) (see Braun Binder).

Not only for users but also for supervisory authorities and the general public, it is important that the treatment of digital technologies, including the use of AI, be generally comprehensible and controllable. In this regard, sufficient transparency is a prerequisite for creating not only trust but also accountability and, in some cases, liability.[55]

6.4 Concentration of Power

Furthermore, the application of law and its outcome are made considerably more difficult by the concentration of power in the IT field.[56] In this regard, the development of AI is becoming increasingly dominated by large IT companies and specialised firms associated with them. Powerful IT companies have managed to keep the development of software and internet-based services, as well as their output, largely unregulated. Although antitrust law, which is commonly used to limit economic power, is applicable to companies with IT business areas,[57] national and EU antitrust law is limited both with respect to its territorial applicability and in

---

[52] See, inter alia, Kroll (2018) and Wischmeyer (2018).
[53] See Leopoldina et al. (2018), p. 50.
[54] See e.g. BGHZ 200, 38 for credit scoring by the German private credit bureau Schufa.
[55] Wischmeyer (2018) and Hoeren and Niehoff (2018).
[56] Welfens et al. (2010); Rolf (2018); Nemitz (2018), pp. 2 et seq.
[57] And has already been so applied—see Körber (2017). For references concerning legal actions, particularly against Google, see Schneider (2018), pp. 156–159.

terms of its substantive reach. Global antitrust law covering the IT sector does not exist.

Moreover, antitrust law is a tool for ensuring the viability of markets, particularly from an economic standpoint, meaning that its usefulness is limited. More substantial concerns involving individual and public interests, such as protection of the right of privacy, freedom from manipulation, fair access to information, and prevention of discrimination, may be jeopardised by power asymmetries and the abuse of power. However, the broad protection of those concerns is normally not the purview of antitrust law, nor is this automatically assured or sufficiently capable of being assured through antitrust measures. Accordingly, there may be a need for supplementary regulatory law and for coordinating it with traditional regulatory law.[58]

6.5 Escaping Legal Constraints

To the extent that national or transnational law can be applied in the IT sector, particularly transnational and even globally operating companies often make efforts—as described above (see Sect. 6.2)—to evade such constraints.[59] Law loses its effectiveness if it can be avoided or ignored, or if it is not implemented, including enforcement by public authorities.

The avoidance of strict legal constraints can occur through a targeted choice of where to incorporate or by shifting activities to other parts of the group if this means that the legal constraints that need to be observed become weaker or if the legal requirements are not implemented in the state concerned and violations are not subject to penalties. Moreover, companies can employ their general business terms and conditions as a tool for exploiting any remaining legal leeway in shaping the general terms and conditions for the use of services, for instance excluding liability.

7 Types of Rules and Regulations

These (and other) difficulties do not mean that the IT sector is a rule-free zone. In addition to (the albeit few) IT-specific regulations employed by state authorities, the legal system as a whole is—as mentioned above—also applicable here. Moreover, there are forms of private rules and regulations, including those whose content state authorities are capable of influencing from a regulatory standpoint in the exercise of their enabling responsibility. In order to illustrate how diverse the possible forms are, the following will describe several types of rules and regulations that are also applied in the IT sector. Although they were not developed with respect to the special risks

---

[58] See Hoffmann-Riem (2018), pp. 72 et seq.
[59] Nemitz (2018), pp. 4 et seq.

and opportunities associated with AI, it is possible to examine the extent to which they can be applied to AI-specific problems or can be reconfigured in such a way that they help to manage the regulatory needs associated with the creation and use of AI (ensuring opportunities, preventing risks, and taking measures to minimise detriments).

7.1 Self-structuring

The area of rules and regulations does not, however, cover an actor's own autonomous conduct, unbound by rules, for achieving self-defined objectives. By means of self-structuring, it is possible for individual companies to manage, for example, the development and use of digital algorithms, as well as the use of AI in connection with this. The same applies to decisions involving the purchase of software developed outside the company. Similarly subject to self-structuring are the business models developed by IT companies, whose implementation often involves the use of AI, and thus largely also the structuring of the relationship with users of services. To the same extent, auditing and monitoring measures and other means of preliminary and accompanying control, as well as compliance, can be created in the course of self-structuring for each company department. Self-structuring measures also consist of guidelines that companies draw up to govern their own conduct. Examples include Deutsche Telekom's 'Guidelines for the Use of Artificial Intelligence' (2018) and Google's 'AI at Google: Our Principles' (2018).

7.2 Self-imposed Rules

The area of autonomous action also includes instances where companies voluntarily comply with non-binding yet collectively established or at least recognised requirements concerning conduct in the IT area, including the use of AI. Such forms—I refer to them as 'self-imposed rules'—have existed in the field of digitalisation for some time. They include informal rules of decorum (as with 'netiquette' in the early days of the internet) as well as rules governing the collaborative development of software (such as open source or open content). Noteworthy are also non-binding codes of conduct and other behavioural rules in the form of morally or ethically based behavioural requirements. Also relevant are technical standards developed by one company that are also accessible to other companies and are used by them without the standards becoming legal binding on third parties.

61   Despite the fact that they are not legally binding and are not subject to legal sanctioning, self-imposed rules may be socially sanctionable (loss of reputation, exclusion from the community, and the like).

7.3 Company Self-regulation

62   I use this term to describe rules that pursue a regulatory purpose going beyond the individual case and that have been made legally binding. To the extent that companies create them without the involvement of public authorities, I refer to this as 'company self-regulation'. This has to do with codes of conduct approved by trade or commercial groups, particularly those that have been developed by associations whose statutes require members to abide by them. Also falling under this heading are technical standards, including those that, while having been developed by a single company, have gained such acceptance on the market as to be essentially binding, e.g. because they are controlling with respect to decisions concerning liability issues (like standards as an expression of the state of art of science and technology).

7.4 Regulated Self-regulation

63   The term 'regulated self-regulation'[60] is intended to describe situations in which public authorities entrust the solution of problems to regulatory efforts undertaken (relatively) autonomously by members of society, especially companies, while seeking to encourage compliance with certain objectives, such as the fulfilment of public interest purposes, either with legally regulated incentives or in a regulatory manner (through binding requirements in substantive law or procedural law). Such encouragement can take place in very different ways, not only in the form of conduct incentives (for instance, procurement directives) but also by establishing structures or institutions for collaborative efforts between private and public actors.

64   Candidates for regulated self-regulation include legal requirements for certification and auditing by private, accredited bodies.[61] These tools, which have a long history in the law of data protection, may also be applicable to intelligent information technology systems in other dimensions. In this regard, such forms of actions do not necessarily need to be made legally binding, i.e. as imperative law. Instead, public authorities can also create incentives to use them, such as the prospect of limitation of liability in the event of compliance with the requirements (see Sect. 5.6).

---

[60]Eifert (2001).

[61]On such forms of action and supervision generally, see Ehmann and Selmayer (2018), margin nos. 26 et seq.

The GDPR, for instance, relies on possibilities for regulated self-regulation. For example, it encourages associations or other bodies to draw up codes of conduct to facilitate its proper and effective application (GDPR, Recitals 77 and 98). This can also include the use of AI, to the extent that the GDPR is applicable to it. Article 40 (2) GDPR lists several topics that may be amenable to specification. The suggestions for specifications are intended as regulatory guidance for codes of conduct, although associations and other bodies are not obligated to enact them. Nor are they obligated to make use of the offer set forth in Article 40(5) to submit the draft to the supervisory authority with the possibility of obtaining approval of it. The European Commission may, by way of implementing acts, even decide that a code of conduct that is applicable in several Member States has general validity within the EU (Article 40(9)). Article 41 GDPR provides for possibilities of accreditation by appropriate bodies for the purpose of monitoring compliance with a code of conduct. Member States are also encouraged to establish certification mechanisms and data protection seals and marks (Article 42 GDPR). Corresponding legal measures can also be developed outside of the scope of the GDPR, including for the use of AI.

Also belonging to the category of regulated self-regulation are instances where certain standards (such as technical ones) that gain acceptance in the private sector are treated in legal norms enacted by public authorities as controlling for the purpose of evaluating whether a course of action is legal, such as for issues of liability in the area of robotics or motor vehicles built for autonomous or automated driving. Through this transfer, they are simultaneously transformed into law. Another example are IT security standards that have been developed by a Bitkom working group.[62] Although they contain only recommendations, they may have legal consequences, such as for the evaluation of negligence in connection with the production of goods.

Furthermore, jurisdiction can contribute to regulated self-regulation. One example, although it does not relate to AI, is the Google Spain decision by the CJEU.[63] The Court ordered Google Inc. to take steps to protect the so-called 'right to be forgotten' in connection with the operation of its search engine. In application of the EU Data Protection Directive (95/46/EC), which is no longer in force, Google was obligated to remove from its search engine in Europe links to information objected to by affected third parties under certain conditions (now further expanded in Article 17 GDPR). This makes it difficult to access the relevant information (which however is not erased as such). Google has the sole power to decide whether to remove the link.[64] The company set up an advisory council with experts from European countries, which has developed recommendations for self-regulative practice.[65]

---

[62] See BITKOM/DIN (2014).

[63] CJEU C-131/12 (13 May 2014), ECLI:EU:C:2014:317.

[64] This is a distinct flaw in the CJEU's decision: The decision to block access to information originating from a third party, which often has far-reaching effects, is placed solely in the hand of a commercially operating, oligopolistic enterprise.

[65] Google Advisory Council (2015).

7.5 Hybrid Regulation

68 By 'hybrid regulation' I mean a rule created by a company in a self-regulatory manner, with state bodies being involved in developing the rule or determining its relevance. This also relates to several of the examples addressed under Sect. 7.4, above.

69 A further example can be found in IT security law. The IT Baseline Protection Catalogs prepared by the German Federal Office for Information Security and updated roughly every 6 months[66] are not legally binding, but they can be used as the basis for certification. Certification serves as evidence that the company has taken appropriate steps, such as safeguards in connection with the use of AI, to protect its IT systems against IT security threats.

70 IT security law aims in particular at preventing and averting threats posed by cybercrime and cybersabotage. While threats sometimes employ AI, they can also be averted using AI. Specifically with respect to so-called 'Critical Infrastructure', the companies concerned are obligated to create appropriate technical and organisation measures aimed at preventing disruptions to the availability, integrity, authenticity, and confidentiality of their information technology systems (section 8a (1) of the German Act on the Federal Office for Information Security (*Gesetz über das Bundesamt für Sicherheit in der Informationstechnik*)). These companies as well as their associations may make proposals for security standards (section 8a (2)). Upon request, the Federal Office establishes whether such standards are suitable for meeting the security requirements. Also possible are security audits and certifications (section 8a (3)).

7.6 Regulation by Public Authorities

71 This term covers norms enacted by public authorities that are directly binding on those to whom they are addressed, i.e. they do not require further intervention through self-regulative acts. Examples include requirements contained in the GDPR concerning the lawfulness of data processing, duties involving information and access to personal data, duties relating to the rectification and erasure of personal data, and prohibitions of discrimination and data usage. Binding requirements may also consist of the duty to carry out impact assessments in the case of high-risk data processing (see Articles 35 and 36 GDPR).

72 Falling under the heading of regulation by public authorities is, in particular, imperative, boundary-setting law, such as in the area of regulations involving IT security or to combat discrimination, which may also be associated with the use of AI.[67] Imperative law is indispensable in the area of threat prevention and

---

[66]On these Catalogs, see e.g. Stetter and Heukrodt-Bauer (2017).
[67]See, inter alia, Bozdag (2013).

aversion, such as requirements for the design and software of self-driving motor vehicles.

By no means have the possibilities been exhausted for using imperative law to limit the risks associated with the use of AI. But it also should not be overlooked that in innovative areas in which the actors need to be creative and willing to cooperate, the application of imperative law can be counterproductive if it needlessly impedes leeway, such as for the development of innovative AI. That said, it should not be the sole aim of legal measures to ensure an environment amenable to innovation. They also need to ensure the responsibility that goes along with innovation.[68]

7.7 Techno-regulation

The formal as well as informal forms of action available in each affected legal area can be used to implement normative requirements. I mention this here only in passing. But I should add that in times of digitalisation, digital algorithms can also be used as decision-makers, as in the case of 'governance by algorithms' referred to previously (see Sect. 4). 'Legal Technology' is the term used to describe the use of digitalisation in setting and applying law as well as the replacement of human decision by algorithms, including through the use of AI.[69] The risks and opportunities associated with it cannot be examined in depth here (see Buchholtz).

8 Replacement or Supplementation of Legal Measures with Extra-Legal, Particularly Ethical Standards

Earlier, I mentioned the interlocking of ethical and legal requirements generally, but also with respect to digitalisation and the use of AI (see Sect. 4). The challenges in configuring the development and use of AI include clarifying the extent to which protective measures should be based on ethical standards alone or instead should also be supported by law and, especially, by binding regulations.

Many institutions have recently been dealing with issues involving the ethics of digitalisation, including with respect to AI,[70] and others are still working on them. For instance, the European Commission has established a 'High-Level Expert Group on Artificial Intelligence'.[71] Also, the German federal government has adopted

---

[68]On these two poles—'Innovationsoffenheit' and 'Innovationsverantwortung'—see Hoffmann-Riem (2016), pp. 28–35.
[69]On Legal Technology, see, inter alia, Buchholtz (2017), Boehme-Neßler (2017), Hartung et al. (2018) and Breidenbach and Glatz (2018).
[70]Nemitz (2018), p. 7 (with further references in footnotes 18 and 19).
[71]European Commission (2018).

cornerstones for an artificial intelligence strategy.[72] It has also set up a data ethics commission and tasked it with addressing certain central questions; the commission has delivered its opinion in October 2019.[73] The German Bundestag has set up an Enquete Commission on artificial intelligence, which also plans to deal with ethical issues.[74] Noteworthy is also that individual companies have established ethics guidelines or principles, such as Google and Deutsche Telekom noted above. In the general public, as well as in academia,[75] there have also been intense discussions about the role of ethics and its relationship to legal rules.[76]

77 In view of the general difficulties associated with legal regulation and implementation in the area of AI, including the particular difficulties of reaching agreement on a transnational legal framework, there is a risk with such discussions that the outcome—if any—will ultimately stick largely to non-binding and often only vaguely formulated ethical principles. In any case, it can be expected that most IT companies, particularly those that dominate on the market, will prefer ethical principles over legal constraints and that they will attempt to thwart as far as possible the creation of laws and penalties so as to preserve the latitude to protect their own interests.[77]

78 It would likely be inconsistent with the state's enabling responsibility to rely solely on ethical principles. In view of the risks associated with digitalisation generally and the use of AI in particular, it is doubtlessly indispensable to have law that is set by state authorities, or in which they at least play a role, and that is furnished with sanctioning options. The verbal acknowledgement of ethical principles must not be used as an alibi for dispensing with legal constraints.

9 On the Necessity of Transnational Law

79 As a result of territorial break-downs, which are also typical for the use of AI (see Sect. 6.2), national efforts, including national legal rules, are often insufficient for solving the problems in this area. What are needed, therefore, are also transnational and globally effective tools that, ideally, are based on corresponding transnational and international agreements, at least where they are intended to take legal form. This includes new concepts, agreements, and institutions of transnational gover-

---

[72]Bundesregierung (2018).

[73]Bundesministerium des Innern, für Bau und Heimat/Bundesministerium der Justiz und für Verbraucherschutz (2018); Data Ethics Commission (2019).

[74]Enquête-Kommission (2018).

[75]Himma and Tavani (2008), Van den Hoven et al. (2015) and Rath et al. (2018).

[76]See, inter alia, Winfield and Jirotka (2018), Cath (2018), Otto and Gräf (2018) and Leonelli (2016).

[77]Nemitz (2018), pp. 3–4; Cath (2018).

nance[78] in which public actors collaborate with the stakeholders concerned, i.e. with associations and companies in the digital economy, but also with NGOs and other entities representing the interests of civil society.[79] In order to have any sustained effect, such transnational agreements require law that is set by state authorities, or in which they at least play a role, and that is coupled with measures for enforcing it.

References

Bafin (2018) Big Data trifft auf künstliche Intelligenz, Herausforderungen und Implikationen für Aufsicht und Regulierung von Finanzdienstleistungen. www.bafin.de/SharedDocs/Downloads/DE/dl_bdai_studie.html

Baumgartner U, Gausling T (2017) Datenschutz durch Technikgestaltung und datenschutzfreundliche Voreinstellungen. Zeitschrift für Datenschutz:308–313

Benz A, Dose N (eds) (2010) Governance – Regierung in komplexen Regelsystemen, 2nd edn. VS Verlag für Sozialwissenschaften, Wiesbaden

Beucher K, Utzerath J (2013) Cybersicherheit – Nationale und internationale Regulierungsinitiativen: Folgen für die IT-Compliance und die Haftungsmaßstäbe. MultiMedia und Recht:362–367

Bishop CM (2008) Pattern recognition and machine learning. Springer-Verlag, Berlin

BITKOM (2017) Künstliche Intelligenz verstehen als Automation des Entscheidens. Leitfaden. www.bitkom.org/sites/default/files/file/import/Bitkom-Leitfaden-KI-verstehen-als-Automation-des-Entscheidens-2-Mai-2017.pdf

BITKOM, DIN (ed) (2014) Kompass der IT-Sicherheitsstandards – Auszüge zum Thema Elektronische Identitäten. www.bitkom.org/sites/default/files/file/import/140311-Kompass-der-IT-Sicherheitsstandards.pdf

Boehme-Neßler V (2017) Die Macht der Algorithmen und die Ohnmacht des Rechts. Wie die Digitalisierung das Recht relativiert. Neue Juristische Wochenschrift 70:3031–3037

Bostrom N (2014) Superintelligence. Paths, dangers, strategies. Oxford University Press, Oxford

Bozdag A (2013) Bias in algorithmic filtering and personalization. Ethics Inf Technol 15:209–227

Breidenbach S, Glatz F (eds) (2018) Rechtshandbuch Legal Tech. Beck, München

Britz G (2007) Freie Entfaltung durch Selbstdarstellung. Mohr Siebeck, Tübingen

Buchholtz G (2017) Legal Tech. Chancen und Risiken der digitalen Rechtsanwendung. Juristische Schulung:955–960

Bundesministerium des Innern, für Bau und Heimat/ Bundesministerium der Justiz und für Verbraucherschutz (2018) Leitfragen der Bundesregierung an die Datenethikkommission vom 5. Juni 2018. https://www.bmjv.de/SharedDocs/Downloads/DE/Ministerium/ForschungUndWissenschaft/DEK_Leitfragen.pdf

Bundesnetzagentur (2017) Digitale Transformation in den Netzsektoren. Aktuelle Entwicklungen und regulatorische Herausforderungen. www.bundesnetzagentur.de/SharedDocs/Downloads/DE/Allgemeines/Bundesnetzagentur/Publikationen/Berichte/2017/Digitalisierung.pdf

Bundesregierung (2018) Eckpunkte der Bundesregierung für eine Strategie künstlicher Intelligenz. www.bmbf.de/files/180718%20Eckpunkte_KI-Strategie%20final%20Layout.pdf

---

[78] One example is the (not binding) NETmundial Multistakeholder Statement of 24 April 2014, which outlines a set of 'Internet Governance Principles' and contains a 'Roadmap for the future evolution of the Internet Governance Ecosystem', available at https://www.alainet.org/images/NETmundial-Multistakeholder-Document.pdf.

[79] See Hoffmann-Riem (2016), pp. 691–693, with further references.

Callies C (2006) Schutzpflichten § 44, in: Merten D/ Papier H-J, Handbuch der Grundrechte in Deutschland und Europa, Band II, Auflage, Heidelberg: 963-991. § 44

Castilla A, Elman J (2017) Artificial intelligence and the law. TechCrunch, Bay Area. techcrunch.com/2017/01/28/artificial-intelligence-and-the-law/

Cath C (2018) Governing artificial intelligence: ethical, legal and technical opportunities and challenges. Philos Trans Royal Soc A 376:20180080. https://doi.org/10.1098/rsta.2018.0080

Chen Y, Cheung ASY (2017) The transparent self under big data profiling: privacy and Chinese Legislation on the Social Credit System. J Comp Law 12:356–378

Cole T (2017) Digitale transformation, 2nd edn. Franz Vahlen, München

Cornils M (2017) Entterritorialisierung im Kommunikationsrecht. Veröffentlichungen der Vereinigung der Deutschen Staatsrechtslehrer 76:391–437

Creemers R (2018) China's social credit system: an evolving practice of control. ssrn.com/abstract=3175792 or https://doi.org/10.2139/ssrn.3175792

Data Ethics Commission (2019) Opinion – executive summary of Oct 23:2019. https://www.bmjv.de/DE/Themen/FokusThemen/Datenethikkommission/Datenethkommission_EN_node.html

Dai X (2018) Toward a reputation state: the social credit system project of China. ssrn.com/abstract=3193577

Deutsche Telekom (2018) Die neun Leitlinien der Telekom zum Einsatz von künstlicher Intelligenz. www.telekom.com/de/konzern/digitale-verantwortung/details/ki-leitlinien-der-telekom-523904

Djeffal C (2018) Normative Leitlinien für künstliche Intelligenz in Regierung und öffentlicher Verwaltung. In: Kar MR et al (eds) (Un-)Berechenbar? Algorithmen und Automatisierung in Staat und Gesellschaft. Fraunhofer-Institut für Offene Kommunikationssysteme, Berlin, pp 493–515

Dolderer M (2000) Objektive Grundrechtsgehalte. Duncker & Humblot, Berlin

Ehmann E, Selmayer M (2018) Datenschutz-Grundverordnung, 2nd edn. Beck, München

Eidenmüller H (2017) The rise of robots and the law of humans. ZEuP 25:765–777

Eifert M (2001) Regulierte Selbstregulierung und die lernende Verwaltung. Die Verwaltung, Beiheft 4:137–157

Enquête-Kommission (2018) Künstliche Intelligenz – Gesellschaftliche Verantwortung und wirtschaftliche, soziale und ökologische Potenziale. www.bundestag.de/blob/574748/7c0ecbc8a847bb8019f2045401c1d919/kuenstliche_intelligenz_1-data.pdf

European Commission (2018) Press Release concerning the appointment of a "High-Level Expert Group on Artificial Intelligence" of Dec 17, 2018. ec.europa.eu/digital-single-market/en/high-level-expert-group-artificial-intelligence

European Group on Ethics in Science and New Technologies (2018) Statement on artificial intelligence, robotics and 'Autonomous' systems. ec.europa.eu/research/ege/pdf/ege_ai_statement_2018.pdf

Fischer-Lescano A (2014) Der Kampf um die Internetverfassung: Rechtsfragen des Schutzes globaler Kommunikationsstrukturen von Überwachungsmaßnahmen. JuristenZeitung 69:965–974

Floridi L (ed) (2015) The Onlife Manifesto. Being human in a hyperconnected World. Springer, Cham

Floridi L (2018) Soft Ethics, the governance of the digital and the General Data Protection Regulation. Philos Trans Royal Soc A 376:20180081. https://doi.org/10.1098/rsta.2018.0081

Franzius C (2009) Gewährleistung im Recht: Grundlagen eines europäischen Regelungsmodells öffentlicher Dienstleistungen. Mohr Siebeck, Tübingen

Gasson MN, Koops B-J (2013) Attacking human implants: a new generation of cybercrime. Law Innov Technol 5:248–277

Goodfellow I et al (2016) Deep Learning. MIT Press, Cambridge

Google (2015) The Advisory Council to Google on the right to be forgotten. drive.google.com/file/d/0B1UgZshetMd4cEI3SjlvV0hNbDA/view?pli=1

Google (2018) AI at Google: Our Principles. blog.google/technology/ai/ai-principles/

Harris D et al (eds) (2018) Law of the European Convention on human rights. Oxford University Press, Oxford

Hartung M, Bues M-M, Halbleib G (eds) (2018) Legal Tech: die Digitalisierung des Rechtsmarkts. Beck, München
Hauser M (2015) Das IT-Grundrecht. Schnittfelder und Auswirkung. Duncker & Humblot, Berlin
Hawking S (2018) Kurze Antworten auf große Fragen. Klett-Cotta, Stuttgart
Hildebrandt M (2015) Smart technologies and the End(s) of Law. Novel entanglements of law and technology. Edward Elgar, Cheltenham
Hildebrandt M (2017) Saved by design? The case of legal protection by design. Nanoethics 11:307–311
Himma KW, Tavani HT (eds) (2008) The handbook of information and computer ethics. John Wiley & Sons, Hoboken
Hoeren T, Niehoff M (2018) KI und Datenschutz – Begründungserfordernisse automatisierter Entscheidungen. Rechtswissenschaft 9:47–66
Hoffmann-Riem W (2016) Innovation und Recht – Recht und Innovation. Mohr, Tübingen
Hoffmann-Riem W (2017) Verhaltenssteuerung durch Algorithmen – eine Herausforderung für das Recht. Archiv des öffentlichen Rechts 142:1–43
Hoffmann-Riem W (2018) Rechtliche Rahmenbedingungen für und regulative Herausforderungen durch Big Data. In: Hoffmann-Riem W (ed) Big Data – Regulative Herausforderungen. Nomos, Baden-Baden, pp 11–78
Jakobs J (2016) Vernetzte Gesellschaft. Vernetzte Bedrohungen. Wie uns die künstliche Intelligenz herausfordert. Cividale, Berlin
Just N, Latzer M (2016) Governance by algorithms: reality construction by algorithmic selection on the Internet. Media Cult Soc:1–21
Kaplan J (2016) Artificial intelligence. Oxford University Press, New York
Knebel SV (2018) Die Drittwirkung der Grundrechte und -freiheiten gegenüber Privaten. Regulierungsmöglichkeiten sozialer Netzwerke. Nomos, Baden-Baden
Kolany-Raiser B, Heil R, Orwat C, Hoeren T (2018) Big Data und Gesellschaft. Eine multidisziplinäre Annäherung. Springer, Wiesbaden
Körber T (2017) Konzeptionelle Erfassung digitaler Plattformen und adäquate Regulierungsstrategien. Zeitschrift für Urheber- und Medienrecht 61:93–101
Kroll J (2018) The fallacy of inscrutability. Philos Trans Royal Soc A 376:20180084. https://doi.org/10.1098/rsta.2018.0084
Kulwin N (2018) The Internet Apologizes . . . Even those who designed our digital world are aghast at what they created. A breakdown of what went wrong – from the architects who built it. nymag.com/intelligencer/2018/04/an-apology-for-the-internet-from-the-people-who-built-it.html
Latzer M et al (2016) The economics of algorithmic selection of the internet. In: Bauer JM et al (eds) Handbook on the economics of the internet. Edward Elgar Publishing, Cheltenham, pp 395–425
Leisterer H (2018) Internetsicherheit in Europa. Mohr Siebeck, Tübingen
Lenzen M (2018) Künstliche Intelligenz. Was sie kann & was uns erwartet. Beck, München
Leonelli S (2016) Locating ethics in data science: responsibility and accountability in global and distributed knowledge production systems. Philos Trans Royal Soc A 374:20160122. https://doi.org/10.1098/rsta.2016.0122
Leopoldina (2018) Nationale Akademie der Wissenschaften, acatech. In: Union der deutschen Akademien der Wissenschaften (ed) Stellungnahme: Privatheit in Zeiten der Digitalisierung. Köthen, Berlin
Luch AD (2011) Das neue "IT_Grundrecht" – Grundbedingung einer "Online-Handlungsfreiheit". MMR 14:75–79
Marauhn T (2015) Sicherung grund- und menschenrechtlicher Standards gegenüber neuen Gefährdungen durch private und ausländische Akteure. Veröffentlichungen der Vereinigung der Deutschen Staatsrechtslehrer 74:373–400
Marsch N (2018) Das europäische Datenschutzgrundrecht. Grundlagen – Dimensionen – Verflechtungen. Mohr Siebeck, Tübingen
Martini M, Nink D (2017) Wenn Maschinen entscheiden. NVwZ Extra 10(2017):1–14

Misselhorn C (2018) Grundfragen der Maschinenethik. Reclam, Ditzingen
Müller AC, Guido S (2017) Einführung in Machine Learning mit Python. O'Reilly, Heidelberg
Nemitz P (2018) Constitutional democracy and technology in the age of artificial intelligence. Philos Trans Royal Soc A 376:20180089. https://doi.org/10.1098/rsta.2018.0089
NETmundial (2014) NETmundial Multistakeholder Statement. www.alainet.org/images/NETmundial-Multistakeholder-Document.pdf
Otto P, Gräf E (eds) (2018) 3TH1CS. Die Ethik der digitalen Zeit. Bundeszentrale für politische Bildung, Bonn
Pagallo U (2016) Even angels need the rules. ECAI 285:209–215
Pfliegl R, Seibt C (2017) Die digitale Transformation findet statt. e&i 134:334–339
Pieper F-U (2018) Künstliche Intelligenz: Im Spannungsfeld von Recht und Technik. Zeitschrift zum Innovations- und Technikrecht:9–15
Precht RD (2018) Jäger, Hirten, Kritiker. Eine Utopie für die digitale Gesellschaft, 3rd edn. Goldmann, München
Rath M, Krotz F, Karmasin M (2018) Maschinenethik. Normative Grenzen autonomer Systeme. Springer VS, Wiesbaden
Rolf A (2018) Weltmacht Vereinigte Daten. Die Digitalisierung und Big Data verstehen. Metropolis-Verlag, Marburg
Roßnagel A (2003) Handbuch Datenschutzrecht. Beck, München
Roßnagel A (2017) Das neue Datenschutzrecht. Beck, München
Ruge R (2004) Die Gewährleistungsverantwortung des Staates und der Regulatory State. Duncker & Humblot, Berlin
Russell S, Norvig P (2012) Künstliche Intelligenz. Ein moderner Ansatz, 3rd edn. Pearson, Hallbergmoos
Sattler A (2017) Schutz von maschinengenerierten Daten. In: Sassenberg T, Faber T (eds) Rechtshandbuch Industrie 4.0 und Internet of Things. Beck, München
Saurwein F et al (2015) Governance of algorithms: options and limitations. info 17(6):35–49
Scherer M (2016) Regulating artificial intelligence systems: risks, challenges, competencies, and Strategies. Harv J Law Technol 29:354–400
Schliesky U et al (2014) Schutzpflichten und Drittwirkungen im Internet: Das Grundgesetz im digitalen Zeitalter. Nomos, Baden-Baden
Schmidt J-H (2017) Social media, 2nd edn. Springer SV, Wiesbaden
Schneider I (2018) Bringing the state back in: big data-based capitalism, disruption, and novel regulatory approaches in Europe. In: Saetnan AR et al (eds) The politics of big data. Routledge, London, pp 129–175
Schulze-Fielitz H (2012) Grundmodi der Aufgabenwahrnehmung. In: Hoffmann-Riem W et al (eds) Grundlagen des Verwaltungsrechts. Col. 1, 2nd edn. Beck, München, § 10
Schuppert GF (2003) The Ensuring State. In: Giddens R (ed) The progressive manifesto. New ideas for the centre-left. Polity Press, Cambridge, p 54 et seq
Schuppert GF (2011) Alles Governance oder was? Nomos, Baden-Baden
Simitis S, Hornung G, Spiecker genannt Döhmann I (eds) (2019) Datenschutzrecht. Nomos, Baden Baden
Smith B (2017) The need for a Digital Geneva Convention (posted Feb. 14, 2017). blogs.microsoft.com/on-the-issues/2017/02/14/need-digital-geneva-convention/
Spiecker genannt Döhmann I (2016) Zur Zukunft systemischer Digitalisierung – Erste Gedanken zur Haftungs- und Verantwortungszuschreibung bei informationstechnischen Systemen. CR 32:698–704
Stetter F, Heukrodt-Bauer S (2017) IT-Grundschutzkataloge des BSI — Last oder Mehrwert? Wirtschaftsinformatik & Management 9(4):62–66
Surden H (2014) Machine learning and law. Washington Law Rev 89:87–114
Tegmark M (2017) Lie 3.0: being a human in the age of artificial intelligence. Knopf, New York
Tutt A (2017) An FDA for algorithms. Adm Law Rev 69:83–123

Van den Hoven et al (eds) (2015) Handbook of ethics, values, and technological design. Springer Reference, Wiesbaden

Veale M, Binns R, Edwards L (2018) Algorithms that remember: model inversion attacks and data protection law. Philos Trans Royal Soc A 376:20180083. https://doi.org/10.1098/rsta.2018.0083

Vesting T (2017) Digitale Entgrenzung. In: Lomfeld B (ed) Die Fälle der Gesellschaft. Eine neue Praxis soziologischer Jurisprudenz. Mohr Siebeck, Tübingen, p 81 et seq

Voßkuhle A, Wischmeyer T (2017) The "Neue Verwaltungsrechtswissenschaft" Against the Backdrop of Traditional Administrative Law Scholarship in Germany. In: Rose-Ackerman S, Lindseth PL (eds) Comparative administrative law, 2nd edn. Edward Elgar Publishing, Cheltenham, p 85 et seq

Wehage J-C (2013) Das Grundrecht auf Gewährleistung der Vertraulichkeit und Integrität informationstechnischer Systeme und seine Auswirkungen auf das bürgerliche Recht. Universitätsverlag Göttingen, Göttingen

Welfens JJ et al (2010) Internetwirtschaft 2010. Perspektiven und Auswirkungen. Physica-Verlag, Heidelberg

Winfield AFT, Jirotka M (2018) Ethical governance is essential to building trust in robotics and artificial intelligence systems. Philos Trans Royal Soc A 376:2018008085. https://doi.org/10.1098/rsta.2018.0085

Wischmeyer T (2017) Informationssicherheitsrecht. IT-Sicherheitsgesetzgesetz und NIS-Richtlinie als Elemente eines Ordnungsrechts für die Informationsgesellschaft. Die Verwaltung 50:155–188

Wischmeyer T (2018) Regulierung intelligenter Systeme. Archiv des öffentlichen Rechts 143:1–66

Wu SS, Goodman M (2013) Neural implants and their legal implications. GPSolo 30:68–69

Yeung K (2008) Towards an understanding of regulating by design. In: Brownsword R, Yeung K (eds) Regulating technologies: legal futures, regulation, frames and technological fixes. Hard Publishing, London

Yeung K (2017) Algorithmic regulation: a critical interrogation. Regul Gov 12:505–523

Part I
Foundations of Artificial Intelligence Regulation

Artificial Intelligence and the Fundamental Right to Data Protection: Opening the Door for Technological Innovation and Innovative Protection

Nikolaus Marsch

Contents

1 The Objective of the Chapter: 'Opening the Door' 34
2 Why a Door Needs to Be Opened 35
   2.1 The Traditional Basic Concept of Data Protection Law: Strict Limits for the Use of AI 35
   2.2 Constitutionalisation of a Non-constitutional Regulatory Model: The Right to Informational Self-determination in Germany as a Limitation for AI Under Constitutional Law 38
   2.3 Interim Conclusion 41
3 How the Door Can Be Opened 42
   3.1 Article 8 CFR as an Obligation of the Legislator to Regulate Data Processing, Not as a Right to Informational Self-determination 43
   3.2 Looking at the CJEU: The Window of Opportunity 47
4 No Door Without a Frame: The Legislator and Legal Scholarship Have a Responsibility 48
   4.1 Legislator: Framing AI 48
   4.2 Legal Scholarship: Plea for More Bottom-up Research 50
References 50

Abstract The use of AI—insofar as personal data are processed—poses a challenge to the current data protection law as the underlying concept of data protection law conflicts with AI in many ways. It is debateable whether this has to be the case from the perspective of fundamental rights. If the fundamental data protection right in Article 8 of the EU Charter of Fundamental Rights (CFR) recognised a right to informational self-determination, to make a personal decision on the use of one's personal data, then the limitations of the legislator, at least with regard to the use of AI by public bodies would be strict—i.e. the use of AI would thus be largely prohibited in this regard. However, it seems to be more convincing to interpret Article 8 CFR as a duty of the legislator to regulate the handling of data by the

N. Marsch (✉)
Rechtswissenschaftliche Fakultät, Saarland University, Saarbrücken, Germany
e-mail: nikolaus.marsch@uni-saarland.de

state—and thus also the use of AI—in such a way that fundamental rights are protected as far as possible. A fundamental right to data protection interpreted in this way would be open to technical innovations, because it would enable the legislature to deviate in parts from the traditional basic concept of data protection law and instead to test innovative protective instruments that could even prove to be more effective. At the same time, it does not leave the individual unprotected, since it obliges the legislator, among other things, to base its regulations on a comprehensive concept for the protection of fundamental rights, which must also take account of data processing by private individuals.

1 The Objective of the Chapter: 'Opening the Door'

1 Artificial Intelligence, big data analytics and machine learning challenge the current law, in particular European data protection law. Like all other technical innovations, AI also raises the question to what extent the current rules still fit the changed reality. If the existing law does not provide answers adequate to the problem, new solutions must be found. Many Chapters in this volume already outline such answers in relation to the technological progress associated with AI.[1]

2 It is questionable, however, what room for manoeuvre national and European legislators still have for new answers. Insofar as personal data are processed, the *national* legislators are primarily bound by European data protection law, namely the General Data Protection Regulation (GDPR). These concepts of ordinary law, i.e. flexible limits, are not the subject of the following Chapter.[2] Instead, the objective of the following is to discuss those limits that are stipulated for the national *and* the European legislators by the fundamental rights, in particular by Article 8 of the EU Charter of Fundamental Rights (CFR). For the first time this article enshrines an explicit fundamental data protection right at European level, which not only binds the institutions of the EU but to a great extent also the national legislators (Article 51(1) CFR).[3]

3 The purpose of this Chapter is to open a door for AI, without leaving the citizen unprotected. This is based on the conviction that technological innovations such as AI cannot be answered unquestioningly with existing legal instruments, but that they regularly demand innovative solutions. According to the conventional interpretation of Article 8 CFR the use of AI (at least by public bodies and if personal data are used) is largely prohibited, which makes it necessary to open a door. In the following, it is

---

[1] See especially Hoffmann-Riem, paras 58–74; see Ernst, paras 31–49; see Wischmeyer, paras 43–48; see Krönke, paras 14–62; see Buchholtz, paras 31–45; see Schemmel, paras 35–46; see Djeffal, paras 15–32.

[2] On this topic, see the articles of Hoeren and Niehoff (2018) and Kamarinou et al., inter alia. (2017) as well as Conrad (2018), pp. 542–545.

[3] Comprehensively in this regard, Marsch (2018), pp. 306–344.

initially explained why the conventional interpretation of Article 8 CFR essentially closes the door for AI (Sect. 2) before explaining how the door can be opened by a reinterpretation of the fundamental right (Sect. 3). As every door also requires a frame, the responsibilities of the legislation and legal scholarship shall be outlined in conclusion in order to define this frame, i.e. the limits for the use of AI, more closely (Sect. 4).

2 Why a Door Needs to Be Opened

So let us first address the question *why* a door must be opened. The reason is that according to the traditional basic concept of data protection law, the use of AI is largely prohibited (Sect. 2.1). At least in Germany, this also represents a constitutional problem because the Federal Constitutional Court has developed the fundamental right to informational self-determination with recourse to data protection law and thus constitutionalised the basic concept thereof (Sect. 2.2). Therefore, an analysis of the development of German law is worthwhile because there are signs of a similar development in the jurisprudence of the Court of Justice of the European Union (Sect. 3.2).

2.1 The Traditional Basic Concept of Data Protection Law: Strict Limits for the Use of AI

From the outset, the aim of data protection law was to structure and limit the processing of personal data and to make it transparent for data subjects. For this purpose section 3 of the Federal Data Protection Act (BDSG) of 1977 already included the prohibition principle, according to which the processing of personal data is principally prohibited unless it is justified by a statutory basis or consent. This standard from 1977 already specified that the requirement of a legal basis or consent applies to each individual phase of processing.[4] This concept, to regulate every single data processing, which also governs the GDPR (namely Article 5 and 6), includes the principle of purpose limitation as a 'cornerstone',[5] according to which personal data may only be processed for specified, explicit purposes (Article 5(1)(b) GDPR).[6] This specification of a purpose for the data processing is associated with a number of other regulations and principles such as e.g. the duty to provide

---

[4]See also Albers (2014), pp. 214–215.
[5]Article 29 Data Protection Working Party (2013), p. 4.
[6]On the development of the principle of purpose limitation at international level, namely in the conventions of the European Council and in the OECD guidelines, see Forgó et al. (2017), pp. 22–25.

information pursuant to Article 13 and 14 GDPR and the principle of necessity in Article 5(1)(c) GDPR. Thus, the conventional objective of the current data protection law is to rationalise data processing by only allowing the personal data to be processed on a statutory basis, for specified purposes and in a transparent manner. In the words of Marion Albers: 'The entire approach is guided by the idea that courses of action and decision-making processes could be almost completely foreseen, planned and steered by legal means.'[7] It is obvious that AI conflicts with this objective of data protection law.

6 Thus the use of the current conventional machine-learning-based AI[8] is based on large data volumes that are used for training and testing purposes.[9] These data have been regularly collected for other purposes, which is why their further use as training and testing data for the use of AI must be justified. Article 6(4) GDPR foresees the possibility of a further use for other purposes if the original and the new purpose are compatible. However, many believe that this is an exception from the purpose limitation principle, which must be interpreted in a strict sense and which at least, as a result of its vague wording, does not create the required legal certainty to be able to justify the use of the data as the basis for AI beyond individual cases.[10] More fundamentally, AI therefore comes into conflict with the basic conception of the current data protection law because in many cases even the programmers—particularly in the case of unsupervised learning—are no longer able to comprehend how AI obtains its results and because it is the data analysis itself that uncovers correlations and thus concretizes ultimately the purpose of the processing.[11] The idea of regulating every data processing step by law is diametrically opposed to such a black box.[12] The concern relating to the loss of control reflected in the data protection law faces the partially uncontrolled and uncontrollable in the form of AI.[13]

7 It becomes clear that AI challenges the basic concept of the current data protection law when one attempts to apply the catalogue of the data protection-related principles listed in Article 5 GDPR to AI. AI comes in conflict with almost all

---

[7]Albers (2014), p. 221.
[8]With regard to the term see Rademacher/Wischmeyer, paras 5–6.
[9]Wischmeyer (2018), pp. 10–11, 14–15.
[10]In this regard—however in relation to big data—Spiecker gen. Döhmann (2017), pp. 58–61; less strict—also with a view to big data—Hornung and Herfurth (2018), pp. 168–169; a general pleading for an understanding of the purpose limitation that is open to innovation is made by Grafenstein (2018).
[11]Conrad (2018), pp. 543–544; Hornung (2018), pp. 85–86.
[12]Also indicated in Conrad (2017), p. 743; on intransparency as a central problem, particularly with a view to the subsequent monitoring Martini (2017), pp. 1018–1019; on the connection between purpose limitation and transparency see Forgó et al. (2017), p. 27 and Trute (2018), p. 317; on the controllability as the aim of transparency Rademacher (2017), pp. 376–377.
[13]Boehme-Neßler (2017) does not only apply this finding to data protection law but to law as a whole, which is challenged in its *limiting* effect by the *lowering of the threshold* effect of digitalisation.

principles,[14] i.e. there is at least a certain tension (which does not mean that all of the principles are violated in all cases). What has been said above illustrates the tensions with the principle of transparency,[15] the purpose limitation[16] and the accountability principle (Article 5(2) GDPR). But also the principles of data minimisation (c) and storage limitation (e) ultimately oppose the idea of big data, to collect as many data as possible for the purpose of pattern recognition.[17] In many cases, a big data user could only satisfy these principles by the fact that he/she as a data processor interprets the purpose of the processing extremely broadly and thus renders it ambiguous (e.g. 'for the purpose of pattern recognition'). Such a broad purpose limitation however, would hardly fulfil its actual objective of protection (limitation and transparency of data processing) and would also hardly be considered 'explicit' in the meaning of Article 5(1)(b).[18] Even the principle of accuracy enshrined in Article 5(1)(c) cannot be reconciled with one of the basic ideas of big data, which is to increase the significance predominantly by the sheer mass of data, even if these are messy and even incorrect in parts.[19]

It is therefore ultimately unsurprising that the GDPR does not take the problems raised by AI into account.[20] This is because this would ultimately require a deviation from the basic conception of European data protection law, at least for the field of AI. Attempts at a solution that remain within the existing framework, such as the anonymization of the data, will only be successful in isolated cases but not in general, since, in view of the efficiency of big data analyses, the risk of de-anonymization has also increased.[21]

8

Thus there are now two ways of reacting to the finding that the use of AI is largely incompatible with current European data protection law[22]: In view of the risks and dangers associated with the use of AI, one may consider this to be correct and dispute the requirement for legislative action.[23] Or if one interprets AI as a challenge to a concept of data protection law that largely stems from the 1970s and therefore no

9

---

[14] The relationship with the principles of integrity and confidentiality enshrined in Article 5 (1) lit. f GDPR is mostly free of conflict.

[15] In this regard see in detail Wischmeyer, paras 1–7.

[16] Very critical in respect of the purpose specification and use limitation principles Cate et al. (2014), p. 11.

[17] Trute and Broemel (2016), p. 53 and Hornung (2018), p. 86, correctly stress that without a determination of the purpose there is also no reference point for the underlying requirement of data minimisation and storage limitation.

[18] In this regard see Forgó et al. (2017), pp. 27–28; in detail on the precision of the purpose limitation as a central problem Grafenstein (2018), pp. 231–295.

[19] With regard to the two characteristics big and messy, see Mayer-Schönberger and Cukier (2013), chapter 2 and 3.

[20] In this respect, see also Hoeren and Niehoff (2018), p. 58.

[21] In this respect Altman et al. (2018), pp. 41–42 and Hoffmann-Riem (2018), p. 56.

[22] Accordingly, Hoffmann-Riem (2018), pp. 45–46.

[23] A tendency to this direction is found in Hornung (2018), p. 87.

longer represents an adequate legal response to the technological progress.[24] However, if one were to take the second position and argue in favour of a reform of data protection law that reasonably controls and limits the use of AI by innovative rules, for which there is much to be said,[25] then the question is raised to what extent the data protection law can still be changed. In other words: which parts of data protection law are mandatory under fundamental rights and therefore not subject to amendment by the legislator? Here we will first take a look at the historically older German right to informational self-determination (Sect. 2.2) before a distinguishing concept of the fundamental right to data protection in Article 8 CFR, which is open to innovation, is developed (Sect. 3).

2.2 Constitutionalisation of a Non-constitutional Regulatory Model: The Right to Informational Self-determination in Germany as a Limitation for AI Under Constitutional Law

Innovation of the Fundamental Rights by Using a Regulatory Model of Ordinary Law

10 In its famous *census judgement*, the German Federal Constitutional Court has deduced a right to informational self-determination from the constitutional general right of personality. The fundamental right to informational self-determination warrants 'the capacity of the individual to determine the disclosure and use of his personal data.'[26] The court substantiated the innovation of the fundamental right derived from the Basic Law[27] as follows:

> Those who cannot know with sufficient certainty which information about them is known in certain parts of their social environment, and who have no way of assessing the knowledge of potential communication partners, can be substantially inhibited in their freedom to make plans or decisions out of their own determination. The right to informational self-determination would not be compatible with a social order and a legal system that would

---

[24]For example Trute and Broemel (2016), p. 50; principally in relation to the need for reform triggered by the algorithmisation Hoffmann-Riem (2018), pp. 13–14.

[25]In this direction for example also Conrad (2017), p. 744 and Hoffmann-Riem (2018), pp. 58–59; Trute (2018), p. 323, also stresses that the employment of a simple regulatory pattern is proscribed here.

[26]German (Federal) Constitutional Court 1 BvR 209, 269, 362, 420, 440, 484/83 'Census Judgment' (15 December 1983) para 155.

[27]Comprehensively on the Fundamental Right Innovations of German Constitutional Law Hornung (2015).

permit such a social order where citizens could no longer identify what is known about them by whom, at what time and on which occasion.[28]

Therefore, according to the court, any processing of personal data by a public body requires

> a (constitutional) statutory basis, the requirements and the scope of the limitations of which are clear and apparent to the citizen, and which thereby correspond to the requirement of a state under the rule of law to provide clarity of legal rules.[29]

11

The Federal Constitutional Court has thereby constitutionalised the historically older regulatory model of the prohibition principle of data protection laws applicable to each phase of data processing.[30] Since, as previously demonstrated, this regulatory model, which has now been enshrined in the fundamental rights, is difficult to reconcile at least with the use of AI by state authorities, at first glance there is much to suggest that it is also largely unconstitutional. However, this conclusion is challenged under a closer inspection of the theoretical basis of the right to informational self-determination.

12

Distinction Between the Legal Construction and the Theoretical Concept: The Right to Informational Self-determination as an Instrumental Preemptive Protection

Over the past 15 years it has been established in the German literature on fundamental rights that the right to informational self-determination must not be misinterpreted as a property right that gives each individual the right to dispose of personal data concerning him or her.[31] In the judgment on the national census, the Federal Constitutional Court already clarified that 'the individual does not have a right in the sense of an absolute, illimitable control over "his" data (quotation marks in the original)'[32] and that 'information, including personal information, represents a reflection of social reality, which cannot be exclusively allocated to the data subject.'[33] *Gabriele Britz* and *Ralf Poscher*, in particular, have established that the right to informational self-determination, as a mere *instrumental* fundamental right, first and foremost has the purpose to protect *other* fundamental rights, the violation of

13

---

[28] German (Federal) Constitutional Court 1 BvR 209, 269, 362, 420, 440, 484/83 'Census Judgment' (15 December 1983) para 154.
[29] German (Federal) Constitutional Court 1 BvR 209, 269, 362, 420, 440, 484/83 'Census Judgment' (15 December 1983) para 157.
[30] Albers (2014), p. 215.
[31] See for example Albers (2014), p. 225; Britz (2010), pp. 566–568; Trute (2003), paras 16–24; Hoffmann-Riem (1998), pp. 519–521.
[32] German (Federal) Constitutional Court 1 BvR 209, 269, 362, 420, 440, 484/83 'Census Judgment' (15 December 1983) para 156.
[33] German (Federal) Constitutional Court 1 BvR 209, 269, 362, 420, 440, 484/83 'Census Judgment' (15 December 1983) para 156.

which should already be prevented *in advance* by the regulation of data processing.[34] *Marion Albers*, who objects to an individualistic interpretation of the right to informational self-determination,[35] goes one step further and stresses that the data protection law protects a whole bundle of interests, which cannot be understood as a uniform legally protected good.[36]

14 In any case the decisive factor for the understanding of the right to informational self-determination is that a distinction must be made between the *legal construction* and the *theoretical concept* underlying the fundamental right.[37] Accordingly, the *construction* of the right to informational self-determination, according to which the processing of personal data by the state constitutes an interference into the right of the individual to determine the processing himself, is not an end in itself[38] but only a means for the purpose of protecting other fundamental rights. *The theoretical concept* lies in this instrumental effect of the right to informational self-determination. German jurisprudence has taken a long time to elaborate on this fundamental differentiation, which may also have been caused by the ambiguous description of the fundamental right by the Federal Constitutional Court as a right to *informational self-determination* and that to date the court has not issued a clear statement on the theoretical principles of the fundamental right. However, in the most recent jurisprudence it is becoming increasingly clear that the Federal Constitutional Court also does not interpret the right to informational self-determination as being strictly individualistic but rather ascribes to it a strong supra-individualistic dimension.

Supra-individualistic Elements in the Jurisprudence of the Federal Constitutional Law

15 This becomes particularly clear in the first decision of the Federal Constitutional Court on Automatic Number Plate Recognition from 2008.[39] The police had set up cameras in two German states (*Länder*), which they used to record the number plates of passing motor vehicles. The recorded number plates were subsequently automatically cross checked with a file containing vehicles which the police were searching for. If this comparison produced a 'hit', this was reported to the police. In all other cases in which the relevant number plate was not included in the search inventory,

---

[34]Britz (2010); Poscher (2012). Oostveen and Irion (2018) discuss an 'enabling right'.
[35]Comprehensively Albers (2005).
[36]In brief Albers (2014), p. 227.
[37]Comprehensively in this regard Marsch (2018), pp. 98–107.
[38]Poscher (2017) succinctly discusses a 'no-right theory'.
[39]German (Federal) Constitutional Court 1 BvR 2074/05, 1254/07 'Automatic Number Plate Recognition Judgment 1' (11 March 2008).

the number plate was automatically erased directly after it was cross checked. This process took no more than a second—depending on the system used.[40]

16   The Federal Constitutional Court initially establishes in its decision that the fundamental right is only infringed with where there are 'hits'.[41] If the number plate, which does not directly identify the keeper or the driver, is erased immediately after it is cross checked without the personal reference being established, then in the opinion of the court these cases do not constitute an infringement of the right to informational self-determination.[42] This initially means that most number plates will be recorded and cross-checked against the search inventory, without this constituting an infringement of the fundamental right. Nevertheless, under the aspect of proportionality, the court has stressed for the—few—hits that the recording of number plates concerns everyone driving past the control point and that they could feel that they are under surveillance, which could result in a chilling effect. Thus, in the proportionality test, the court also draws upon the non-hits as an argument, which it does not consider to be an infringement of the fundamental rights. This is not a logical break but the recognition by the court that the right to informational self-determination must not be interpreted in a purely individualistic sense but that it contains a strong supra-individual dimension resulting in objective requirements for the handling of information by the state.[43]

2.3   Interim Conclusion

17   Thus, with the right to informational self-determination, the Federal Constitutional Court has constitutionalised the historically older regulatory model of statutory data protection law. Therefore, in the same way as for the data protection law, the finding of *Marion Albers* established with regard to data protection processes also applies to the right to informational self-determination. 'The idea that these processes could be almost completely foreseen, planned and steered by legal means has turned out to be too simple.'[44] The regulatory model dating back to the 1970s and thus to the age of mainframe computers, which was adopted by the Federal Constitutional Court, may have fulfilled its purpose at that time. However, in the age of smart phones,

---

[40]On more modern examples of the use of intelligent video surveillance, see Rademacher, paras 3–5.
[41]German (Federal) Constitutional Court 1 BvR 2074/05, 1254/07 'Automatic Number Plate Recognition Judgment 1' (11 March 2008) paras 69–74.
[42]German (Federal) Constitutional Court 1 BvR 2074/05, 1254/07 'Automatic Number Plate Recognition Judgment' (11 March 2008) para 68; this is now explicitly overridden by a recent judgement of the German (Federal) Constitutional Court 1 BvR 142/15 'Automatic Number Plate Recognition Judgment 2' (18 December 2018) paras 41–53, in which the Court decides that there is also an infringement of the right of informational self-determination, when there is no hit.
[43]Comprehensively in this regard, Marsch (2018), pp. 116–124.
[44]Albers (2014), p. 232.

ubiquitous computing, the Internet of things and the increased use of AI, it is proving to be outdated, detrimental to innovation and additionally barely suitable to ensure adequate protection of the individual. Whether the further development and the strengthening of supra-individualistic elements can remedy this seems questionable. If one realizes that the legal construction of the right to informational self-determination must be distinguished from the underlying theoretical concept and therefore also from its protective goals then this raises the question whether the right to informational self-determination as a construct requires an update. The starting point for this would have to be the protective purposes—thus the theoretical concept—not the legal construction, which is historically contingent. Using the outdated construction and the conventional regulatory model of data protection law to respond to the progress associated with AI would be as unsatisfactory as subjecting modern aviation to the rules of road traffic by arguing that in both cases it is traffic and the aim is to protect life and limb.

18   This poses a problem to the Federal Constitutional Court. It is one thing to infer innovative fundamental rights from the constitutional text with a reference to the idea of a living constitution. It is entirely another, however, to fundamentally question one's own innovations in fundamental rights and to construct them anew. However, a constitution must not only be adaptable with regard to the question of *whether* it provides protection against new threats; it must also be adaptable with regard to *how* it provides the required protection. Even if the constitutional courts shy away from changes in the jurisprudence for good reasons, the Federal Constitutional Court will have to answer the question in the coming years as to how the right to informational self-determination must be developed further in view of the technological progress. The CJEU has it a little easier in this regard—as will be demonstrated in the following section.

3   How the Door Can Be Opened

19   Thus, while the fundamental right, which was concretized by the Federal Constitutional Court based on the regulatory model of data protection law more than 35 years ago, currently largely prohibits the use of AI by government bodies, the CJEU has the chance that Article 8 CFR, an innovative fundamental right, which has only been in force since 2009, forms the standard of review of its jurisprudence. This proves to be more flexible and more open to innovation than the right to informational self-determination of the Basic Law and thus offers a more up-to-date protection against the threats to the fundamental rights by the new technologies (Sect. 3.1). However, it is anticipated that in the long term the CJEU may interpret Article 8 CFR in line with the conventional regulatory model of data protection law and thus in line with the outdated right to informational self-determination of the Basic Law, so the window of opportunity for a more modern interpretation of Article 8 CFR could be closed soon (Sect. 3.2).

3.1 Article 8 CFR as an Obligation of the Legislator to Regulate Data Processing, Not as a Right to Informational Self-determination[45]

However, how must Article 8 CFR, which is decisive for the use of AI, be interpreted? Contrary to the opinion of most authors in Germany,[46] there is much to oppose the interpretation of the same as a European 'right to informational self-determination'. To be precise, the wording and the history of legislation (section 'Wording and History of Legislation'), the structure of Article 8 CFR (section 'Structure') and the criticism of the purely individualistic understanding of the German right to informational self-determination (section 'Article 8 as a Modern Fundamental Right to Data Protection: Combination of Openness to Innovation and Effective Protection') already outlined above, speak against the assumption of such a legal transplant.

Wording and History of Legislation

Let us first discuss the wording of Article 8 CFR. It states relatively openly that 'everyone has the right to the protection of personal data concerning him or her.' While the wording does not say much at this point, it has a certain significance in the context of the history of its origin. For in the Convention on Fundamental Rights—after the draft committee had initially made a proposal largely corresponding to the current version—a proposal by the German Convention member *Jürgen Meyer* had meanwhile been discussed. With the support of the German President of the European Convention, *Roman Herzog,* he had proposed to use the following wording: 'Everyone has the right to determine for himself whether his personal data may be disclosed and how they may be used.'[47] This literal adoption of the German right to informational self-determination, however, did not meet with the approval of the Convention, in fact it was heavily criticised, as many Convention members feared an unacceptably severe impairment of government action. The Convention on Fundamental Rights therefore returned to its original wording, according to which individuals have a *right to protection* of personal data concerning him or her. The wording and the history of the Convention's origin therefore do not indicate that Article 8 CFR establishes a right to informational self-determination based on the German model.

---

[45]The following section is based on considerations, which I made on Article 8 CFR in the central chapter of my habilitation thesis, Marsch (2018), chapter 3.

[46]This is explicitly addressed in Bernsdorff (2014), n° 13–14; Kingreen (2016), n° 1., for example.

[47]In detail and with evidence of the history of origin Marsch (2018), pp. 74–75.

Structure

22 This opinion is reinforced by the internal structure of Article 8, namely by the subdivision of the paragraphs 1 and 2. The latter states that

> such data must be processed fairly for specified purposes and on the basis of the consent of the person concerned or some other legitimate basis laid down by law.

23 The German literature predominantly views this as a special limitation clause,[48] which is intended to concretise the general limitation clause of Article 52(1) CFR, without displacing it.[49] However, this interpretation is not convincing because on the one hand it is peculiar that Article 8(2) repeats the requirement of a legal basis, which is also enshrined in Article 52(1). On the other hand, the fundamental rights of the data subject are precisely not infringed in the event of consent and therefore there is no other limitation, which also gives rise to doubts about the theory that Article 8(2) is a limitation clause. However, if Article 8(2) does not contain a limitation clause, what does it actually regulate? This question cannot be answered in isolation, without including paragraph 1.

24 In this regard *González Fuster* and *Gutwirth*[50] provide a first answer. In their lucid article they distinguish between two different understandings of the fundamental right to data protection in Article 8 CFR: The understanding, which is held in the German literature almost without exception, according to which paragraph 1 purportedly contains a right to informational self-determination and paragraph 2 contains a limitation clause, is described by them as a *prohibitive concept*. According to this concept the processing of personal data is prohibited from the outset (paragraph 1) unless it is permitted on the basis of a relevant statutory basis in accordance with paragraph 2 or consent (as an exception). The authors contrast this *prohibitive* concept with a *permissive or regulatory* concept. Accordingly, data processing does not generally constitute an infringement of fundamental rights; it is in principle admissible, however, it must take the requirements of paragraph 2 into consideration. According to this understanding, the actual core of the guarantee of the fundamental rights lies in paragraph 2.[51] In this way paragraph 2 acquires a meaning that it would not have in the prohibitive concept. However, if the core of the guaranteed fundamental rights is to be located in paragraph 2 of Article 8 CFR, what is the significance of paragraph 1 of this provision?

---

[48]For example Siemen (2006), pp. 283–284; Cornils (2015), p. 27.
[49]Cornils (2014), n° 46–47; Kingreen (2016), n° 14.
[50]González Fuster and Gutwirth (2013), pp. 532–533.
[51]In this regard Marsch (2018), pp. 137–139.

Article 8 as a Modern Fundamental Right to Data Protection: Combination of Openness to Innovation and Effective Protection

The first two paragraphs of Article 8 CFR can be reconciled by interpreting paragraph 1 as a mandate to the legislator to regulate the processing of personal data so that the fundamental rights and interests of the citizens are adequately protected. The fundamental right to data protection thus requires the legislators in paragraph 1 to enact rules that are adequate to fundamental rights and contains specified requirements in paragraph 2, which much be taken into consideration in the legislation. However, it is permitted to deviate from these requirements while observing the principle of proportionality if an adequate protection of the fundamental rights is ensured by other protective mechanisms.[52] Such an understanding also has the advantage that it can apply to the entire paragraph 2 and not just to the first sentence. This is because the second sentence of paragraph 2 contains two central rights of data protection law, the right of access and the right to rectification, which have since ever been limited by the legislator in particular constellations and must undisputedly be limited.[53] This interpretation is also confirmed by the explanations related to the Charter, which pursuant to Article 52(7) CFR must be taken into account by the courts when interpreting the Charter and in which it is stated that

> the above-mentioned Directive [95/46/EC] and Regulation [45/2001] contains *conditions and limitations* for the exercise of the right to the protection of personal data (highlighted by the author).

In contrast to the right to informational self-determination of the Basic Law, a fundamental right to data protection interpreted in this way is more open to innovation, since it does not force the continuation of outdated data protection concepts but enables the legislator to respond to the technological progress with new regulatory concepts that are suitable for the problem. Simultaneously, it obligates the legislator to take action and in this way it potentially allows a more effective protection than previous concepts could provide. This normative openness also corresponds to the multitude of very different interests that data protection law aims to protect. The basic data protection law therefore designates the processing of personal data as an issue requiring attention from a fundamental rights perspective. Simultaneously, it does not exempt the legislator from any restrictions but, for example, demands that the legislator bases its regulatory considerations on a concept (in this regard Sect. 4.1).

However, despite the limitations derived from Article 8 and the principle of proportionality which governs the legislator in its design, a fundamental right to data protection interpreted in this way could lead to the anticipation that it does not guarantee a robust protection of the fundamental rights. However, there is no reason for such fears. In addition to the basic data protection right in Article 8 CFR, Article

---

[52]Comprehensively in this regard, Marsch (2018), pp. 190–196.
[53]See Article 23 GDPR and Article 13 Data Protection Directive 95/46/EC.

7 of the Charter contains a right to the protection of a private life. Pursuant to the coherence clause in Article 52(3) CFR, this right must be interpreted in accordance with Article 8 ECHR, whereby the case law of the ECHR must also be taken into account.[54] The right to respect for one's private life under Article 8 ECHR also infers an—albeit limited—right to the protection of personal data: Accordingly, the processing of data by public bodies shall constitute an infringement of Article 8 ECHR, if the data concern the private life of individuals[55] or if they have been 'systematically collected'—in particular by the police or intelligence services.[56] This jurisprudence of the ECtHR was widely accepted by the CJEU, even before the Charter of Fundamental Rights became binding.[57] Since the Charter became binding, the CJEU has created a 'fundamental rights combination' from Articles 7 and 8 of the CFR, which has acted as a counterpart to the ECtHR's data protection case law. When the CJEU refers to the 'right to respect for private life with regard to the processing of personal data, recognised by Articles 7 and 8 of the Charter'[58] since the decision in *Schecke* in established case-law, it thus establishes coherence with the ECHR and the ECtHR. For data processing operations which have a particularly high risk potential and which are therefore regarded by the ECtHR as an infringement of Article 8 ECHR, Article 8 CFR in conjunction with Article 7 CFR is reinforced to a prohibitive right in the terminology of *González Fuster* and *Gutwirth*.

The interpretation of the fundamental right to data protection presented here thus combines the concepts identified by the two authors by interpreting Article 8 (1) CFR, as a duty of the legislator, to enact and structure data protection regulations in a way that is compatible with fundamental rights taking into account the principles enshrined in paragraph 2. In addition to this flexible and innovative protection, the fundamental rights combination of the Articles 7 and 8 provides more robust but also less flexible protection for data processing operations with a particularly close link to private life or systematic data processing by the police and secret services.

---

[54]Naumann (2008), pp. 425–426.

[55]ECtHR 9248/1 'Leander/Sweden' (26 March 1987) para 48, ECtHR 27798/95 'Amann/Switzerland' (16 February 2000) paras 66–67.

[56]ECtHR 28341/95 'Rotaru/Romania' (4 May 2000) para 43, ECtHR 44787/98 'P. G. and J. H./ United Kingdom' (25 September 2001) para 57. Contrary to the assumption of some authors, the ECtHR did not derive however from the right to privacy a general right to informational self-determination, since it has not yet judged in any decision that *without exception every* processing of personal data constitutes an encroachment on Article 8 ECHR, see here the analysis of the case-law of the ECtHR at Marsch (2018), pp. 8–17.

[57]See in particular the decision of the CJEU C-465/00 in conjunction with C-138/01 and C-139/01 'ORF' (20 May 2003).

[58]CJEU C-92/09 in conjunction with C-93/09 'Schecke' (9 November 2010) para 53, CJEU C-468/10 in conjunction with C-469/10 'ASNEF' (24 November 2011) para 42, CJEU C-291/12 'Schwarz' (17 October 2013) para 46.

3.2 Looking at the CJEU: The Window of Opportunity

However, looking at the more recent jurisprudence of the CJEU, it raises the concern that the CJEU intends to deduce a comprehensive right to informational self-determination based on the German model from the Charter of Fundamental Rights. Initially, the Court of Justice had been hesitant to stipulate the exact content of Article 8(1) and the relationship between Article 8(2) and Article 52(1).[59] For example, in the decision in *Schecke* it had initially applied the combined fundamental right that it had created from Article 7 and 8 CFR, in order to establish coherence with the ECtHR jurisprudence and without commenting on whether it considers every processing of personal data to be an infringement of fundamental rights. In the decision in *Schwarz,* the Court then cautiously states in reference to Articles 7 and 8 CFR that

> it follows from a joint reading of those articles that, *as a general rule*, any processing of personal data by a third party *may* constitute a threat to those rights (highlighted by the author).[60]

Only in the decision in *Digital Rights Ireland* does the CJEU perceive the Directive on the Retention of Data to be

> an interference with the fundamental right to the protection of personal data guaranteed by Article 8 of the Charter because it provides for the processing of personal data.[61]

However, in the following examination as to whether the infringement of fundamental rights is justified, Article 7 CFR represents the focal point, whereas Article 8 largely appears as a fundamental right containing a technical form of data protection.[62] In the decision in *Google Spain* and in *Schrems* once again the CJEU does not differentiate between Article 7 and 8 CFR, but refers to them cumulatively as standard of review[63]; additionally Article 7 CFR is in the forefront of the decision in *Schrems*.[64] In its opinion on the *EU-Canada PNR Agreement*, the CJEU appears to wish to consolidate its case law towards a right to informational self-determination, by stating that

> those operations also constitute an interference with the fundamental right to the protection of personal data guaranteed in Article 8 of the Charter since they constitute the processing of personal data.[65]

---

[59]With regard to the following, see in detail Marsch (2018), pp. 132–134 and 136–137.
[60]CJEU C-291/12 'Schwarz' (17 October 2013) para 25.
[61]CJEU C-293/12 in conjunction with C-594/12 'Digital Rights Ireland' (8 April 2014) para 36.
[62]CJEU C-293/12 in conjunction with C-594/12 'Digital Rights Ireland' (8 April 2014) paras 66–68.
[63]CJEU C-131/12 'Google Spain' (13 May 2014) paras 38, 69, 80, CJEU C-362/14 'Schrems' (6 October 2015) para 91.
[64]CJEU C-362/14 'Schrems' (6 October 2015) paras 92–94.
[65]CJEU Opinion 1/15 'EU-Canada PNR agreement' (26 July 2017) para 126.

32   The window of opportunity, during which the CJEU could be convinced not to give away the innovation potential that is inherent in Article 8 CFR, is thus at risk of slowly closing.

4 No Door Without a Frame: The Legislator and Legal Scholarship Have a Responsibility

33   In order to convince the CJEU that an alternative understanding of Article 8 CFR is not only innovative for the benefit of the data processors, but also offers a more innovative protection to the data subjects, the legislators and academics should therefore develop proposals as quickly as possible to demonstrate what this kind of protection could look like. This is because the interpretation of Article 8 CFR presented here as an obligation to regulate is not designed to provide *less* protection, but rather to open the door for the legislator to be able to provide a *different form* of protection. The frame of this door, i.e. in the first step the type and nature of protection, is determined by the legislator, however, the adequacy thereof can be reviewed by the courts and in particular by the CJEU in a second step and, if necessary, it can be declared inadequate.

4.1 Legislator: Framing AI

34   Therefore, the first and foremost duty of the legislator is to regulate and limit the use of AI. Insofar as personal data are used, the structural principles of Article 8(2) CFR provide guidelines for regulation. These are primarily aimed at the structuring, limitation and transparency of data processing and thus ultimately at securing the confidence of the data subjects.[66] However, this does not mean that their application is absolute. Rather, they may be deviated from in the public interest if and to the extent that a consideration makes this appear necessary and appropriate, in particular because other security mechanisms ensure adequate protection.

35   The GDPR already contains a whole series of such general security instruments, which could be adapted and tailored to the use of AI in special regulations. Principles such as data protection by design (Article 25 GDPR), but also procedural rules such as the data protection impact assessment (Article 35 GDPR) and the designation of data protection officers (Article 37–39 GDPR) as well as self-regulatory mechanisms such as the development of approved codes of conduct by data processing companies (Article 40–41 GDPR) and the establishment of data protection certification mechanisms and of data protection seals and marks (Article 42–43 GDPR), can serve as models for specific AI regulations. Furthermore, a number of other instruments

---

[66]With regard to the latter, see Eichenhofer (2016).

are discussed which can ensure the use of AI to protect fundamental rights, such as the establishment of an internal or external ethics board or committee,[67] the assurance of compliance by technical means[68] such as supervision algorithms[69] and the development of explainable AI (XAI) as well as the enactment of adequate liability rules by the legislator.[70] Such security instruments could then also justify exceptions based on the model of exceptions for public and private research (Article 6(1)(c) and Article 6(4) in conjunction with Article 5(1)(a) GDPR).

The list of proposals for regulatory instruments is by no means exhaustive, but could even be extended. With regard to the legislator, however, it is not the quantity of regulatory instruments that is important, but that they fit into a legislative concept that promises adequate protection of fundamental rights. This concept also represents the starting point for judicial control which, as in the decision of the CJEU in *Schecke*, is linked to the reasons of the respective legal act (see Article 296 (2) TFEU). In this decision, the CJEU had first begun to examine the proportionality of the EU regulation on the publication of the names of recipients of agricultural subsidies.[71] Within that examination, however, the Court of Justice subsequently moves from a substantive examination to a procedural examination and declares the regulation null and void essentially on the grounds that

36

> it does not appear that the Council and the Commission sought to strike such a balance between the European Union's interest in guaranteeing the transparency of its acts and ensuring the best use of public funds, on the one hand, and the fundamental rights enshrined in Articles 7 and 8 of the Charter, on the other.[72]

A duty of the legislator to draw up a comprehensive concept and to include it (at least partly) in the reasoning of the legal act is suitable to compensate the rather weak material ties, which follow from Article 8 CFR, procedurally.[73] Additionally, the legislative concept—as demanded by *Wolfgang Hoffmann-Riem*[74]—can take greater account of the outcome and impact of a regulation of the use of AI.

37

Finally, the approach presented here has the advantage that the limitations of the use of AI do not have to be derived from the Charter of Fundamental Rights in an abstract form, which is likely to result in inadequately fitting solutions, but that it is the task of the legislator to develop solutions adapted to the specific subject area.

38

---

[67]In accordance with the Guidelines on the Protection of Natural Persons in the Processing of Personal Data in a world of big data of Council of Europe's Consultative Committee of Convention 108 (2017), n° 1.3 and the proposal of the UK Information Commissioner's Office (2017), n° 176–178, 196 (see also with regard to this proposal Butterworth 2018).

[68]Kroll et al. (2017).

[69]Martini (2017), p. 1022; Rost (2018), p. 561.

[70]In this regard Martini (2017), pp. 1024–1025.

[71]CJEU C-92/09 in conjunction with C-93/09 'Schecke' (9 November 2010) para 72 et seqq.

[72]CJEU C-92/09 in conjunction with C-93/09 'Schecke' (9 November 2010) para 80; see also paras 81–83.

[73]Comprehensively in this regard, Marsch (2018), pp. 196–203.

[74]See Hoffmann-Riem, para 7.

This is because, according to *Marion Albers*, data protection law must be a 'reflexive law' which, through instruments such as experimental legislation, ensures that learning processes and advancements remain possible.[75] Legal scholarship in particular can and must support this process.

4.2 Legal Scholarship: Plea for More Bottom-up Research

39   The legal scholarship have previously discussed the topic of AI with increasing intensity. The majority of contributions have initially approached AI in an abstract way, attempting to describe problems and to outline legal solutions in a generalized manner. As important as this is in the first phase of scientific penetration of a new topic, also in order to initially collect potential perspectives and to access problems, a bottom-up approach, which also characterizes a number of contributions in this volume, will be required in the future.[76] Based on the (possible) use of AI in specific areas, a second phase of the legal analysis of AI should intensively research which regulatory instruments offer an adequate level of protection of fundamental rights in specific areas such as health care.[77] The findings to be gained in the individual fields of application of AI would then have to be organized in a third phase and could ultimately be integrated into a scientifically sound regulatory proposal for a general part of an AI framework.[78]

References

Albers M (2005) Informationelle Selbstbestimmung. Nomos, Baden-Baden
Albers M (2014) Realizing the complexity of data protection. In: Gutwirth S, Leenes R, De Hert P (eds) Reloading data protection: multidisciplinary insights and contemporary challenges. Springer, Dordrecht, Heidelberg, London, New York, pp 213–235
Altman M, Wood A, O'Brien DR, Gasser U (2018) Practical approaches to big data privacy over time. Int Data Priv Law 8:29–51
Article 29 Data Protection Working Party (2013) Opinion 03/2013 on purpose limitation (2.4.2013). http://ec.europa.eu/justice/article-29/documentation/opinion-recommendation/files/2013/wp203_en.pdf. Accessed 18 Sept 2018
Bernsdorff N (2014) Art. 8. In: Meyer J (ed) Charta der Grundrechte der Europäischen Union, 4th edn. Nomos, Baden-Baden
Boehme-Neßler V (2017) Die Macht der Algorithmen und die Ohnmacht des Rechts. Neue Juristische Wochenschrift 70:3031–3037

---

[75] Albers (2014), p. 232.
[76] See in particular the contributions in part II 'Governance of and through AI'.
[77] Especially for this see Molnár-Gábor and see Jabri.
[78] The development of the ReNEUAL model rules on EU administrative procedure could be exemplary in this respect, see Craig et al. (2017).

Britz G (2010) Informationelle Selbstbestimmung zwischen rechtswissenschaftlicher Grundsatzkritik und Beharren des Bundesverfassungsgerichts. In: Hoffmann-Riem W (ed) Offene Rechtswissenschaft: Ausgewählte Schriften von Wolfgang Hoffmann-Riem mit begleitenden Analysen. Mohr Siebeck, Tübingen, pp 561–596

Butterworth M (2018) The ICO and artificial intelligence: the role of fairness in the GDPR framework. Comput Law Secur Rev 34:257–268

Cate FH, Cullen P, Mayer-Schönberger V (2014) Data protection principles for the 21st century: revising the 1980 OECD guidelines. https://www.oii.ox.ac.uk/archive/downloads/publications/Data_Protection_Principles_for_the_21st_Century.pdf

Conrad CS (2017) Künstliche Intelligenz — Die Risiken für den Datenschutz. Datenschutz und Datensicherheit 41:740–744

Conrad CS (2018) Kann die Künstliche Intelligenz den Menschen entschlüsseln? — Neue Forderungen zum Datenschutz. Datenschutz und Datensicherheit 42:541–546

Cornils M (2014) Schrankendogmatik. In: Grabenwarter C (ed) Enzyklopädie Europarecht II: Europäischer Grundrechtsschutz. Nomos, Baden-Baden, § 5

Cornils M (2015) Der grundrechtliche Rahmen für ein (trans-)nationales Datenschutzrecht im digitalen Zeitalter. In: Hain K-E, Peifer K-N (eds) Datenschutz im digitalen Zeitalter – global, europäisch, national: Vortragsveranstaltung des Instituts für Rundfunkrecht an der Universität zu Köln vom 16. Mai 2014. Beck, München, pp 11–50

Council of Europe's Consultative Committee of Convention 108 (2017) Guidelines on the protection of individuals with regard to the processing of personal data in a world of Big Data. https://rm.coe.int/CoERMPublicCommonSearchServices/DisplayDCTMContent?documentId=09000016806ebe7a

Craig PP, Hofmann H, Schneider J-P, Ziller J (eds) (2017) ReNEUAL model rules on EU administrative procedure. Oxford University Press, Oxford, New York, NY

Eichenhofer J (2016) Privatheit im Internet als Vertrauensschutz: Eine Neukonstruktion der Europäischen Grundrechte auf Privatleben und Datenschutz. Der Staat 55:41–67

Forgó N, Hänold S, Schütze B (2017) The principle of purpose limitation and big data. In: Corrales M, Fenwick M, Forgó N (eds) New technology, big data and the law, vol 17. Springer, Singapore, pp 17–42

González Fuster G, Gutwirth S (2013) Opening up personal data protection: a conceptual controversy. Comput Law Secur Rev 29:531–539

Grafenstein M (2018) The principle of purpose limitation in data protection laws: the risk-based approach, principles, and private standards as elements for regulating innovation. Nomos, Baden-Baden

Hoeren T, Niehoff M (2018) KI und Datenschutz – Begründungserfordernisse automatisierter Entscheidungen. RW 9:47–66

Hoffmann-Riem W (1998) Informationelle Selbstbestimmung in der Informationsgesellschaft: Auf dem Wege zu einem neuen Konzept des Datenschutzes. Archiv des öffentlichen Rechts 123:513–540

Hoffmann-Riem W (2018) Rechtliche Rahmenbedingungen für und regulative Herausforderungen durch Big Data. In: Hoffmann-Riem W (ed) Big Data - Regulative Herausforderungen. Nomos, Baden-Baden, pp 9–78

Hornung G (2015) Grundrechtsinnovationen. Mohr Siebeck, Tübingen

Hornung G (2018) Erosion traditioneller Prinzipien des Datenschutzrechts durch Big Data. In: Hoffmann-Riem W (ed) Big Data - Regulative Herausforderungen. Nomos, Baden-Baden, pp 79–98

Hornung G, Herfurth C (2018) Datenschutz bei Big Data: Rechtliche und politische Implikationen. In: König C, Schröder J, Wiegand E (eds) Big Data: Chancen, Risiken, Entwicklungstendenzen. Springer VS, Wiesbaden, pp 149–183

Information Commissioner's Office (2017) Big data, artificial intelligence, machine learning and data protection. https://ico.org.uk/media/for-organisations/documents/2013559/big-data-ai-ml-and-data-protection.pdf. Accessed 18 Sept 2018

Kamarinou D, Millard C, Jatinder S (2017) Machine learning with personal data. In: Leenes R, van Brakel R, Gutwirth S, de Hert P (eds) Data protection and privacy: the age of intelligent machines. Bloomsbury Publishing PLC, Oxford, Portland, pp 89–114

Kingreen T (2016) Art. 8 GRC. In: Calliess C, Ruffert M (eds) EUV/AEUV: Das Verfassungsrecht der Europäischen Union mit Europäischer Grundrechtecharta – Kommentar, 5th edn. München

Kroll JA, Huey J, Barocas S, Felten EW, Reidenberg JR, Robinson DG, Yu H (2017) Accountable algorithms. Univ Pa Law Rev 165:633–705

Marsch N (2018) Das europäische Datenschutzgrundrecht: Grundlagen - Dimensionen - Verflechtungen. Mohr Siebeck, Tübingen

Martini M (2017) Algorithmen als Herausforderung für die Rechtsordnung. JuristenZeitung 72:1017–1025

Mayer-Schönberger V, Cukier K (2013) Big data: a revolution that will transform how we live, work, and think. Houghton Mifflin Harcourt, Boston

Naumann K (2008) Art. 52 Abs. 3 GrCh zwischen Kohärenz des europäischen Grundrechtsschutzes und Autonomie des Unionsrechts. Europarecht 43:424–435

Oostveen M, Irion K (2018) The golden age of personal data: how to regulate an enabling fundamental right? In: Bakhoum M, Conde Gallego B, Mackenrodt M-O, Surblytė-Namavičienė G (eds) Personal data in competition, consumer protection and intellectual property law: towards a holistic approach? Springer, Berlin, pp 7–26

Poscher R (2012) Die Zukunft der informationellen Selbstbestimmung als Recht auf Abwehr von Grundrechtsgefährdungen. In: Gander H-H, Perron W, Poscher R, Riescher G, Würtenberger T (eds) Resilienz in der offenen Gesellschaft. Nomos, Baden-Baden, pp 167–190

Poscher R (2017) The right to data protection: a no-right thesis. In: Miller RA (ed) Privacy and power: a transatlantic dialogue in the shadow of the NSA-Affair. Cambridge University Press, Cambridge, pp 129–141

Rademacher T (2017) Predictive Policing im deutschen Polizeirecht. Archiv des öffentlichen Rechts 142:366–416

Rost M (2018) Künstliche Intelligenz. Datenschutz und Datensicherheit 42:558–565

Siemen B (2006) Datenschutz als europäisches Grundrecht. Duncker & Humblot, Berlin

Spiecker gen. Döhmann I (2017) Big und Smart Data: Zweckbindung zwecklos? Spektrum der Wissenschaften Spezial:56–62

Trute H-H (2003) Verfassungsrechtliche Grundlagen. In: Roßnagel A (ed) Handbuch Datenschutzrecht: Die neuen Grundlagen für Wirtschaft und Verwaltung. Beck, München, Kap. 2.5

Trute H-H (2018) Rechtliche Herausforderungen der Digitalisierung. In: Bär C, Grädler T, Mayr R (eds) Digitalisierung im Spannungsfeld von Politik, Wirtschaft, Wissenschaft und Recht: 2. Volume: Wissenschaft und Recht. Springer Gabler, Berlin, pp 313–330

Trute H-H, Broemel R (2016) Alles nur Datenschutz? Zur rechtlichen Regulierung algorithmenbasierter Wissensgenerierung. Berliner Debatte Initial 27:50–65

Wischmeyer T (2018) Regulierung intelligenter Systeme. Archiv des öffentlichen Rechts 143:1–66

Artificial Intelligence and Autonomy: Self-Determination in the Age of Automated Systems

Christian Ernst

Contents

1 Introduction and Practical Applications 54
   1.1 Health or Life Insurance and Health Status 54
   1.2 Financial Transactions and Financial Creditworthiness 55
   1.3 Chinese Social Credit System and Personal Behaviour in General 56
2 Potential Risks from Automated Systems on Self-Determination 57
   2.1 The Function of Automated Systems 57
   2.2 Concrete Structures of Risks 58
3 Legal Framework Conditions: Individual Self-Determination 62
   3.1 Legally Affected Rights 62
   3.2 Requirement of Legal Regulation or Personal Responsibility? 63
4 Possibilities for Legal Responses 64
   4.1 Instruments with Direct Effect 64
   4.2 Instruments with Indirect Effect 70
References 71

Abstract The use of automated (decision-making) systems is becoming increasingly widespread in everyday life. By, for example, producing tailor-made decisions or individual suggestions, these systems increasingly penetrate—intentionally or unintentionally, openly or covertly—a sphere that has long been reserved for individual self-determination. With the advancing digitalisation of everyday life and the increasing proliferation of such systems, it can become more and more difficult for those affected to recognize the impact of these systems or to avoid their influence. This Chapter illustrates the risks that such systems may pose for individual self-determination and possible ways out.

C. Ernst (✉)
Helmut-Schmidt-Universität/Universität der Bundeswehr Hamburg, Hamburg, Germany
e-mail: christian.ernst@hsu-hh.de

© Springer Nature Switzerland AG 2020
T. Wischmeyer, T. Rademacher (eds.), *Regulating Artificial Intelligence*,
https://doi.org/10.1007/978-3-030-32361-5_3

1 Introduction and Practical Applications

The digital revolution and the development of artificial intelligence are putting the relationship between humans and machines to the test in various ways. Fortunately, occasionally expressed fears—sometimes even apocalyptical—of machines replacing humans have not become reality so far. This is, however, no reason to sit back and relax. It is already evident today that automated systems can have a considerable impact on the way individuals shape their lives—although this often takes place with supposedly good intentions and in a subtle way.

1.1 Health or Life Insurance and Health Status[1]

One example is the 'Vitality' programme offered by various insurance companies in different versions worldwide. While the Vitality programme itself is operated independently of the insurance company, the performance of a member in the Vitality programme can influence the conditions offered by the insurance company. Vitality was developed by the South African insurance company Discovery in 1997 and has since been adopted by other companies.[2] In Germany, the Generali Group has offered a Vitality programme since July 2016.[3] Vitality analyses the initial health status of a policyholder by means of various tests. On this basis, certain goals are proposed to the member. The member receives Vitality points for the achievement of these goals. Members can also collect points for, for example, completing further tests and examinations, visiting a gym or transmitting data from a fitness tracker. The more points collected, the higher the member's Vitality status. The higher the status, the more likely is an impact on the premium to be paid or the profit participation within the framework of the associated insurance relationship. In addition, members receive financial benefits from several partner companies.

The Vitality model launched by US insurer John Hancock in autumn 2018, is even more extensive.[4] The private health insurance policy offered by the company will be available only in combination with simultaneous Vitality membership and under the condition that the policyholder uses a fitness tracker.[5] The data collected by the device, which may comprise for example sleeping habits, the number of steps taken each day, whether or not the person has exercised or the development of the pulse level over a day must be transferred to the insurance company. These data are incorporated into the design of the concrete insurance tariffs and other benefits of the Vitality programme. In the event of underperformance or non-achievement of the

---

[1] See also Tischbirek, paras 10 et seq.
[2] See Krohn and Linder (2018).
[3] See www.generalivitality.de/vmp/.
[4] See www.johnhancockinsurance.com/vitality-program.html.
[5] Krohn and Linder (2018).

fitness goals, John Hancock's insurance may even request subsequent payments for the fitness tracker, which the policyholder initially purchased at a discount from the insurer. The collection and evaluation of health data within the framework of insurance relationships by means of automated data processing and decision-making systems can be positively motivating for the individual but can also be perceived negatively as coercion and pressure. In any case, it influences autonomous decision-making of the individual.

1.2 Financial Transactions and Financial Creditworthiness

In the case of life or health insurances, the connection with health data is substantively comprehensible and generally recognisable for those affected. This may be different with scoring in business transactions. Scoring is a method by which a probability value is calculated for the future conduct of a person in order to support the decision on the conclusion, form or termination of a contractual relationship.[6] Regularly it is a matter of quantifying the creditworthiness of a person when deciding about a loan application or other long-term contractual relationships such as rent. An automated system calculates the creditworthiness using certain criteria and information about the person in question. It does not consider only past business behaviour, but may also take into account the place of residence and in some cases, it has even been reported that the name of the person concerned can play a role.[7]

Through the extensive use of machine learning-based systems and big data, the traditional scoring procedure is now being further developed. Companies such as the German start-up Kreditech do not concentrate primarily on past behaviour, but expand the range of factors assessed to include social graphs such as connections and activities in social networks, data from devices or the concrete process for completing questionnaires.[8] Kreditech even believes to have discovered that people who do not pay back their loan would use a very specific font on their computer—it is said to be a font that is only used by casino and poker programmes.[9] The evaluation of personal behaviour thus increasingly draws upon sources of

---

[6] See the definition in Section 31 German Federal Data Protection Act (BDSG). According to the GDPR, scoring is a subset of profiling pursuant to Article 4(4) GDPR. The GDPR follows a comprehensive approach, see Selmayr and Ehmann (2018), para 75 et seq.; Schantz (2018), para 8; Pötters (2018), para 24. So, it is doubtful whether the national legislator is allowed to enact a rule like Section 31(1) BDSG that is more restrictive for scoring than Article 22 GDPR. Whether or not Section 31 BDSG can still be considered a 'suitable measure to safeguard the data subject's rights and freedoms and legitimate interests' in the sense of Article 22(2)(b) GDPR, is an open question, see Krämer (2018), para 3; skeptical Buchner (2018), paras 4 et seq.; Moos and Rothkegel (2016), p. 567.
[7] Hockling (2013).
[8] Sachverständigenrat für Verbraucherfragen (2018), p. 62; Hartlmaier (2018).
[9] Seibel (2015).

information that are not directly related to the subject of the evaluation procedure. There is a danger for those affected that the evaluation of their behaviour becomes opaque and incomprehensible.

1.3 Chinese Social Credit System and Personal Behaviour in General[10]

6   There has always existed a concrete occasion for using evaluation procedures in the examples described so far, such as determining the conditions of insurance or loans. However, this might evolve in the future. Looking to China, where a social credit system is currently being tested in some cities on a voluntary basis, can provide an idea of how the mechanisms described may work if they are extended to all aspects of everyday life.[11] From 2020, the system is to be made mandatory and comprehensive in some locations, for example in Beijing.[12] The system aims to improve honesty in social interaction through comprehensive monitoring. Specifically, it targets social sincerity, commercial sincerity, judicial credibility but also government affairs sincerity.[13] For this purpose, government and private data on the individual citizen are to be merged. This includes, for example, financial creditworthiness, information from the criminal register and other data from private corporations, as well as personal behaviour, preferences and interpersonal relationships.[14] The personal score of the individual, which increases and decreases as a result of this data, can have a significant impact on the way the people live their day-to-day lives; it is reported to have an impact on career opportunities, on the access of one's own children to certain schools, on booking air travel and high-speed trains or on the speed of internet access.[15] For companies, which are also rated, state subsidies, public procurement or credit terms may depend upon it.[16] In addition to these direct consequences, social interaction will also be highly influenced by the score of an individual score. Social prestige and position will become quantifiable, measurable and visible to everyone.

---

[10]See also Hoffmann-Riem, para 10.
[11]See comprehensive State Council (2014), State Council (2016).
[12]Holland (2018).
[13]State Council (2014).
[14]Botsman (2017).
[15]Botsman (2017).
[16]Meissner (2017), p. 3.

2 Potential Risks from Automated Systems on Self-Determination

Automated systems can put pressure on the legal position of individuals in a variety of ways.[17]

2.1 The Function of Automated Systems

The function of automated systems sets individual self-determination under pressure.[18] From a functional perspective, it is crucial that automated (decision-making) systems identify and analyse human behaviour patterns at a level of depth and detail that was previously impossible to achieve and that they are also able to exploit these patterns.[19] Individual self-determination is endangered by the ever-increasing decoding of conscious or unconscious behaviour by someone else and the open or concealed use of this knowledge by the other party in (legal) relationships to improve their own position, e.g., by evaluating the individual when exchanging goods, services or information. This has always been a goal in business and social relations, but this process is taking on a new quality under the conditions of digitalisation. Automated systems offer the possibility to process a multitude of very different data, to recognize correlations between them and to derive new information from an area that was previously closed to human perception in general. Knowledge about the behaviour of another person reaches a new level. It is due to the use of automated systems that a credit institution has identified a connection between the font used on a computer and financial creditworthiness (although this does not yet answer the question of whether this connection is reliable or should be taken into account[20]). The new quality of this process also arises from the fact that automated systems can be used systematically and in a way that is not possible for human beings. Therefore, the consequences of these systems cannot regularly be overlooked in their entirety by the individual affected. For example, the transmission of heart rate data to a health insurance company does not only provide information about the pulse and condition of the heart. In combination with data on movement and the daily routine of the affected person, further information about the general state of health and lifestyle can be generated. The user of automated systems sometimes may know more about an individual than the individual her- or himself and can use this knowledge without the counterpart being aware of it.

---

[17]See Ernst (2017a), pp. 1032 et seq.
[18]For a general definition of artificial intelligence see Wischmeyer and Rademacher, paras 5–6.
[19]Broemel and Trute (2016), p. 59.
[20]See paras 38 et seq. and paras 41 et seq.

9 The study of automated systems and their impact is complicated by the diversity of actual applications. This chapter focuses on the use of automated systems by private actors. The use of such systems by public authorities is subject to additional requirements which are not analysed here.

2.2 Concrete Structures of Risks

Potential to Influence Automated Decisions in General

10 The risk automated systems pose to individual self-determination is largely due to the significantly increased granularity of these systems.[21] An analysis of actual life circumstances regarding personal and environmental characteristics as well as their correlation opens up possibilities to exert influence that has not been available until now.

11 Automated systems can meanwhile be used to assess the personality of individuals in detail, for example with regard to character and cognitive traits or other personal aspects.[22] These data allow that certain needs and goals may be presented, suggested or disclosed to the individual which she or he would not have considered without this influence.[23] This becomes particularly problematic when these needs and goals become important because they are the needs and goals of the source of the influence. In this case, the goals of the individual are steered and shaped and become a goal precisely because they benefit others. Autonomy becomes heteronomy and the self-image is replaced by perception by others.

12 The influence on which this is based can be exerted in a variety of ways and through different techniques. For example, influencing another person can aim to change their automated, intuitive behaviour or target conscious and reflective decision-making structures, whereby the influence can be recognisable or non-transparent in both variants.[24] In the case of nudging, to which a significant overlap exists, a distinction is made between 'system 1 nudges' and 'system 2 nudges'.[25] An abstract analysis of the potential of automated systems to influence people is further complicated by the fact that influencing other persons can be the

---

[21] von Grafenstein et al. (2018), p. 46.

[22] Ebers (2018), pp. 423 et seq.

[23] O'Neil (2016), pp. 194 et seq.; Calo (2014), pp. 1015 et seq.; Ebers (2018), p. 423; Wolff (2015), p. 202.

[24] Sunstein (2016), pp. 124 et seq.; Hansen and Jespersen (2013), pp. 14 et seq.; Lindstrom (2014); von Grafenstein et al. (2018), p. 69; Wolff (2015), pp. 202 et seq.; Seckelmann and Lamping (2016), pp. 191 et seq.

[25] Sunstein (2016), pp. 124 et seq.; Hansen and Jespersen (2013), pp. 14 et seq.; Lindstrom (2014); von Grafenstein et al. (2018), p. 69; Weber and Schäfer (2017), pp. 578 et seq.; Seckelmann and Lamping (2016), pp. 191 et seq.

purpose of using automated systems or can occur unintentional.[26] The latter may often be the case in the field of digitalisation, for example, when data subjects are no longer able to assess which information and data about themselves are known to others and how they are used.[27]

Concrete influencing mechanisms are manifold and can only be presented here exemplarily.[28] It is possible, for instance, that affected persons receive feedback about their performance through the automated system and that the presentation of their performance by processed data will influence their future behaviour. This is an essential function of wearables and health data. Confrontation with focused and seemingly objective presentation of individual aspects of one's own way of life causes a change in behaviour.[29] The data can additionally be put in relation to the performance of other persons. The human impulse to seek comparison with others, not to attract negative attention or to compete with others then can be exploited.[30] The performance profile can also be transferred to third parties for control purposes, who in turn, e.g., in their function as superiors or contractual partners, may exert influence. Lastly, automated systems can individually and openly request certain behavioural changes or independently define new tasks and goals for the individual, which are based on previous performance.

One might be inclined to reject a risk to individual self-determination if the potential for influence develops positive effects for the person concerned. In fact, many practical applications have such effects and pursue beneficial change. At this point, however, it is less important whether the use of an automated system has positive or negative consequences for the person concerned, but who decides on the use of the system, its decision architecture, the generated and used data as well as the possible consequences of the use. A risk is not absent if the use of the automated system has a positive effect, but only if this positive effect is achieved in a self-determined manner. Under this condition, an automated system can, for example, provide meaningful indications of the misconduct of the individual, which would otherwise not have attracted her or his attention. Such a system can also provide valuable advice according to guidelines defined by the user her- or himself, such as risk-averse decisions for risk-averse users. The prerequisite for this, however, is that the user at all times and with regard to every essential aspect of content decides her- or himself whether to use the system.

---

[26]von Grafenstein et al. (2018), p. 45.
[27]German Federal Constitutional Court 1 BvR 209/83 et al. 'Volkszählung' (15 December 1983), BVerfGE 65 p. 43; 1 BvR 256/08 et al. 'Vorratsdatenspeicherung' (2 March 2010), BVerfGE 125 p. 232.
[28]In detail von Grafenstein et al. (2018), p. 20; see also Weber and Schäfer (2017), pp. 569 et seq.; Purnhagen and Reisch (2016), pp. 637 et seq.
[29]See Viseu and Suchman (2010).
[30]Thaler and Sunstein (2009), pp. 53 et seq.; Wolff (2015), pp. 201 et seq.; Zillien et al. (2015), p. 87.

Approximation and Standardisation

15 The potential for influence of automated systems often also has a content-related effect. With the proliferation of automated decisions, there is a risk of standardisation, so that the individual behaviour of a large number of people will be aligned and more uniform as a result. On the one hand, this can be due to the fact that by means of an automated system, system operators (or autonomously the system itself) can set standards, which then can be uniformly and effectively applied to a variety of situations.[31] These standards can thus be applied on a broad scale that would hardly be possible without the means of digital mass management.

16 On the other hand, the decisions of an automated system can have a self-reinforcing effect. An essential factor for determining the concrete content of a decision often are the previous decisions of the contractual partners or users. People tend to align their own behaviour with that of others.[32] For the individual the approval by the masses can make a decision option appear trustworthy but can also create an obstacle not to deviate. Decisions that seem to have been met with broad acceptance in the past will therefore continue to be taken into account increasingly by automated systems in the future. Past acceptance nourishes the expectation of future acceptance. In addition, such decisions, which are based on previous behaviour, also have an independent potential for influence, which further reinforces the effect.

17 If an automated system primarily suggests and recommends a specific decision, alternative options become less visible. An availability heuristic can occur, so that present possibilities are more likely to be chosen. If, however, the individual chooses an alternative option, there is a risk that this will result in higher costs or will require a larger effort. These alternatives therefore tend not to be pursued further.

18 The framework within which such a process of approximation and standardisation can develop is subject to wide variations. Alignment can take place within society or in groups tailored to specific criteria if the decision-making options made for an individual are based on the behaviour of society or the behaviour of group members. This generally affects the relationship between the individual case and typing as well as the possibility of taking individual circumstances into account and enforcing them.[33] The process of approximation and standardisation can even concern only the behaviour of a particular individual, so that only that individual's decision-making options and range of behaviour are reduced. The latter demonstrates that alignment may take place not only with respect to the content of decisions but also over time. Particularly, when using old data, the development of individual self-determination is also put under pressure by one's own previous behaviour. The operational modalities of the automated system are crucial for the framework of the alignment process.

---

[31] See von Grafenstein et al. (2018), pp. 35 et seq.

[32] Schultz (2007), and von Grafenstein et al. (2018), pp. 39 et seq.

[33] Ernst (2017b), pp. 72 et seq.

Depending on the design of the AI system, there may be a concentration of behaviour patterns and a convergence of individuals. The sum of options available to the individual may tend to be reduced and focused on mainstream behaviour and decisions. The realisation of individuality can then require greater effort and higher costs and even lead to social separation.

Lack of Comprehensibility

These risks are accompanied and intensified by a further circumstance, which is also symptomatic of the current use of automated systems and should be considered here independently.

Automated systems are increasingly able to identify, evaluate and link different criteria and thus compare different situations. In this way, automated systems can determine the characteristics, inclinations, goals and intentions of individuals in previously unknown depth and detail and thus calculate predictions about their future behaviour.[34] Human cognitive abilities cannot keep up with this, so that the human ability to actually comprehend the concrete decision-making processes of automated systems reaches its limits. This problem is exacerbated by the fact that automated systems also use data from the past without reflection, which have lost their context in the meantime or which fail to reflect a recent development of the individual in question.[35] If an automated system identifies a certain context and bases its decision on it, there is a danger that the automated procedure will no longer be easily comprehensible for humans. Even if the concrete connection identified by an automated system cannot be understood by a human observer, the result may nevertheless be true but so far just has not been recognizable for humans. The possibilities of individual self-determination are impaired if the individual is always uncertain which criteria are used by an automated system.[36]

The individuals concerned are therefore often unable to adequately comprehend how the decisions, specifications or proposals of automated systems come about. As a result, the criteria and factors upon which decisions about a person have been made often remain unclear.[37] Individuals hardly know the circumstances of other people in comparable situations. This can reduce the value of a declared consent, not only from a legal point of view.[38] The lack of knowledge about the development of behavioural options, based on the operation of automated systems, makes it considerably more difficult for the individual to deviate.

---

[34] Ebers (2018), p. 423; Broemel and Trute (2016), p. 59.
[35] See Tischbirek, paras 9 et seq.
[36] See Constitutional Court 'Volkszählung' (see note 27), p. 42; Martini (2014), p. 1483; Broemel and Trute (2016), p. 57.
[37] See Wischmeyer; see Hoffmann-Riem, paras 51 et seq.
[38] Hermstrüwer (2016), pp. 227 et seq.; Radlanski (2016), pp. 11 et seq.; Broemel and Trute (2016), p. 53.

23   A special kind of information asymmetries may stand behind this process.[39] Conventional information asymmetries are generally based on an information advantage concerning the beneficiary's own sphere, for example, the beneficiary's additional knowledge about the characteristics of a contractual object offered by her or him. However, the use of automated systems can lead to an information asymmetry, in which the advantage of one person results precisely from information about and against the other person.[40] The superior knowledge refers to the sphere and person of the potential business partner. The use of automated systems makes it possible to assess which individual needs and goals the person concerned has or can be provided with, regardless of whether she or he is aware of her or his own needs and goals.

3 Legal Framework Conditions: Individual Self-Determination

24   The fundamental right to freedom of individual self-determination is an essential condition for the fulfilment of personality.

3.1 Legally Affected Rights

25   In German law, individual self-determination is an expression of the general right of personality pursuant to Article 2(1), 1(1) of the Basic Law. The free development of one's personality and one's independent way of life are protected, taking into account one's own individuality.[41] On the one hand, this refers to an inner-freedom, which ensures that decisions can be made free from the influences of others.[42] The impairment of individual autonomy through automated systems must not result in third-party control replacing self-determination protected by fundamental rights.[43] This should also include the possibility for the individual to adapt her or his actions to the behaviour of third parties and to influence her or his own fate.

26   On the other hand, individual self-determination further protects the ability to behave in accordance with one's own decisions and thus to perceive actual external influence.[44] In a strictly liberal sense, this can also include the freedom to make mistakes. This addresses a form of authenticity that ensures that one perceives

---

[39]See Hoffmann-Riem, paras 54 et seq.
[40]Ebers (2018), p. 423.
[41]Di Fabio (2001), para 147; Broemel and Trute (2016), pp. 57 et seq.
[42]Britz (2007), p. 24; von Grafenstein et al. (2018), p. 54.
[43]Petrlic (2016), p. 96; see Jandt (2016), p. 571; Di Fabio (2001), para 107.
[44]See von Grafenstein et al. (2018), p. 54 with further references.

oneself as the author of one's own actions.[45] If, however, one cannot identify which criteria and factors shape one's everyday life, the possibility of ascertaining one's own position—not only from a legal point of view, but also from a social and personal point of view—is put at risk.[46] However, such self-assessment is of essential importance as a basis for self-determined decision-making. Only with an extensive knowledge of one's own position and possibilities is it possible to influence one's own life in a self-determined way.

3.2 Requirement of Legal Regulation or Personal Responsibility?

Self-determination arguably also covers surrendering oneself to external and foreign determination. This approach, which is based upon fundamental rights, principally justifies demanding acceptance and respect from the legal system for subordinating oneself to the will of others. This leads to a basic problem in dealing with individual self-determination. Do the amenities and benefits that individuals may gain from automated systems cause individual autonomy to abolish itself? Conversely, the question arises as to whether the safeguarding of autonomy may be left to the individual. In fact, even following a positively intended external control can turn out to be disadvantageous.

This leads to the question of who determines what is best for the individual.[47] This is also discussed within the framework of the justifiability and accountability of nudging. There, for example, the focus can be on whether the induced decision has a greater benefit, whether the persons concerned are guided to better decisions based on their own standards or whether their original behaviour is biased and flawed.[48] From a content-paternalistic or societal perspective, it may be easier to assign the decision of what is best for someone to a third party. However, from a point of view that respects individual self-determination, this decision basically remains with the person concerned. For this reason, 'system 2 nudges', which are intended to influence conscious and reflective decision structures, will probably be more broadly accepted than 'system 1 nudges', which aim to exploit intuitive regular cognitive and sensitive automatisms.[49]

A comparable situation arises for the preliminary/initial decision to renounce autonomy and to surrender to the influence of others. In particular, the use of AI

---

[45] See von Grafenstein et al. (2018), p. 54 with further references.
[46] Ernst (2017b), p. 72.
[47] See Huster (2015), pp. 24 et seq.; Wolff (2015), pp. 209 et seq.; Weber and Schäfer (2017), pp. 572 et seq.
[48] Thaler and Sunstein (2009), pp. 5 et seq.; see Weber and Schäfer (2017), pp. 575 et seq.; Wolff (2015), pp. 209 et seq. with further references.
[49] Sunstein (2016).

systems often results in an asymmetry of information in favour of the user and thus in an imbalance between the user and the individual concerned.[50] A renunciation of the exercise of self-determination is also possible in such cases, but there is always the danger that the renunciation takes place without complete knowledge of all relevant circumstances and not according to an autonomous informed decision. It must therefore be ensured that the renunciation of self-determination takes place in a self-determined manner.

4 Possibilities for Legal Responses

30   Legal responses to the risks described here can be divided into instruments with direct and indirect effects.

4.1 Instruments with Direct Effect

31   Legal instruments with direct effect concentrate primarily on the potential of AI systems to influence other people.

Preliminary Question: The Legal Relevance of Influencing People

32   The fundamental question here is to ascertain when such a potential for influence is legally relevant. When must it therefore be regarded by the legal system as a risk to individual self-determination? Such legal relevance appears conceivable at least if the person concerned decides otherwise than is suggested to her or him by the automated system, and therefore direct legal or considerable actual consequences occur, including the concrete form of a legal transaction.

33   This cannot, however, be affirmed in general terms for all conceivable influencing potentials, nor can it be determined in abstract terms. There are two reasons for this. First, the individual can practically not escape actual moments of influence anyway. This becomes evident when one considers that the influence on persons is exerted through information. Information can be understood as a fact which can be perceived by a recipient and which is capable of influencing the condition or behaviour of the recipient.[51] The question as to whether the recipient intends to have access to a certain fact or not is irrelevant here. At most, this, like other factors, can have an influence on the probability that the information leads to a change in behaviour and is

---

[50]Ebers (2018), p. 423.

[51]See Kloepfer (2002), § 1 para 60; Vesting (2001), pp. 220 et seq.; Druey (1995), pp. 26 et seq.

not ignored by the recipient.[52] As a result, any information, not only through automated systems, can influence the behaviour of the individual. For this reason, a "database" for nudges, which some scholars have proposed,[53] is unlikely to be feasible.

Second, the intensity of an influencing potential can only be determined individually. A perceived pressure to change behaviour is significantly influenced by individual experiences and can hardly be typified. The mere idea of the recipient that an automated system provides her or him with more optimal, knowledgeable or individual information may increase the probability of influence but cannot generally imply that the threshold for legal relevance is met.[54] Not every influence on human behaviour by automated systems generally possesses such legal significance that the possibility of state regulation is opened up or even required. Although the individuality and accuracy of an influencing potential is an aspect that can increase the quality of the legal risk. Also, the awareness of the data subjects, that their own data that are presented to them is contrasted to data of other persons is in itself no reason to categorise this process as legally relevant. Yet here, too, such a comparison with other persons can increase the potential for influence and the pressure exerted to such an extent that legal intervention is more likely to be possible. This applies in particular if the data about the data subject is also made accessible to third parties and anonymity is lacking.

Illegal Influences in the Sense of the Unfair Commercial Practices Directive

A general inadmissibility of the use of automated systems to influence other persons may arise on the basis of Article 2(j), Article 5(4), Article 8 and Article 9 of Directive 2005/29/EC (Unfair Commercial Practices Directive). Under these rules, national legislators must prohibit unfair commercial practices.[55] Unfair commercial practices include, inter alia, the use of aggressive commercial practices, which in turn are to be assumed in the case of undue influence. Article 2(j) Directive 2005/29/EC stipulates that undue influence is the exploitation of a position of power in relation to the consumer so as to apply pressure, even without using or threatening to use physical force, in a way which significantly limits the consumer's ability to make an informed decision. According to Article 8 of Directive 2005/29/EC, this must result in the average consumer being likely to be induced by the undue influence to take a transactional decision which she or he would not have taken otherwise.

---

[52] See von Grafenstein et al. (2018), p. 82.
[53] See von Grafenstein et al. (2018), p. 111.
[54] See Duttweiler and Passoth (2016), pp. 12 et seq.; Crawford et al. (2015), p. 492; von Grafenstein et al. (2018), p. 38.
[55] In Germany see Section 4a UWG.

36 The decisive hurdle in the use of automated systems is the exertion of pressure. The consumer must be under the impression that she or he is threatened with disadvantages outside the intended transaction which go beyond the failure to conclude the transaction if she or he deviates from the decision option which is suggested to her or him.[56] This is certainly possible for the constellations of interest here, but cannot generally be assumed.[57] While the user of an automated system typically has a special position of power, it is of informational nature. Influencing with automated systems develops its special effect unconsciously, manipulatively and on the basis of personality decoding and can dispense with the use of perceptible pressure. However, the risk to freedom of decision and freedom of conduct cannot therefore be underestimated. The legislator should therefore supplement the scope of unfair commercial practices with a variant of the exploitation of personal information asymmetries. Instead of the exertion of pressure, a manipulative effect could build the standard.

37 Alternatively, a prohibition based on the general clause, as provided for in Article 5(2) of Directive 2005/29/EC, can also be considered. Accordingly, a commercial practice is unfair and prohibited if it materially distorts or is likely to materially distort the economic behaviour with regard to the product of the average consumer whom it reaches or to whom it is addressed, or of the average member of the group when a commercial practice is directed to a particular group of consumers. This, however, requires the average consumer to be taken into account. The average consumer is reasonably well-informed and reasonably observant and circumspect according to the case law of the ECJ and the recitals of the Directive.[58] However, the mechanisms with which automated systems operate work on a different level.[59] The available consumer information, which normally provides sufficient services in business life, is a component of the problematic information asymmetry when confronted with automated systems. And even the critical attention of the average consumer is regularly inferior to hidden influencing mechanisms. It is not only the average consumer who is part of the problem, but the Directive also requires that there be a material distortion of the economic behaviour. According to Article 2(e) of Directive 2005/29/EC, this is the case when the use of a commercial practice appreciably impairs the consumer's ability to make an informed decision, thereby causing the consumer to take a transactional decision that he or she would not have taken otherwise. Influencing one's counterpart is an inseparable part of everyday business life and as such not inadmissible per se.[60] However, a special situation may

---

[56] Köhler (2019), para 1.59; Picht (2016), para 27; Götting (2016), para 14; Ebers (2018), p. 424.

[57] Ebers (2018), p. 424.

[58] CJEU C-178/84 'Reinheitsgebot für Bier' (12 March 1987), 1987 E.C.R. 1227, paras 31–36; C-362/88 'GB-Inno-BM/Confédération du commerce luxembourgeois' (7 March 1990), 1990 E.C.R. I-667, paras 13–19; C-220/98 'Estée Lauder' (13 January 2000), 2000 E.C.R. I-117, paras 27 et seq.; recital 18 of Directive 2005/29/EC; see Weber and Schäfer (2017), p. 579.

[59] Ebers (2018), pp. 423 et seq.

[60] Sosnitza (2016), para 36.

arise due to the constantly increasing capabilities of evaluation systems and access to personal data. The more personal data automated systems use to influence behaviour, the less transparent they appear, and the more they affect unconscious and irrational cognitive or intentional human processes, the more likely it is an impermissible act within the meaning of Article 5(2) of Directive 2005/29/EC.

Randomly Appearing Criteria: Relevance of a Reasonable Expectation Horizon

These legal prohibitions may also prevent the use of automated systems in individual cases. The use of randomly appearing criteria can justify a prohibition of automated influence on individual self-determination. Such criteria, that are used by automated systems for decision-making, are not in any obvious relation to the content and purpose of the decision in question. The evaluation of such randomly appearing criteria is therefore only possible when taking the purpose of the decision into account. **38**

This idea is based on the expanded knowledge possibilities and deviating decision-making structures of automated systems in comparison to humans. As already explained, it is possible that a connection that is identified by an automated system and taken into account for a decision is not comprehensible to humans.[61] This raises the question of which benchmark should be decisive for the legal assessment. While the lack of comprehensibility of automated decisions can lead to humans reaching the limits of their actual cognitive ability, this factual finding cannot be transferred to the legal situation because the legal system has always been based on human capabilities and decision-making structures. In this sense, the use of automated systems is (still) always attributable to a natural or legal person.[62] This human standard is therefore also decisive for the procedure of AI systems, so that the legality of AI systems does not depend on what is arithmetically necessary or not necessary for an AI system. **39**

For the assessment of randomly acting decision criteria, the knowledge horizon of an informed third party and its expectations must therefore be considered. The more unexpected, less comprehensible and coincidental a criterion is from the point of view of an informed third party in light of the purpose of the automated system, the more likely it is that its use is inadmissible. The use of criteria that are not predictable and comprehensible according to the current human expectation horizon is therefore **40**

---

[61] See para 22.
[62] German Federal Supreme Court X ZR 37/12 (16 October 2012), BGHZ 195, 126 para 17; VI ZR 269/12 (14 May 2013), BGHZ 197, 213 para 17; District Court Cologne 9 S 289/02 (16 April 2003), MMR 2003, 481 et seq.; Schulz (2018), para 18. See also Schirmer, paras 16 et seq.

Factual Criteria: Profiling and Consent

41 If the knowledge horizon of an intelligent third party forms the basis, it is not always possible to draw a clear dividing line between criteria with and criteria without a comprehensible factual context.[64] The former are referred to as factual decision-making criteria. Their assumption must also be based on the knowledge horizon and expectations of an informed third party, so that this is the counterpart to randomly acting decision criteria.

42 However, the existence of a factual criterion does not necessarily mean that the use of such criteria is always permissible. The use of factual criteria can also significantly impair individual self-determination. There is also a wide range of consequences, that are hardly comprehensible for the person concerned, when using factual criteria. And if the consequences are comprehensible, another effect arises: If perceived coincidences create a diffuse feeling of insecurity in the persons concerned because it is unclear what information about them is available and used, then comprehensibility intensifies the pressure to comply because the persons concerned find it harder to refuse the reasonable conclusion and the pressure to change behaviour.

43 Nevertheless, consent is often given in such contexts. However, when considering day-to-day practice, the impression arises that the instrument of consent is subject to considerable ineffectiveness.[65] This can have a variety of causes, such as the fact that the individual is unable to understand the various consequences of using data with algorithms or is confronted with them in a timely manner. The constitutional positions concerned must therefore be updated within the framework of fundamental rights protection. The effectiveness of consent depends on whether there is an appropriate balance of power between the parties involved. In the light of fundamental rights, consent may be precluded by mandatory law if there is no longer balance of power between the parties involved and therefore the independent design

---

[63]In German law regarding General Terms and Conditions, Section 305c BGB (Civil Code) contains a rule according to which clauses which are surprising for the contractual partner are not valid. Only such contractual conditions shall be legally effective that are expected. This ensures the protection of confidence and takes into account that general terms and conditions are regularly so complex that they are not completely comprehensible for an average consumer, see Basedow (2019), para 1. This protective effect is comparable to the proposal made here. See Hoffmann-Riem, para 23.

[64]An illustrative example of the delimitation difficulties that may be associated with this is the consideration of the font in connection with the granting of loans, as described above see para 5.

[65]Hermstrüwer (2016), p. 227; Radlanski (2016), pp. 11 et seq.; Broemel and Trute (2016), p. 53.

of one's own (legal) relationships is no longer guaranteed.[66] Early decisions by the Federal Constitutional Court on commercial agent agreements, sureties, marriage contracts or clauses from inheritance contracts can be a model for this.[67]

Further protection for affected persons is offered by Article 22 General Data Protection Regulation (GDPR), which contains provisions for profiling. Profiling in this sense requires that a decision based exclusively on an automated processing legally affects a person or impairs it considerably in a similar way. According to Article 4(4) GDPR, 'profiling' means any form of automated processing of personal data consisting of the use of personal data to evaluate certain personal aspects relating to a natural person, in particular to analyse or predict aspects concerning that natural person's performance at work, economic situation, health, personal preferences, interests, reliability, behaviour, location or movements. Although such profiling takes place regularly in the constellations discussed here, it is unlikely that such profiling and the influence of automated systems based upon it will always lead to a decision with legal effect or comparable factual effects. Instead, the persons concerned are only encouraged to make certain decisions.

In view of the resulting risks to individual self-determination, it seems appropriate to loosen this link that occurs from data protection law between profiling and decisions with legal effect. It should rather be viewed the procedural role of profiling it has in practice. If one were to dispense with the requirement of a 'decision with legal effect' in the context of the data protection and extend Article 22 GDPR in this respect, this might render the handling of the regulation practicably becoming impossible in view of the variety and prevalence of automated decision processes. It seems more sensible to consider profiling not only in connection with data protection law but also in connection with unfair commercial practices. In this sense, one could also assume an 'undue influence' according to Article 2(j) of Directive 2005/29/EC, which so far requires a position of power to exert pressure, for cases in which an informational position of power exists on the basis of profiling. The use of automated profiling could also be included as an additional category of commercial practices that could lead to a significant influence on the economic behaviour of the consumer within the meaning of Article 2(e) of Directive 2005/29/EC.

This illustrates a current fundamental legislative challenge. At present, it still seems to be difficult to assign concrete regulatory approaches in an objective and functionally appropriate manner to certain areas of legislative.[68] Also, the central provision of Article 22 GDPR does not pursue strictly the purpose of data-protection. The rule does not concern the question which kind of data is used, but

---

[66] German Federal Constitutional Court 1 BvR 567/89, 1044/89 'Bürgschaftsverträge' (19 October 1993), BVerfGE 89, p. 233.

[67] See German Federal Constitutional Court 1 BvR 26/84 'Handelsvertreter' (7 February 1990), BVerfGE 81, p. 242; 'Bürgschaftsverträge' (see note 66), BVerfGE 89 p. 214; 1 BvR 2248/01 'Erbvertrag' (22 March 2004), NJW 2004, p. 2008.

[68] See Hoffmann-Riem, para 14; see Marsch, para 8.

in which way decisions may be made. Despite the progressing actual digitalisation, no adequate regulation environment exists for questions like that so far.[69] Even if the data protection content of this provision is limited, it is attached to the data protection law for lack of alternatives.

4.2 Instruments with Indirect Effect

47   In addition, indirect mechanisms can be used to counter the risks posed by AI systems. These aim at the transparency of the functioning of AI systems, for example, through disclosure rules or guidance to persons concerned.[70] They aim at strengthening the ability to exercise individual self-determination. Besides, and at least as importantly, they also aim at activating the democratic process in order to find social consensus on the areas of application and permissible possibilities of automated systems. These mechanisms are therefore primarily aimed at the problem of harmonisation and standardisation as well as insufficient comprehensibility.

48   In order to achieve this purpose for automated (decision-making) systems, Article 14(2)(g) and Article 13(2)(f) GDPR can be used. According to these provisions, data subjects have the right to be informed by the user about the existence of automated decision-making, including meaningful information about the logic involved as well as the scope and intended effects. In view of the affected legal positions, it is necessary that 'information on the logic involved' be interpreted in such a way that, in the case of an automated system, at least the decision and assessment criteria used are revealed. Considering the complexity of such assessment and decision-making structures, it does not appear necessary and in fact hardly possible to name each individual criterion. Rather, it is decisive that abstract generic terms are formed for decision criteria, which are based on, for example, the categories of Article 9 (1) GDPR. It is crucial that data subjects get an appropriate overview and impression of the criteria used to assess their person. This is the only way for the persons concerned to effectively protect their rights and interests.

49   In order to generate the necessary public discussion on the use of AI systems, system operators should meet further information obligations. In the case of the automated presentation of decision options, the presentation of alternative options should be considered, which are based on the treatment of other persons or groups. One could also consider the compulsory inclusion of a decision option which is identical for all persons concerned without taking individual criteria into account and thus represents a kind of 'normal case'. Depending on the decision-making structure, randomisation may also be considered.

---

[69]Bachmeier (1995), p. 51; Wuermeling (1996), p. 668; Kamlah (2013), para 2; Ernst (2017a), p. 1031.
[70]See Wischmeyer, paras 25 et seq.

References

Bachmeier R (1995) EG-Datenschutzrichtlinie – Rechtliche Konsequenzen für die Datenschutzpraxis. RDV 11:49–52

Basedow J (2019) § 305c BGB. In: Säcker FJ et al (eds) Münchener Kommentar zum Bürgerlichen Gesetzbuch, 8th edn. C.H. Beck, München

Botsman R (2017) Big data meets Big Brother as China moves to rate its citizens. WIRED. 21 October 2017. www.wired.co.uk/article/chinese-government-social-credit-score-privacy-invasion

Britz G (2007) Freie Entfaltung durch Selbstdarstellung. Mohr Siebeck, Tübingen

Broemel R, Trute H-H (2016) Alles nur Datenschutz? Zur rechtlichen Regulierung algorithmenbasierter Wissensgenerierung. Berliner Debatte Initial 27(4):50–65

Buchner B (2018) § 31 BDSG. In: Kühling J, Buchner B (eds) DS-GVO, 2nd edn. C.H. Beck, München

Calo R (2014) Digital Market Manipulation. George Wash Law Rev 82:995–1051

Crawford K et al (2015) Our metrics, ourselves: a hundred years of self-tracking from the weight scale to the wrist wearable device. Eur J Cult Stud 18:479–496

Di Fabio U (2001) Art. 2(1) GG. In: Maunz T et al (eds) Grundgesetz. Kommentar, 39th edn. C.H. Beck, München

Druey JN (1995) Information als Gegenstand des Rechts. Schulthess, Zürich

Duttweiler S, Passoth J-H (2016) Self-Tracking als Optimierungsprojekt? In: Duttweiler S et al (eds) Leben nach Zahlen: Self-Tracking als Optimierungsprojekt?, pp 9–42

Ebers M (2018) Beeinflussung und Manipulation von Kunden durch Behavioral Microtargeting – Verhaltenssteuerung durch Algorithmen aus der Sicht des Zivilrechts. MMR 21:423–428

Ernst C (2017a) Algorithmische Entscheidungsfindung und personenbezogene Daten. JuristenZeitung 72:1026–1036

Ernst C (2017b) Die Gefährdung der individuellen Selbstentfaltung durch den privaten Einsatz von Algorithmen. In: Klafki A et al (eds) Digitalisierung und Recht. Bucerius Law School Press, Hamburg, pp 63–81

Götting H-P (2016) 4a UWG. In: Götting H-P, Nordemann A (eds) UWG. Kommentar, 3rd edn. Nomos, Baden-Baden

Hansen PG, Jespersen AM (2013) Nudge and the manipulation of choice: a framework for the responsible use of the nudge approach to behaviour change in public policy. Eur J Risk Reg 4:3–28

Hartlmaier B (2018) Überwachung: Umfassendes Social Scoring wie in China ist auch bei uns möglich. WIRED. 9 November 2018. www.wired.de/article/ueberwachung-umfassendes-social-scoring-wie-in-china-ist-auch-bei-uns-moeglich

Hermstrüwer Y (2016) Informationelle Selbstgefährdung. Zur rechtsfunktionalen, spieltheoretischen und empirischen Rationalität der datenschutzrechtlichen Einwilligung und des Rechts auf informationelle Selbstbestimmung. Mohr Siebeck, Tübingen

Hockling S (2013) Manche Namen senken Scorewert für Kreditwürdigkeit. Die Welt. 23 March 2013. www.welt.de/finanzen/verbraucher/article114709366/Manche-Namen-senken-Scorewert-fuer-Kreditwuerdigkeit.html

Holland M (2018) "Social Scoring": Ab 2020 Punktesystem für vorbildliches Verhalten in Peking. heise online. 23 November 2018. www.heise.de/newsticker/meldung/Social-Scoring-Ab-2020-Punktesystem-fuer-vorbildliches-Verhalten-in-Peking-4231644.html

Huster S (2015) Selbstbestimmung, Gerechtigkeit und Gesundheit. Nomos, Baden-Baden

Jandt S (2016) Smart Health. Wird die DSGVO den dynamischen Herausforderungen gerecht? DuD 40:571–574

Kamlah W (2013) § 6a BDSG. In: Plath K-U (ed) BDSG. Kommentar, 2nd edn. Dr. Otto Schmidt, Köln

Kloepfer M (2002) Informationsrecht. C.H. Beck, München

Köhler H (2019) § 4a UWG. In: Köhler H et al (eds) Gesetz gegen den unlauteren Wettbewerb. Kommentar, 39th edn. C.H. Beck, München

Krämer W (2018) § 31 BDSG. In: Wolff HA, Brink S (eds) BeckOK Datenschutzrecht, 25th edn. C.H. Beck, München

Krohn P, Linder R (2018) Lebensversicherer verlangt, dass Kunden Fitness-Tracker nutzen. FAZ. 20 September 2018. www.faz.net/aktuell/wirtschaft/diginomics/lebensversicherung-bei-john-hancock-nur-mit-fitness-tracker-15798146.html

Lindstrom L (2014) So, when is it legitimate to nudge? The Swedish Nudging Network. 5 November 2014, theswedishnudgingnetwork.com/2014/11/05/so-when-is-it-legitimate-to-nudge

Martini M (2014) Big Data als Herausforderung für den Persönlichkeitsschutz und das Datenschutzrecht. DVBl 129:1481–1489

Meissner M (2017) Chinas gesellschaftliches Bonitätssystem. www.merics.org/sites/default/files/2017-09/China%20Monitor_39_SOCS_DE.pdf

Moos F, Rothkegel T (2016) Nutzung von Scoring-Diensten im Online-Versandhandel. ZD 9:561–567

O'Neil C (2016) Weapons of math destruction. Allen Lane, Penguin, London

Petrlic R (2016) Das vermessene Selbst. Von der Selbst-Überwachung zur Fremd-Bestimmung. DuD 40:94–97

Picht P (2016) § 4a UWG. In: Harte-Bavendamm H, Henning-Bodewig F (eds) Gesetz gegen den unlauteren Wettbewerb (UWG). Kommentar, 4th edn. C.H. Beck, München

Pötters S (2018) Art. 1 DS-GVO. In: Gola P (ed) DS-GVO, 2nd edn. C.H. Beck, München

Purnhagen K, Reisch L (2016) "Nudging Germany"? Herausforderungen für eine verhaltensbasierte Regulierung in Deutschland. ZEuP 24:629–655

Radlanski P (2016) Das Konzept der Einwilligung in der datenschutzrechtlichen Realität. Mohr Siebeck, Tübingen

Sachverständigenrat für Verbraucherfragen (2018) Verbrauchergerechtes Scoring. Berlin 2018

Schantz P (2018) Art. 1 DSGVO. In: Wolff HA, Brink S (eds), BeckOK Datenschutzrecht, 25th edn. C.H. Beck, München

Schultz PW et al (2007) The constructive, destructive, and reconstructive power of social norms. Psychol Sci 18:429–434

Schulz S (2018) Art. 22 DS-GVO. In: Gola P (ed) Datenschutz-Grundverordnung. Kommentar, 2nd edn. C.H. Beck, München

Seckelmann M, Lamping W (2016) Verhaltensökonomischer Experimentalismus im Politik-Labor. DÖV 69:189–200

Seibel K (2015) Gegen Kreditech ist die Schufa ein Schuljunge. Die Welt. 17 April 2015. www.welt.de/finanzen/verbraucher/article139671014/Gegen-Kreditech-ist-die-Schufa-ein-Schuljunge.html

Selmayr M, Ehmann E (2018) Einführung. In: Selmayr M, Ehmann E (eds) DS-GVO, Kommentar, 2nd edn. C.H. Beck, München

Sosnitza O (2016) § 4a UWG. In: Ohly A, Sosnitza O (eds) Gesetz gegen den unlauteren Wettbewerb. Kommentar, 7th edn. C.H. Beck, München

State Council (2014) Planning Outline for the Construction of a Social Credit System (2014–2020). http://chinacopyrightandmedia.wordpress.com/2014/06/14/planning-outline-for-the-construction-of-a-social-credit-system-2014-2020

State Council (2016) State Council Guiding Opinions concerning Establishing and Perfecting Incentives for Promise-keeping and Joint Punishment Systems for Trust-Breaking, and Accelerating the Construction of Social Sincerity. http://chinacopyrightandmedia.wordpress.com/2016/05/30/state-council-guiding-opinions-concerning-establishing-and-perfecting-incentives-for-promise-keeping-and-joint-punishment-systems-for-trust-breaking-and-accelerating-the-construction-of-social-sincer

Sunstein C (2016) People prefer System 2 nudges (kind of). Duke Law J 66:121–168

Thaler RH, Sunstein C (2009) Nudge: improving decisions about health, wealth and happiness. Penguin Books, London

Vesting T (2001) Die Bedeutung von Information und Kommunikation für die verwaltungsrechtliche Systembildung. In: Hoffmann-Riem W et al. (eds). Grundlagen des Verwaltungsrechts, Band. 2, Informationsordnung – Verwaltungsverfahren – Handlungsformen, 2nd edn. C.H. Beck, München

Viseu A, Suchman L (2010) Wearable augmentations: imaginaries of the informed body. In: Edwards J, Penny H, Wade P (eds) Technologized images, technologized bodies. Berghahn, New York, pp 161–184

von Grafenstein M et al. (2018) Nudging – Regulierung durch Big Data und Verhaltenswissenschaften, ABIDA Gutachten. Berlin, 2018

Weber F, Schäfer H-B (2017) "Nudging", Ein Spross der Verhaltensökonomie. Der Staat 56:561–592

Wolff J (2015) Eine Annäherung an das Nudge-Konzept. Rechtswissenschaft 6:194–222

Wuermeling U (1996) Umsetzung der Europäischen Datenschutzrichtlinie, DB 49:663–671

Zillien N et al (2015) Zahlenkörper. Digitale Selbstvermessung als Verdinglichung des Körpers. In: Hahn K, Stempfhuber M (eds) Präsenzen 2.0. Medienkulturen im digitalen Zeitalter. Springer, Wiesbaden, pp 77–94

Artificial Intelligence and Transparency: Opening the Black Box

Thomas Wischmeyer

Contents

1 Introduction 76
2 Generating Knowledge Through Access to Information 79
    2.1 Epistemic Constraints 80
    2.2 Normative Constraints 82
    2.3 Functional Constraints 85
3 Creating Agency Through Explanations 87
    3.1 Causal Explanations 88
    3.2 Counterfactual Explanations 90
    3.3 Explanations in Context 92
4 The Way Forward 93
    4.1 Principles 93
    4.2 Practice 94
References 97

Abstract The alleged opacity of AI has become a major political issue over the past few years. Opening the black box, so it is argued, is indispensable to identify encroachments on user privacy, to detect biases and to prevent other potential harms. However, what is less clear is how the call for AI transparency can be translated into reasonable regulation. This Chapter argues that designing AI transparency regulation is less difficult than oftentimes assumed. Regulators profit from the fact that the legal system has already gained considerable experience with the question of how to shed light on partially opaque decision-making systems—human decisions. This experience provides lawyers with a realistic perspective of the functions of potential AI transparency legislation as well as with a set of legal instruments which can be employed to this end.

T. Wischmeyer (✉)
Faculty of Law, University of Bielefeld, Bielefeld, Germany
e-mail: thomas.wischmeyer@uni-bielefeld.de

1 Introduction

1 In light of AI's growing impact on society, there is broad agreement that those who regulate, employ or are affected by AI-based systems should have an adequate understanding of the technology. A steady stream of policy papers, national planning strategies, expert recommendations, and stakeholder initiatives frames this objective in terms of AI transparency.[1] While one should not forget that AI analyzes patterns much faster and far more accurately than humans ever could, and that AI-based systems are therefore typically deployed to shed light on matters which are too complex for human minds to understand,[2] these transparency *enhancing* capabilities are not at the center of the discourse on AI transparency. Rather, it is the alleged opacity of AI itself which has become a major political issue over the past few years. Opening the black box, so it is argued, is indispensable to identify encroachments on user privacy (see Marsch, paras 5 et seq.), to detect biases or AI discrimination (see Tischbirek, para 19) and to prevent other potential harms (see Hermstrüwer, para 45; Rademacher, para 31).[3]

2 While transparency has always been a general principle of data protection (cf. Article 5(1)(a) General Data Protection Directive—GDPR), law-makers around the globe are currently starting to experiment with specific transparency requirements for automated decision-making systems (ADMs), including AI-based systems. In 2017, law-makers in New York City proposed to oblige any city agency 'that uses, for the purposes of targeting services to persons, imposing penalties upon persons or policing, an algorithm or any other method of automated processing system of data' to, inter alia, 'publish on such agency's website, the source code of such system'.[4] In 2018, the German Conference of Information Commissioners called for new laws which would make it mandatory for public authorities and private actors employing ADMs to publish detailed information on the 'logic' of the system, the classifiers and weights applied to the input data and the level of

---

[1] Cf. only National Science and Technology Council Committee on Technology (2016), OECD Global Science Forum (2016), Asilomar Conference (2017), European Parliament (2017), Harhoff et al. (2018), Singapore Personal Data Protection Commission (2018), Agency for Digital Italy (2018), House of Lords Select Committee on Artificial Intelligence (2018), Villani (2018), European Commission (2018) and Datenethikkommission (2018).

[2] Bundesanstalt für Finanzdienstleistungsaufsicht (2018), pp. 144–145. See also Hermstrüwer, para 3, Hennemann, para 37.

[3] Important contributions to this debate include Mayer-Schönberger and Cukier (2013), pp. 176 et seq.; Zarsky (2013); Pasquale (2015); Burrell (2016); Diakopoulos (2016); Zweig (2016); Ananny and Crawford (2018).

[4] The initial proposal (Int. 1696–2017) would have added the text cited above to Section 23-502 of the Administrative Code of the City of New York. However, the law that was finally passed only established a task force which is designated to study how city agencies currently use algorithms. For a detailed account of the legislative process see legistar.council.nyc.gov/LegislationDetail.aspx?ID=3137815&GUID=437A6A6D-62E1-47E2-9C42-461253F9C6D0.

expertise of the system administrators.[5] Also in 2018, a task force set up by the Conference of German State Justice Ministers suggested a general duty to notify the public about the use of ADMs.[6] In the EU, the Commission introduced the Regulation on Promoting Fairness and Transparency for Business Users of Online Intermediation Services in 2018, which foresees disclosure obligations for ranking algorithms.[7] Similar proposals are also under discussion in Germany for 'media intermediaries' (see Krönke, para 55).[8] For certain ADM-based financial activities, notification requirements are already in place (see Schemmel, para 25).[9]

The call for transparency is, to a certain extent, generic in debates on new technologies,[10] as is its critique. The objections first address technical feasibility. According to some, meaningful transparency regulation will inevitably fail, because the decision-making processes of AI-based systems are—as Jenna Burrell has put it—inherently 'opaque in the sense that the person affected by a decision can hardly ever comprehend how or why a certain input of data has been categorized and produced a certain output' (see paras 10 et seq.).[11] A second line of criticism highlights the faulty normative assumptions underlying transparency regulations, which only create an illusion of accountability (see paras 23 et seq.).[12] A third group of scholars argues that the problem is actually less AI's lack of transparency, but—here the discourse gets a bit fuzzy—its poor 'explainability', 'intelligibility', 'comprehensibility', 'understandability', or 'foreseeability', or vice versa the 'secrecy', 'inscrutability' or 'non-intuitiveness' of AI-based systems (see paras 25 et seq.).[13]

However, while having a right to look at the source code or the database of an AI-based system will not be very enlightening for laypersons and, while sunshine laws alone do not guarantee accountability, promoting AI transparency remains nevertheless a necessary and worthwhile enterprise. To paraphrase a statement of the Article 29 Data Protection Working Party, technological complexity is no excuse for not providing vital information.[14] Even if its value is primarily instrumental, transparency is still an indispensable element of any accountability framework.

---

[5]Konferenz der Informationsfreiheitsbeauftragten (2018), p. 4.

[6]Arbeitsgruppe "Digitaler Neustart" (2018), p. 7.

[7]COM/2018/238 final—2018/0112 (COD).

[8]Rundfunkkommission der Länder (2018), pp. 25–26.

[9]As of January 2018, investment service providers in Germany are subject to notification requirements, if they engage in algorithmic trading within the meaning of Section 80(2) of the *Wertpapierhandelsgesetz* (WpHG—Securities Trading Act). This provision implements the EU Markets in Financial Instruments Directive II (MiFID II).

[10]Cf. Mittelstadt et al. (2016), p. 6: 'transparency is often naïvely treated as a panacea for ethical issues arising from new technologies.' Similarly, Neyland (2016), pp. 50 et seq.; Crawford (2016), pp. 77 et seq.

[11]Burrell (2016), p. 1.

[12]Cf. Ananny and Crawford (2018), p. 983. For an extensive discussion of this point see Tsoukas (1997); Heald (2006), pp. 25–43; Costas and Grey (2016), p. 52; Fenster (2017).

[13]For references see Selbst and Barocas (2018), pp. 1089–1090.

[14]Article 29 Data Protection Working Party (2018), p. 14.

Especially for public authorities, decision-making procedures must be 'generally visible and understandable', as the German Federal Constitutional Court (FCC) has put it.[15] Here, the call for transparency is ultimately based on the rule of law and the principle of democratic government. But transparency also serves a vital function in the private sector. There, transparency regulation is used to reduce the costs of market entry, to re-balance structural and harmful information asymmetries, e.g., between businesses and consumers. Transparency requirements for private AI can thus create or sustain competition in the increasing number of markets in which AI-based technologies are deployed.[16]

5   But how can the call for AI transparency be translated into reasonable regulation? This paper argues that designing AI transparency regulation may be complicated, but it is less difficult than oftentimes assumed. Regulators profit from the fact that the legal system has already gained considerable experience with the question of how to shed light on partially opaque decision-making systems—human decisions. This experience provides lawyers with a realistic perspective of the functions of potential AI transparency legislation as well as with a set of legal instruments which can be employed to this end.

6   With regard to the *functions*, past attempts to open the human black box have shown that 'full' transparency is neither possible nor desirable. Instead, transparency regulations in a broad sense should aim at two things: First, to provide different groups of stakeholders—citizens, consumers, the media, parliaments, regulatory agencies, and courts—with the knowledge each of them needs to initiate or conduct an administrative or judicial review of a decision or to hold the decision-maker otherwise accountable. Second, transparency regulation can and should impart a sense of agency to those who are directly affected by a decision in order to generate trust in the decision-making process.

7   With regard to the *regulatory toolbox*, transparency regulation can either grant access to information about the system and its operations, or it can require system operators to explain their decisions to those affected. Both types of regulations serve the above-mentioned functions and therefore strengthen AI accountability, but the quality and kinds of information which system operators need to provide in response to these obligations or the exercise of the corresponding rights differs.

8   Being realistic about the functions and the instruments helps to avoid two common misconceptions of AI transparency regulation. Section 2 of this Chapter shows that it is not primarily epistemic reasons—the black box issue—

---

[15]Bundesverfassungsgericht 2 BvR 2134, 2159/92 'Maastricht' (12 October 1993), BVerfGE 89, p. 185; 2 BvR 1877/97 and 50/98 'Euro' (31 March 1998), BVerfGE 97, p. 369. On the values of transparency cf. Scherzberg (2000), pp. 291 et seq., 320 et seq., 336 et seq.; Gusy (2012), § 23 paras 18 et seq.; Scherzberg (2013), § 49 paras 13 et seq.

[16]Cf. CJEU C-92/11 'RWE Vertrieb AG v Verbraucherzentrale Nordrhein-Westfalen eV' (21 March 2013), ECLI:EU:C:2013:180; CJEU C-26/13 'Árpád Kásler and Hajnalka Káslerné Rábai v OTP Jelzálogbank Zrt' (30 April 2014), ECLI:EU:C:2014:282. See also Busch (2016). For a critical perspective on disclosure obligations in U.S. private law and in privacy law see Ben-Shahar and Schneider (2011) and Ben-Shahar and Chilton (2016).

Artificial Intelligence and Transparency: Opening the Black Box 79

which make the production of knowledge about AI a difficult case for regulators. Rather, it is especially the legitimate interests of the system operators in AI secrecy which make individual access to information rights in this field a delicate balancing act (less so, however, an obligation to explain). Secondly, the inability of (some) AI-based systems to 'explain' themselves, in the sense of telling us what the causal determinants for their decisions are, is less relevant in terms of individual agency than the current lack of resources of regulatory agencies and courts to process the information which the systems and their operators already can and do provide. Therefore, as discussed in Sect. 3, AI 'explainability' is not a matter of technology design, as recent initiatives on Explainable AI (XAI) assume, but first and foremost an institutional challenge for the administration and the judiciary. Against this backdrop, Sect. 4 sketches a way forward for meaningful AI transparency regulation.

2 Generating Knowledge Through Access to Information

Under the epistemic conditions of modern social organization, knowledge is generated not in isolation, but in critical and open discussions.[17] In society, openness enables creativity, encourages criticism and prevents cognitive and other biases, while for governments it ensures responsivity, efficiency and accountability and thus contributes to good governance.[18] Standard regulatory tools to create openness and thus to foster the growth of knowledge include individual access to information rights, mandatory disclosure rules or investigatory authorities granted to public authorities.[19] Whether in the case of AI such rights and obligations—which are grouped together here under the umbrella term of 'access to information regulation'—are able to increase transparency depends first and foremost on the alleged opacity of AI technology (Sect. 2.1). Whether such rules can be designed in a necessary and proportionate manner must also be considered in light of the normative positions of those negatively affected by transparency regulations (Sect. 2.2). Finally, when deciding on the enactment and the scope of access to information regulation for AI, regulators should take pragmatic considerations into account, including, but not limited to, the capacity of individual stakeholders to process the knowledge obtained through such regulation (Sect. 2.3).

---

[17]Merton (1968), pp. 71–72.
[18]Cf. Fassbender (2006), § 76 para 2; Hood and Heald (2006); Florini (2007).
[19]Sometimes, transparency regulation is identified with granting individual rights to information. However, such individual rights are only one element within a larger regulatory structure that governs the flow of information in society, see Part 4.

2.1 Epistemic Constraints

10 Current discussions on AI transparency tend to emphasize the epistemic constraints, which AI-based decision-making systems pose for external observers. And, indeed, from the perspective of a layperson, these constraints are obvious. Only a small fraction of the population can read computer code and the vast majority is unable to analyze even the most primitive machine learning algorithm. The same is true for public officials. And due to the high degree of specialization, in the IT industry, even IT experts who have been trained in the field might not understand all methods used in a complex AI-based system.[20]

11 However, these difficulties should not overshadow the fact that the technology and the logic behind AI—defined here as the application of a class of statistical methods and algorithms usually subsumed under the generic term of machine learning to potentially very large and often heterogeneous sets of data (big data)—are generally well-understood, in fact much better than many other natural or social phenomena such as climate change, nanotechnology, or financial markets. Moreover, the software industry has developed various control tools over the past decades which are regularly employed to test complex systems,[21] including AI-based systems.[22] To this end, an expert team of auditors can check the code, reconstruct the underlying algorithms, analyze the training processes, evaluate the training and the result databases, feed dummy data etc.[23]

12 Although our understanding of AI is thus quite advanced in theory, the literature on AI transparency points to three serious challenges that AI audits face in practice. The *first* concerns the fact that the greater the volume, variety and velocity of data processing, the more difficult it becomes to understand and predict the behavior of a system or to re-construct the computed correlations.[24] However, this problem is not specific for AI-based systems. Even fully deterministic programs today process a

---

[20] On the difficulty to identify the 'boundaries' of AI-based systems, which further complicates the quest for transparency, see Kaye (2018), para 3; Ananny and Crawford (2018), p. 983.

[21] Outside the specific context of AI, error detection and avoidance has become the subject of sophisticated research activities and extensive technical standardization efforts, cf. the international standard ISO/IEC 25000 'Software engineering—Software product Quality Requirements and Evaluation (SQuaRE)" (created by ISO/IEC JTC 1/SC 07 Software and systems engineering). The German version 'DIN ISO/IEC 25000 Software-Engineering – Quality Criteria and Evaluation of Software Products (SQuaRE) – Guideline for SQuaRE' is maintained by NA 043 Information Technology and Applications Standards Committee (NIA) of the German Institute for Standardization.

[22] A much cited paper in this context is Sandvig et al. (2014), pp. 1 et seq.

[23] Recently, Munich Re and the German Research Centre for Artificial Intelligence (DFKI) have collaborated in auditing the technology behind a startup which uses AI to detect fraudulent online payments. After the audit, which comprised a check of the data, the underlying algorithms, the statistical models and the IT infrastructure of the company, was conducted successfully, the startup was offered an insurance.

[24] Tutt (2017), pp. 89–90, describes several instances, in which forensic experts from IBM and Telsa were unable to reconstruct ex post the reasons for a malfunction of their systems.

potentially unlimited number of valuables and properties in an extremely short time. Moreover, in many instances, computing technology also provides a solution to the problem, since at least parts of the audit can be automated. Even specialized AI can be used to this end.[25] Whether or not data-based systems are easily accessible depends therefore less on the 'bigness' of data, but rather on the way they are processed in the system under review, i.e., on the algorithms.

The algorithms are at the core of the *second* challenge. At least for some algorithms used in AI-based systems it is practically—not theoretically—impossible to retroactively connect a specific input to a specific output and vice versa.[26] Oftentimes it is assumed that all AI-based systems using machine learning algorithms elude such causal explanations. However, machine learning is not a monolithic concept, but it comprises a variety of techniques, which range from traditional linear regression models over support vector machines and decision tree algorithms to different types of neural networks. The difficulty to establish a causal nexus *ex post* between a specific input and a specific output differs considerably between these techniques.[27] While decision tree algorithms, which can be used both for regression and classification problems and are employed, e.g., in financial forecasting or in loan application programs, allow causal explanations once a tree has been built, this is not necessarily true for artificial neural networks, which are employed primarily for the purposes of pattern recognition, such as speech or image recognition or natural language processing. Here, the re-construction problem is serious, because even with complete information about the operations of a system, an *ex post* analysis of a specific decision may not be able to establish a linear causal connection which is easily comprehensible for human minds. Instead, the analysis will present a decision rule, which is a probability function over a large number of weighted variables, which is sometimes even further modified in order to optimize calculation time. Even if it is theoretically still possible to write down or to re-calculate this function, there remains a 'mismatch between mathematical optimization in high-dimensionality characteristic of machine learning and the demands of human-scale reasoning and styles of semantic interpretation.'[28]

The 'opacity' of neural networks might be unsatisfactory from an engineer's point of view. However, the difficulty to identify causal relations in neural networks does not prove the futility of—mandated or voluntary—AI audits for neural networks and even less so for other forms of AI, because it does not affect the possibility to collect information about the system and its operations. Incrementally seeking explanations for opaque phenomena by gathering data and by testing a series of

---

[25] See supra note 2.
[26] For the following see only Hildebrandt (2011), pp. 375 et seq.; van Otterlo (2013), pp. 41 et seq.; Leese (2014), pp. 494 et seq.; Burrell (2016), pp. 1 et seq.; Tutt (2017), pp. 83 et seq.
[27] For a detailed discussion see Bundesanstalt für Finanzdienstleistungsaufsicht (2018), pp. 188 et seq.
[28] Burrell (2016), p. 2.

hypotheses is the standard way to produce knowledge and to comprehend the data in science and in society. And, as we will discuss shortly, it is one of the main objectives of access to information regulation (Sect. 2.3).

The *third* challenge concerns the high dynamic of AI development in general and the dynamic performance of AI-based systems in particular.[29] An increasing number of AI-based systems, following the example of IBM's Watson, possesses in-built feedback loops, which allow them to constantly adjust the weight of their variables depending on the effects of their algorithms on the users.[30] Thus, ideally, every operation of the system trains and updates the system. Factors which had the impact x at t_0 may therefore lead to a different decision y at t_1. In such a dynamic architecture, explanations are only valid for a brief moment in time. Therefore, even 'if an algorithm's source code, its full training data set, and its testing data were made transparent, it would still only give a particular snapshot of its functionality.'[31] However, this observation also refutes neither the possibility of AI audits nor the need for access to information regulation, because a single snapshot can still contain valuable information. From a regulatory perspective, the third challenge thus only means that transparency regulation needs to be complemented by documentary obligations, which ensure that access to information remains possible (see para 48).

2.2 Normative Constraints

There are thus no strong epistemic reasons which would make it a priori unreasonable for regulators to oblige the operators of AI-based systems to grant supervisory authorities and other third parties, including auditors, access to the code, the databases, the statistical models, the IT infrastructures etc. At present, however, no access to information regulation exists, which would require such far-reaching disclosures. Most jurisdictions do not even stipulate a duty to notify the public about AI-based systems, which are deployed for decision-making purposes, let alone a right to access the code etc. One much-discussed exception is the French Digital Republic Act from October 7, 2016, which provides that, in the case of state actors taking a decision 'on the basis of algorithms', individuals have a right to be informed about the 'principal characteristics' of a decision-making system.[32] The French Act

---

[29]Even many conventional algorithms are constantly updated, which makes an ex-post evaluation difficult, cf. Schwartz (2015).

[30]Cf. IBM (2018).

[31]Ananny and Crawford (2018), p. 982. See also Diakopoulos (2016), p. 59.

[32]Loi n° 2016-1321 du 7 octobre 2016 pour une République numérique. As further laid out Article R311-3-1-2, created through Article 1 of the Décret n° 2017-330 du 14 mars 2017 relatif aux droits des personnes faisant l'objet de décisions individuelles prises sur le fondement d'un traitement algorithmique (available at www.legifrance.gouv.fr/affichTexte.do?cidTexte=JORFTEXT000034194929&categorieLien=cid), the administration needs to provide information about (1) the degree and the way in which algorithmic processing contributes to the

was inspired by the provisions on 'automated decision-making systems' (ADMs) in Articles 12a and 15 of the 1995 EU Data Protection Directive (DPD), which were replaced in 2018 by Articles 13–15 and 22 GDPR. According to Articles 13(2)(f) and 14(2)(g) GDPR, all data controllers in the EU now must provide data subjects with information about the 'the existence of automated decision-making, including profiling' and 'meaningful information about the logic involved,' while Article 15(1)(h) GDPR grants data subjects a corresponding right of access to this information. The GDPR rights, however, are limited to cases of ADM within the meaning of Article 22 GDPR, which only applies to decisions which are based 'solely' on automated processing and have 'legal effects' or 'similarly significantly affect' a person.[33] Thus, AI-based systems which only support humans in decision-making are beyond the scope of the provision.[34] Furthermore, where Article 22 GDPR applies, the information which needs to be provided to the data subject according to Articles 13 to 15 GDPR is limited. For the DPD and the implementing legislation in the EU Member States, including Sections 6a and 28b *Bundesdatenschutzgesetz 2001* (BDSG—German Federal Data Protection Act of 2001), which have been replaced by the almost identical Sections 31 and 37 BDSG 2018, the courts decided that detailed information on the decision in the individual case was unnecessary and that a description of the abstract design of the system was generally sufficient.[35] There has been no case in which a court has held that the data controller must provide access to the raw data, the code, etc. of an automated system.

There is little ground to assume that this jurisprudence will change significantly under the GDPR. The reason for this is not that lawmakers and courts underestimate the importance of ADM transparency. Rather, there are important legal grounds which make more ambitious disclosure requirements a difficult issue. This includes the protection of intellectual property rights and of trade and business secrets, which

---

decision making, (2) which data are processed and where they come from, (3) according to which variables the data is treated and, where appropriate, how they are weighed, (4) which operations are carried out by the system—all of this needs to be presented, however, "sous une forme intelligible et sous réserve de ne pas porter atteinte à des secrets protégés par la loi." There is also a national security exception to the law. For more details see Edwards and Veale (2017).

[33]For details cf. von Lewinski (2018), paras 7 et seq.; Martini (2018), paras 16 et seq., 25 et seq.

[34]Cf. Martini and Nink (2017), pp. 3 and 7–8; Wachter et al. (2017), pp. 88, 92; Buchner (2018), para 16; Martini (2018), paras 16 et seq.; von Lewinski (2018), paras 16 et seq., 23 et seq., 26 et seq.

[35]For Article 12a DPD see CJEU, C-141/12 and C-372/12, paras 50 et seq. For the German Data Protection Act, which contained (and still contains) a special section on credit scoring, the Bundesgerichtshof decided that brief statements on the design of credit scoring systems are sufficient and that system operators need only to explain the abstract relationship between a high credit score and the probability of securing credit. Detailed information on the decision or the system, in an individual case, was not deemed to be necessary, cf. Bundesgerichtshof VI ZR 156/13 (28.1.2014), BGHZ 200, 38, paras 25 et seq. In the literature there are numerous diverging views on what exact information has to be disclosed in order to adequately inform about the logic involved. For an overview of the different positions see Wischmeyer (2018a), pp. 50 et seq.

Recital 63 sentence 5 GDPR explicitly recognizes as limits for transparency.[36] Additionally, privacy and law enforcement interests can be negatively affected by transparency requirements.[37] These claims to 'AI secrecy' have so far not been treated in a systematic manner. A full account of the issue, which would need to distinguish between various kinds of 'legal secrets' (Kim Scheppele) as well as between public and private operators of AI,[38] is beyond the scope of this Chapter.[39] Here, I will only point out how the need to protect strategic and fiduciary secrets influences AI transparency regulation on a general level.

18   *Strategic* secrecy seeks to stabilize information asymmetries in order to reach competitive advantages. In the private sector, strategic secrets are the rule rather than the exception, because the obligation to grant a third party access to information infringes upon fundamental rights and needs to be justified. Therefore, most transparency regulations for the private sector—also outside the IT sector—only grant access to aggregated or abstract information, as in the case of credit scoring (see para 16); more ambitious obligations are still a rare exception. For public officials acting under freedom of information laws, it is secrecy which needs to be justified in light of the citizens' interests in transparency. However, most freedom of information laws recognize that state actors also need to act strategically under certain circumstances, e.g., for law enforcement purposes, in tax law, competition law or financial market regulation. If citizens had access to the databases and algorithms used by the state in such cases, this might frustrate enforcement efforts or enable competent actors to 'play' the system. For this reason, e.g., Section 88(5) sentence 4 *Abgabenordnung* (AO—German Fiscal Code) expressly excludes access to information about the tax authority's risk management systems insofar as a publication 'could jeopardize the uniformity and legality of taxation.'[40]

19   The protection of *fiduciary* secrets takes into account that in social interactions parties regularly exchange information which they do not want to disclose to the public or to third parties. The exchange of secret information deepens cooperation, facilitates coordinated strategic behavior and stabilizes trust. The wish to keep

---

[36]Cf. Hoffmann-Riem (2017), pp. 32–33. On the 'risk of strategic countermeasures' see Hermstrüwer, paras 65–69.

[37]See only Leese (2014), pp. 495 et seq.; Mittelstadt et al. (2016), p. 6.

[38]While the rule of law and the principle of democratic governance commit public actors to transparency and therefore limit administrative secrecy (see para 4), transparency requirements for private actors need to be justified in light of their fundamental rights. However, considering the public interests at stake and the risky nature of the new technology, the interests of private system operators will hardly ever prevail in toto. Moreover, the legislator needs also to protect the fundamental rights of those negatively affected by AI-based systems, which typically means that parliament must enact laws which guarantee an effective control of the technology. However, lawmakers have considerable discretion in this regard. For certain companies which operate privatized public spaces ('public fora') or have otherwise assumed a position of power that is somehow state-like, the horizontal effect of the fundamental rights of the data subjects will demand a more robust transparency regulation.

[39]For a theory of 'legal secrets' see Scheppele (1988), Jestaedt (2001) and Wischmeyer (2018b).

[40]See Braun Binder, paras 12 et seq. See also Martini and Nink (2017), p. 10.

information secret may also be based on the confidential nature of the relationship or the specific kind of data exchanged, e.g., in the case of personal data. The latter is particularly relevant for the databases of AI-based systems working with personal data. Here, the public interest in transparency and the need to protect privacy and the integrity of the personal data collide.[41] A similar conflict exists if state actors use private proprietary systems. Here, the interest in making public decision-making procedures 'visible and understandable' collides with the rights of those private actors who have invested in the development of their systems (see para 17).

Even legitimate claims to AI secrecy do not justify blanket exceptions (cf. Recital 63 sentence 6 GDPR). Laws such as Section 88(5) sentence 4 AO, which completely seal off the government's internal processes from external scrutiny, are overly rigid. Similarly, the *Bundesgerichtshof*'s near absolute position with regard to the protection of trade secrets for credit scoring (see para 16) can only be justified as long as the practical effects of a negative score are limited. In order to balance the competing interests in transparency and secrecy the regulatory toolbox contains various instruments, which can be employed to ensure the protection of truly sensitive data, while still providing valuable information about the system and its operations. These include (1) multi-tiered access regimes for sensitive information, which distinguish between notification duties, rights of access to raw or to aggregated data (see paras 22 et seq.), (2) temporal restrictions for access rights, (3) the employment of information intermediaries, (4) procedural safeguards, such as in-camera-proceedings, etc.[42] In many cases, these instruments will increase overall transparency without negatively affecting the secrecy interests of the system operators. However, if the interests in transparency outweigh the claims to secrecy and a reasonable balance cannot be reached, this is an important reason for not using AI-based systems in that particular context.[43]

2.3 Functional Constraints

Typically, access to information regulation grants different kinds of access to different kinds of stakeholders. The press can usually rely on statutory rights which are less restrictive than the general freedom of information laws, which again differ from the powers of courts and agencies to access or generate information. This granular approach accommodates the distinctive normative status of the

---

[41]This problem concerns all forms for transparency regulation, see Holznagel (2012), § 24 para 74; von Lewinski (2014), pp. 8 et seq.
[42]Wischmeyer (2018b), pp. 403–409.
[43]This has been discussed for cases where sensitive private proprietary technology is deployed for criminal justice or law enforcement purposes, cf. Roth (2017), Imwinkelried (2017) and Wexler (2018). For this reason, the police in North-Rhine Westphalia has developed a predictive policing system which does not use neural networks, but decision tree algorithms, cf. Knobloch (2018), p. 19.

stakeholders, but it also takes functional aspects into account, such as the relevance of the data for a stakeholder. If citizens seek information not only out of a general interest, but because they are negatively affected by a particular decision, their right to access is usually stronger. Another assumption underlying this regime is that individual citizens do not necessarily possess—nor do they need to develop—the competence to evaluate complex matters on their own. Rather, they can and should rely on experts and public institutions, especially the courts, to which they can bring their complaints and which can exercise their more far-reaching investigatory powers.[44]

22   For AI regulation, this means that we should stop looking for a one-size-fits-all solution. Not everyone needs unlimited access to all information. Instead, regulators are well advised to follow the traditional approach and consider the individual interests involved, the status of the stakeholders and the legal nature of those operating the system, which can be a public authority or a private party, the sensitivity and criticality of the sector, in which the system will be used, when designing an access to information regime for AI (see Sect. 4).

23   The functional approach also allows us to address a common criticism of access to information regulation for AI. It has been remarked many times that access to the source code generates no added value for the vast majority of citizens, while access to simplified information, e.g., to an abstract description of the system, a list of statistically significant factors or to aggregated output data, only allows for the identification of obvious mistakes, but not of truly problematic faults such as algorithmic discrimination or data protection violations.[45] But does this necessarily mean that AI transparency regulation creates only an illusion of accountability or even obscures the situation (see para 3)? This line of critique focuses mostly on individual information rights, such as the rights and obligations in Articles 13 to 15 GDPR. Indeed, the mixed experiences with access to information rights show that individual rights are no panacea.[46] In the worst case, such rights can be even used to externalize a social problem through subjectivisation, while the actual policies remain opaque and unchanged. Nevertheless, in the general discourse on transparency regulation hardly anyone questions today that individual information rights are able to serve a vital function in a democratic society, if they are understood as one component within a larger structure of information flow regulation and are accompanied by regulations which guarantee that individuals can use the information they have received to initiate a more thorough review of the system, especially through regulatory agencies or the courts (see para 4).

24   Still, from an access to information perspective, the role of the individual citizen is primarily instrumental. By claiming their rights, citizens contribute to the general growth of knowledge in society about AI. However, various authors have pointed to

---

[44]See, however, on the (potentially prohibitive) costs of expertise Tischbirek, para 41.

[45]Datta et al. (2017), pp. 71 et seq.; Tene and Polonetsky (2013), pp. 269–270.

[46]For a nuanced account of the strengths and weaknesses of access to information regulation see Fenster (2017).

the fact that the promise of transparency is actually more ambitious. If transparency is to be seen as a cornerstone of AI accountability, this requires 'not just seeing inside any one component of an assemblage but understanding how it works as a system.'[47] While access to information regulation tries to let stakeholders look inside the black box, it is not immediately concerned with making the information understandable. In order to avoid the fallacy that seeing equals understanding, the access to information framework therefore needs to be complemented by a different instrument which focuses specifically on the perspective of individuals affected by the deployment of AI-based systems.[48]

3 Creating Agency Through Explanations

As we have seen, if individuals feel overwhelmed or even objectified[49] by a loan refusal, a tax audit or a search order that is issued or recommended by an AI-based system, granting them unrestricted access to the source code will hardly restore their trust in the technology. It is therefore widely acknowledged that transparency regulation must not limit itself to providing information, but it also should impart those affected by the decision in question with a sense of agency. This means that the information those affected receive should enable them to react to a decision in a meaningful way—either by challenging it (exit), by changing their behavior (loyalty) or by initiating a debate on whether the criteria they were subjected to are acceptable in a democratic society (voice). To a similar end, Article 12(1) GDPR and other laws demand that data controllers provide information to data subjects 'in a concise, transparent, intelligible and easily accessible form, using clear and plain language.' The same conviction is also the starting point for those who argue that the debate on AI transparency should focus less on access to information and rather consider how to increase the 'intelligibility', 'comprehensibility', 'understandability', 'foreseeability', or 'explainability' of AI-based systems.[50]

However, the proliferation of terms and concepts indicates that it is not entirely clear how individual agency can be created through information. For many, explainability—this term will be used here to denote the challenge of creating a sense of agency through transparency—is associated with causality. Much recent work of computer scientists on Explainable AI (XAI) is therefore directed at

---

[47]Ananny and Crawford (2018), p. 983.
[48]Ananny and Crawford (2018), p. 982.
[49]The purpose of Article 22 GDPR is frequently defined as preventing the degradation of 'the individual to a mere object of a governmental act of processing without any regard for the personhood of the affected party or the individuality of the concrete case' (Martini and Nink (2017), p. 3) (translation T.W.). Similarly, von Lewinski (2014), p. 16.
[50]See supra note 13. See also Doshi-Velez and Kortz (2017), p. 6: '[E]xplanation is distinct from transparency. Explanation does not require knowing the flow of bits through an AI system, no more than explanation from humans requires knowing the flow of signals through neurons.'

identifying the factors that have caused an AI-based decision and at presenting those factors in an accessible manner (Sect. 3.1). However, this approach has its natural limitations, because, in many instances, causal explanations will be unavailable or too complex to be easily accessible for those affected. For this reason, alternative theories of explanations have recently experienced a renaissance in the literature on AI transparency, building, in particular, on David Lewis' work on counterfactuals (Sect. 3.2).[51] However, counterfactuals, too, cannot escape the trade-off between explainability and fidelity, which has to be made in every explanation. Therefore, this Chapter suggests shifting perspective and understanding explanations not solely as an act of providing information to an individual, but also as a social practice that is embedded in a specific institutional setting and that creates individual agency also in and through social and legal institutions (Sect. 3.3).

3.1 Causal Explanations

27 In the philosophy of science, an 'explanation' is understood primarily as the identification of factors that have caused an event or a decision.[52] From an ethical perspective, causal explanations can generate agency, because they help individuals to recognize how they can modify their behavior or which factors they must challenge in order to change the outcome. It is assumed that learning why one was classified in a particular manner means knowing how to avoid such a classification in the future. In this sense, strengthening AI explainability means developing analytical tools which equip AI-based systems with the ability to observe and analyze their own operations, to identify the causally determinant factors and present them to those affected in a way that is comprehensible for human beings. Numerous projects are currently operating in this field of Explainable AI (XAI).[53] Legal regulation could mandate the deployment of such tools.

28 Some scholars have argued that Article 22(3) GDPR already contains such an obligation.[54] The provision requires operators of ADMs to implement 'suitable measures to safeguard the data subject's rights' in cases in which automated

---

[51] Especially Wachter et al. (2018) draw on the work of Lewis, in particular on Lewis (1973a, b).

[52] While there exists 'considerable disagreement among philosophers about whether all explanations in science and in ordinary life are causal and also disagreement about what the distinction (if any) between causal and non-causal explanations consists in [...], virtually everyone [...] agrees that many scientific explanations cite information about causes' (Woodward 2017). See also Doshi-Velez and Kortz (2017), p. 3.

[53] Cf. Russell et al. (2015); Datta et al. (2017), pp. 71 et seq.; Doshi-Velez and Kim (2017); Fong and Vedaldi (2018). Despite recent progress, research in this field is still in its infancy. In 2017, a DARPA project on Explainable AI was initiated, see www.darpa.mil/program/explainable-artificial-intelligence.

[54] Goodman and Flaxman (2016). For additional references see Wachter et al. (2017), pp. 76–77.

processing is allowed according to Article 22(2)(a) and (c) GDPR.[55] However, a close reading of the provision shows that Article 22 GDPR—following in the footsteps of the 1995 Data Protection Directive—does not require the operators of ADMs to provide information about what has caused a decision in a specific case. Rather, abstract information on the logic of the system suffices (see para 20). This also applies to the notification duties in Articles 13(2)(f) and 14(2)(g) and the access to information right in Article 15(1)(h) GPDR. During the legislative drafting, a more ambitious 'right to explanation' had been discussed, but it was not implemented in the final version of the Regulation.[56]

It is worth considering whether, even if the GDPR or other laws would grant such a right to causal explanation, it would be technically feasible and if individuals would benefit from it. This has been doubted for the reasons discussed above (see paras 10 et seq.), in particular the difficulty to identify causal relations in some—not all—AI-based systems. Current research on XAI is making progress in this regard.[57] However, a tool that would allow observers to identify a causal relationship between a given input variable and a specific output is still not available for deep neural networks. Moreover, the complexity of many AI-based systems makes it impossible to present the causal factors which have led to a decision in a way that is comprehensible for laypersons. The more intricately connected factors a system takes into account when making its decisions—and increasing these numbers is typically the very purpose of employing AI instead of human intelligence[58]—, the less accessible their presentation becomes. This is true not only for AI, but it is a feature of all decision-making systems which take a multitude of interdependent factors into account. Assuming further innovations in XAI, a deep learning system might eventually be able to list all factors that have influenced its decision-making process and rank them according to their statistical significance for the specific case. However, if the number of listed features with all their interrelations exceeds the individual's capacity to process the information, such a list will be as meaningless for the addressee as the code itself.[59]

The machine learning community has made various innovative proposals to address this issue, including Locally Interpretable Model Agnostic Explanations (LIME), Bayesian Decision Lists (BDL) or Black Box Explanations through Transparent Approximations (BETA), which all enable observers to test the reliability of

---

[55]On the narrow scope of the provision cf. supra note 33.

[56]For a detailed analysis of the legislative process see Wachter et al. (2017), p. 81; Wischmeyer (2018a) pp. 49–52.

[57]For example, scholars recently proposed a mechanism to establish a relation of order between classifiers in a deep neural network which was used for image classifying thus making a significant step forward in offering a causal model for the technology: Palacio et al. (2018). Cf. also Montavon et al. (2018).

[58]Cf. Hermstrüwer, paras 70–74.

[59]Ribeiro et al. (2016), sec. 2: 'if hundreds or thousands of features significantly contribute to a prediction, it is not reasonable to expect any user to comprehend why the prediction was made, even if individual weights can be inspected.'

the classifiers in a machine learning system in order to find out whether they can trust the model or not. Currently, these models support experts in developing a better understanding of the technology. Whether they are also helpful for laypersons is still an open question.[60] In any event, the approaches are again confronted with the fact that there is an inherent tension between the attempt to reduce the complexity of an AI-based decision-making process to a level which can be comprehended by a layperson and the goal to preserve the informative value of the explanation. Technology can try to optimize the trade-off between fidelity and interpretability, but it cannot escape it.[61]

3.2 Counterfactual Explanations

31   If only a precise causal analysis of the decision-making process would count as an explanation, the fidelity/interpretability trade-off would threaten the very project of creating agency through explanation. However, while identifying all 'real determinants of a decision'[62] might support explainability, it is neither a necessary nor a sufficient condition for the way in which explanations are commonly understood and operationalized in societal practice. Otherwise, the insistence on explanations would make little sense in a society that, from an epistemic point of view, has always been a 'symphony of opacity' (Niklas Luhmann).[63] Especially collective (human) decisions would be structurally un-explainable, because, in most cases, it is impossible to reconstruct them in a way that makes the 'really' motivating causes visible.[64] But also for many individual decisions, the search for the true causes usually does not lead us very far.[65]

32   Nevertheless, we still insist that individuals and groups explain their actions. In the legal system, explanations are mandatory for most decisions of public authorities, precisely in order to create a sense of agency for citizens (see para 37). This suggests that the concept of explanation, as it is grounded in everyday practice and

---

[60]Wachter et al. (2018), p. 851.

[61]On this trade-off see Lakkaraju et al. (2013), sec. 3; Ribeiro et al. (2016), sec 3.2. Wachter et al. (2018), p. 851, even speak of a 'three-way trade-off between the quality of the approximation versus the ease of understanding the function and the size of the domain for which the approximation is valid.'

[62]Bundesverfassungsgericht 2 BvR 1444/00 (20 February 2001), BVerfGE 103, pp. 159–160.

[63]Luhmann (2017), p. 96.

[64]Wischmeyer (2015), pp. 957 et seq.

[65]Tutt (2017), p. 103. Cf. Lem (2013), pp. 98–99: 'Every human being is thus an excellent example of a device that can be used without knowing its algorithm. Our own brain is one of the "devices" that is "closest to us" in the whole Universe: we have it in our heads. Yet even today, we still do not know how the brain works exactly. As demonstrated by the history of psychology, the examination of its mechanics via introspection is highly fallible and leads one astray, to some most fallacious hypotheses.'

actually performed in society, is conceptually different from the scientific search for causes.[66] This intuition is shared by a growing community of scholars who try to find alternative means of generating AI transparency through explanations. Among the more prominent proposals is the idea of 'hypothetical alterations', which Danielle Citron and Frank Pasquale have introduced to the discussion on credit scoring and which would allow consumers to access and (hypothetically) modify their credit histories in order to analyze the effects.[67]

Similarly, Sandra Wachter, Brent Mittelstadt and Chris Russell have recently introduced the idea of 'counterfactual explanations', according to which only those factors of an AI-based decision-making process must be disclosed that would need to change in order to arrive at a different outcome.[68] In the case of a failed loan application, the individual applicant would thus be presented a counterfactual showing which data would need to be altered or amended for receiving a favorable result. Such information, they argue, would enable the applicant to modify their behavior or to contest a negative decision.[69] Because the hypothetical shows a concrete alternate future, its motivational capacity may indeed be greater than in the case of 'mere' causal explanations. Following Wachter et al., system operators could therefore be obliged to compute and disclose counterfactuals at the time a decision is made or at a later time either automatically or in response to specific requests lodged by individuals or a trusted third-party auditor.[70]

33

The concept of counterfactuals is attractive, because it builds on the insight that, in society, explanations hardly ever require a precise reconstruction of the decision-making processes. Instead, explanations typically focus only on those facts that have made a difference to the decision. Moreover, the theory acknowledges that AI-based systems will to some extent necessarily remain 'black boxes' for laypersons (see para 10). Finally, it bypasses the balancing procedure between transparency and secrecy interests (see para 20), because it only observes the performance of a system from the outside.

34

However, in addition to other serious limitations,[71] counterfactuals do not escape the trade-off between fidelity and interpretability.[72] As Wachter et al. acknowledge,

35

---

[66]That humans can interact with each other even if they do not know exactly what is causing the decisions of other persons, may have an evolutionary component: Yudkowsky (2008), pp. 308 et seq.
[67]Citron and Pasquale (2014).
[68]Wachter et al. (2018). See also Doshi-Velez and Kortz (2017), p. 7. For philosophical foundations see Lewis (1973a, b) and Salmon (1994).
[69]Wachter et al. (2018), p. 843.
[70]Wachter et al. (2018), p. 881.
[71]Cf. Wachter et al. (2018), p. 883: 'As a minimal form of explanation, counterfactuals are not appropriate in all scenarios. In particular, where it is important to understand system functionality, or the rationale of an automated decision, counterfactuals may be insufficient in themselves. Further, counterfactuals do not provide the statistical evidence needed to assess algorithms for fairness or racial bias.'
[72]Similarly Hermstrüwer, paras 45–48.

the greater the complexity of a decision-making system becomes, the more counterfactuals are needed in order to illustrate which factors the data subject can tweak in order to produce a different outcome.[73] Counterfactuals are therefore good at supporting data subjects in developing a general understanding of moderately complex AI-based systems. Its main beneficiaries, however, are the operators of such systems, which can provide information about the system without granting the data subjects or third parties deep access.

3.3 *Explanations in Context*

36 As long as explanations are understood solely as a specific form in which information about a decision is presented to the addressee, the trade-off between fidelity and interpretability is unavoidable. However, what is missing in almost all theories of AI 'explainbility' is the institutional setting in which explanations typically take place. This setting is important, because institutions can take part of the burden of interpretation off the individual's shoulders and thus reduce the need to compromise fidelity in order to preserve interpretability.

37 In the legal system, institutional aspects are an integral part of the theory of explanation or, even more specifically, of reason-giving. The purpose of reason-giving requirements in law is not only to inform individuals about a decision, but also to enable them to set in motion the complex machinery of the rule of law in order to protect their rights.[74] The German Federal Administrative Court (*Bundesverwaltungsgericht*) has emphasized this connection between reason-giving and access to justice by holding 'that a citizen whose rights the administration affects must be informed of the relevant reasons because he or she is only then in a position to adequately defend his or her rights.'[75]

38 Understanding explanation in this sense as a social practice which is embedded in an institutional context—an explanation is only the first step of a collaborative control process—does not negate the importance of providing causal or counterfactual information. Rather, it shifts the perspective and draws attention to the fact that

---

[73] Wachter et al. (2018), p. 851: 'The downside to this is that individual counterfactuals may be overly restrictive. A single counterfactual may show how a decision is based on certain data that is both correct and unable to be altered by the data subject before future decisions, even if other data exist that could be amended for a favourable outcome. This problem could be resolved by offering multiple diverse counterfactual explanations to the data subject.'

[74] (Causal) explanations and (semantic) reasons are not identical. However, both explanations and reason-giving require an institutional framework in order to be effective. Reason-giving requirements exist primarily for public authorities. However, the functions of reason-giving as described by courts and scholars are applicable for private parties, too. On the following in more detail Kischel (2003), pp. 88 et seq.; Wischmeyer (2018a), pp. 54 et seq. For a comparative analysis cf. Saurer (2009), pp. 382–383.

[75] Bundesverwaltungsgericht 2 C 42.79 (7 May 1981), DVBl 1982, pp. 198–199.

agency is generated not only through knowledge about the causes of the decision or potential alternatives, but also in and through institutions which support the individual in interpreting and scrutinizing the decision. This institutional approach allows the legal system to escape the fidelity/interpretability dilemma by essentially distinguishing two different elements of every explanation:

The first tries to make sure that the addressee is able to recognize that he or she has been subjected to a decision and can choose whether to accept the outcome or to seek legal remedies by involving a superior authority or the courts; if the addressee does not fully understand the explanation, he or she is expected to seek legal advice.[76] The second element addresses the supervisory authorities. For them, an explanation must be as complex as necessary in order to exercise effective control. It therefore depends on the circumstances of the case, and not on the capacities of the affected individuals, to what extent an explanation is accessible for a layperson. In his typical sober and ironic manner, Niklas Luhmann has described this as follows:

> Thus, in practice, the explanatory statement is written by lawyers for lawyers, for the superior authority or for the court; and it is encoded in an effort to be correct and error-free in such a way that the recipient often cannot understand it and can only decipher it with the help of experts.[77]

In this model, the success of an explanation depends both on the capacity of the individual to decipher that he or she has been subjected to a decision as well as on the integrity and the level of expertise of the control institutions. Now, applying this model to AI encounters a serious obstacle: While the existing legal control institutions are equipped to deal with many complex issues, this is so far not true for AI. Currently, administrative agencies or the courts have only little experience with analyzing complex AI-based systems. For this reason, developing and strengthening these capacities must become an integral part of every theory of AI transparency as well as of every serious political initiative in this field.

4 The Way Forward

4.1 Principles

The discussion on AI transparency needs to overcome false absolutes. Neither are all AI-based systems inscrutable black boxes nor does transparency all by itself guarantee accountability.[78] Rather, the value of AI transparency regulation consists of generating knowledge and sparking debate about the technology, motivating individuals to contest AI-based decisions and—eventually in the long run—

---

[76]Stelkens (2018), § 39 VwVfG, paras 41, 43.
[77]Luhmann (1983), p. 215 (translation T.W.).
[78]For a comprehensive discussion of AI's accountability problem, of which transparency is one dimension, cf. Busch (2018).

strengthening societal acceptance of the new technology.[79] To what extent regulation can actually achieve these goals depends on many factors. However, it seems at least plausible that the existence of robust access to information regulation and the introduction of explanation-giving requirements, which are embedded in a larger collaborative control process, will positively contribute to realizing these objectives, while the refusal to provide information or to explain decisions might provoke resistance and undermine trust.[80] Transparency regulation should therefore be considered as a means to counteract the widespread ignorance and the diffuse sense of disenfranchisement that accompanies the rise of AI.

42 Important for the future design of this architecture is the distinction between access to information and explanation, which has been discussed extensively in the previous Parts. Equally fundamental is the distinction between the public or private nature of the operators of AI-based systems, which would need further elaboration in a comprehensive theory of AI transparency (see paras 17 et seq.). Additionally, regulators need to take the following factors into account when balancing the competing interests in AI transparency and AI secrecy: (1) The criticality of the sector in which the system is employed; (2) the relative importance of the system operator for this sector; (3) the quality and weight of the individual and collective rights which are affected by the deployment of the system; (4) the kind of data concerned (especially whether or not special categories of personal data in the sense of Article 9 GDPR are concerned); (5) how closely the technology is integrated into individual decision-making processes—much suggests that AI transparency laws should move past the formalist approach of Article 22 GDPR, which requires that automated processing has 'legal effects' or 'similarly significantly affects' data subjects, and include all AI-based systems operating with personal data that contribute to decision-making processes[81]; (6) and, finally, whether and how it is possible to protect the legitimate interest of the system operators in AI secrecy through organizational, technical or legal means.

4.2 Practice

43 Transparency is the informational dimension of accountability and, as such, both a precondition for and a product of the control framework for decision-making processes. Transparency regulation is therefore a multi-faceted issue. In the 'analog' world, various instruments are employed to make decisions of public actors transparent, including the prohibition of secret laws, procedural transparency requirements for administrative and judicial actions and the different constitutional and

---

[79]This last aspect is particularly prominent in EU and US constitutional law, cf. Saurer (2009), pp. 365 and 385.
[80]Mittelstadt et al. (2016), p. 7.
[81]See supra note 34. For a similar appeal see Wachter et al. (2018), p. 881.

statutory rights to information for parliamentarians, the press and citizens. The same is true for AI transparency regulation. Individual rights to information or explanation are therefore only one element within a larger regulatory and supervisory structure. Technology—transparency by design—is another important part of this architecture, but, again, not the only answer. Against this backdrop, a meaningful transparency strategy should include at least the following five interlocking measures.

The *first* and probably least controversial step is the duty to disclose the existence of AI-based systems as well as the duty to notify the competent authorities and, eventually, the data subjects of their deployment.[82] In some sectors, such disclosure and notification requirements are already in place or currently under discussion.[83] For public authorities, the disclosure should include 'details about its purpose, reach, potential internal use policies or practices, and implementation timeline'.[84] Because notification and disclosure are basic requirements of the rule of law, exceptions can only be justified in special circumstances.[85] For private actors, it depends, inter alia, on the sector in which the system is employed and the quality and intensity in which the rights of the data subjects are affected, whether such requirements can be enacted. However, the information presented in such abstract statements is rarely particularly sensitive, which gives the legislator a certain margin of appreciation in this regard.

If AI-based systems are used for individual decision-making purposes, the notification can be combined with a right to explanation, the *second* level in the transparency architecture. As described in Sect. 3, explanations are not about giving the addressee an exact description of the system or providing him or her with a list of all causes or counterfactuals. Rather, the information that is presented in an explanation needs to be carefully calibrated in light of the overriding purposes of explanation-giving requirements, i.e., to enable citizens to realize their rights to administrative or judicial control of a decision as well as to support courts and supervisory agencies in exercising this control. This might entail information on (1) the data basis of the system; (2) the models and the decision logic; (3) (data) quality standards implemented by the system operators; (4) the reference groups or profiles used by the system; (5) actual or potential inferences made by the system with regard to the individual concerned; etc.[86] The exact content of such an

---

[82]Martini (2017), p. 1020; Busch (2018), pp. 58–59.
[83]Cf supra notes 4 to 9.
[84]Reisman et al. (2018), p. 9.
[85]Cf. Bundesverfassungsgericht 1 BvR 256, 263, 586/08 'Vorratsdatenspeicherung' (2 March 2010), BVerfGE 125, pp. 336–337.
[86]Cf. Busch (2018), pp. 59–60; Sachverständigenrat für Verbraucherfragen (2018), pp. 122, 162–163; Zweig (2019).

explanation cannot be defined in the abstract, but it needs to be determined in each case individually.[87]

46 The *third* step consists of creating individual access to information rights. Such rights allow data subjects or researchers, even if they are not personally affected by decisions of an AI-based system, an assessment of the system and its operations and can be used to prepare judicial or administrative actions against the data controller or simply to spark a debate about the system. In the case of public authorities, the natural way to create such rights is to extend the scope of the existing freedom of information laws to include AI-based systems.[88] For private actors, access to information rights are still an underdeveloped and under-researched matter. As discussed in Sect. 2.2, access to information rights are not absolute. Current freedom of information laws contain exceptions, which will also apply to AI secrecy, e.g., if the administration uses a system for airport security or for tax fraud detection. For private actors, the right to secrecy is typically stronger in order to prevent that access to information rights are being misused by competitors. Here, a reasonable balance between the competing interests must be achieved through a careful design of the exceptions to the right of access (see para 20).

47 While these exceptions might diminish the practical effectiveness of information rights, the accountability of the systems can be guaranteed by other means as well. In particular, supervisory agencies and courts can be granted access to information, too. Such investigatory authorities for public agencies are the *fourth* step towards a comprehensive AI transparency regime. In the private sector, public investigatory authorities are a standard instrument of administrative control. And if public agencies themselves use AI-based systems, a higher or a specialized supervisory authority or the courts need to have access to the system in order to review the legality of a decision (cf. Article 19(4) *Grundgesetz*—German Basic Law). While secrecy interests must also be taken into account in these constellations, they usually can be accommodated more easily than in the case of individual information rights, because the information remains within the sphere of the state. How rigorous the supervisory mechanisms need to be depends on the factors discussed in Sect. 4.1. Especially, where individual access to information rights are not granted, supervisory control has a compensatory function and must therefore be performed more thoroughly and more frequently. Whether the investigatory authorities for AI-based systems should be vested in one specialized agency[89] or distributed among various agencies, which each supervise the deployment of AI-based systems within their respective domain, will depend on the constitutional requirements as well as on the administrative culture within a country (see Hoffmann-Riem, para 39). In technical terms, operators

---

[87]Cf supra note 38.

[88]According to some scholars, such a requirement was introduced in France through the Digital Republic Law (Loi n°2016-1321 pour une République numérique), which has amended the definition of the administrative document in Article 300-2 of the Code des relations entre le public et l'administration by the words 'codes sources'. For details see Jean and Kassem (2018), p. 15.

[89]Cf. Tutt (2017).

of AI-based systems will need to set up appropriate technical interfaces (APIs) for the agencies.

The *fifth* and final step includes various accompanying measures, such as the duty to document the operations of AI-based systems (see para 16).[90] Moreover, courts and agencies must build up the necessary level of expertise for the control of AI-based systems. To this end, governments should participate in expert networks, set up specialized agencies and standardization processes, create a framework for certification and auditing etc.[91] Obviously, this is a difficult and long-term task that moves past the realm of transparency regulation. However, it is indispensable for any serious attempt to 'open the black box'.

References

Agency for Digital Italy (2018) White Paper on artificial intelligence at the service of citizens. www.agid.gov.it/en/agenzia/stampa-e-comunicazione/notizie/2018/04/19/english-version-white-paper-artificial-intelligence-service-citizen-its-now-online

Ananny M, Crawford K (2018) Seeing without knowing: limitations of the transparency ideal and its application to algorithmic accountability. New Media Soc 20(3):973–989

Arbeitsgruppe "Digitaler Neustart" (2018) Zwischenbericht der Arbeitsgruppe "Digitaler Neustart" zur Frühjahrskonferenz der Justizministerinnen und Justizminister am 6. und 7. Juni 2018 in Eisenach. www.justiz.nrw.de/JM/schwerpunkte/digitaler_neustart/zt_fortsetzung_arbeitsgruppe_teil_2/2018-04-23-Zwischenbericht-F-Jumiko-2018%2D%2D-final.pdf

Article 29 Data Protection Working Party (2018) Guidelines on automated individual decision-making and Profiling for the purposes of Regulation 2016/679 (wp251rev.01). ec.europa.eu/newsroom/article29/item-detail.cfm?item_id=612053

Asilomar Conference (2017) Asilomar AI principles. futureoflife.org/ai-principles

Ben-Shahar O, Chilton A (2016) Simplification of privacy disclosures: an experimental test. J Legal Stud 45:S41–S67

Ben-Shahar O, Schneider C (2011) The failure of mandated disclosure. Univ Pa Law Rev 159:647–749

Buchner B (2018) Artikel 22 DSGVO. In: Kühling J, Buchner B (eds) DS-GVO. BDSG, 2nd edn. C.H. Beck, München

Bundesanstalt für Finanzdienstleistungsaufsicht (2018) Big Data trifft auf künstliche Intelligenz. Herausforderungen und Implikationen für Aufsicht und Regulierung von Finanzdienstleistungen. www.bafin.de/SharedDocs/Downloads/DE/dl_bdai_studie.html

Burrell J (2016) How the machine 'thinks': understanding opacity in machine learning algorithms. Big Data Soc 3:205395171562251. https://doi.org/10.1177/2053951715622512

---

[90]Data controllers need to make the documented data available to individuals or supervisory authorities in 'a structured, commonly used and machine-readable format' (cf. Article 20 GDPR). For this requirement in a different context see Bundesverfassungsgericht 1 BvR 1215/07 'Antiterrordatei' (24 April 2013), BVerfGE 133, p. 370 para 215.

[91]Cf. Kaushal and Nolan (2015); Scherer (2016), pp. 353 et seq.; Martini and Nink (2017), p. 12; Tutt (2017), pp. 83 et seq. On government knowledge in general see Hoffmann-Riem (2014), pp. 135 et seq.

Busch C (2016) The future of pre-contractual information duties: from behavioural insights to big data. In: Twigg-Flesner C (ed) Research handbook on EU consumer and contract law. Edward Elgar, Cheltenham, pp 221–240

Busch C (2018) Algorithmic Accountablity, Gutachten im Auftrag von abida, 2018. http://www.abida.de/sites/default/files/ABIDA%20Gutachten%20Algorithmic%20Accountability.pdf

Citron D, Pasquale F (2014) The scored society: due process for automated predictions. Washington Law Rev 89:1–33

Costas J, Grey C (2016) Secrecy at work. The hidden architecture of organizational life. Stanford Business Books, Stanford

Crawford K (2016) Can an algorithm be agonistic? Ten scenes from life in calculated publics. Sci Technol Hum Values 41(1):77–92

Datenethikkommission (2018) Empfehlungen der Datenethikkommission für die Strategie Künstliche Intelligenz der Bundesregierung. www.bmi.bund.de/SharedDocs/downloads/DE/veroeffentlichungen/2018/empfehlungen-datenethikkommission.pdf?__blob=publicationFile&v=1

Datta A, Sen S, Zick Y (2017) Algorithmic transparency via quantitative input influence. In: Cerquitelli T, Quercia D, Pasquale F (eds) Transparent data mining for big and small data. Springer, Cham, pp 71–94

Diakopoulos N (2016) Accountability in algorithmic decision making. Commun ACM 59(2):56–62

Doshi-Velez F, Kim B (2017) Towards a rigorous science of interpretable machine learning. Working Paper, March 2, 2017

Doshi-Velez F, Kortz M (2017) Accountability of AI under the law: the role of explanation. Working Paper, November 21, 2017

Edwards L, Veale M (2017) Slave to the algorithm? Why a 'Right to an Explanation' is probably not the remedy you are looking for. Duke Law Technol Rev 16(1):18–84

European Commission (2018) Artificial intelligence for Europe. COM(2018) 237 final

European Parliament (2017) Resolution of 16 February 2017 with recommendations to the Commission on Civil Law Rules on Robotics. 2015/2103(INL)

Fassbender B (2006) Wissen als Grundlage staatlichen Handelns. In: Isensee J, Kirchhof P (eds) Handbuch des Staatsrechts, vol IV, 3rd edn. C.F. Müller, Heidelberg, § 76

Fenster M (2017) The transparency fix. Secrets, leaks, and uncontrollable Government information. Stanford University Press, Stanford

Florini A (2007) The right to know: transparency for an open world. Columbia University Press, New York

Fong R, Vedaldi A (2018) Interpretable explanations of Black Boxes by meaningful perturbation, last revised 10 Jan 2018. arxiv.org/abs/1704.03296

Goodman B, Flaxman S (2016) European Union regulations on algorithmic decision-making and a "right to explanation". arxiv.org/pdf/1606.08813.pdf

Gusy C (2012) Informationsbeziehungen zwischen Staat und Bürger. In: Hoffmann-Riem W, Schmidt-Aßmann E, Voßkuhle A (eds) Grundlagen des Verwaltungsrechts, vol 2, 2nd edn. C.H. Beck, München, § 23

Harhoff D, Heumann S, Jentzsch N, Lorenz P (2018) Eckpunkte einer nationalen Strategie für Künstliche Intelligenz. www.stiftung-nv.de/de/publikation/eckpunkte-einer-nationalen-strategie-fuer-kuenstliche-intelligenz

Heald D (2006) Varieties of transparency. Proc Br Acad 135:25–43

Hildebrandt M (2011) Who needs stories if you can get the data? Philos Technol 24:371–390

Hoffmann-Riem W (2014) Regulierungswissen in der Regulierung. In: Bora A, Reinhardt C, Henkel A (eds) Wissensregulierung und Regulierungswissen. Velbrück Wissenschaft, Weilerswist, pp 135–156

Hoffmann-Riem W (2017) Verhaltenssteuerung durch Algorithmen – Eine Herausforderung für das Recht. Archiv des öffentlichen Rechts 142:1–42

Holznagel B (2012) Informationsbeziehungen in und zwischen Behörden. In: Hoffmann-Riem W, Schmidt-Aßmann E, Voßkuhle A (eds) Grundlagen des Verwaltungsrechts, vol 2, 2nd edn. C.H. Beck, München, § 24

Hood C, Heald D (2006) Transparency. The key to better Governance? Oxford University Press, Oxford

House of Lords Select Committee on Artificial Intelligence (2018) AI in the UK – Ready, willing and able? publications.parliament.uk/pa/ld201719/ldselect/ldai/100/100.pdf

IBM (2018) Continuous relevancy training. console.bluemix.net/docs/services/discovery/continuous-training.html#crt

Imwinkelried E (2017) Computer source code. DePaul Law Rev 66:97–132

Jean B, Kassem L (2018) L'ouverture des données dans les Universités. openaccess.parisnanterre.fr/medias/fichier/e-tude-open-data-inno3_1519834765367-pdf

Jestaedt M (2001) Das Geheimnis im Staat der Öffentlichkeit. Was darf der Verfassungsstaat verbergen? Archiv des öffentlichen Rechts 126:204–243

Kaushal M, Nolan S (2015) Understanding artificial intelligence. Brookings Institute, Washington, D.C. www.brookings.edu/blogs/techtank/posts/2015/04/14-understanding-artificial-intelligence

Kaye D (2018) Report of the Special Rapporteur on the promotion and protection of the right to freedom of opinion and expression 29 August 2018. United Nations A/73/348

Kischel U (2003) Die Begründung. Mohr Siebeck, Tübingen

Knobloch T (2018) Vor die Lage kommen: Predictive Policing in Deutschland, Stiftung Neue Verantwortung. www.stiftung-nv.de/sites/default/files/predictive.policing.pdf (19 Jan 2019)

Konferenz der Informationsfreiheitsbeauftragten (2018) Positionspapier. www.datenschutzzentrum.de/uploads/informationsfreiheit/2018_Positionspapier-Transparenz-von-Algorithmen.pdf

Lakkaraju H, Caruana R, Kamar E, Leskovec J (2013) Interpretable & explorable approximations of black box models. arxiv.org/pdf/1707.01154.pdf

Leese M (2014) The new profiling: algorithms, black boxes, and the failure of anti-discriminatory safeguards in the European Union. Secur Dialogue 45(5):494–511

Lem S (2013) Summa technologiae. University of Minnesota Press, Minneapolis

Lewis D (1973a) Counterfactuals. Harvard University Press, Cambridge

Lewis D (1973b) Causation. J Philos 70:556–567

Luhmann N (1983) Legitimation durch Verfahren. Suhrkamp, Frankfurt am Main

Luhmann N (2017) Die Kontrolle von Intransparenz. Suhrkamp, Berlin

Martini M (2017) Algorithmen als Herausforderung für die Rechtsordnung. JuristenZeitung 72:1017–1025

Martini M (2018) Artikel 22 DSGVO. In: Paal B, Pauly D (eds) Datenschutz-Grundverordnung Bundesdatenschutzgesetz, 2nd edn. C.H. Beck, München

Martini M, Nink D (2017) Wenn Maschinen entscheiden... – vollautomatisierte Verwaltungsverfahren und der Persönlichkeitsschutz. Neue Zeitschrift für Verwaltungsrecht Extra 36:1–14

Mayer-Schönberger V, Cukier K (2013) Big data. Houghton Mifflin Harcourt, Boston

Merton R (1968) Social theory and social structure. Macmillan, New York

Mittelstadt B, Allo P, Taddeo M, Wachter S, Floridi L (2016) The ethics of algorithms. Big Data Soc 3(2):1–21

Montavon G, Samek W, Müller K (2018) Methods for interpreting and understanding deep neural networks. Digital Signal Process 73:1–15

National Science and Technology Council Committee on Technology (2016) Preparing for the future of artificial intelligence. obamawhitehouse.archiv es.gov/sites/default/files/whitehouse_files/microsites/ostp/NSTC/preparing_for_the_ future_of_ai.pdf

Neyland D (2016) Bearing accountable witness to the ethical algorithmic system. Sci Technol Hum Values 41(1):50–76

OECD Global Science Forum (2016) Research ethics and new forms of data for social and economic research. www.oecd.org/sti/inno/globalscienceforumreports.htm

Palacio S, Folz J, Hees J, Raue F, Borth D, Dengel A (2018) What do deep networks like to see? arxiv.org/abs/1803.08337

Pasquale F (2015) The Black Box Society: the secret algorithms that control money and information. Harvard University Press, Cambridge

Reisman D, Schultz J, Crawford K, Whittaker M (2018) Algorithmic impact assessments: a practical framework for public agency accountability. ainowinstitute.org/aiareport2018.pdf

Ribeiro M, Singh S, Guestrin C (2016) "Why Should I Trust You?" Explaining the predictions of any classifier. arxiv.org/pdf/1602.04938.pdf

Roth A (2017) Machine testimony. Yale Law J 126:1972–2259

Rundfunkkommission der Länder (2018) Diskussionsentwurf zu den Bereichen Rundfunkbegriff, Plattformregulierung und Intermediäre. www.rlp.de/fileadmin/rlp-stk/pdf-Dateien/Medienpolitik/04_MStV_Online_2018_Fristverlaengerung.pdf

Russell S, Dewey S, Tegmark M (2015) Research priorities for robust and beneficial artificial intelligence. arxiv.org/abs/1602.03506

Sachverständigenrat für Verbraucherfragen (2018) Technische und rechtliche Betrachtungen algorithmischer Entscheidungsverfahren. Gutachten der Fachgruppe Rechtsinformatik der Gesellschaft für Informatik e.V. http://www.svr-verbraucherfragen.de/wp-content/uploads/GI_Studie_Algorithmenregulierung.pdf

Salmon W (1994) Causality without counterfactuals. Philos Sci 61:297–312

Sandvig C, Hamilton K, Karahalios K, Langbort C (2014) Auditing algorithms: research methods for detecting discrimination on internet platforms. www.personal.umich.edu/~csandvig/research/Auditing%20Algorithms%20%2D%2D%20Sandvig%20%2D%2D%20ICA%202014%20Data%20and%20Discrimination%20Preconference.pdf

Saurer J (2009) Die Begründung im deutschen, europäischen und US-amerikanischen Verwaltungsverfahrensrecht. Verwaltungsarchiv 100:364–388

Scheppele K (1988) Legal secrets. University of Chicago Press, Chicago

Scherer M (2016) Regulating artificial intelligence systems. Harv J Law Technol 29:353–400

Scherzberg A (2000) Die Öffentlichkeit der Verwaltung. Nomos, Baden-Baden

Scherzberg A (2013) Öffentlichkeitskontrolle. In: Hoffmann-Riem W, Schmidt-Aßmann E, Voßkuhle A (eds) Grundlagen des Verwaltungsrechts, vol 3, 2nd edn. C.H. Beck, München, § 49

Schwartz B (2015) Google: we make thousands of updates to search algorithms each year. www.seroundtable.com/google-updates-thousands-20403.html

Selbst A, Barocas S (2018) The intuitive appeal of explainable machines. Fordham Law Rev 87:1085–1139

Singapore Personal Data Protection Commission (2018) Discussion paper on artificial intelligence and personal data. www.pdpc.gov.sg/-/media/Files/PDPC/PDF-Files/Resource-for-Organisation/AI/Discussion-Paper-on-AI-and-PD%2D%2D-050618.pdf

Stelkens U (2018) § 39 VwVfG. In: Stelkens P, Bonk H, Sachs M (eds) Verwaltungsverfahrensgesetz, 9th edn. C.H. Beck, München

Tene O, Polonetsky J (2013) Big data for all: privacy and user control in the age of analytics. Northwest J Technol Intellect Prop 11:239–273

Tsoukas H (1997) The tyranny of light. The temptations and paradoxes of the information society. Futures 29:827–843

Tutt A (2017) An FDA for algorithms. Adm Law Rev 69:83–123

van Otterlo M (2013) A machine learning view on profiling. In: Hildebrandt M, de Vries K (eds) Privacy, due process and the computational turn. Routledge, Abingdon-on-Thames, pp 41–64

Villani C (2018) For a meaningful artificial intelligence – towards a French and European Strategy. www.aiforhumanity.fr/pdfs/MissionVillani_Report_ENG-VF.pdf

von Lewinski K (2014) Überwachung, Datenschutz und die Zukunft des Informationsrechts. In: Telemedicus (ed) Überwachung und Recht. epubli GmbH, Berlin, pp 1–30

von Lewinski K (2018) Artikel 22 DSGVO. In: Wolff H, Brink S (eds) Beck'scher Online-Kommentar Datenschutzrecht. C.H. Beck, München

Wachter S, Mittelstadt B, Floridi L (2017) Why a right to explanation of automated decisionmaking does not exist in the general data protection regulation. Int Data Priv Law 7:76–99

Wachter S, Mittelstadt B, Russell C (2018) Counterfactual explanations without opening the Black Box: automated decisions and the GDPR. Harv J Law Technol 31:841–887

Wexler R (2018) Life, liberty, and trade secrets: intellectual property in the criminal justice system. Stanf Law Rev 70:1343–1429

Wischmeyer T (2015) Der »Wille des Gesetzgebers«. Zur Rolle der Gesetzesmaterialien in der Rechtsanwendung. JuristenZeitung 70:957–966

Wischmeyer T (2018a) Regulierung intelligenter Systeme. Archiv des öffentlichen Rechts 143:1–66

Wischmeyer T (2018b) Formen und Funktionen des exekutiven Geheimnisschutzes. Die Verwaltung 51:393–426

Woodward J (2017) Scientific explanation. In: Zalta E (ed) The Stanford encyclopedia of philosophy. Stanford University, Stanford. plato.stanford.edu/archives/fall2017/entries/scientific-explanation

Yudkowsky E (2008) Artificial intelligence as a positive and negative factor in global risk. In: Bostrom N, Ćirkovic M (eds) Global catastrophic risks. Oxford University Press, New York, pp 308–345

Zarsky T (2013) Transparent Predictions. Univ Ill Law Rev 4:1503–1570

Zweig K (2016) 2. Arbeitspapier: Überprüfbarkeit von Algorithmen. algorithmwatch.org/de/zweites-arbeitspapier-ueberpruefbarkeit-algorithmen

Zweig K (2019) Algorithmische Entscheidungen: Transparenz und Kontrolle, Analysen & Argumente, Digitale Gesellschaft, Januar 2019. https://www.kas.de/c/document_library/get_file?uuid=533ef913-e567-987d-54c3-1906395cdb81&groupId=252038

Artificial Intelligence and Discrimination: Discriminating Against Discriminatory Systems

Alexander Tischbirek

Contents

1	Introduction	104
2	Discriminatory Systems?	104
	2.1 Flawed Data Collection	105
	2.2 Flawed Data Aggregation	106
	2.3 Normative Unresponsiveness	106
3	Current Antidiscrimination Law Doctrine and AI	109
	3.1 From Causality to Correlations	109
	3.2 Statistics on Statistics	113
4	Towards a Paradigm of Knowledge Creation	115
	4.1 A Need for Concepts	115
	4.2 A Need for Facts	116
	4.3 Statistics in Court	117
5	Conclusion	118
References		119

Abstract AI promises to provide fast, consistent, and rational assessments. Nevertheless, algorithmic decision-making, too, has proven to be potentially discriminatory. EU antidiscrimination law is equipped with an appropriate doctrinal tool kit to face this new phenomenon. This is particularly true in view of the legal recognition of indirect discriminations, which no longer require certain proofs of causality, but put the focus on conspicuous correlations, instead. As a result, antidiscrimination law highly depends on knowledge about vulnerable groups, both on a conceptual as well as on a factual level. This Chapter hence recommends a partial realignment of the law towards a paradigm of knowledge creation when being faced with potentially discriminatory AI.

The basic argument of this contribution stems from Tischbirek (2019).

A. Tischbirek (✉)
Faculty of Law, Humboldt-Universität zu Berlin, Berlin, Germany
e-mail: tischbirek@rewi.hu-berlin.de

© Springer Nature Switzerland AG 2020
T. Wischmeyer, T. Rademacher (eds.), *Regulating Artificial Intelligence*,
https://doi.org/10.1007/978-3-030-32361-5_5

1 Introduction

1 Insecurity and caprice, prejudice and ignorance, hatred and anxiety have been key obstacles to implementing a society of equals. Hence, what better solution could there be than having computers make our decisions for us?[1] Computers are fast. Their decisions are consistent and purely based on naked facts.[2] Particularly, computers have no concept of race, sex, disability, religion, or sexual orientation, one might think. So does technological progress side with the non-discrimination principle? Will intelligent systems ultimately even deprive anti-discrimination laws of their subject matter?

2 Raising such a question in the beginning of a Chapter with still a couple of pages to come implies an answer in the negative: As intelligent systems, too, do produce discriminatory results (Sect. 2), anti-discrimination law needs to be reconsidered. I will argue that anti-discrimination law can draw on past doctrinal developments, which—in principle—allow for a proper legal assessment of discriminatory AI (Sect. 3). The central thesis of this Chapter is, however, that the law needs to be realigned towards a paradigm of knowledge creation when it comes to matters of discriminatory AI. This sheds new light on classic conceptual controversies in anti-discrimination law as much as it challenges some basic assumptions in data protection law and procedural law (Sect. 4).

2 Discriminatory Systems?

3 Data mining specialists, sociologists, and legal scholars alike have come to question the rationality and objectivity of automated decision-making. Especially the discriminatory potential of *Big Data*-driven AI has been of growing interest.[3] So how can AI turn racist or sexist given that it merely performs statistical operations?

4 Conceptually, the phenomenon of discriminatory AI can be traced back to three different kinds of insufficiencies: flawed data collection (Sect. 2.1), flawed data aggregation (Sect. 2.2), and normative unresponsiveness (Sect. 2.3). To be clear, programmers and users of AI may deliberately make use of any of these insufficiencies, if they intend to (covertly) discriminate. Scholars have referred to such a use of AI as *masked* discrimination.[4] However, the picture becomes much more

---

[1] On AI's potential to rationalize administrative decision making processes see Hermstrüwer, paras 3 et seq.

[2] In contrast, see Danziger et al. (2011) for an empirical study on the effects of a lunch break on (human) decision-making in court.

[3] See, *inter alia*, Calders and Žliobaitė (2013), Barocas and Selbst (2016), Žliobaitė and Custers (2016), O'Neil (2016), Caliskan et al. (2017), Kroll et al. (2017), Hacker (2018); for an early account, see Friedman and Nissenbaum (1996).

[4] Barocas and Selbst (2016), pp. 692–693.

complicated when taking into account that AI may very well exhibit discriminatory behavior even though nobody ever intended any harm. This latter variant of discriminatory AI shall be of particular concern, here, for AI is even capable to circumvent certain built-in safeguards against discrimination, as we will see.

2.1 Flawed Data Collection

A common reason for insufficient or even discriminatory results in AI decision-making is flawed training data.[5] Biased input data is likely to produce biased output data.[6] Such an 'input bias' may stem from either an under- or an overrepresentation of a protected group[7]: if police habitually patrols non-white neighborhoods more often than white neighborhoods, crime statistics will show a disproportionately high number of non-white offenders simply because people of color are overrepresented in the original sample of controlled citizens. If AI is being fed with such data, it is likely to reproduce that bias. Hence, AI-supported *predictive policing* applications will calculate a higher risk score for future crime in non-white neighborhoods.[8] If police now gears its operations towards neighborhoods with the highest computed risk scores and plays data from these operations back into the system, this may result in a highly problematic feedback loop. The initial statistical distortions become bigger and bigger, for patrols are increasingly directed into certain parts of town, where they detect more crime, which will again push the neighborhood's risk score. At the same time, the algorithm's distortions are hard to detect, since they do lead police to effective—albeit non-efficient and, of course, racist—patrols.

Inversely, an underrepresentation of a protected group may provoke a detrimental reproduction of bias, too. New Zealand's passport authorities employed an automated system in order to check passport photographs. The system regularly rejected people with Asian descent, claiming their photographs to be invalid because the pictures allegedly showed the applicants with their eyes closed.[9] Once again, the biased automated decision was a direct result from a flawed initial data collection: as the system had been set up with training data of mostly non-Asian test subjects, it performed badly with people that did not fit the system's simplistic model.

---

[5]For a good introduction, see O'Neil (2016), pp. 15–31.
[6]See Hermstrüwer, paras 21–38.
[7]Calders and Žliobaitė (2013), p. 51.
[8]Ferguson (2015), pp. 401–403; for German police law see Rademacher, paras 35 et seq. and Rademacher (2017), p. 376.
[9]Regan (2016).

2.2 Flawed Data Aggregation

7 Another reason for discriminatory AI is flawed data aggregation. Here, the initial training data as such is representative, but a bias is introduced later on in the process. This can again occur in different ways. Firstly, AI may be trained through an initial step of manual data aggregation.[10] Inconsistencies in data labelling during this period of manual training may now serve as examples for subsequent automated decisions and, hence, continue to affect AI behavior. If in consumer credit decisions the label 'creditworthy' was denied to people of color who fall behind on three credit card repayments while other (mostly white) people could fall in arrears with four repayments without being labelled as 'defaulting', AI is likely to treat future cases of 'creditworthiness' accordingly.[11]

8 Secondly, inconsistencies may still be introduced even after the initial training period. When googling 'professional hairstyles for work' and 'unprofessional hairstyles for work' the engine showed mostly pictures of white women with blond hair for the first and pictures of black women for the second search.[12] Hypothetically, if an employer decided to let AI scan job applications and sort out those with 'unprofessional' looks, this could again add up to a legally relevant, full-fledged racial discrimination. The reason for the different aggregations however stem from Google's user behavior, which is played back into the system as input data for machine learning, and the information that the algorithm can find in the internet. If a disproportionate number of pictures showing black women is surrounded by words that are associated with the notion of 'unprofessional', and if users click the black women's photo when researching 'unprofessional looks', the system will correlate the two even stronger. Again, this entails the problem of a feedback loop; and again, AI's results cannot be better than the data that it was fed with. If a bias is (subsequently) inscribed in the data and the way we interpret it, AI is likely to reproduce and, hence, to reinforce it.

2.3 Normative Unresponsiveness

9 This points to another more fundamental problem of AI-based decision-making: AI is about statistics, it can assess the future only with a view of the past. Normative considerations, on the other hand, are driven by the contra-factual.[13] Consequently, it can be highly challenging to translate such considerations into a language that is understood by AI. Let me illustrate this by reference to one last example, which will

---

[10]Calders and Žliobaitė (2013), p. 50.
[11]Barocas and Selbst (2016), p. 681, with reference to Hand (2006), p. 10; see Ernst, paras 4–5.
[12]Wolfangel (2017).
[13]Möllers (2015), pp. 13–17.

directly lead us into the legal implications of discriminatory AI and, hence, shall be reported in some greater detail here.

In one of the most influential anti-discrimination law rulings of the past decade, the CJEU in the case of *Association belge des Consommateurs Test-Achats* has declared that insurance tariffs that differentiate as to the gender of the client violate the EU's nondiscrimination principle.[14] The CJEU's ruling thereby is a textbook example of how a normative prescription, by its very nature, might have to fight the (present-day) facts for the benefit of a different, future reality; for in view of state-of-the-art statistical knowledge, insurance companies have every reason to compute gender-specific tariffs. Statistically, men are much more likely to cause car accidents that involve significant damage.[15] Then again, the average life expectancy of women is several years higher than the life expectancy of men.[16] Finally, women will generally face more pregnancy-related costs. Consequently, one would expect car insurance and life insurance plans to be more expensive for men than for women, whereas one would expect women's health insurance tariffs to be higher than men's. In other words: if the numbers are right—and nothing suggests that they are not—statistical knowledge urges insurance companies to the use of sex as an actuarial factor.[17] Said statistical knowledge and its consequences are however subject to political evaluation and, ultimately, to legal structuring. A strong case can be made that the costs of pregnancy should be split equally between men and women instead of yielding gender-specific health insurance tariffs: protecting motherhood is even a constitutional obligation in many countries and, arguably, the succession of generations is of concern for society at large. Moreover, as the Advocate General in *Test-Achats* has pointed out, the 'principle of causation' surely calls for an equal taxing of costs between the sexes in the case of pregnancy. Similarly, even divergent life expectancies of men and women can be perceived as a common concern, which implies full insurance.[18]

Normative conclusions like the CJEU's requirement of unisex tariffs are however challenged when AI comes into play.[19] Even if an insurance company did not

---

[14]CJEU C-236/09 'Association belge des Consommateurs Test-Achats ASBL et al. v. Conseil des ministres' (1 March 2011), 2011 E.C.R. 773, paras 30–32. To be precise: the Court invalidated Article 5(2) of Council Directive 2004/113/EC, (2004) O.J. L 373 37–43, which allowed for gender-specific tariffs under certain procedural conditions. It held that such (permanent) exemptions to the non-discrimination clause of Article 5(1) of the Directive constituted a violation of Articles 21 and 23 of the EU Charter of Fundamental Rights.

[15]For Germany, see Statistisches Bundesamt (2017), pp. 12, 21.

[16]The World Bank (2017).

[17]For an attempt to statistically and sociologically justify gender-specific insurance tariffs in the U.K. see The Social Issues Research Center Oxford (2004).

[18]In *Test-Achats*, the CJEU only referred to the problem of differences in life expectancy since Article 5 (3) of Council Directive 2004/113/EC explicitly prohibits to actuarially impose the costs of pregnancy on women alone.

[19]For discussions of *Test-Achats* in light of AI decision making, cf. Gellert et al. (2013), pp. 79–81; Hacker (2018), pp. 1166–1167.

positively know about an applicant's sex, it could still come to a quite precise guess by tracking down a variant of apparently unsuspicious proxies. Friends lists on Facebook, shopping habits on Amazon and search histories on Google easily translate into a high probability of a user's sex. Obviously, there are even easier ways for insurance companies to find out: simply by checking the 'Mr./Mrs.' box in the application form, most applicants might freely give away the information in the first place. In many cases, the applicant's first name will furthermore reveal the person's sex.

12   However, by the use of AI, the correlations become much more complex. As the system is constantly fed with data, it continuously expands its set of patterns and learns to come up with new models of grouping the data in order to make ever more refined group-specific risk assessments.[20] When being fed with data concerning shopping habits, AI can easily learn to cluster people along categories labelled A and B. These clusters might correspond quite accurately with people's sex, although the system may be programmed to disregard any *direct* data about the applicant's sex. AI can learn that category A people spend more money on hard liquor and cigarettes than category B people. It might also learn that category B people are more likely to spend money on pregnancy-related medication. After being fed with the insurance company's customer data, the algorithm will quickly unveil other quite relevant correlations—even if the customer data are fully anonymized. The algorithm might learn, for example, that people who are being treated for alcohol abuse are cheaper clients in health insurance (because they usually die younger) than people who give birth at a hospital at least once in their life time. As all of these dots are being connected automatically, there is no one to grow suspicious of these correlations. AI only knows to differentiate between clusters A and B. It does not have any concept of gender whatsoever. Still, the result of all that math is likely to be an insurance plan that is much cheaper for cluster A people than for the cohort of group B. Moreover, since the algorithm is constantly growing and developing, it may soon be capable to arrive at much more sophisticated correlations than the ones we just outlined. As these correlations increase in complexity, they also grow more and more opaque. Even its programmers—let alone the average applicant to an insurance plan—may no longer be able to retrace its calculations at reasonable expense.[21]

13   For all of these reasons, this last example of discriminatory AI is the ultimate test case for the effectiveness of antidiscrimination law doctrine and the legal structuring of AI-driven processes in general. Technical solutions to the problem are hampered, since there is—strictly speaking—no technical problem: the input data are

---

[20] For a discussion of 'vitality' programs in health insurance see Ernst, paras 2–3.

[21] See Wischmeyer, paras 9 et seq.; reverse-engineering may even be undesired by the users of AI in order to prevent gaming, see Hermstrüwer, paras 65–69.

representative and complete. No bias is fed into the system in the sense that the detrimental factors, i.e. differences in life expectancy and in the 'risk' of pregnancy, are indeed unequally distributed between the sexes. A correction of training data is hardly possible, because the training data are correct in the first place. Moreover, simply taking the sensitive attribute—in our case: gender—out of the equation is not promising, either, for AI may 'learn' about the applicant's sex anyhow, as we have seen. At the same time, the ever-changing, dynamic configuration of the algorithm makes it extremely hard—if not impossible—to retrospectively identify all decisive factors in the computation of a specific insurance tariff.[22]

3 Current Antidiscrimination Law Doctrine and AI

Antidiscrimination law in its present state of development is not powerless in the face of discriminatory AI.[23] It particularly benefits from a fundamental doctrinal shift that occurred long before discriminatory systems could give rise to legal problems (Sect. 3.1). Notably, after said shift, conventional doctrine provides a valid starting point in legally assessing modern forms of AI (Sect. 3.2).

3.1 From Causality to Correlations

EU antidiscrimination law's doctrinal reorientation from a pure paradigm of causality towards a paradigm of correlation proves to be a pivotal prerequisite for confronting discriminatory systems. Such an enhancement of antidiscrimination law doctrine can be observed in several instances.

According to classic doctrine, a forbidden discrimination presupposes causation between an outlawed ground of discrimination and a specific disadvantage.[24] Any act or failure to act with the open intent to unfavorably distinguish between people on the grounds of sex or race etc. hence qualifies as a (direct) discrimination. Likewise, even in the absence of discriminatory intent, any direct concatenation between a forbidden ground and a less favorable treatment falls within the scope of classic doctrine.[25]

On this matter, both US and EU antidiscrimination law resemble one another, although the early landmark decisions of the U.S. Supreme Court and the CJEU very much differed in the particular issues at stake. While gender equality is the

14

15

16

17

---

[22]Cf. Wischmeyer (2018), pp. 42–46.

[23]For a more skeptical assessment of current antidiscrimination law doctrine, see Barocas and Selbst (2016), and Hacker (2018).

[24]Fredman (2011), p. 203.

[25]Ellis and Watson (2012), pp. 163–165; Thüsing (2015), § 3 AGG at para 9.

paradigmatic model for EU antidiscrimination law and racial equality has been at the core of American equality case law,[26] the two legal orders have respectively taken this causal structure as a doctrinal starting point. Famously, in *Brown v Board of Education* the key question was whether racial segregation caused disadvantages in the personal development of black primary school children.[27] Correspondingly, in the CJEU's early *Defrenne* cases, the Court had to assess openly gender-based differences in pay.[28]

Imputed Causality

18   The traditional causality model of antidiscrimination law however proved to be incapable of confronting other more complex issues of discrimination. Especially phenomena of tacit or structural discrimination could hardly be addressed by classic doctrine alone. A first intermediary step away from a pure doctrine of causality are enhanced burden of proof regimes: if a restaurant owner puts out a sign stating that her staff would not wait on people of color, or if the police admittedly stops and frisks only dark-skinned persons without probable cause, it is fairly easy to establish an infringement of antidiscrimination law. In particular, it is very well feasible to demonstrate a causal relation between, first, the restaurant owner's and the police's motives of action, second, the skin-color of the person wishing to get dinner at the restaurant or passing by the police patrol and, third, the difference in treatment. This is especially true, when the restaurant owner does not remove the sign and the police has documented an internal order that calls for enhanced patrolling against a certain ethnic minority. However, there might be another restaurant owner, who does not put humiliating signs at her door but only hires white staff outside of the kitchen, because she believes that her customers were deterred by people of color. Moreover, there might still be a police officer who considers it to be more effective to 'stop and frisk' only dark-skinned citizens even without any corresponding order from the head of operations. Whereas these latter cases undoubtedly exhibit a racist behavior, too, it is much harder to effectuate the non-discrimination principle, because the forbidden motive has not been explicitly voiced.

19   Here, antidiscrimination lawsuits are faced with serious problems of evidence. The specific extra-legal knowledge that is required to win the case is non-transparent. Again, there is a causal relation between the police officer's and the restaurant owner's motives, the skin color of a person who applied for a job in that restaurant or who is asked by the officer to show his identity card and the detrimental difference in treatment. Causality is at work, but it is not obvious.

---

[26]Mangold (2016), p. 223.
[27]U.S. Supreme Court 'Brown v. Board of Education' (17 May 1954), 347 U.S. 483.
[28]CJEU 80/70 'Defrenne v. Sabena I' (25 May 1971), 1971 E.C.R. 445; 43/75 'Defrenne v. Sabena II' (8 April 1976), 1976 E.C.R. 455; 149/77 'Defrenne v. Sabena III' (15 June 1978) 1978 E.C.R. 1365.

Antidiscrimination doctrine has reacted to this problem by lowering and even partially shifting the burden of proof. Article 8 of Council Directive 2000/43/EC, for example,[29] requires Member States to ensure that

> when persons who consider themselves wronged because the principle of equal treatment has not been applied to them establish, before a court or other competent authority, facts from which it may be presumed that there has been direct or indirect discrimination, it shall be for the respondent to prove that there has been no breach of the principle of equal treatment.

Antidiscrimination law does not yet abandon any notion of causality, here. However, it recognizes the considerable difficulties of generating necessary case-specific knowledge in court due to severe information asymmetries on the side of the plaintiff.[30] It does so by introducing legal fictions. The plaintiff wins her case, if she merely presents pieces of circumstantial evidence to the court that the respondent cannot adequately rebut. The rejected candidate for employment can therefore establish an illegal discrimination by showing that the restaurant owner had previously fired all dark-skinned staff, while keeping most white employees, when she bought the place a couple of years ago. Accordingly, racial profiling can be proven, if the plaintiff was able to demonstrate that only dark-skinned persons were 'stopped and frisked' without probable cause in a certain police operation.[31] Unless the respondent on her part presents hard evidence that no racist motive controlled her course of action, both, the forbidden motive and its causality for the plaintiff's unequal treatment, are legally assumed.

Indirect Discrimination

The doctrinal shift from causation towards mere correlations was completed when courts began to scrutinize 'indirect' discriminations (which is known in U.S. antidiscrimination law as the doctrine of 'adverse effect'): in many instances, even a lowering of the burden of proof alone is insufficient in order to legally sanction unequal treatment. This is especially true for communities with a long history of discrimination, for certain well-established routines and traditional structures may have a strong ongoing disadvantageous effect on the very minority group

---

[29]Council Directive 2000/43/EC, [2000] O.J. L 180 22–26. Corresponding provisions can be found in Article 10(1) of Directive 2000/78/EC, [2000] O.J. L 303 16–22, Article 9(1) of Directive 2004/113/EC and Article 19(1) of Directive 2006/54/EC, [2006] O.J. L 204 23–36.
[30]Ellis and Watson (2012), pp. 157–163.
[31]It must be mentioned that police action is generally beyond the scope of Council Directive 2000/43/EC. The same is not necessarily true for Article 21 of the Charter of Fundamental Rights, however, and a shift in the burden of proof can also result from constitutional law or even conventional administrative law doctrine without any reference to the EU anti-discrimination directives.

that had historically been a victim of discrimination.[32] What makes things complicated is that these routines and structures seem neutral when looked at in isolation from their specific workings in society. They are neutral on the face, but discriminatory in effect.[33] Moreover, in this field, discriminatory conduct may more often than not be driven by implicit biases, which are embedded in certain routines and may even be due to unconscious mental processes.[34]

23 A certain assessment or decision may feel 'right' precisely because it reinforces patterns that are fully internalized, that help to reduce complexity and sustain existing conditions. Nevertheless, these assessments and decisions may have a substantial discriminatory effect, which—as opposed to its tacit reasons—is no longer concealed.

24 These tacit reasons, after all, threaten to overstress even antidiscrimination laws with enhanced burden of proof regimes. A provision like the abovementioned Article 8 of Council Directive 2000/43/EC still demands for certain circumstantial evidence that suggests a forbidden discrimination. With tacit reasons at play, even this exceptionally low burden of proof may still inhibit the effective implementation of the law's substantial non-discrimination principle, for most frequently, the only feasible circumstantial evidence will amount to demonstrating the undesired discriminatory effect itself. Tacit reasons and implicit bias, on the other hand, lack a central prerequisite for any legal conversation: they do not adhere to the law's general expectation of intersubjectivity.[35] While they might still be causal for a certain assessment, decision, or action, said deficit in intersubjectivity inevitably also hinders any account of causality in these particular cases.

25 The doctrinal answer to this difficulty in European and American antidiscrimination law alike has been the concept of indirect discrimination. A famous line of CJEU court rulings received the concept in matters of gender equality from the early 1980s on. And again, U.S. antidiscrimination law doctrine which aimed at fighting racial discrimination served as a model for EU law.[36] In *Griggs et al. v. Duke Power Co.*, the U.S. Supreme Court had famously ruled that certain seemingly neutral employment prerequisites violated the Civil Rights Act of 1964, because they exhibited a disparate impact on black applicants.[37] Some 10 years later, the CJEU—while directly referring to *Griggs*[38]—first relied on a disparate impact argument in an antidiscrimination case concerning employment law: in *Jenkins*

---

[32]This is referred to as 'structural' or 'institutional' discrimination. See Delgado and Stefancic (2017), pp. 31–35. For structural discriminations concerning two or more 'intersecting' categories, see Crenshaw (1989).

[33]Fredman (2011), pp. 177–189, 203–204.

[34]Krieger (1995), and Jolls and Sunstein (2006).

[35]Cf. the classic conception of 'tacit knowledge' by Polanyi (1966), p. 4: 'we can know more than we can tell'.

[36]Tourkochoriti (2017).

[37]U.S. Supreme Court 'Griggs et al. v. Duke Power Co.' (8 Mar 1971) 401 U.S. 424.

[38]See the direct quotation in the Opinion of Advocate General Warner to CJEU 96/80 'Jenkins v. Kinsgate' (delivered 28 January 1981), 1981 E.C.R. 911, 936.

v. Kinsgate, the CJEU held that differences in payment between full-time workers and part-time workers can amount to an indirect sex discrimination as women statistically far more often than men occupy part-time jobs.[39] In *Jenkins*, the CJEU may still have been particularly suspicious, because Kinsgate, the respondent, had always paid women lower wages and only switched to the distinction between full-time and part-time work when Britain enacted its Equal Pay Act.[40] Hence, *Jenkins* might rather be an example of covert sexism than of misguided tacit motivations. In later cases, however, the CJEU had no reason to assume covert discriminatory behavior, but nevertheless it stuck to its doctrine of indirect discrimination precisely because it was confronted with the *structural* problem of the gender pay gap. The respondents' (tacit) motivations were no longer made a subject of the decisions—and rightly so, as they overstrain the cognitive framework of the law. In *Bilka v. Weber von Hartz,* the CJEU thus only stressed the difference in treatment between full-time and part-time employees as well as the obvious assumption, 'that a much lower proportion of women than of men work full time'.[41] Correlation had superseded causation. Part-time work served as a proxy for gender, for statistically the former was found to largely correspond with the latter. By using this proxy itself, the court could overcome the 'tacit dimension' because a different treatment of part-time and full-time work—other than the opaque grounds for structural sex discrimination—ranged on this side of the line between the explicit and the tacit.

3.2 Statistics on Statistics

Both enhancements to antidiscrimination law doctrine, imputed causality and the notion of indirect discrimination, now constitute an important first step in capturing discriminatory AI from a legal perspective. In this context, AI bears significant similarities to the much older phenomena of tacit knowledge and implicit bias. This may be surprising at first, since AI's Big Data Analytics are purely mathematical and, hence, utterly rational operations, whereas the notions of tacit knowledge and implicit bias are marked irrational, emotional and closely linked to the *condicio humana*.[42]

However, mental processes that include implicit bias and discriminatory AI arguably stem from structurally similar insufficiencies as much as they confront antidiscrimination law doctrine with identical challenges. In both cases, learned but unquestioned discriminatory structures from the past guide present decisions and, thus, tend to be reinforced. In both cases, distorted assumptions are difficult to detect as they are being processed within a 'black box', about which even the decision-

---

[39]CJEU 96/80 'Jenkins v. Kinsgate' (31 March 1981), 1981 E.C.R. 911, para 13.
[40]CJEU 96/80 'Jenkins v. Kinsgate' (31 March 1981), 1981 E.C.R. 911, 913.
[41]CJEU 170/84 'Bilka v. Weber von Hartz' (13 May 1986), 1986 E.C.R. 1607, para 29.
[42]See, for example, Fassbender (2006), pp. 248–249.

maker herself cannot provide comprehensive information. Therefore, in both cases, causalities are obfuscated,[43] which is particularly true from the perspective of a potential victim of discrimination.

28   In light of these parallels, present-day antidiscrimination law can face not just implicit bias, but also AI. The classic doctrine of direct, open discriminations will rarely apply to discriminatory AI: it is uncertain, whether AI exhibits anything (functionally) equivalent to intent. AI's programmers and/or users usually do not act maliciously in cases of discriminatory AI, as we have seen. Establishing causality is—for the most part—impossible. However, both imputed causality through enhanced burden of proof regimes and the concept of indirect discriminations once again promise to be effective tools.[44] If statistics showed, for example, that an insurance company's algorithm computed—on average—higher tariffs for women than for men, this could firstly be recognized as circumstantial evidence in the sense of Article 8 of Council Directive 2000/43/EC. Secondly, it would satisfy the first prong of the CJEU's disparate impact test. Consequently, it is then on the users of AI decision mechanisms—in our case: the insurance company—to demonstrate exculpatory evidence and justification.

29   More specifically, a verified disparate impact will not automatically be justified through proportionality analysis, at least when it comes to EU antidiscrimination law. Although the use of AI will most regularly follow a rationale of economic efficiency, it is far from clear, that economic interests must always outweigh the non-discrimination principle.[45] At least in cases of severe adverse effects for a protected group, the non-discrimination principle, which the CJEU has repeatedly labelled an important general principal of European law,[46] must prevail.

30   Hence, in principal, the language of antidiscrimination law doctrine can effectively deal with the non-language of AI. The key to opening the 'black box' of AI decision making thereby is the acceptance of statistical arguments in law. AI, which is entirely about statistics itself, thus can only be contained by statistical knowledge. What is needed are 'statistics on statistics' and the detection of 'correlations between correlations'.

---

[43]See Wischmeyer, paras 13–14.

[44]See for U.S. law: Barocas and Selbst (2016), pp. 701–702; for EU law: Hacker (2018), pp. 1152–1154.

[45]Hacker (2018), pp. 1160–1165, by contrast, believes proportionality to offer a 'relatively straightforward route to justification' on economic grounds at least when it comes to cases of proxy discrimination.

[46]Most recently, see CJEU C-68/17 'IR v. JQ' (11 September 2018), ECLI:EU:C:2018:696, para 67.

4 Towards a Paradigm of Knowledge Creation

This very practical need for (statistical) knowledge has some implications that reach even beyond the field of antidiscrimination law: it sheds new light on fundamentally differing conceptions in U.S. and EU antidiscrimination law (Sect. 4.1), and it questions some basic assumptions in data-protection law (Sect. 4.2) as well as in procedural law (Sect. 4.3).

4.1 A Need for Concepts

One might argue that antidiscrimination law aims at stripping any (legal) significance from categories such as race, ethnicity, gender, sexual orientation, and disability; for the non-discrimination principle states that, ultimately, such matters *shall not* matter.[47] Moreover, some of these categories are heavily contested on a conceptual level. This holds especially true for the notions of race, disability, and gender. In all of these cases, any biologistic and essentialist understanding must be dismissed.[48] In view of race, Recital 6 of the abovementioned EU Council Directive 2000/43/EC accordingly states:

> The European Union rejects theories which attempt to determine the existence of separate human races. The use of the term 'racial origin' in this Directive does not imply an acceptance of such theories.

Similarly, in the UN Convention on the Rights of Persons with Disabilities, the member states committed themselves to a 'dynamic' understanding of disability, which responds to social barriers instead of exclusively focusing on certain physical restrictions.[49] Finally, rigid binary concepts of gender are increasingly being challenged as many Constitutional orders recognize not just intersex identities, but also the possibility of more complex variances and even changing gender identities, which take self-conception as a starting point instead of extrinsic sex assignment.[50]

Nevertheless, the notions of race, disability, gender etc. are justified as *sociological* categories. As such, they provide antidiscrimination law with the indispensable vocabulary to depict discriminatory structures in the first place. This does not go uncontested—notably more so in European than in American antidiscrimination law scholarship. It is inevitable, that simply by making use of these concepts, antidiscrimination law itself threatens to deepen a divisive way of thinking along the very lines that it actually wishes to combat. It is for this dilemma, that France,

---

[47] Cf. Baer (2009).
[48] For the category of race, see most recently Feldmann et al. (2018).
[49] Preamble lit. e and Article 1 (2) of the UN Convention on the Rights of People with Disabilities.
[50] Cf. Ainsworth (2015).

above all, has committed itself to a policy of 'race-blindness'.[51] This most recently even included a Constitutional amendment in order to discard the term 'race' from Article 1 of the Constitution of the Fifth Republic, which had formerly proclaimed 'the equality of all citizens before the law, without distinction of origin, race or religion'. In Germany, too, the use of race as a legal term is highly contested.[52] The alternative, however, is a threat of antidiscrimination law's voicelessness.[53] This entails consequences for cases of discriminatory AI as well. If a claimant wanted to show that an actuarial algorithm disadvantaged people of color in computing insurance tariffs, the very prerequisite of her claim is the legal recognition of the (sociological) concept of race. If the law lacks the concepts for pointing at discriminations, the non-discrimination principle cannot effectively be implemented.

4.2 A Need for Facts

35 As antidiscrimination law must heavily lean on disparate impact doctrine when being confronted with discriminatory AI, concepts alone do not suffice to effectuate non-discrimination, nor do the case-specific facts of a particular incident. Instead, the law is in need for general empirical knowledge about the everyday realities of protected groups. Such knowledge will regularly be formed and transferred by way of statistics. Again, the French policy of 'race-blindness' illustrates, firstly, how the formation of the necessary knowledge can be impeded, when the French *Conseil Constitutionnel* opposed any studies on ethnic and racial origins on behalf of the equality principle.[54]

36 Secondly, apart from these very fundamental objections, the formation of empirical knowledge on discriminating structures is subject to strict data protection legislation. In particular, the EU has prominently committed itself to—amongst others—the principles of 'purpose limitation', 'data minimization', and 'storage limitation' in Article 5 No. 1 lit. b, c and e of the General Data Protection Regulation (GDPR).[55] More specifically, the GDPR sets especially rigid standards in view of personal data that involve the categories of antidiscrimination law in Article 9 GDPR.

37 Of course, by acknowledging that race or ethnicity, sexual orientation or religious belief are sensitive information, and by recognizing a right to privacy, data protection law ultimately tries to render such information irrelevant in the public sphere.

---

[51]For a critical account, see Keaton (2010).
[52]Cf. Liebscher et al. (2012).
[53]Barskanmaz (2011).
[54]Conseil Constitutionnel Decision CC 2007-557 DC concerning the constitutionality of the *Loi relative á la maîtrise de l'immigration, á l'intégration et á l'asile* (15 November 2007), ECLI:FR: CC:2007:2007.557.DC.
[55]Regulation 2016/679, (2016) O.J. L 119 1–88.

Hence, privacy is as much about (normative) equality as it is about autonomy and dignity.[56] Therein, privacy laws are first of all another important pillar of antidiscrimination law themselves. At the same time, not just the doctrine of indirect discrimination, but also legal provisions containing so-called 'positive measures' (i.e. affirmative action) or the above-mentioned 'dynamic' notion of a disability fall on stony ground if they cannot be fed with empirical knowledge about some vulnerable groups. Article 9 (2) GDPR offers a number of exemptions from the prohibition of the processing of sensitive personal data. They include cases of 'explicit consent', processing that is 'necessary for the establishment, exercise or defense of legal claims or whenever courts are acting in their judiciary capacity', and necessary processing 'for archiving purposes in the public interest, scientific or historical research purposes or statistical purposes'. Nevertheless, it is important to see that even under these exemption clauses the principles of data minimization, purpose limitation, and storage limitation apply and, thus, put restrictions on statistical research and knowledge accumulation concerning the realities of discrimination.

4.3 Statistics in Court

Finally yet importantly, the phenomenon of discriminatory AI challenges the procedural embedding of antidiscrimination law. The doctrinal switch from causation to correlation entails a shift in focus from 'adjudicative' to 'legislative' facts. According to the famous distinction in U.S. legal scholarship, the processing of extra-legal knowledge is inherently different in courts and legislatures.[57] Traditionally, courts—especially in private law cases—settle disputes between two individuals. Litigation is party-initiated and party-controlled. The court is summoned to retrospectively assess a specific incident that has occurred between the litigants. Classic civil procedure mechanisms of generating and digesting the necessary extra-legal knowledge are narrowly tailored to serve this purpose. Hence, in court, the generating of facts is almost exclusively left to the parties, who need to bring the evidence that supports their respective claim. This is justified not least because of the parties' particular proximity to the facts of the case. It furthermore reflects the traditional perception of the (civil) courts as neutral arbiters that are made available to the individual market participants in order to enhance private ordering.

Statistics, to the contrary, are of a different cognitive structure than conventional 'adjudicative' facts. From the point of departure, they do not concern a single incident of the past. Statistics for the most part contain general information that makes a statement about a multitude of different cases. Moreover, statistics are not

---

[56]Cf. Arthur Glass (2010), pp. 65–68; on the concepts underlying European privacy law see also Marsch, paras 5 et seq.
[57]Davis (1942), pp. 402–403; Chayes (1976), pp. 1282–1283.

necessarily retrospective, but more often than not, they suggest depicting present times or even aspire to predict the future. Structurally, for one, statistics are rather to be associated with the legislative or executive than with the judicative function.[58] Thus, anti-discrimination adjudication—which happens to be largely civil adjudication—faces the challenge of having to process general, rather 'legislative' extra-legal knowledge by means of a procedure that is much rather geared towards case-specific facts.

40   This tension, again, becomes evident by example of an actuarial algorithm that is suspected to compute gender-specific tariffs. According to the principles of civil procedure, it is generally to the plaintiff who claims a sex discrimination to demonstrate the facts that support her argument. As we have seen, she may only be able to make her case by reference to striking statistical correlations and disparate impact doctrine. However, whilst individual case-specific facts are usually quite accessible to the plaintiff, having to produce solid statistical data on 'AI behavior' might easily ask too much of her as she will regularly lack information that do not directly concern here individual insurance application. Furthermore, a scientifically sound data preparation is likely to overstrain the plaintiff unless she is a trained statistician.

41   The usual answer of civil procedure to such a lack of knowledge is a court order for an expert opinion. In our case, this however hardly provides relief. Even though it may address the plaintiff's lack of mathematical and sociological expertise, the costs of calling in experts remain high. This is all the more so, when experts, too, still have to collect and interpret the data. Here, the high financial risks of litigation have a potentially prohibitive effect. This effect is especially problematic in matters of antidiscrimination law, as certain minority groups are disproportionally deterred from entering into legal disputes and accessing the court system, anyhow.[59]

5 Conclusion

42   EU antidiscrimination law is, at first glance, equipped with an appropriate doctrinal tool kit to face the new phenomenon of discriminatory AI. This is particularly true in view of the legal recognition of indirect discriminations, which no longer require certain proofs of causality, but put the focus on conspicuous correlations, instead. Herein, antidiscrimination law doctrine and decision making through AI show some astonishing structural parallels—yielding an 'arms race' in the forming of correlations, for both AI's discriminatory 'conduct' as such and its (legal) substantiation are ultimately based on statistical data.

43   The effectiveness of antidiscrimination law hence directly relies on enhanced extra-legal knowledge. However, the formation of such knowledge is not only conceptually and methodologically challenging, but it also encounters legal barriers,

---

[58]Ladeur (2012), pp. 77–80, 82–86.
[59]Berghahn et al. (2016), pp. 101, 161–162.

particularly in data protection law, civil procedure, and even antidiscrimination law itself. The very recent phenomenon of discriminatory AI therefore sheds new light on some familiar debates.

Proposals to strengthen the non-discrimination principle here will have to be geared towards a paradigm of knowledge creation. They may include the introduction and broadening of mechanisms of collective action in antidiscrimination lawsuits,[60] AI 'audits'[61] or even additional competences of antidiscrimination and/or data protection agencies.[62] All of these measures must however inevitably revert to thorough empirical knowledge on AI and—equally important—on the everyday realities of the very groups that antidiscrimination law intends to protect. Legal doctrine's need for empirical knowledge may then, in turn, have repercussions on the law itself. Hence, discriminatory AI poses a challenge for both the legal and the social sciences. Both will have to go hand in hand in guarding the non-discrimination principle against new forms of social marginalization in the digital world.

References

Ainsworth C (2015) Sex redefined. Nature 518:288–291. https://doi.org/10.1038/518288a

Baer S (2009) Chancen und Grenzen positiver Maßnahmen nach § 5 AGG. www.rewi.hu-berlin.de/de/lf/ls/bae/w/files/ls_aktuelles/09_adnb_baer.pdf. Accessed 4 Feb 2019

Barocas S, Selbst AD (2016) Big data's disparate impact. Calif Law Rev 104:671–732

Barskanmaz C (2011) Rasse - Unwort des Antidiskriminierungsrechts. Kritische Justiz 44:382–389

Berghahn S, Klapp M, Tischbirek A (2016) Evaluation des Allgemeinen Gleichbehandlungsgesetzes. Reihe der Antidiskriminierungsstelle des Bundes. Nomos, Baden-Baden

Calders T, Žliobaitė I (2013) Why unbiased computational processes can lead to discriminative decision procedures. In: Custers B, Calders T, Schermer B, Zarsky T (eds) Discrimination and privacy in the information society. Studies in applied philosophy, epistemology and rational ethics. Springer, Berlin, pp 27–42

Caliskan A, Bryson JJ, Narayanan A (2017) Semantics derived automatically from language corpora contain human-like biases. Science 356:183–186. https://doi.org/10.1126/science.aal4230

Chayes A (1976) The role of the judge in public law litigation. Harv Law Rev 89:1281–1316. https://doi.org/10.2307/1340256

Crenshaw K (1989) Demarginalizing the intersection of race and sex: a black feminist critique of antidiscrimination doctrine, feminist theory and antiracist politics. Univ Chicago Legal Forum 1989:139–167

Danziger S, Levav J, Avnaim-Pesso L (2011) Extraneous factors in judicial decisions. Proc Natl Acad Sci USA 108:6889–6892

Davis KC (1942) An approach to problems of evidence in the administrative process. Harv Law Rev 55:364–425. https://doi.org/10.2307/1335092

---

[60]Cf. Berghahn et al. (2016), pp. 101–102.

[61]Barocas and Selbst (2016), p. 719; see Wischmeyer, paras 10–15.

[62]Hacker (2018), pp. 1177–1179.

Delgado R, Stefancic J (2017) Critical race theory, 3rd edn. New York University Press, New York
Ellis E, Watson P (2012) EU anti-discrimination law. Oxford EU law library, 2nd edn. Oxford University Press, Oxford
Fassbender B (2006) Wissen als Grundlage staatlichen Handelns. In: Isensee J, Kirchhof P (eds) Handbuch des Staatsrechts, vol IV, 3rd edn. C.F. Müller, Heidelberg, pp 243–312
Feldmann D, Hoffmann J, Keilhauer A, Liebold R (2018) "Rasse" und "ethnische Herkunft" als Merkmale des AGG. Rechtswissenschaft 9:23–46
Ferguson A (2015) Big data and predictive reasonable suspicion. Univ Pa Law Rev 163:327–410
Fredman S (2011) Discrimination law. Clarendon law series, 2nd edn. Oxford University Press, Oxford
Friedman B, Nissenbaum H (1996) Bias in computer systems. ACM Trans Inf Syst 14:330–347. https://doi.org/10.1145/230538.23056
Gellert R, de Vries K, de Hert P, Gutwirth S (2013) A comparative analysis of anti-discrimination and data protection legislations. In: Custers B, Calders T, Schermer B, Zarsky T (eds) Discrimination and privacy in the information society. Studies in applied philosophy, epistemology and rational ethics. Springer, Berlin, pp 61–88
Glass A (2010) Privacy and law. In: Blatterer H, Johnson P (eds) Modern privacy. Palgrave Macmillan, London, pp 59–72
Hacker P (2018) Teaching fairness to artificial intelligence: existing and novel strategies against algorithmic discrimination under EU law. Common Mark Law Rev 55:1143–1186
Hand DJ (2006) Classifier technology and the illusion of progress. Stat Sci 21:1–14. https://doi.org/10.1214/088342306000000060
Jolls C, Sunstein CR (2006) The law of implicit bias. Calif Law Rev 94:969–996
Keaton TD (2010) The politics of race-blindness: (anti)blackness and category-blindness in contemporary France. Du Bois Rev Soc Sci Res Race 7:103–131. https://doi.org/10.1017/S1742058X10000202
Krieger LH (1995) The content of our categories: a cognitive bias approach to discrimination and equal employment opportunity. Stanford Law Rev 47:1161–1248
Kroll JA, Huey J, Barocas S, Felten EW, Reidenberg JR, Robinson DG, Yu H (2017) Accountable algorithms. Univ Pa Law Rev 165:633–795
Ladeur K-H (2012) Die Kommunikationsinfrastruktur der Verwaltung. In: Hoffmann-Riem W, Schmidt-Assmann E, Voßkuhle A (eds) Grundlagen des Verwaltungsrechts, vol 2. C.H. Beck, München, pp 35–106
Liebscher D, Naguib T, Plümecke T, Remus J (2012) Wege aus der Essentialismusfalle: Überlegungen zu einem postkategorialen Antidiskriminierungsrecht. Kritische Justiz 45:204–218
Mangold AK (2016) Demokratische Inklusion durch Recht. Habilitation Treatise, Johann-Wolfgang von Goethe-Universität, Frankfurt a.M
Möllers C (2015) Die Möglichkeit der Normen. Suhrkamp, Berlin
O'Neil C (2016) Weapons of math destruction. How big data increases inequality and threatens democracy. Crown, New York
Polanyi M (1966) The tacit dimension. The University of Chicago Press, Chicago
Rademacher T (2017) Predictive Policing im deutschen Polizeirecht. Archiv des öffentlichen Rechts 142:366–416
Regan J (2016) New Zealand passport robot tells applicant of Asian descent to open eyes. Available via Reuters. www.reuters.com/article/us-newzealand-passport-error/new-zealand-passport-robot-tells-applicant-of-asian-descent-to-open-eyes-idUSKBN13W0RL. Accessed 10 Oct 2018
Statistisches Bundesamt (2017) Verkehrsunfälle: Unfälle von Frauen und Männern im Straßenverkehr 2016. Available via DESTATIS. www.destatis.de/DE/Publikationen/Thematisch/TransportVerkehr/Verkehrsunfaelle/UnfaelleFrauenMaenner5462407167004.pdf?__blob=publicationFile. Accessed 10 Oct 2018
The Social Issues Research Center Oxford (2004) Sex differences in driving and insurance risk. www.sirc.org/publik/driving.pdf. Accessed 10 Oct 2018

The World Bank (2017) Data: Life expectancy at birth. data.worldbank.org/indicator/SP.DYN.LE00.MA.IN (male) and data.worldbank.org/indicator/SP.DYN.LE00.FE.IN (female). Accessed 10 Oct 2018

Thüsing G (2015) Allgemeines Gleichbehandlungsgesetz. In: Säcker FJ (ed) Münchener Kommentar zum BGB, vol 1, 7th edn. Beck, München, pp 2423–2728

Tischbirek A (2019) Wissen als Diskriminierungsfrage. In: Münkler (ed) Dimensionen des Wissens im Recht. Mohr Siebeck, Tübingen, pp 67–88

Tourkochoriti I (2017) Jenkins v. Kinsgate and the migration of the US disparate impact doctrine in EU law. In: Nicola F, Davies B (eds) EU law stories. Cambridge University Press, Cambridge, pp 418–445

Wischmeyer T (2018) Regulierung intelligenter Systeme. Archiv des öffentlichen Rechts 143:1–66. https://doi.org/10.1628/aoer-2018-0002

Wolfangel E (2017) Künstliche Intelligenz voller Vorurteile. Available via NZZ. www.nzz.ch/wissenschaft/selbstlernende-algorithmen-kuenstliche-intelligenz-voller-vorurteile-ld.1313680. Accessed 10 Oct 2018

Žliobaitė I, Custers B (2016) Using sensitive personal data may be necessary for avoiding discrimination in data-driven decision models. Artif Intell Law 24:183–201. https://doi.org/10.1007/s10506-016-9182-5

Artificial Intelligence and Legal Personality: Introducing "Teilrechtsfähigkeit": A Partial Legal Status Made in Germany

Jan-Erik Schirmer

Contents

1 Introduction 124
2 The 'Dual Dilemma' 125
  2.1 The Case for Agency 125
  2.2 The First Dilemma 127
  2.3 The Case for Legal Personality 128
  2.4 The Second Dilemma 132
3 A 'Halfway Status' Made in Germany: Introducing *Teilrechtsfähigkeit* 133
  3.1 Teilrechtsfähigkeit 133
  3.2 *Teilrechtsfähigkeit* for Intelligent Agents 136
4 Of Mice and Machines 139
5 Conclusion 140
References 141

Abstract What exactly are intelligent agents in legal terms? Are we just looking at sophisticated objects? Or should such systems be treated as legal persons, somewhat similar to humans? In this article I will argue in favor of a 'halfway' or 'in-between' status that the German civil law has to offer: *Teilrechtsfähigkeit*, a status of partial legal subjectivity based on certain legal capabilities. When applied, intelligent agents would be treated as legal subjects as far as this status followed their function as sophisticated servants. This would both deflect the 'autonomy risk' and fill most of the 'responsibility gaps' without the negative side effects of full legal personhood. However, taking into consideration the example of animals, it is unlikely that courts will recognize *Teilrechtsfähigkeit* for intelligent agents on their own. This calls for the lawmaker to come up with a slight push, which I call the 'reversed animal rule': It should be made clear by statute that intelligent agents are not persons, yet that they can still bear certain legal capabilities consistent with their serving function.

J.-E. Schirmer (✉)
Faculty of Law, Humboldt-Universität zu Berlin, Berlin, Germany
e-mail: jan-erik.schirmer@rewi.hu-berlin.de

1 Introduction

1   On April 19, 2015, more than 20 years after her death, Audrey Hepburn was reborn in a laboratory in Hong Kong. The scientists did an outstanding job, one could think she had just returned from Hollywood's Golden Age. Something about her appearance was slightly different, though. Where one would have expected her characteristic dark brown hair, only a transparent skull cap covering electric cables and circuit boards existed. And instead of Audrey, she insisted on being called Sophia.

2   What happened in Hong Kong was not another milestone for modern medicine. It was a demonstration of state-of-the-art technology. The scientists did not bring Audrey Hepburn back to life, they created a technical twin, a doppelganger robot named Sophia. Just like the real actress, Sophia is capable of imitating gestures and facial expressions. Thanks to artificial intelligence, visual data processing, and facial recognition, she can walk, sustain eye contact, and engage in small talk.[1] And she is a public figure as well: The United Nations Development Program nominated Sophia as the first-ever Innovation Champion for Asia and the Pacific. She made the front pages of several magazines and even appeared on TV shows.[2] The latest highlight followed in 2017, when Sophia became a citizen of the kingdom of Saudi Arabia, being the first robot to receive citizenship of any country.[3]

3   But Sophia is just the most prominent example. A number of her siblings are out there. Virtual assistants, such as Amazon's Echo or Apple's Siri, are able to shop online, order pizza, or request an Uber ride for their users. The Georgia Institute of Technology designed the robot Curi for the purpose of organizing an entire dinner—starting with grocery shopping, proceeding to prepare the meal, and ending with choosing the right wine.[4] The kitchen will by no means be the last place intelligent agents will take over. By the end of the next decade, experts assume that autonomous cars will rule our roads, while humans take the backseat.[5]

4   Naturally, such a profound transformation does not come without difficulties. The law as well will not remain unaffected by these challenges. Just consider the examples mentioned: How do smart assistants conclude binding contracts? Who is responsible if someone is injured by an autonomous car? Is it possible to grant robots citizenship? All of these issues face unique problems in and of themselves. Nonetheless, in the end these boil down to the same fundamental question, which I call the 'status question': What exactly are intelligent agents in legal terms? Are we just

---

[1] www.bbc.com/future/story/20170906-how-it-feels-to-meet-sophia-a-machine-with-a-human-face.
[2] www.asia-pacific.undp.org/content/rbap/en/home/presscenter/pressreleases/2017/11/22/rbfsingapore.html.
[3] www.cnbc.com/2017/12/05/hanson-robotics-ceo-sophia-the-robot-an-advocate-for-womens-rights.html.
[4] www.theatlantic.com/technology/archive/2014/03/the-dream-of-intelligent-robot-friends/284599.
[5] See Wachenfeld et al. (2016), p. 9; Matthaei et al. (2016), p. 1519.

looking at sophisticated objects? Or should such systems be treated as legal persons, somewhat similar to humans? In this article I will argue in favor of a functional approach: *Teilrechtsfähigkeit*—a *partial legal status* based on *specific legal capacities*.[6]

2 The 'Dual Dilemma'

The status question is typically approached from two sides: Philosophically or sociologically speaking, one could ask if intelligent agents should be considered agents in a strict sense. This would entail treating intelligent agents as acting and accountable subjects just as humans. Legally speaking the main question is whether it is necessary to grant intelligent agents legal personality for doctrinal or practical reasons. This section will illustrate that both approaches eventually lead to a 'dual dilemma': While there are good arguments in favor of granting such a status, acknowledging legal personality leads to a slippery slope.

2.1 The Case for Agency

Especially in continental philosophy, agency is traditionally linked to attributes such as free will, reason, and self-awareness. Due to these characteristics, agents are able to make moral judgments and can be held accountable for their actions. This distinguishes agents from objects, which are driven by natural forces and lack the ability to think and reflect—animals being the classic example. Unlike agents, objects are not, as Kant put it, an end in themselves, instead they are a means to an end. Hence, subjects act upon objects or wield power over them.[7]

With that in mind, the answer to the status question appears to be a no-brainer: Neither smart assistants nor driverless cars have a free will or self-awareness. They do not reflect on what is 'right' or 'wrong'. Intelligent agents simply follow a certain protocol, acting according to a subject's—the programmer's, user's etc.— instructions. Many scholars do not even consider their ability to 'think' and 'learn' to be a gamechanger.[8] Despite promising results in the last years, these scholars argue that human intelligence still outperforms artificial intelligence, particularly when it comes to creativity and originality. Moreover, there are some fundamental objections to equating intelligent agents to human beings. Namely computer scientists stress that not only the term 'intelligent agent' but the comparison with human agents

---

[6]For an earlier version of this approach see Schirmer (2016), p. 660.
[7]See Hew (2014), p. 197 and Schirmer (2016), p. 661.
[8]A good overview is given by Hew (2014), p. 198.

in general is misleading because they are structured discordantly and will never think and act like humans.⁹

Although this line of reasoning might sound convincing, it is not in any way helpful in answering the status question. Based on the traditional concept of agency, it is no surprise that intelligent agents are excluded: they are simply not human. The classic concept of agency—especially with its underlying assumptions of free will, reason, self-awareness etc.—is tailored to fit us. It was created to explain why humans are moral subjects. In other words, one can not answer the status question without challenging the concept of status itself.¹⁰ Consequently, progressive philosophers do not attempt to find the human aspects in machines, instead they try to reconstruct agency in a far more abstract and, therefore open sense. In Germany, one of the most prominent advocates for this approach is Andreas Matthias. He conceptualizes moral agency not as a matter of free will or reason, but as the ability to control one's own behavior.¹¹ Along with this ability, he argues, comes accountability, and with accountability comes subjectivity. In his opinion this inference is applicable to intelligent agents: They act with 'intentionality' because the code underlying their decisions does not determine the concrete path, i.e. how—and through which interim goals—they reach the ultimate target. In addition, Matthias points out that intelligent agents are receptive both to external reasons ('responsiveness') and to internal 'second-stage desires'. For instance, intelligent agents can wish to run a certain work process, but at the same desire to change that process in order to save battery power.¹²

The same result can be achieved when agency is not understood in an ontological sense but as an act of social attribution achieved through communication. Niklas Luhmann developed this concept with his famous systems theory. Gunter Teubner, one of Germany's leading legal sociologists, applies this theory to intelligent agents: Just like corporate entities, intelligent agents develop their own hierarchies of preferences, needs and interests. According to Teubner they differentiate themselves from other actors through communication, and by virtue of social attribution, they are eventually perceived as independent actors themselves.¹³ This concept of attribution through communication is, I think, what Ryan Calo had in mind, when claiming robots had social valence: '[t]hey feel different to us, more like living agents.'¹⁴ However, Teubner's comparison to corporations shows that this perception is not just true for anthropomorphic technology such as robots. In other words, humans do not treat a non-human entity as an agent only because it has a physical presence. Although there is strong empirical evidence corroborating the fact that

---

⁹See, for instance, the classic critique by Fodor (1983), p. 114. For more details on the debate see Calo (2015), p. 529.
¹⁰See generally Gruber (2012), p. 134; Teubner (2018), p. 172.
¹¹Matthias (2008), p. 45. For an English summary of Matthias' theory see Matthias (2004), p. 175.
¹²Here Matthias refers to Harry Frankfurt's famous concept.
¹³Teubner (2018), p. 166. For an earlier version of his theory Teubner (2006), p. 14.
¹⁴Calo (2015), p. 532.

Artificial Intelligence and Legal Personality   127

physical resemblance enhances the attribution process,[15] the example of corporations demonstrates how humans are equally comfortable with treating intangible constructs like themselves, as long as they can perceive and address this 'something' as a 'separate communicative something'.[16] When people feel affection for Siri or other digital assistants, they do not project their feelings onto the device; it is the communicative counterpart, the replying unphysical 'something', they hold dear.[17] This assessment strengthens the systems theory's assumption that communication is the decisive factor. And communication is an attribute not only robots share, but one that is essential for all intelligent agents.[18]

2.2 The First Dilemma

All of these elements provide strong arguments for treating intelligent agents as acting subjects. Once one is willing to adjust the classic agency concept to fit other entities besides humans, both the technical capabilities of intelligent agents as well as other actors' perceptions push for subjectivity. Yet this leads to another fundamental question: Should we really *allow* this to happen? If in the end it is a matter of conceptualization, then it is in our hands whether or not we include intelligent agents. Because humans are, at least for now, the gatekeepers of agency, we could keep everyone else out. In the end, the status question comes down to a decision, but one that we eventually have to make.[19]   10

And there are, no doubt, good reasons to have second thoughts. For one, treating intelligent agents as accountable subjects could shift the focus away from human responsibility. Jack Balkin has a point when he argues that the discussion about agency is misleading for this very reason; not the 'obedient Golem', as he puts it, but his master, 'the Rabbi', is to blame when the Golem steps out of line.[20] Yet aside from allocating responsibilities, the status question has a much more essential underlying issue: Where would granting agency leave us (see Ernst, para 7 et seq.)? It is just a small step from agency to personhood. Once this point is reached, intelligent agents would effectively join the ranks of humans.[21] In other words, we should ask ourselves if we are willing to put pressure on the unique status of humans   11

---

[15]See, for instance, Kahn et al. (2011), p. 125.

[16]Historian Yuval Noah Harari (2014), p. 86, describes this concept in his impressive study on the history of humankind as the 'inter-subjective reality', which 'exists within the communication network linking the subjective consciousness of many individuals.'

[17]See www.nytimes.com/2014/10/19/fashion/how-apples-siri-became-one-autistic-boys-bff.html. Spike Jonze's 2013 movie 'Her' is another (fictional) example, see also Balkin (2015), p. 56.

[18]See Teubner (2018), pp. 166 and 174.

[19]See also Wagner (2018), p. 20.

[20]See Balkin (2016), p. 1223 '('homunculus fallacy').

[21]See Eidenmüller (2017), p. 776 ('So, treating robots like humans would dehumanize humans, and therefore we should refrain from adopting this policy.').

in society by bringing in a new player. This is an especially pressing question because we are not talking about a clumsy rookie, but a big time player that will eventually outperform us without even breaking a sweat (see Hoffmann-Riem, para 1).[22] On the other hand, missing the right moment or not considering agency at all, could also be the wrong choice because at some point intelligent agents could demand subjectivity and eventually personhood by force. I admit, this might sound like a poor Hollywood script. However, in the past many oppressed minority groups had to resort to force in order to obtain their rights. In fact, the very concept of human agency is an intellectual revolt against oppression, an enlightenment by those who were kept in the dark for too long.[23]

12   What then are we to do? In my opinion, there are equally good arguments for both sides, but either of them involves high risks. This leaves us with the first dilemma: Agency or no agency—apparently there is no right choice.

2.3   The Case for Legal Personality

13   The question of legal personality is related to the agency discourse. However, at least in Europe and especially in Germany, it is approached from a different angle. Most scholars are concerned about the disruptive effects in law: Intelligent agents no longer acting deterministically leads to a high degree of unpredictability. This in turn brings about a novel 'autonomy risk' (*Autonomierisiko*). According to these scholars the autonomy risk in turn requires answers the existing law is unable to provide, ultimately creating so-called 'responsibility gaps' (*Verantwortungslücken*)—legal vacuums that need to be filled by new legal rules specifically crafted for intelligent agents. And for many authors, legal personality provides the most promising solution.[24]

14   In 2017, the European Parliament joined this line of argument. The legislative body of the European Union appealed to the European Commission to adopt EU-wide new civil law rules on 'robots, bots, androids and other manifestations of artificial intelligence'. According to the European Parliament, the use of intelligent agents is about to 'unleash a new industrial revolution, which is likely to leave no stratum of society untouched' and that will cause 'legal and ethical implications and effects' legislatures have to address.[25] In the long run, it will be necessary to create 'a specific legal status [...], so that at least the most sophisticated autonomous robots

---

[22]Just take Google's AlphaGo Zero algorithm, which reached superhuman level in just a couple of days of training and five million games of self-play, see Silver et al. (2017), p. 354. Another example is Hitachi's swinging robot that learned to swing better than humans in a few minutes, see www.youtube.com/watch?v=q8i6wHCefU4.

[23]See, for instance, Winkler (2016), p. 157.

[24]See, among others, Mayinger (2017), p. 166; Günther (2016), p. 251.

[25]European Parliament (2017), sec. B.

Artificial Intelligence and Legal Personality

could be established as having the status of electronic persons responsible for making good any damage they may cause, and possibly applying electronic personality to cases where robots make autonomous decisions or otherwise interact with third parties independently.'[26] If this recommendation will ever be implemented, is hard to say. However, even if the European Commission takes the proposal into further consideration, the process of drafting and implementing would take years if not decades.[27]

But what are these 'responsibility gaps' that both legal scholars and the European Parliament are referring to? In the following I will illustrate the problem by referring to two prominent examples in German civil law: contract formation and torts.

Contract Formation

Just as under most other national civil laws, contracts are concluded by a meeting of the minds. In Germany this is referred to as 'corresponding declarations of intent' (*übereinstimmende Willenserklärungen*).[28] If I enter a pizzeria and order a pepperoni pizza, I submit a declaration of intent (*Willenserklärung*) that is intended to trigger a legal consequence—a legally binding offer to buy a pizza. But what if I instruct my smart assistant to 'order food' without making any further specifications? What if, say, the assistant ends up ordering salad because it concludes, based on the time of day, previous meals and my diet, that I have had enough pizza already? Can the order still be considered my declaration of intent, was a valid contract concluded?

Some argue that an intelligent agent's declaration always has to be treated as the declaration of its user.[29] This pragmatic approach, however, is problematic since it conflicts with the long-standing contract formation doctrine. In the above-mentioned example of ordering food, it is in fact the smart assistant which transforms my instruction to 'order food' into a legally binding offer. The assistant chooses what to order, at which restaurant and at what price. In other words, the smart assistant alone defines the essential terms of the sales contract (*essentialia negotii*).[30] Taking it even further, my instructions themselves lack everything required for a binding offer because they are not detailed enough to trigger any legal consequences without my assistant's specifications. This example illustrates clearly what the European Parliament had in mind when stating that traditional rules are made inapplicable 'insofar as machines designed to choose their counterparts, negotiate contractual terms, conclude contracts and decide whether and how to implement them'.[31]

---

[26]European Parliament (2017), sec. 59 f).
[27]See Lohmann (2017), p. 168.
[28]Markesinis et al. (1997a), p. 47.
[29]See Spindler (2014), p. 64: 'Einstweilen geklärt'; Müller-Hengstenberg and Kirn (2017), p. 139; Arbeitsgruppe Digitaler Neustart (2017), p. 103.
[30]Markesinis et al. (1997a), p. 48.
[31]European Parliament (2017), sec. AG.

18 Therefore, it is more consistent to apply the law of agency (*Stellvertretungsrecht*).[32] The advantage of this approach being that the declaration could be classified for what it is, i.e. the intelligent agent's own declaration. At the same time precise solutions could be possible with respect to the 'autonomy risk': The declaration would not strictly bind the user. The agent's declaration would only produce binding effect if it was acting within its scope of authority (*Vertretungsmacht*). The existing rules could also provide solutions for mistakes (*Irrtümer*).[33]

19 In order to apply the law of agency, however, one would have to consider the agent's declaration a *declaration of intent*—the problem being that these are conceptually reserved for human beings alone, as only they can trigger legal consequences by virtue of their free will. In other words, applying the law of agency seems to depend on granting intelligent agents a legal personality similar to that of humans: Without legal personality no declaration of intent would exist, and without a declaration of intent the law of agency is not applicable. Indeed, that is one major reason why the European Parliament calls for an 'electronic personality'. This could help solve 'cases where robots make autonomous decisions or otherwise interact with third parties independently'.[34]

Torts

20 Despite some forms of strict liability, the German tort system is conceptually based on fault. Plaintiffs only succeed if they can prove the tortfeasor injured a legally protected right (*Rechtsgut*) intentionally or negligently.[35] Unlike under common law, no vicarious liability rule exists, i.e. superiors are not strictly liable for wrongful acts of their subordinates; instead, plaintiffs must prove the superiors themselves acted intentionally or negligently.[36] This short introduction alone illustrates the difficulties plaintiffs would face in making a tort case involving an intelligent agent. What if, say, I instructed my consistently reliable smart assistant to water the flowers on my balcony and it misinterpreted an input signal, running the water throughout the night, which lead to the destruction of my neighbor's valuable roses one floor below? Would I be held liable for my smart assistant's act?

---

[32] See Teubner (2018), p. 177; Specht and Herold (2018), p. 42; Schirmer (2016), p. 664.
[33] Schirmer (2016), p. 664.
[34] European Parliament (2017), sec. 59 f).
[35] See generally Markesinis et al. (1997b), p. 35.
[36] Sec. 831 para. 1 German Civil Code states: 'A person who uses another person to perform a task is liable to make compensation for the damage that the other unlawfully inflicts on a third party when carrying out the task. Liability in damages does not apply if the principal exercises reasonable care when selecting the person deployed and, to the extent that he is to procure devices or equipment or to manage the business activity, in the procurement or management, or if the damage would have occurred even if this care had been exercised.' See generally Markesinis et al. (1997b), p. 676.

21   The plaintiff could only try to make a claim for negligence since there are obviously no indications for intent on my behalf. Under German tort law, the plaintiff must show that the tortfeasor breached a *Verkehrspflicht*, a duty of care that arises once someone is engaged in a potentially dangerous activity. In my example, some scholars would argue that a duty of care had been breached. In their view, I would have failed to properly monitor and control my smart assistant.[37] Just as in the contractual context, however, this pragmatic approach fails to reflect the essential element of intelligent agents, as defendants can rely on the concept of the 'autonomy risk' as a defense: The damage was not foreseeable. 'Malfunctions' can hardly be prevented even with the best possible monitoring in place. In fact, damages like the destruction of my neighbor's roses are the very essence of the 'autonomy risk': By allowing intelligent agents to interact with their environment autonomously, erroneous decisions are to a certain extent inevitable.[38] Most tort cases involving intelligent agents will simply lack any basis for a presumtion of negligence (for the 'lack of transparency' see generally Hoffmann-Riem, para 51). Anyone who opposes this view in fact argues for strict vicarious liability—yet such rule does not exist under German civil law.[39]

22   To fill the responsibility gap, some scholars try to tackle the problem at the source by allocating liability to the intelligent agent itself.[40] Of course this would require a pool of assets from which damages could be disbursed. However, this is rather a technical than a conceptual problem: The intelligent agent could either be equipped with some sort of equity, which could even increase through commissions payed for each of its regular activities. Or compulsory insurance or liability funds could cover the damage.[41] The conceptual issue runs deeper: Assigning tort responsibility to intelligent agents as a necessary first step requires the ability to be a tortfeasor. Yet under German civil law only persons can be tortfeasors.[42] At least for now, one must say. The European Parliament's appeal to implement a'status of an electronic person' aims to overcome this hurdle so that intelligent agents could be held responsible 'for making good any damage they may cause'.[43]

---

[37] See, for instance, Spindler (2014), p. 70; Arbeitsgruppe Digitaler Neustart (2017), p. 111.
[38] See Schirmer (2018), p. 462.
[39] See Teubner (2018), p. 190; Schirmer (2016), p. 665.
[40] See Mayinger (2017), p. 244.
[41] For this approach see European Parliament (2017), sec. 59 and Wagner (2018), p. 22.
[42] Sec. 823 para 1 states: 'A person who, intentionally or negligently, unlawfully injures the life, body, health, freedom, property or another right of another person is liable to make compensation to the other party for the damage arising from this.'; see generally Markesinis et al. (1997b), p. 35.
[43] European Parliament (2017), sec. 59 f).

2.4 The Second Dilemma

23   In summary, granting intelligent agents legal personality could indeed have a positive impact on German (and most other continental) civil law. Once intelligent agents are considered persons under the law, the 'responsibility gaps' many civil law systems face today would be filled. Moreover, the 'legal [...] implications and effects' of the 'new industrial revolution',[44] would suddenly seem manageable—a single change of the law would bring many existing frameworks such as the law of agency or torts back to life.

24   But there is a catch. Granting intelligent agents legal personality would most likely end in what I call the 'humanization trap'[45]: The status as a legal person indicates a significant normative upgrading. The law would not only move a formerly marginal occurrence to the center of attention, but also address intelligent agents as independent actors. Intelligent agents would be placed at the same level as other legal subjects, bringing it very close to the most prominent representative—the human being. And once an entity reaches this point, the trap snaps shut. It gets harder to justify why this person should not enjoy the same rights and privileges natural persons enjoy. The experience in dealing with corporate entities is a good (and warning) example: Many German jurists claim that legal entities hold the general right to personality because *as persons* they should enjoy the same rights as other persons.[46] Similarly, in the United States a formalistic interpretation of the word 'person' in the fourteenth amendment entailed granting corporations the right to free speech. This has had wide ranging consequences for the legal system and society as a whole.[47] In other words, just as with legal entities, it would be hard to justify why intelligent agents, although recognized as persons under the law, should not hold certain rights such as worker protection or even constitutional rights.[48] To be clear, I am not saying that intelligent agents should not enjoy these rights at all. I just think it is important to determine their ability to be rightsholders for each right specifically. Yet in bestowing intelligent agents with legal personality, the debate could be over before it even begins.

25   So once again, we are stuck in a dilemma: Granting legal personality seems crucial to close the 'responsibility gaps' created by the 'autonomy risk'. But at the same time, it will put us on a slippery slope.

---

[44]European Parliament (2017), sec. B.

[45]Schirmer (2016), p. 662.

[46]See generally Schirmer (2015), p. 201.

[47]First National Bank of Boston v. Bellotti, 435 U.S. 765 (1978). See generally Scofield (1979), p. 1225.

[48]But see, for example, Kersten (2017), p. 14, who argues in favor of a constitutional right to privacy. In other words, the kind of issues that would arise were robots to 'wake up' are of an entirely other order.

3 A 'Halfway Status' Made in Germany: Introducing *Teilrechtsfähigkeit*

Many scholars share the underlying concern of the 'humanization trap'. Ryan Calo, for instance, argues that intelligent agents might use their legal status to claim the right to procreate or desire democratic representation. Following psychologist Peter Kahn and colleagues in their suggestion of a new ontological category, he proposes to create 'a new category of a legal subject, halfway between person and object.'[49] Jack Balkin supports this approach because it matches people's unstable and incomplete perception of intelligent agents: 'People may treat the robot as a person (or animal) for some purposes and as an object for others.' By assigning a 'halfway-status' the law could not only reflect this view but open a path to 'contextual [...], and, above all, opportunistic' solutions.[50]

Calo and Balkin seem to have found the way out of the dilemma. Instead of treating the status question as a matter of 'either/or', they propose an equidistant solution. Yet, such an in-between category is rather unusual. Traditionally, law distinguishes between person and non-person. Something is either an active legal subject with rights and obligations, or an inactive, subordinated object. Nevertheless, Calo believes that the dichotomy has come to an end; the establishment of a 'halfway status' must start now and 'the law will have to make room for this category'.[51]

Neither Calo nor Balkin, however, offer a theory for a 'halfway-status'. Without a theoretical concept, though, the new status stays vague and offers, I think, not much help. For the remainder of this article I will try to outline what such a theory could look like. The good news is, I do not have to start from scratch: German law offers exactly such a 'halfway category'. We call it *Teilrechtsfähigkeit*—partial legal capacity.

3.1 *Teilrechtsfähigkeit*

Under German law, legal capacity describes the ability to have rights and obligations. Historically, one could either have full legal capacity or no legal capacity at all. For human beings, for example, the legal capacity began with the completion of birth and ended with death, while before and after these events humans could not exercise rights or have obligations at all.[52] The same was true for corporations. Upon

---

[49]Calo (2015), p. 549.
[50]Balkin (2015), p. 57; similar Wagner (2018), p. 20: 'Entity status is no black- and-white decision but allows for graduation; the accordance of legal status in one context need not lead to an award of the same status in another.'
[51]Calo (2015), p. 549.
[52]The very first section of the German Civil Code states: 'The legal capacity of a human being begins on the completion of birth.'

registration they were recognized as legal persons entailing full legal capacity, whereas before registration or after liquidation they were legally inexistent. Put simply, it was a system of all or nothing—either one had the potential to have all rights and obligations the legal system had to offer, or one was treated as a complete nobody.[53]

30   Such a structure has a huge benefit. It is an easy binary code, yes or no, black or white. Even in Germany, though, reality comes in shades of gray. Soon the question arose how the law should deal with entities during the process of formation. For instance, how should the law protect the unborn life (so-called *nasciturus*) or cope with unregistered but already operating companies if neither of them had any rights or obligations? For Eugen Ehrlich the answer was to expand the understanding of legal capacity. In his 1909 published book '*Die Rechtsfähigkeit*', he argued that the whole idea of a two-tier system of legal capacity was flawed. By pointing out examples, such as the concept of slavery in ancient Rome or the treating of minors in modern civil law systems, he concluded that at all times legal capacity came in plurals—the binary code was a theoretical illusion, in reality many sorts of legal capacities and therefore many legal statuses existed.[54] In the 1930s, Hans-Julius Wolff transformed Ehrlich's observation into the concept of *Teilrechtsfähigkeit*. He determined *Teilrechtsfähigkeit* to be the status applicable to a human or an association of humans having legal capacity only according to specific legal rules, but otherwise not bearing duties and having rights.[55] According to Wolff, an entity could have legal capacity with regard to some areas of law, whereas at the same time it could be excluded from others.

31   During the Nazi-Regime, however, *Teilrechtsfähigkeit* was used in a way that neither Ehrlich nor Wolff had envisioned.[56] Namely Karl Larenz, one of the leading jurists of the Third Reich, heavily relied on the idea of gradated legal capacities to justify the exclusion of Jewish citizens from civil liberties, while at the same time making Jews subject to various obligations.[57] This abuse was a hard blow for the concept. After the war many argued—ironically one of them being Larenz himself— that the whole idea of a 'halfway status' was flawed and the law should return to the classic binary system.[58] Yet, the idea of *Teilrechtsfähigkeit* prevailed eventually, in particular because German courts adopted it in various forms.[59] In the 1970s, Germany's Federal Constitutional Court acknowledged the state's duty to protect the unborn life. Building on this, the Federal Court of Justice found that a sales

---

[53]See generally Lehmann (2007), p. 226.

[54]Ehrlich (1909), passim.

[55]The idea appears first in Wolff (1933), p. 200 and, more detailed, in his later works on administrative law (*Verwaltungsrecht*).

[56]Both of them were Jewish. Wolff had to flee Germany for Panama in 1935, Ehrlich died years before the *Machtergreifung*.

[57]See generally Jakobs (1993), p. 813.

[58]Fabricius (1963), pp. 21, 35.

[59]Fabricius (1963), pp. 5, 111; Behme (2018), paras 4 et seq.

contract or a donation agreement could also be concluded in favor of such an unborn child.[60] Like under English common law, the unborn child was considered a legal subject whenever this was consistent with the idea of a human being in the making. The same is true for the preliminary company (*Vorgesellschaft*). It is considered a legal entity of its own kind (*Rechtsform sui generis*) subject only to the rules of the articles of association and the statuary laws governing the company, insofar as those laws do not require registration.[61] The same applies to certain company types such as the company constituted under civil law (*Gesellschaft bürgerlichen Rechts*) or the homeowner's association (*Wohnungseigentümergemeinschaft*).[62] All of these entities have partial legal capacity. That is to say, whereas they are not legal persons with full legal capacity, they are still legal subjects, yet the range of their subjectivity is limited by their specific functions. The courts' inference were always quite similar: Even in the case of the unborn child the courts were not primarily motivated by a need to provide protection. Rather, the courts predominantly acknowledged *Teilrechtsfähigkeit* for practical and doctrinal reasons. The addressability as a legal actor solved certain legal issues, such as the question how donation agreements with an unborn child are concluded or how pre-companies as such purchased goods.[63]

Conceptually, the notion of *Teilrechtsfähigkeit* as it is understood today represents a third way of comprehending legal subjectivity. Put simply, it is the Bauhaus School in law—form follows function. *Teilrechtsfähigkeit* is not so much a matter of morality. It stands for the sense that law itself can mold its actors according to its own particular terms and conditions.[64] In other words, creating an addressable subject is just another doctrinal way of solving problems, yet a way that is always limited in scope. The main difference to legal personality can best be illustrated by picturing a candy jar: For a person the jar is full, generally persons can have all rights and obligations the law has to offer. This does not mean, of course, that they actually do have all those rights and obligations. But there is a presumption in their favor that persons have not only an abstract legal capacity, but also in regard to specific rights and obligations.[65] Thus, there is an urging need for justification whenever certain rights and obligations are excluded from persons. Taking candy out of a jar, presupposes a defense. For subjects with only partial legal capacity it is a different story. They start off with an empty jar. Candy is placed into the jar only with respect to their specific function. Again, this does not mean that the glass will always stay at

---

[60]Bundesverfassungsgericht 1 BvF 1 - 6/74 (Feb 25, 1975), BVerfGE 39, p. 1; Bundesgerichtshof XII ZR 29/94 (May 3, 1995), BGHZ 129, p. 297.

[61]Behme (2018), paras 9.

[62]For the GbR see Bundesgerichtshof II ZR 331/00 (Jan 21, 2001), BGHZ 146, p. 344 ('beschränkte Rechtssubjektivität'); for WEG see Bundesgerichtshof V ZB 32/05 (June 2, 2005), BGHZ 163, p. 158 ('Teilrechtsfähigkeit'); see generally Lehmann (2007), p. 231.

[63]Regarding the nasciturus see Bundesgerichtshof XII ZR 29/94 (May 3, 1995), BGHZ 129, p. 305.

[64]Gruber (2012), pp. 134, 154; Kersten (2017), p. 9; Schirmer (2016), p. 662; see generally Luhmann (1993), p. 54.

[65]See Behme (2018), para 5. In essence, this presumption goes back to Kant's concept of subjective rights, see Habermas (1992), p. 131.

that level. But each new candy placed into the jar has to be justified. In other words, the burden to sustantiate the allocation of legal capacities is the exact opposite—legal personhood deals with subtracting, while *Teilrechtsfähigkeit* is concerned with adding rights and obligations. And those different starting points make a huge difference.

3.2 **Teilrechtsfähigkeit** *for Intelligent Agents*

33   Now that we know what the concept is all about, how could *Teilrechtsfähigkeit* work for intelligent agents? As pointed out, partial legal capacity follows function. The primary question hence becomes what function intelligent agents take on. By looking at the areas of application, it is fair to say that intelligent agents are sophisticated servants. Jack Balkin puts it well when he speaks of a 'substitution effect': Intelligent agents take on activities which persons are either unwilling to perform or incapable of.[66] At least for now they do not act in their own interest. Their job is to provide support for both natural and legal persons.[67] An autonomous car does not drive for driving's sake, it drives to transport its occupant to a certain destination. A trading algorithm does not trade on its own account, but on the account of the person who deploys it. In other words, we are looking at the typical 'master-servant situation', in which the servant acts autonomously, but at the same time only on the master's behalf.

34   Thus, intelligent agents should be treated as legal subjects insofar as this status reflects their function as sophisticated servants. Although scenarios are imaginable in which intelligent agents need protection particularly from their masters, this is, I think, not a matter of urgent concern.[68] The focus currently lies on practical and doctrinal ease: In which case can the status as a 'servant' help solve legal problems that arise due to the 'autonomy risk'?

Contract Formation and Torts

35   In the before-mentioned examples of contract formation and torts, the concept of *Teilrechtsfähigkeit* can provide a viable solution. Regarding contracts, intelligent agents would not be able to conclude contracts on their own. Their legal subjectivity would be limited to the status of contractual agents. Due to their function as sophisticated servants, there is no need to assign intelligent agents all capabilities

---

[66]Balkin (2015), p. 59.
[67]See Teubner (2018), p. 162; Schirmer (2016), p. 665.
[68]But see Kersten (2017), p. 14.

contract law has to offer. It is merely necessary to grant them the capabilities needed to conclude and execute their master's contracts.[69]

The same considerations are applicable to torts. Following function, the key question is not whether the intelligent agent itself should be held liable. The intelligent agent supports its master, the harm is not done in its own but in its master's interest. In other words, since the tort is performed within the scope of deployment, liability should, as usual, address the person who profits from the deployment—the master (see Schemmel, para 36; see Hennemann, para 38).[70] In common law jurisdictions, the obvious solution would be to apply the *respondeat superior* rule, which states that the master is strictly liable for acts of his or her agents. Doctrinally, however, the *repondeat superior* rule requires a negligent act of the agent. This implies that intelligent agents need to be considered potential tortfeasors—yet this problem could be solved by expanding its legal subjectivity and treating it not only as a contractual but also as a tortious agent. Due to the fact that German civil law does not foresee the concept of strict vicarious liability, this approach naturally would not suffice. Consequently, Gunter Teubner recently argued for the implementation of a master-servant rule based on the intelligent agent's wrongful decisions (*digitale Assistenzhaftung*).[71]

Although this solution surely looks appealing from a doctrinal standpoint, I would argue against applying (or implementing) the *respondeat superior* rule for one simple reason: The concept's weak point is its need for a servant's negligent action.[72] A negligent act necessitates a breach of a duty of care. The intelligent agent's behavior must, therefore, lag behind a standard of reasonable care, i.e. the intelligent agent, as a minimum, has to perform poorer than other comparable intelligent agents. Moreover, both in common and civil law systems, the harm or injury has to be foreseeable to some extent. But just as the master cannot foresee the harmful act, the intelligent agent itself cannot foresee it. Again, in allowing intelligent agents to interact with their environment autonomously, decisions that turn out to be wrong are to a certain extent inevitable. Unforeseeable harms are the very essence of the 'autonomy risk'. Even when deploying the most sophisticated intelligent agents, wrongful decisions can never be avoided completely without abandoning the technical concept of machine autonomy as a whole.[73] Consequently, it becomes difficult to speak of the intelligent agent's behavior as breaching a duty of care. Applying the *respondeat superior* doctrine would therefore not fill the 'responsibility gap': Most cases would lack the prerequisite of negligence and, therefore, the master's liability could not be triggered.

---

[69] See Teubner (2018), p. 182; Schirmer (2016), p. 664.
[70] See Teubner (2018), p. 190; Schirmer (2016), p. 665.
[71] See Teubner (2018), p. 193.
[72] See Schirmer (2018), p. 470.
[73] Schirmer (2018), p. 470.

38 A true strict liability for intelligent agents avoids this problem.[74] Because it does not presuppose an illicit and culpable behavior, strict liability would hold the user liable for every damage caused by the intelligent agent, relieve the plaintiff from proving that the intelligent agent acted negligently, and fill the 'responsibility gap' after all.

Side Note: Criminal Law

39 So far, I have only provided examples pertaining to civil law. The benefits of the construct of *Teilrechtsfähigkeit*, however, do not end here. I want to illustrate this with a heavily debated issue under criminal law related to the famous 'trolley problem'[75]: Assume, an autonomous car faces a situation, in which it must decide whether to hit and kill five people by going straight or kill just one person by making a sharp turn. Only these two options are available. The autonomous car cannot, say, perform a safety stop or sacrifice its passengers—it has the choice between killing five or killing one. Assume further, the autonomous car's algorithm is programed to follow the principle of maximum utility, meaning that it will make the turn and kill one person to spare four lives. This raises two questions: Will the autonomous car's passengers giving the instruction to start driving, face criminal charges? Can the person programming the algorithm be held responsible?

40 Most scholars answer both questions in the negative. To arrive at this conclusion, however, takes a considerable amount of reasoning. It is often argued that both the passenger and the programmer fulfill all elements of a (negligent) homicide but can rely on an extraordinary emergency defense (*übergesetzlicher Notstand*). Roughly speaking, this extra-legal justification is only available in extreme cases, in which great harm can only be prevented by sacrificing someone's life—it is the last resort when the law has no justifications left.[76]

41 Treating the autonomous car as a partial legal subject, however, would make life much easier. If we considered an intelligent agent to be a potential tortfeasor, one could argue that both the passenger and the programmer did not even commit any elements of the crime. Taking into consideration the proximate cause test—Germans speak of *objektive Zurechnung*—both acts caused the harm. Nonetheless, the argument could be made that both the act of the programmer and the passenger were not proximate enough to the harm to be legally valid because the car itself broke the causal chain by autonomously performing the turn—just as a human taxi driver would have broken it. Similar to the torts case, however, this does not necessitate holding the car itself criminally liable. In fact, it is hard to even find a

---

[74]See Spindler (2015), p. 775; Arbeitsgruppe Digitaler Neustart (2017), p. 116; Gifford (2018), pp. 124, 140.
[75]See, for instance, Engländer (2016), p. 608; Ethik-Kommission (2017), p. 17.
[76]Engländer (2016), p. 614.

reason for such an assessment.[77] If, say, an autonomous car repeatedly broke traffic laws or harmed others, maybe because its machine learning got out of hand, it should be possible to reprogram its software or, if ineffective, shut it down. Under criminal law, the notion of *Teilrechtsfähigkeit* just means that an intelligent agent should be treated as a legal subject insofar as it is capable of breaking the causal chain by performing a tortious act. From this capability, of course, does not follow that the intelligent agent will always break the chain and the programmer and the passenger will never be held responsible. Partial legal subjectivity simply provides a different line of argument for those cases in which there is no reason to press criminal charges.

4 Of Mice and Machines

These examples make a strong case for *Teilrechtsfähigkeit*. Partial subjectivity based on specific legal capacities brings us quite close to the ideal solution for intelligent agents. The 'double dilemma' that arises both from agency and personhood can be avoided. With *Teilrechtsfähigkeit* we can, indeed, have it both ways: Legal subjectivity without the slippery slope. Avoiding the status as a person with all its undesired consequences while at the same time still being able to allocate rights and obligations. 42

Yet one question has been left unanswered thus far: Who should assign *Teilrechtsfähigkeit*? As mentioned above, courts in Germany traditionally recognize partial legal capability.[78] Regarding intelligent agents, one could therefore argue that courts will sooner or later follow suit, all we have to do is wait.[79] However, there are good reasons to doubt this assumption. First, courts have been very reluctant in the past when it came to acknowledging legal subjectivity for non-human actors. The classical example would be animals: While courts have had no difficulties in granting soon-to-be humans or human associations partial legal status, only very few courts took a similar approach regarding orangutans or chimpanzees, although there are many good arguments supporting the notion to treat animals as legal subjects.[80] Intelligent agents, therefore, will most likely share the same fate. Moreover, recognizing a partial legal status for machines or lines of software code is an even bigger step. To my mind, most courts will consider it too big a task to take on by themselves. 43

I would argue, therefore, in favor of pushing the courts in the right direction. In order to achieve this goal, the lawmaker should implement a rule that I call the 44

---

[77] See generally Wagner (2018), p. 21; but see Seher (2016), p. 45.
[78] See infra 3.1.
[79] In this sense Teubner (2018), pp. 162 and 182. I have argued along these lines in the past, see Schirmer (2016), p. 664.
[80] See, for instance, Peters (2016), p. 25.

'reversed animal rule'. What I mean by that becomes clearer when looking at sec. 90a of the German Civil Code, which came into force in 1990 and states:

> Animals are not things. They are protected by special statutes. They are governed by the provisions that apply to things, with the necessary modifications, except insofar as otherwise provided.

45 What sounds confusing is, in fact, a smart piece of legislation. Sec. 90a creates a legal fiction, a technique quite common under German civil law. Animals *are* no longer objects by the means of the law, but for practical and doctrinal reasons they are *treated* as if this were the case. In other words, animals and chairs are legally not the same thing, yet to a large extent the law treats them the same. This approach, when applied reversely, could also work for intelligent agents. I am thinking of a rule similar to this one:

> Intelligent agents are not persons. Consistent with their serving function, they are governed by the provisions that apply to agents, with the necessary modifications, except insofar as otherwise provided.

46 From this rule, one can infer several things: First, it is made perfectly clear that intelligent agents are not persons, which avoids the slippery slope of legal personality. Second, the rule states that intelligent agents can still have certain legal capabilities consistent with their functions leaving it up to courts and scholars to identify and justify those capabilities. Third, the rule implies that intelligent agents remain objects for most of the time. This means, for instance, that they can be sold like any other good.

5 Conclusion

47 In this article I developed three major arguments. First, the discussion about agency and personhood leads to what I call the 'dual dilemma': On one hand, the conceptual and practical arguments for a status similar to that of humans cannot be ignored. Yet at the same time, acknowledging such a status will put the exclusive status of humans under pressure and lead to a situation, in which one has to justify why certain rights and obligations are being withheld from intelligent agents. The ideal solution therefore must be a 'halfway' or 'in-between' status.

48 Second, German civil law offers a template for such a 'halfway solution'—the concept of *Teilrechtsfähigkeit*, a status of partial legal subjectivity based on certain legal capabilities. When applied, intelligent agents would be treated as legal subjects insofar as this status followed their function as sophisticated servants. This would both deflect the 'autonomy risk' and fill most of the 'responsibility gaps' without the negative side effects of personhood.

49 Third, taking into consideration the example of animals, it is unlikely that courts will recognize *Teilrechtsfähigkeit* for intelligent agents on their own. This calls for the lawmaker to come up with a slight push, which I call the 'reversed animal rule': It

should be made clear that intelligent agents are not persons, yet that they can still bear certain legal capabilities consistent with their serving function.

Naturally, I am unsure whether this approach provides the best solution. However, it buys us some time, at the least. For now, the concept of *Teilrechtsfähigkeit* can be a powerful tool to solve most of the urgent problems involving intelligent agents without taking too much of a risk. Since we do not know where artificial intelligence will eventually lead us, it might not be the worst idea, as Germans would say, *auf Sicht zu fahren*—to pick a speed at which we remain in control for as long as we can.

References

Arbeitsgruppe Digitaler Neustart der Konferenz der Justizministerinnen und Justizminister der Länder (2017) Bericht vom 15. Mai
Balkin JM (2015) The path of robotics law. Calif Law Rev Circ 6:45–59
Balkin JM (2016) Sidley Austin distinguished lecture on big data law and policy: the three laws of robotics in the age of big data. Ohio State Law J 5:1217–1241
Behme C (2018) § 1 BGB. In: Hager J (ed) beck-online. GROSSKOMMENTAR BGB, C.H. Beck
Calo R (2015) Robotics and the lessons of cyberlaw. Calif Law Rev 103:513–563
Ehrlich E (1909) Die Rechtsfähigkeit. Puttkammer & Mühlbrecht, Berlin
Eidenmüller H (2017) The rise of robots and the law of humans. ZEuP 4:765–777
Engländer A (2016) Das selbstfahrende Kraftfahrzeug und die Bewältigung dilematischer Situationen. ZIS 9:608–618
Ethik-Kommission Automatisiertes und Vernetztes Fahren (2017) Bericht Juni, Berlin
European Parliament (2017) Resolution of 16 February with recommendations to the Commission on Civil Law Rules on Robotics (2015/2103(INL))
Fabricius F (1963) Relativität der Rechtsfähigkeit. C.H. Beck, München
Fodor J (1983) The modularity of mind. MIT Press, Cambridge
Gifford DG (2018) Technological triggers to tort revolutions: steam locomotives, autonomous vehicles, and accident compensation. J Tort Law 1:71–143
Gruber M-C (2012) Rechtssubjekte und Teilrechtssubjekte des elektronischen Geschäftsverkehrs. In: Beck S (ed) Jenseits von Mensch und Maschine. Nomos, Baden-Baden, pp 133–160
Günther J-P (2016) Roboter und rechtliche Verantwortung: Eine Untersuchung der Benutzer- und Herstellerhaftung. Herbert Utz Verlag, München
Habermas J (1992) Faktizität und Geltung. Suhrkamp, Frankfurt am Main
Harari YN (2014) A brief history of Humankind. Random House, New York
Hew PC (2014) Artificial moral agents are infeasible with foreseeable technologies. Ethics Inf Technol 3:197–206
Jakobs HH (1993) Karl Larenz und der Nationalsozialismus. JuristenZeitung 17:805–815
Kahn PH, Reichert AL, Gary HE, Kanda T, Ishiguro H, Shen S, Ruckert JH, Gill B (2011) The new ontological category hypothesis in human-robot interaction. In: Proceedings of the 6th ACM/IEEE International Conference on Human-Robot interaction, pp 159–160
Kersten J (2017) Relative Rechtssubjektivität. ZfRSoz 37:8–25
Lehmann M (2007) Der Begriff der Rechtsfähigkeit. AcP 2:225–255
Lohmann M (2017) Ein europäisches Roboterrecht – überfällig oder überflüssig? ZRP 6:168–171
Luhmann N (1993) Das Recht der Gesellschaft. Suhrkamp, Frankfurt am Main
Markesinis BS, Lorenz W, Dannemann G (1997a) The German law of obligations: the law of contracts and restitution: a comparative introduction. Clarendon Press, Oxford

Markesinis BS, Lorenz W, Dannemann G (1997b) The German law of obligations: the law of torts: a comparative introduction. Clarendon Press, Oxford

Matthaei R, Reschka A, Rieken J, Dierkes F, Ulbrich S, Winkle T, Maurer M (2016) Autonomous driving. In: Winner H, Hakuli S, Lotz F, Singer C (eds) Handbook of driver assistance systems: basic information, components and systems for active safety and comfort. Springer, Switzerland, pp 1519–1556

Matthias A (2004) The responsibility gap: ascribing responsibility for the actions of learning automata. Ethics Inf Technol 3:175–183

Matthias A (2008) Automaten als Träger von Rechten: Plädoyer für eine Gesetzesänderung. Logos-Verlag, Berlin

Mayinger SM (2017) Die künstliche Person: Untersuchung rechtlicher Veränderungen durch die Installation von Softwareagenten im Rahmen von Industrie 4.0, unter besonderer Berücksichtigung des Datenschutzrechts. Recht Und Wirtschaft, Frankfurt am Main

Müller-Hengstenberg C, Kirn S (2017) Rechtliche Risiken autonomer und vernetzter Systeme, Eine Herausforderung. De Gruyter, Oldenbourg

Peters A (2016) Liberté, Égalité, Animalité: human–animal comparisons in law. Transnl Environ Law 1:25–53

Schirmer J-E (2015) Das Körperschaftsdelikt. Mohr Siebeck, Tübingen

Schirmer J-E (2016) Rechtsfähige Roboter? JuristenZeitung 13:660–666

Schirmer J-E (2018) Robotik und Verkehr – Was bleibt von der Halterhaftung? Die Rechtswissenschaft 4:450–472

Scofield GW (1979) Bellotti-Corporations' Freedom of Speech. Louisiana Law Rev 4:1225–1239

Seher G (2016) Intelligente Agenten als "Personen" im Strafrecht? In: Gless S, Seelmann K (eds) Intelligente Agenten und das Recht. Nomos, Baden-Baden, pp 45–60

Silver D, Schrittwieser J, Simonyan K, Antonoglou I, Huang A, Guez A, Hubert T, Baker L, Lai M, Bolton A, Chen Y, Lillicrap T, Hui F, Sifre L, van den Driessche G, Graepel T, Hassabis D (2017) Mastering the game of go without human knowledge. Nature 550:354–359

Specht L, Herold S (2018) Roboter als Vertragspartner? Gedanken zu Vertragsabschlüssen unter Einbeziehung automatisiert und autonom agierender Systeme. MMR 1:40–44

Spindler G (2014) Zivilrechtliche Fragen beim Einsatz von Robotern. In: Hilgendorf E, Beck S (eds) Robotik im Kontext von Recht und Moral. Nomos, Baden-Baden, pp 63–80

Spindler G (2015) Roboter, Automation, künstliche Intelligenz, selbststeuernde Kfz – Braucht das Recht neue Haftungskategorien? CR 12:766–776

Teubner G (2006) Elektronische Agenten und große Menschenaffen: Zur Ausweitung des Akteursstatus in Recht und Politik. ZfRSoz 27:5–30

Teubner G (2018) Digitale Rechtssubjekte? Zum privatrechtlichen Status autonomer Softwareagenten. AcP 2–3:155–205

Wachenfeld W, Winner H, Gerdes JC, Lenz B, Maurer M, Beiker S, Fraedrich E, Winkle T (2016) Use cases for autonomous driving. In: Maurer M, Gerdes JC, Lenz B, Winner H (eds) Autonomous driving: technical, legal and social aspects. Springer, Berlin

Wagner G (2018) Robot Liability (working paper, June 19). ssrn.com/abstract=3198764 or https://doi.org/10.2139/ssrn.3198764

Winkler HA (2016) Geschichte des Westens: Von den Anfängen in der Antike bis zum 20. Jahrhundert. C.H. Beck, München

Wolff HJ (1933) Organschaft und juristische Person. Untersuchungen zur Rechtstheorie und zum öffentlichen Recht. Juristische Person und Staatsperson. Heymanns, Berlin

Part II
Governance of and Through Artificial Intelligence

Artificial Intelligence and Social Media

Christoph Krönke

Contents

1 Of Arms Races and Filter Biases 146
2 Phenomenology 149
    2.1 Key Features of Social Media 149
    2.2 Social Media AI 150
3 Concepts of Social Media Regulation 151
4 Protective Social Media Regulation 152
    4.1 Communication Through AI As an Exercise of Fundamental Rights 153
    4.2 Restricting AI-Based Communication on Social Media Services 155
    4.3 Responsibilities of Social Media Providers 159
5 Facilitative Social Media Regulation 166
    5.1 Purposes and Instruments of Facilitative Regulation of Social Media AI 167
    5.2 Constitutional Framework of Facilitative Regulation of Social Media AI 168
6 Conclusion 170
References 171

Abstract This article examines the legal questions and problems raised by the increasing use of artificial intelligence tools on social media services, in particular from the perspective of the regulations specifically governing (electronic) media. For this purpose, the main characteristics of social media services are described, and the typical forms of AI applications on social media services are briefly categorized. The analysis of the legal framework starts with the introduction of 'protective' and 'facilitative' media regulation as the two basic concepts and functions of media law in general and of the law governing information society services in particular. Against this background, the major legal challenges associated with the use of AI on social media services for both protective and facilitative media regulation are presented. With respect to protective media regulation, these challenges include the fundamental rights protection of AI-based communication on social media services, legal options to restrict such forms of communication and the

---

C. Krönke (✉)
Institute for Public Policy and Law, Ludwig Maximilian University of Munich, Munich, Germany
e-mail: christoph.kroenke@jura.uni-muenchen.de

© Springer Nature Switzerland AG 2020
T. Wischmeyer, T. Rademacher (eds.), *Regulating Artificial Intelligence*,
https://doi.org/10.1007/978-3-030-32361-5_7

responsibilities of social media providers in view of unwanted content and unwanted blocking of content. As a major objective of facilitative regulation of social media AI, the regulatory handling of potential bias effects of AI-based content filtering on social media users is discussed, including phenomena commonly referred to as 'filter bubble' and 'echo chamber' effects.

1 Of Arms Races and Filter Biases

If you want to get a first glimpse of how important the use of intelligent systems[1] in social media has already become, you should take a look at the statements that Mark Zuckerberg made in the European Parliament on 22 May 2018. In a hearing before members of parliament he addressed, among other things, the problems faced by the social network *Facebook* with regard to the integrity of the content disseminated in the network. In fact, the reason for the hearing itself is a good first illustration of how artificial intelligence (AI) is used in social media: At that time, *Facebook* was heavily criticized in public after it had become known that *Cambridge Analytica*, a company which had used AI to offer political microtargeting[2] of certain social media users in the run-up to the US presidential elections, temporarily had access to the personal data of millions of users on the network. This shows that AI plays an important role *for organized users*[3] *of social media*, i.e. for the users with a strong commercial or political background. Companies and organizations can use data-based profiling in order to engage in intelligent content marketing[4] or content

---

[1]For the purpose of this article, the terms 'artificial intelligence' (or 'AI', as references to a certain concept) and 'intelligent systems' (or 'AI systems', or 'AI tools', as references to a certain technology) are used in a rather broad sense without referring to a particular branch of AI (such as rule-based AI or machine learning systems). I will follow the definition developed by Scherer (2016), p. 362, who refers to AI as meaning 'machines that are capable of performing tasks that, if performed by a human, would be said to require intelligence' (as opposed to tasks that can be performed 'mechanically'). This definition includes—at least in my view—not only data-driven AI but also rule-based AI, as long as the respective system is sufficiently sophisticated and leaves the concrete decisions made by the system hard or even impossible to foresee. In contrast, I do not think that—for the purpose of this article—the AI system's decision-making process needs to be independent of human programming. From a regulatory perspective, sophisticated systems with a fixed set of pre-defined rules can raise the same legal problems as machine learning systems (with its 'own' experience as the determining factor in the decision-making process).

[2]'Political microtargeting' is a term used to describe the personalized addressing of an individual for political purposes on the basis of behavior- and personality-based user profiles that are created by algorithmic evaluation of personal data. Cf. O'Neil (2016), pp. 194 et seq.

[3]In this article, the term 'organized users' shall refer to persons who use social media specifically for commercial and/or political purposes.

[4]Similar to political microtargeting, 'intelligent content marketing' (or 'behavioral marketing') is marketing (or advertising) 'that is based on the observation of the behaviour of individuals over time [...] (repeated site visits, interactions, keywords, online content production, etc.)' and

curation,[5] or, in case they pursue political objectives like *Cambridge Analytica*'s clients did, to address certain user groups with specific (dis)information by means of political targeting. A specific technique of commercial or political targeting is the use of social bots, i.e. accounts operated by software, which—either openly or disguised as human users—share information with relevant user groups.[6]

Quite obviously, social media providers cannot leave these developments unanswered. Considering the fact that social media are flooded with inappropriate content even without the involvement of 'AI opponents', *platform providers*, too, feel the need to resort to intelligent means of control in order to cope with the increasing amount of unwanted and critical content in their networks, including coordinated and automated misinformation operations. With respect to the situation on *Facebook*, Zuckerberg stated in the hearing of 2018 that

> we're using new technology, including AI, to remove fake accounts that are responsible for much of the false news, misinformation and bad ads that people can see on Facebook. In the run-up to the 2017 French Presidential Election, our systems found and took down, more than 30.000 fake accounts.[7]

It becomes clear in his statement that, taking into account the technological possibilities of organized users, the implementation of these 'new technologies' is no longer just a matter of convenience for the network, but of necessity:

> We'll never be perfect on this. You know our adversaries, especially on the election side, people who are trying to interfere, will have access to some of the same AI tools that we will. So, it's an arms race, and we'll need to constantly be working to stay ahead. But our vision for how we should manage the system is going to move from one of reactive management, as people in our community flag things, to one where we're more proactively having systems look through content [and] flag things (...), and we're already making significant progress in doing that.

These descriptions give the impression that underneath the attractive, brightly colored surface of commercial social media services, a real social media war seems to rage, carried out between (rogue) users and social media providers who are highly armed with AI weapons.

---

conducted 'in order to develop a specific profile and thus provide data subjects with advertisements tailored to match their inferred interests', Article 29 Working Party (2010), p. 4. See also e.g. Calo (2014), pp. 1015 et seq.; Ebers (2018), passim.

[5]The term 'content curation' is used ambiguously. It is sometimes referred to as synonym for content filtering and blocking of illegal content carried out by platform providers, see e.g. Hoffmann-Riem (2017), p. 18. In the specific context of social media marketing, (intelligent) content curation means 'filtering through all the interesting content across the web and sharing the best news, articles, videos and infographics on your social channels' (and targeting users based on their individual preferences), cf. Deeran (2013). In the latter sense, intelligent content curation is a specific form of intelligent online marketing.

[6]Cf. Schröder (2018), p. 465.

[7]There is no written record of the hearing. The statements quoted here were taken from the video recordings of the hearing, available—for example—at www.youtube.com/watch?v=bVoE_rb5g5k (via CNBC's YouTube channel).

5   All in all, the events and statements around the *Cambridge Analytica* scandal draw the picture of a social media environment that is being massively designed and shaped by AI. This picture is complemented by the observation that social media providers use AI techniques not only to preserve the integrity of the content on their services. They also use AI to improve those services and, most importantly, for commercial reasons and in the interest of other user groups, to display content to individual users that matches their personal preferences as closely as possible and to arrange the content accordingly. In many of these cases, personal data are processed and analyzed on the basis of profiling; however, due to the public significance of social media, these business models could (!) raise problems that might go far beyond mere data protection issues. AI-based content filtering could lead to users no longer being confronted with content (i.e. commercial offers, but also factual information and opinions) outside their own communication environment, or to users only coming into contact with content that corresponds to the preferences of the majority. In the long run, this could result in the infamous 'filter bubbles'[8] or 'echo chambers'[9] for users, to a fragmentation of the democratic public sphere as a whole or even to a 'dictatorship' of the respective majority opinion—in short: the use of AI might cause publicly significant *filter biases.*

6   In this article, I would like to examine the legal questions and problems raised by the increasing use of AI tools on social media services, in particular from the perspective of the regulations specifically governing (electronic) media.[10] For this purpose, I will first describe the characteristics of social media and briefly categorize the typical forms of AI applications on social media services (see Sect. 2). I will then introduce protective and facilitative regulation as the two basic functions of media regulation in general and of the law governing information society services[11] in particular (see Sect. 3). Against this background, the major legal challenges associated with the use of AI on social media services for both protective (see Sect. 4) and facilitative (see Sect. 5) media regulation can be discussed.

---

[8]Pariser (2011), passim.

[9]Sunstein (2017), p. 9 and passim.

[10]Other (important) regimes which are also affected, in whole or in parts, by the use of AI in social media, such as data protection law (see Marsch), general competition law and antitrust law in particular (see Hennemann), will not be covered in this article.

[11]The term 'information society service' is defined in Article 1(b) of the Directive (EU) 2015/1535 of the European Parliament and of the Council of 9 September 2015 laying down a procedure for the provision of information in the field of technical regulations and of rules on Information Society services (codification) as 'any service normally provided for remuneration, at a distance, by electronic means and at the individual request of a recipient of services'. I will use the term equivalently to the terms 'electronic media' and 'telemedia'. The 'law governing information society services' (or: the 'law of electronic media', or: 'telemedia law') will be considered as a specific branch of media law in general.

2 Phenomenology

2.1 *Key Features of Social Media*

While the different types of social media[12] definitely show a certain heterogeneity, they actually share at least two specific features which are elementary to the far-reaching impact of these services and to the key role of their providers:

First, social media enable the individual user to communicate information[13] in a certain way[14] to a large number of other users and to react by way of communication to the content published by other users. This feature constitutes the social character of social media, and it has significantly changed the very structure not only of private and individual communication, but also of public and mass communication.[15] It also contributes substantially to the fact that online and offline worlds are increasingly amalgamating.[16]

As a *second* characteristic feature, social media allow this form of communication on the basis of and within the framework of internet-based, virtual *platforms* on which the communicated contents are conveyed and arranged in a certain manner. The platforms are provided by social media providers, mostly private companies. Because of their technical means to shape and influence the flow and arrangement of information, platform providers *de facto* play a key role in social media, they are the 'bottlenecks' of communication.[17] Hence, when it comes e.g. to preserving the integrity of content disseminated in social media, it is first and foremost the social media providers who are increasingly called for (more) legal responsibility for the content on their services, even if in most cases they do not disseminate their own content.

7

8

9

---

[12]A distinction can be made between social networks (e.g. Facebook), multimedia platforms (e.g. YouTube), microblogs (e.g. Twitter) and wikis (e.g. Wikipedia), cf. Schmidt (2013), pp. 11 et seq. Of course, each individual business model has certain variations and may carry characteristics of more than one 'genre'.

[13]In most social media, communication is open to text, photo and video.

[14]Depending on the design of the social medium, the information is communicated and received by other users in different ways, e.g. in a general news feed (Facebook) or on demand (YouTube), permanently (Twitter) or on a temporary basis only (Snapchat).

[15]See for example Hoffmann-Riem (2016), pp. 626–629; Ingold (2017), pp. 506–517.

[16]Some others suggest that we should use the term 'onlife' in order to illustrate the merger of online and offline, cf. Floridi (2015), pp. 87 et seq.; Hildebrandt (2015), pp. 41 et seq.; Hoffmann-Riem (2017), p. 6.

[17]See for example Eifert (2017), p. 1450.

2.2 Social Media AI

10 It follows from what has already been said that basically two groups of actors can use and implement AI technologies: the providers of social media and certain organized users of their services.

11 The *providers* use AI technologies (1) to check the contents on their services for communication amounting to violations of the applicable *laws* (e.g. to take down illegal hate speech or dissemination of child pornography) or violations of the provider's individual *community standards* (e.g. to block or remove fake accounts, false news and bad ads, in the future possibly also to monitor certain discussion standards[18]) as well as to prevent *other interferences and threats* resulting from or related to the use of their services (e.g. the use of recognition software to detect suicide intentions). Such communication can be either *blocked* (*ex ante* or *ex post*), *removed* (*ex post*), *labelled* (*ex ante* or *ex post*) in a specific manner (e.g. as 'not verified') or *reported* to the competent authorities.[19] Another purpose of the implementation of AI by providers is (2) the use as tools for intelligent *control of access* to information for individual users, in particular for greater (targeted) *personalization*.[20] While this can certainly be considered, at least in parts, as a means of individualizing and hence optimizing user experience, a major reason for social media providers to control the individual user's access to information is also to generate more user activity and thus ultimately more (advertising) revenue.

12 For certain users who use social media specifically for commercial and/or political purposes (i.e. *organized users*), AI can open up possibilities for intelligent content marketing and content curation.[21] On the basis of behavioral targeting, users can be (1) addressed according to their individual preferences (*individualization* of machine-generated communication). Somewhat more specific, but also increasingly widespread, is the use of social bots, i.e. accounts controlled (openly or disguisedly) by software, which conduct consultation or advertising conversations with individual users (as 'chat bots'), specifically place advertisements, generate trending topics or disseminate certain information or disinformation. In this way, AI can be used (2) to (consciously or unconsciously) create the appearance of human authorship of the respective communication and thus strengthen the recipients' trust in the quality of that communication (*humanization* of machine-generated communication). In quantitative terms, too, automated accounts and intelligent marketing can quickly (3) create the impression of a large number of users disseminating a

---

[18] The AI-based service 'Perspectives' developed by Google is already capable of filtering out discussion contributions with a 'toxic' effect for discussions on social networks and reporting them to the operators. For more information see www.perspectiveapi.com.

[19] A rather theoretical (and problematical) option for social media providers would be to discretely modify or manipulate unwanted communication. There are no indications, however, that concealed modifications are actually performed.

[20] Cf. for example Paal and Hennemann (2017), p. 644.

[21] For an explanation of these terms see above in notes 4 and 5.

certain piece of information or representing an opinion (*multiplication* of machine-generated communication).

3 Concepts of Social Media Regulation

These phenomena encounter more or less developed legal frameworks in different countries. While this article will be referring to regulations in Germany and Europe, the regulatory issues as such shall be discussed in an abstract way. Therefore, we will not simply work through the specific media law regimes applicable in Germany and Europe. Rather, we will use German and European media regulations as examples and illustrations of how the general regulatory issues raised by social media AI could or should (not) be addressed.

Based on the two most fundamental functions of law, media regulation in general and content regulation of information society services in particular can be divided into two categories: protective content regulation and facilitative social media regulation.[22] The role that AI (can) play for regulation lies crosswise to these two regulatory concepts: in both concepts, AI can be the *object* ('regulation *of* AI'), but also the *means* of regulation ('regulation *through* AI').[23]

Intuitively, the regulation of electronic media is primarily perceived as protective regulation. Legislators and courts are first and foremost dealing with questions of how users and/or third parties can be *protected* from certain contents disseminated in media. From the perspective of media law, protective content regulation covers avoiding, eliminating or at least labelling unwanted or even illegal content, and attributing responsibility (in the sense of liability) for such content to certain actors (users or providers). At the same time, protective content regulation can also be about the protection of permissible communication. In the US, for example, the protection of free speech in electronic media has long been recognized as a distinct and highly relevant *topos*,[24] and in Germany, too, the undue 'overblocking' of content in social media is increasingly perceived as a pressing problem—at least

13

14

15

---

[22]Cf. similar Eifert and Hoffmann-Riem (2011), pp. 689 et seq., who distinguish media regulation for the purpose of (1) managing conflicts between the freedom of communication and other legal interests (here: 'protective media regulation') and of (2) ensuring the exercise of the freedom of communication (here: 'facilitative media regulation').

[23]See also Hoffmann-Riem, para 16, who distinguishes between 'governance *of* algorithms' and 'governance *by* algorithms'.

[24]For example, in the famous and groundbreaking Yahoo! case (2000–2006) which has become an integral part of the history of internet law, the argumentation of the US courts (in contrast to the reasoning of the French courts) focused primarily on the question of whether the obligation imposed by French courts on the company Yahoo! to block certain inadmissible contents could 'survive' in view of the 'strict scrutiny required by the First Amendment [i.e. freedom of speech]', cf. Yahoo! Inc. v. LICRA, 169 F. Supp. 2d 1181, 1189 and 1193 (N.D. California 2001). See also Kohl (2010), pp. 199 et seq.

since the Network Enforcement Act (NEA) was introduced in 2017.[25] Besides these issues, media law also deals with consumer-protection concerns and provides, for example, imprint obligations and specific advertising rules for electronic media services (e.g. the principle of separation of content and advertising). Again, the discussion increasingly focuses on the protection of permissible commercial communication as well.

16 In view of the social significance of media, especially those with a considerable broad impact, there is yet another function in addition to the protective function of media regulation: the facilitative function of media law. The facilitative function aims at ensuring that public media produce a sufficient level of diversity of opinions. This should *facilitate* that every citizen can form his opinion in freedom and on the basis of sufficient information. At least in the German legal system, the facilitative function of media regulation is mainly realized in the field of classical broadcasting. However, many German authors argue that we ought to consider whether or not the facilitative function of media regulation should also be extended to information society services, particularly to social media and search engines.[26] Recognizing such a facilitative function would mean that on information society services too, diversity of opinions needs to be ensured. A general obligation of certain powerful social media providers to safeguard diversity, for example, could restrict algorithm-based personalization on social media services. Facilitative media regulation could even include an obligation to actively provide for content reflecting diverse opinions. Some minor but initial steps towards a facilitative social media regulation can be found in the draft Media State Treaty of August 2018.[27]

4 Protective Social Media Regulation

17 As stated above, in its protective function media law aims to protect users of social media, third parties and/or common goods *from dangers and risks* that may emanate from unwanted content on social media services, and, vice versa, to protect users of social media *from being unduly restricted* in their freedom to distribute content in social media.

18 These two dimensions of protective media law particularly affect the activities of organized social media users who operate with AI tools. On the one hand, these activities principally fall within the scope of fundamental rights (in particular: the freedom of speech and expression) and must hence be respected and protected by

---

[25]See for example Paal and Hennemann (2017), pp. 650–651; Feldmann (2017), p. 295; Nolte (2017), pp. 555 et seq.; Lang (2018), pp. 232–237.

[26]Cf. Drexl (2016), pp. 13 et seq. with an accurate overview over the discussion on how media regulators should react to digitization.

[27]See below in para 35 and in para 58 for a legal discussion of the measures proposed in the draft treaty.

media regulation (see Sect. 4.1). On the other hand, media law sets limits to these activities in order to protect the interests of others (see Sect. 4.2). Possible addressees of legal obligations are not only those persons or instances directly endangering the protection of the rights and interests. Due to their far-reaching possibilities of influencing the flow of information on their platforms, especially through AI, it is also the social media providers who come into consideration as addressees of protective regulation (see Sect. 4.3).

4.1 Communication Through AI As an Exercise of Fundamental Rights

Although there is discussion about restricting AI-based communication in social media, especially with respect to the operation of social bots and fake accounts (see below in Sect. 4.2), communication through AI is itself covered by several fundamental rights and freedoms and is therefore subject to specific protection under (constitutional) media law. Hence the exact scope of fundamental rights protection for the use of AI in social media needs to be examined in the first place.

In principle, it makes no difference whether a person exercises his or her fundamental rights and freedoms in person or by using technical aids, at whatever stage of the exercise of rights. From a legal point of view, it seems therefore irrelevant whether a person forms and/or expresses his or her opinion or relevant facts personally, or whether he or she leaves this up to an AI system which he or she controls. As long as the output of the system is ultimately attributable to his or her actions and hence qualifies as his or her 'anticipated' expression of opinion,[28] the operation of the system will be regarded as a specific exercise of the freedom of speech and expression. The same rules apply to other fundamental rights, e.g. the freedom of occupation, in case the operation of the AI tool is part of the operator's professional activities.

Moreover, the concrete results of the exercise of the fundamental right do not have to be taken note of individually by the holder of the fundamental right concerned. For this reason it is not relevant that the operator of an AI-based communication system is likely to be unaware of the system's individual output in most cases. With respect to the freedom of expression in particular, it is sufficient that the output is meant as an act of communication towards one or more human recipients. Legal protection for a machine-generated expression of opinion could only be denied in cases in which the communication is not addressed to human recipients but to machines. A 'conversation between machines', i.e. a pure exchange

19

20

21

---

[28]The term 'anticipated' expression of opinion ('antizipierte Meinungsäußerung') is used by Milker (2017), p. 217, who argues that the operation of social bots is an exercise of the freedom of speech and expression.

22 of data between machines, can certainly not be classified as a communicative act within the scope of application of the right to free expression.[29]

For the German legal system, these principles were confirmed in the *Autocomplete* decision of the German Federal Court of Justice (FCJ) in 2013. In this decision, the FCJ qualified *Google*'s autocomplete-function—most certainly a powerful AI application—as falling within the scope of *Google*'s freedom of speech (Article 5 of the Basic Law) and its economic freedom of action (Article 2 of the Basic Law).[30]

23 In certain cases, however, it might be necessary to deny fundamental rights protection to AI-based distribution of content in social networks if the activity amounts a priori to an *abusive use* of fundamental rights. Such an exception is discussed, for example, with regard to telemedia providers who operate with social bots under pseudonyms (or as 'fake accounts') and hence falsely pretend that the accounts are actually run by (a large number of) human beings. Moreover, organized users who conduct coordinated (mis)information campaigns on the basis of AI controlled targeting could also fall within this exclusion.

24 Exempting certain activities *a priori* from fundamental rights protection is not something entirely unusual. According to the settled case-law of the German Federal Constitutional Court (FCC), a provably or knowingly untrue factual claim does not fall within the scope of the freedom of speech under Article 5 of the Basic Law, as long as they are not intrinsically linked to a statement of opinion.[31] In a similar way, invoking the freedom of occupation (Article 12 of the Basic Law) is excluded in the case of activities that are as such disapproved of by the legal system,[32] in the context of electronic media for example for someone who operates a service for the distribution of digital pirated copies.[33]

25 However, these considerations can only be applied to the use of AI tools in social media within very narrow limits. The FCC's case-law only refers to the *content* of statements, not to its *modalities*. Choosing a false username may violate the terms of use of the respective service provider, but it is not per se an abusive exercise of fundamental rights. Quite to the contrary: According to the FCC, freedom of expression includes the right of the person making a statement to choose the form and the circumstances for his or her statement, ensuring that the statement has the greatest possible effect.[34] This does not only entail the right to explicitly state one's

---

[29]Cf. Schröder (2018), p. 467, who refers to Bundesverfassungsgericht 2 BvR 1345/03 'IMSI-Catcher' (22 August 2006), BVerfGK 9, p. 74.

[30]Bundesgerichtshof VI ZR 269/12 'Autocomplete' (14 May 2013) BGHZ 197, p. 222.

[31]Cf. Bundesverfassungsgericht 1 BvR 797/78 'Böll' (3 June 1980), BVerfGE 54, p. 219, and 1 BvR 1376/79 'NPD Europas' (22 June 1982), BVerfGE 61, p. 8.

[32]See Bundesverfassungsgericht 1 BvR 1054/01 'Sportwetten' (28 March 2006), BVerfGE 115, p. 301.

[33]See for example Bundesgerichtshof I ZR 18/11 'Alone in the Dark' (12 July 2012), NJW 2013, p. 785.

[34]Bundesverfassungsgericht 1 BvR 131/96 'Missbrauchsbezichtigung' (24 March 1998), BVerfGE 97, pp. 397–400, on the right to expressly state one's name.

own name but also the right to express an opinion anonymously, in order to avoid sanctions or other negative effects that might prevent the person from expressing his or her opinion.[35]

If we accept this 'freedom to choose the modalities'[36] of an expression of opinion and take it seriously, we will have to reject most arguments that could be put forward against the need for fundamental rights protection of AI-based communication. This concerns in particular arguments related to (1) the ability of AI-controlled communication systems to address users according to their respective preferences—i.e. user targeting, some might say: manipulation—, as well as (2) the enormous scatter and impact of such communication. According to the logic described above, the choice of the modalities of expressions of opinion (and the factual assertions associated with them) is supposed to enable the holders of fundamental rights to *maximize the effect of their expressions*. If they do so by relying on a particularly sophisticated communication tailored to the psychological situation of the addressees, this may be subject to certain limits (e.g. restrictions resulting from the addressees' right to data protection). In principle, however, the choice of powerful data analytics tools is legitimate and covered by the freedoms of communication and occupation. Similarly, it is generally permissible to enhance the effect of an expression by creating the impression that it is backed by a greater mass of people than is actually the case—for example, when a large number of intelligent chatbots are used to spread certain content.

Against the background of these considerations, it is clear that *prima facie* most forms of AI-based communication on social media services do qualify, in principle, as a legitimate exercise of fundamental rights by their providers. In most cases they must not be precluded *a priori* from invoking their fundamental rights and freedoms.

4.2 Restricting AI-Based Communication on Social Media Services

The fact that machine-generated, AI-based communication on social media services principally falls within the scope of protection of fundamental rights, especially the freedom of speech and expression as well as the freedom of occupation, does not mean that restricting these freedoms is not permissible at all. The primary consequence is merely that any restriction of a guaranteed freedom requires distinct *legal justification*. Several reasons actually speak in favor of restricting certain forms of AI-based communication in social media as such (paras 29–32). For this purpose, different means of restriction can be used (paras 33–35).

---

[35]See Bundesgerichtshof VI ZR 196/08 'Spickmich' (23 June 2009), BGHZ 181, pp. 341–342 (on the 'right to anonymously express an opinion'); Kersten (2017), p. 242.
[36]Steinbach (2017), p. 103 ('Modalitätsfreiheit').

Grounds for Restriction

29 With regard to the non-commercial, rather politically motivated use of AI on social media services, the protection of the *democratic process* as a whole is often cited as the main reason for restriction (*de lege ferenda*).[37] At first glance, the argumentation in favor of restriction seems plausible: As described above, AI allows for disseminating information in social media (1) under the pretense of human communication, (2) on a large scale and/or (3) with specific tailoring to the preferences of individual users. These 'artificial' modalities of communicating (politically relevant) information could be contrasted with 'authentic' communication modalities. One could argue that, on the traditional 'market of opinions', (1) human authorship is clearly recognizable as such and ensures a special degree of authenticity and effectiveness, especially if the person making a statement appears by name and does not hide behind anonymity.[38] Likewise, (2) artificial majorities cannot easily be created, and reproductions are generally recognizable as such. And finally, it could be argued that, in the traditional political discourse, (3) information needs to be placed and utilized objectively and convincingly; psychological means that address the individual psychological situation of citizens are only available to a very limited extent.

30 At second glance, however, a restriction on the basis of these considerations would appear to be problematic. There is no prototype of a democratic public sphere or a fixed model of public communication that would be appropriate for the democratic process. The social foundations of the classic normative concepts of the public sphere and of public communication such as the one proclaimed by *Jürgen Habermas*[39] had changed long before the advent of digitization,[40] and even more so with it: The digital transformation has triggered ongoing developments from one-to-one and one-to-many towards many-to-many communication, from information shortage towards information overload and from individual and collective activities towards behavioral structures such as emergent and/or 'swarm' activities which are increasingly independent of the actions of individuals.[41] In view of these fluctuations, constitutions and their concepts of democracy must be interpreted as being open to a development of the public sphere and of public communication. Constitutions and their institutions are not supposed to preserve any particular state of society. For this reason, restrictions on new forms of communication for the

---

[37] See for example Steinbach (2017), p. 104; Schröder (2018), p. 470.

[38] The FCC has recognized this thought in Bundesverfassungsgericht 1 BvR 131/96 'Missbrauchsbezichtigung' (24 March 1998), BVerfGE 97, pp. 398–399, in a slightly different context: 'The effect of an expression of opinion on a third party essentially depends on whether its author is recognizable or not. Anonymous statements often lack the authenticity that is necessary in order to have the intended impact or to provoke reactions.'

[39] See Habermas (1962), passim.

[40] Cf. Vesting (2015), pp. 151–164, with a critique of Habermas's concept of the public sphere.

[41] See Ingold (2017), pp. 506–521.

purpose of protecting[42] the democratic process must not be promoted prematurely, on the basis of a traditional understanding of democracy and of the democratic public sphere. Rather, information society regulation must take account of the fact that it is these new forms of communication too that are shaping the democratic public sphere (s) and their functional conditions, i.e. the conditions that are commonly proposed as grounds for restriction. After all, restricting new forms of communication such as AI-controlled communication for the purpose of protecting the 'democratic public sphere' as a distinct common good mostly prove to be circular. In view of constitutional law, the protection of the democratic process is not a suitable legal basis for restricting AI-generated communication. The same must apply to similarly abstract regulatory goals such as the 'integrity of social media' or the 'objectivity of discourse'. Social media operators can certainly include these targets in their terms of use in order to maintain a certain quality of service or to appeal to a certain user audience, but they do not constitute acceptable grounds for *regulatory* restrictions of AI-based communication.

There is yet an alternative reason for restricting certain forms of disseminating content based on AI. Since they concern specific modalities of communicating on social media services with other individual users, one should consider other instances where media law regulates communication modalities for the protection of individual addressees. At the level of European Union law, for example, Article 6 (a) of the E-Commerce Directive[43] provides that commercial communications which are part of or constitute an information society service shall be clearly identifiable as such. With regard to advertising in particular, Section 58(1) of the State Treaty on Broadcasting and Telemedia concluded between the German federal states stipulates that advertising in electronic media must be clearly identifiable as such and clearly separated from the rest of the content; moreover, no subliminal techniques may be used in advertising. These regulations are based on the following idea. The users of electronic media usually place a greater degree of trust in editorial content than in information coming from a commercial undertaking or from advertisers, because they assume that editorial content is created with greater objectivity and not driven by subjective commercial interests.[44] For this reason, regulations such as Article 6 (a) of the E-Commerce Directive and Section 58(1) of the State Treaty on Broadcasting and Telemedia are supposed to protect the users of electronic media from misleading communication. Users shall have the opportunity to position themselves

31

---

[42]Of course, the legislator is not precluded from shaping the public sphere and the corresponding media order by means of facilitative regulation. This, however, is a distinct dimension of media regulation and will be discussed below in Sect. 5.

[43]Directive 2000/31/EC of the European Parliament and of the Council of 8 June 2000 on certain legal aspects of information society services, in particular electronic commerce, in the Internal Market.

[44]Cf. for these and the following considerations Smid (2015), p. 5.

in a critical distance from commercial and advertising content in order to form a free will and opinion.[45]

32 Regulation of AI-driven communication on social media services could build on this idea from consumer protection in electronic commerce and aim at the protection of (1) the individual right to form a free opinion and (2) the individual right to form a free will with regard to legal transactions. Since we have seen that users usually place particular trust in authentic human communication, both freedoms can be impaired or at least endangered if information on social media services is disseminated by means of AI (1) under the mere pretense of human communication, (2) on an artificially large scale, and/or (3) with specific tailoring to the preferences of individual users. On the basis of these considerations, restrictions of AI communication would not rest upon an abstract and blanket concept of the democratic public sphere(s) that can hardly be defined. Rather, they would protect very concrete individual rights and legal interests.

Means of Restriction

33 The fact that there are certain legitimate grounds for legislators to restrict the use of AI tools on social media services does not mean that these tools should simply be banned. Possible means of restricting AI tools also include obligations of users to *label* accounts controlled by and information generated and/or disseminated by software based on AI technologies. In view of the principle of proportionality, labelling obligations should be legislators' first choice in order to restrict the implementation of AI tools. In contrast, obligations to *limit* the use of AI-driven (as regards the quantity or quality of the information) or to *refrain* from implementing AI tools on social media services should definitely be the last resort for a regulation of AI. Obligations to *report* the intended use of AI technologies to the authorities or to obtain a specific *license* or *certificate* would also be less invasive than banning the use entirely, but these options would probably not be practically feasible, considering the sheer multitude of users recurring to machine-generated communication.

34 Against the background of the limited number of legitimate grounds for restricting the use of AI tools in social media, a *ban* of these tools would only be admissible in exceptional cases and with respect to specific implementations, for example the implementation for the purpose of massive defamation or targeted misinformation. Of course, this would not only affect the AI-based dissemination of information but all forms of abusive communication. The major problem for this

---

[45]See for example Heidel (1988), p. 168; Bosman (1990), p. 548, who explicitly argue that the separation of commercial communication and advertising from other contents aims at protecting the right to freely form an opinion. Other authors, for example Micklitz and Schirmbacher (2015b), p. 22, consider misleading communication as a violation of the freedom of decision in commercial contexts. In any case, these statements illustrate that the regulations clearly have a constitutional background.

kind of regulation would certainly be to determine in fact and in law whether there is a provably or knowingly untrue factual claim in a particular case.[46]

In most cases, the principle of proportionality will only allow for *labelling obligations* for the use of AI-driven communication.[47] It is therefore not surprising that the draft for a new Media State Treaty, worked out by the German federal states and published in August 2018, also contains a provision on the labelling of automatically generated content.[48] According to Section 55(3) of the draft treaty, providers of telemedia services in social networks are obliged to label content or messages created automatically by means of a computer program if the account used for this purpose has been made available for use by natural persons. The shared content or message has to be accompanied by a clear indication that it has been automatically created and sent using a computer program.

4.3 Responsibilities of Social Media Providers

While it is obvious that content providers are legally responsible that the content and modalities of their own communication published on social media services complies with all applicable legal requirements, the vast number of content providers, many of whom operate anonymously and from abroad, renders the practical enforcement of legal requirements, including possible restrictions on the use of AI, quite difficult and in many cases even impossible.[49] For this reason, the legal responsibility of social media providers for the content distributed in their networks, for the *output* of their services ('output-responsibility'), is of great practical importance, especially in view of the possibilities of platform providers to use AI in order to detect contents that do not comply with the applicable legal requirements (paras 37–45). As described above in Sect. 1, social media providers are actually very active when it comes to blocking or removing unwanted content on their services, and for this purpose they constantly improve their AI-based technologies. However, since users of social media do not only require protection from certain forms of communication but also from unjustified blocking of their own communication (and of information shared by other users which might be of interest for them), social media providers are also responsible, to a certain extent, that their AI-driven systems do not unduly block user communication, i.e. the *input* in their services ('input-responsibility'), (paras 46–54).

---

[46]Cf. Bundesverfassungsgericht 1 BvR 797/78 'Böll' (3 June 1980), BVerfGE 54, p. 219, and 1 BvR 1376/79 'NPD Europas' (22 June 1982), BVerfGE 61, p. 8.

[47]Cf. with a similar result Brings-Wiesen (2016); Milker (2017), p. 221.

[48]The draft is available in German on www.rlp.de/fileadmin/rlp-stk/pdf-Dateien/Medienpolitik/ Medienstaatsvertrag_Online_JulAug2018.pdf.

[49]Cf. Schröder (2018), p. 471.

Responsibility for Unwanted Content ('Output-Responsibility')

37   In practice, many social media providers already take on responsibility when it comes to keeping communication on their services 'clean'. Facebook's 'Community Standards', for example, contain detailed specifications for the content that may be distributed in the network. According to these standards, content that supports violence or criminal acts, the offering of prohibited objects (firearms, drugs, etc.), harassment, bullying, violations of privacy, the distribution of pornographic content, hate speech, depictions of violence and nudity, misrepresentations and false reports, as well as copyright infringing content are not permitted.[50] Certainly some of these conditions go even further than the applicable legal requirements, and one might ask whether it is not obsolete to demand *legal* responsibility from the operators in addition to their *voluntary* efforts to ensure the integrity of their services. However, holding providers liable for content disseminated in their networks gives users and third persons who are affected by unwanted content enforceable claims, and it urges the operators to issue strict community standards in the first place and to effectively implement content-related requirements, including for instance the labelling obligations described above in paras 33–35.[51] For this reason, provider liability remains an important issue.

38   With respect to user content, social media providers usually count as 'host providers' in the sense of Article 14 of the E-Commerce Directive, i.e. providers offering a service that consists of the storage of information provided by a recipient of the service. Within the European Union, some basic principles governing the responsibility of host providers for information stored on their platforms are contained in regulations at the European level, in particular in Articles 12 to 15 of the E-Commerce Directive. The details, however, are a matter of domestic law.

39   Under German law (or more specifically: under German media law, copyright law and competition law), a host provider can only be held responsible for third-party content if he or she has violated a 'duty to inspect' the information shared on his or her services.[52] Courts have developed certain criteria for determining whether or not a host provider should have noticed that a certain piece of information was wrongfully published and hence was obligated to block or delete that information. The various criteria include inter alia the practical cognitive resources of the provider,[53]

---

[50]The standards are available on www.facebook.com/communitystandards.

[51]Consequently, the draft Media State Treaty of August 2018 provides in Section 53d(4) that social media operators must take appropriate steps in order to ensure compliance of users with the labelling obligation under Section 55(3).

[52]Cf. with certain variations in the details Bundesgerichtshof I ZR 18/04 'Jugendgefährdende Medien bei eBay' (12 July 2007), BGHZ 173, p. 201 (competition law); Bundesgerichtshof I ZR 121/08 'Sommer unseres Lebens' (12 March 2010), BGHZ 185 p. 335 et seq. (copyright law); Bundesgerichtshof VI ZR 93/10 'Blog-Eintrag' (25 October 2011), BGHZ 191, p. 226 (media law). See also Hennemann, paras 43–47, who discusses the transfer of this liability concept (as a 'duty to maintain safety') to competition law.

[53]Cf. Bundesgerichtshof VI ZR 93/10 'Blog-Eintrag' (25 October 2011), BGHZ 191, p. 227.

his or her (passive or active) role on the individual social media platform,[54] the risks associated with his or her business model,[55] financial benefits for the provider from storing the wrongful information[56] and—last but not least—the existence, effectiveness and cost of monitoring measures, in particular the use of filtering software.[57]

This last group of criteria related to the implementation of monitoring measures is particularly interesting in the context of AI tools. It is true that German courts generally emphasize that host providers cannot be expected to comply with any *proactive* filtering obligations in the sense of general, future-oriented monitoring or investigation obligations.[58] This corresponds with Article 15(1) of the E-Commerce Directive ('No general obligation to monitor'), which stipulates that EU Member States shall not impose a general obligation on providers, when providing host services, to monitor the information which they store, nor a general obligation actively to seek facts or circumstances indicating illegal activity. *De lege lata*, this provision hinders national lawmakers from legally requiring host providers such as social media operators to proactively search for unwanted content using AI tools on their services.

However, it should be noted that the E-Commerce Directive dates from a time when the 'siege' of information society services by organized and/or commercial users with highly effective technological tools, including AI, was not yet foreseeable. Rather, the E-Commerce Directive focused on promoting service providers by exempting them from excessive liability.[59] Recent developments at European and national level show that this 'promotive' attitude is gradually changing and that the need for greater involvement of service providers in order to preserve the legality of social media content is increasingly coming to the fore.

In Germany, for example, the Network Enforcement Act (NEA) of 2017 considerably tightened the obligations of operators of social networks to block certain illegal content. While the NEA does not formally provide for general monitoring obligations, one can raise the question as to whether operators will be able to fulfil their strict duties of conduct without any proactive, AI-supported filtering of the content.

The European institutions are even more progressive when it comes to the implementation of AI technologies for filtering purposes. For example, in its

40

41

42

43

---

[54]Cf. Bundesgerichtshof I ZR 251/99 'Ambiente' (17 May 2001), BGHZ 148, p. 19 and I ZR 131/10 'Regierung-oberfranken.de' (27 October 2011), NJW 2012, p. 2280.

[55]Cf. Bundesgerichtshof I ZR 80/12 'File-Hosting-Dienst' (15 August 2013), NJW 2013, p. 3247.

[56]Cf. Bundesgerichtshof I ZR 304/01 'Rolex' (11 March 2004), BGHZ 158, p. 252 and I ZR 155/09 'Sedo' (18 November 2010), GRUR 2011, p. 620.

[57]Cf. Bundesgerichtshof I ZR 35/04 'Internet-Versteigerung II' (19 April 2007), BGHZ 172, p. 134 and I ZR 139/08 'Kinderhochstühle im Internet' (22 July 2010), GRUR 2011, p. 155.

[58]See for example Bundesgerichtshof I ZR 18/11 'Alone in the Dark' (12 July 2012), NJW 2013, p. 785.
Cf. Bundesgerichtshof I ZR 57/09 'Stiftparfüm' (17 August 2011), BGHZ 191, pp. 26–27 and I ZR 18/11 'Alone in the Dark' (12 July 2012), NJW 2013, p. 785.

[59]Cf. Micklitz and Schirmbacher (2015a), p. 2.

Communication on 'Tackling Illegal Online Content' of 2017,[60] the European Commission at least encouraged service providers to use AI tools to proactively detect illegal content. On the one hand, the Commission emphasized that such an approach would not lead to providers adopting the filtered content as their own (thereby losing their liability privileges as host providers). On the other hand, the Commission concluded its remarks on 'Detecting and Notifying Illegal Content' with an appeal:

> Online platforms should do their utmost to proactively detect, identify and remove illegal content online. The Commission strongly encourages online platforms to use voluntary, proactive measures aimed at the detection and removal of illegal content and to step up cooperation and investment in, and use of, automatic detection technologies.

44 Moreover, in the specific field of EU copyright law, the use of such automatic detection technologies, including AI tools, is likely to become mandatory. Certainly, in contrast to the Commission's original proposal, Article 17 of the EU Copyright Directive will not explicitly demand the 'use of effective content recognition technologies'. Nevertheless, in the current draft version of the Directive, Article 17 (4) provides, inter alia, that 'online content sharing service providers shall be liable for unauthorised acts of communication to the public (...) of copyright-protected works' unless the service providers demonstrate that they have 'made, in accordance with high industry standards of professional diligence, best efforts to ensure the unavailability of specific works' for which the rightholders have provided sufficient information.[61] As a result, this call for 'best efforts' will most likely result in a *de facto* obligation to introduce effective 'recognition technologies'.

45 After all, we must conclude that the availability of AI suggests that in the foreseeable future operators of social networks will have to proactively filter at least certain content out of their systems. All the signs are pointing to a protective content regulation through AI. However, it would be wrong to prematurely view this trend towards comprehensive AI-based filters as a 'total censorship' of content published in social media or to polemicise that user-generated content would thus be placed under 'general suspicion'.[62] In view of the above-mentioned 'armament' of organized users with AI for the dissemination of (also) unwanted content, the use of AI-controlled filter systems simply corresponds to the practical necessity of keeping social media usable and 'clean'. If the legal positions of users, who (allegedly) are wrongly prevented from publishing their content, are also sufficiently taken into account, the use of such filter systems does not raise as such serious legal concerns.

---

[60] Communication of 28 September 2017 on 'Tackling Illegal Content Online', COM(2017) 555 final.

[61] Directive (EU) 2019/790 of the European Parliament and of the Council of 17 April 2019 on copyright and related rights in the Digital Single Market and amending Directives 96/9/EC and 2001/29/EC. In the draft proposal, the provisions of Article 17 of the final directive were contained in Article 13.

[62] See e.g. the 'Article 13 open letter' on the proposal for the new copyright directive, available on www.liberties.eu/en/news/delete-article-thirteen-open-letter/13194. The letter was signed by 57 human rights and digital rights organizations.

Responsibility for Unwanted Blocking ('Input-Responsibility')

As described above, we can expect that social media operators will be increasingly involved in the protection of users and third parties as well as the general public against unwanted content, not only voluntarily, for their own economic interests but also because of legal obligations. AI will be a key technology for this. The central role played by platform operators in social media for the flow of communication will thus be further expanded. At the same time, this increases the probability that information will be blocked or removed by the operators before or after their publication for protective purposes. This brings to the fore the question of whether and to what extent affected users can defend themselves against AI-based filtering measures carried out by providers.

So far, only few authors in Germany discuss input-responsibility as a distinct legal issue.[63] Certainly, 'overblocking' is considered as a problem, but it is rather discussed in the context of whether or not provider liability should be intensified (with the consequence that providers are inclined to block or delete contents).[64] This is quite remarkable because logically, the question of whether providers are in principle responsible for publishing user contents (and for not unduly suppressing them) somewhat precedes the question of whether they 'overly' block these contents.

Under German law, provider liability can result from contractual claims[65]—the use of social media is based on platform or network contracts concluded between users and providers—as well as from non-contractual claims—users may (also) be entitled to claims for injunctive relief against the blocking or deletion of their content.[66] Certainly, social media providers usually include specific blocking and deletion clauses in their contracts for cases in which user generated content is allegedly not in compliance with their community standards and legal obligations. Many of these clauses contain substantial margins of appreciation for social media providers to determine in fact and in law whether or not a certain content is actually in line with the applicable standards.[67] Ultimately, however, these blocking and deletion clauses and the measures taken on their basis have to be in conformity with the fundamental rights and freedoms of the affected users, including their freedom of speech and expressions as well as their freedom of occupation (in the context of

---

[63]Three of the few authors are Guggenberger (2017), p. 2581; Holznagel (2018), passim; Peukert (2018), p. 575; see also Müller-Franken (2018), p. 12; Peifer (2018), p. 20 in the context of the German NEA.

[64]For references see note 24.

[65]Cf. Holznagel (2018), p. 370, who compares the constellation with ebay traders' claims against the platform for access to their accounts. For ebay cases see e.g. OLG Brandenburg 7 U 169/04 (18 May 2005) and KG Berlin 13 U 4/05 (5 August 2005).

[66]Cf. LG Berlin 31 O 21/18 (23 March 2018); LG Frankfurt 2-3 O 182/18 (14 May 2018); LG Offenburg 2 O 310/18 (26 September 2018). At least in the latter two cases, the claims were based on Section 1004 of the German Civil Code.

[67]Cf. Holznagel (2018), p. 372.

commercial activities). While fundamental rights norms were designed to (directly) apply within the relationship between the State and its citizens only, it is common ground (even) in German legal scholarship and under the settled case-law of the FCC that fundamental rights have also (indirect) effects on the relationships between two private persons. As a consequence, both the contractual rights of social media users[68] and their non-contractual claims[69] have to be interpreted in light of their fundamental rights and freedoms. These rights and freedoms speak prima facie for a legitimate interest in the unhindered publication of the contents.

49 Of course, in the legal relationship between the social media provider and the user, not only the interests of the user in the distribution of his communication are to be taken into account, but also the interests of affected third parties and the general public as well as the rights of the providers. This means that, similar to protective regulatory restrictions of communicative user rights (see above in Sect. 4.2) and to holding social media services providers accountable for user generated content (see above paras 37–45), decisions on the claims of users against providers that their content be published require a careful balancing of the rights and interests of the different stakeholders.

50 However, the legal assessment of whether users have (or should have) the right to publish their content vis-à-vis social media providers differs structurally from both the considerations of protective regulatory restrictions on the freedom of communication of users for the benefit of third parties or the general public and from the reflections on provider liability for user contents. The claim of the user is fundamentally different from the claim in the case of regulatory restrictions of his or her communication and in the case of provider liability. In the latter constellations, it is the *regulator* who *interferes* with the rights and freedoms of the persons concerned, either by restricting communication on social media services or by holding providers legally responsible for the conduct of others. In the case of input-responsibility, however, the user *demands* a positive action, and not from the State but from a *private undertaking*.

51 Both aspects, the user's *demanding* position and the *private* nature of the legal relationship between the user and the provider, have an impact on the balancing of the conflicting legal interests to be carried out when examining a user's civil law claim. In principle, the *private* operator of a social media platform has considerable autonomy in shaping the terms of use of his platform due to his own fundamental rights. On the one hand, this autonomy of platform providers concerns the *material* standards for user generated content. Providers do not necessarily have to stick to demanding only compliance with the law. They can also formulate more far-reaching requirements for the content shared by users (e.g. objectivity of

---

[68]Pursuant to Section 242 of the German Civil Code, an obligor has the duty to perform according to the requirements of good faith. This is commonly regarded as a 'gateway' for courts to consider the fundamental rights of the contract parties.

[69]Pursuant to Section 1004 of the German Civil Code, a claim for injunctive relief requires that the respondent 'interferes' with the rights of the claimant and that the claimant is not 'obliged to tolerate the interference'. When interpreting these terms, courts must respect the parties' fundamental rights.

contributions). On the other hand, *procedural* aspects can in principle also be determined unilaterally by social media providers. For example, the provider may determine the scope for evaluation when determining the facts relevant for a deletion or blocking or refer to certain procedures for the recognition of inadmissible content. This may apply in particular to the use of AI. A provider could explicitly refer, for example, to the use of intelligent recognition software which shall be 'entrusted' with checking each individual act of communication for unwanted content, and the provider could limit its own activities to taking measures to ensure the proper functioning of the recognition software (e.g. maintenance of a risk management system). This approach would be in the legitimate interest of the provider to rationalize its activities.

The social media providers' autonomy is strengthened by the fact that users are in a *demanding* position with regard to the providers' input-responsibility. After all, social media operators *provide* services. They *offer* users positive options for activities, i.e. communication with other users, their services do *not impair* the activities of users in the first place. While it is generally legitimate for users to demand that unwanted impairments be removed, users cannot simply demand a specific service from providers, for example the publication of a specific content in a specific form. **52**

Now, there are certainly *limits* to social media provider's autonomy in particular constellations for reasons of constitutional law.[70] When balancing the interests of users and providers, we should bear in mind that it is not just *any* service that social media operators provide to their users. As described above in see Sect. 2, social media nowadays have an outstanding significance for society as a whole. Numerous users define themselves through their self-representations and their 'social standing' in social media, which is above all shaped by the contents they communicate and publish. In this respect, social media have assumed a central function for the participation of people in social life. Taking account of the importance of sharing content on social media services for users, and considering that the operators of social media profit from their role to a significant extent economically,[71] the providers can be expected to thoroughly reflect the interests of the users when deciding on whether or not to block or delete their contents. As to the concrete obligations of social media providers to consider the interests of users,[72] it seems impermissible for **53**

---

[70]The following considerations are primarily based on the ideas developed by the FCC in Bundesverfassungsgericht 1 BvR 3080/09 'Stadionverbot' (11 April 2018), NJW 2018, p. 1669, on the constitutional obligations of football stadium operators following from fundamental rights. In its decision, the FCC stated that stadium operators open to a large public access to sporting events, and that this access 'decides to a considerable extent on the participation in social life of those affected. By setting up such an event, a private individual also acquires a special legal responsibility under the constitution'.

[71]For the relevance of this criterion see e.g. Bundesgerichtshof I ZR 304/01 'Rolex' (11 March 2004), BGHZ 158, p. 252 and I ZR 155/09 'Sedo' (18 November 2010), GRUR 2011, p. 620.

[72]The following concrete obligations were emphasized by the FCC in Bundesverfassungsgericht 1 BvR 3080/09 'Stadionverbot' (11 April 2018), NJW 2018, p. 1670. The same principles can be applied to access rights of social media users, see also Holznagel (2018), p. 372.

providers, for example, to *arbitrarily* block or delete content. Rather, they need a proper reason for this. Moreover, it will be necessary that affected users are given a sufficient *explanation* for the blocking or deletion of their content.[73] For the use of AI, this means that automated filtering of content is only permissible if reasons can be given for individual cases of blocking or deletion, i.e. a form of 'explainable AI' (XAI) is required.[74]

54   We have thus determined the scope of social media provider obligations with regard to the distribution of user generated content. However, with regard to the implementation of AI tools for filtering content, it still needs to be clarified which principles should apply to the liability of providers for violations of those obligations. At least in the German legal system, the principles developed by the FCC in its *Autocomplete* decision can (again) be used.[75] As in that decision, social media providers are considered to have *directly* breached their obligations with regard to the publication of user content, even though the breach was 'committed' by the AI they used for filtering content. Normally, therefore, providers would be directly liable for the breach. However, in its *Autocomplete* decision, the FCC relied on the principles of provider liability for *indirect* breaches and imposed only *reactive* obligations on providers. This relatively mild liability can be justified by the legitimate interest of operators in using AI to rationalize content management on their services. For the wrongful filtering out of user-generated content by AI-controlled systems, this means—in concrete terms—that in such a case the provider cannot in principle be directly held liable. The provider can only be indirectly held liable if it has subsequently failed to examine objections raised by users to the allegedly inadmissible blocking or deletion of his or her communication, and if it has failed, if necessary, to correct the error made by its AI.[76]

5 Facilitative Social Media Regulation

55   In contrast to protective social media regulation, which already exists to a large extent at the national and/or European level and has concrete effects on the use of AI technologies in social media, the implementation of substantial *facilitative* regulation in general and with regard to the use of AI in particular is not yet advanced. Nevertheless, regulatory options for action are being discussed and, at least in Germany, are already being introduced in small steps. The following Part will

---

[73] Eifert (2017), p. 1453, even argues that social media providers should be obliged to make the reasoning of their blocking practice publicly available.

[74] See e.g. Rademacher (2017), p. 377 (with further references in footnote 59).

[75] For the following considerations cf. Bundesgerichtshof VI ZR 269/12 'Autocomplete' (14 May 2013), BGHZ 197, pp. 222–224.

[76] For a similar liability standard in case of competition law infringements caused by AI see Hennemann, paras 43–47.

therefore briefly explain the possible purposes of facilitative regulation, insofar as this can also become relevant for the use of AI in social media (see Sect. 5.1), and use examples of possible facilitative AI regulation in social media to analyze the particularities that can arise when assessing the conformity of facilitative regulation of social media AI with constitutional law (see Sect. 5.2).

5.1 Purposes and Instruments of Facilitative Regulation of Social Media AI

As mentioned above, traditional facilitative media regulation which aims at ensuring diversity of opinion only concerns *broadcasting*. Broadcasting is defined in Section 2(1) of the German State Treaty on Broadcasting and Telemedia as any *linear* distribution of offers in (moving) picture and/or sound along a transmission schedule, intended for the general public and for simultaneous reception.[77] Since most[78] information society services, including social media and services offered in social media, do not qualify as linear within the meaning of this definition, most facilitative elements of media regulation do not apply to them. There has been a constant debate for many years as to whether and how information society services in general and social media services in particular require facilitative media regulation in order to ensure diversity of opinion on these services as well. Of course, this discussion cannot be reproduced here. The main topics of the debate include dropping the distinction between (linear) broadcasting and (non-linear) telemedia, the readjustment of media concentration control in relation to the overall market, the expansion of platform regulation to virtual platforms, an increase of the activities of public service broadcasting in the field of telemedia as well as the introduction of a specific regulation to ensure *accessibility of information*, *transparency* and *non-discrimination*, especially for information intermediaries.[79] It is first and foremost the latter aspect that concerns social media, in particular the use of intelligent systems to organize and arrange distributed content.

56

The implementation of intelligent filtering systems on social media services is said to have various bias effects on social media users. It has become one of the great narratives of the digital media world that the individual user, thanks to algorithmic

57

---

[77]See also Article 1(1)(e) of Directive 2010/13/EU of the European Parliament and of the Council of 10 March 2010 on the coordination of certain provisions laid down by law, regulation or administrative action in Member States concerning the provision of audiovisual media services (Audiovisual Media Services Directive).

[78]In 2017, German authorities found that certain livestreaming services on YouTube and Twitch qualified as 'broadcasting' and asked the operators to apply for a broadcasting license. The decisions were assessed extremely critically in public media and in jurisprudence, see for example Bodensiek and Walker (2018), passim.

[79]Cf. for example Paal and Hennemann (2017), pp. 645–646 and pp. 651–652; Cornils (2018), p. 377.

and AI-controlled personalization and filtering of the content displayed to him or her, is trapped in a bubble reflecting his or her own preferences, and that other contents are hidden from him or her ('filter bubble effect').[80] Another great narrative is that, as a consequence of intelligent personalization, people are less and less confronted with opinions and values that deviate from their own ideas, as a result of which they are more and more encouraged by the echo of their own attitudes and inclined to political radicalism ('echo chamber effect').[81]

58   Various proposals have been made to address these and other risks of intelligent filtering of information and content in social media. The draft Media State Treaty of 2018, for example, contains provisions on *transparency* (Section 53d) as well as on *non-discrimination* (Section 53e) in social networks. Pursuant to Section 53d(1) (2) of the draft treaty, providers of larger social networks are obliged to disclose the main criteria of aggregation, selection and presentation of content and their weighting, including information on the functioning of the algorithms used for this purpose. In order to 'safeguard the diversity of opinions', Section 53e(1) of the draft treaty requires that social network providers must not hinder or treat differently, without objective justification, journalistically edited content if they have a particularly high influence on the perceptibility of the content. Another category of proposals discussed by authors and commentators concerns *positive obligations* of information intermediaries to ensure diversity of opinions through their AI-controlled filter systems, including e.g. a definition of the criteria by which the content is aggregated, selected and presented,[82] demanding 'opposing viewpoint buttons' which allow people 'to click on them and receive uncongenial perspectives' as well as 'serendipity buttons' which expose people 'to unanticipated, unchosen material on their News Feed',[83] or even constituting must-carry obligations in favor of certain 'general interest media'.[84]

5.2 Constitutional Framework of Facilitative Regulation of Social Media AI

59   However, these measures for the facilitative regulation of social media AI appear to be problematic from a legal point of view. There is no question that the proposed measures interfere with the rights of social media providers and thus require a solid legal basis. Certainly, the purpose of ensuring 'diversity of opinions' is as such a

---

[80]Pariser (2011), passim.

[81]Sunstein (2017), p. 9 and passim. Cf. also Lischka (2018), p. 391, for a distinction between these two effects.

[82]See for example Danckert and Mayer (2010), p. 221, who propose the definition of objective search engine criteria.

[83]Sunstein (2017), pp. 215, 231 and 232.

[84]Cf. Cornils (2018), p. 381, who merely reproduces this proposal but rejects it immediately.

legitimate ground for regulatory action. Nevertheless, the justification of the interference with the providers' rights is a very delicate task because the proposals are based on a rather *uncertain empirical foundation*. In particular, recent studies conducted by communication scientists show quite clearly that both the filter bubble effect and the echo chamber effect can hardly be empirically confirmed, or at least only to a very limited extent.[85]

The constitutional assessment of the individual measures for the facilitative regulation of social media can certainly not be carried out here in detail. A few fundamental remarks must suffice. It is particularly important to consider the difference between measures of facilitative and protective regulation of social media AI. In the mode of *protective* media regulation, the regulator protects a specifically endangered legal asset and interferes with the media-related rights of individuals. This is the classical constellation in which the fundamental rights of the persons affected by this interference set limits to the state intervention. In this constellation, the requirements for the justification of the intervention are relatively strict.

In the mode of *facilitative* media regulation, however, the legislator aims at something else. The aim is to create, shape and maintain the concrete conditions for citizens as users of social media to make use of their freedom of communication.[86] Regulation thus does not serve to protect freedom of communication from threats, but rather its *configuration*. Configurative regulation within the scope of application of fundamental rights, including the freedoms of communication, is a well-recognized *topos* in German jurisprudence and also in the case-law of the FCC,[87] in particular with respect to 'facilitative' regulation enabling citizens to make use of their fundamental rights. The legal consequence of the classification of a certain regulation as configurative is primarily an extended margin of appreciation of the legislator with regard to the assessment of actual circumstances and future developments. This is based on the following consideration: Legislation should not be subject to excessive constitutional boundaries when deciding on systemic issues, even if the configuration may impair individual rights as an unintended secondary effect.

Bearing this in mind, the fact that the assumed negative impacts of intelligent filtering systems used by social media providers on users are difficult to prove empirically at the moment does not per se preclude the legislator to enact facilitative media regulations in order to prevent these negative impacts. Against this background, *moderate interferences* with the rights of social media providers (caused e.g. by transparency or non-discrimination obligations as provided by the draft

---

[85] Cf. Lobigs and Neuberger (2018), p. 75 (with references to further studies in footnote 215); the uncertain empirical foundations of the filter bubble and echo chamber 'theories' are being increasingly acknowledged by legal scholars as well, cf. for example Hoffmann-Riem (2016), p. 629 ('The impact of the filtering on the contents displayed on Facebook is disputed.'); Drexl (2017), pp. 531–532; for these and for further references see also Cornils (2018), p. 381.

[86] Similarly, see Hoffmann-Riem, paras 23–25, argues that the state has an 'enabling responsibility' to create a framework for safeguarding the exercise of fundamental rights.

[87] Cf. Cornils (2005), passim; Krönke (2015), pp. 790–794.

Media State Treaty) can still be justified, despite the uncertain empirical foundation of the facilitative measures. Particularly *intense interferences* (such as obligations to disclose the algorithms used for the filtering systems[88] or 'positive obligations' of social media providers as described above in see Sect. 5.1), however, would require a more profound empirical basis and are hence not permissible—at least not at the moment. The fact that configurative (facilitative) regulation exempts from strict constitutional restraints does not mean that there are no such constitutional restraints at all.

6 Conclusion

63 At the beginning of our reflections, the findings on AI and social media were rather worrying. While organized users are going to war with the providers of social media, using more or less sophisticated AI weapons in order to disseminate illegal content and misinformation, the providers themselves also use intelligent systems to select, arrange and display content according to economic factors rather than for the purpose of ensuring diversity of opinion.

64 The analysis of the constitutional framework has shown, however, that communication on the basis of AI technologies is itself legally protected and must therefore not be prevented without a sufficient legal basis. Instead, legitimate reasons are necessary for a protective regulation of social media AI. To this end, less emphasis should be placed on the protection of the conditions for a (hardly definable, abstract) healthy democratic public sphere than on the (concrete) rights of individual users to form their own opinions and wills freely. Furthermore, a general exclusion of AI-based communication may rarely be considered; in contrast, labelling obligations, as provided for in the draft Media State Treaty of the German federal states, are certainly permitted.

65 We have also seen that it is above all the private providers of social media services who should be involved in protecting the integrity of social media from unwanted content. With further progress in the development of AI technologies, it will become more likely that the providers will also be obliged *de lege ferenda* to live up to their responsibility by using such technologies. The prerequisite for this, however, is that sufficient account is taken of the protection of the users affected by automated filtering measures.

66 Finally, regulators are in principle also entitled to introduce facilitative regulations in order to safeguard diversity of opinion in the long term. To this end, they can take particular account of the widespread fears that the economically driven use of AI for the targeted selection, arrangement and display of content by providers might lead to serious bias effects on social media users, at least in the long run. The draft

---

[88]For a thorough analysis of the legal standard for justifying obligations to disclose algorithms (which amount to business secrets) see Wischmeyer.

Media State Treaty will therefore legitimately address providers or social networks with transparency obligations and prohibitions of discrimination. The fact that the empirical foundations of the bias effects of AI-based content selection on users are still relatively uncertain does not stand in the way of such moderate facilitative regulation. The regulator has a relatively broad margin of appreciation in 'configurating' the freedom of communication through facilitative regulation.

All in all, it has become clear that the dangers and risks of the use of AI in social media can definitely be dealt with by means of regulation. Within the applicable constitutional framework, there is no need to be afraid of any 'arms races' or 'filter biases'.

67

References

Article 29 Data Protection Working Party (2010) Opinion 2/2010 on online behavioural advertising. ec.europa.eu/justice/article-29/documentation/opinion-recommendation/files/2010/wp171_en.pdf
Bodensiek K, Walker M (2018) Livestreams von Gaming Video Content als Rundfunk? Notwendigkeit einer verfassungskonformen Auslegung der Rundfunkzulassungspflicht. MMR 18:136–141
Bosman W (1990) Rundfunkrechtliche Aspekte der Trennung von Werbung und Programm. Zeitschrift für Urheber-und Medienrecht 90:545–556
Brings-Wiesen T (2016) Meinungskampf mit allen Mitteln und ohne Regeln? Blog post. www.juwiss.de/93-2016/
Calo R (2014) Digital market manipulation. George Washington Law Rev 14:995–1051
Cornils M (2005) Die Ausgestaltung der Grundrechte. Mohr Siebeck, Tübingen
Cornils M (2018) Vielfaltssicherung bei Telemedien. AfP 18:377–387
Danckert B, Mayer FJ (2010) Die vorherrschende Meinungsmacht von Google. Bedrohung durch einen Informationsmonopolisten? MMR 10:219–222
Deeran S (2013) What is social media content curation. Blog post. www.huffingtonpost.com/stefan-deeran/what-is-social-media-cont_b_3383706.html
Drexl J (2016) Economic efficiency versus democracy: on the potential role of competition policy in regulating digital markets in times of post-truth politics. Max Planck Institute for Innovation and Competition Research Paper No. 16-16, Munich 2016
Drexl J (2017) Bedrohung der Meinungsvielfalt durch Algorithmen. Wie weit reichen die Mittel der Medienregulierung? Zeitschrift für Urheber-und Medienrecht 17:529–543
Ebers M (2018) Beeinflussung und Manipulation von Kunden durch Behavioral Microtargeting. Verhaltenssteuerung durch Algorithmen aus der Sicht des Zivilrechts. MMR 18:423–428
Eifert M (2017) Rechenschaftspflichten für Soziale Netzwerke und Suchmaschinen. Zur Veränderung des Umgangs von Recht und Politik mit dem Internet. Neue Juristische Wochenschrift 17:1450–1454
Eifert M, Hoffmann-Riem W (2011) Telekommunikations- und Medienrecht als Technikrecht. In: Schulte M, Schröder R (eds) Handbuch des Technikrechts, 2nd edn. Springer, Berlin, pp 667–719
Feldmann T (2017) Zum Referentenentwurf eines NetzDG: Eine kritische Betrachtung. K&R 17:292–297
Floridi L (2015) Die 4. Revolution. Wie die Infosphäre unser Leben verändert. Suhrkamp, Berlin
Guggenberger N (2017) Das Netzwerkdurchsetzungsgesetz in der Anwendung. Neue Juristische Wochenschrift 17:2577–2582

Habermas J (1962) Strukturwandel der Öffentlichkeit: Untersuchungen zu einer Kategorie der bürgerlichen Gesellschaft. Luchterhand, Neuwied

Heidel T (1988) Verfassungsfragen der Finanzierung von Privatfunk durch Werbung. Nomos, Baden-Baden

Hildebrandt M (2015) Smart technologies and the End(s) of law. Elgar, Cheltenham

Hoffmann-Riem W (2016) Innovation und Recht – Recht und Innovation. Recht im Ensemble seiner Kontexte. Mohr Siebeck, Tübingen

Hoffmann-Riem W (2017) Verhaltenssteuerung durch Algorithmen – Eine Herausforderung für das Recht. Archiv des öffentlichen Rechts 17:1–42

Holznagel D (2018) Overblocking durch User Generated Content (UGC)-Plattformen: Ansprüche der Nutzer auf Wiederherstellung oder Schadensersatz? Computer und Recht 18:369–378

Ingold A (2017) Digitalisierung demokratischer Öffentlichkeiten. Der Staat 17:491–533

Kersten J (2017) Schwarmdemokratie. Mohr Siebeck, Tübingen

Kohl U (2010) Jurisdiction and the internet. Cambridge University Press, Cambridge

Krönke C (2015) Ausgestaltung der Koalitionsfreiheit durch das Tarifeinheitsgesetz. DÖV 15:788–794

Lang A (2018) Netzwerkdurchsetzungsgesetz und Meinungsfreiheit. Zur Regulierung privater Internet-Intermediäre bei der Bekämpfung von Hassrede. Archiv des oeffentlichen Rechts 18:220–250

Lischka K (2018) Wie Algorithmen Öffentlichkeit strukturieren. Grundlagen, Folgen, Lösungsansätze. AfP 18:388–391

Lobigs F, Neuberger C (2018) Meinungsmacht im Internet und die Digitalstrategien von Medienunternehmen. Neue Machtverhältnisse trotz expandierender Internet-Geschäfte der traditionellen Massenmedien-Konzerne. VISTAS, Leipzig

Micklitz H-W, Schirmbacher M (2015a) Commentary on Section 4 of the German Telemedia Act. In: Spindler G, Schuster F (eds) Recht der Elektronischen Medien, Kommentar, 3rd edn. C.H. Beck, Munich

Micklitz H-W, Schirmbacher M (2015b) Commentary on Section 6 of the German Telemedia Act. In: Spindler G, Schuster F (eds) Recht der Elektronischen Medien, Kommentar, 3rd edn. C.H. Beck, Munich

Milker J (2017) Social-Bots' im Meinungskampf. Zeitschrift für Urheber-und Medienrecht 17:216–222

Müller-Franken S (2018) Netzwerkdurchsetzungsgesetz: Selbstbehauptung des Rechts oder erster Schritt in die selbstregulierte Vorzensur? – Verfassungsrechtliche Fragen. AfP 18:1–14

Nolte G (2017) Hate-Speech, Fake-News, das 'Netzwerkdurchsetzungsgesetz' und Vielfaltsicherung durch Suchmaschinen. Zeitschrift für Urheber-und Medienrecht 17:552–565

O'Neil C (2016) Weapons of math destruction: how big data increases inequality and threatens democracy. Crown, New York

Paal BP, Hennemann M (2017) Meinungsbildung im digitalen Zeitalter. Regulierungsinstrumente für einen gefährdungsadäquaten Rechtsrahmen. JuristenZeitung 17:641–652

Pariser E (2011) Filter Bubble. What the Internet is Hiding from You. Penguin, London

Peifer K-N (2018) Netzwerkdurchsetzungsgesetz: Selbstbehauptung des Rechts oder erster Schritt in die selbstregulierte Vorzensur? – Zivilrechtliche Aspekte. AfP 18:14–23

Peukert A (2018) Gewährleistung der Meinungs- und Informationsfreiheit in sozialen Netzwerken. Vorschlag für eine Ergänzung des NetzDG um sog. Put-back-Verfahren. MMR 18:572–578

Rademacher T (2017) Predictive Policing im deutschen Polizeirecht, in: Archiv des öffentlichen Rechts. Archiv des öffentlichen Rechts 17:366–416

Scherer MU (2016) Regulating Artificial Intelligence Systems: Risks, Challenges, Competences, and Strategies. Harv J Law Technol 16:353–400

Schmidt J-H (2013) Social media. Springer, Berlin

Schröder M (2018) Rahmenbedingungen der staatlichen Regulierung von Social Bots. Deutsches Verwaltungsblatt 18:465–472

Smid J (2015) Commentary on § 58 of the State Treaty on broadcasting and telemedia. In: Spindler G, Schuster F (eds) Recht der Elektronischen Medien, Kommentar, 3rd edn. C.H. Beck, Munich

Steinbach A (2017) Social Bots im Wahlkampf. ZRP 17:101–105

Sunstein C (2017) #republic. Divided democracy in the age of social media. Princeton University Press, Princeton

Vesting T (2015) Die Medien des Rechts: Computernetzwerke. Velbrück Wissenschaft, Weilerswist

Artificial Intelligence and Legal Tech: Challenges to the Rule of Law

Gabriele Buchholtz

Contents

1 Introduction 176
2 Fields of Application 177
   2.1 Definitions 177
   2.2 Legal Tech in Private Use: Status Quo and Trends 179
   2.3 Legal Tech in Public Use: Status Quo and Trends 180
3 Conceptual Differences Between 'Law' and 'Code' 182
   3.1 Application of the Law As a Social Act 182
   3.2 Code As a Technical Act 183
   3.3 Misconceptions of 'Code' 184
   3.4 Need for Regulation 185
4 Constitutional Framework 185
   4.1 Rule of Law and Democracy 185
   4.2 Right to Privacy 187
   4.3 Right to Non-discrimination 189
5 Proposals for 'Regulation by Design': A Balancing Act 190
   5.1 Regulatory Realignment 190
   5.2 Legal Protection by Design As a Starting Point 191
   5.3 Regulatory Guidelines 192
   5.4 The 'Human Factor' 194
   5.5 Balancing Act 194
6 Conclusion 195
References 196

Abstract Artificial intelligence is shaping our social lives. It is also affecting the process of law-making and the application of law—coined by the term 'legal tech'. Accordingly, law-as-we-know-it is about to change beyond recognition. Basic tenets of the law, such as accountability, fairness, non-discrimination, autonomy, due process and—above all—the rule of law are at risk. However, so far, little has been said about regulating legal tech, for which there is obviously considerable demand. In this article, it is suggested that we reinvent the rule of law and graft it

G. Buchholtz (✉)
Bucerius Law School, Hamburg, Germany
e-mail: gabriele.buchholtz@law-school.de

onto technology by developing the right standards, setting the right defaults and translating fundamental legal principles into hardware and software. In short, 'legal protection by design' is needed and its implementation must be required by law—attributing liability where necessary. This would reconcile legal tech with the rule of law.

> The computer programmer is a creator of universes for which he alone is the lawgiver. No playwright, no stage director, no emperor, however powerful, has ever exercised such absolute authority to arrange a stage or field of battle and to command such unswervingly dutiful actors or troops.[1]

1 Introduction

AI is shaping our social lives. And it is also deeply affecting the process of law-making and the application of law—coined by the term 'legal technology', or 'legal tech'. Accordingly, law-as-we-know-it is about to change beyond recognition. Basic tenets of the law, such as accountability, fairness, non-discrimination, autonomy, due process and—above all—the rule of law are at risk. These concerns are closely intertwined with a 'language barrier': traditionally, 'law needs language as a fish needs water'.[2] But algorithms follow a different logic than human language. Despite—or perhaps because of—these challenges, little has been said about regulating legal tech so far, for which there is obviously considerable demand. The question is not whether legal tech should be regulated, but whether the existing legal framework needs to be adjusted or refined. Lawmakers today bear an enormous responsibility; they shape the initial regulatory conditions. These decisions are crucial, because they will create path dependencies.[3] According to Lawrence Lessing we must 'build, architect, or code cyberspace to protect values that we believe are fundamental.'[4] It is time to move on from words to deeds.

In this article, it is suggested that we reinvent the rule of law and graft it onto technological infrastructures by 'developing the right standards', 'setting the right defaults' and translating fundamental legal principles into hardware and software. In short, 'legal protection by design' is in demand aiming to safeguard our human ability to challenge automated decision systems, 'by providing time and space to test and contest the workings of such systems'.[5] And its implementation must be required by law—attributing liability where necessary. Ultimately, this will reconcile legal tech with the rule of law. The initial hypothesis claims that the law remains

---
[1]Weizenbaum (1976), p. 115.
[2]Isensee (1990), p. 52.
[3]Eidenmüller (2017); Hartzog (2018), p. 76.
[4]Lessing (2006), p. 3.
[5]Hildebrandt (2018), p. 35.

relevant as long as algorithms do not ensure effective minority protection and the common good. However, the law must reinvent itself under the increasing influence of digitalisation: It must become familiar with the logic of a digital world. Legal solutions can be found only in cooperation with different academic disciplines, in particular, technology and sociology. Only then will the law keep up with the digital world.

This article is structured as follows: In part two, an overview of legal tech in public and private use will be provided. In part three conceptual differences between 'law' and 'code' will be explained in order to illustrate why regulation is needed. In the fourth part of this article, the constitutional framework will be sketched and in the fifth part, proposals for legal tech regulation will be made. The objectives of this article are threefold: firstly, it provides an overview of legal tech in public and private use, secondly, it examines the legal challenges raised by recent technological developments and thirdly, develops guidelines for future legal tech regulation, with a focus on the European and Anglo-American legal sphere. The proposals are based on the idea of 'legal protection by design'—aiming to bring legal tech in line with the rule of law.

2 Fields of Application

In a broad sense, legal tech covers all information technology used in the legal field—and it is inextricably tied to data. Legal tech is an umbrella term for any algorithm-based technology in legal matters—private and public use included.[6] In order to create a basic understanding of the main operating principles of legal tech, some further definitions and categorisations will be provided.

2.1 Definitions

An 'algorithm' is a process or set of rules defining a sequence of operations to be followed in order to solve a certain problem. Starting from an 'input', 'the instructions describe a computation that, when executed, proceeds through a finite number of well-defined successive states, eventually producing an "output"'.[7] In other words, an algorithm is a step-by-step procedure to perform a specific task or function.[8] 'Code' is the concrete implementation of the respective algorithm.[9]

---

[6]Grupp (2014), p. 660.
[7]https://en.wikipedia.org/wiki/Algorithm.
[8]Sharma et al. (2018), p. 479.
[9]Schmidt (2016), § 1, para 2.

5   Based on these definitions, the scope of potential legal tech applications is enormous. In particular with the rise of 'big data' and 'AI' disruptive changes have come about in the legal landscape. 'Big data' on the one hand, is defined as '[...] high-volume, high-velocity and high-variety information assets that demand cost-effective, innovative forms of information processing for enhanced insight and decision making.'[10] It has rightly been noted that we are living in a time of data-driven enthusiasm given, for example, the investments that are made by governments, universities, and private entities to collect and store data and to extract new knowledge from these ever growing databases.[11] 'AI' on the other hand '[...] refers to the analysis of data to model some aspect of the world. Inferences from these models are then used to predict and anticipate possible future events.'[12] AI enables machines to learn from experience, thereby steadily progressing to imitate human cognitive abilities. It is ultimately about '[...] giving computers behaviours which would be thought intelligent in human beings.'[13] One of the fastest growing AI-approaches is 'machine learning'. This set of techniques and tools allows computers to 'think' and solve problems 'independently and efficiently'.[14] By definition, 'machine learning is a subset of AI—a powerful application of AI technology' where machines are exposed to large datasets and provided with mechanisms to learn independently and become incrementally 'smarter'.[15]

6   To find an analytical access to legal tech it is essential to break the concept down into different categories. For regulatory purposes, a first distinction is drawn between private and public use of legal tech. There is a difference, for example, between the way legal tech is applied by a private law firm and the way it is applied by the police. Whereas private entities are driven by economic motives, state authorities must serve the public interest. For regulatory purposes this differentiation is highly relevant. A second differentiation concerns the application of legal tech as an 'investigative prediction tool' used in a decision-making process to generate new knowledge, or as a 'decision substitute' (requiring no further human intervention). These two differentiations are important when it comes to regulating legal tech. Which different standards and rationales apply, will be elaborated on in the fifth part of this article. In the following an overview of private and public use of legal tech is provided which (given the rapidity of technological developments) can, of course, only be a 'snapshot'.

---

[10]Gartner IT Glossary (2018).
[11]Medina (2015), p. 1005.
[12]Government Office for Science (UK) (2016), p. 5.
[13]Society for the Study of Artificial Intelligence and Simulation of Behaviour (2011).
[14]Frese (2015), p. 2090; Hoffmann-Riem (2017), p. 3; Mainzer (2016), p. 3; Stiemerling (2015), p. 765.
[15]Pfeifer (2018).

2.2 Legal Tech in Private Use: Status Quo and Trends

So far as the private use of legal tech is concerned, there are numerous potential benefits for lawyers as well as consumers. The technical possibilities have long since gone beyond electronic data management by electronic databases such as lexisnexis and Westlaw (for the common law jurisdictions) and Beck online or juris (for Germany). With the help of so-called knowledge-based expert systems users can check any individual document (contracts, administrative acts or other matters) partially or fully automatically.[16] Apart from that, 'smart contracts' have become almost commonplace—first proposed by Nick Szabo, who coined the term in 1994.[17] Smart contracts are computerised transaction protocols intended to digitally execute the terms of a contract. They allow the performance of credible transactions without third parties. Likewise, newer applications are on the market that can handle (minor) legal cases independently, such as disputes over flight compensation or traffic accidents.[18] And for some time now, there has been legal tech software on the market that uses machine learning—especially in the field of contract analysis.[19] Moreover, legal tech is used in online dispute resolution (ODR).[20] In January 2016 the online dispute resolution regulation[21] came into effect allowing the application of ODR in cases initiated by consumers resident in the EU against businesses in the EU.

While the technical developments in Germany and Europe are traditionally cumbersome, in the US 'AI-driven' robot lawyers have already entered the stage. In 2016, for example, the world's first artificially intelligent lawyer was hired by the US law firm BakerHostetler. They have agreed to license 'Ross-Intelligence', which was developed by IBM based on its Watson engine, for use in its bankruptcy, restructuring and creditors' rights team.[22] These robot lawyers are deployed principally in the areas of document searches and classification discovery. Another AI-trend driving the legal industry is 'predictive analytics' or 'big data analytics'. This method involves the analysis of large datasets through statistical or mathematical applications in order to identify meaningful relationships in the data.[23] Beneficiaries could be lawyers, insurers or consumers. However, in the European legal landscape there is (still) a lack of reliable data on the outcome of legal disputes: what is needed is an established case law database containing not only the upper court's decisions, but also the decisions of the district and regional courts.

---

[16]Frese (2015), p. 2090; Stiemerling (2015), p. 765.
[17]Szabo (1994).
[18]Frese (2015), p. 2092.
[19]Legal Technology Journal, Smart Contracts (2017).
[20]Grupp (2014), p. 660; Shackelford and Raymond (2014), p. 615.
[21]Regulation (EU) No 524/2013 of the European Parliament and the Council of 21 May 2013.
[22]Chowdhry (2016).
[23]Aletras et al. (2016).

2.3 Legal Tech in Public Use: Status Quo and Trends

9   So far as the public use of legal tech is concerned, law enforcement has assumed a pioneering role—not only in the US, but also on this side of the Atlantic.[24] In several European countries the police have implemented new 'big data' technology that is intended to help them predict future crimes before they materialise—an initiative called 'predictive policing'. In England, predictive policing was recently backed by the High Court[25] and the German police have also introduced this new technology. Many German federal states are testing software called Precobs (Pre Crime Observation System) or SKALA (System zur Kriminalitätsanalyse und Lageantizipation) that will use certain characteristics of a burglary (crime scene, victims, etc.) to estimate a person's likelihood of returning to a crime. The 'crime forecasting'-system displays risk levels for different areas and applies them to heat maps. Policemen can then be on the ground before the next crime occurs.[26] Proponents of the technical tools argue that these kinds of analyses are more accurate and less biased than the results humans can provide, and ultimately make it easier to focus on pre-emptive policing and prevention.[27]

10   Of course, the application of legal tech in public administration is not limited to predictive policing. It extends to many fields: namely, AI-applications are used in the administrative management of road traffic. In particular, intelligent traffic control systems on highways gather various data via sensors and regulate the traffic accordingly, for example by indicating overtaking bans or speed limits. Based on the collected data, automated administrative acts are issued. Likewise, AI is used in tax proceedings. In Germany, for example, AI-driven risk identification has already become, as it seems, part of regular tax management systems, which decide who must submit their supporting documents for tax audits (see Braun Binder, paras 16–18).

11   Even in the judiciary, legal tech is now being used. Automated debt collection procedure is a first simple example in Germany. Unsurprisingly, the US is much further ahead in this respect, using software that will become the basis for decision-making in a later court proceeding. COMPAS (Correctional Offender Management Profiling for Alternative Sanctions), for example, has been implemented in several US states and was also introduced in 2012 by the Department of Corrections (DOC) in Wisconsin. The system aims to reliably predict the risk of criminal re-offending. For each offender COMPAS calculates an individual 'risk score' which will have an impact on the subsequent sentence. The underlying logic is simple: if the software scores a high risk for a defendant on a scale of 1 to 10, the judge does not allow probation, but imposes a prison sentence.[28] While this software has been highly

---

[24] For an overview on AI and Law Enforcement see also Rademacher, paras 3–12.
[25] Brown v BCA Trading Ltd [2016] EWHC 1464 (Ch) (17 May 2016).
[26] Rademacher (2017), p. 366.
[27] Angwin et al. (2016) and Dressel and Farid (2018).
[28] Pasquale (2017).

criticised by some, who reject the idea of an algorithm helping to send a person to prison,[29] others praise COMPAS as a reliable machine learning tool.[30] Further studies have been initiated by the proponents to provide convincing proof of the benefits: based on datasets of about 150,000 US felony cases, a policy simulation shows that a release rule according to machine learning predictions would reduce the jail population by 42% with no increase in crime rates, or reduce crime rates by 25% without changing the jail population.[31] What should we think of these promises? Can we trust AI to decide impartially—without having an insight into the inner workings of a system like COMPAS? How might judges and juries use evidence produced by AI? And to what extent should courts rely on AI as a tool to regulate behaviour when it comes to crucial decisions such as criminal sentencing? What is at stake when AI applications fail? Critical answers will be given below.

These examples show that the legal landscape will dramatically change as AI steadily progresses to imitate human cognitive abilities.[32] Legal tech is no longer just about digitising the work environment and providing individual efficiency-enhancing tools, it is about enabling machines to take on core legal activities in the private and public sphere.[33] The question therefore arises if the 'cybercourt' and the 'robot lawyer' are not just science fiction any more, but a realistic picture of what the future might bring. The answer is no, probably not. Stakeholders from different areas—ranging from government authorities, academics[34] to corporations—have rejected the idea that AI has attained 'superhuman, wholly autonomous capabilities' so far.[35] However, the technological development continues and legal tech will be an ever-greater challenge for the law in the years to come.[36] Today, the legal tech industry has grown to about 700 companies worldwide, of which around 100 are active in the German market.[37] They develop IT applications which aim to master more and more complex tasks.[38] These promising applications fall on fertile ground. Not only does legal tech provide answers to the increasing efficiency and cost pressures in the legal industry, it can also help to improve access to justice—at least potentially. However, it is quite a different matter as to whether legal tech will be able to tackle complicated regulatory problems that require careful consideration. On this point, skepticism is warranted.[39] The problems which may occur will be examined below.

---

[29] Pasquale (2017).
[30] Kleinberg et al. (2017), p. 2.
[31] Kleinberg et al. (2017).
[32] Susskind (2013).
[33] Wagner (2018), pp. 2–3.
[34] Bostrom (2014); Goertzel (2015), p. 55; La Diega (2018), paras 10 et seq.
[35] Stevens (2017).
[36] Wischmeyer (2018), p. 3.
[37] Tobschall and Kempe (2017), p. 10.
[38] Wagner (2018), p. 3.
[39] Eidenmüller (2017).

3 Conceptual Differences Between 'Law' and 'Code'

13 It has been mentioned that differences in 'law' and 'code' call for different regulatory concepts. In this section, operating principles of 'law' and 'code' will be juxtaposed, in order to detect problems and regulatory needs. Technical and dogmatic aspects must be considered equally. Attention will also be drawn to the sociological question as to what it really means to set and apply law.[40]

3.1 Application of the Law As a Social Act

14 First of all, attention shall be drawn to the seemingly trivial fact that (written) legal norms are 'human work' and 'social acts'—and so is the application and interpretation of law in every individual case.[41] Applying a legal norm is a demanding process: First, a concretisation step is required, because legal norms are usually drafted in general terms.[42] This process is usually more challenging the more abstract a provision is. Consider, for example, the principle of 'good faith' codified in § 242 in the German Civil Code. After concretisation the norm can be applied to a particular case.[43]

15 It is fundamental to realise that law can only exist 'in language and through language'[44] which brings with it an openness to interpretation.[45] However, the act of statutory interpretation is not a 'straightforward mechanical operation of textual analysis'.[46] It is far more complex and requires complementary knowledge, especially where there is room for discretion.[47] Take, for example, the field of legal risk prevention, which relies on technical expertise, or the legal sphere of immigration and asylum law, which cannot do without social-scientific knowledge. In particular in administrative law, the real-life implications of a legal provision must be given serious consideration: if the law shall serve as an instrument of behavioural control, the lawyer must pay attention not only to the immediate effects, but also to the long-term social consequences.[48] In other words, legal practitioners and

---

[40] See Buchholtz (2017), p. 956.
[41] Hoffmann-Riem (2017), p. 26; Hoffmann-Riem (2016a), p. 37.
[42] Riehm (2006), p. 21.
[43] Bydlinski (1982), pp. 395–396.
[44] Becker (2014), p. 19; Großfeld (1985), p. 1577; Isensee (1990), p. 52; Kotsoglou (2014), p. 1101.
[45] Hoffmann-Riem (2016a), pp. 80 et seq.; Kotzur (2014), § 260 para 23.
[46] La Diega (2018), para 11.
[47] Hoffmann-Riem (2017), p. 26.
[48] Ehlers (2015), § 3 para 102; Hoffmann-Riem (2016b), p. 5.

lawmakers must not turn a blind eye to the consequences of law.[49] To conclude, the application of law is an independent act of 'legal production'. In each individual case, law is recreated as a 'social product'.[50]

3.2 Code As a Technical Act

How do basic assumptions about the application of law change when computers replace lawyers? Of course, algorithms are made by humans; they are 'social acts' in the first place.[51] This seemingly obvious fact has far-reaching consequences. Melvin Kranzberg gets to the point by claiming: 'Technologies are neither good nor bad, nor neutral.'[52] Apart from that, 'law' and 'code' differ significantly in their application. Algorithms are not written in a natural, but in a technical language: a binary code maps information through the sequences of the two symbol-system '1' and '0'. Thus, coding a legal tech software consists of two key translation challenges. First, 'law' must be converted into binary code, and secondly, it must be translated back into natural language. Driven by this logic, algorithms translate social reality into binary code: drawn from random inferences, however, they can only identify correlations, not causalities.[53] All AI-driven software is limited to this binary logic. However, advanced forms of AI-driven systems—so called learning-systems—are able to transform new data (input) into decisions (output) without significant human intervention.[54] 'Responsive systems' can even dynamically modify the previous decision patterns.[55] Thus, the decision-making process is conditioned by the learning experiences of an AI-driven system. That, in turn, can lead to structurally unpredictable decisions.[56] However, the impossible remains impossible: algorithms lack 'common sense' and 'soft' decision factors such as intuition, value judgment or holistic thinking.[57] Machines cannot think, nor can they answer deep philosophical questions, best expressed in prose by Goethe: 'Only mankind can do the impossible: he can distinguish, he chooses and judges [...]'.[58]

---

[49]Ehlers (2015), § 3 para 102.
[50]Bryde (2015), p. 129; Hoffmann-Riem (2016b), pp. 12 et seq.
[51]Hoffmann-Riem (2017), pp. 28–29.
[52]Kranzberg (1986), p. 547.
[53]Martini (2017), p. 1018; Rademacher (2017), p. 389.
[54]Wischmeyer (2018), p. 3.
[55]Wischmeyer (2018), p. 13.
[56]Wischmeyer (2018), p. 3.
[57]Grupp (2014), p. 664.
[58]Goethe (2008), p. 256.

3.3 Misconceptions of 'Code'

17 As already indicated, legal tech is based on the notion that legal norms can be formalised and fully translated into computer language. To verify this claim, one must reveal the different operating principles of 'law' and 'code'. Traditionally, the application of law is not perceived as a strictly formalised process, especially with increasing discretional power of lawyers and judges. A lawyer or a judge is not a 'Subsumtionsautomat'[59] who applies law in a formal-mathematical sense, but rather in a dialectical sense.[60] The process of applying and interpreting a legal norm requires value judgments, intuitive knowledge and holistic thinking.[61] However, algorithms lack any of these human qualities—and there is little prospect that software programmers will ever be able to bridge this gap.[62] While machines may in the near future perform some of the repetitive legal tasks, we are far away from replacing nuanced value judgement and expertise and perhaps we never will.[63]

18 Another critical question arises: Can natural language be transformed into the binary language of a computer system at all? Although natural language has a certain inherent logic due to its grammar, the meaning of a word may vary significantly depending on the context ('context variance').[64] Linguistic distinctions are not entirely predictable or programmable.[65] Only in straightforward simple cases is formalisation imaginable (however, it is hard to determine ex ante whether a case is easy or complex),[66] but in a difficult legal or factual situation, formalisation fails.[67] In conclusion, it is quite obvious that the formalisation of the legal language is neither semantically possible nor is it desirable.[68] Yet, the law needs to be flexible to cope with complex technical or social phenomena—in the best interests of society. The necessary degree of flexibility is provided by human language.[69] At this point, a categorial difference between 'law' and 'code' becomes manifest—calling for new forms of regulation. More on this later.

---

[59]Weber (2002), p. 826.
[60]Jandach (1993), pp. 105–106.
[61]La Diega (2018), para 11.
[62]Engel (2014), p. 1097.
[63]Kotsoglou (2014), p. 455; La Diega (2018), para 11; Pfeifer (2018).
[64]Kotsoglou (2014), p. 453.
[65]Engel (2014), p. 1098; Kotsoglou (2014), pp. 453–454.
[66]La Diega (2018), para 11.
[67]Engel (2014), p. 1097.
[68]Kotsoglou (2014), p. 454.
[69]Buchholtz (2017), p. 958.

3.4 Need for Regulation

Why is legal regulation necessary in the digital world? The answer is simple. The societal function of law is, above all, to serve the common good and minority protection. But neither category matters in digital 'code'. As long as this situation persists, public law remains an indispensable instrument of control and regulation.[70] In other words: The state matters.[71] As has been illustrated above, computers lack an understanding of social norms and language.[72] Mireille Hildebrandt comments: 'The mode of existence of meaningful information in human society builds on the spoken word, and on handwritten and printed text.'[73] How can lawmakers bridge these gaps? Situations where conflicts with basic constitutional principles occur, will be analysed in the following section.

4 Constitutional Framework

This section will outline the constitutional guidelines for legal tech software development and application. As a first step, this section will examine why legal tech might pose a risk for the rule of law and democracy (Sect. 5.1). As a second step, potential conflicts between legal tech and the right to privacy as set out in the respective national constitutions and at EU-level will be highlighted (Sect. 5.2). Finally, this section will analyse why legal tech might conflict with the right to non-discrimination (Sect. 5.3).

4.1 Rule of Law and Democracy

First of all, serious criticism of legal tech concerns the (legal) conditions under which software is developed. This process takes place far beyond state control.[74] It has rightly been criticised that 'software development, even open source, is opaque, and concentrated in a small programming community, many of whom are employed by few oligopolistic corporations directly accountable to no external party.'[75] This procedure does not offer any possibilities for potentially affected people to intervene or even participate.

---

[70]Boehme-Neßler (2017), p. 3034.
[71]Medina (2015), p. 1018.
[72]Wischmeyer (2018), pp. 17–18.
[73]Eisenstein (2005); Goody (1986); Hildebrandt (2018), pp. 12–35; Ong (1982).
[74]Schmidt (2016), § 1 para 1 ff.
[75]O'Hara (2017), p. 101.

22   Under current law software developers even enjoy trade secret protection and do not have to reveal their algorithms.[76] The resulting lack of control can have serious consequences: While software developers are certainly willing to be neutral and objective,[77] they can never fully escape bias, customs, culture, knowledge and context when developing algorithms.[78] It has rightly been stated that '[c]ode is not purely abstract and mathematical; it has significant social, political, and aesthetic dimensions.'[79] Computation might even deepen and accelerate processes of sorting, classifying and differentially treating rather than reforming them.[80] This is because algorithms lack the ability—unlike human beings—to balance biases in interpretation of datasets by a conscious attention to redress bias.[81] Moreover, most algorithms are deliberately created for purposes that are far from neutral: to generate revenue, 'to nudge behaviour and structure preferences in a certain way', and to identify, sort and classify people.[82] As set out in the introduction, 'the computer programmer is a creator of universes for which he alone is the lawgiver. No playwright, no stage director, no emperor, however powerful, has ever exercised such absolute authority.'[83] Rightly put! Software developers will become 'quasi-legislators' without accountability or democratic control, if lawmakers do not manage to shape the regulatory conditions in the best interests of society.

23   Apart from that, undemocratic software development—especially the lack of transparency—triggers a variety of concerns about the rule of law.[84] In this context, the rule of law should be interpreted as 'government by law' requiring 'that all people and institutions are subject to and accountable to law that is fairly applied and enforced'.[85] A crucial element is the right to contest the application and validity of a legal norm, typically before a court.[86] In short: The rule of law is about accountability, fairness and due process.

24   When turning from software development to the application of legal tech software, the situation is even more critical: The rule of law is exposed to serious potential risks, especially when legal tech is applied by state authorities which—as has been pointed out—must serve the public interest. Recall, for example, that judges increasingly rely on AI-driven systems in order to determine a person's risk for recidivism. As long as the inner workings of AI technologies are shielded from public view, people will be unable to contest any suspected infringement or manipulation of their rights. This 'dehumanisation of decision-making' calls into question

---

[76]For details see La Diega (2018), para 31 ff.
[77]Porter (1995).
[78]Kitchin (2017), p. 18.
[79]Montfort et al. (2012), p. 3.
[80]Pasquale (2017), p. 5.
[81]La Diega (2018), para 18.
[82]Kitchin (2017), p. 18.
[83]Weizenbaum (1976), p. 115.
[84]Hoffmann-Riem (2017), p. 31; see Wischmeyer, paras 3 et seq.
[85]https://www.dictionary.com/browse/rule-of-law.
[86]Hildebrandt (2015), p. 10.

due process, and the ability to meaningfully appeal an adverse decision.[87] Another objection concerns the above-mentioned differentiation between legal tech used as an 'investigative prediction tool' in a judge's decision-making process or as a 'decision substitute' replacing a judge's decision (see Sect. 2.1). This was at issue in Eric Loomis' case who had been charged with five felony counts in a drive-by shooting in 2013. At his sentencing, the trial court judge merely referred to Loomis' score on the COMPAS assessment. On appeal, the Wisconsin Supreme Court held that a judge relying on closed-source recidivism assessment software in sentencing does not necessarily violate the constitutional 'due process rights even though the methodology used to produce the assessment was disclosed neither to the court nor to the defendant'. However, the judge must not rely on the risk score exclusively.[88] The US Supreme Court refused to hear the case in June 2017.[89] The decision might have serious consequences: if judges gradually exchange ordinary verbal reasoning for AI-driven methods, they undermine the complexity of a judgment. The principle of due process gives defendants a right to understand what they are accused of, and what the evidence against them is. This right, however, is at stake when courts or other state authorities (partly or even entirely) base their sentences solely on secret algorithms. While it might be useful that judges rely on algorithms 'to improve the quality and consistency of their decisions, they shall not let algorithms decide in their stead'.[90]

As has been indicated above, algorithms 'lack an ethical compass'.[91] The question thus arises to what extent government must ensure that the rule of law and democratic participation become quality features of a 'good' algorithm.[92] But how much government intervention is appropriate? Lawmakers are faced with an intricate balancing act: Should private or state software developers disclose their source code for public inspection, or should they be subject to some type of control? A challenging task! Answers will be developed in the fifth part of this article.

4.2 Right to Privacy

As already indicated, legal tech might entail serious risks for the right to privacy—both in public and private use. Without any insight into the inner workings of legal tech software people have little control over how the respective applications collect and store their personal data. The situation has become even more precarious with the rise of data-driven analytics.

---

[87]La Diega (2018).
[88]State of Wisconsin v. Eric Loomis, 7. 881 N.W.2d 749 (Wis. 2016).
[89]Eric Loomis v. State of Wisconsin No. 16-6387.
[90]La Diega (2018), para 117.
[91]Martini (2017), p. 1018.
[92]Hoffmann-Riem (2017), p. 36.

27 What is meant when talking about 'privacy' and where are the constitutional limits for legal tech? According to a common notion, the right to privacy is about choice, autonomy, and individual freedom. It encompasses the right to determine what a particular person will keep hidden and what, how, when and to whom this person will disclose personal information. The terms 'privacy', 'information privacy', 'data privacy' and 'data protection' are often used synonymously in order to emphasize the right to control the collection and processing of personal data by state governments and private entities. Likewise, the German Constitutional Court 'invented' the basic right of informational self-determination as a sub-group of the general right of personality in its ground-breaking 1983 judgment.[93] This right to informational self-determination provides the legal basis for data protection in the German constitution. The court ruled that: '[...] the protection of the individual against unlimited collection, storage, use and disclosure of his/her personal data is encompassed by the general personal rights in the German constitution. This basic right warrants in this respect the capacity of the individual to determine in principle the disclosure and use of his/her personal data. Limitations to this informational self-determination are allowed only in the event of an overriding public interest.'[94]

28 Other than the German constitution, Article 8 of the EU Charter of Fundamental Rights (CFR)—which is decisive for the use of AI—does not stipulate a right to informational self-determination per se, but rather serves as a modern fundamental right to data protection.[95] Based on these constitutional requirements the General Data Protection Regulation (GDPR), implemented on 25 May 2018, introduces uniform standards for processing personal data in the EU. Most of these requirements apply to private and state authorities. The central idea is to give consumers effective control over their personal data. To comply with EU data protection rules, businesses and other (state) organisations must follow key principles of data processing set out in Article 5 GDPR, namely transparency, purpose limitation, data minimisation, accuracy, storage limitation, integrity and confidentiality. In particular, they must provide information where personal data are collected from the data subject (Article 13 GDPR)—a provision that is highly relevant when it comes to big data analytics. Moreover, the GDPR requires operators to be transparent and understandable in communication with users. Also, they are obliged to respond to users' requests for access to their data, its rectification or erasure (Articles 15–17 GDPR). In addition, Article 21 of the GDPR entails the right to object, allowing individuals to ask a company to stop processing their personal data. But the GDPR is also very explicit that the right to object is not absolute; like other civil rights it can be restricted when conflicting with the public interest. Another provision that is particularly important when it comes to legal tech and big data analyses is

---

[93] Cf. Marsch and Rademacher, paras 15–18.
[94] Bundesverfassungsgericht 1 BvR 209, 269/83 'Volkszählung' (15 October 1983), BVerfGE 65, p. 1.
[95] See also Marsch, paras 20–28.

Article 22(1) GDPR ('Automated individual decision-making, including profiling') providing that the data subject shall have the right not to be subject to a decision based solely on automated processing (any operation or set of operations which is performed on personal data or on sets of personal data, whether or not by automated means), including profiling (any form of automated processing of personal data consisting of the use of personal data to evaluate certain personal aspects relating to a natural person), which produces legal effects concerning or similarly significantly affecting him or her. Furthermore, Article 22(4) GDPR provides that automated decisions shall generally not be based on 'sensitive data' (ethnicity, political views, religion, trade union membership, health status, sexual orientation, genetic and biometric data) referred to in Article 9(1) GDPR.

4.3 Right to Non-discrimination

The aforementioned objections against legal tech—especially the lack of transparency—might also entail negative side-effects on the right to non-discrimination.[96] These concerns are related to the fact that algorithm-driven software will possibly deepen and accelerate processes of sorting and classifying people—without any possibility of control for those who are potentially affected. Discrimination can be defined as any unfair treatment of an individual because of his or her membership of a particular group, e.g. race, gender, etc.[97] The right to non-discrimination is enshrined in the normative framework of the EU; it is explicitly provided for in Article 21 CFR, Article 14 of the European Convention on Human Rights, and in Articles 18–25 of the Treaty on the Functioning of the European Union.[98]

Measured against these standards, the use of legal tech might, in a certain sense, be considered as inherently discriminatory[99]: Recall, for example, the use of predictive policing. A study found that the software COMPAS predicts that defendants of black skin colour will have higher risks of recidivism than they actually do, while white defendants have lower rates than they actually do.[100] Although the data used by COMPAS do not contain a person's race, other aspects of the collected data might be correlated to race that can entail racial disparities in the predictions.[101] These results show: 'machine learning depends upon data that has been collected from society', and to the extent that society contains inequality, exclusion or discrimination, these social grievances will exist in the data. Even more so, machine learning can perpetuate existing patterns of discrimination—'if they are found in the training

---

[96] Cf. Wischmeyer, paras 3 et seq.
[97] Altman (2015).
[98] Goodman and Flaxman (2017).
[99] Cf. Tischbirek, paras 3–13.
[100] Angwin et al. (2016).
[101] Dressel and Farid (2018).

dataset, then by design an accurate classifier will reproduce them'.[102] In fact, the legal tech might be even 'worse' than human lawyers—due to the lack of transparency and accountability. Where datasets are relied upon without any further (human) review and control, the computer will exacerbate biases.[103] What is the root of the problem? The fundamental principle of non-discrimination is not a relevant category in 'code'. Recall the fact that algorithms 'lack an ethical compass'.[104] What is needed? As Alexander Tischbirek rightly states, AI and legal sciences 'have to go hand in hand in guarding the non-discrimination principle against new forms of social marginalization in the digital world'.[105]

5 Proposals for 'Regulation by Design': A Balancing Act

31 In the following section some thoughts will be presented on how existing regulatory rules can be brought in line with the aforementioned constitutional principles. Although, this exploration is not exhaustive, it will serve as an invitation to participate in interdisciplinary research and as a guideline for future legal tech regulation. The strategy is twofold: First, we must ensure that AI technologies develop so as to guarantee societal norms. Second, we must find ways to incorporate these principles into technology.

5.1 Regulatory Realignment

32 What is important from a regulatory point of view? Existing regulatory tools must be complemented with innovative means in order to handle the rapid technological developments. For this purpose, the traditional 'command and control'-approach must be rejected as inappropriate. Instead, legal regulation must redesign its accustomed unilateral and deterministic control structures and move on to 'communication'. What is meant here is the communication between lawyers and software developers in order to learn from each other's discipline[106]—an effort that has been associated with the notion of 'legal protection by design' in the last few years.[107]

---

[102]Goodman and Flaxman (2017).
[103]La Diega (2018), para 116.
[104]Martini (2017), p. 1018.
[105]See Tischbirek, para 25.
[106]Scherzberg (2004), p. 226.
[107]Hildebrandt (2017), p. 308.

5.2 Legal Protection by Design As a Starting Point

For a long time, lawmakers have overlooked the power of design, but recently the phrase 'legal protection by design' has attained great popularity. According to sociological findings, design is powerful. It can influence societal norms and expectations.[108] Based on this knowledge, law should guide the design of information technology to protect our constitutional values.[109]

What exactly is meant when talking about 'legal protection by design' or 'by default'? The concept is inspired by Article 25(1) of the GDPR ('Data protection by design and by default'). According to this provision the controller shall, both at the time of the determination of the means for processing and at the time of the processing itself, implement appropriate technical and organisational measures, such as pseudonymisation, which are designed to implement data-protection principles, such as data minimisation, in an effective manner and to integrate the necessary safeguards into the processing in order to protect the rights of the data subject. Moreover, according to Article 25(2) GDPR, the controller shall implement appropriate technical and organisational measures for ensuring that, by default, only personal data which are necessary for each specific purpose of the processing are processed. In particular, such measures shall ensure that by default personal data are not made accessible without the individual's intervention to an indefinite number of natural persons. Correspondingly, recital 78 sentence 2 provides that the controller should adopt internal policies and implement measures which meet in particular the principles of data protection by design and data protection by default.

The rationale behind 'data protection by design' is that data protection and privacy principles must be embedded into technology. This brings up the term 'design' which describes 'how a system is architected, how it functions, how it communicates, and how that architecture, function, and communication affects people'. 'Good design' cannot be achieved without the participation and respect of all stakeholders, including engineers, executives, users and lawyers. Protection by design is a proactive ex ante approach to consider and protect privacy and other societal norms in the development of a group (e.g. business), action (e.g. information or collection), or thing (e.g. technology). Oftentimes, the (worse) alternative is responding to privacy harm (ex post) after it occurred.[110]

With the concept of 'protection by design', communication between lawyers and software developers is necessary, and it is manageable. If lawmakers decide to care about design, they will not have to reinvent the wheel or master the task on their own. There is a robust and well-established software development discipline dedicated to privacy-protective design. Government regulators must not overlook the expertise 'of those already committed to leveraging technological design to protect our privacy' and social values. Apart from that, the lessons learned from design

---

[108] See Hartzog (2018), pp. 8, 21 et seq.
[109] Hartzog (2018), pp. 5 et seq.
[110] Hartzog (2018), pp. 11–12.

regulation in other legal fields and jurisdictions might be helpful when regulating legal tech.[111]

37 In a nutshell, what are the key issues? 'Ignoring design is dangerous, but so is overregulating it, and an important balance must be struck.'[112] How can this be done? In the following section, core elements of 'legal protection by design' will be presented. Partly, existing provisions must be reformed; partly, they must be completely redefined and revised. Thereby, typological and regulatory distinctions between public and private use of legal tech will be considered.

5.3 Regulatory Guidelines

38 As has been demonstrated in the previous sections, a lack of transparency and control might prevent people from fully exercising their rights (especially privacy and non-discrimination). However, where fundamental rights are restricted by legal tech, normative justification is required; where state officials apply legal tech, transparency is a fundamental rule of law principle.[113] To what extent does current law already meet these requirements and what reforms are needed?

39 Article 22(1) of the GDPR ('Automated individual decision-making, including profiling') expresses the need that any data subject shall have the right not to be subject to a decision based solely on automated processing, including profiling, which produces legal effects concerning him or her, or which significantly affects him or her. In addition, private and state software developers must meet information requirements where personal data are subject to automated decision-making (where a decision is made solely by automated means and without any human involvement). Pursuant to Article 13(2) lit. f GDPR the controller shall, at the time when personal data are obtained from the data subject, provide them with information necessary to ensure fair and transparent processing about: the existence of automated decision-making, including profiling, referred to in Article 22(1) and (4) GDPR and, at least in those cases, meaningful information about the logic involved, as well as the significance and the envisaged consequences of such processing for the data subject. Likewise, according to Article 14(2) lit. g GDPR, where personal data have not been obtained from the data subject, the controller shall inform the data subject about the existence of automated decision-making, including profiling, referred to in Article 22(1) and (4) GDPR.

40 The idea behind these provisions is 'individual empowerment'[114]: People shall be kept informed about and protected from automated decision-making wherever possible.[115] Therefore, pursuant to Article 22(1) GDPR, it must be guaranteed that

---

[111] See also Hartzog (2018), pp. 86 et seq.
[112] Hartzog (2018), p. 6.
[113] Wischmeyer (2018), p. 22.
[114] Kuner (2012), p. 1.
[115] Martini (2017), p. 1020; cf. Wischmeyer, para 46.

an automated-decision is reviewed by a human being who 'takes account of other factors in making the final decision'.[116] But fabricating any human involvement is not sufficient according to the 'Article 29 Data Protection Working Party'. If, for example, a human employee routinely rubber-stamps automatically generated profiles without any actual influence on the result, this would not meet the requirements under Article 22 GDPR.[117] 'Meaningful' oversight is needed by 'someone who has the authority and competence to change the decision.'[118] Yet, the question arises, if and to what extent human reviewing will finally deviate from a prior automated decision. In practice, it is unlikely that human oversight will actually go beyond a mere plausibility check.[119] Despite all criticism of Article 22 GDPR, regulation is required to provide transparency and prevent discrimination. In particular, people must be informed about AI-driven data processing—in an easily comprehensible format which allows them to react to a decision in a meaningful way.[120] However, a general duty to reveal a software's programme code would be disproportionate with regard to the legitimate interests of software developers. But it has rightly been demanded that software developers shall be obliged to disclose the basic decision-making structures of their software[121] in order for the (potentially) affected people to understand guiding principles of a decision-making process.[122]

Moreover, in order to balance out knowledge asymmetries (due to the complexity of datasets) collective control mechanisms must be implemented: It has been suggested that software with potential impact on sensitive data must undergo government admission control.[123] This 'algorithm check' shall not only cover the programme code itself, but also the quality and reliability of the software training programme. This inspection should be mandatory for any state application of legal tech with potential impact on sensitive data. Judges, for example, should not use software like COMPAS if there is no external quality assurance. Apart from a mandatory admission control, learning systems must undergo continuous control with their subsequent implementation, because learning algorithms change the decision-making structures frequently.[124] Government control must extend to the validity and the accuracy of the database. Control algorithms might help to systematically analyse automated decision-making processes, particularly in order to uncover bias and discrimination. Moreover, software developers must be obliged to set up risk management systems, in order to make sure that software applications will not produce discriminatory or biased decisions. So far, current legislation does

---

[116]Article 29 Data Protection Working Party (2018), p. 21.
[117]Article 29 Data Protection Working Party (2018), pp. 9–10.
[118]Article 29 Data Protection Working Party (2018), p. 10.
[119]Hoffmann-Riem (2017), p. 36.
[120]Martini (2017), p. 1020; see Wischmeyer, para 25.
[121]Mayer-Schönberger and Cukier (2013), pp. 179 et seq.
[122]Martini (2017), p. 1020.
[123]Martini (2017), p. 1021.
[124]Martini (2017), p. 1021.

not require software developers to establish risk management systems. However, such an obligation would be useful to give potentially affected people a fair chance to rightly assess and identify privacy risks ex ante. Eventually, each legal tech system ought to be designed to give users and other subjects of the system the ability to assess the system's accountability through algorithms and datasets. Moreover, transparency and accountability must be guaranteed for those who are potentially affected. Only then, people would have the ability to 'reject any insidious nudging' and they would be able to 'challenge the legal consequences of any such technological process'.[125] We will see whether these mechanisms will be put into practice. A substantial contribution of these proposals, however, is to show that fundamental constitutional values can be embedded in algorithms. Properly applied, AI-driven technology will not only make more accurate predictions, but provide greater transparency and fairness compared to its human counterparts. And another lesson to be learned: a sound design of technology requires intense cooperation between technical and legal experts.[126]

5.4 The 'Human Factor'

42   Finally, some comments should be made on legal education. As has been demonstrated above, 'legal protection by design' requires interdisciplinary effort. The technological change that lawyers have witnessed brings in its wake an obligation for legal scholars to become familiar with opportunities and consequences of AI-driven tools (see, mutatis mutandis, Molnár-Gábor, paras 13 et seq.). Solutions must be developed to apply technology in the best interests of society.[127] By recognising technological limits lawyers will find a greater clarity about their profession and their 'ethical compass'. 'And we shall find [...] that our intuitive expertise, irreducible to rules, casts the weight on the side of the human mind as we try to establish a new balance between ourselves and our even more powerful, yet perhaps perpetually limited, machines.'[128]

5.5 Balancing Act

43   Ultimately, legal tech regulation requires an intricate balancing act, especially between the privacy related interests of consumers and the economic interests of

---

[125] Stevens (2017); see Wischmeyer, para 41.
[126] Goodman and Flaxman (2017).
[127] Shackelford and Raymond (2014), p. 633.
[128] Dreyfus and Dreyfus (1986), p. XV.

software developers.[129] Moreover, regulators must take into account the effects of regulation on innovation as well as the implications of technical change for the rationale and design of regulation. The interplay between regulation and innovation is mutual and dynamic.[130] Yet, the proposals on 'legal protection by design' put forward in this article provide an appropriate balance. It has to be emphasized, however, that 'legal protection by design' must be required by law, or as Mireille Hildebrandt rightly puts it: 'Legal protection by design' must be turned 'from an ethical choice into a legal requirement.' Only then, we can make sure that legal tech will be effectively brought in line with the rule of law.[131]

6 Conclusion

'The state matters if we want to create technologies that benefit the wider citizenry.'[132] Legal tech can be brought in line with the rule of law only by means of law. Thereby, a focus of technological design must lie on privacy protection if we are willing to build systems that safeguard human freedom—'the lack of privacy protection in our current systems is a choice'.[133] Moreover, we need to develop 'mechanisms not only for greater algorithmic transparency but also for democratic control'.[134] This will generate trust which is, incidentally, an essential ingredient for commerce and a flourishing society. So if we are striving to improve commerce, our search for self-definition, and our society in general, we need better legal protection by design.[135]

Lawmakers and legal scholars have to be aware of their responsibilities. Interdisciplinary communication and research is needed. Only when they are in place can government regulators find the right equilibrium between privacy related and economic interests. In this sense, 'legal protection by design' will serve the rule of law and the best interests of society. If we start to think critically of AI from an interdisciplinary perspective, society can make full use it. And possibly, society will be more 'human' through AI.

---

[129]Martini (2017), p. 1021.
[130]Blind (2012), p. 391; Martini (2017), p. 1025.
[131]Hildebrandt (2017), p. 311.
[132]Medina (2015), p. 1018.
[133]Medina (2015), p. 1018.
[134]Medina (2015), p. 1018.
[135]See Hartzog (2018), p. 9.

References

Aletras N, Tsarapatsanis D, Preoţiuc-Pietro D, Lampos V (2016) Predicting judicial decisions of the European Court of Human Rights: a natural language processing perspective. Peer J Comp Sci 2:e93. https://doi.org/10.7717/peerj-cs.93
Altman A (2015) Discrimination. In: Zalta EN (ed) The Stanford encyclopedia of philosophy. Stanford University, Stanford. Winter 2016 edn. plato.stanford.edu/archives/win2016/entries/discrimination. Accessed 4 Oct 2018
Angwin J, Larson J, Mattu S, Kirchner L (2016) Machine bias. ProPublica, New York. www.propublica.org/article/machine-bias-risk-assessments-in-criminal-sentencing. Accessed 4 Oct 2018
Article 29 Data Protection Working Party (2018) Guidelines on automated individual decision-making and Profiling for the purposes of Regulation 2016/679, 17/EN, WP251rev.01, adopted on 3 October 2017, as last revised and adopted on 6 February 2018
Becker C (2014) Was bleibt? Recht und Postmoderne. Nomos, Baden-Baden
Blind K (2012) The influence of regulations on innovation: a quantitative assessment for OECD countries. Res Policy 41:391–400
Boehme-Neßler V (2017) Die Macht der Algorithmen und die Ohnmacht des Rechts. Neue Juristische Wochenschrift 42:3031–3037
Bostrom N (2014) Superintelligence – paths, dangers, strategies. Oxford University Press, Oxford
Bryde BO (2015) Richterrecht und Gesetzesbindung. Sozialrecht 5:128–132
Buchholtz G (2017) Legal Tech – Chancen und Risiken der digitalen Rechtsanwendung. Juristische Schulung 2017:955–960
Bydlinski F (1982) Juristische Methodenlehre und Rechtsbegriff. Springer, Wien
Chowdhry A (2016) Law Firm BakerHostetler hires a 'digital attorney' namend Ross. Forbes, New York. www.forbes.com/sites/amitchowdhry/2016/05/17/law-firm-bakerhostetler-hires-a-digital-attorney-named-ross. Accessed 4 Oct 2018
Dressel J, Farid H (2018) The accuracy, fairness, and limits of predicting recidivism. Sci Adv 4(1): eaao5580. https://doi.org/10.1126/sciadv.aao5580
Dreyfus H, Dreyfus SE (1986) Mind over machine. Free Press, New York
Ehlers D (2015) Verwaltungsrecht. In: Ehlers D, Pünder H (eds) Allgemeines Verwaltungsrecht, 15th edn. De Gruyter, Berlin, § 3
Eidenmüller H (2017) The rise of robots and the law of humans. ZeuP 2017:765–777
Eisenstein EL (2005) The printing revolution in early modern Europe. Cambridge University Press, Cambridge
Engel M (2014) Algorithmisierte Rechtsfindung als juristische Arbeitshilfe. JuristenZeitung 69:1096–1100
Frese Y (2015) Recht im zweiten Maschinenzeitalter. Neue Juristische Wochenschrift 68:2090–2092
Gartner IT Glossary (2018) 'Big Data'. www.gartner.com/it-glossary/big-data. Accessed 4 Oct 2018
Goertzel B (2015) Superintelligence: fears, promises and potentials. J Evol Technol 24(2):55–87
Goethe JW (2008) Das Göttliche. Fischer, Frankfurt am Main, pp 258–258
Goodman B, Flaxman S (2017) European Union regulations on algorithmic decision-making and a 'Right to Explanation'. AI Magazine 38(3):50–57. https://doi.org/10.1609/aimag.v38i3.2741
Goody J (1986) The logic of writing and the Organization of Society. Cambridge University Press, Cambridge
Government Office for Science (UK) (2016) Artificial intelligence: opportunities and implications for the future of decision making. assets.publishing.service.gov.uk/government/uploads/system/uploads/attachment_data/file/566075/gs-16-19-artificial-intelligence-ai-report.pdf. Accessed 4 Oct 2018
Großfeld T (1985) Sprache, Recht, Demokratie. Neue Juristische Wochenschrift 28:1577–1586

Grupp M (2014) Legal Tech – Impulse für Streitbeilegung und Rechtsdienstleistung. Anwaltsblatt 2014:660–665

Hartzog W (2018) Privacy's blueprint. Harvard University Press, Cambridge

Hildebrandt M (2015) Smart technologies and the End(s) of Law, novel entanglements of law and technology. Edward Elgar Publishing, Cheltenham

Hildebrandt M (2017) Saved by design? The case of legal protection by design. Nanoethics 11:307–311

Hildebrandt M (2018) Law as computation in the Era of artificial legal intelligence. Speaking law to the power of statistics. Toronto Law J 68:12–35

Hoffmann-Riem W (2016a) Innovation und Recht – Recht und Innovation. Mohr Siebeck, Tübingen

Hoffmann-Riem W (2016b) Außerjuridisches Wissen, Alltagstheorien und Heuristiken im Verwaltungsrecht. Die Verwaltung 49:1–23

Hoffmann-Riem W (2017) Verhaltenssteuerung durch Algorithmen – Eine Herausforderung für das Recht. Archiv des öffentlichen Rechts 142:1–42

Isensee J (1990) Unsere Sprache: Die Sicht des Juristen. In: Großfeld B (ed) Unsere Sprache. VS Verlag für Sozialwissenschaften, Wiesbaden, pp 52–78

Jandach T (1993) Juristische Expertensysteme. Springer, Berlin

Kitchin R (2017) Thinking critically about and researching algorithms. Inf Commun Soc 20 (1):14–29

Kleinberg J, Lakkaraju H, Leskovec J, Ludwig J, Mullainathan S (2017) Human decisions and machine predictions, National Bureau of economic research. Working Paper 23180. www.nber.org/papers/w23180. Accessed 4 Oct 2018

Kotsoglou KN (2014) Subsumtionsautomat 2.0 reloaded? – Zur Unmöglichkeit der Rechtsprüfung durch Laien. Juristenzeitung 69:1100–1103

Kotzur M (2014) Thematik des Verfassungsgesetzes. In: Isensee J, Kirchhof P (eds) Handbuch des Staatsrechts XII, 3rd edn. Müller, Heidelberg, § 260

Kranzberg M (1986) Technology and history: Kranzberg's Laws. Technol Cult 27(3):544–560

Kuner C (2012) The European Commission's proposed data protection regulation: a Copernican revolution in European data protection law. Bloomberg BNA Privacy and Security Law Report, pp. 1–15

La Diega GN (2018) Against the dehumanisation of decision-making – algorithmic decisions at the crossroads of intellectual property, data protection, and freedom of information. J Inellect Prop Inf Technol Electron Commerce Law 9(1):3–34

Legal Technology Journal, Smart Contracts (2017) Von der Smart Factory zum Smart Contract. legal-technology.net/von-smart-factory-zu-smart-contract. Accessed 4 Oct 2018

Lessing L (2006) Code: and other law of cyberspace, Version 2.0. Basic Books, New York

Mainzer K (2016) Künstliche Intelligenz – wann übernehmen die Maschinen? Springer, Heidelberg

Martini M (2017) Algorithmen als Herausforderung für die Rechtsordnung. JuristenZeitung 72:1017–1072

Mayer-Schönberger V, Cukier K (2013) Big data. John Murray, London

Medina E (2015) Rethinking algorithmic regulation. Kybernetes 44:1005–1019. https://doi.org/10.1108/K-02-2015-0052

Montfort N, Baudoin P, Bell J, Bogost I, Douglass J, Marino MC, Mateas M, Reas C, Sample M, Vawter N (2012) 10 PRINT CHR$ (205.5 + RND (1)); : GOTO 10. MIT Press, Cambridge, MA

O'Hara K (2017) Smart contracts – dumb idea. IEEE Internet Comput 21(2):97–101. https://doi.org/10.1109/MIC.2017.48

Ong WJ (1982) Orality and literacy: the technologizing of the word. Routledge, London

Pasquale F (2017) Secret algorithms threaten the rule of law. MIT Technology Review. www.technologyreview.com/s/608011/secret-algorithms-threaten-the-rule-of-law. Accessed 4 Oct 2018

Pfeifer J (2018) The data-driven lawyer and the future of legal technology. www.lawtechnologytoday.org/2018/01/the-data-driven-lawyer. Accessed 4 Oct 2018

Porter TM (1995) Trust in numbers: the pursuit of objectivity in science and public life. Princeton University Press, Princeton

Rademacher T (2017) Predictive Policing im deutschen Polizeirecht. Archiv des öffentlichen Rechts 142:366–416

Riehm T (2006) Abwägungsentscheidungen in der praktischen Rechtsanwendung. Beck, München

Scherzberg A (2004) Risikosteuerung durch Verwaltungsrecht – Ermöglichung oder Begrenzung von Innovationen. Vereinigung der deutschen Staatsrechtslehrer 63:214–263

Schmidt (2016) Programmierung, Dokumentation und Test von Software. In: Auer-Reinsdorff A, Conrad I (eds) Handbuch für IT- und Datenschutzrecht, 3rd edn. Beck, München, § 1

Shackelford SJ, Raymond AH (2014) Building the virtual courthouse: ethical considerations for design, implementation, and regulation in the World of ODR. Wisconsin Law Rev 3:615–657

Sharma S, Mishra P, Mittal M (2018) S-Array: high scalable parallel sorting algorithm. In: Mittal M, Balas VE, Hemanth DJ, Kumar R (eds) Data intensive computing applications for big data. IOS Press BV, Amsterdam

Society for the Study of Artificial Intelligence and Simulation of Behaviour (2011) What is artificial intelligence? www.aisb.org.uk/public-engagement/what-isai. Accessed 4 Oct 2018

Stevens Y (2017) The promises and perils of artificial intelligence: why human rights and the rule of law matter. medium.com/@ystvns/the-promises-and-perils-of-artificial-intelligence-why-human-rights-norms-and-the-rule-of-law-40c57338e806. Accessed 4 Oct 2018

Stiemerling O (2015) Künstliche Intelligenz – Automatisierung geistiger Arbeit, Big Data und das Internet der Dinge. Computer und Recht 31(12):762–765

Susskind R (2013) Tomorrow's Lawyers: an introduction to your future. Oxford University Press, Oxford

Szabo N (1994) Smart contracts. www.fon.hum.uva.nl/rob/Courses/InformationInSpeech/CDROM/Literature/LOTwinterschool2006/szabo.best.vwh.net/smart.contracts.html. Accessed 4 Oct 2018

Tobschall D, Kempe J (2017) Der Deutsche Legal-Tech-Markt. Neue Juristische Wochenschrift – Sonderheft: Innovationen & Legal Tech, pp 10–13

Wagner J (2018) Legal Tech und Legal Robots: Der Wandel im Rechtsmarkt durch neue Technologien und künstliche Intelligenz. Springer, Wiesbaden

Weber M (2002) Wirtschaft und Gesellschaft, 5th edn. Mohr Siebeck, Tübingen

Weizenbaum J (1976) Computer power and human reason: from judgement to calculation. W. H. Freeman & Co, Oxford

Wischmeyer T (2018) Regulierung intelligenter Systeme. Archiv des öffentlichen Rechts 143:1–66

Artificial Intelligence and Administrative Decisions Under Uncertainty

Yoan Hermstrüwer

Contents

1 Introduction 200
2 Frictions: Machine Learning Versus Administrative Law 201
   2.1   Investigation 202
   2.2   Prediction 203
   2.3   Decision 204
3 Challenges: Machine Learning and Administration Under Uncertainty 205
   3.1   Generalizability 206
   3.2   Counterfactual Reasoning 210
   3.3   Error Weighting 213
   3.4   Proportionality 214
   3.5   Gaming 217
   3.6   Complexity 218
4 Conclusion 219
Appendix 220
References 221

Abstract How should artificial intelligence guide administrative decisions under risk and uncertainty? I argue that artificial intelligence, specifically machine learning, lifts the veil covering many of the biases and cognitive errors engrained in administrative decisions. Machine learning has the potential to make administrative agencies smarter, fairer and more effective. However, this potential can only be exploited if administrative law addresses the implicit normative choices made in the design of machine learning algorithms. These choices pertain to the generalizability of machine-based outcomes, counterfactual reasoning, error weighting, the proportionality principle, the risk of gaming and decisions under complex constraints.

Y. Hermstrüwer (✉)
Max Planck Institute for Research on Collective Goods, Bonn, Germany

Transatlantic Technology Law Forum, Stanford Law School, Stanford, CA, USA
e-mail: hermstruewer@coll.mpg.de

1 Introduction

1 For centuries, administrative agencies have relied on human judgement and the decisions of their civil servants, flesh-and-blood human beings.[1] While evolution has programmed humans to learn and adapt quickly, administrative agencies are not notorious for their adaptiveness. It is part of the administrative rationale to stick with the status quo or use some heuristic akin to habit ('We've always done it that way').[2] Such heuristics guide many administrative decisions under risk and uncertainty in the Knightian sense.[3]

2 Artificial intelligence challenges the role of human conviction underlying administrative decisions that are subject to uncertainty and complex constraints. How should artificial intelligence guide these decisions? And how can the requirements of the rule of law and the practical advantages of smart machines be reconciled? While I do not claim to provide a definitive answer, I propose three arguments – mainly with respect to machine learning.

3 First, I argue that the black box concerns often raised against machine learning are partly misplaced.[4] As Herbert Simon observed, lawyers and civil servants are subject to various cognitive and motivational biases.[5] Machine learning lifts the veil covering these biases and the implicit normative choices underlying administrative decisions. Machine learning will rationalize the administrative decision making process, but only if lawmakers and administrative lawyers take an active role in shaping the technology. This requires an in-depth understanding of the implicit normative choices embedded in the technology.[6] If off-the-shelf machine learning is used without questioning the underlying assumptions and shaping algorithmic design, administrative agencies will be prone to erroneous conclusions. I will therefore focus on technical issues, specifically the potential and pitfalls of machine learning.

4 Second, I argue that machine learning may help to reduce some of the biases that administrative agencies are subject to, shape the exercise of discretion, and sometimes reduce the margin of appreciation that administrative agencies have when making decisions under uncertainty. Predictions based on machine learning may shape both the interpretation of vague statutory conditions (*unbestimmte Rechtsbegriffe*) and the exercise of discretionary power (*Ermessen*), but only if the pitfalls of the algorithms are well understood. It is important to note, however, that machine learning refers to a 'zoo' of techniques rather than a homogeneous 'class' of

---

[1] I would like to thank Christoph Engel, Timo Rademacher and Thomas Wischmeyer for valuable comments on an earlier draft of this chapter.
[2] Simon (1997), pp. 99–100; for an example, see Joh (2017), pp. 290 et seq.
[3] While *risk* usually refers to situations where the probability of an outcome is known, *uncertainty* is usually assumed when probabilities cannot be quantified. See Knight (1921) and Vermeule (2015).
[4] Also see Rademacher, para 31 and Wischmeyer, para 6. For an account of these concerns, see Pasquale (2015); Citron and Pasquale (2014); Hogan-Doran (2017), pp. 32–39.
[5] Simon (1955, 1997); for a recent account of biases among judges, see Spamann and Klöhn (2016).
[6] For a similar approach, see Lehr and Ohm (2017); see also Rademacher, paras 36–38.

techniques. Therefore, any attempt to distill the normative challenges of machine learning is susceptible to overgeneralization. While I admittedly overgeneralize in this chapter, legal scholarship might soon need a sharper analytical framework to domesticate some of the 'wilder animals' in the zoo of machine learning.

Third, I argue that uncertainties relating to both facts and the application of administrative law are likely to dwindle over time. If the exercise of discretion and the application of administrative law stringently follow machine-based predictions of regulatory problems, the structural nexus between the identification of a regulatory problem and the adoption of administrative measures to solve that very problem may become more transparent and calculable. If it gets easier to calculate the outcomes of administrative law, it will also get easier to game the legal system. Hence, Ronald Dworkin's notorious claim that law is not like chess may lose some ground.[7] At least, it seems that machine learning shifts the law somewhat more into the direction of chess, that is, a system of rules that can be calculated and anticipated. The gains in *predictive accuracy* might therefore—paradoxical as it may seem—induce administrative agencies to capitalize on *legal indeterminacy*. Specifically, as predictions become predictable, administrative agencies might have to engrain some uncertainty element in the application of administrative law in order to prevent the risk of strategic countermeasures.[8]

2 Frictions: Machine Learning Versus Administrative Law

Administrative law is primarily determined by a classification of facts under an abstract legal definition, at least in continental jurisdictions.[9] Machine learning denotes a class of statistical methods aimed at detecting patterns or correlations between dependent and independent variables (classification) or predicting an outcome (prediction).[10] Against this backdrop, the advent of machine learning will enable administrative agencies to identify regularities with respect to facts and the law.

To impose some structure on the following arguments, I suggest a distinction on two dimensions. On the one hand, it makes sense to distinguish between reasoning about law and reasoning about facts as a condition of applying the law.[11] On the other hand, it makes sense to distinguish between the stages of an administrative

---

[7]Dworkin (1965), p. 682. A note of precision is warranted: the use of machine learning algorithms by administrative agencies will of course not entail a formal modification of existing legal rules. Rather, it will alter the factual classifications and predictions required to apply existing legal rules. As far as machine learning effectively reduces factual errors when applying the law, the law itself is likely to become somewhat more predictable as well.

[8]For an analysis of the virtues of legal uncertainty, see Baker et al. (2004).

[9]For an analysis in the context of common law, see Sunstein (2001).

[10]For an overview, see Athey and Imbens (2017), pp. 22–27.

[11]Also see Buchanan and Headrick (1970), pp. 47 et seq.

procedure: investigation, prediction, and decision. With these distinctions in mind, I shall discuss some of the frictions arising between principles of administrative law and machine learning.

2.1 Investigation

8 Each administrative procedure begins with an investigation of the facts.[12] In cases involving risk and uncertainty, the administration is only required to gather sufficient information prompting the reasonable conclusion that a legally protected interest (e.g. physical integrity) is at stake and that this interest may be infringed upon with some probability.

9 While the administration is largely free to use computing tools in the investigation, it is also required to investigate the singularities and specificities of the case at hand.[13] In other words, administrative law requires that each case be treated as unique. This requirement cannot easily be met in an investigation directed with the aid of machine learning based-predictions, since these predictions are based on statistical regularities. Current algorithms target a class or subset of cases with generalizable properties rather than singular cases.[14]

10 This points at a fundamental tension between machine learning and the requirement to investigate the specific case. Administrative law and doctrine will need to accommodate the tendency of machine learning to override the singularities of the case. This will become easier over time, as predictions will become more and more granular, eventually allowing for personalized investigations. In the long run, machine learning is likely to let the pendulum swing back towards a system of administrative practices that consider the specificities of each single case without touching upon the generality of the respective legal rules. Therefore, the potential move towards personalized investigations should not be conflated with a system of legal rules targeted at regulating individual behavioral idiosyncrasies ('personalized administrative law'). Such a system would not only require a personalized investigation based on *abstract-general rules* but a set of *concrete-individual rules* stipulating different legal prescriptions for different (heterogeneous) types of persons.[15]

---

[12]See § 24(1) VwVfG—Verwaltungsverfahrensgesetz.

[13]See § 24(2) VwVfG—Verwaltungsverfahrensgesetz.

[14]Note that machine learning algorithms also quantify the *confidence* one may have in the prediction or classification, which mitigates the concerns raised here.

[15]However, there is a grey area: Consider the likely case that machine learning yields better predictions for some groups than for others (e.g. a better prediction of statutory non-compliance). In that case, personalized investigations will impose higher burdens on the group for which a better prediction is available, since administrative agencies will be more likely to target that group and apply the respective administrative rules to it even though these rules may be formally abstract and general. Abstract and general legal rules can therefore have similar effects as *formal personalized law* if the machine-based predictions entail a different (e.g. more stringent) application of the law for

2.2 Prediction

Predicting risks is one of the core tasks of the administrative state.[16] Roughly speaking, such predictions are required in most areas of administrative law that aim at reducing or preventing the probability of some socially harmful outcome, including police law (crime risks), restaurants law (health risks), environmental law (environmental risks), and financial law (financial risks). While administrative law does not prescribe how predictions should be generated, it contains some rules on how to determine a legally relevant risk. One such rule is the so-called 'the more, the less' rule (*Je-desto-Formel*), basically an application of expected utility theory to the law of risk regulation.[17] According to this rule, a legally relevant risk is determined by the product of the level of harm H and its probability p, that is, the expected value of harm $E(H) = p \cdot H$. The higher the level of harm, the lower the probability required to assume a legally relevant risk, and vice versa. The operation underlying the determination of risk, however, is less rational than this rule suggests. The reasons are twofold.

First, continental administrative law doctrine can be considered as being *quantification-averse*.[18] Neither the level of harm nor the corresponding probability distributions are usually translated into any quantifiable metric.[19] Instead, risks are considered as a fundamentally normative problem. While scientific insights will often guide the administrative decision, the risk is ultimately determined by a civil servant engaging in some qualitative assessment of the facts. The epistemic model underlying this view of the law is that legally relevant risks are social constructs based on some kind of implicit human agreement rather than measurable phenomena.[20]

Second, the conditions enshrined in administrative statutes—even those qualified as bright-line rules—are usually too vague to allow for precise quantification. Therefore, the interpretation of the law is often considered to be impossible without some human interposition that aims at making vague statutes operational. Consider the debarment of unreliable business persons. Under German public business law, a business person shall partly or entirely be debarred in case of facts indicating that the business person is unreliable.[21] The determination of unreliability is based on an evaluation of specific facts and a prediction of future non-compliance with statutory

---

groups about which more is known (*de facto personalized law*). For an overview of personalized law approaches, see Pasquale (2018), pp. 7–12.

[16]See Coglianese and Lehr (2017), pp. 1160 et seq.; Cuéllar (2016), pp. 10 et seq.

[17]While the rule is a specificity of German administrative law, similar ideas can be found in US law and cost benefit analysis applied to law. For the foundations of expected utility theory, see von Neumann and Morgenstern (1944).

[18]US law is somewhat different in that respect, see Sunstein (2018), pp. 3 et seq.

[19]For an informal application of probability theory to police law, see Poscher (2008), pp. 352 et seq.

[20]See also Buchholtz, paras 13 et seq.

[21]§ 35(1) GewO—Gewerbeordnung.

rules. According to case law, predictors are previous crimes and misdemeanors, tax debts, an excess level of private debts, or the non-compliance with social security regulations.[22]

14 The interpretation of many such administrative statutes requires predictions based on some proxy variable. No fundamental objection against the use of other—better—proxies as those uncovered by machine learning algorithms can be derived from legal principles. However, if administrative predictions are based on machine-based predictions, this will likely entail a significant shift in the proxies used by administrative agencies and accepted by administrative courts, thus entirely reshaping legal doctrine.[23]

2.3 Decision

15 Most of the frictions arise with respect to the legal principles governing the question of how an administrative decision should be made given a specific prediction. Two such frictions are particularly relevant.

16 The first relates to the justification of the administrative decision. The administration has to give reasons for its decision, the main functions being self-control of the administration, control through the citizens, the guarantee of trust and the recognition as a human being with a right to be subject to a human decision.[24] Since it is almost impossible for any human to reconstruct and fully understand the intricacies of a machine learning algorithm, any attempt to articulate the reasons for observing a specific predicted outcome is subject to severe constraints.[25] While administrative law does not require an econometrically solid identification of the causes for a decision, it does require some description of the things that the person concerned would have to change in order to obtain a different decision.

17 The second relates to the question whether machine learning should be used as a *complement* (a decision aid) or as a *substitute* to human administrative decisions.[26] The answer depends on the degree of discretionary power conferred to the administrative agency. On a doctrinal view, administrative law can be seen as a set of

---

[22]Marcks (2018), paras 35–62. Similar rules can be found in German restaurants law, see §§ 15(1), (2), 4(1) Nr. 1 GastG—Gaststättengesetz. For an overview, see Ehlers (2012), paras 21 et seq.

[23]If machine-based proxies are better at predicting the reliability of business persons than proxies based on human judgement, there is no obvious reason for sticking to the latter. In fact, business persons who are disadvantaged by human-made proxies may try to invoke equal protection rights and argue that sticking to human-made proxies constitutes an unjustified discrimination. All this depends on the interpretation of what 'reliability' exactly means under administrative law (a dummy for existing human-made proxies or a concept that is open to new interpretations).

[24]§ 39 VwVfG; for an analysis, see Coglianese and Lehr (2017), pp. 1205 et seq.; Wischmeyer (2018), pp. 56–59.

[25]See Wischmeyer, paras 9 et seq.

[26]Cuéllar (2016); for a computer science perspective, see Parkes and Wellman (2015).

conditional statements (if-then-statements): if certain statutory conditions are met, then an administrative decision is to be taken according to the program set out by the then-statement. Depending on the statute, discretion may be exercised in the if-statement, the then-statement, or both. With respect to machine learning, we may distinguish between a weak case and a hard case.

The weak case occurs when the if-statement contains a specific description of measurable conditions and the then-statement compels the administrative agency to take a specific decision. In such a case, no compelling argument against the use of machine learning as a substitute can be derived from administrative law. This squares with the rationale of the new German administrative procedure law.[27] Accordingly, a fully automated administrative decision is allowed if there is a statutory basis and there is room for discretion neither with the interpretation of the statutory conditions nor as to the decisions to be taken if the statutory conditions are met.

The hard case occurs when some discretionary power is conferred to the administrative agency. In these cases, machine learning might serve as a *complementing* micro-directive in the exercise of discretion.[28] In some cases, it may even serve as a *substitute* ('algorithmic discretion'). This, however, is only possible within the bounds set by privacy law (cf. Article 22 EU-GDPR) and constitutional law. The stronger machine learning-generated outputs interfere with individual rights, the more the EU and constitutional law impose an obligation on the legislative branch to determine the normatively relevant technical choices according to various types of non-delegation doctrines.[29]

18

19

3 Challenges: Machine Learning and Administration Under Uncertainty

In what follows, I will mainly refer to supervised machine learning.[30] It is useful to distinguish between the labelling, training, validating, testing and implementation phases. In the labelling phase, an output variable representing the outcome to be predicted (e.g. 'cat') is given a label that represents the true value of the output variable ('cat').[31] This label is usually based on human judgement and decision

20

---

[27] § 35a VwVfG—Verwaltungsverfahrensgesetz, see Djeffal, paras 20 et seq.

[28] Alarie et al. (2017); Alarie et al. (2018), pp. 117–124.

[29] Coglianese and Lehr (2017), pp. 1177–1184; Cuéllar (2016). A similar doctrine is known as *Wesentlichkeitslehre* in German constitutional law; see also Rademacher, paras 14, 18.

[30] It is difficult to interpret the results of unsupervised machine learning without any parameter for normative weight. This problem is particularly acute in the analysis of legal texts, see Talley (2018). Most legal applications are based on supervised machine learning, see Lehr and Ohm (2017), p. 676.

[31] Technically, the output variable is the dependent variable, while the input variable is the independent variable.

making. In the training phase, some algorithm is fed with pairs of input variables and labelled output variables included in a *training data* set. The algorithm is then trained to distinguish between the true values ('cats') and the other values ('non-cats') of the output variables and predict them based on input variables. In the validation phase, the errors made by the algorithm are evaluated on *validation data*. The parameters are adjusted to reduce error rates. In the test phase, the algorithm is exposed to a *test data* set for the first time in order to test the generalizability and accuracy of the model on an unknown sample. Eventually, the algorithm is implemented to make predictions in the wild.

3.1 Generalizability

21 Administrative agencies need predictions that are generalizable over the class of cases requiring a decision. This is only guaranteed if the algorithm trained on a test sample accurately predicts data from another sample. Administrative agencies are likely to encounter two problems here: the neglect of selection effects and bias aversion.

Neglect of Selection Effects

22 Random sampling is crucial to allow for an accurate prediction. Random sampling, however, requires that selection effects can largely be eliminated.[32] Suppose a procurement agency wants to minimize the probability of cost overruns in a public infrastructure project to award a public contract 'on the most economically advantageous tender' under Article 67(1) of the EU Procurement Directive 2014/24/EU. If the algorithm used to predict the risk of cost overruns is trained on data of past cost overruns, the prediction will not be generalizable.

23 The reason is that data on past cost overruns only consider firms that submitted a bid in the procurement procedure and were awarded the project. Those who were not awarded the project and those who did not submit a bid will not be considered; the data is contaminated by a selection effect. If past non-winning bidders substantively differ from past winning bidders on some dimension, the machine learning algorithm will fail to make an accurate prediction for bidders sharing the characteristics of past non-winning bidders. In such cases, the risk of violating equality rights is particularly high, since those sharing the characteristics of past non-winning bidders will likely not be considered in the procurement procedure, even if their risk of overrunning costs is in fact lower.[33]

---

[32] Berk (2017), pp. 159 et seq.
[33] For a related argument, see Barocas and Selbst (2016), pp. 677 et seq.

Similar problems may arise when some observations are not considered because   24
some data is missing or when the administrative agency that generated the training
data consisted of biased civil servants.[34] Missing observations can be a problem if
they are tied with some rare characteristics. Even when only a relatively small
number of observations displaying these characteristics are excluded, the prediction
will not be generalizable.

The Bias-Variance-Tradeoff and Bias Aversion

While the objective of traditional regression models is to estimate effects rather than   25
goodness of fit, machine learning is usually used to compare different models and
operate a data-driven selection of the model with the best fit. The common feature of
many traditional regression techniques and machine learning is that they minimize
some kind of error. Traditionally, the ordinary least squares (OLS) method is used to
estimate the unknown parameters in linear regression models.[35] With respect to
machine learning (e.g. random forests, neural networks, deep learning), an algorithm
is trained on data in order to minimize an *objective function*, also called *loss function*.
The objective function denotes a formal expression of accuracy.[36] On a legal view, it
would be fatal to simply accept the objective function as given. In fact, the choices
made to define the objective function are fundamentally normative. They require
value judgements that should be subject to legislative, administrative or judicial
scrutiny.

On the one hand, the objective function maps the *variance* of the estimator.   26
Metaphorically, variance is a measure of how scattered the shots are on a target.[37] On
the other hand, the objective function considers *bias*. Metaphorically, bias is a
measure of how far off the average shot is from the center of a target that represents
the true value.[38] The degree of variance and bias in a model will not only determine
the fit of the model but also the risk of overfitting. In case of overfitting, the model
will respond flexibly to idiosyncratic features in the data set at hand (e.g. predict with
an accuracy of 100% on the training data), but predictions will not be generalizable
to a different and unknown sample (e.g. predict with the accuracy of a coin toss on
the test data). While overfitting is a problem for any kind of econometric analysis,
machine learning is particularly prone to the risk of overfitting.

When a linear model is estimated using OLS, the risk of overfitting is usually low,   27
since the number of observations n is usually relatively high compared to the number

---

[34] Lehr and Ohm (2017), pp. 681–683; Joh (2017), pp. 290 et seq.

[35] For a formal description, see Appendix A.1.

[36] For a formal description, see Appendix A.2.

[37] For a formal description, see Appendix A.3. Also see Ramasubramanian and Singh (2017), p. 489.

[38] For a formal description, see Appendix A.4. Also see Ramasubramanian and Singh (2017), p. 489.

of features or dimensions p measured per individual ($n > p$). The sparsity of the model used to analyze the data (e.g. experimental data) works against overfitting if the sample is sufficiently large. With machine learning, however, the risk of overfitting is often not negligible. The reason is that the number of features and dimensions used by machine learning algorithms typically exceeds the number of observations ($p > n$). In that case, the in-sample-prediction is likely to fit very well. The out-of-sample prediction, however, may be way off.

28 The reason for this problem is related to a phenomenon often referred to as the curse of dimensionality.[39] Machine learning models are rich and thus include many variables and interactions.[40] A correct generalization gets exponentially more difficult as the number of dimensions grows more rapidly than sample size. The more dimensions the input variables have, the less variance can be explained by each single input variable, especially if all input variables are correlated. And the higher the number of variables processed by the algorithm, the bigger the sample size required or the higher the need for dimensionality reduction. If $p > n$, a dimensionality reduction is indispensable to obtain a generalizable estimate.

29 On a normative view, this analysis shows that meaningful prediction requires simplification. This simplification process is normative, since there is no econometric logic for reducing the model on some dimensions rather than others. It is a choice about those dimensions that are seen as *irrelevant* when making a prediction, and if administrative law compels administrative agencies to ignore some dimensions, these prescriptions should be reflected in the process of dimensionality reduction. Dimensionality reduction notwithstanding, the administrative agency using a machine learning algorithm needs to make the model simpler, but not too simple. In fact, it is not possible to optimize the predictive model for sparsity, since minimizing the loss function requires a bias-variance-tradeoff: a tradeoff between the sparsity of the model and its fit.[41] On the one hand, as the model gets richer in parameters, the bias declines, but the variance and the risk of overfitting increase. On the other hand, as the model gets sparser, the variance declines, but the bias and the risk of failure to generalize increase.

30 Intuition may push some lawyers to argue in favor of preventing bias at all cost, even if this implies an increase of variance. Since administrative lawyers are trained and even compelled to assess the singularities of each individual case, they may be 'overfitters' by *déformation professionelle*.[42] The argument may be that it is better to

---

[39]Domingos (2012), p. 81.

[40]Note, however, that we should be careful with general statements about the properties of machine learning algorithms. Some machine learning algorithms have low bias, but high variance (decision trees, k-nearest neighbors, support vector machines). Other models used in machine learning generate outcomes with high bias, but low variance (linear regression, logistic regression, linear discriminant analysis).

[41]Athey (2018), p. 4; Ramasubramanian and Singh (2017), pp. 488–492; Domingos (2012), pp. 80–81; Lehr and Ohm (2017), p. 697.

[42]Camerer (2018), p. 18, states more generally that 'people do not like to *explicitly* throw away information.'

be inconsistently entirely right than consistently somewhat wrong. To support this argument, one might claim that on average even a model with higher variance can be expected to make useful predictions.

This intuition is based on what I call *bias aversion*. There are good normative reasons to fear bias, particularly so when it coincides with discrimination based on illegal characteristics.[43] The problem, however, is that if the administration optimizes for low bias, there is a risk of failure to generalize.[44] In this case, too much weight would be put on variation in the data and accurate predictions would become difficult. The guesswork required to decide unknown (out-of sample) cases would then increase, calling into doubt the usefulness of machine-based predictions. If no other data sets are available, what matters is the performance of the machine learning algorithm on the *available* data. But if an administrative agency wants to predict unknown cases, it indeed faces a severe problem: it cannot obtain the best general prediction for *unknown* data and entirely minimize the risk of discrimination at the same time.

There are several methods to tackle the bias-variance-tradeoff.[45] In Random Forests, for example, replications of the initial training data are created by using random selection with replacement (resampling of trees).[46] At the end of a specified number of iterations, the results of all replications are averaged in order to asymptotically reduce variance.[47] A related technique to counter the curse of dimensionality is feature selection.[48] The goal of feature selection is to reduce the risk of overfitting without sacrificing the accuracy of the prediction. The underlying idea is to reduce the set of variables up to the point where a further reduction would also entail a reduction of predictive power.[49] The prediction thus contains as little noise due to correlations in variables as possible.

How should administrative law cope with these problems? Administrative agencies are bound by statutory law and fundamental rights. The choices that need to be made when addressing the aforementioned tradeoffs have immediate normative implications. Therefore, it is not enough if the aforementioned tradeoffs are addressed by computer scientists without further legal guidance. Administrative agencies carry a legal responsibility to take part in defining objective functions, restricting the set of input variables and reducing the set of dimensions to be used.[50]

---

[43] See Tischbirek.
[44] For a similar argument, see Lehr and Ohm (2017), p. 714.
[45] These methods include: cross-validation, see Berk (2017), pp. 33 et seq.; pruning in classification and regression trees (CART), see Berk (2017), pp. 157 et seq.; Random Forests, a method that relies on bagging or boosting, see Lehr and Ohm (2017), pp. 699–701. The latter technique resembles bootstrapping, a procedure used under more conventional types of econometric analyses.
[46] Berk (2017), pp. 205 et seq.
[47] Lehr and Ohm (2017), pp. 693–694; Berk (2017), pp. 187 et seq., 195–196.
[48] Alpaydin (2014), pp. 109 et seq.; in the legal context, see Barocas and Selbst (2016), pp. 688–692.
[49] Lehr and Ohm (2017), pp. 700–701.
[50] Thanks to Krishna Gummadi for his insights on the definition of objective functions. Hildebrandt (2018), p. 30, argues that lawyers should 'speak law to the power of statistics.'

33   Two arguments support this view. First, civil servants are likely to have superior knowledge about typical cases, contexts, institutions and the law.[51] This knowledge is required to design machine-learning systems that are tailored to the needs of administrative agencies and the restrictions of the law, for example those falling within the scope of equality rights and antidiscrimination laws. Second, *ex ante* monitoring of algorithmic design will prevent administrative agencies from too many *ex post* corrections of machine-based predictions, thus reducing the risk of disparate treatment through the backdoor of correction.

3.2 *Counterfactual Reasoning*

34   Machine learning algorithms entail two distinct, but related problems of incomplete or asymmetric information. The first relates to the lack of knowledge about how machine learning algorithms fare in comparison to human judgement. The second relates to the lack of information about the reasons why a prediction or decision was made, on what factual grounds it can be contested and how behavior may be changed to alter future decisions.

Experimental Administration

35   It is usually unknown whether machine learning algorithms generate more or less bias than human discretion when making legal decisions. Consider the case of bail decisions under US criminal law.[52] Assume that it is known that some defendants were arrested. What is not known is whether they would have committed a crime or fled if they had been released. It may well be that judges observe characteristics that the algorithm does not observe and only arrest a subset of persons with these characteristics. Hence, there is no access to the counterfactual where the machine learning algorithm releases the defendant, but the judge would not.

36   Do machine-based predictions cause a difference in legal decision making as compared to human judgement? A potential answer can be found in randomization. One solution is to exploit the close-to-random assignment of defendants to judges and compare the decisions of lenient and strict judges with the outcome of the machine learning algorithm.[53] The objective of this technique is to determine the marginal impact of the machine learning algorithm using a counterfactual scenario. This comparison requires to determine the subgroup of persons that would be treated differently (marginal group)—most persons will be treated the same way

---

[51]For a related argument, see Lehr and Ohm (2017), p. 675.
[52]Kleinberg et al. (2018).
[53]See Kleinberg et al. (2018), pp. 255 et seq.; for a similar method, see Amaranto et al. (2018).

(non-marginal group)—under a different intervention (counterfactual).[54] In such cases, supervised machine learning can even reduce bias that is observable in the training data collected from human decisions if there is a sufficient level of inconsistency and noise in the data.[55]

The problem is that close-to-random assignment will often not be available to administrative agencies. Consider the case of unreliability in German public business law.[56] The administration may choose to either tackle the risks associated with an unreliable business person and intervene or not do anything. If the intervention is based on machine learning, we only observe the machine-based outcome Y_M, but we do not know the hypothetical and alternative human-based outcome Y_H.

In such cases, other techniques are needed to measure the percentage and distribution of decisions that would have been different (e.g. more accurate or more biased) if the decision had been based on human judgement rather than machine learning. One solution is to replace machine learning with human judgement randomly for a sufficiently large sample. The administrative agency would *randomly* determine a group of persons that would be tackled by the administrative intervention if the decision was machine-based and apply human judgement to them instead. Such a counterfactual comparison would enable the agency to measure the impact of the covariates that drive the differences between human judgement and machine learning and affect the marginal business person.

Some lawyers might argue that this idea of 'experimental administration' is incompatible with equality rights. This argument, however, seems flawed: Assume that human civil servants discriminate between legally prohibited categories, such as race. If it is *ex ante* unknown whether there is a difference between machine-based decisions and human decisions, and if the only sound way of eliciting such a difference is randomization, equality rights may even require a random assignment to administrative interventions. Of course, experimental administration requires careful handling and circumspect tests in areas where the disparate impact of differential treatment can be considered as harmless.

Pseudo-Causal Explanations

Citizens often do not and cannot know what the machine learning algorithm does, how it generates predictions and why. In that regard, claims for transparency of the machine learning algorithm, its functional form, variables and parameters go somewhat astray. Nobody, not even developers of machine learning algorithms, could understand the precise inner workings of the respective algorithms. This type of transparency would be merely formal and useless, even more so for lay persons.

---

[54]Pearl and Mackenzie (2018), pp. 362 et seq.; Bottou et al. (2013).
[55]Cowgill and Tucker (2017), p. 2.
[56]§ 35(1) GewO—Gewerbeordnung.

41 Many scholars have therefore developed arguments in favor of interpretable machine learning.[57] Proposals to provide counterfactual explanations without opening the black box go in a similar direction.[58] The idea is to grant citizens a right to explanation (cf. Recital 71 EU-GDPR) without disclosing information about the training data or impinging on the secrecy of the algorithm. Given that someone displays a characteristic x_i, a counterfactual explanation would take the form: 'The outcome Y was generated, because you display characteristic x_i. If you displayed characteristic $\neg x_i$, the outcome Y' would be generated.' Similar approaches are suggested to establish an alignment of human and machine-based outputs. Under a method called counterfactual faithfulness, the comparison of Y_H and Y_M is used to determine whether $Y_H \sim Y_M$, and only if this is the case and if this result is robust to smaller changes of the covariates, counterfactual faithfulness is established.[59]

42 While these approaches have great merit, they are unlikely to bolster due process rights. First, it is very difficult to know the smallest set of variables that is to be changed in a model to reach a different outcome.[60] Even if such a closest possible different state of the world can be determined, the corresponding information will often not be helpful for citizens, for example, if it only refers to immutable characteristics—variables that cannot be influenced through behavior—or if an exogenous change of the relevant variable is unforeseeable. Second, counterfactual explanations do not provide useful information about the structural differences between two different administrative decision-making techniques.[61] A single observation does not enable citizens to determine what the marginal group exactly is. It is possible, for example, that some machine learning algorithms put negative weight on certain characteristics, but that human judgement puts even more weight on them.[62] In such cases, counterfactual explanations may trigger misleading intuitions and induce citizens to refrain from litigation where it would be legally appropriate, and vice versa.

43 Lawmakers should consider specific rules compelling the administration to make counterfactual assessments in the initial phase of a new machine learning rollout. The objective of such rules should be to partly compensate the transparency deficits resulting from the impossibility to disclose the algorithmic specifications in a meaningful way. In addition, the deficits in transparency might be compensated through accountable supervisory bodies.

---

[57] Selbst and Barocas (2018), pp. 1099 et seq.; Doshi-Velez and Kim (2017).
[58] Wachter et al. (2017, 2018); for a related approach, see Doshi-Velez and Kortz (2017), pp. 6–9.
[59] Doshi-Velez and Kortz (2017), p. 7.
[60] This is also acknowledged by Wachter et al. (2018), p. 845.
[61] For a related argument, see Cowgill and Tucker (2017), p. 2.
[62] Cowgill (2017).

3.3 Error Weighting

The human mind is fallible. Civil servants make errors. This holds for predictions based on observations, conclusions drawn from predictions, and decisions based on conclusions. But the law contains some general rules telling the administration and courts on which side to err. These legal rules ascribe normative weights to false positives and false negatives, but the problem is that these error weights can only provide a cognitive anchor when applying the law. Despite the fact that human errors and biases may be hard-wired into many data sets currently used, machine learning has the potential to make the administration less error-prone.[63] Specifically, machine learning helps to make human biases or errors more visible and may be accommodated to deal with asymmetric weights that the law puts on specific types of errors.

Suppose an agency wants to decide whether to install CCTV cameras. Assume that the main goal of the intervention is to deter crime and a machine learning algorithm is used to predict the deterrent effect. A false positive error (Type-1-error) occurs when a result indicates that the camera deters, while in fact it does not. A false negative error (Type-2-error) occurs when a result indicates that the camera does not deter, while in fact it does. To assess the accuracy of a prediction, it is sensible to plot the true positive rate $P(D_+|Pr_+)$ and the false positive rate $P(D_-|Pr_+)$ on a Receiver Operating Characteristic Curve.[64] Such methods should be used by administrative agencies to get a sense of the reliability of the prediction.

If confidence in the prediction is established, the machine learning algorithm can be constrained to reflect the normative error weights. While it is not possible to equalize false positive errors and false negative errors across different categories of people (e.g. young and old, male and female), it is possible to put weight on specific types of errors, for example, by assigning a privilege to false negatives or false positives.[65]

Suppose an intelligence service (in charge of *information gathering*) or the police (in charge of *prevention*) have to decide about whether to identify a terrorist sleeper. The agency will need to balance the cost of false negatives against the costs of false positives. The costs of false negatives—failing to identify a sleeper—are likely to be higher than the costs of false positives—wrongly identifying someone as a sleeper. In the law of criminal procedure, a body of law targeted at *repression*, the principles *in dubio pro reo* and the presumption of innocence require the opposite asymmetric cost ratio.

Asymmetric cost ratios can be implemented via a change of the specification of the objective function.[66] They are constraints that can be imposed on the machine learning algorithm.[67] If, for example, the law values false negatives as ten times

---

[63]For a related argument, see Alarie et al. (2017).
[64]For an example, see Talley (2018), pp. 198–199.
[65]Athey (2018), p. 9.
[66]Berk (2017), pp. 147 et seq., pp. 274 et seq.
[67]See Witten et al. (2016), pp. 179–183; see also Lehr and Ohm (2017), p. 692.

more costly than false positives, an asymmetric cost ratio of 10:1 can be imposed as a constraint.[68] As a consequence, the algorithm will penalize false positives and compute the predictions such that for every false positive there are ten false negatives.

49 One of the beneficial properties is that this kind of ratio increases the confidence into a prediction of outcomes when the error to predict this outcome has been penalized. With a false negative/false positive ratio of 10:1, strong evidence is needed to predict the positive outcome, which should increase confidence in a positive prediction.

50 Since asymmetric cost ratios result from a normative judgement, this judgement should be reflected in the practice of administrative law. Embedding this judgement in the algorithm itself has several advantages. First, it makes the normative error weighting visible. Second, it guarantees a uniform application of error weights for decisions targeted at the same categories of persons. Hence, it may allow for more consistent compliance with equality rights.[69] Third, it creates a basis for a much more specific legal discussion about the legally admissible distribution of errors.

3.4 Proportionality

51 Predictions will often not allow for an immediate conclusion as to what should be done under the law. The reason is that the administration faces multidimensional uncertainty. Facing this type of uncertainty, there is no easy way to make a proportionate administrative decision without making further—sometimes strong—assumptions. Under the predominant version of the proportionality principle, an administrative decision has to meet four requirements: (1) it has to pursue a legitimate goal, (2) it has to be adequate to achieve this goal (*adequacy*), (3) it has to be the least restrictive among all equally effective interventions (*necessity*), and (4) its weight may not exceed the weight of the legitimate goal in a balancing operation (*proportionality strictu sensu*).[70]

52 Suppose the administration needs to decide whether to conduct an inspection of a restaurant under public health law.[71] Assume that a machine-based prediction of the probability of non-compliance is available.[72] The mere prediction only allows for the normative conclusion that control is warranted. Under administrative law, *discretion*

---

[68]For an application to predictions of domestic violence, see Berk et al. (2016), pp. 103–104.

[69]Article 3 GG—Grundgesetz; Article 21 EU Charter of Fundamental Rights.

[70]For a discussion, see Petersen (2013). Note that *necessity* can be seen as a version of pareto-efficiency: the administration is not authorized to pick a measure that makes the population worse off than another equally effective measure.

[71]§ 22(1), (2) GastG—Gaststättengesetz.

[72]Kang et al. (2013) use Yelp reviews for Seattle restaurants over the period from 2006 to 2013.

to act (*Entschließungsermessen*) would be reduced: The administration would be compelled to do something.

However, the prediction does not allow for a conclusion as to what the agency should do, that is, how *instrumental discretion* (*Handlungsermessen*) should be exercised to meet the requirements of the proportionality principle. In the example above, the administrative agency may intervene based on the assumption that the behavior of the controlled entity remains constant over time and that the costs of the administrative intervention are homogeneous across all entities.[73] Unobserved or patterned heterogeneity in the population, however, pose a real challenge for the proportionality principle.

Suppose that a machine learning algorithm classifies a single entity as high-risk and ten entities as low-risk. Assume that all risks are additive and that the potential harm resulting from the sum of high-risk entities exceeds the potential harm from the single low-risk entity. Restricting the administrative intervention to the high-risk entity could hardly be proportionate if the costs or the intensity of the intervention against the high risk entity largely exceeded the costs or intensity of the intervention against the low-risk entities. Structurally, this resembles the problems faced by companies when managing the risk of customer churn. The identification of customers with a high risk of churning does not warrant the conclusion that targeting these customers is an effective remedy against churn.[74]

These considerations shed light on an important pitfall when applying the proportionality principle: a discrepancy between the heterogeneity of identified risks and the heterogeneity in behavioral responses to the administrative interventions used to address the risks. This kind of *layered heterogeneity* poses puzzling normative problems, especially fairness problems. If an administrative agency identifies entities posing a high risk, this does not necessarily imply that the administrative intervention should be addressed against any of these entities. Instead, according to the necessity requirement of the proportionality principle, the intervention should probably target those entities that are most sensitive to the intervention and most likely to change their behavior.[75] But of course, considering *sensitivity* to the intervention rather than *causation* of the risk as the legally decisive variable, is likely to trigger unfair interventions.[76] Administrative agencies need to consider this problem when deciding what to do (*Handlungsermessen*) and whom to target (*Störerauswahlermessen*).

---

[73] For a discussion of the problem, see Athey (2017), p. 484.

[74] Ascarza (2018).

[75] For a similar conclusion in a different context, see Ascarza (2018), p. 2.

[76] Consider a small group of high-risk persons (e.g. engaging in grand corruption) who are non-sensitive to an intervention and a large group of low-risk persons (e.g. engaging in petty corruption) who are sensitive to an intervention. Is it proportionate to intervene against the latter only if the purpose of the intervention is to reduce the total amount of risks (e.g. the social costs of corruption)? To the best of my knowledge, this problem has not been analyzed systematically, neither in cost-benefit analysis nor in public law doctrine.

56	This relates to a deeper normative problem arising from the potential mismatch between the specification of the variables used by machine learning algorithms, the predictive goals, and the normative goals embedded in administrative law. In the restaurants case, for example, it is very difficult to directly measure health risks. Instead, a proxy outcome variable is needed. The level of confidence in the prediction will then depend on the plausibility of specific causal assumptions. If past inspections are used to predict health risks, an implicit assumption would be that the assessment of health risks by the administration reflects the condition of the restaurant and not the condition of the civil servant.[77] If causes cannot be empirically identified, there is a risk of falling prey to fatal errors when making the adequacy assessment required by the proportionality principle.
57	Consider the question whether search-based sales ads work. One of the approaches is to predict sales through clicks. For eBay, return on investment, measured by the ratio of sales due to clicks and the cost of clicks, was estimated to 1400% under this approach. Using a *difference-in-difference approach* and the comparison of a treatment group with a control group of cities,[78] a recent study suggests that return on investment is—63%.[79] The choice of a *prima facie* plausible proxy variable obfuscates the truth of reverse causality: Users do not purchase because they click, but click because they are intent on purchasing. The problem is that the identification of causes rests on the parallel trend assumption—the assumption that the difference between the control group and the treatment group is constant over time.
58	One method used to overcome these shortcomings is the *instrumental variables approach*.[80] Under this method, no random assignment to treatment X is needed. Instead, it is sufficient if another variable—the instrumental variable I—has a monotonic effect on the independent variable X (*montonicity assumption*) and if I is not correlated with the dependent variable Y other than through its effect on X (*exclusion restriction*).[81] One of the main problems here is that the exclusion restriction is not testable. It is posited as an assumption of being exogenous. Since most variables used to prepare an administrative decision are likely to be somehow interdependent, the exclusion restriction is unlikely to be met.
59	This shows that the causality-related questions prompted by the proportionality principle cannot be solved on purely empirical or machine-based grounds. Some

---

[77] For a related argument, see Ho (2017), p. 32; Joh (2017), pp. 290 et seq.

[78] The difference-in-difference approach compares the average change of an output variable for an untreated group over a specified period and the average change of an output variable for a treatment group over a specified period.

[79] Blake et al. (2015); for a discussion of the diff-in diff approach in the legal context, see Spamann (2015), pp. 140–141.

[80] This approach is used when random assignment—a controlled experiment—is not possible to identify a causal relationship between an input variable and an output variable. The instrumental variable has an effect on the input variable but no independent effect on the output variable.

[81] Angrist and Pischke (2009); Spamann (2015), p. 142; for further analysis, see Athey and Imbens (2017), pp. 14–15.

proxy variable has to be chosen, some assumption about the world has to be made. Human-generated mental representations of the world and latent constructs of social phenomena will remain key in the application of administrative law. Administrative agencies will have to die one death in making assumptions, but they will be able to choose which one.

3.5 Gaming

As administrative agencies will increasingly use machine learning algorithms, the law will need to tackle another substantive risk: the risk of gaming (strategic countermeasures). The mechanics underlying the risk of strategic countermeasures are straightforward: Machine learning algorithms can be reverse-engineered.[82] In cases where such a black box reverse-engineering occurs, algorithms become vulnerable to gaming. There is a risk that administrative decisions will become too predictable if they solely rely on machine-generated predictions. While predictability can be considered a virtue under due process principles,[83] it can also hamper the effectiveness of administrative decisions and ultimately work against the public interest.

First, an excess level of predictability may result in the production of counter-information. Automated agents can be used to generate information that feeds into the algorithm used by the administration. Information may be generated through machine learning-based agents or bots programmed by malicious actors in order to distort and bias the output generated by the machine learning-algorithm used by the administration.[84]

Second, too much predictability may result in behavioral adaptation. Predictable predictions and decisions based on such predictions alter strategic incentives. If a person anticipates that she faces a lower probability of being monitored than others she will likely reduce her efforts to comply with the law. Consider the case of the British Columbia Ministry of Forests that wanted to use the bids in timber auctions as a predictor of stumpage fees for long-term public tenures.[85] In such a procedure, licensees have an incentive to engage in strategic bidding and reduce their bids in the auction or their demand for logs from bidders to lower the predicted fees and increase their revenue from stumpage fees.[86]

---

[82]Tramèr et al. (2016).

[83]Article 19(4) GG – Grundgesetz; Article 47 EU Charter of Fundamental Rights.

[84]For a related argument, see Lodge and Mennicken (2017), pp. 4–5.

[85]Athey et al. (2002).

[86]Of course, gaming the system in that case requires collusion, which is rather unlikely when the market is thick or when antitrust law is effectively enforced. For an account of legal remedies against collusion in procurement auctions, see Cerrone et al. (2018).

63 How should such risks be mitigated? The gaming argument rests on the assumption that machine learning is used as a substitute for human administrative decisions, meaning that the outcome of the decision is not blurred by human judgement or noise. When human judgement is involved, predictions will usually be noisy. And noise implies that the prediction is less predictable. These considerations point at a normative tradeoff.

64 Administrative agencies can either opt for consistent prediction and high predictive accuracy embracing a higher vulnerability to gaming. Or they can reduce predictive power by adding human judgement or noise to the decision, thereby maintaining a level of opacity that makes it difficult to game the system. At least for now, the risk of gaming provides an argument against purely machine-based decisions. Human judgement—either through error or intended noise—may increase the level of strategic uncertainty, generate positive compliance effects, and prevent gaming. In the long run, administrative agencies might have to make a choice between waging a war of the algorithms with the private sector or adding grains of human salt when making decisions under risk and uncertainty.

3.6 Complexity

65 When facing complex constraints, administrative agencies usually make their decision based on some kind of heuristic that works reasonably well. While administrative courts exercise some control over such decisions in some areas of the law, they usually grant a margin of appreciation to administrative agencies. The main reason for judicial self-restraint may be the lack of technical expertise within administrative courts and the irresolvable uncertainty in some technical areas of the law. This kind of uncertainty often involves complex combinatorial optimization problems—such as the allocation of spectrum in telecommunications law—or uncertainty about the population subject to administrative decisions. These are the areas where machine learning will probably most sharply reduce the scope of human discretion.

66 Machine learning can and should be used by administrative agencies to solve very complex problems, especially a class of problems called NP-complete or NP-hard.[87] P denotes the general class of problems that can be solved by an algorithm in polynomial time; these problems can be *solved* easily. NP denotes the general class of problems that can be verified in polynomial time once they are solved; these problems can be *verified* easily.[88] A problem p in P is NP-complete if every other problem s in NP can be reduced to p in polynomial time. If $P \neq NP$, there are problems that are more difficult to solve than to verify.

67 NP-hard problems can be exemplified with the traveling salesman problem: A number of cities and the distance between each of them are known. What is the

---

[87] For an introduction to the P versus NP problem, see Fortnow (2009).
[88] NP stands for *nondeterministic polynomial time*.

shortest route that allows for a stop at each city and links the point of departure with the point of arrival? Simple heuristics or *greedy algorithms* of the kind 'Go to the closest city next' cannot optimally minimize the length of the route. The FCC faced a similar NP-complete problem when implementing the reallocation of spectrum in the 2012 reverse incentive auction.[89] The major constraint was that pairs of close stations cannot be assigned the same frequency without creating broadcast interference.[90] If the efficient allocation of scarce frequencies is defined as a goal of telecommunications law, machine learning will likely reduce discretion in the design of allocation mechanisms.[91]

Similarly complex problems arise when refugees need to be assigned to resettlement locations. A combination of machine learning and optimal matching algorithms can be used to maximize the likelihood of integration (e.g. measured by employment probabilities) even under burden-sharing constraints in a federal state.[92]

The legal conclusion is not that such systems should replace human judgement. Yet they may be used as micro-directives guiding the exercise of administrative discretion and the definition of property rights. Administrative agencies might be compelled to justify decisions overriding the machine-based solution. In addition, machine learning will reduce the uncertainty about the population to be addressed in complex procedures. For example, one problem in the design of revenue-maximizing auctions is that the corresponding models simply assume that the bidders' valuations are drawn from some known probability distribution.[93] When implementing a procurement auction, most administrative agencies will usually not have access to this kind of information. If some information about bidders is available and the sample is sufficiently large, machine learning can be used to predict information about unknown bidders and conduct a procurement procedure that minimizes public expenditures.[94] In the long run, this could reduce civil servants' incentives to maximize their budget out of mere precaution and induce a more efficient allocation of public resources.

4 Conclusion

In this article, I have shed light on the potential and pitfalls that administrative agencies will need to consider when using machine learning in support of their decisions. Can machine learning be used to improve administrative decisions under

---

[89]Milgrom and Tadelis (2019); Milgrom (2017), pp. 26 et seq.; Leyton-Brown et al. (2017).
[90]Milgrom (2017), pp. 33–37.
[91]For an overview of §§ 55(10), 61(4) TKG—Telekommunikationsgesetz, see Eifert (2012), paras 113 et seq.
[92]Bansak et al. (2018).
[93]Balcan et al. (2005).
[94]For such an approach, see Feng et al. (2018).

uncertainty? Yes, it can. On a normative view, it probably should be used, since it has the potential to improve the quality of predictions and reduce human biases. But neither the pitfalls I have discussed nor human judgement should be left out of the equation. At least for now, human judgement in administrative agencies has an important function. The use of machine learning algorithms requires normative decisions that should not be decided upon by computer scientists. As I have shown, administrative discretion can even be seen as a prerequisite for a sensible implementation of machine learning. Since a sensible use of machine learning requires tremendous technical expertise it should be used very carefully and be subject to democratic or judicial scrutiny.

As far as supervised machine learning is concerned, an important administrative task will be to supervise the training phase and embed basic normative constraints in the objective functions used by machine learning algorithms. Administrative agencies will need to conduct a process of conceptual disambiguation in order to bridge the gap between technology and legal doctrine. Machines are just as good as their input. Humans in administrative agencies are one of the main sources of their input. The democracy principle will require technology-sensitive legal rules to steer these inputs and push the cognitive boundaries of administrative decision making.

Appendix

1. An ordinary least squares regression takes the functional form:

$$y_i = \beta_0 + \beta_1 x_{1i} + \ldots + \beta_n x_{ni} + \varepsilon_i$$

2. The objective function usually used for regression algorithms is to minimize the mean squared error (MSE) between the vector of observed values Y_i and the vector of predicted values $\widehat{Y}_i$ given a set of n observations:

$$MSE = \frac{1}{n} \sum_{i=1}^{n} \left(Y_i - \widehat{Y}_i\right)^2$$

The closer MSE is to zero, the higher the accuracy of the predictor.

3. Technically, variance describes the difference between estimates of a value in one sample from the expected average estimate of the value if the algorithm were retrained on other data sets:

$$V = E\left[\left(\widehat{f}(x) - E\left[\widehat{f}(x)\right]\right)^2\right]$$

4. Technically, bias is the difference between the expected average prediction of the machine learning and the true value that the model is intended to predict:

$$B = E\left[\widehat{f}(x) - f(x)\right]$$

References

Alarie B, Niblett A, Yoon A (2017) Regulation by machine. J Mach Learn Res W&CP:1–7
Alarie B, Niblett A, Yoon A (2018) How artificial intelligence will affect the practice of law. Univ Toronto Law J 68(Supplement 1):106–124
Alpaydin E (2014) Introduction to machine learning, 3rd edn. MIT Press, Cambridge
Amaranto D et al (2018) Algorithms as prosecutors: lowering rearrest rates without disparate impacts and identifying defendant characteristics 'Noisy' to human decision-makers. Working Paper, January 28, 2018
Angrist J, Pischke J-S (2009) Mostly harmless econometrics. Princeton University Press, Princeton
Ascarza E (2018) Retention futility: targeting high-risk customers might be ineffective. J Market Res 55:80–98
Athey S (2017) Beyond prediction: using big data for policy problems. Science 355:483–485
Athey S (2018) The impact of machine learning on economics. Working Paper, January 2018
Athey S, Imbens GW (2017) The state of applied econometrics: causality and policy evaluation. J Econ Perspect 31:3–32
Athey S, Cramton P, Ingraham A (2002) Auction-based timber pricing and complementary market reforms in British Columbia. Manuscript, 5 March 2002
Baker T, Harel A, Kugler T (2004) The virtues of uncertainty in law: an experimental approach. Iowa Law Rev 89:443–487
Balcan MF et al (2005) Mechanism design via machine learning. In: Proceedings of the 46th Annual IEEE Symposium on Foundations of Computer Science, pp 605–614
Bansak K et al (2018) Improving refugee integration through data-driven algorithmic assignment. Science 359:325–329
Barocas S, Selbst AD (2016) Big data's disparate impact. Calif Law Rev 104:671–732
Berk RA (2017) Statistical learning from a regression perspective, 2nd edn. Springer International, Basel
Berk RA, Sorenson SB, Barnes G (2016) Forecasting domestic violence: a machine learning approach to help inform arraignment decisions. J Empir Legal Stud 13:94–115
Blake T, Nosko C, Tadelis S (2015) Consumer heterogeneity and paid search effectiveness: a large-scale field experiment. Econometrica 83:155–174
Bottou L et al (2013) Counterfactual reasoning and learning systems: the example of computational advertising. J Mach Learn Res 14:3207–3260
Buchanan BG, Headrick TE (1970) Some speculation about artificial intelligence and legal reasoning. Stanf Law Rev 23:40–62
Camerer CF (2018) Artificial intelligence and behavioral economics. In: Agrawal AK, Gans J, Goldfarb A (eds) The economics of artificial intelligence: an agenda. University of Chicago Press, Chicago
Cerrone C, Hermstrüwer Y, Robalo P (2018) Debarment and collusion in procurement auctions. Discussion papers of the Max Planck Institute for Research on Collective Goods Bonn 2018/5
Citron DK, Pasquale F (2014) The scored society: due process for automated predictions. Washington Law Rev 89:1–33

Coglianese C, Lehr D (2017) Regulating by robot: administrative decision making in the machine-learning era. Georgetown Law J 105:1147–1223

Cowgill B (2017) Automating judgement and decisionmaking: theory and evidence from résumé screening. Working Paper, May 5, 2017

Cowgill B, Tucker C (2017) Algorithmic bias: a counterfactual perspective. Working paper: NSF Trustworthy Algorithms, December 2017

Cuéllar MF (2016) Cyberdelegation and the administrative state. Stanford Public Law Working Paper No. 2754385

Domingos P (2012) A few useful things to know about machine learning. Commun ACM 55:78–87

Doshi-Velez F, Kim B (2017) Towards a rigorous science of interpretable machine learning. Working Paper, March 2, 2017

Doshi-Velez F, Kortz M (2017) Accountability of AI under the law: the role of explanation. Working Paper, November 21, 2017

Dworkin RM (1965) Philosophy, morality and law – observations prompted by Professor Fuller's Novel Claim. Univ Pa Law Rev 113:668–690

Ehlers D (2012) § 20 Gaststättenrecht. In: Ehlers D, Fehling M, Pünder H (eds) Besonderes Verwaltungsrecht, Bd. 1, Öffentliches Wirtschaftsrecht. C.F. Müller, Heidelberg

Eifert M (2012) § 23 Telekommunikation. In: Ehlers D, Fehling M, Pünder H (eds) Besonderes Verwaltungsrecht, Bd. 1, Öffentliches Wirtschaftsrecht. C.F. Müller, Heidelberg

Feng Z, Narasimhan H, Parkes DC (2018) Deep learning for revenue-optimal auctions with budgets. In: Proceedings of the 17th International Conference on Autonomous Agents and Multiagent Systems (AAMAS 2018), pp 354–362

Fortnow L (2009) The status of the P versus NP problem. Commun ACM 52:78–86

Hildebrandt M (2018) Law as computation in the era of artificial legal intelligence: speaking law to the power of statistics. Univ Toronto Law J 68(Supplement 1):12–35

Ho DE (2017) Does peer review work? An experiment of experimentalism. Stanf Law Rev 69:1–119

Hogan-Doran D (2017) Computer says "no": automation, algorithms and artificial intelligence in Government decision-making. Judicial Rev 13:1–39

Joh EE (2017) Feeding the machine: policing, crime data, & algorithms. William Mary Bill Rights J 26:287–302

Kang JS et al (2013) Where not to eat? Improving public policy by predicting hygiene inspections using online reviews. In: Proceedings of the 2013 conference on empirical methods in natural language processing, pp 1443–1448

Kleinberg J et al (2018) Machine learning and human decisions. Q J Econ 133:237–293

Knight F (1921) Risk, uncertainty and profit. Houghton Mifflin, Boston

Lehr D, Ohm P (2017) Playing with the data: what legal scholars should learn about machine learning. UC Davis Law Rev 51:653–717

Leyton-Brown K, Milgrom P, Segal I (2017) Economics and computer science of a radio spectrum reallocation. PNAS 114:7202–7209

Lodge M, Mennicken A (2017) The importance of regulation of and by algorithm. In: Andrews L et al (eds) Algorithmic regulation. London School of Economics and Political Science, London, Discussion Paper 85:2–6

Marcks P (2018) § 35 GewO. In: Landmann/Rohmer (ed) Gewerbeordnung, 78th edn. C.H. Beck, München

Milgrom P (2017) Discovering prices: auction design in markets with complex constraints. Columbia University Press, New York

Milgrom PR, Tadelis S (2019) How artificial intelligence and machine learning can impact market design. In: Agrawal AK, Gans J, Goldfarb A (eds) The economics of artificial intelligence: an agenda. University of Chicago Press, Chicago

Parkes DC, Wellman MP (2015) Economic reasoning and artificial intelligence. Science 349:267–272

Pasquale F (2015) The Black Box Society: the secret algorithms that control money and information. Harvard University Press, Cambridge
Pasquale F (2018) New economic analysis of law: beyond technocracy and market design. Crit Anal Law 5:1–18
Pearl J, Mackenzie D (2018) The book of why: the new science of cause and effect. Basic Books, New York
Petersen N (2013) How to compare the length of lines to the weight of stones: balancing and the resolution of value conflicts in constitutional law. German Law J 14:1387–1408
Poscher R (2008) Eingriffsschwellen im Recht der inneren Sicherheit. Die Verwaltung 41:345–373
Ramasubramanian K, Singh A (2017) Machine learning using R. APress, New York
Selbst AD, Barocas S (2018) The intuitive appeal of explainable machines. Fordham Law Rev 87:1085–1139
Simon HA (1955) A behavioral model of rational choice. Q J Econ 69:99–118
Simon HA (1997) Administrative behavior: a study of decision-making processes in administrative organizations, 4th edn. The Free Press, New York
Spamann H (2015) Empirical comparative law. Ann Rev Law Soc Sci 11:131–153
Spamann H, Klöhn L (2016) Justice is less blind, and less legalistic, than we thought. J Legal Stud 45:255–280
Sunstein CR (2001) Of artificial intelligence and legal reasoning. Univ Chicago Law School Roundtable 8:29–35
Sunstein CR (2018) The cost-benefit revolution. MIT Press, Cambridge
Talley EL (2018) Is the future of law a driverless car?: Assessing how the data-analytics revolution will transform legal practice. J Inst Theor Econ 174:183–205
Tramèr F et al (2016) Stealing machine learning models via prediction APIs. In: Proceedings of the 25th USENIX security symposium, pp 601–618
Vermeule A (2015) Rationally arbitrary decisions in administrative law. J Legal Stud 44:S475–S507
von Neumann J, Morgenstern O (1944) Theory of games and economic behavior. Princeton University Press, Princeton
Wachter S, Mittelstadt B, Floridi L (2017) Why a right to explanation of automated decisionmaking does not exist in the general data protection regulation. Int Data Priv Law 7:76–99
Wachter S, Mittelstadt B, Russell C (2018) Counterfactual explanations without opening the Black Box: automated decisions and the GDPR. Harv J Law Technol 31:841–887
Wischmeyer T (2018) Regulierung intelligenter Systeme. Archiv des öffentlichen Rechts 143:1–66
Witten IH et al (2016) Data mining: practical machine learning tools and techniques, 4th edn. Elsevier, Amsterdam

Artificial Intelligence and Law Enforcement

Timo Rademacher

Contents

1 Introduction: Smart Law Enforcement 226
2 The Status Quo of Smart Law Enforcement 227
   2.1 'Watching' 227
   2.2 'Reading' 229
   2.3 'Listening' 231
   2.4 'Smelling' 231
   2.5 ... Everywhere, Always, and Remembering It All 232
3 Constitutional Frameworks 232
   3.1 Germany 233
   3.2 European Union 236
   3.3 United States 238
4 Three Core Issues 241
   4.1 A Challenge: State-of-the-Art Information or Undemocratic In-Formation? 243
   4.2 A Chance: Biased Enforcement or Transparent Biases? 246
   4.3 A Choice: Human or 'Perfect' Enforcement of the Law? 247
5 Conclusion 250
References 250

Abstract Artificial intelligence is increasingly able to autonomously detect suspicious activities ('smart' law enforcement). In certain domains, technology already fulfills the task of detecting suspicious activities better than human police officers ever could. In such areas, i.e. if and where smart law enforcement technologies actually work well enough, legislators and law enforcement agencies should consider their use. Unfortunately, the German Constitutional Court, the European Court of Justice, and the US Supreme Court are all struggling to develop convincing and clear-cut guidelines to direct these legislative and administrative considerations. This article attempts to offer such guidance: First, lawmakers need to implement regulatory provisions in order to maintain human accountability if AI-based law enforcement technologies are to be used. Secondly, AI law enforcement should be used, if

T. Rademacher (✉)
Faculty of Law, University of Hannover, Hannover, Germany
e-mail: timo.rademacher@jura.uni-freiburg.de

and where possible, to overcome discriminatory traits in human policing that have plagued some jurisdictions for decades. Finally, given that smart law enforcement promises an ever more effective and even ubiquitous enforcement of the law—a 'perfect' rule of law, in that sense—it invites us as democratic societies to decide if, where, and when we might wish to preserve the freedom to disobey the rule(s) of law.

1 Introduction: Smart Law Enforcement

The police are trying to get 'smarter', too. That is to say that police forces and other law enforcement agencies all around the world are trying to enhance their visual capacities, hearing abilities, senses of smell, and their memories by means of AI and big data technologies. The aim of this Chapter is to first give an overview of the status quo of such 'smart' law enforcement technologies as they are applied in Germany, the EU, and the US (Sect. 2).[1] Section 3 will examine the relevant constitutional frameworks in these three jurisdictions and corresponding jurisprudence. This analysis will show that, at least in my opinion, the courts have not yet asked (all) the right questions in order to advise the legal and political discourse on whether or not to use AI for law enforcement purposes. In building on the specific features distinguishing smart law enforcement from human law enforcement, I will attempt, in Sect. 4, to formulate these questions and to also offer some—admittedly preliminary—answers.

Before we turn to the status quo of smart law enforcement, some specific definitions are necessary.[2] For the purpose of this Chapter, I shall define smart law enforcement as the *automated detection of suspicious behavior*. Behavior is *suspicious* in this sense if it indicates, with sufficient accuracy, precision, and probability, that some form of non-compliance with legal rules[3] has occurred, is occurring, or will occur in the future. In the definition of *detecting* I will only include those technologies public authorities deploy to draw attention to previously unrecognized suspicious activities. Not included are those technologies used to merely consolidate suspicion that has already been pre-established by other means.[4] Finally, *automation*

---

[1]In doing so, this Chapter also complements the more specific analyses provided by Buchholtz, Schemmel, paras 32–46, and Braun Binder, paras 16 et seq., on legal tech, financial market regulation, and tax law enforcement, respectively.

[2]For the general definition of artificial intelligence informing this Book cf. Rademacher and Wischmeyer, paras 5–6.

[3]Or some other incident requiring state interference, e.g. an attempted suicide or the identification of a person for whom an arrest warrant is issued.

[4]That excludes more 'traditional' big data technologies such as breathalyzers, field testing kits, or DNA analyses. This definition is similar to the one proposed by Rich (2016), pp. 891–892, who correctly notes that even though '[t]hese traditional technologies can be exceptionally helpful to

means that the respective indications are not detected through human means, i.e. officers patrolling the streets, hearing cries for help, or reading through financial transaction files. Instead, big data technologies are used to identify these indicators. In a first step, these technologies rely on machine learning[5] to detect patterns representative of unlawful conduct from records of past infringements; then, in step two, they apply these patterns to real life, constituting—on an admittedly high level of abstraction—a functional equivalent to a human officer watching, reading, listening, and/or smelling.

2 The Status Quo of Smart Law Enforcement

2.1 'Watching'

While still heavily contested by human rights advocacy groups,[6] the reliability of intelligent video surveillance software appears to have made significant progress in recent years.[7] Law enforcement officials in the US[8] and in the UK are already extensively testing or regularly making use of facial recognition systems in particular.[9] Mostly for historical reasons, Germany is more reluctant to deploy video surveillance, be it 'smart' or not.[10] However, even in Germany, federal police conducted a pilot project at a Berlin train station in 2017/2018. According to the Federal Ministry of the Interior, facial recognition technology passed the test with

---

police in establishing the "historical facts" of what happened', they cannot analyze on their own 'groups of disparate facts together and [draw] conclusions about the probability of an individual' non-compliance. It is the specific feature of smart law enforcement technologies—called 'automated suspicion algorithms' by Rich—that they attempt to apply patterns that are woven with such density that a 'match' qualifies, per se, as indicative of suspicious activity (cf. para 29). Furthermore, the definition also excludes so-called 'impossibility structures', i.e. technology which not only detects suspicious activity, but at a more sophisticated level aims at making illegal conduct physically impossible (cf. Rich 2013, pp. 802–804; see also, with a different terminology, Cheng 2006, p. 664: 'Type II structural controls', Mulligan 2008, p. 3: 'perfect prevention', and Rosenthal 2011, p. 579: 'digital preemption').

[5]Cf., for a definition, in this Book Rademacher and Wischmeyer, and the thorough explanation offered by Rich (2016), pp. 880–886, esp. 883.

[6]See, e.g., Big Brother Watch (2018), pp. 25–33; Chaos Computer Club (2018).

[7]Compare to the technical limitations still described by Candamo et al. (2010), esp. p. 215. For video summarization technologies cf. Thomas et al. (2017).

[8]Ferguson (2017), pp. 88–90.

[9]Big Brother Watch (2018), pp. 25–30; on the current legal framework governing the use of CCTV and comparable surveillance technologies in the UK cf. McKay (2015), paras 5.181 et seq.

[10]The historical sensitivity, of course, translates into a rather restrictive interpretation of constitutional rules when it comes to video surveillance, cf. Wysk (2018), passim; Bier and Spiecker gen Döhmann (2012), pp. 616 et seq., and *infra*, paras 17–18.

'impressive' results.[11] False positives, i.e. alerts falsely indicating a 'hit', are said to be reducible to 0.00018%.[12]

4   Systems of so-called behavior recognition are supposed to detect patterns of suspicious movements, such as an ongoing robbery, drug trafficking, lies,[13] or persons in need of help.[14] A particularly comprehensive system of behavioral recognition called 'Domain Awareness System' appears to be in full operation in New York City.[15] It connects and records video feeds from approximately 9000 CCTV cameras installed across Manhattan and informs officers of—ideally—still ongoing suspicious activities. Officers can then review the video footage that caused the alarm. If the alert proves to be correct, they can intervene in real-time to prevent further harm or damage. As recordings are stored for one month,[16] police may also trace suspects for punitive purposes after infringements have occurred.

5   Ultimately, any other form of image recognition technology constitutes a functional equivalent to human 'watching'. One hotly debated example of *almost* state-ordered use of such technology for the purposes of proactive law enforcement is ex Article 13(1) of the EU's Commission proposal for a new Directive on copyright in the Digital Single Market. The regulation therein expressly encouraged 'information society service providers' to apply 'content recognition technologies' in order 'to prevent the availability' of protected work on service provider websites (upload-filters). However, following successful lobbying by advocacy groups and parts of the media industry, the European Parliament rejected this initiative.[17]

---

[11] Bundesministerium des Innern (2018). But cf. Chaos Computer Club (2018), rebutting the Ministry's optimistic evaluation. Similar RWI (2018).

[12] Bundespolizeipräsidium (2018), p. 35.

[13] The EU-funded iBorderCtrl-project (www.iborderctrl.eu) is testing software that is to detect persons lying at border controls; see, for a first assessment, Algorithm Watch (2019), pp. 36–37.

[14] E.g. Bouachir et al. (2018): video surveillance for real-time detection of suicide attempts.

[15] Davenport (2016); Joh (2014), pp. 48–50; for further examples see Capers (2017), pp. 1271–1273. Comparable systems are being tested in Germany, too, cf. Djeffal, para 9, and Wendt (2018).

[16] Ferguson (2017), p. 86.

[17] In the final version of what is now Directive (EU) 2019/790 the explicit reference to content recognition technologies has been removed (cf. Article 17 of the Directive). If that effectively avoids a de facto obligation on information service providers to apply such filter technologies remains to be seen. For an early discussion of technological means of 'automatic enforcement' see Reidenberg (1998), pp. 559–560. See also Krönke, para 44, who expects a 'de facto obligation' of service providers to apply recognition software.

2.2 'Reading'

In the US, big data technology complements or replaces human officers when it comes to filtering social media posts,[18] police[19] and commercial[20] databases, financial transaction and tax files,[21] as well as metadata from hotline calls requesting help[22] or reporting child abuse.[23] All of these activities are aimed at proactively finding suspicious patterns indicating past, ongoing, or various kinds of future infringements.[24] Particular attention has recently been paid to *place*-based predictive policing, which is used both in the US[25] and in Germany.[26] The term '*place*-based predictive policing' refers to software that 'mines' field reports of past burglaries or car thefts for patterns that—according to criminological theories confirmed by big data analyses—predict future crimes of the same kind ('near-repeats'). Algorithms trained for the task of so-called data mining can be equated with human 'reading' inasmuch as textual data (instead of image data, see paras 3 et seq.) are analyzed.

Again, in contrast to their US counterparts, German legislators are much more hesitant to allow law enforcement agencies to rely on data mining as soon as *person*-based data is analyzed.[27] Informed by the concept of 'informational separation of

---

[18]Ferguson (2017), pp. 114–118. For the Israeli intelligence agencies' reportedly extensive and successful use of social media monitoring in detecting terrorists cf. Associated Press (2018); on terrorism in general see also Pelzer (2018).

[19]Including well-established techniques such as fingerprint and DNA analysis. Cf. for a rather critical overview of 'new' technologies Murphy (2007), pp. 726–744; on more modern projects see Ferguson (2017), pp. 116–118.

[20]Ferguson (2017), p. 118.

[21]Rich (2016), p. 872; for an up-to-date account on that technology see Schemmel, para 32 and Throckmorton (2015), pp. 86–87; on data mining aimed at predicting tax avoidance see Lismont et al. (2018) and Braun Binder and with an example from Australia see Djeffal, para 11.

[22]E.g. the private Polaris Project, which analyzes telephone calls for help in cases of human trafficking, to reveal places, routes, and even financial cash flows worthy of police attention.

[23]See Eubanks (2018), for a critical report on software predicting child abuse tested in Allegheny County; see Spice (2015), reporting on a DARPA funded software to detect sex trafficking by screening online advertisements.

[24]To some extent that includes misconduct within police forces as well, cf. Ferguson (2017), pp. 143–162.

[25]Cf. Ferguson (2017), pp. 63–69. Commercial applications used in the US include HunchLab, Risk Terrain Modelling (RTM, cf. Caplan and Kennedy 2016, and Ferguson 2017, pp. 67–68), and PredPol.

[26]For an up-to-date overview of place-based predictive policing in Germany cf. Seidensticker et al. (2018) and, for a criminological evaluation, Singelnstein (2018), pp. 3–5; for a comprehensive approach, which includes other forms of big data policing, cf. Rademacher (2017), pp. 368–372.

[27]For the constitutional constraints German police has to respect see para 18. A second reason for the German reluctance might also be that big data driven proactive 'rasterizing' proved spectacularly inefficient when German police applied it in the aftermath of 9/11, cf. German Constitutional Court 1 BvR 518/02 'Rasterfahndung' (4 April 2006), BVerfGE 115, pp. 327–331.

powers'[28] (see para 14), German agencies usually store personal data in different data 'silos'. These are established for specific purposes and, in principle, willfully disconnected from one another. Data are deleted as soon as the specific purpose they were collected for has been met. Additionally, German law enforcement agencies rarely make use of social media monitoring, network analysis, and data mining—comparable to the (in)famous Chicago 'Heat List'[29]; all of these being instruments implemented in order to identify individual persons likely to become perpetrators or victims of future crimes. Recently, these limitations on (automated) data sharing and—consequently—data mining have met heavy criticism following several terrorist attacks in Germany. Notably, one incident in Berlin from December 2017 is said to be attributable, in part, to insufficient data sharing between various law enforcement agencies. The *Land* Hesse is the first federal state to have reacted to this criticism by purchasing American intelligence technology.[30] The software, designed and implemented by Palantir Inc., enables police to perform integrated searches on a specific individual across several police databases, including social media data received from US authorities. Even though this form of automated data sharing might indeed mark a significant break with German tradition,[31] it is not a move towards smart law enforcement as defined in this Chapter's second paragraph: AI technology is still used, it appears, merely as an instrument to *consolidate* individual suspicion rather than to detect suspicious activities.

8 Interestingly, the German legislature does not display the same reluctance vis-à-vis person-based data mining performed by private entities for law enforcement purposes. As an example of privately executed, but state ordered big data analysis, one can point to the German Money Laundering Act. It requires banks to monitor any financial transaction for evidence indicating the financing of terrorism activities or money laundering.[32] For further examples of German and EU legislation that, even though not *expressly* requiring private entities to monitor or filter their business activities, will hardly be complied with *without* relying on proactive filter technologies (Krönke, paras 40–42).

9 Taking into account the principle of primacy of EU law, Germany might also have to reconsider, at least in specific fields, its restrictive application of law enforcement agencies' use of pattern analyses. For instance, Article 6(2) lit. c of the EU's Passenger Name Record (PNR) Directive requires EU Member States to

---

[28]Cf. Burkert (2012), p. 101: 'aimed at erecting Chinese walls within the executive'. This conception replaced the former idea of informational 'Einheit der Verwaltung' (executive unity), which prevailed, approximately, until the 1970s, cf. Oldiges (1987), pp. 742–743.

[29]Rather negatively evaluated by Saunders et al. (2016), but reported to have improved significantly since 2015, cf. Ferguson (2017), p. 40.

[30]Brühl (2018). On the federal 'Polizei 2020' program aimed at establishing an integrated database for all German police agencies, cf. Bundesministerium des Innern (2016).

[31]Brühl (2018). The legal basis for this data mining is presumably Section 25a(1), (2) Hessisches Gesetz über die öffentliche Sicherheit und Ordnung (HSOG), in force since 4 July 2018.

[32]Section 10 Geldwäschegesetz; cf. for a case study on anti-money laundering technology Demetis (2018); see also Schemmel, para 12.

authorize national law enforcement agencies to analyze PNR data 'for the purpose of updating or creating new criteria to be used [...] in order to identify any persons who may be involved in a terrorist offence or serious crime'.[33] Germany implemented this obligation in Section 4 *Fluggastdatengesetz* (German Law on Passenger Name Records). That statute allows the Federal Criminal Police Office to apply pattern analyses to all flights leaving or arriving in Germany in order to detect specific past or future felonies.[34]

2.3 'Listening'

In comparison to image recognition and text mining, scholars are less focused on software that 'listens' for suspicious acoustic patterns (aural surveillance).[35] Nonetheless, it is already in use. For instance, according to the New York Times, up until August 2018 90 US cities applied ShotSpotter, the leader in gunfire detection software.[36] This software is supposed to react to gunshots and to alert police faster than human witnesses. ShotSpotter cooperates with Verizon Inc., which is planning on connecting its software to Verizon's Light Sensory Network, a system installed in streetlights across the US. This could significantly increase the availability of and reliance on 'listening' AI.[37]

2.4 'Smelling'

The assessment made on software that 'listens' for infringements is even more true for surveillance technology that has the ability to 'smell'. So far, such technologies seem to be deployed only rarely. However, recent newspaper articles suggest significant improvements in the field of odor recognition software capable of 'smelling' diseases.[38] It does not need much imagination to see 'sniffing' devices replace dogs at airports or other public places trained to discover drugs, explosives, or contraband.

---

[33] Directive (EU) 2016/681 of 27 April 2016 on the use of passenger name record (PNR) data for the prevention, detection, investigation and prosecution of terrorist offences and serious crime. For an evaluation against the backdrop of EU and German constitutional law cf. Rademacher (2017), pp. 410–415.
[34] For a status quo report on German PNR-analyses cf. Bundestag (2018).
[35] See, for a rare example, Ferguson (2017), p. 88.
[36] Schlossberg (2015).
[37] For an early instance of aural surveillance cf. Zetter (2012).
[38] Saracco (2017); see also May (2018), on AI designed to detect doping athletes.

2.5 ... *Everywhere, Always, and Remembering It All*

12 The comparisons just drawn between human policing and machine learning highlight that smart law enforcement is, *functionally* speaking, not groundbreaking. Of course, the similarities must not be overstated. Significant differences exist. Above all, deficiencies are inherent in the technique,[39] which will be further discussed in Sect. 4 of this Chapter. One difference, however, stands out and is ultimately the central reason for smart law enforcement technologies to be rolled out in the first place: Technology can handle big data, humans cannot. Given the proliferation of sensor technology, smart law enforcement is, again figuratively speaking, able to 'watch', 'read', and 'listen' everywhere and anytime.[40] AI is able to interconnect and store the information thus retrieved for law enforcement purposes and subsequent judicial review infinitely.[41] While human officers are still much better at understanding and contextualizing *small* data (and are therefore called upon to confirm any suspicion discovered by AI-based surveillance, see paras 31–34), they are unable, simply for practical reasons, to be everywhere at the same time and to connect and remember[42] all the data that would be gathered. Smart law enforcement might be able, one day, to be and to do exactly that, provided that data sources are sufficiently interconnected.[43]

3 Constitutional Frameworks

13 The following analysis will try to flesh out how the highest courts in Germany, the EU, and the US have tried to apply their respective constitutional provisions—all *not* adopted in the computer-age—to modern smart law enforcement technologies. On the one hand, the analysis reveals significant differences; perhaps not surprisingly, German and EU law is much less permissive vis-à-vis state surveillance than its American cousin. On the other hand, all three courts actually do rely on quite similar lines of arguments to deal with the chances and challenges of smart law enforcement, albeit with different results.

---

[39]Cf. Rademacher (2017), pp. 373–393; Rich (2016), pp. 880–886, 895–901.

[40]Joh (2019), p. 179.

[41]Henderson (2016), p. 935: '[W]hen it comes to criminal investigation, time travel seems increasingly possible.'

[42]If police tried 'to see into the past' (Ferguson 2017, p. 98) before the rise of big data policing, they usually had to rely on human eye witnesses—who are notoriously unreliable.

[43]See Barret (2016), reporting on technology that could connect up to 30 million CCTV cameras in the US.

3.1 Germany

The starting point in German constitutional law is clear: officers do not need specific legislative authorization to watch, listen, or read, if the information is in some form publicly available.[44] Officers *do* need specific legislative authorization, adopted by parliament, if they want to enter, search, or monitor certain 'rooms' (apartments,[45] hard disks[46]); if they want to intercept ongoing communication; or if they begin to systematically collect data on specific individuals.[47] In order for legislation and the subsequent concrete use of surveillance technology to be constitutional in these cases, several criteria need to be met. One of them being that legislation must require the police to demonstrate some form of individualized place- or person-based suspicion[48] *already detected* before the surveillance is deployed.

The conditions for deeming *automated* detection of suspicious activity constitutional, appear to be less clear. The German Constitutional Court's jurisprudence on automated systems of surveillance (sometimes) seems contradictory[49] and (most of the times) excessively fine-tuned. This judicial fine-tuning roots in the 1983 'census judgment' (*Volkszählungsurteil*). In this judgment, the Court 'found' an unwritten constitutional right to informational self-determination in the German Basic Law. It was defined as the right of an individual to decide who does or does not have knowledge of and may use personal data.[50] Conceptually, this right is based on the assumption that no data concerning an individual are 'unimportant'—in the sense of: all personal data have the potential to be dangerous—if electronically collected,

14

15

---

[44]Cf. German Constitutional Court 1 BvR 370/07 'Onlinedurchsuchung' (27 February 2008), BVerfGE 120, pp. 344–346, concerning intelligence agents performing website searches.

[45]Article 13 Grundgesetz (German Basic Law).

[46]Fundamental right to confidentiality and integrity of IT systems, developed by the Constitutional Court in 'Onlinedurchsuchung' (see note 44), pp. 302–315. On that right cf. Heinemann (2015), pp. 147–171; Hoffmann-Riem (2008), pp. 1015–1021; Böckenförde (2008).

[47]Constitutional Court 'Onlinedurchsuchung' (see note 44), p. 345.

[48]E.g. German Constitutional Court 1 BvR 2074/05 'KFZ-Kennzeichenkontrollen' (11 March 2008), BVerfGE 120, p. 431; cf. Rademacher (2017), pp. 403–405, 406–407.

[49]See, e.g., German Constitutional Court 'KFZ-Kennzeichenkontrollen' (see note 48), p. 430 with p. 399: Although an ALPR-scan was said to *not* count as an interference with A's right to informational self-determination, *if* A's license plate number does not produce a match in the database and the image was therefore deleted immediately, *A's* potential privacy fear ('chilling effect' due to a feeling of constant observation') still should render the interference with *B's* right to informational self-determination—whose license plate number had produced a 'hit'—unconstitutional. Just after the Federal *Administrative* Court confirmed that irritating jurisprudence, the Constitutional Court reversed it, now holding that any form of video surveillance amounts to an interference with the right to informational self-determination, see Constitutional Court 1 BvR 142/15 'KFZ-Kennzeichenkontrollen 2' (18 December 2018), paras 45. Cf. Marsch (2012), pp. 605–616.

[50]German Constitutional Court 1 BvR 209/83 'Volkszählung' (15 December 1983), BVerfGE 65, p. 42: '[...] right of individuals to decide in principle themselves when and within what limits personal matters are disclosed'. Author's translation.

processed and/or stored by the state.[51] After all, the state (or rather: state employees gone rogue) might be tempted to combine that data with other information to create personality profiles and, consequently, an Orwellian Big Brother state ('chilling effect'). This doctrine superseded the older *Sphärentheorie* (theory of different personality spheres),[52] which is to some degree comparable to common law curtilage.[53]

16   In the years following the 1983 decision, much of the Court's jurisprudence and respective legal scholarship on state surveillance and informational rights was concerned with 'trimming back' those overly broad assumptions and their consequences.[54] It took some time to realize that the right to informational self-determination was much more a mandate directed at legislators, requiring them to design a legal framework adapted to modern information processing, and was much less about the creation of individual rights similar to property.[55]

17   However, the vast amount of German jurisprudence and scholarship devoted to the automated processing of personal data obscures the fact that decisions concerning software *detecting* suspicious evidence by means of pattern analysis is rare. There are two Constitutional Court decisions on automated license plate readers (ALPRs) from 2008 and now from 2018,[56] and one on dragnet investigations (Rasterfahndung) from 2006.[57] Therefore, one should be careful about drawing general conclusions. What can be said safely is that whether a given smart system of law enforcement is constitutional or not always depends on a proportionality test. This test on the one hand takes into account the degree of the interference with the right to informational self-determination, and the weight of the objectives pursued by the state on the other hand.[58] Clearly, as with most balancing approaches under constitutional law, that test offers little guidance. The Constitutional Court's decisions on smart law enforcement, therefore, have become hardly predictable. Nonetheless, in taking a step back, three recurrent arguments emerge from the Court's jurisprudence that have effectively shaped the use of modern surveillance technologies in Germany. First, a strong case against proportionality can be made if the technology does not work well, i.e. produces too many false positives, subjecting

---

[51]Cf. Constitutional Court 'Volkszählung' (see note 50), p. 45: 'in that respect, "unimportant" data no longer exist in the context of automated data processing'. Author's translation.

[52]The *Sphärentheorie* offered, in principle, heightened protection from surveillance for information that could be categorized as intimate or private, and did not protect, again in principle, information that was considered social or public.

[53]Cf. Ferguson (2014), pp. 1313–1316.

[54]Cf. Poscher (2017), pp. 131–134; Marsch (2018), pp. 116–124.

[55]Cf. Marsch, paras 15–16. Ditto Poscher (2017), p. 132.

[56]Constitutional Court 'KFZ-Kennzeichenkontrollen' (see note 48), and 'KFZ-Kennzeichenkontrollen 2' (see note 49).

[57]Constitutional Court 'Rasterfahndung' (see note 27).

[58]Cf. Staben (2016), pp. 160, 162 for a broad overview, listing most, if not all, the criteria the Constitutional Court so far has weighed against modern surveillance technologies.

individuals to intensified *human* scrutiny without good cause.[59] Conversely, and to some extent paradoxically, some of the Court's decisions suggest that a negative factor for the use of smart surveillance technology is that (or if) it is more powerful, efficient, and effective than human surveillance (see para 12).[60] Finally, technologically enhanced surveillance is still said, due to that superhuman efficacy, to create 'chilling effects', suppressing not only behavior that is illegal, but also behavior that is permitted or even socially desirable[61]—'you never know', so to speak (see para 15).[62]

Whereas the first argument will diminish in strength as big data policing becomes more accurate and specific,[63] it seems difficult to appease the two other concerns in some rational, i.e. judicially reviewable, manner (arguably, they are not judicial, but political and even emotional in nature). Still, as it was not an option for the Court to ban *all* forms of automated surveillance, it simply expanded the constitutional protections originally provided only for apartments and ongoing communication (see para 14), to encompass almost all forms of technologically enhanced surveillance. That means that for smart law enforcement to be constitutional, first, a specific legislative basis is required. Secondly, the respective statute may only allow the use of the technology if police can demonstrate, beforehand, some form of person- or place-based suspicion that crimes or other infringements of the law might occur or might have occurred, in the given circumstances, with sufficient likelihood.[64] Finally, surveillance must not be allowed to be 'flächendeckend',[65] i.e. locally all-encompassing. Obviously, the second limb of that approach results in a tension with the very idea of smart law enforcement that is difficult to be resolved: as such technologies are at their best when it comes to detecting suspicious patterns where

18

---

[59]See, esp., the decision on dragnet investigations, Constitutional Court 'Rasterfahndung' (see note 27), pp. 354, 356–357.

[60]Constitutional Court 'KFZ-Kennzeichenkontrollen' (see note 48), pp. 401, 407.

[61]Constitutional Court 'Volkszählung' (see note 50), p. 43; Constitutional Court 'KFZ-Kennzeichenkontrollen' (see note 48), pp. 402, 430; Constitutional Court 'KFZ-Kennzeichenkontrollen 2' (see note 49), paras 51, 98.

[62]The Constitutional Court's recurrence to this line of argument ('risks of abuse', see e.g. Constitutional Court 'KFZ-Kennzeichenkontrollen' (see note 48), p. 402) has been harshly criticized by German legal scholarship for being empirically unfounded, cf. Trute (2009), pp. 100–101.

[63]See also Hermstrüwer, paras 10, 19.

[64]Whether that being an imminent risk of harm to an individual's health, life, or liberty, or whether police experience regarding a specific place (crime hot spots) or activity suffices (see for examples of the latter Constitutional Court 'KFZ-Kennzeichenkontrollen 2' (see note 49), para 94, and Rademacher 2017, pp. 401–410), depends on the 'invasiveness' of the respective means of surveillance. Obviously, that again requires a proportionality test, the outcome of which is hard to predict. In specific areas, such as tax law (see Braun Binder) and financial regulation (see Schemmel, paras 10–12 and para 32 for US law), state databases are 'rasterized' routinely, thus implementing a limited form of generalized suspicion (Generalverdacht) or so-called 'anlasslose Kontrolle' (cf. Constitutional Court 'KFZ-Kennzeichenkontrollen 2' (see note 49), para 94).

[65]Constitutional Court 'KFZ-Kennzeichenkontrollen' (see note 48), p. 378, recital 4.

humans, for practical reasons, fail to do so (see para 12), requiring police to demonstrate suspicion *for the technology to be deployed*, is problematic.[66]

3.2 European Union

19 With the coming into force of the EU's Charter of Fundamental Rights (CFR) in 2009, the Court of Justice of the European Union (CJEU) has begun to intensify scrutiny of Member State and EU legislation in the areas of law enforcement and public security. Earlier case law was closely aligned with the jurisprudence of the European Court of Human Rights, and consequently marked by a relatively high degree of judicial (self-)restraint vis-à-vis legislators.[67] However, recently the CJEU made its intention clear to introduce a right to informational self-determination into EU law very much along the lines of the German *Volkszählungsurteil* and the corresponding proportionality test (see paras 15 and 17).[68] It is important to bear in mind that, with the broad reach of EU secondary legislation in the field of data protection,[69] almost all Member State legislation concerning law enforcement, be it pro-active or punitive, falls within the scope of application of the CFR.

20 The CJEU's new approach transfers the German jurisprudence's unpredictability into EU law. Yet again, the CJEU's case law regarding smart law enforcement contains two EU-specific aspects. The first one appears to be consolidated by now: EU or Member State authorities may neither retain personal data *solely* for future, as of today unknown, law enforcement purposes. Nor may respective legislation require private entities, especially providers of electronic communication services, to retain personal data in such a scenario. This means that data retention for law enforcement purposes within the EU requires, to be lawful, at least some indication,

---

[66]Rademacher (2017), pp. 401–403.

[67]Marsch (2018), pp. 17–30. Cf. for an up-to-date account of the ECtHR's jurisprudence on surveillance technology Bachmeier (2018), pp. 178–181.

[68]Most recently confirmed in CJEU Case C-207/16 'Ministerio Fiscal' (2 October 2018) para 51. The respective jurisprudence is mainly based on Article 8 CFR [Right to data protection]. For a detailed analysis of that provision and the shift in the CJEU's jurisprudence towards an understanding similar to the German right to informational self-determination cf. Marsch, paras 29–32.

[69]See, above all, Regulation (EU) 2016/679 of 27 April 2016 on the protection of natural persons with regard to the processing of personal data and on the free movement of such data (General Data Protection Regulation); Directive (EU) 2016/680 of 27 April 2016 on the protection of natural persons with regard to the processing of personal data by competent authorities for the purpose of the prevention, investigation, detection or prosecution of criminal offences or the execution of criminal penalties, and on the free movement of such data; and Directive (EG) 2002/58 of 12 July 2002 concerning the processing of personal data and the protection of privacy in the electronic communications sector (ePrivacy Directive). Cf. Dimitrova (2018).

be it place- or person-based, that such data might contain suspicious information.[70] Of course, there is nothing 'smart' in indiscriminately retaining data. Yet, as some patterns based on respective technologies will 'stretch over time',[71] *some* storing of initially unsuspicious activity will certainly be necessary for them to work properly.[72]

That leads us to the second decision relevant for our purposes, i.e. the Court's Opinion No. 1/15 on the *EU-Canada PNR Agreement*. Similar to Article 6(2) of the EU's PNR Directive (see para 9) the Agreement would have required air carriers departing from an EU airport towards Canada to provide personal data on passengers to Canadian authorities. The authorities in turn would be entitled to apply 'models and criteria' to that data. The aim was to detect data indicating specific future or past offences. Additionally, Canada would have been allowed to retain data for five years, irrespective of the outcome of the initial screening. The CJEU, in line with its previous case law, did not accept this latter provision on data retention. According to the Court it was not proportionate,[73] as the EU could not demonstrate why five years of data retention should be necessary even though the initial screening had not resulted in a 'match'.[74] This argumentation naturally raises the question of whether the Agreement *would have* passed the proportionality test if the retention period had been aligned with the temporal requirements of the respective 'models and criteria'. It is important to note that the obligation of air carriers to provide personal data for pattern analysis *as such* was, under the given circumstances, considered lawful under EU law, provided the respective technology was reliable.[75] In Opinion No. 1/15 the CJEU accepted the mere fact that a border crossing took place as sufficient *place-based* suspicion. Consequently justifying, under its weighing approach, the

21

---

[70]Cf. CJEU Case C-203/15 'Tele2 Sverige' (21 December 2016) para 111: '[N]ational legislation [requiring private companies to store communications data] must be based on objective evidence which makes it possible to identify a public whose data is likely to reveal a link, at least an indirect one, with serious criminal offences [...].' Confirmed by CJEU Opinion No. 1/15 'Passenger Name Record' (26 July 2017), para 191. But cf. the referrals submitted under Article 267 TFEU by the Investigatory Powers Tribunal London (C-623/17), the French Conseil d'État (C-512/18), and the Belgian Constitutional Court (C-520/18), rather critically scrutinizing the CJEU's data protection-friendly approach. See also ECtHR Case-No. 35252/08 'Big Brother Watch v. United Kingdom' (13 September 2018), para 112.

[71]Take, for instance, 'intelligent' video surveillance that is supposed to alert to pickpocketing at train stations. Certainly, it will need to indiscriminately record at least some minutes of what happens on the platform to distinguish suspicious behavior from people just strolling around waiting for their trains.

[72]Additionally, the data will be needed to train new algorithms and evaluate algorithms which are already applied, cf. CJEU 'Passenger Name Record' (see note 70), para 198.

[73]'[N]ot [...] limited to what is strictly necessary', CJEU 'Passenger Name Record' (see note 70), para 206.

[74]CJEU 'Passenger Name Record' (see note 70), paras 204–209.

[75]Meaning that the 'models and criteria' applied by Canada must be 'specific and reliable, making it possible [...] to arrive at results targeting individuals who might be under a "reasonable suspicion" of participation in terrorist offences or serious transnational crime', cf. CJEU 'Passenger Name Record' (see note 70), para 172.

22 collection and subsequent 'rasterizing' of personal data, i.e. the interference with the right of informational self-determination.[76]

23 Compared to German law, one should be even more careful when drawing general conclusions from the CJEU's still fragmented jurisprudence on the right to informational self-determination.[77] However, even if we take into account the casuistic nature of its proportionality approach, it appears from Opinion No. 1/15 that the CJEU might actually be more open than its German counterpart for EU and Member State legislators[78] to deploy smart surveillance technology. The CJEU's jurisprudence allows their use in defined areas, by regarding a comparably low and abstract degree of initial suspicion as sufficient.[79]

3.3 United States

Compared to German and EU law, until recently the legal standard in the US was marked by an almost complete 'absence of constitutional protection from ordinary observational surveillance in public'.[80] Generally, the Fourth Amendment as the sole constitutional protection against surveillance,[81] does not apply in public. Following the Supreme Court's decision in *Katz v. United States*, citizens did not have a legitimate expectation of privacy with regard to public conduct.[82] Therefore, US

---

[76] See CJEU 'Passenger Name Record' (see note 70): 'The transfer of that data to Canada is to take place regardless of whether there is any objective evidence permitting the inference that the passengers are liable to present a risk to public security in Canada.' [para 186] '[T]hat processing is intended to identify the risk to public security that persons, who are not, at that stage, known to the competent services, may potentially present, and who may, on account of that risk, be subject to further examination. In that respect, the automated processing of that data, before the arrival of the passengers in Canada, facilitates and expedites security checks, in particular at borders.' [para 187] According to para 191 et seq., that suffices to 'establish a connection between the personal data to be retained and the objective pursued'. Cf. Rademacher (2017), pp. 412–413.

[77] That is especially true as the CJEU's reasoning in its 'Passenger Name Record' decision (see note 70) is premised on public international law concerning air traffic and respective border controls, cf. para 188. However, public international law is only one line of argument in favor of the agreement the Court has accepted, cf. para 187.

[78] Due to the interference with the fundamental right to informational self-determination, in any case a specific legal basis is required, see Article 52(1) CFR.

[79] See also CJEU 'Ministerio Fiscal' (see note 68), paras 54, 56–57.

[80] Ferguson (2017), p. 98; ditto Wittmann (2014), pp. 368–369. See also Joh (2016), p. 17: 'Unlike arrests or wiretaps, the decision to focus police attention on a particular person, without more, is unlikely to be considered a Fourth Amendment event.'

[81] Cf. Ferguson (2014), p. 1333: 'In a government truly of limited powers, police would not have the surveillance powers to invade privacy or security unless there was a law specifically allowing it. Such is not the current reality under the Fourth Amendment.' But cf. Ferguson (2017), p. 116, suggesting that social media monitoring and respective storage of data could interfere with the First Amendment as well.

[82] Katz v. United States, 389 U.S. 347 (1967), p. 361 (Harlan, J., concurring).

law enforcement authorities are, in principle, allowed to enhance their visual capacities, hearing abilities or senses of smell, and their memories by means of technology, as long as the data thus processed is in some form public.[83] Consequently, legal scholarship in the US dedicated to smart surveillance is less concerned with the question of whether or not such surveillance is constitutional.[84] Instead, most scholars focus on assessing whether suspicion that *has been* generated automatically may or may not constitute 'probable cause' under the Fourth Amendment.[85] 'Probable cause' would justify those more intrusive interferences with one's privacy (searches, wiretaps, arrests, thermal observations[86]). These are deemed, under the traditional interpretation of the Fourth Amendment, as worthy of constitutional[87] protection. The rationale behind the 'legitimate expectation of privacy' doctrine was controversial from the beginning.[88] Nonetheless, from the perspective of smart law enforcement and compared to German and EU law, this doctrine provides a test that is relatively straightforward. At the same time, this test is highly permissive. That explains why most of the big data technologies described in Sect. 2 of this Chapter are being tested or used in the US.

It was the 2012 decision in *United States v. Jones* that is said to have 'upended the Fourth Amendment doctrine'.[89] The issue presented before the Supreme Court was clear-cut: The police had installed a GPS device in Mr. Jones' car, tracking his movements for 28 days without fulfilling the conditions laid down in the Fourth Amendment. Although almost all his movements took place in public, the Supreme Court unanimously held the police had thus violated Jones' rights under the Fourth Amendment. For the majority, the decisive fact was that the GPS device had been *physically* attached to the underside of the car. According to Justice Antonin Scalia, writing for five Justices, there could be no doubt 'that such a physical intrusion

---

[83]'Public' is defined quite broadly, encompassing any communication that is directed to third parties, cf. Smith v. Maryland, 442 U.S. 735 (1979); for an in-depth analysis of the Court's case law see Wittmann (2014), pp. 146–328; arguably, Carpenter v. United States has destabilized the third party doctrine, too (cf. note 99).

[84]Joh (2016), p. 18, notes that '[s]urprisingly, there is little discussion of these decisions that the police make about individuals before any search, detention, or arrest takes place. Rather, current unresolved issues of police technology have focused on whether a particular use is a Fourth Amendment search requiring a warrant and probable cause.'

[85]Rich (2016), pp. 895–901; Ferguson (2015), pp. 388–409; Joh (2014), pp. 55–65, but see pp. 66–67: 'Beyond the Fourth Amendment'.

[86]Cf. Kyllo v. United States, 533 U.S. 27 (2001), pp. 34–35.

[87]That does not mean that legislators could not step in and implement more restrictive requirements for surveillance that fall short of constituting an interference under the Fourth Amendment. According to Ferguson (2017), p. 101, however, such legislative restrictions or clarifications are, to date, missing. The new California Consumer Privacy Act (CCPA), which has received great attention in the EU, too, limits its scope of application to data processing by private entities (cf. Cal. Civ. Code § 1798.140(c)).

[88]Cf. Ferguson (2014), p. 1305, identifying seven 'values' discussed as underlying the Fourth Amendment case law.

[89]Ferguson (2014), p. 1307.

would have been considered a "search" within the meaning of the Fourth Amendment when it was adopted', as the 'Government [had] physically occupied private property for the purpose of obtaining information'.[90] Basically, the judgement relied on a concept of privacy that roots in the long-established common law principle of trespass ('traditional property-based rationale'[91]).

25 Justice Samuel Alito, joined by Justices Ginsburg, Breyer and Kagan, instead opted for an update of the Fourth Amendment doctrine in accordance with the reality of '21st-century surveillance technique'. He criticized the majority as 'unwise' for having decided the 'case based on 18th-century tort law'.[92] Yet, arguably, the core of Justice Alito's argument appears historical, too.[93] It is based on the assumption that '[f]or [most] offenses, society's expectation has been that law enforcement agents and others would not—and indeed, in the main, simply could not—secretly monitor and catalogue every single movement of an individual's car for a very long time'.[94] In contrast, society would recognize 'short-term monitoring of a person's movements on public streets' as reasonable, even without prior probable cause. The same *could* be true for long-term secret surveillance as well, if it were adopted 'in the context of investigations involving extraordinary offenses'.[95] Conceptually, these four Justices referred to a societal expectation that different types of offenses, simply due to limited resources, i.e. as a matter of *fact*, had been subjected to different forms of enforcement efficacy in the past and will continue to be so in the future, albeit now as a matter of law, in the age of modern surveillance technologies. This approach is empirical in nature, as it is premised on societal expectations, yet was not supported by any empirical evidence, at least not in *Jones* itself. Justice Alito compensated for this shortcoming, to some extent, by devoting a substantial part of his opinion to the uncertainty und instability of privacy expectations in light of new technologies, expressly inviting legislators to define respective standards.[96]

26 Remarkably, with the exception of Justice Sonia Sotomayor, who proposed to apply a more modern test *in addition* to the property-based rationale preferred by Justices Roberts, Thomas, Scalia and Kennedy, none of the Justices referred to the

---

[90] United States v. Jones, 565 U.S. 400 (2012), p. 404.

[91] Cf. Ferguson (2014), p. 1308.

[92] United States v. Jones (see note 90), p. 418 (Alito, J., concurring). But see also Justice Sotomayor's opinion, ibid, at p. 414, consenting to the majority that 'the Government's physical intrusion on Jones' Jeep supplies a [...] basis for decision' in any case.

[93] A similarly historical approach applies to surveillance technology that is able to 'explore details of the home that would previously have been unknowable without physical intrusion' (Kyllo v. United States (see note 86), p. 40—such surveillance *does* constitute a search within the meaning of the Fourth Amendment; see also Florida v. Jardines, 133 S.Ct. 1409 (2013), p. 1419 (Kagan, J., concurring)).

[94] United States v. Jones (see note 90), p. 430 (Alito, J., concurring).

[95] Ibid.

[96] Ibid, pp. 429–430 (Alito, J., concurring).

Artificial Intelligence and Law Enforcement

famous unintended chilling effects which surveillance could have on *lawful* conduct.[97]

Based on the three different threads visible in *Jones* it is hard to predict if and how the Supreme Court will eventually 'update' the Fourth Amendment doctrine to 21st-century surveillance. As Andrew Ferguson observed, five of the nine Supreme Court Justices opted for such an update, indicating that US police forces might be obliged, in the future, to demonstrate probable cause even for surveillance technology that 'watches', 'reads', etc. data that is in some form public. So far, however, a different Supreme Court majority only once adopted this update. In *Carpenter v. United States* the Court raised the question of whether or not police needed 'probable cause' to access cell-site records kept by a wireless carrier (i.e. by a third party[98]). Those records documented Mr. Carpenter's movements for over 127 days. The Court answered that question in the affirmative, explicitly referring to Justice Alito's efficacy-based reasoning in *Jones*.[99] At the same time however, the Court stressed that the 'decision today is a narrow one' (four Justices dissented) and would not 'call into question conventional techniques and tools, such as security cameras'.[100] In comparison to the German Constitutional Court's jurisprudence, the approach suggested by the Supreme Court still appears to be much more permissive towards smart law enforcement being used without prior suspicion.

27

4 Three Core Issues

The previous analyses in Sect. 2 revealed an ever-increasing use of pattern recognition technologies in the process of detecting suspicious activities that might justify state interference. At the same time courts, both in the EU and in the US, appear to find it difficult to 'update' their respective constitutional frameworks to accommodate smart law enforcement technologies with established concepts of individual rights, especially the right to privacy. The following Sect. 4 will *not* attempt to examine which of the different lines of judicial arguments described in Sect. 3 is most convincing or even the 'correct' one under the applicable constitutional law. Instead, I will try to flesh out three specific features of smart law enforcement that

28

---

[97]Ibid, pp. 416–417 (Sotomayor, J., concurring). See also paras. 18 and 42. Cf. Staben (2016), pp. 67–68: the argument of chilling effects *does* appear in the Supreme Court's jurisprudence, but usually regarding the First Amendment.

[98]Thus, at least under traditional interpretation of the Fourth Amendment, constituting public disclosure; see also notes 83 and 99.

[99]The crime in question in *Carpenter* was robbery. Interestingly, Justice Alito dissented, arguing that the majority's decision would be 'revolutionary' inasmuch as it ignored established case law according to which the Fourth Amendment would not apply to 'an order merely requiring a [third] party to look through its own records and produce specific documents' (Carpenter v. United States, 585 U.S. ___ (2018), p. 12 (Roberts, C. J., for the majority).

[100]Ibid, p. 18 (Roberts, C. J., for the majority).

differentiate it from human policing and which therefore require and deserve, in my view, the attention of legislators, courts, and most of all scholars.

29 Before we turn to those features, it makes sense to state the obvious: Smart law enforcement must *function well* if it is to be deployed on a large scale. That means that the machine learned patterns applied to reality must be 'woven' densely, allowing for sufficiently[101] individualized,[102] precise, and accurate[103] predictions that unlawful conduct might be imminent or has already happened. Certainty cannot and must not be required.[104] Much like drug-sniffing dogs,[105] the technology must be tested on a regular basis.[106] Deploying patterns is otherwise entirely prohibited under German and EU constitutional law (see paras 17 and 21). Under US law, patterns that have *not* proven reliable at least on test data would not meet the

---

[101] Obviously, the degree of precision and accuracy that is required will vary depending on the intrusiveness of the surveillance measure itself, the availability of less intrusive means, and the severity of the crime or threat in question.

[102] It is a mistake to conclude that the application of machine learned patterns could not result in individualized predictions (cf. Ferguson 2017, p. 127: 'generalized suspicion'). As soon as data concerning a specific individual is used as input data for the prediction, the result is individualized *by definition*. The question that really matters is, whether it is individualized *enough*, i.e. whether the pattern in question relies on more than just one or two predictors such as place of birth, education etc. (cf. Hermstrüwer, para 10, and also paras 30–34 on the converse risk of *excessive* individualization ('overfitting')). One should bear in mind that all police suspicion, be it detected by human or technological means, starts with and relies on some form of pattern recognition, i.e. the application of previously learned information to new situations. For details cf. Rademacher (2017), pp. 373–377, 381–383, and Harcourt and Meares (2011), p. 813: 'In reality, most individuals arouse suspicion because of the group-based-type behavior that they exhibit or the fact that they belong to readily identifiable groups—sex and age are two examples—rather than because of unique individual traits. Typically, individuals come to police attention because they are young, or are male, or are running away from the police, or have a bulge in their pocket'.

[103] See, for further details on the methods of evaluating predictive algorithms and on the difference between precision and accuracy, Degeling and Berendt (2017), esp. 3.2.

[104] All forms of suspicion are probabilistic in nature, be it human or technological. By definition, reliance on 'suspicion' accepts that any actions based thereon are made in a state of possible incompleteness of information (cf. Rich 2016, p. 898; Rademacher 2017, p. 383) and should—consequently—be open to ex post rectification.

[105] Interestingly, American scholars suggest comparing smart law enforcement to drug dogs rather than to humans, e.g. Rich (2016), pp. 913–921. On the law of drug dogs see esp. Rodriguez v. United States, 575 U.S. __ (2015), pp. 5–6 (Ginsburg, J., for the majority), finding that police may perform investigations (like dog sniffs) *unrelated* to a roadside detention (which itself requires 'probable cause' under the Fourth Amendment), but only if that investigation does not prolong the stop. In Florida v. Jardines (see note 93), the Supreme Court held, in a 5 to 4 decision, that a dog sniff *does* amount to a search within the meaning of the Fourth Amendment when it is performed on property surrounding the home of a person (so-called curtilage, in that specific case: a front porch), *if* that property had been entered with the intention of performing that investigation. On the other hand, Justice Scalia reaffirmed that 'law enforcement officers need not "shield their eyes" when passing by the home "on public thoroughfares"' (at p. 1423).

[106] Ferguson (2017), p. 198: '"Here is how we test it" may be a more comforting and enlightening answer than "here is how it works."' For a detailed analysis of up-to-date testing mechanisms cf. Kroll et al. (2017), pp. 643–656.

'probable cause' standard under the Fourth Amendment to justify the adoption of more intrusive surveillance measures (see para 23).[107] Perhaps even more importantly, and simply as a matter of fact, police should not *want* to use patterns that alert to too many activities that finally prove harmless (false positives) or use patterns that 'overlook' too many actually dangerous and/or criminal situations (false negatives).[108] After all, human resources to evaluate the findings of smart law enforcement technologies and to act on those findings are limited. Additionally, an excessive number of false positives or negatives would eventually undermine popular approval of smart law enforcement technologies, which could lead to a statutory ban.

If what has just been said is axiomatic, what crucial issues should legislators, courts, and scholars then discuss amongst each other and, even more importantly, with data scientists, police forces, and human rights groups?[109] To me it seems that there are three characteristics of smart law enforcement technologies that distinguish them from human policing and, therefore, deserve foremost attention. The first one represents a challenge (see paras 31 et seq.); the second one a chance (see paras 35 et seq.); and the third one a hard choice (see paras 39 et seq.).

4.1 A Challenge: State-of-the-Art Information or Undemocratic In-Formation?

Much has been written in recent years about the need of algorithms to be 'transparent', so as to allow for public and judicial scrutiny.[110] The call for algorithmic transparency, however, misses the point—at least if it refers to, as it usually does,[111] transparency of the source code.[112] For instance, it is not *really* important for a judge to understand the science that lies behind DNA analysis.[113] Even with expert explanation, only very few judges will be able to make sense of the respective

---

[107] Cf. Rich (2016), pp. 913–921, premised on the comparability of smart law enforcement ('automated suspicion algorithms') with drug dogs.

[108] Cf. Hermstrüwer, paras 52–55, who correctly notes that acceptability of false positives or false negatives depends on whether AI is applied for information gathering, or for preventive or punitive purposes.

[109] Cf. Kroll et al. (2017), pp. 695–705, for detailed 'recommendations' to lawmakers, policymakers, and computer scientists to 'foster' interdisciplinary collaboration.

[110] Ibid, pp. 657–658.

[111] See, e.g., Bieker et al. (2018), p. 610, referring to Article 13 of the EU's General Data Protection Regulation (see para 69).

[112] Ditto see Hermstrüwer, paras 3, 45–47, and Kroll et al. (2017), p. 657: a 'naïve solution to the problem'; Ferguson (2017), pp. 137, 138: 'The issue [...] is not the transparency of the algorithm [...] but the transparency of how the program is explained to the public and, of course, what is done with the information'. See also Wischmeyer, passim, and esp. paras 24 et seq. and 30.

[113] Cf. Joh (2014), pp. 50–55.

data themselves, be it made transparent to them or not. Still, the results of DNA analyses may serve as decisive evidence in a murder case. Likewise, it is not necessary to have neuro-images of a dog's brain from the moment when it alerts to drugs in order to assess whether or not the respective alert amounted to 'probable cause' in the meaning of the Fourth Amendment.[114] These two—very different—examples should suffice to show that we must not reject technological innovation to help optimize the process of information gathering *just* because the data processing that occurs between the input and output stages is not transparent to the police officer, the judge, or the public.

32 On the other hand, Mireille Hildebrandt has quite rightly observed that there is a difference between 'information as the object of cognition' and 'information as an agent that in-forms and thus transforms our cognition'.[115] The latter phenomenon is problematic.[116] Whereas a democratic society should require state authorities to act on the best information available, i.e. make well-*in*formed decisions harnessing the opportunities offered by modern technology, it should prevent information technology—in Hildebrandt's words—from becoming an agent on its own that in-*forms*, i.e. directs, state action. After all, the technology has not been elected and it cannot be held accountable for its 'mistakes' by means of criminal or administrative law.

33 The challenge, therefore, is to create an 'institutional setting' (see Wischmeyer, para 36) for the use of smart law enforcement technologies, which preserves human accountability. To that end, officers who are called to base investigatory actions on the results of such technologies must be placed in a position in which they are able to assume substantial responsibility for the actions they are going to take. At the same time, the rules that govern the process of technology-based decision-making must take into account that most state representatives will not hold a degree in computer science. Algorithmic transparency, therefore, is neither needed nor sufficient to prevent undemocratic in-*formation* of police conduct.[117] Instead, accountability requires disclosure and human re-evaluation of the input data triggering the alarm, e.g. by showing officers the recorded video footage the 'smart' surveillance camera identified as drug trafficking.[118] If the input information stems from a variety of sources, perhaps by combining 'reading', 'listening' etc., the software should provide officers with the specific pieces of input data proven *decisive* for triggering the alarm, displayed in a form and manner that is comprehensible to the specific

---

[114]Cf. Rich (2016), p. 919.

[115]Hildebrandt (2016), pp. 3, 21–22; see also Marks et al. (2017), pp. 714–715: 'automatic criminal justice'.

[116]On the need to (re)establish human agency cf. Wischmeyer, paras 24 et seq.

[117]See also Kroll et al. (2017), pp. 657–660, Ferguson (2017), pp. 137–138, and, for an up-to-date overview of the accountablity discussion, Andrews (2019). This is *not* to say that specific public officials should not have the right to scrutinize source codes, training and test data etc. *if* circumstances, especially procedures of judicial review require that kind of additional transparency. See for details Wischmeyer, esp. para 47.

[118]For techniques to preserve privacy in the course of human re-evaluation of video data cf. Birnstill et al. (2015).

addressee.[119] Ideally, this disclosure occurs *before* the police acts on an automated alarm. Then, *if* human officers can reconstruct the suspicion according to established human standards—taking into account all the traditional sources of knowledge like police experience, expert testimony etc.[120]—and if they could, eventually, defend their conclusions under judicial review (requiring the capacity to *give reasons* for their actions as defined by Wischmeyer, paras 36–39, esp. para 37), police should be allowed to act on the alarm as if the suspicious conduct had been detected by human means.[121] Otherwise, i.e. if human officers cannot reconstruct a suspicious case on their own, they cannot assume responsibility and must consequently refrain from taking action.

An exception to this principle should apply if an alert *cannot* be re-evaluated by human means for biological or cognitive reasons, e.g. because it exceeds the human sense of smell (analogous to drug dogs) or because time is too pressing for a thorough re-evaluation of suspicious social media posts. In such cases, accountability standards inevitably are called into question. However, analogous to the use of drug dogs,[122] police reactions based on patterns that haven proven accurate and precise in the past (see para 28), should still be considered legitimate *if* such reactions are limited to further investigations and/or provisional measures, which require lower levels of accountability.

34

---

[119]Ditto Rich (2016), p. 920, who, however, appears to be skeptical as to the practicality of such systems of disclosure: 'theoretically solvable'. See also Wischmeyer, esp. para 27. The respective techniques are called explainable AI (short form: XAI), cf. Waltl and Vogl (2018) and Samek et al. (2017).

[120]Eventually also including 'counterintuitive' insights, cf. Ferguson (2017), pp. 117, 136–140; for a critical account under EU law cf. Rademacher (2017), pp. 388–391.

[121]It is important to note that in this case it is irrelevant that the software itself is limited to detecting correlations and is not able to 'understand' casual links. To Ferguson (2017), p. 119, the difference between correlation and causation is one of the 'fundamental questions' behind big data policing. I disagree: The lack of understanding, which is inherent in machine learning, would only constitute a case against the use of smart law enforcement technologies, if we were to require the *software* to be held accountable, i.e. require it to explain itself and be subject, eventually, to disciplinary or electoral sanctions. Instead, what we need, is to establish a regulatory framework that preserves *human* accountability. Therefore, the software itself does not need to 'understand' the correlations it searches for. See also, from a private law perspective, Eidenmüller (2017), p. 13: 'Treating robots like humans would dehumanize humans, and therefore we should refrain from adopting this policy.'

[122]Cf. Rich (2016), pp. 911–924 for a detailed analysis of the law on drug dogs (in the US) and its suitability for being applied, by way of analogy, to 'automated suspicion algorithms'; see also note 105.

4.2 A Chance: Biased Enforcement or Transparent Biases?

35 Machine learning technologies 'learn' from the past (see para 2). Consequently, they do not and cannot promise a 'clean start' or 'neutral output'.[123] If the data stems from past events fraught with human biases, the software will, if applied without modifications, reflect and eventually reproduce such biases.[124] Therefore, it is hardly surprising that legal tech software ('COMPAS') trained on US police data turned out to be biased against black people.[125]

36 However, the answer to avoiding the continuation or even perpetuation of biased law enforcement is *not* to ban smart law enforcement technologies. The solution, instead, is to make human biases that have transcended into the technology transparent[126]; and then to cleanse the technology from such biases. Inasmuch as such cleansing is feasible, smart law enforcement actually does offer the opportunity of a 'clean start'. Unlike human brains, machines can be manipulated so as *not* to equal '[y]oung + [b]lack + [m]ale' to '[p]robable [c]ause'.[127] That is not to say that it will be easy to reveal biases in machine learned patterns and to remove them (although it is—fortunately—easier than to actively cleanse human brains from biases and prejudices).[128] For instance, it is not sufficient to remove those predictors from the patterns that are *directly* discriminatory, such as race, sexual orientation, gender, or religion.[129] Instead, it is also necessary to search for so-called proxies for discriminatory features. 'Proxy' describes data that—without being illegitimate themselves—implicitly *encode* sensitive or prohibited classes of information. One often mentioned proxy for race is the place of birth and/or residence.[130] The good news is that there is a growing body of literature concerned with the development of 'technical tools for nondiscrimination'.[131] Even better, several of those instruments

---

[123] Ferguson (2017), p. 133.

[124] Cf. Tischbirek, paras 5 et seq.

[125] See Buchholtz, para 30; Hacker (2018), pp. 1143–1144; but see also Brantingham et al. (2018), p. 1: 'We find that there were no significant differences [...] by racial-ethnic group between the control and treatment conditions.' For a detailed account of comparable software being tested in the criminal justice system of the UK, cf. Scantamburlo et al. (2019), esp. pp. 58 et seq.

[126] See Hermstrüwer, paras 3–4; see also Bennet Capers (2017), pp. 1242, 1271: 'I am a black man. [...] I am interested in technology that will lay bare not only the truth of how we police now but also how those of us who are black or brown live now.'

[127] The example is taken from Bennet Capers (2017), p. 1242, who uses this equation to describe his perception of the status quo of *human* law enforcement in the US.

[128] Ditto Hacker (2018), pp. 1146–1150.

[129] Cf. Kroll et al. (2017), p. 685; see Tischbirek, para 13. For an up-to-date catalogue of sensitive predictors under EU law see Article 21 CFR.

[130] Ferguson (2017), pp. 122–124; Kroll (2017), p. 685; see Tischbirek, paras 11–12.

[131] Current research is summed up by Kroll et al. (2017), pp. 682–692. For an account of *legal* tools to reveal discriminatory algorithms see Hacker (2018), pp. 1170–1183.

can be applied to test software for procedural and substantive fairness without the need for algorithmic transparency.[132]

Unfortunately, there is bad news, too: Some of the most effective tests for revealing and eventually suppressing proxies for sensitive information require the *training* data to contain sensitive information, i.e. data on race, religion, sexuality and so on.[133] Otherwise, it becomes difficult to identify those seemingly innocuous categories of data like a home address, which might eventually turn out to be a proxy for sensitive information. So, perhaps counterintuitively, color blindness, or non-bias towards class or religion in the process of developing and training smart law enforcement software may lead to more, not less biased systems.

Nevertheless, smart law enforcement technologies provide us with an opportunity. If they are checked carefully for explicit *and* implicit biases, and if they are deployed with proper explanation to the public and appropriate judicial supervision,[134] smart law enforcement might eventually increase the perception of law enforcement's legitimacy especially in those areas of law and society, where today's *human* law enforcement has gained a bad reputation for being guided by illegitimate human prejudice.[135]

4.3 A Choice: Human or 'Perfect' Enforcement of the Law?

No society, be it democratic or not, has ever had sufficient policing or judicial resources to guarantee a full implementation of the law or, so-to-speak, a *perfect* enforcement or rule of the law. Instead, implementation traditionally depended much more on compliance than on enforcement.[136] Not surprisingly, that has often led to complaints about implementation deficits in such areas of the law where compliance was low, for whatever reason.[137] So far, many of those deficits simply *could* not be overcome by any system of law enforcement due to the human gap that always existed between the *unconditional* demand of the legal order for legal compliance on the one hand, and the *limited* possibilities of humans to enforce such compliance on the other hand. Smart law enforcement technologies are about to bridge that gap between law and law enforcement: Whereas it would have been impossible for human officers to police all the streets of a city, or to review every bank account

---

[132]Kroll et al. (2017), p. 674 (procedural fairness), pp. 690–692 (nondiscrimination). See also Hermstrüwer, paras 41–43.

[133]The approach has therefore been labelled 'fairness through awareness', cf. Dwork et al. (2011). See also Tischbirek, paras 31 et seq.: 'towards a paradigm of knowledge creation'.

[134]Ferguson (2017), p. 137.

[135]See, e.g., Bennet Capers (2017), pp. 1268–1283, 1285, with a strong plea for the replacement of (biased) human policing by (hopefully) less biased policing by technology.

[136]Cf. Tyler (1990), pp. 3–4; Hoffmann-Riem (2017), pp. 33–34.

[137]See, e.g., Cheng (2006), pp. 659 et seq.

(let alone the internet), such ubiquitous surveillance becomes possible with smart law enforcement technologies (cf. para 12). Increasingly, technology can be used to detect and to sanction *any* instance of illegal conduct. With so-called 'impossibility structures'[138] technology might even be deployed to physically prevent such conduct.[139]

40 To some, these prospects might appear attractive, at least in a democracy. After all, the technology promises a ubiquitous and (finally) equal,[140] i.e. a *perfect* enforcement of *legitimate* law. Yet, I assume that most readers will also find these prospects *un*attractive. The traditional way of fending off ubiquitous surveillance is to refer to '1984'[141] or, nowadays, the 'Social Credit System',[142] i.e. to evoke the threat of the Orwellian or Chinese surveillance state that might abuse personal data to suppress individualism.[143] Due to its possibility of abuse, comprehensive surveillance is said to inhibit not only illegal, but also legal behavior (see para 17: 'chilling effect').[144] However, to me, this line of argument appears to weaken over time. The more we surround ourselves with smart devices (such as smart phones, smart homes, autonomous cars, or even smart cities[145]), or allow software to regulate our everyday lives (think of AI-based personal assistants, smart trading, smart bank accounts), the more we *invite* technology into our lives that *must* be able to surveil us, simply to work properly. So if it were true that the presence of surveillance technology really created 'chilling effects', then why do we not feel 'chilled' by all the cameras, microphones, and filter technologies we *willingly* let into our private lives?[146] I believe that the reason for our calmness is that we—or at least many of us—actually *do* expect state authorities to intervene if private actors misuse our data, and—more importantly—do *not* expect state authorities to *illegally* gain access to and abuse such technologies. To put it differently, it seems that we—or again: at least many of us—expect to live within states that, by and large, play by the constitutional and democratic rules.

---

[138] See note 4 and Rich (2013), pp. 802–804; for more recent reflections on impossibility structures or 'embedded law' cf. Rademacher (2019) and Becker (2019), respectively.

[139] See, for a plea for preventive regulation of financial markets, Schemmel, para 46.

[140] Cf. Bennet-Capers (2017), pp. 1282–1283, 1285–1291.

[141] Orwell (1949).

[142] Cf. Oganesian and Heermann (2018).

[143] For a more sophisticated attempt to explain 'The Dangers of Surveillance' cf. Richards (2013), esp. pp. 1950–1958, 1962–1964. See Timan et al. (2018), pp. 744–748, for an interdisciplinary attempt to reconcile the insights of 'surveillance studies' with legal reasoning, quite rightly asking for 'more legal scholarship' that 'views surveillance as generally good and bad at the same time, or as good or bad depending on the situation'.

[144] Solove (2007), pp. 758, 765; Richards (2013), p. 1961; for a thorough analysis from the German perspective see Staben (2016) and Oermann and Staben (2013).

[145] Joh (2019), p. 178: '[A]s cities become "smarter", they increasingly embed policing itself into the urban infrastructure.'

[146] See also Timan et al. (2018), p. 738: 'increasing blend of governmental and corporate surveillance infrastructures' and 'an increase of citizen-instigated forms of surveillance can be witnessed'.

If what has just been said is true, then the notion of a 'chilling effect' is about to become but an easy excuse for another sentiment that underlies the uneasiness with which I and—if I am right—many of the readers regard the promise of a 'perfect' enforcement or, in that sense, a 'perfect' rule of the law. The real reason, I submit, is encapsulated in the opinion offered by Justice Alito in *Jones*: It does not meet 'society's expectation' if *any* form of illegal conduct is detectable by state authorities—and thus inhibited or 'chilled' due to a fear of sanctions—with the *same* high level of efficacy (see para 25). To put it differently, it seems that law enforcement may become too effective to be perceived as fair.[147] The state-wide ban on traffic enforcement cameras recently approved by the Senate of Iowa[148] provides an illustrative example of a legislator bowing to a popular wish to have 'a sporting chance'[149] to get away with a specific violation. So even if there may be no 'freedom to commit crimes', there definitely is a widespread expectation that at least with regard to some rules it must be up to the individual citizen to decide whether or not to obey them—and, consequently, to have a chance to get away with disobedience.[150]

The prospect of a perfect enforcement of the law,[151] as it is provided by smart law enforcement technology that can 'watch, read, listen, and smell' and can do so 'everywhere, always, and remembering it all' (see para 12) is antithetical to that expectation. Therefore, regarding some forms of illegal conduct, that oxymoronic 'freedom to commit crimes' perhaps deserves preservation, by preferring human—i.e. imperfect—mechanisms of law enforcement over smart—i.e. potentially perfect—law enforcement.[152] Courts are not well equipped to establish when that expectation deserves attention and when it must be discarded as illegitimate. So in that regard, too, Justice Alito may be right: 'In circumstances involving dramatic technological change, the best solution to privacy concerns may be legislative'.[153] Or, to put it differently: it is a matter of (societal) choice more than a matter of (constitutional) law to identify those legal rules that actually require unconditional compliance, and to

---

[147]Cf. Rich (2013), p. 810. This sentiment might actually deserve some form of legal, perhaps even constitutional recognition. The reason for that is that we live in what I would call 'imperfect democracies'. I.e. in societies that *try* very hard to balance out majority rule on the one hand and the individual's rights to self-determination and political participation on the other hand—by providing a plethora of fundamental and political rights in order to protect minorities—but which fail, and will continue to fail in the future, to *fully* provide such balance for many practical reasons. So as long as even democratic laws cannot claim to be perfectly legitimate with regard to *each and every paragraph*, there is good reason to argue that such laws on their part may not claim perfect compliance.

[148]Petroski (2018).

[149]Cheng (2006), pp. 682–688, with a critical account of legislation respecting that wish.

[150]See also Hartzog et al. (2015), esp. pp. 1778–1792, advocating for automated law enforcement to be consciously 'inefficient' to prevent 'perfect enforcement'.

[151]Mulligan (2008), p. 3.

[152]See also Timan et al. (2018), p. 747, citing J Cohen: 'importance of room for play'.

[153]United States v. Jones (see note 90), p. 429; see also note 55 for the German discussion.

distinguish them from rules that should not be subjected to smart law enforcement so as to preserve the freedom to (dis)obey them.[154]

5 Conclusion

Artificial intelligence is increasingly able to autonomously detect suspicious activities. These activities in turn might warrant further inquiry and eventually trigger preventive or repressive action by law enforcement agencies (Sect. 2). In certain areas, technology already fulfills the task of detecting suspicious activities better than human police officers ever could, especially in quantitative terms—and computer capacities are likely to improve significantly in the years to come.

So, if AI technologies actually work well enough—with the standard of 'enough' being dependent on the respective field of application—then legislators and law enforcement agencies should consider their use. So far, the German Constitutional Court, the Court of Justice of the European Union, and the US Supreme Court are all struggling to develop convincing and clear-cut guidelines to direct these legislative and administrative considerations (Sect. 3). Section 4 tries to offer such guidelines: First, lawmakers should implement regulatory provisions in order to maintain human accountability (Sect. 4.1). This at least applies to law enforcement operating within democratic societies, as democracy is premised on the delegation and exercise of power to (and respectively by) *humans*. Secondly, AI law enforcement should be used, if and where possible, to overcome discriminatory traits in human policing that have plagued some jurisdictions for decades (Sect. 4.2). Finally, and perhaps somewhat counterintuitively, the prospect of a 'perfect' rule of law, in the sense of an ever more effective, perhaps even ubiquitous enforcement of the law, is not an entirely attractive prospect (Sect. 4.3). Therefore, the availability of technology to implement perfect law enforcement forces us to decide if, where, and when society might wish to preserve the freedom to *disobey* the rule(s) of law.

References

Algorithm Watch, BertelsmannStiftung (2019) Automating Society. Taking stock of automated decision-making in the EU. www.bertelsmann-stiftung.de/de/publikationen/publikation/did/automating-society. Accessed 21 Feb 2019

Andrews L (2019) Algorithms, regulation, and governance readiness. In: Yeung K, Lodge M (eds) Algorithmic regulation. Oxford University Press, Oxford, pp 203–223

---

[154]See also Rich (2013), pp. 804–828; Hartzog et al. (2015), pp. 1786–1793; Hoffmann-Riem (2017), p. 34; Rademacher (2017), pp. 398, 403–410.

Associated Press (2018) Israel claims 200 attacks predicted, prevented with data tech. CBS News. www.cbsnews.com/news/israel-data-algorithms-predict-terrorism-palestinians-privacy-civil-liberties. Accessed 29 Nov 2018

Bachmeier L (2018) Countering terrorism: suspects without suspicion and (pre-)suspects under surveillance. In: Sieber U, Mitsilegas V, Mylonopoulos C, Billis E, Knust N (eds) Alternative systems of crime control. Duncker&Humblodt, Berlin, pp 171–191

Barret B (2016) New surveillance system may let cops use all of the cameras. Wired. www.wired.com/2016/05/new-surveillance-system-let-cops-use-cameras. Accessed 16 Nov 2018

Becker M (2019) Von der Freiheit, rechtswidrig handeln zu können. Zeitschrift für Urheber- und Medienrecht 64:636–648

Bieker F, Bremert B, Hansen M (2018) Verantwortlichkeit und Einsatz von Algorithmen bei öffentlichen Stellen. Datenschutz und Datensicherheit:608–612

Bier W, Spiecker gen Döhmann I (2012) Intelligente Videoüberwachungstechnik: Schreckensszenario oder Gewinn für Datenschutz. Computer und Recht:610–618

Big Brother Watch (2018) Face off. The lawless growth of facial recognition in UK policing. https://www.bigbrotherwatch.org.uk/wp-content/uploads/2018/05/Face-Off-final-digital-1.pdf. Accessed 29 Nov 2018

Birnstill P, Ren D, Beyerer J (2015) A user study on anonymization techniques for smart video surveillance. IEEE. https://ieeexplore.ieee.org/stamp/stamp.jsp?tp=&arnumber=7301805. Accessed 29 Nov 2018

Böckenförde T (2008) Auf dem Weg zur elektronischen Privatsphäre. JuristenZeitung 63:925–939

Bouachir W, Gouiaa R, Li B, Noumeir R (2018) Intelligent video surveillance for real-time detection of suicide attempts. Pattern Recogn Lett 110:1–7

Brantingham PJ, Valasik M, Mohler GO (2018) Does predictive policing lead to biased arrests? Results from a randomized controlled trial. Stat Public Policy 5:1–6

Brühl J (2018) Wo die Polizei alles sieht. Süddeutsche Zeitung. www.sueddeutsche.de/digital/palantir-in-deutschland-wo-die-polizei-alles-sieht-1.4173809. Accessed 26 Nov 2018

Bundesministerium des Innern (2016) 'Polizei 2020'. www.bmi.bund.de/DE/themen/sicherheit/nationale-und-internationale-zusammenarbeit/polizei-2020/polizei-2020-node.html. Accessed 7 Dec 2018

Bundesministerium des Innern (2018) Pressemitteilung. Projekt zur Gesichtserkennung erfolgreich. www.bmi.bund.de/SharedDocs/pressemitteilungen/DE/2018/10/gesichtserkennung-suedkreuz.html. Accessed 29 Nov 2018

Bundespolizeipräsidium (2018) Teilprojekt 1 'Biometrische Gesichtserkennung'. Abschlussbericht. www.bundespolizei.de/Web/DE/04Aktuelles/01Meldungen/2018/10/181011_abschlussbericht_gesichtserkennung_down.pdf;jsessionid=2A4205E1606AC617C8006E65DEDD7D22.2_cid324?__blob=publicationFile&v=1. Accessed 29 Nov 2018

Bundestag (2018) Antwort der Bundesregiegung auf die Kleine Anfrage 'Umsetzung der EU-Richtlinie zur Vorratsdatenspeicherung von Fluggastdaten'. BT-Drucksache 19/4755

Burkert H (2012) Balancing informational power by information power, or rereading Montesquieu in the internet age. In: Brousseau E, Marzouki M, Méadel C (eds) Governance, regulations and powers on the internet. CUP, Cambridge, pp 93–111

Candamo J, Shreve M, Goldgof D, Sapper D, Kasturi R (2010) Understanding transit scenes: a survey on human behavior recognition algorithms. IEEE Trans Intell Transp Syst 11:206–224

Capers IB (2017) Race, policing, and technology. N C Law Rev 95:1241–1292

Caplan J, Kennedy L (2016) Risk terrain modeling. University of California Press, Oakland

Chaos Computer Club (2018) Biometrische Videoüberwachung: Der Südkreuz-Versuch war kein Erfolg. www.ccc.de/de/updates/2018/debakel-am-suedkreuz. Accessed 26 Nov 2018

Cheng E (2006) Structural laws and the puzzle of regulating behavior. Northwest Univ School Law 100:655–718

Davenport T (2016) How Big Data is helping the NYPD solve crime faster. Fortune. fortune.com/2016/07/17/big-data-nypd-situational-awareness. Accessed 29 Nov 2018

Degeling M, Berendt B (2017) What is wrong about Robocops as consultants? A technology-centric critique of predictive policing. AI & Soc 33:347–356

Demetis D (2018) Fighting money laundering with technology: a case study of Bank X in the UK. Decis Support Syst 105:96–107

Dimitrova D (2018) Data protection within police and judicial cooperation. In: Hofmann HCH, Rowe GC, Türk AH (eds) Specialized administrative law of the European Union. Oxford University Press, Oxford, pp 204–233

Dwork C, Hardt M, Pitassi T, Reingold O, Zemel R (2011) Fairness through awareness. arXiv.org/pdf/1104.3913.pdf. Accessed 29 Nov 2017

Eidenmüller H (2017) The rise of robots and the law of humans. Oxford Legal Studies Paper. Ssrn.com/abstract=2941001. Accessed 29 Nov 2018

Eubanks V (2018) A child abuse prediction model fails poor families. Wired. www.wired.com/story/excerpt-from-automating-inequality. Accessed 29 Nov 2018

Ferguson AG (2014) Fourth amendment security in public. William Mary Law Rev 55:1283–1364

Ferguson AG (2015) Big data and predictive reasonable suspicion. Univ Pa Law Rev 163:327–410

Ferguson AG (2017) The rise of big data policing. New York University Press, New York

Hacker P (2018) Teaching fairness to artificial intelligence: existing and novel strategies against algorithmic discrimination under EU law. Common Mark Law Rev 55:1143–1186

Harcourt B, Meares T (2011) Randomization and the fourth amendment. U Chi L Rev 78:809–877

Hartzog W, Conti G, Nelson J, Shay LA (2015) Inefficiently automated law enforcement. Mich State Law Rev:1763–1796

Heinemann M (2015) Grundrechtlicher Schutz informationstechnischer Systeme. Schriften zum Öffentlichen Recht, vol 1304. Duncker & Humblot, Berlin

Henderson SE (2016) Fourth amendment time machines (and what they might say about police body cameras). J Constit Law 18:933–973

Hildebrandt M (2016) Law as information in the era of data-driven agency. Mod Law Rev 79:1–30

Hoffmann-Riem W (2008) Der grundrechtliche Schutz der Vertraulichkeit und Integrität eigengenutzer informationstechnischer Systeme. JuristenZeitung 63:1009–1022

Hoffmann-Riem W (2017) Verhaltenssteuerung durch Algorithmen – Eine Herausforderung für das Recht. Archiv des öffentlichen Rechts 142:1–42

Joh E (2014) Policing by numbers: big data and the fourth amendment. Wash Law Rev 89:35–68

Joh E (2016) The new surveillance discretion: automated suspicion, big data, and policing. Harv Law Policy Rev 10:15–42

Joh E (2019) Policing the smart city. International Journal of Law in Context 15:177–182

Kroll JA, Huey J, Barocas S, Felten EW, Reidenberg JR, Robinson DG, Yu H (2017) Accountable algorithms. Univ Pa Law Rev 165:633–705

Lismont J, Cardinaels E, Bruynseels L, De Goote S, Baesens B, Lemahieu W, Vanthienen J (2018) Predicting tax avoidance by means of social network analytics. Decis Support Syst 108:13–24

Marks A, Bowling B, Keenan C (2017) Automatic justice? In: Brownsword R, Scotford E, Yeung K (eds) The Oxford handbook of law, regulation, and technology. Oxford University Press, Oxford, pp 705–730

Marsch N (2012) Die objektive Funktion der Verfassungsbeschwerde in der Rechtsprechung des Bundesverfassungsgerichts. Archiv des öffentlichen Rechts 137:592–624

Marsch N (2018) Das europäische Datenschutzgrundrecht. Mohr Siebeck, Tübingen

May J (2018) Drug enforcement agency turns to A.I. to help sniff out doping athletes. Digital trends. https://www.digitaltrends.com/outdoors/wada-artificial-intelligence-doping-athletes. Accessed 23 Oct 2019

McKay S (2015) Covert policing. Oxford University Press, Oxford

Mulligan CM (2008) Perfect enforcement of law: when to limit and when to use technology. Richmond J Law Technol 14:1–49

Murphy E (2007) The new forensics: criminal justice, false certainty, and the second generation of scientific evidence. Calif Law Rev 95:721–797

Oermann M, Staben J (2013) Mittelbare Grundrechtseingriffe durch Abschreckung? DER STAAT 52:630–661

Oganesian C, Heermann Th (2018) China: Der durchleuchtete Mensch – Das chinesische Socia-Credit-System. ZD-Aktuell:06124

Oldiges M (1987) Einheit der Verwaltung als Rechtsproblem. Neue Zeitschrift für Verwaltungsrecht 1987:737–744

Orwell G (1949) Nineteen eighty-four. Secker & Warburg, London

Pelzer R (2018) Policing terrorism using data from social media. Eur J Secur Res 3:163–179

Petroski W (2018) Iowa Senate OKs ban on traffic enforcement cameras as foes predict more traffic deaths. Des Moines Register. https://eu.desmoinesregister.com/story/news/politics/2018/02/27/traffic-enforcementcameras-banned-under-bill-passed-iowa-senate/357336002. Accessed 23 Oct 2019

Poscher R (2017) The right to data protection. In: Miller R (ed) Privacy and power. Cambridge University Press, Cambridge, pp 129–141

Rademacher T (2017) Predictive Policing im deutschen Polizeirecht. Archiv des öffentlichen Rechts 142:366–416

Rademacher T (2019) Wenn neue Technologien altes Recht durchsetzen: Dürfen wir es unmöglich machen, rechtswidrig zu handeln? JuristenZeitung 74:702–710

Reidenberg J (1998) Lex Informatica: the formulation of information policy rules through technology. Tex Law Rev 76:553–593

Rich M (2013) Should we make crime impossible? Harv J Law Public Policy 36:795–848

Rich M (2016) Machine learning, automated suspicion algorithms, and the fourth amendment. Univ Pa Law Rev 164:871–929

Richards NM (2013) The dangers of surveillance. Harv Law Rev 126:1934–1965

Rosenthal D (2011) Assessing digital preemption (and the future of law enforcement?). New Crim Law Rev 14:576–610

RWI Essen (2018) "Erfolgreiche" Gesichtserkennung mit hunderttausend Fehlalarmen. http://www.rwi-essen.de/unstatistik/84. Accessed 29 Nov 2018

Samek W, Wiegand T, Müller K-R (2017) Explainable artificial intelligence: understanding, visualizing and interpreting deep learning models. arXiv:1708.08296v1. Accessed 25 Oct 2019

Saracco R (2017) An artificial intelligence 'nose' to sniff diseases: EIT Digital. https://www.eitdigital.eu/newsroom/blog/article/an-artificial-intelligence-nose-to-sniff-diseases. Accessed 29 Nov 2018

Saunders J, Hunt P, Hollywood JS (2016) Predictions put into practice: a quasi-experimental evaluation of Chicago's predictive policing pilot. J Exp Criminol 12:347–371

Scantamburlo T, Charlesworth A, Cristianini N (2019) Machine decisions and human consequences. In: Yeung K, Lodge M (eds) Algorithmic regulation. Oxford University Press, Oxford, pp 49–81

Schlossberg T (2015) New York police begin using ShotSpotter system to detect gunshots. The New York Times. https://www.nytimes.com/2015/03/17/nyregion/shotspotter-detection-system-pinpoints-gunshot-locations-and-sends-data-to-the-police.html. Accessed 29 Nov 2018

Seidensticker K, Bode F, Stoffel F (2018) Predictive policing in Germany. http://nbn-resolving.de/urn:nbn:de:bsz:352-2-14sbvox1ik0z06. Accessed 29 Nov 2018

Singelnstein T (2018) Predictive Policing: Algorithmenbasierte Straftatenprognosen zur vorausschauenden Kriminalintervention. Neue Zeitschrift für Strafrecht:1–9

Solove DJ (2007) 'I've got nothing to hide' and other misunderstandings of privacy. San Diego Law Rev 44:745–772

Spice B (2015) Carnegie Mellon developing online tool to detect and identify sex traffickers. www.cmu.edu/news/stories/archives/2015/january/detecting-sex-traffickers.html. Accessed 24 Oct 2019

Staben J (2016) Der Abschreckungseffekt auf die Grundrechtsausübung. Internet und Gesellschaft, vol 6. Mohr Siebeck, Tübingen

Thomas S, Gupta S, Subramanian V (2017) Smart surveillance based on video summarization. IEEE. https://ieeexplore.ieee.org/document/8070003. Accessed 29 Nov 2018

Throckmorton CS, Mayew WJ, Venkatachalam M, Collins LM (2015) Financial fraud detection using vocal, linguistic and financial cues. Decis Support Syst 74:78–87

Timan T, Galic M, Koops B-J (2018) Surveillance theory and its implications for law. In: Brownsword R, Scotford E, Yeung K (eds) The Oxford handbook of law, regulation, and technology. Oxford University Press, Oxford, pp 731–753

Trute HH (2009) Grenzen des präventionsorientierten Polizeirechts in der Rechtsprechung des Bundesverfassungsgerichts. Die Verwaltung 42:85–104

Tyler TR (1990) Why people obey the law. Yale University Press, New Haven and London

Waltl B, Vogl R (2018) Increasing transparency in algorithmic decision-making with explainable AI. Datenschutz und Datensicherheit:613–617

Wendt K (2018) Zunehmender Einsatz intelligenter Videoüberwachung. ZD-Aktuell:06122

Wittmann P (2014) Der Schutz der Privatsphäre vor staatlichen Überwachungsmaßnahmen durch die US-amerikanische Bundesverfassung. Nomos, Baden-Baden

Wysk P (2018) Tausche Freiheit gegen Sicherheit? Die polizeiliche Videoüberwachung im Visier des Datenschutzrechts. Verwaltungsarchiv 109:141–162

Zetter K (2012) Public buses across country quietly adding microphones to record passenger conversations. Wired. www.wired.com/2012/12/public-bus-audio-surveillance. Accessed 26 Nov 2018

Artificial Intelligence and the Financial Markets: Business as Usual?

Jakob Schemmel

Contents

1. AI in the Financial Markets 256
   1.1 Business-Customer-Relations: 'Robo-advisers' 256
   1.2 Financial Markets and Institutions: 'Cyborg Finance' 258
   1.3 Compliance: 'RegTech I' 260
   1.4 New Players: 'FinTech' 261
2. Regulatory Approaches Towards AI in the Financial Markets 262
   2.1 Global Level 262
   2.2 European Level 263
   2.3 National Level 264
3. Governance Through and of AI in the Financial Markets 267
   3.1 Regulation and Supervision Through AI: 'RegTech II' 268
   3.2 Vital Aspects of Future AI Governance 269
4. AI and the Financial Markets: To a New Tomorrow 272
   4.1 First-Mover Advantages 273
   4.2 Yesterday's Mistakes 273
References 274

Abstract AI and financial markets go well together. The promise of speedy calculations, massive data processing and accurate predictions are too tempting to pass up for an industry in which almost all actors proceed exclusively instructed by a profit maximising logic. Hence, the strong mathematical prerequisites of financial decision-making give rise to the question: Why do financial markets require a human element anyway? The question is largely of a rhetorical nature due to the lack of complexity of most current AI tools. However, AI tools have been used in finance since the early 1990s and the push to overcome faulty computing and other shortcomings has been palpable ever since. Digitalization has amplified efforts and possibilities. Institutions with business models based on AI are entering the market by the hundreds; banks and insurers are either spinning off their AI expertise to foster its growth or paying billions

---

J. Schemmel (✉)
Institute for Staatswissenschaft and Philosophy of Law, Albert-Ludwigs-University Freiburg, Freiburg, Germany
e-mail: jakob.schemmel@jura.uni-freiburg.de

© Springer Nature Switzerland AG 2020
T. Wischmeyer, T. Rademacher (eds.), *Regulating Artificial Intelligence*,
https://doi.org/10.1007/978-3-030-32361-5_11

to acquire expertise. There is no way around AI—at least in certain parts of the financial markets. This article outlines the developments concerning the application of AI in the financial markets and discusses the difficulties pertaining to its sudden rise. It illustrates the diverse fields of application (Sect. 1) and delineates approaches, which major financial regulators are taking towards AI (Sect. 2). In a next step governance through and of AI is discussed (Sect. 3). The article concludes with the main problems that a reluctant approach towards AI results in (Sect. 4).

1 AI in the Financial Markets

When discussing the changes that AI is bringing to the financial markets, most observers are not afraid of overstating its importance. There is talk of a new era[1] and of the new physics of financial services.[2] However, there is also no doubt that the profound transformation is still in its nascent phase.[3] In particular, the development is far from consistent and varies from sector to sector. As of now, there certainly are some AI applications, which have almost completely substituted human labour. In other areas, however, AI support does not amount to more than a promising blueprint.

1.1 Business-Customer-Relations: 'Robo-advisers'

One of the more advanced areas in employing AI tools is customer relations. The potential to reduce costs for service personnel spurred a remarkable growth in interactive algorithms which are not only used in the financial services.[4] In the business-customer-relation, AI is mostly employed to assist both customers and institutions with complex decisions.

A high number of institutes are already using AI to provide personalised **investment advice** and enable monitoring of investments in the retail financial services through so called 'robo-advisers'.[5] Even though most of the robo-advisors in use are still overseen by human investment advisors, there is a clear trend towards independent robo-advising.[6] The wide range of programs is still in an early stage and used by

---

[1] BaFin (2018), p. 19.
[2] WEF (2018).
[3] FSB (2017a), p. 1.
[4] Edwards, pp. 97 et seq.: the most common being advice algorithms that compute not only market data but also the personal information of users in order to give guidance to consumers when they engage in business with a firm.
[5] Lightbourne (2017), pp. 652 et seq.
[6] KPMG (2016), p. 3.

both costumers and advisors to tailor investment decisions according to certain strategies and risk appetites. Most programs operate in a rather basic manner: The AI assesses the investment strategy of the user by asking predefined questions about her risk profile.[7] It then interprets current market information and calculates the most feasible investment for the detected investment strategy. In most cases, the AI is fed information on investment products, risk classifications and market predictions to conduct its assessment.[8] It is however not only the superior computing power of AI which has been identified as a major benefit. AI investment support purportedly increases accessibility of financial services,[9] lowers transaction costs,[10] and provides sound and well-supported investment advice. Yet, empirical evaluations show that robo-advisers are still far away from fulfilling all of these high expectations. Even in the stable environment of ETF-trading, AI tools dealing with the same risk characteristics delivered highly diverse returns.[11] Algorithm development as well as information support still seem to remain a challenging task.

Another prominent application of AI in the retail sector is **consumer lending**—a field which has a traditional affiliation with algorithms. Credit scores are the result of a complex calculus factoring in a few dozen data points. AI tools are able to include a multiple thereof.[12] Since 2006, marketplace lenders and other lending companies in the US have therefore utilised machine learning to conduct the credit scoring of potential lenders.[13] However, as important as the computing power of AI tools to this business model is the massive amount of personal digital data that has become available in the last decades. The personal data used ranges from club memberships to social media activity and texting habits.[14] In contrast to 'robo-advisers' which are also employed by big commercial banks most of AI credit scoring is conducted by smaller businesses. These financial technology ('FinTech') companies have filled the space left vacant by the banking industry when they pulled out of lending in the wake of the financial crisis in and after 2008.[15] Even though the sector of marketplace lending is growing remarkably fast, it exhibits all traits of a nascent financial industry: Consumer complaints over loan processing, adjustable rates, and even fraudulent behaviour or identity fraud are not uncommon.[16]

In contrast to retail trading, AI is not yet indispensable in the core business of the **insurance sector**.[17] Opportunities however seem ample: Insurers could use AI to

---

[7]Robo-advisers are not necessarily chatbots; on their utilization see Hennemann, para 12.
[8]Chiu (2016), p. 88.
[9]Bradley (2018), p. 74.
[10]Chiu (2016), p. 89.
[11]Lightbourne (2017), pp. 663 et seq.
[12]On the potential influence of flawed data aggregation see Tischbirek, para 7.
[13]Bruckner (2018), p. 13.
[14]Odinet (2018), p. 785. About the implications of such algorithm decisions on a persons autonomy see Ernst, paras 4–5.
[15]Odinet (2018), pp. 783, 800 et seq.
[16]Odinet (2018), pp. 829 et seq.
[17]Portfolio management however still is a central function of insurers.

model new risks that could not be accurately modelled due to missing historical data, develop modularized policies including dynamic pricing and automated underwriting, and implement dynamic individual pricing for its customers.[18] Big insurance companies are especially interested in dynamic (i.e. behavioral) pricing models that have been tested in a number of projects. Indeed this particular application seems to hold enormous potential: The change from proxy to individual data for respective consumers would enhance accuracy of risk assessment drastically. Projections are accordingly (over-)optimistic: Some observers even speak of a prospective seismic shift.[19]

1.2 Financial Markets and Institutions: 'Cyborg Finance'

6   Algorithms have supported buying and selling on financial markets since decades. The steady expansion of machine trading has been propelled by the same reasons as the development of robo-advisors: higher efficiency, lower costs, fewer errors, quicker execution, and extended data computing. The market environment nowadays is shaped by 'supercomputers'.[20] In the digital age, trading without algorithmic support seems at the very least imprudent.

7   Most selling and buying in the financial markets is therefore done by algorithmic or **automated traders**.[21] Almost all of these machines are directed by unsupervised algorithms. In contrast to most robo-advisors, they are able to execute trades on their own. They can sell, buy, and hold positions without human confirmation or direction. Coding therefore is key. The basic data points used are: what assets to trade, products to create, width of spread to identify before unloading, sizes of positions to hold, and broker-dealers to deal with or avoid. All algorithms also feature crucial limiting parameters. Most automated traders however have a much more sophisticated setup.[22] They integrate certain economic model assumptions and are able to compute what politics, traffic, weather, or other events mean for risk assessment; they can detect market sentiments and trends; and they can update and act on market predictions in seconds. Until recently, this required highly complex operations that were laid down in algorithms coded by human back offices. To capture this close interconnectedness between human coding and algorithmic execution the literature has coined the term 'cyborg finance'.[23] Yet algorithmic trades remained limited to events that coders could think of. AI however lifts these constraints. Regulators therefore predict a larger expansion of AI use in the foreseeable future.[24]

---

[18]WEF (2018), p. 111.
[19]E.g. Balasubramanian et al. (2018).
[20]Ling (2014), p. 568.
[21]Yadav (2015), pp. 1618 et seq.
[22]Narang (2013), pp. 8 et seq.
[23]Ling (2014), p. 572.
[24]BaFin (2018), p. 11.

A prominent field of automatic trading that already employs artificial intelligence is **high frequency trading** (HFT). HFT is a form of automated trading that generates profits by competing on speed, rapid turnover and a high order-to-trade ratio.[25] Automated traders buy and sell comparatively small amounts of assets frequently and with a very short investment horizon to profit from price movements (directional trading). HFT was a dominant form of trading with revenues in the billions until the financial crisis. However, the high profitability of HFT lead to an arms race between competitors. As a result, advantages levelled and profits fell.[26] To re-establish a competitive edge, traders have turned to models developed by deep learning networks or Deep Neural Networks (DNNs) to more accurately predict price movements.[27] 'Neural Networks' are designed to mimic the information processing capabilities of the human brain[28] and have been used in finance since the early 1990s.[29] Artificial Neural Networks (ANNs) consist of interconnected processors that can perform a weighted aggregation of multiple input signals. They are capable of identifying complex patterns in high dimensional spaces and extracting critical information.[30] However, ANNs only have a few layers of processing units and therefore input is limited.[31] Deep ANNs or DNNs on the other hand can be characterized as more sophisticated and complex forms of ANNs since they use multiple hidden layers. While passing through each layer, data is processed and dimensions are reduced until patterns can be identified. This design enables DNNs to handle significantly more input, i.e. to deal with raw data. Recent developments in the fields of unsupervised and supervised machine learning have made the results of DNNs more reliable and increased the number of hidden layers that can be engaged.

8

AI is also becoming more and more important when it comes to **portfolio management**. Portfolio or asset management describes the balancing, restructuring and allocation of financial assets to maintain certain (long-term) target dimensions. Complexity and variance of the respective targets are usually high and demand multi-layered data analytics. In this field, AI is already used to identify new signals on price movements. It is detecting correlations and hidden developments in data sets to predict volatility and price levels over different time horizons.[32] Especially hedge funds are employing AI tools to structure investments. Fully automated AI structured assets are however rare to find. For example, it is estimated that unsupervised AI instructs only about 2.5% of mutual funds' global market liquidity.[33]

9

---

[25] Seddon and Currie (2017), p. 300.
[26] Osipovich (2017).
[27] Seddon and Currie (2017), p. 305.
[28] Kaastra and Boyd (1996), p. 234.
[29] Trippi and DeSieno (1992), pp. 27 et seq.
[30] Arévalo et al. (2016), p. 424.
[31] Schmidhuber (2015), p. 85.
[32] FSB (2017a), p. 18.
[33] FSB (2017a), p. 19.

1.3 Compliance: 'RegTech I'

10   Financial institutes have been facing a toughening of regulative requirements after the financial crisis. The European Union in particular overhauled most of its financial markets law. Some of the new rules are criticized as being too extensive and overly burdensome to the institutions. AI, however, could help lifting some of the compliance burden by an autonomous application of rules.

11   One of the more prominent reforms is part of **prudent regulations** and concerns institutional requirements, which aim to ensure the stability of banks: capital requirements. As of now, most countries have implemented the vital Basel III instrument.[34] The Basel accords require that banks need to maintain a certain risk-based capital ratio.[35] This ratio determines the level of regulatory capital to be held by the banks. Risk assessment constitutes the most important factor in the ratio-equation since risk weight assets represent the most important share of a banks' capital.[36] Basel III allows banks to take an internal ratings-based approach towards credit risks to reduce the reliance on external credit ratings. It has been discussed for quite some time now whether banks should employ AI to more precisely capture risk relations and developments.[37] Some banks are already using AI to validate the outputs of their internal risk models or detect anomalous projections generated by internal stress testing models.[38]

12   A second field in which AI might help to make compliance more cost-effective is **market conduct regulation**—in particular recently established anti money-laundering rules.[39] These rules require banks, inter alia, to gather and store certain key information about their clients ('know your costumer' or KYC)[40] and have proven challenging to comply with since they severely increased costs and personnel demands. The current KYC-processes are dominated by a high level of manual and data intensive tasks that seem ineffective to combat money laundering: identities must be verified, suspicious activities need to be detected, connections between actors must be established.[41] Many observers agree that a KYC-AI would not only reduce costs significantly but also increase the overall quality of money laundering detection.[42] In recent years, an increasing number of banks therefore have

---

[34] FSB (2017b), p. 3.

[35] BCBS (2011), pp. 12 et seq. For a short summary of its legal status Schemmel (2016), pp. 460 et seq.

[36] For a discussion of the relation between risk-weighted bank capital and the minimum leverage ratio that is not risk weighted and was introduced by Basel III as a backstop to risk-based capital requirements see Gambacorta and Karmakar (2016), pp. 3 et seq.

[37] Angelini et al. (2008) and Danielsson et al. (2017).

[38] FSB (2017a), p. 16.

[39] Anagnostopoulos (2018).

[40] 31 CFR 103.121 (USA). Article 8 Directive 2005/60/EC (European Union)—sometimes referred to as 'customer due diligence'.

[41] Craig (2018).

[42] Aziz and Dowling (2018), p. 10. On other possible applications Neufang (2017).

implemented machine learning to either support or conduct KYC and money laundering identification.[43] Since AI can perform only as well as the quality of data it is fed, some banks are discussing common databases. Recently the five biggest banks of Scandinavia, DNB Bank, Danske Bank, Nordea, Handelsbanken and SEB, created 'Nordic KYC Utility'—a platform for sharing business costumer data to ease the KYC-burden for clients and banks.[44]

1.4 New Players: 'FinTech'

AI and its manifold applications in the financial sectors have propelled a significant growth in the financial start up sector. FinTech businesses have become the new primary driving force reshaping the financial sectors. The involvement of FinTech in the financial services industry can be described by using three stages of integration: (i) They may act as data brokers assembling and licensing out assembled data or results of AI analytics (data broker); (ii) they may offer services to a limited range of businesses guiding their credit decisions by AI analytics (vertical integration); (iii) they may act as full service financial institutions using AI to offer services and products (horizontal diversification).[45]

In specific, horizontally diversified FinTech has had a great impact on the business models of traditional financial service providers. Their advantages are cost-effectiveness, easy accessibility and customer friendly services that seem to meet all requirements of the digital era. Conventional financial services usually collectivize investment management and sell large quantities of packaged products for consumer-based risk management[46]: To be cost-effective service providers need to pool customer savings into collective investments. Consumers invest in funds and abstract financial products and do not know the recipient or borrower of their money. Traditional service providers also tend to offer package deals to their customers. The one-stop-shop mentality has significant cost benefits for providers but also creates perverse incentives for service advisors. In contrast to that, FinTech businesses offer tailored services adapted to customer specification or profiles. Early stage products such as **peer-to-peer financial services** or **online crowdfunding** also convey a sense of consumer empowerment.

However, even though FinTech businesses seem to bolster disintermediation by cutting out the middleman, i.e. commercial banks, their effect in that regard is rather limited.[47] Most observers agree that intermediation is a vital part of financial markets or services and cannot be eliminated since supply and demand must be matched and

---

[43]Milne (2018).
[44]Nordea (2018). On the competition implications of data power see Hennemann, paras 20 et seq.
[45]Zetsche et al. (2018), p. 410.
[46]For further discussion of the following see Chiu (2016), pp. 71 et seq.
[47]Chiu (2016), pp. 83 et seq.

16 costumer friendly products need to be created. FinTech therefore leads to re-intermediation or disaggregated value chains[48] and rather exchanges the middlemen.[49]

16   Whereas these developments seem rather conventional from a regulatory perspective, the advent of **data broker FinTech** companies might prove challenging: They introduce a new structure of knowledge distribution into the highly regulated financial services. Providers of AI tools are not necessarily financial service providers themselves. Laws governing financial services therefore do not apply to all of them. Furthermore technological development in the recent years rather led to monopolization of providers. If this will be the case with AI as well, providers could quickly accrue systematic relevance.[50]

2 Regulatory Approaches Towards AI in the Financial Markets

17   It is common that regulators of the financial markets act only hesitantly when it comes to new technological developments. The same seems to hold true for this case: Since most of the described applications of AI are still in the early stage of development, most regulators have not yet taken action. Algorithmic trading—as the only form of machine supported trading that has existed for decades—seems to be the exception to that rule. However, regulators around the globe take notice of AI tools and are monitoring developments with growing scrutiny.

2.1 Global Level

18   The **Financial Stability Board** (FSB), a group consisting of G20 government and central bank officials that assesses and monitors the systemic risk of the global financial markets, recently published a report on AI and machine learning in financial services.[51] The FSB concludes that AI shows substantial promise if its specific risks are properly managed. Its potential to enhance efficiency of information processing can strengthen the information function of the financial markets.[52] As a consequence, prices would reflect more accurately the intrinsic value of traded assets. Furthermore, AI has the potential to enhance profitability of financial institutions, reduce costs for market participants in various areas, and may at the same

---

[48] BaFin (2018), pp. 65 et seq.
[49] Lin (2015a), p. 655.
[50] Lin (2016), pp. 168 et seq.
[51] FSB (2017a).
[52] On the following see FSB (2017a), pp. 24 et seq.

time benefit costumers.[53] The FSB even identifies potential improvements in regulatory compliance and supervision.[54] However, the report also identifies grave risks linked to AI applications. Network effects and scalability may give rise to unregulated third party dependencies. At the same time, AI might lead to 'unexpected' forms of interconnectedness between financial markets and institutions.[55] Last but not least, it is the lack of auditability that concerns the Board. AI tools used by financial institutions are 'black boxes' that do not explain their decisions.[56] The widespread use of such opaque models could result in a heavily reduced ability to assess and maintain financial stability.[57]

2.2 European Level

The **European Supervisory Authorities** for the financial markets recently concluded an analysis on the benefits and risks of AI and big data.[58] In comparison to the FSB, this European report strikes a much more reserved tone. Even though the reservations might be the result of the reports' specific perspective that views big data analytics as a separate technology and not as an AI application, the conclusions match the diction: AI is seen as not mature enough to even make a prediction on how it will develop. However, the report acknowledges that AI is a key tool to improve discovering patterns on captured data, classification, evaluation and prediction.[59]

The European Commission has taken a more optimistic stance. In its FinTech Action Plan the Commission recognises AI as one of the main driving forces changing the European financial industry and identifies certain regulatory challenges—such as paper-based disclosure requirements—for further technological development.[60] To prevent a lack of regulatory certainty and guidance from becoming a major hurdle for AI and other FinTech the Commission has created an **EU FinTech Lab**. The Lab aims to build capacity and knowledge among regulators and supervisors about technological developments and their market implications. The European Banking Authority has implemented a similar initiative.[61] First meetings have focussed on data issues such as cloud outsourcing.

---

[53]Cf. see paras 6 et seq. and 2 et seq.
[54]Cf. see paras 10 et seq.
[55]FSB (2017a), p. 1.
[56]On so-called 'explainable AI' see Wischmeyer, paras 27 et seq., Rademacher, para 33.
[57]FSB (2017a), p. 2.
[58]Joint Committee (2018).
[59]Joint Committee (2018), p. 22.
[60]European Commission (2018).
[61]EBA (2018).

21   The only area the EU has regulated and in which AI finds relevant application is algorithmic trading and HFT. The amending directive on markets in financial instruments and the respective regulation (MiFID II/MiFIR)[62] lay down certain ground rules. Algorithmic traders are required to ensure that their systems are resilient and sufficiently equipped.[63] They also need to inform their supervisory authority and trading venue that they engage in algorithmic trading[64] and keep information on trades of the algorithms, details on the person overseeing an algorithm, and records on compliance and risk systems in place at the disposal of the authorities for five years.[65] Trading venues are required to install systems that can limit algorithmic trading when it leads to market disorder. These include mechanisms to limit the ratio of unexecuted orders, slow down order flow and enforce minimum tick sizes.[66] Institutions engaging in HFT are regulated in a similar way but need to file additional information: They are required to store information on placed orders, including cancellations of orders, executed orders and quotations on trading venues.[67]

2.3 National Level

22   The cautious international approach towards regulating AI can also be found on the national level. Countries with traditionally strong financial markets embrace the new technology as a competitive advantage whereas others tend to observe developments. This distinction holds true even in the EU despite its efforts to create a single market.

United States

23   As home of the biggest financial market, the USA naturally takes the lead when it comes to regulating and supervising new financial technology. Recently, government and authorities have shown strong interest in AI applications due to the current administration's focus on fostering 'economic growth and vibrant financial markets'.[68] As a part of these endeavours the US Department of the Treasury recently presented a report on 'Nonbank Financials, Fintech, and Innovation'.[69] The report

---

[62] Directive 2014/65/EU. Regulation Nr. 600/2014.
[63] See on the following Čuk and Waeyenberge (2018).
[64] Article 17 Directive 2014/65/EU.
[65] Article 26 para. 3 Regulation Nr. 600/2014.
[66] Article 48 Directive 2014/65/EU.
[67] Article 17 para 2 subpara 5.
[68] Article 1 lit. c Executive Order 13772 on Core Principles for Regulating the United States Financial System.
[69] US Treasury (2018).

details investment trends in AI, current applications of technology and forecasts concerning its future use. As issues associated with AI applications the report discusses the development of high concentrations amongst market providers, potential circumvention of fraud detection, lack of auditability, job loss and data privacy concerns.[70] Against this background, the final recommendations are rather unexpected: 'The Treasury recommends that financial regulators [...] emphasize use-cases and applications in the financial services industry, including removing regulatory barriers to deployment of AI-powered technologies.'[71] In this vein the Financial Industry Regulatory Authority (FINRA) is currently inviting comments of the industry on how regulatory requirements interfere with AI.[72]

This course of action fits the current administration's stance on HFT. The sheer endless discussion as to whether the SEC should amend rule 15b9-1[73] to extend its oversight over HF traders—thereby catching up with European regulations—have yet to bear fruit.[74] The short-lived HFT regulation proposal of the Commodity Futures Trading Commission (CFTC) that was discussed during the Obama administration and even involved access for supervisory authorities to the algorithms of HF traders are only a distant memory.[75]

Germany

As a Member State of the European Union it transposed the European rules concerning HFT into national law. Therefore institutions engaging in HFT need an authorization (§§ 32(1) 1, (1a) No. 4 lit. d Banking Act [*Kreditwesengesetz*— KWG]), and need to tag trades executed by algorithms (§ 16(3) No. 2 Stock Exchange Act [Börsengesetz—BörsG]). Other Requirements applying to all algorithmic trading have been transposed by § 80(2) Securities Trading Act (*Werpapierhandelsgesetz*—WpHG).[76] According to § 80(2) Financial Service Providers (FSP) entertaining algorithmic trading must ensure sufficient resilience and capacity of the trading system (§ 80(2) 3 No 1 WpHG), prevent faulty orders (§ 80 (2) 3 No 2 WpHG), and guarantee that algorithmic trading cannot be used for market abuse or other illegal purposes (§ 80(2) 3 No 3 WpHG). In addition FSP need to establish distress measures and report keeping which enable not only an immediate suspension of trade but also subsequent investigations (§ 80(2) 4, (3) WpHG). Finally, § 80(2) 5 WpHG requires FSP that engage in algorithmic trading to register

---

[70]US Treasury (2018), pp. 56 et seq.
[71]US Treasury (2018), p. 59.
[72]FINRA (2018), pp. 6 et seq.
[73]17 CFR 240.15b9-1. On the political background see Bain (2018).
[74]On the most recent proposal Morelli (2017), pp. 220 et seq. For a summary of the events leading to the current system Poirier (2012).
[75]BaFin (2018).
[76]Cf. see para 21.

with their competent supervisory authority as well as the respective trading venue.[77] This approach towards the regulation of algorithmic trading leaves the specific measures to the FSP. The broad wording of the respective clauses allows for a substantial autonomy of FSP.[78] Compliance will take numerous shapes.[79] Additional requirements must be met by FSP using algorithmic trading for Market-Making. Due to their crucial role in market liquidity, they must notify the respective trading venue and enter into a contract which specifies scope and type of markets as well as features of traded instruments. To honor such agreements, FSP will have to adapt their Market-Maker algorithms according to the agreed items.

26   However, the overall regulatory strategy of Germany seems more balanced or—depending on one's perspective—cautious. A rather technical study of the German *Bundesanstalt für Finanzdienstleistungsaufsicht* (Federal Financial Supervisory Authority) introduces the issue of AI as follows: 'It must be clear to everyone involved that BDAI [Big Data/Artificial Intelligence] brings with it risks as well as opportunities. These risks must be understood and actively addressed.'[80] Certainly, the report also states opportunities arising from AI. However, it conveys the sense that these opportunities are only relevant for private institutions, whereas the authority is mainly interested in risks and regulatory questions. It is telling that the Strategy on Artificial Intelligence of the German Government does not mention financial markets at all.[81] The difference to the approach of the US Treasury and FINRA is striking.

United Kingdom

27   The UK shows that the cautious German course does not stem from its EU-membership. As the financial centre of Europe, the UK pursues a strategy that aims to further increase the use of AI and FinTech in the financial markets.

28   One of the most successful UK undertakings furthering this approach is the **'regulatory sandbox'**. The concept of a 'sandbox' as a testing environment has been developed by the computer sciences. It describes a testing environment for new or unknown software. Programmes are run isolated from the main operating program or server to mitigate the spreading of damaging events. The regulatory sandbox of the UK Financial Conduct Authority (FCA) operates under a similar designation and is currently accepting applicants for its fifth cohort.[82] During the first four cohorts,

---

[77]This requirement was established to transpose the almost equally worded Article 17(2) 1 Directive 2014/65/EU. The registration duty exists to enable supervisory authorities to make use of their auditing powers under Article 17(2) 2 Directive 2014/65/EU; § 4(1) WpHG.

[78]Even though the European Securities and Markets Authority (ESMA) has already published guidelines further specifying some of the requirements: Guideline 2 ESMA/2012/122 (EN). On guidelines and their (quasi-)legal effect Schemmel (2016), pp. 459 et seq.

[79]This borders on a principle based approach, see Schemmel (2016), pp. 487 et seq.

[80]BaFin (2018), p. 3.

[81]Bundesregierung (2018). For a comparison see House of Lords (2017).

[82]On the following FCA (2018a).

six AI applications were tested. In contrast to its role model, the regulatory sandbox operates in a live market environment and is not isolated from it.[83] However, a strict registration process, limited authorizations, and so-called sandbox tools are designated to protect consumers from financial harm. Applicants must have a (i) well-developed testing plan as well as a (ii) genuinely innovative product (iii) intended for the UK market that (iv) benefits consumers but (v) does not easily fit the current regulatory framework. Sandbox tools also ensure a close exchange between FCA and sandbox businesses. They receive individual guidance by a specifically assigned case officer that may not only provide informal steering but can also waive certain regulatory requirements altogether.[84] EU law however constitutes limits to the sandbox concessions. European rules do not allow for lifting application requirements. Member State authorities must apply EU law and cannot grant exemptions. The FCA claims that this regulatory environment contributes to mutual learning and understanding and enables the agency to build appropriate consumer protection safeguards into new products and services.[85] The main goal is to establish and maintain the competitive advantage of the UK as a financial hub.

The most smashing export hit until now however is the sandbox itself. It served as model for similar endeavours in other jurisdictions[86] and even in the US demands for similar projects are voiced.[87] The FCA however has even bigger plans: In collaboration with eleven financial regulators, it founded the Global Financial Innovation Network (GFIN) which aims to create a 'global regulatory sandbox'.[88]

3 Governance Through and of AI in the Financial Markets

The advent of AI not only holds the promise of a more lucrative future, it also renews an old promise—a levelled playing field for both: regulators and industry. Regulatory and supervising authorities that have been outnumbered and outspent for decades may even catch up with financial institutions.[89]

---

[83]FCA (2017a), pp. 4 et seq. Arner et al. (2017), p. 371: A better term might therefore be 'clinical trial'.
[84]On the concept of umbrella sandbox Zetsche et al. (2017), pp. 85 et seq.
[85]FCA (2017a), pp. 6 et seq.
[86]E.g. Australia, Singapore, Switzerland, Hong Kong, Thailand, Abu Dhabi and Malaysia. On this with further references Arner et al. (2017), p. 371.
[87]Thomas (2018); rather hesitant Peirce (2018).
[88]FCA (2018b).
[89]On challenges of digitalisation Lin (2017), pp. 1253 et seq.

3.1 Regulation and Supervision Through AI: 'RegTech II'

31   This hope rests on the shoulders of AI applications that put par of industry and supervisors within reach through superior data processing performance, high efficiency, and abilities to anticipate market developments as well as compliance breaches.[90]

Supervision: 'Robocops'

32   AI is currently employed by a number of supervisors including the FCA, the Australian Securities and Investments Commission, and the Monetary Authority of Singapore. It enables supervisors to potentiate their data processing abilities.[91] In particular, the US Securities and Exchange Commission has made no secret of its current use of AI tools to detect potential **market misconduct**.[92] Natural language processing through unsupervised AI is currently used to analyse most filings to the Commission (prospectuses, tips, complaints, and referrals). Furthermore, Enforcement and Examination are using AI tools to assist with their work. Processing financial documents and filings AI has been able to identify potential misconduct or fraudulent institutions and traders and thereby help to efficiently deploy resources. Even though human work is currently still needed at every stage of examinations, the SEC seems to aim for completely automatic examinations.[93]

Regulation: 'Machine Readable and Executable Rulebook'

33   The regulation of financial markets post 2007 relies heavily on reported data to assess macro- and micro-economic risks. These reporting requirements are a massive cost driver for financial institutions. To ease the burden of compliance and enhance quality and accuracy of the data, FCA and the Bank of England are evaluating as to whether reporting duties of the main rulebooks—the FCA's Handbook and the Prudential Regulatory Authority's Handbook—can be adapted to enable an automatic reporting by machines.[94] The project is still in its early stages and core elements, such as from what data such programmes would gather information to report, still need to be addressed. However, FINRA has already indicated a similar interest.[95]

---

[90]On certain specifics of AI based agency supervision see Hermstrüwer, paras 20 et seq.
[91]Broeders and Prenio (2018), p. 10.
[92]Bauguess (2017).
[93]Bauguess (2017); for an account of constitutional frameworks and major issues concerning AI and law enforcement in general see Rademacher, paras 13 et seq.
[94]FCA (2017b).
[95]FINRA (2018), pp. 8 et seq. (machine-readable rulebook).

Another more ambitious avenue of development currently discussed amongst scholars is **dynamic regulation**.[96] The argument is straightforward: Financial markets law is quickly out-dated by market developments and therefore regulations must become adaptive: Quick and counter-cyclical. This holds true in particular when one considers the developments of financial activities driven by AI and Big Data. It therefore seems to be a rather obvious idea that FinTech must be met with RegTech. AI computing and data processing would be employed to monitor financial markets and institutions constantly while AI-regulators engage in flagged trades and impede predicted market failures. This could free crucial working capacities for 'big picture' regulatory decisions.[97] However, such a development needs an independent and highly complex AI that takes into account regulatory purposes.[98]

3.2 Vital Aspects of Future AI Governance

AI will transcend the possibilities of current financial institutions. Nevertheless, the technologically neutral approach taken by most regulators until now must be further pursued until it proves not to be sufficient any longer. Future regulation will have to adapt to the issues the respective AI creates but certain key points can already be identified.[99]

Assigning Responsibility

It will be crucial that AI governance and accountability remains with its users.[100] Even though coding and backstopping of AI may be outsourced, when it is applied in the financial markets, the user institution must remain responsible for the compliance of its dealings to not give rise to a massive moral hazard. In most cases, technological neutrality and a strict application of existing rules will be sufficient.[101] However, in other cases the following—rather obvious—rule of thumb should apply: Unsupervised AI trading must be subject to rules that entail liability concerns, duties to inform investors, and authority reporting. Trading losses should be borne by the institution employing AI or the investor who made the informed decision to delegate her investment to AI.

---

[96] On the following Baxter (2016), pp. 589 et seq.; Guihot et al. (2017), pp. 436 et seq. For a discussion of innovative regulation with regard to legal tech see Buchholtz, paras 32 et seq.
[97] Baxter (2016), p. 603.
[98] On financial service regulation as path-breaker Fenwick et al. (2017).
[99] A central AI-Agency seems therefore impractical, suggesting this Scherer (2016), pp. 395 et seq.
[100] For a discussion of liability attribution under competition law see Hennemann, paras 31 et seq.
[101] On the enforcement policies of the CTFC Scopino (2015), pp. 279 et seq.

Redefining Systemic Relevance

37   AI will most likely lead to a change in development distribution. As of now, financial institutions are designing their own algorithms. However, the high complexity of AI and its (currently) high development costs will presumably lead to outsourcing. As most digital developments have resulted in high market concentration and quasi monopolies, the same is to be expected with financial markets AI. This does not only carry implications for competition law but might also bear systemic relevance. Depending on the market penetration of AI a glitch in the code could have disastrous results. Regulators should therefore keep an eye on developments concerning AI distributors. If a significant share of financial markets AI is developed by a contractor that is not a financial institution, relevant market conduct and prudential regulations should be extended to it.

Insisting on Auditability

38   One of the greatest challenges of AI is its lack of auditability. Regulation and supervision of financial markets depend on the rational and assessable behaviour of its participants. The more opaque the models are, which are shaping investment decisions, the harder it becomes to accurately evaluate the state of markets. Even though there are technical limits to the replicability of automated decisions, it will be of crucial importance to insist on rudimentary explanation at the very least.[102] If therefore an AI shows glitches, causes crashes or behaves irrationally, it and similar AI should be banned from market interaction unless reasonable explanation for the error is presented, and recurrence can be ruled out.

39   Furthermore, current AI is introduced into a steady market environment. How AI interacts with highly volatile and crisis driven markets, however, will be key to market stability.[103] AI should therefore demonstrate how well it performs under crisis circumstances before being integrated into algorithms that cannot simply be switched off. The same applies to low liquidity market environments.

Adapting Reporting and Disclosure

40   Data is a central resource when it comes to AI. Reporting and disclosure rules should therefore be adapted to make for a smarter AI. This would also induce long overdue reforms. Current reporting is not only inapt because it is paper-based.[104] It also does not equip supervisors with the information needed to understand current trading.[105]

---

[102] On agency through explanation see also Wischmeyer, paras 25 et seq., and see Rademacher, para 33.

[103] See also Wall (2018). Cf. Hermstrüwer, paras 65–69 for proposals on how AI might be used to improve administrative procedures in dealing with regulatory complexity.

[104] On additional challenges Packin (2018), pp. 211 et seq.

[105] On the normative constraints of information regulation see Wischmeyer, paras 16 et seq.

FinTech Labs as initiated by the European Commission or the FCA's sandbox are first steps to keep up with these developments but they are not sufficient. Supervisors need a coherent and complete picture of the trading environments they are monitoring. There should be a requirement to report employed supervised and unsupervised AI every six months. Autonomously executing (i.e. non-auditable) AI should be reported in shorter intervals specifying traded amounts, assets, prices and other significant data points.[106] Finally, authorities should identify data points that RegTech AI will need to perform basic monitoring and supervising duties. According to the results, reporting duties to the authorities should be changed.

Furthermore, disclosure rules must be reformed.[107] Disclosures seem permanently stuck in the early twentieth century. Their elaborated texts and flowery language do not fit into an era, in which numbers dominate and investors rather read balance sheets than annual accounts. Therefore, to advance a well-informed market environment and lower entry levels for well-informed AI disclosure, rules should be amended.

41

Reducing Regulatory Arbitrage

Financial innovation does not stop at borders. If a technology promises higher margins, it will find its way onto other national and international markets. Legislators seldom possess the stature to pass up profit opportunities of its domestic industries and the respective tax gains. Regulators that approach AI hesitantly should therefore proactively engage in discussions with their more dynamic colleagues to prevent a regulatory race to the bottom. There will certainly be no global approach, but an agreement about main issues among the members of the FSB[108] seems possible.

42

Consumer Protection

During the next years of adaption, AI will be applied to almost all fields of the financial services. Minor errors and crashes will be accepted in the hope of more efficient markets and higher margins. Whereas this might be acceptable if institutions bear the costs of their dealings, consumers need to be guarded from such events. A minimum precaution should be that AI trading or advising is clearly stated and that it is indicated in short and understandable language what the risks of AI trading are, i.e. complete loss of all investments.[109] Also, consumers should be made aware of the fact that AI cannot, in line of principle,[110] explain its investment decisions.

43

---

[106]See also Wischmeyer, paras 22 in favor of a tailor made approach.
[107]Lin (2015b), pp. 508 et seq.
[108]See para 18.
[109]On the question as to whether consumers should also be informed about non-personalized results see Ernst, para 48.
[110]See para 18, esp. note 53.

44 **Discrimination** constitutes another issue that AI gives rise to. AI is bound to internalise stereotypes and act accordingly.[111] It therefore will be of outmost importance to either set clear rules on which characteristics may influence an automated decision or educate AI in a way that essentially prevents discrimination. Either way, supervision will be key.

45 Furthermore, it will be crucial to watch how financial institutions will be dealing with consumer data. Since AI learns the quickest if it is fed well-structured data, the incentive to use consumer data is high. This leads to several issues. For example, it must be ensured that this data cannot be extracted from the AI again if another institution buys it.[112]

Regulatory Independence

46 Last but certainly not least, it is crucial that regulatory and supervising authorities remain independent when assessing AI. Regulators need to build an independent expertise in this promising field. Claims for **self-regulation** should be rejected.[113] How AI will develop, what volume it will turn over and how it will change financial markets cannot be predicted. It is essential that regulators remain in control over developments and are equipped to halt undesired developments. In most cases, financial markets regulation will need to switch from an ex-post to an ex-ante regulation.[114] This becomes particularly important when AI will be more and more confronted with financial markets regulations. How AI interacts with rules and whether it will show circumventing behaviour will be crucial to its impact on financial markets. Certain rules will need to be source-coded into AI to guarantee the stability of the financial system.

4 AI and the Financial Markets: To a New Tomorrow

47 It has already been said that observers are not afraid to overstate the importance of AI for the financial markets' future. And indeed, its promises are breath-taking: They render **truly efficient markets** possible—markets that compute all available information, display intrinsic value of assets, and distribute capital accordingly.[115] With AI, there finally exists the (remote) chance of the textbook version of financial

---

[111] See the detailed account Tischbirek, paras 3 et seq.

[112] On the General Data Protection Regulation and AI see Marsch, paras 7–9.

[113] On this Guihot et al. (2017), pp. 431 et seq. On the responsibility of public actors and possible types of regulation see Hoffmann-Riem, paras 21 et seq., 58 et seq.

[114] Lee et al. (2018).

[115] On the perspective of existing idealized economic models Parkes and Wellman (2015) (discussing the 'homo economicus').

markets becoming a reality.[116] However, such a state will not ensue by itself. It will need a proactive and international regulatory approach.

4.1 First-Mover Advantages

Germany takes a rather hesitant approach towards financial markets AI. Whether this is the case because German regulators are sceptical about AI's impact on financial markets or because they do not rate their expertise on this matter as high as—for instance—the UK is unclear. It can, however, be noted that the USA and UK do not display similar restraints. They decisively foster growth and innovation in the area of financial markets AI. Security and systemic concerns are noted but are viewed as being of secondary importance. This will be reflected in the fundamentals of the AI that is currently coded and instructed. AI, however, needs ex-ante regulation. Regulators that follow the approach of Germany or the European Supervisory Authorities should be aware that a cautious course of action relinquishes the first-mover advantage—the advantage to influence developments significantly and at a fracture of the effort that will be necessary to achieve comparable results in the decades to come. Future bailouts must be prevented now. AI has the potential to systematically change financial markets and will therefore gain systematic relevance automatically.[117]

48

4.2 Yesterday's Mistakes

Leaving regulatory guidance for the development of financial markets AI to other jurisdictions will not delay its advance. As has been mentioned above, financial innovation does not stop at borders. In a global financial environment that is more interlinked than ever before it is likely that AI already instructs a significant amount of trading and investment in the EU, and that European institutions hold massive investments that are fully or partially controlled by AI. The last financial crisis took many supervisors by surprise because the scale of interlinked investments had not been correctly assessed.[118] This is a mistake not to be repeated. There are no *national* developments in the financial services industry. In this regard there is no difference between AI and Credit Default Swaps or Collateralized Debt Obligations.

49

---

[116]Mutatis mutandis, i.e. discussing the promises of 'perfect law enforcement' via AI, see Rademacher, paras 39–42.
[117]On the importance of system protection see Hoffmann-Riem, paras 29 et seq.
[118]See report of the German Parliament Deutscher Bundestag (2009), p. 91 and passim.

References

Anagnostopoulos I (2018) Fintech and regtech: impact on regulators and banks. J Econ Bus. https://doi.org/10.1016/j.jeconbus.2018.07.003

Angelini E, di Tollo G, Roli A (2008) A neural network approach for credit risk evaluation. Q Rev Econ Finance 48:733–755

Arévalo A, Niño J, Hernández G, Sandoval J (2016) High-frequency trading strategy based on deep neural networks. In: Huang D, Han K, Hussain A (eds) Intelligent computing methodologies – 12th International Conference (ICIC 2016), Proceedings Part III. Springer, Basel, pp 424–436

Arner DW, Barberis JN, Buckey RP (2017) FinTech, RegTech, and the reconceptualization of financial regulation. Northwest J Int Law Bus 37:371–413

Aziz S, Dowling MM (2018) AI and machine learning for risk management. https://doi.org/10.2139/ssrn.3201337

Bain B (2018) Flash-boys regulation fight returns to U.S. derivatives agency. https://www.bloomberg.com/news/articles/2018-02-14/flash-boys-regulation-fight-returns-to-u-s-derivatives-agency. Accessed 7 Feb 2019

Balasubramanian R, Libarikian A, McElhaney D, McKinsey&Company (2018) Insurance 2030—the impact of AI on the future of insurance. https://www.mckinsey.com/industries/financial-services/our-insights/insurance-2030-the-impact-of-ai-on-the-future-of-insurance. Accessed 7 Feb 2019

Basel Committee on Banking Supervision [BCBS] (2011) Basel III: a global regulatory framework for more resilient banks and banking systems. https://www.bis.org/publ/bcbs189.pdf. Accessed 7 Feb 2019

Bauguess SW (2017) The role of big data, machine learning, and AI in assessing risks: a regulatory perspective. https://www.sec.gov/news/speech/bauguess-big-data-ai. Accessed 7 Feb 2019

Baxter LG (2016) Adaptive financial regulation and RegTech: a concept article on realistic protection for victims of bank failures. Duke Law J 66:567–604

Bradley CG (2018) FinTech's double edges. Chi-Kent Law Rev 93:61–95

Broeders D, Prenio J (2018) Innovative technology in financial supervision (suptech) – the experience of early users. FSI Insights on policy implementation No 9. https://www.bis.org/fsi/publ/insights9.pdf. Accessed 7 Feb 2019

Bruckner MA (2018) The promise and perils of algorithmic lenders' use of big data. Chi-Kent Law Rev 93:3–60

Bundesanstalt für Finanzdienstleistungsaufsicht [BaFin] (2018) Big Data meets artificial intelligence. Challenges and implications for the supervision and regulation of financial services. https://www.bafin.de/SharedDocs/Downloads/EN/dl_bdai_studie_en.pdf?__blob=publicationFile&v=.11. Accessed 7 Feb 2019

Chiu I (2016) Fintech and disruptive business models in financial products, intermediation and markets – policy implications for financial regulators. J Technol Law Policy 21:55–112

Craig P, Ernst&Young (2018) How to trust the machine: using AI to combat money laundering. https://www.ey.com/en_gl/trust/how-to-trust-the-machine%2D%2Dusing-ai-to-combat-money-laundering. Accessed 7 Feb 2019

Čuk T, Waeyenberge A (2018) European legal framework for algorithmic and high frequency trading (Mifid 2 and MAR): a global approach to managing the risks of the modern trading paradigm. Eur J Risk Regul 9:146–158

Danielsson J, Macrae R, Uthemann A (2017) Artificial intelligence, financial risk management and systemic risk. SRC Special Paper 13

Deutsche Bundesregierung (2018) Eckpunkte der Bundesregierung für eine Strategie Künstliche Intelligenz. https://www.bmbf.de/files/180718%20Eckpunkte_KI-Strategie%20final%20Layout.pdf. Accessed 7 Feb 2019

Deutscher Bundestag (2009) Beschlussempfehlung und Bericht des 2. Untersuchungsausschusses nach Artikel 44 des Grundgesetzes, BT-Drucks. 16/14000. https://dip21.bundestag.de/dip21/btd/16/140/1614000.pdf. Accessed 7 Feb 2019

European Banking Authority [EBA] (2018) https://www.eba.europa.eu/financial-innovation-and-fintech/fintech-knowledge-hub. Accessed 7 Feb 2019
European Commission (2018) FinTech Action plan: for a more competitive and innovative European financial sector. COM(2018) 109 final. https://eur-lex.europa.eu/legal-content/EN/TXT/HTML/?uri=CELEX:52018DC0109&from=EN. Accessed 7 Feb 2019
FCA (2017a) Regulatory sandbox lessons learned report. https://www.fca.org.uk/publication/research-and-data/regulatory-sandbox-lessons-learned-report.pdf. Accessed 7 Feb 2019
FCA (2017b) Model driven machine executable regulatory reporting TechSprint. https://www.fca.org.uk/events/techsprints/model-driven-machine-executable-regulatory-reporting-techsprint. Accessed 7 Feb 2019
FCA (2018a) Regulatory sandbox. https://www.fca.org.uk/firms/regulatory-sandbox. Accessed 7 Feb 2019
FCA (2018b) Global Financial Innovation Network. https://www.fca.org.uk/publications/consultation-papers/global-financial-innovation-network. Accessed 7 Feb 2019
Fenwick M, Kaal WA, Vermeulen EPM (2017) Regulation tomorrow: what happens when technology is faster than the law. Am Univ Bus Law Rev 6:561–593
Financial Industry Regulatory Authority [FINRA] (2018) Technology based innovations for regulatory compliance ("RegTech") in the securities industry. https://www.finra.org/sites/default/files/2018_RegTech_Report.pdf. Accessed 23 Oct 2019
Financial Stability Board [FSB] (2017a) Artificial intelligence and machine learning in financial services. Market developments and financial stability implications. http://www.fsb.org/wp-content/uploads/P011117.pdf. Accessed 7 Feb 2019
Financial Stability Board [FSB] (2017b) Implementation and effects of the G20 financial regulatory reforms. 3rd Annual Report. http://www.fsb.org/wp-content/uploads/P030717-2.pdf. Accessed 7 Feb 2019
Gambacorta L, Karmakar S (2016) Leverage and risk weighted capital requirements. BIS Working Papers No 586. https://www.bis.org/publ/work586.pdf. Accessed 7 Feb 2019
Guihot M, Matthew A, Suzor N (2017) Nudging robots: innovative solutions to regulate artificial intelligence. Vand J Entertain Technol Law 20:385–439
House of Lords (2017) AI in the UK: ready, willing and able?, Report of Session 2017–19. https://publications.parliament.uk/pa/ld201719/ldselect/ldai/100/100.pdf. Accessed 7 Feb 2019
Joint Committee of the European Supervisory Authorities (2018) Joint Committee Final Report on Big Data, JC/2018/04. https://www.esma.europa.eu/sites/default/files/library/jc-2018-04_joint_committee_final_report_on_big_data.pdf. Accessed 7 Feb 2019
Kaastra I, Boyd M (1996) Designing a neural network for forecasting financial and economic time series. Neurocomputing 10:215–236
KPMG (2016) The expansion of robo-advisory in wealth management. https://www2.deloitte.com/content/dam/Deloitte/de/Documents/financial-services/Deloitte-Robo-safe.pdf. Accessed 7 Feb 2019
Lee KY, Kwon HY, Lim JI (2018) Legal consideration on the use of artificial intelligence technology and self-regulation in financial sector: focused on robo-advisors. In: Kang BB, Kim T (eds) Information security applications. 18th international conference – WISA 2017. Springer, Basel, pp 323–335
Lightbourne J (2017) Algorithms & fiduciaries: existing and proposed regulatory approaches to artificially intelligent financial planners. Duke Law J 67:651–679
Lin TCW (2015a) Infinite financial intermediation. Wake Forest Law Rev 50:643–664
Lin TCW (2015b) Reasonable investor(s). Boston Univ Law Rev 95:461–518
Lin TCW (2016) Compliance, technology, and modern finance. Brook J Corp Finan Commer Law 11:159–182
Lin TCW (2017) The new market manipulation. Emory Law J 1253:66–1314
Ling TCW (2014) The new financial industry. Ala Law Rev 65:567–623
Milne R (2018) Nordic banks in anti-money laundering tie-up. https://www.ft.com/content/86e4e4e2-64a6-11e8-90c2-9563a0613e56. Accessed 7 Feb 2019

Morelli M (2017) Implementing high frequency trading regulation: a critical analysis of current reforms. Mich Bus Entrep Law Rev 6:201–229

Narang RK (2013) Inside the black box: a simple guide to quantitative and high frequency trading, 2nd edn. Wiley, Hoboken

Neufang S (2017) Digital Compliance – Wie digitale Technologien Compliance-Verstöße vorhersehen. IRZ 2017:249–255

Nordea (2018) Nordic banks to explore common KYC joint venture. https://mb.cision.com/Main/434/2535839/851433.pdf. Accessed 7 Feb 2019

Odinet CK (2018) Consumer Bitcredit and Fintech Lending. Ala Law Rev 69:781–858

Osipovich A (2017) High-frequency traders fall on hard times. http://www.wsj.com/articles/high-frequency-traders-fall-on-hard-times-1490092200. Accessed 7 Feb 2019

Packin NG (2018) RegTech, compliance and technology judgment rule. Chi-Kent Law Rev 93:193–218

Parkes DC, Wellman MP (2015) Economic reasoning and artificial intelligence. Science 349:267–272

Peirce HM (2018) Beaches and Bitcoin: remarks before the Medici Conference. https://www.sec.gov/news/speech/speech-peirce-050218. Accessed 7 Feb 2019

Poirier I (2012) High-frequency trading and the flash crash: structural weaknesses in the securities markets and proposed regulatory responses. Hastings Bus Law J 8:445–471

Schemmel J (2016) The ESA guidelines: soft law and subjectivity in the European financial market - capturing the administrative influence. Ind J Glob Leg Stud 23:455–504

Scherer MU (2016) Regulating artificial intelligence systems: risks, challenges, competencies, and strategies. Harv J Law Technol 29:353–400

Schmidhuber J (2015) Deep learning in neural networks: an overview. Neural Networks 61:85–117

Scopino G (2015) Do automated trading systems dream of manipulating the price of futures contracts? Policing markets for improper trading practices by algorithmic robots. Fla Law Rev 67:221–293

Seddon JJJM, Currie WL (2017) A model for unpacking big data analytics in high-frequency trading. J Bus Res 70:300–307

Thomas LG (2018) The case for a federal regulatory sandbox for Fintech companies. N C Bank Inst 22:257–281

Trippi RR, DeSieno D (1992) Trading equity index futures with a neural network. J Portf Manag 19:27–33

U.S. Department of the Treasury (2018) A financial system that creates economic opportunities: nonbank financials, Fintech, and innovation. Report to President Donald J. Trump Executive Order 13772 on Core Principles for Regulating the United States Financial System. https://home.treasury.gov/sites/default/files/2018-08/A-Financial-System-that-Creates-Economic-Opportunities%2D%2D-Nonbank-Financials-Fintech-and-Innovation_0.pdf. Accessed 7 Feb 2019

Wall LD (2018) Some financial regulatory implications of artificial intelligence. J Econ Bus. https://doi.org/10.1016/j.jeconbus.2018.05.003

World Economic Forum [WEF] (2018) The new physics of financial services. Understanding how artificial intelligence is transforming the financial ecosystem. http://www3.weforum.org/docs/WEF_New_Physics_of_Financial_Services.pdf. Accessed 7 Feb 2019

Yadav Y (2015) How algorithmic trading undermines efficiency in capital markets. Vand Law Rev 68:1607–1702

Zetsche D, Buckley RP, Arner DW, Barberis JN (2017) Regulating a revolution: from regulatory sandboxes to smart regulation. Fordham J Corp Financ Law 23:31–103

Zetsche D, Buckley RP, Arner DW, Barberis JN (2018) From Fintech to Techfin: the regulatory challenges of data-driven finance. N Y Univ J Law Bus 14:393–430

Artificial Intelligence and Public Governance: Normative Guidelines for Artificial Intelligence in Government and Public Administration

Christian Djeffal

Contents

1. A Design Challenge for Government and Administration in Germany 278
   1.1 The Definition of Artificial Intelligence 278
   1.2 AI Applications in Government and Administration 280
2. Points of Reference: Between Ethics and Politics 282
3. Guidelines 283
   3.1 Law 283
   3.2 Technology 286
   3.3 Organization 286
   3.4 Strategies 288
   3.5 Visions 289
4. Outlook 290
References 290

Abstract This chapter discusses normative guidelines for the use of artificial intelligence in Germany against the backdrop of international debates. Artificial intelligence (AI) is increasingly changing our lives and our social coexistence. AI is a research question and a field of research producing an ever-increasing number of technologies. It is set of technologies that are still evolving. These are driven and influenced by guidelines in the form of laws or strategies. This chapter examines AI systems in public administration and raises the question of what guidelines already exist and what trends are emerging. After defining AI and providing some examples from government and administration, identify ethics and politics as possible points of reference for guidelines. This chapter presents the law, technology, organization, strategy and visions as possible ways to influence and govern AI along with describing current developments. The chapter concludes with a call for

---

This contribution is based on Djeffal (2018b).

C. Djeffal (✉)
Munich Center for Technology in Society, Technical University of Munich, Munich, Germany
e-mail: christian.djeffa@tum.de; https://www.mcts.tum.de/en/people/christian-djeffal/

interdisciplinary research and moderate regulation of technology in order to enhance its positive potential.

1 A Design Challenge for Government and Administration in Germany

1 Although AI technologies have been around for some time already, the effects are increasingly apparent today and will become even more so in the future. Risk management systems now guide decisions in many areas, on issues such as who has to present receipts to justify their tax returns.[1] Intelligent traffic control systems plot and direct flows. Automated lethal weapon systems are another emergent area of application. It is as if our computers are growing arms and legs, or developing capacities we cannot even imagine. While these changes are imminent, it is often forgotten that AI is a product of human activity and conscious design decisions. It is we humans who the development of technology at different levels and through different means. There are, for this reason, numerous constraints on and governance of AI. This chapter not only presents various guidelines in this regard, but also discusses current trends and developments appurtenant to AI applications, especially in government and administration.

2 Government and administration face particular challenges in managing and governing artificial intelligence. This is because they fulfil different roles in relation to technological change. First of all, they are users when they adopt AI technologies to perform specific tasks. In addition, they also directly support the technology, be it through infrastructure services, research funding or award criteria. Governments and public administrations are decisive in the regulation of technology. It is up to them to protect individual rights and the public interest. In terms of the application, promotion and regulation of AI, the particular challenge for governments and administrations derives from the uncertainties they face.[2] In light of these uncertainties, the question arises as to whether the guidelines need to be adapted to new developments or whether traditional approaches are sufficiently robust.

1.1 The Definition of Artificial Intelligence

3 AI is a research question and area of research that is today dealt with by a whole sub-discipline of computer science. It aims to create intelligent systems, i.e. those which, according to Klaus Mainzer's working definition, can 'solve problems efficiently on

---

[1] See also Braun-Binder.
[2] Mandel (2017).

their own'.[3] Even the inventors of the computer had systems in mind that were intended to perform intelligent actions; one of their first projects could be described as a big data venture for predicting the weather.[4] The term artificial intelligence itself was coined by a group of computer scientists in a proposal to the Rockefeller Foundation to fund a seminar. They described their central research concern as follows:

> We propose that a 2 month, 10 man study of artificial intelligence be carried out during the summer of 1956 at Dartmouth College in Hanover, New Hampshire. The study is to proceed on the basis of the conjecture that every aspect of learning or any other feature of intelligence can in principle be so precisely described that a machine can be made to simulate it. An attempt will be made to find how to make machines use language, form abstractions and concepts, solve kinds of problems now reserved for humans, and improve themselves. We think that a significant advance can be made in one or more of these problems if a carefully selected group of scientists work on it together for a summer.[5]

In its origin, the concept of AI was thus broad and reflected the intention to replace human intelligence with machines. Alan Turing foresaw that such projects would meet with contradictions in his epochal essay 'Computing Machinery and Intelligence'.[6] In this essay, he dealt with the question of whether machines can think. His hypothesis was that humans will no longer be able to distinguish between human and machine intelligence after a certain point in time and that the question will thus lose relevance. So far, this has not happened; instead, two camps have formed. Some have pursued the so-called 'strong AI thesis' according to which AI can and will reproduce human intelligence, while others, supporters of the 'weak AI thesis', the possibility and refer to the capacity of machines to solve certain problems rationally. There is thus the fundamental disagreement in computer science about the goals and possibilities of AI research.

However, if the goals of the technologies are controversial, their development and eventual areas of application are not predetermined. This is reflected in the dispute as to whether AI should serve to automate human tasks or augment humans. This was already discussed in the early years of the AI debate.[7] Like other technologies, one could describe AI as 'multistable'. This means that the scope and meaning of a technology in a society is only developed in the course of time and in its application, and that these are not defined by the technology itself.[8] This concept of multistability can be applied very well to AI technologies. What's more, AI is a general purpose technology.[9] By its nature, its purposes and its societal and individual consequences are contingent and dependent on its use.

Since AI technologies are flexible per se, they open up a new dimension of technical possibilities for action and reaction. Not for nothing is the system highlighted as an

---

[3]Mainzer (2016), p. 3.
[4]Dyson (2014).
[5]McCarthy et al. (1955).
[6]Turing (1950).
[7]Grudin (2017), p. 99.
[8]Ihde (2012).
[9]Djeffal (2019).

'agent' from a computer science point of view.[10] As mentioned above, you could say that computers acquire arms and legs and eyes and ears via AI. Conversely, you could also say that cameras, microphones, loudspeakers and machines are acquiring a brain.

If seeking to contrast AI with other fundamental innovations, one might meaningfully compare it with the 'invention' of iron. Iron is not a tool itself, but it is the basis for many different tools. A human can forge swords or ploughshares from it. Iron also forms the basis for other technologies, be it the letterpress or steam engines. It is precisely for this reason that it is very difficult to speak generally of the opportunities and risks of AI. For what is seen as an opportunity and what as a risk often depends on how AI is specifically developed and used.[11]

1.2 AI Applications in Government and Administration

Many AI systems are already being used in public administration. Sometimes AI contributes to the evolutionary development of existing systems. Traffic control systems are an example of this. Such systems influence the behavior of road users in various ways based on the evaluation of traffic and weather data.[12] In order to ensure the flow and safety of traffic, public administration may adopt legal measures such as bans on overtaking and speed limits. Traffic can also be affected by detour recommendations or temporary hard shoulder releases. Decisions are then no longer taken by people, but by the system, even if, as with road signs, traffic signs are legally binding administrative acts.[13]

The purposes, opportunities and risks of AI are contingent. The systems can help to achieve very different purposes. AI is a general purpose technology. As a consequence, it is not possible to simply state that AI is necessarily associated with certain opportunities and risks. AI is generally seen as a danger to informational self-determination, as exemplified by various applications of intelligent video surveillance, such as those being tested in Germany. At the Südkreuz train station in Berlin, the German Federal Police has been carrying out an experiment with cameras using intelligent face recognition. The aim is to use pattern recognition technologies to unambiguously identify people in order to filter them out.[14] Another experiment in Mannheim has even been trying to enable the AI-supported recognition of social situations. A camera system informs the police when it detects actions that could be considered as assault and battery or theft. It is then possible to track the people involved throughout the entire camera system.[15] Both these examples illustrate the possible data protection issues attaching to AI.

---

[10] Poole and Mackworth (2011).

[11] For structural challenges see Hoffmann-Riem, esp. paras 42 et seq.

[12] Bundesanstalt für Straßenwesen.

[13] Administrative acts in German law are legally binding decisions by the administration towards individuals or non-public legal persons.

[14] Bundespolizei (2017). See also Rademacher, para 3.

[15] Sold (2017). See also Rademacher, para 4.

On the other hand, AI can also be used to further data protection. In many municipalities, intelligent parking space monitoring systems are currently being set up. Various sensors can show the number and location of free parking spaces in an app or on display boards. If images are captured via cameras, AI systems can anonymize the images in real time. For example, faces and vehicle number plates can be made so unrecognizable that the driver and vehicle can no longer be identified. Also, chatbots are currently being developed that learn about the attitudes of users as concerning data protection in order to automatically change all data protection settings in the internet. These are instances of AI actually realizing data protection.

AI is believed to have the ability to ensure greater efficiency and effectiveness through automation. This was also one of the motives behind the Act to Modernize the Taxation Procedure, which has now been passed and, among other things, enables tax assessments to be issued automatically (§ 155 (4) of the Tax Code). This was in response to problems encountered by the tax administration, which had to deal with so many procedures that the uniformity and quality of decisions suffered.[16] The legislators emphasized that automation should not only serve to save resources. Rather, the resources should be used for cases that need to be dealt with more intensively, so that fair and just decisions are made. One could say that administration was intended to become more humane through automation.[17] Efficiency is achieved through AI management, for example, at border controls with the EasyPASSsystem. This system can identify people and verify their identity. With this system it is possible to reduce the number of border guards. It is also possible to avoid long queues since a few guards can serve many lines at once.

10

The Australian government, which is known for many successful digitization projects, experienced a disappointment with the 'online compliance intervention'. It was supposed to facilitate the collection of tax debts but ultimately resulted in a political scandal. An algorithm matches various tax-relevant data. If it finds contradictions, it notifies the citizen by letter and SMS. If the citizens do not object, a payment notice is issued to which the addressees can object.[18] The algorithm used is very error-prone and in many cases produced obviously false decisions. As a result of automation, up to 50 times more administrative proceedings against citizens were initiated than before. Because it was no longer possible to answer citizens' enquiries, temporary workers were hired and telephone contact with citizens was outsourced to a private call center. People from weaker societal strata were particularly negatively affected as well as especially vulnerable or disadvantaged population groups who could not defend themselves against the decision. The actual number of wrongfully issued notifications remains controversial. The example shows what negative effects AI can have in public administration when flawed systems are used without considering the social context. As a result, promises of effectiveness and efficiency may never be borne out in fact.

11

---

[16]See Braun Binder, paras 3 et seq.
[17]Djeffal (2017a), p. 813; see also Buchholtz, para 45.
[18]Commonwealth Ombudsman (2017).

Table 1 Comparisons of ethics and politics as normative reference points

Ethics	Politics
Experts	Politician
Good/right	Contingent
Expertise	Legitimation
Discovery	Accountability

2 Points of Reference: Between Ethics and Politics

12 Normative guidelines for technologies differ in their points of reference and are differently 'framed'. In this section, I contrast these points of reference in ideal typical terms as ethics and politics. For example, the discourse concerning 5G infrastructure is framed as political discourse. Discussions on genetic engineering are framed as ethical questions.

13 As far as AI is concerned, the discussion is based on both points of reference. In science and politics, AI is often portrayed as an ethical issue, leading, for example, to discussions about the 'ethics of algorithms'.[19] At the same time, dealing with AI is also understood as part of a political debate and, therefore, as something that can be handled by the strategies and decisions of the democratic legislature. The choice of the normative reference point has important implications, as can be seen from this comparison.

14 To frame something as an ethical question consciously places it outside political realm.[20] This is already illustrated by the people involved. While experts engage with questions of ethical design, political decisions are made by persons usually legitimized to do so. So, political decisions are often prepared by the government and the administration and debated and decided in parliament, whereas the ethical framework is often set by special institutions such as ethics councils. While experts can refer to what is good and right, contingent decisions are made in the political process that are fundamentally open. The justification for decisions also differs, in that it is based on ethical expertise on the one hand, and on the democratic legitimacy and accountability of the decision-makers on the other hand. These decision-makers justify their decisions, while experts tend to discover the right and good on the basis of their expertise (Table 1).

---

[19]Mittelstadt et al. (2016).
[20]Hilgartner et al. (2017), p. 830.

3 Guidelines

3.1 Law

Motivation, Limitation and Design

The law offers binding guidelines for the development of artificial intelligence. It sets boundaries for technology to ensure individual rights and safeguards public interests. But this is not the only function of law in the development of technology. The functions of law can also be described as relating to motivation, limitation and design.[21]

The law's role in motivating the development of technology can take different forms. It can motivate the development, advancement and application of technology by the administration or even make it compulsory. Mandatory legal obligations can result from statutory but also from constitutional law. Such a 'right to AI' could, for example, be derived from Article 41 of the European Charter of Fundamental Rights, which grants the right to good administration. Paragraph 1 sets out that '[e]very person has the right to have his or her affairs handled impartially, fairly and within a reasonable time by the institutions, bodies, offices and agencies of the Union'. If algorithms perform certain tasks much faster, more easily and better, Art. 41 of the European Charter of Fundamental Rights could require the introduction of AI. There might be even an obligation to use algorithms. Such an obligation can also be found in the United Nations Convention on the Rights of Persons with Disabilities. Art. 4 para. 1 (g) obliges states to undertake or promote research and development of, and to promote the availability and use of new technologies, including information and communications technologies, mobility aids, devices and assistive technologies, suitable for persons with disabilities, giving priority to technologies at an affordable cost. As a member state of the Convention, this obligation also applies to the German government and administration. Direct obligations to implement AI systems for the administration can also result from statutory law. For example, the Federal Office for Information Security (BSI) is responsible for the protection of federal communications technology. The Federal Office for Information Security Law grants the power to detect anomalies in federal agencies' data traffic. According to the law, without cause the BSI may only evaluate data automatically. Only if AI has detected an anomaly that indicates malware or a lack of security may data be processed by human agents.[22]

As mentioned above, it is one of the functions of the law to *limit* AI in public administration. We find such limits for example in § 114 para. 4 of the Federal Civil Servants Act (Bundesbeamtengesetz). According to this provision, decisions relating to civil servants may not be taken by automatic systems exclusively. However, this only applies to the processing of personal data. While this provision refers specifically to automated systems, AI applications must also comply with general provisions. For example, IT security law is applicable to all IT systems, such as Art.

---

[21]Djeffal (2017a), pp. 811–815.
[22]This applies under the condition that there is no other reason—such as a hint.

11 para. 1 of the Bavarian E-Government Act. This stipulates that the security of IT systems must be guaranteed. This means AI may only be used in public administration if it can be adequately secured. Public administrations must take measures towards safeguarding their IT systems.

18   In addition, the law also has a *design function*. In this capacity, it influences the process of development, advancement and application of technologies in society.[23] The law not only limits and promotes technology, it also merges legal requirements with what is technically possible and desirable. AI applications make technology flexible and independent. They open technical systems to a certain degree to design according to the purposes of the laws. An increase of rules concerning technology design in public administration can be expected. In European data protection law, for example, there are obligations to implement data protection and data security through technology design. For the authorities responsible for security or criminal prosecution, this obligation follows from § 71 of the new Federal Data Protection Act (BDSG), which is based on Directive (EU) 2016/680[24]: when the controller determines the means for data processing and when he carries out the processing, he must take precautions to ensure a data protection-friendly design.

19   When 'new' technologies meet the 'old' laws, some scholars and practitioners speak of gaps in the legislation and obstacles caused by the law. There is a gap if something should be regulated but is not.[25] Thus, if a new technology threatens individual rights or the protected general interest without legal regulations for effective enforcement, there might be a gap. Such gaps can be closed in a number of ways: either by the legislature adopting new rules or by the administration and judiciary developing the law through evolutive interpretation within their mandate. However, the opposite might hold; namely that there are barriers to innovation and application.[26] Obstacles arise in particular when existing legal categories do not adequately address new technologies or their impacts. For example, special legal regimes have been created all over the world for automobile traffic. If damage is caused by a motor vehicle, the person using the car on a regular basis must be liable regardless of his actual fault. This modifies the general rule that only those who are responsible for damage, i.e. who act intentionally or negligently, are liable. The question of liability has also been negotiated within the framework of artificial intelligence.[27] In this area of conflict, AI is a challenge for the law. Questions arise whether and how the law should be developed.[28]

---

[23]Djeffal (2017b), p. 103; Hildebrandt (2015).

[24]Directive (EU) 2016/680 of the European Parliament and of the Council of 27 April 2016 on the protection of natural persons with regard to the processing of personal data by competent authorities for the purposes of the prevention, investigation, detection or prosecution of criminal offences or the execution of criminal penalties, and on the free movement of such data, and repealing Council Framework Decision 2008/977/JHA OJ L 119, 4.5.2016, pp. 89–131.

[25]Canaris (1983).

[26]Hoffmann-Riem (2016), p. 33.

[27]Hilgendorf (2012). See Molnár-Gábor.

[28]Martini (2017).

The New Legislation on Automated Administrative Decisions

One development that has to be highlighted in this context is the new law on automated administrative decisions. The German Parliament introduced this law in the context of reforming and modernizing tax administration in 2015.[29] It introduced a new provision in § 35a in the Code of Administrative Procedure which reads as follows:

> An administrative act may be adopted entirely by automatic devices, provided that this is permitted by a legal provision and that there is neither discretion nor margin of appreciation.[30]

This provision makes it clear that fully automated decisions are legally possible.[31] It also establishes two legal requirements that have to be met.[32] First, the decision by an automated system has to be permitted by law. In German law, the terminology used suggests that there must be either an act of parliament or a statutory ordinance, i.e. a general norm issued by the executive, which is legitimized by an act of parliament. The second criterion is that there must be neither discretion nor a margin of appreciation. In the terminology of German administrative law, the term discretion refers to instances in which parliament empowers administrative bodies to decide whether to act and what measures to take. In contrast to that, the margin of appreciation signifies instances in which expert bodies are competent to determine whether certain requirements of the law are met. The margin of appreciation in its administrative sense is only to be applied in situations in which bodies have a specific competence to make certain judgments. This applies, for example, to the evaluation of civil servants, and to the process of choosing applicants for civil service.[33]

The aim of the provision is twofold. Firstly, it provides clarity on how to implement systems that can take fully automated decisions. Secondly, it specifies the requirements for lawful fully automated decisions, which make automated decisions also subject to the rule of law. The fact that a legal provision is necessary links every automated decision back to a decision of parliament. While there is no requirement regarding what the legal provision ought to include, it will be up to parliament to legitimize automated administrative decisions. In line with the state of the art of research, it is at the moment hardly conceivable that instances in which there is a margin of appreciation can be replaced by machines. In contrast, automated decisions have already been justified by provisions granting discretion to public administrations. Take, for example, § 45 German Road Traffic Order Regulations.

---

[29]Braun Binder (2016a, b).

[30]This was translated by the author. The original reads: 'Ein Verwaltungsakt kann vollständig durch automatische Einrichtungen erlassen werden, sofern dies durch Rechtsvorschrift zugelassen ist und weder ein Ermessen noch ein Beurteilungsspielraum besteht'.

[31]For a reflection on the functions of this provision see Berger (2018), p. 1262.

[32]For a detailed interpretation see Prell (2016).

[33]Decker (2019) paras 35–36.

Intelligent traffic systems are already imposing enforceable speed limits based on this provision. Automated systems, therefore, exercise discretion on behalf of public administrations. The fact that there are many systems that currently prohibit automated decisions has been criticized.[34] From a legal standpoint, a simple solution to this problem has been found. Whenever there is a legal provision allowing for an automated decision, this provision is said to be specific to the general rule in § 35a. The specific rule trumps § 35a and the included 'prohibition of automated discretion'. This pragmatic solution has not yet been tested in courts. What is more, it adds very little to the purpose of harmonising AI systems with legal principles. In order to do that, simply allowing or forbidding automated decisions based on discretion would not be enough. It would be necessary to give guidance on how to effectively safeguard human rights and legitimate interests in situations where automated systems exercise discretion.[35]

3.2 Technology

23   It should be mentioned briefly that the technology itself can also serve as a guideline for further development. Scholars have referred to the normative effects of technology, not least under the catchword 'Code is Law'.[36] Even assuming that the future of technology is fundamentally open, its actual development can still give it a certain direction.[37] The future development of the technology concerned can be influenced by certain system architectures or programming methods. The large program libraries developed for AI are a good example. Larger applications can be taken directly from these libraries. The data sets used in the process of training can have a huge impact on the algorithms. For this reason, the Mozilla Foundation has published a data set for speech recognition that is particularly representative and freely available to all.[38] This conscious work on data sets shows that decisions taken now can impact next generation technologies.

3.3 Organization

24   Guidelines for technology development can also arise from the organization of government and administration.[39] The establishment of authorities with certain

---

[34]Stegmüller (2018).
[35]Djeffal (2017a), p. 814.
[36]Lessig (2006) and Schulz and Dankert (2016).
[37]Arthur (1989); David (1992), p. 134.
[38]White (2017).
[39]Hood and Margetts (2007), p. 169.

duties and powers can have a sustainable impact on the development of technologies. An obvious example are the data protection officers, who must be emplaced under certain circumstances mandatorily in government and administration, but also in companies.[40] Especially in the area of internet governance, a multistakeholder approach has been developed that brings different actors together.[41] Thus, organization should have a positive impact on technology development.

In the field of AI, we can observe both ideas and initiatives on how technology can be influenced by the design of organizations. An example of this is the Ethics Commission on Automated and Connected Driving. It was set up by the German Federal Minister of Transport and Digital Infrastructure and has issued a report on autonomous driving, which has become the basis for further measures and legislative proposals by the ministry.[42] This model follows the state ethics commissions, which are particularly common in the field of medical ethics and bioethics.[43] In 2018, there was an interesting proliferation of such entities created by the German government. Parliament founded a Study Commission 'Artificial Intelligence – Social Responsibility and Economic Potential', which is comprised of 19 Members of Parliament and 19 experts.[44] It aims to study future impacts of AI. The federal government has also installed a Data Ethics Commission comprised of 16 members with the mandate to draw up ethical guidelines for a data policy. The Federal Government also assembled a digital council that should give guidance on digitization. Two new agencies were founded in order to enhance digital innovations. One agency will support disruptive innovation, the other agency aims at strengthening innovations in the field of IT security.

At the European Union level, various proposals for institutions with a strong link to artificial intelligence are currently being discussed. A resolution of the European Parliament calls for an Agency for Robotics and AI to be set up to work in a multidisciplinary way across different sectors.[45] The Agency's duty is not only to advise the European institutions, but also to create a register of advanced robots. In his famous European speech, French President Emmanuel Macron called for the creation of an 'agency for disruptive innovation'.[46] The only technology he mentioned in this context is AI. The Chinese government's announcement that it would build a US$ 2 billion technology park in Beijing within five years, where companies and universities will jointly research AI, also in this direction.[47] The United Arab

---

[40]See Art. 37 section 1 of the European General Data Protection Directive and § 38 of the German Data Protection Law.
[41]Hofmann (2016).
[42]Ethik-Kommission Automatisiertes und Vernetztes Fahren (2017).
[43]Braun et al. (2010), pp. 8 et seq.
[44]Deutscher Bundestag (2018).
[45]European Parliament resolution of 16 February 2017 with recommendations to the Commission on Civil Law Rules on Robotics (2015/2103(INL)).
[46]Macron (2017).
[47]Yamei (2018).

Emirates made headlines with the appointment of a minister for AI. According to the minister, one of his main tasks is to promote the development of AI by creating an adequate legal framework.[48] With regard to the organizations, the distinction between a formative and control function is particularly important. In the discourse characterized by the idea of AI regulation, monitoring organizations like the so-called algorithm watchdog are being discussed. However, it should be kept in mind that it is most important to ensure legal and ethical compliance in the design process. Retrospective oversight is limited in its capacity to identifying problems and solving them.[49]

3.4 Strategies

27 State guidelines for the development and application of technologies are often found in implicit or explicit strategies. They define a goal, the resources needed to achieve it, and the environment in which the goal is pursued.[50] It is, therefore, a question of how goals can actually be achieved in a particular situation. Strategies are characterized by the fact that they make goals explicit.

28 In the international debate, strategic considerations about AI have received much attention. Russian President Vladimir Putin told pupils at a conference that AI was the future and whoever takes the lead in this technology will rule the world.[51] The Chinese government's aim to make China the leading country in terms of AI by 2030 also attracted much media attention.[52] This behavior by various states was seen by commentators as the possible beginning of a new cold war.[53] Recently, the rhetoric has become friendlier and more cooperative. The European Union has proposed a strategy built also on connectedness and collaboration.[54] The declaration on AI leading to the strategy also included Norway, which is not a member of the European Union. China's Vice President stressed that China was actively seeking cooperation in developing AI.[55] The new German strategy on AI includes collaboration with other partners and technology transfer to developing states.

29 However, AI is not always the object of strategies, but a strategic tool itself. AI can also be found in smart city concepts aimed at achieving various goals such as environmental protection or improving the quality of life. For example, Berlin's smart city strategy explicitly refers to intelligent applications of the so-called Internet

---

[48]Tendersinfo (2017).
[49]See also Jabri, paras 34 et seq.
[50]Raschke und Tils (2013), p. 127.
[51]Russia Insider (2017).
[52]New York Times (2017).
[53]Allen and Husain (2017).
[54]Djeffal (2018a).
[55]Knight (2018).

of Things.[56] AI will appear in many strategies in the future, both as a resource to achieve goals and as a design goal, where the technology itself will be shaped by the strategy. Such combinations can also be described as 'visions' (Leitbilder).

3.5 Visions

Visions or mind frames are concepts that have the potential for agenda setting or framing of an issue. They influence the way certain issues are perceived and interpreted. Visions result from concepts and can have an impact on further development.[57] Not only do they have a descriptive function, but also the potential to shape development.[58] In the field of administrative modernization, some concepts have gained such importance, such as 'New Public Management', that they can also be described as visions. The German federal government coined the term 'Industry 4.0' and thus successfully created a vision for technology-driven industrial modernization that has been recognized internationally. This has been imitated by public administrations. Therefore, the catchword 'industry 4.0 needs administration 4.0' has become popular.[59]

30

The question about a vision for the design of AI has, in any case, remained unresolved within the German and European context, apart from a few initial approaches. Technology can certainly have a constitutional dimension, as can be seen from questions about a constitution for the Internet.[60] In the same regard, one could also ask about the constitutional dimension of AI. An interesting starting point for the practical handling of constitutions with these phenomena could be a provision from the Constitution of the Free Hanseatic City of Bremen which states in Article 12 (1):[61]

31

Man is higher than technology and machine.[62]

This is a unique provision in German constitutional history, which was inserted into the constitution of Bremen after the Second World War in view of the effects of industrialization, but which has yet to be applied in courts. However, it could provide some guidance on how generally to deal with AI.

32

---

[56]Senatsverwaltung für Stadtentwicklung und Umwelt (2016) Senate Department for Urban Development and Environment, 2016.
[57]Baer (2006), p. 83; Voßkuhle (2001) pp. 506ff; von Braun (2015).
[58]Koselleck (2010), pp. 61–62.
[59]Kruse and Hogrebe (2013).
[60]Pernice (2015).
[61]Artikel 12 Landesverfassung der Freien Hansestadt Bremen vom 21. Oktober 1947 in der Fassung vom 14. Oktober 1997.
[62]The original reads: 'Der Mensch steht höher als Technik und Maschine'.

4 Outlook

33   It is already apparent today that AI has fundamentally changed social coexistence, both on a large and small scale, and will continue to do so. This is another reason why it is so important to influence the development of these technologies positively through guidelines. But since these are emergent technologies, this is a particular challenge for science, business, politics and society. Guidelines cannot just be created and adopted; they must be constantly renewed. Just as it is not possible to accurately predict the impact and development of technologies, it is also not possible to accurately assess the impact of guidelines. In this process of 'reciprocal becoming'[63], it is not appropriate to think that all existing ideas and rules should be thrown overboard in the face of the new technologies. But it is just as wrong to think that nothing will change. Our understanding of what AI technologies can mean for our social coexistence in its infancy. Therefore, it is appropriate to look at these developments from different perspectives and with different assumptions. The possible outcomes and consequences of this technology can only be conceived when AI is simultaneously understood as an opportunity and a danger, when it is simultaneously developed from a technical and social point of view, and when it is viewed from the perspective of the humanities, social sciences and natural sciences. Then we will be able to construct a picture of a socially desirable and good AI. It might then be possible to create a more human and humane society through automation.

References

Allen JR, Husain A (2017) The next space race is artificial intelligence: and the United States is losing. Retrieved from foreignpolicy.com/2017/11/03/the-next-space-race-is-artificial-intelligence-and-america-is-losing-to-china. Accessed 9 Dec 2019
Arthur WB (1989) Competing technologies, increasing returns, and lock-in by historical events. Econ J 99:116–131
Baer S (2006) "Der Bürger" im Verwaltungsrecht: Subjektkonstruktion durch Leitbilder vom Staat. Mohr Siebeck, Tübingen
Berger A (2018) Der automatisierte Verwaltungsakt: Zu den Anforderungen an eine automatisierte Verwaltungsentscheidung am Beispiel des § 35a VwVfG. Neue Zeitschrift Für Verwaltungsrecht 37:1260–1264
Braun Binder N (2016a) Ausschließlich automationsgestützt erlassene Steuerbescheide und Bekanntgabe durch Bereitstellung zum Datenabruf: Anmerkungen zu den § 88 Abs. 5, § 122a, § 150 Abs. 7 n.F., § 155 Abs. 4 n.F. und § 173a AO. Deutsche Zeitschrift für Steuerrecht:526–534
Braun Binder N (2016b) Vollständig automatisierter Erlass eines Verwaltungsaktes und Bekanntgabe über Behördenportale: Anmerkungen zu den §§ 24 Abs. 1 Satz 3, 35a und 41 Abs. 2a VwVfG. Die Öffentliche Verwaltung 69:891–898

---

[63]Kloepfer (2002).

Braun K, Herrmann SL, Könninger S, Moore A (2010) Ethical reflection must always be measured. Sci Technol Hum Values 35:839–864

Bundesanstalt für Straßenwesen. Anlagen zur Verkehrsbeeinflussung auf Bundesfernstraßen. Retrieved from www.bast.de/DE/Verkehrstechnik/Fachthemen/v5-verkehrsbeeinflussungsanlagen.html. Accessed 9 Dec 2019

Bundespolizei (2017) Test zur Gesichtserkennung am Bahnhof Berlin Südkreuz gestartet. Retrieved from www.bundespolizei.de/Web/DE/04Aktuelles/01Meldungen/2017/08/170810_start_videotechnik.html. Accessed 9 Dec 2019

Canaris C-W (1983) Die Feststellung von Lücken im Gesetz: eine methodologische Studie über Voraussetzungen und Grenzen der richterlichen Rechtsfortbildung praeter legem, 2nd edn. Duncker und Humblot, Berlin

Commonwealth Ombudsman (2017) Centrelink's automated debt raising and recovery system. Retrieved from www.ombudsman.gov.au/__data/assets/pdf_file/0022/43528/Report-Centrelinks-automated-debt-raising-and-recovery-system-April-2017.pdf. Accessed 9 Dec 2019

David PA (1992) Heroes, herds and hysteresis in technological history: Thomas Edison and 'The Battle of the Systems' Reconsidered. Ind Corp Change 1:129–180

Decker A (2019) § 114. In: Posser H, Wolff H (eds) Beck'scher Online Kommentar VwGO. C.H. Beck, München

Deutscher Bundestag (2018) Study Commission "Artificial Intelligence – Social Responsibility and Economic Potential". Retrieved from www.bundestag.de/en/committees/bodies/study/artificial_intelligence. Accessed 9 Dec 2019

Djeffal C (2017a) Das Internet der Dinge und die öffentliche Verwaltung: Auf dem Weg zum automatisierten Smart Government? Deutsches Verwaltungsblatt:808–816

Djeffal C (2017b) Leitlinien der Verwaltungsnovation und das Internet der Dinge. In: Klafki A, Würkert F, Winter T (eds) Digitalisierung und Recht, Band 31. Bucerius Law School Press, Hamburg, pp 83–112

Djeffal C (2018a) Harnessing Artificial Intelligence the European Way. Advance online publication. https://verfassungsblog.de/harnessing-artificial-intelligence-the-european-way/. Accessed 9 Dec 2019

Djeffal C (2018b) Normative Leitlinien Für Künstliche Intelligenz in Regierung und Verwaltung. In: Mohabbat Kar R, Thapa B, Parycek P (eds) (Un)Berechenbar? Algorithmen und Automatisierung in Staat und Gesellschaft. OEFIT, Berlin, pp 493–515

Djeffal C (2019) Künstliche Intelligenz. In: Klenk T, Nullmeier F, Wewer G (eds) Handbuch Verwaltungsdigitalisierung. Springer, Wien

Dyson G (2014) Turings Kathedrale: Die Ursprünge des digitalen Zeitalters, 2nd edn. Propyläen, Berlin

Ethik-Kommission Automatisiertes und Vernetztes Fahren (2017) Bericht. Retrieved from www.bmvi.de/SharedDocs/DE/Anlage/Presse/084-dobrindt-bericht-der-ethik-kommission.pdf?__blob=publicationFile. Accessed 9 Dec 2019

Grudin J (2017) From tool to partner: the evolution of human-computer interaction. Synthesis lectures on human-centered informatics. Morgan & Claypool, London

Hildebrandt M (2015) Smart technologies and the end(s) of law: novel entanglements of law and technology. Edward Elgar Publishing, Cheltenham, UK, Northampton, MA, USA

Hilgartner S, Prainsack B, Hurlbut BJ (2017) Ethics as governance in genomics and beyond. In: Felt U, Fouché R, Miller CA, Smith-Doerr L (eds) The handbook of science and technology studies. The MIT Press, Cambridge, Massachusetts, London, England

Hilgendorf E (2012) Können Roboter schuldhaft handeln? In: Jenseits von Mensch und Maschine. Nomos, Baden-Baden, pp 119–132

Hoffmann-Riem W (2016) Innovation und Recht – Recht und Innovation. Mohr Siebeck, Tübingen

Hofmann J (2016) Multi-stakeholderism in Internet governance: putting a fiction into practice. J Cyber Policy 1:29–49

Hood CC, Margetts HZ (2007) The tools of government in the digital age. Palgrave Macmillan, Houndmills

Ihde D (2012) Experimental phenomenologies: multistabilities. SUNY Press, Albany

Kloepfer M (2002) Technik und Recht im wechselseitigen Werden: Kommunikationsrecht in der Technikgeschichte. Schriften zum Technikrecht. Duncker und Humblot, Berlin

Knight W (2018) China's leaders are softening their stance on AI. MIT Technology Review. 18 September 2018. Retrieved from www.technologyreview.com/s/612141/chinas-leaders-are-calling-for-international-collaboration-on-ai/. Accessed 9 Dec 2019

Koselleck R (2010) Die Geschichte der Begriffe und Begriffe der Geschichte. In: Koselleck R (ed) Begriffsgeschichten: Studien zur Semantik und Pragmatik der politischen und sozialen Sprache. Suhrkamp, Frankfurt am Main, pp 56–76

Kruse W, Hogrebe F (2013) "Industrie 4.0" braucht "Verwaltung 4.0": Globaler Wettbewerb, demographischer Wandel, Schuldenbremse. Behörden Spiegel 29:1–2

Lessig L (2006) Code and other laws of cyberspace: version 2.0, 2nd edn. Basic Books, New York

Macron E (2017) Sorbonne Speech. Retrieved from international.blogs.ouest-france.fr/archive/2017/09/29/macron-sorbonne-verbatim-europe-18583.html. Accessed 9 Dec 2019

Mainzer K (2016) Künstliche Intelligenz – Wann übernehmen die Maschinen? Technik im Fokus. Springer, Heidelberg

Mandel N (2017) Legal evolution in response to technological change. In: Brownsword R, Scotford E, Yeung K (eds) The Oxford handbook of law, regulation, and technology. Oxford University Press, Oxford

Martini M (2017) Algorithmen als Herausforderung für die Rechtsordnung. JuristenZeitung 72:1017–1025

McCarthy J, Minsky M, Shannon C (1955) A proposal for the Dartmouth Summer Research Project on Artificial Intelligence. Retrieved from http://www-formal.stanford.edu/jmc/history/dartmouth/dartmouth.html. Accessed 9 Dec 2019

Mittelstadt BD, Allo P, Taddeo M, Wachter S, Floridi L (2016) The ethics of algorithms: mapping the debate. Big Data Soc 3:1–21

Mozur P (2017) Beijing wants A.I. to be made in China 2030. New York Times. 20 July 2017. Retrieved from www.nytimes.com/2017/07/20/business/china-artificial-intelligence.html. Accessed 9 Dec 2019

Pernice I (2015) Global constitutionalism and the internet. Taking People Seriously. HIIG Discussion Paper Series

Poole DL, Mackworth AK (2011) Artificial intelligence: foundations of computational agents. Cambridge University Press, Cambridge

Prell L (2016) § 35a. In: Bader J, Ronellenfitsch M (eds) Verwaltungsverfahrensgesetz: Mit Verwaltungszustellungsgesetz und Verwaltungs-Vollstreckungsgesetz, 2nd edn. C.H. Beck, München

Raschke J, Tils R (2013) Politische Strategie: Eine Grundlegung, 2nd edn. VS Verlag für Sozialwissenschaften, Wiesbaden

Russia Insider (2017) Whoever leads in AI will rule the world!: Putin to Russian children on Knowledge Day. Retrieved from www.youtube.com/watch?v=2kggRND8c7Q. Wiesbaden

Schulz W, Dankert K (2016) Governance by things' as a challenge to regulation by law. Internet Policy Rev 5

Senatsverwaltung für Stadtentwicklung und Umwelt (2016) Smart City-Strategie Berlin. Retrieved from www.berlin-partner.de/fileadmin/user_upload/01_chefredaktion/02_pdf/02_navi/21/Strategie_Smart_City_Berlin.pdf. Accessed 9 Dec 2019

Sold R (2017) Automatischer Alarm bei Taschendiebstahl. Frankfurter Allgemeine Zeitung. 29 December 2017, p 2

Stegmüller M (2018) Vollautomatische Verwaltungsakte – eine kritische Sicht auf die neuen § 24 I 3 und § 35a VwVfG. Neue Zeitschrift Für Verwaltungsrecht:353–358

Tendersinfo (2017) United Arab Emirates: Minister of Artificial Intelligence Minister delivers talk on AI at DPC event. Retrieved from www.tendersinfo.com/. Accessed 9 Dec 2019

Turing A (1950) Computing machinery and intelligence. Mind Q Rev Psychol Philos 59:433–460
von Braun J (2015) Leitbilder im Recht. Mohr Siebeck, Tübingen
Voßkuhle A (2001) Der "Dienstleistungsstaat": Über Nutzen und Gefahren von Staatsbildern. Der Staat:495–523
White S (2017) Announcing the Initial Release of Mozilla's Open Source Speech Recognition Model and Voice Dataset. Retrieved from https://blog.mozilla.org/blog/2017/11/29/announcing-the-initial-release-of-mozillas-open-source-speech-recognition-model-and-voice-dataset/. Accessed 9 Dec 2019
Yamei (2018) Beijing to build technology park for developing artificial intelligence. Xinhuanet. 3 January 2018. Retrieved from www.xinhuanet.com/english/2018-01/03/c_136869144.htm. Accessed 9 Dec 2019

Artificial Intelligence and Taxation: Risk Management in Fully Automated Taxation Procedures

Nadja Braun Binder

Contents

1 Introduction 296
2 Legal Bases 296
   2.1 Fully Automated Taxation Procedure 296
   2.2 Risk Management Systems 298
   2.3 Compatibility of Confidentiality Requirements with Basic Data Protection Regulations 299
3 The Use of AI Within RMS 300
   3.1 Suitability of AI Within RMS 301
   3.2 Controlling AI-based RMS 303
4 Conclusion 304
References 304

Abstract On January 1, 2017, the Taxation Modernization Act entered into force in Germany. It includes regulations on fully automated taxation procedures. In order to uphold the principle of investigation that characterizes German administrative law, a risk management system can be established by the tax authorities. The risk management system aims to detect risk-fraught cases in order to prevent tax evasion. Cases identified as risk-fraught by the system need to be checked manually by the responsible tax official. Although the technical details of risk management systems are kept secret, such systems are presumably based on artificial intelligence. If this is true, and especially if machine learning techniques are involved, this could lead to legally relevant problems. Examples from outside tax law show that fundamental errors may occur in AI-based risk assessments. Accordingly, the greatest challenge of using artificial intelligence in risk management systems is its control.

N. Braun Binder (✉)
Faculty of Law, University of Basel, Basel, Switzerland
e-mail: nadja.braunbinder@unibas.ch

1 Introduction

1 Provisions for fully automated taxation procedures have existed in Germany since January 1, 2017. The corresponding legal basis was established by the Taxation Modernization Act.[1] Thus, tax assessments can be issued completely automatically, i.e., without any human involvement. Full automation, however, inevitably involves cutbacks in the principle of investigation, which is enshrined in Section 88 *Abgabenordnung* (AO—German Fiscal Code).[2] This is to be compensated for by the *use of risk management systems* (RMS).[3] The principle of case-by-case assessment is replaced by automation-based risk assessment. This article first outlines the relevant legal bases of fully automated taxation procedures in Germany (Sect. 2). Second, it examines which requirements arise for the use of AI from the applicable legal bases (Sect. 3). The final section (Sect. 4) summarizes the main findings and results.

2 Legal Bases

2 The legal bases for fully automated taxation procedures in Germany (Sect. 2.1) are summarized below. Particular attention is given to the regulation of RMS (Sect. 2.2) and to the confidentiality requirements regarding the details of RMS (Sect. 2.3).[4]

2.1 Fully Automated Taxation Procedure

3 Since January 1, 2017, tax assessments as well as the offsetting of withholding tax and advance tax payments are allowed to be processed automation-based, provided no reason exists for a case to be handled by public officials (Section 155(4) sentence 1 AO). The same applies to administrative acts and decisions pertaining to tax assessments as well as the offsetting of withholding tax and advance payments (Section 155(4) sentence 2 no. 1 AO). According to the explanatory notes, the wording 'based solely on automated processing' means that data are not examined

---

[1] Law of July 18, 2016 (BGBl I p. 1679); see also the draft bill dated February 3, 2016 of the Federal Government on the modernization of the taxation procedure, BT-Drs. 18/7457; recommended decision and report of the Finance Committee dated May 11, 2016, BT-Drs. 18/8434; second and third sessions of the Bundestag dated May 12, 2016, minutes of the plenary session of the Bundestag 18/170, pp. 16773C–16783D; approval of the Federal Council dated June 17, 2016, BR-Drs. 255/16.
[2] Tax Code in the version published on October 1, 2002 (BGBl. I p. 3866; 2003 I p. 61), last amended by Article 6 of the Law of July 18, 2017 (BGBl. I p. 2745).
[3] BT-Drs. 18/7457, pp. 48–49 and 69–70.
[4] The deliberations in see paras 3 et seq. and see paras 9 et seq. are based on Braun Binder (2016), pp. 526 et seq. Those in see paras 12 et seq. are based on Braun Binder (2019).

by public officials.[5] Accordingly, these new regulations pertain to procedures in which all administrative steps are performed at all times without any human involvement.

The correction of tax assessments as well as the offsetting of withholding tax and advance tax payments and/or of administrative acts and decisions connected with these may also be carried out fully automatically in the future (Section 155(4) sentence 1 or 2 respectively AO). In addition, ancillary provisions to the administrative act (Section 120 AO) may also be issued based solely on automated processing, insofar as this is based on an administrative directive issued either by the Federal Ministry of Finance or by the supreme financial authority of a federal state (Section 155(4) sentence 2 no. 2 AO). If such an administrative directive means that no discretionary scope (Section 5 AO) exists for taking decisions on the ancillary provision (i.e., reduction of discretionary powers to zero), it may be issued fully automatically.[6]

In some cases, tax returns must be processed manually. Human processing may be initiated by the RMS (Section 88(5) sentence 3 nos. 1 and 2 AO), by the selection through a public official (Section 88(5) sentence 3 no. 3 AO), or by the taxpayer entering text into a 'qualified free-text field' (Section 155(4) sentence 3 in association with Section 150(7) sentence 1 AO).[7] The latter permits data input that does not fit the tax return input mask that only permits for clearly structured, unambiguous data input.

The fully automated procedure is based on the data provided by the taxpayer in the electronic tax return and on the information already available to the tax authorities (Section 155(4) sentence 1 AO). The second category also includes data transmitted by third parties to the tax authorities (Section 93c AO). The data transmitted by third parties are considered taxpayer data unless the taxpayer states otherwise in a data field provided for this purpose on the tax return (Section 150 (7) sentence 2 AO). If the taxpayer makes divergent statements in the field provided for this purpose, this leads to the sorting out of the tax return from fully automated processing and thus to its examination by public officials.[8]

The fully automatically generated tax administrative act is not required to contain any indication that it was issued based solely on automated processing. No such indication is necessary according to the relevant explanatory notes of the Federal Government, since no other legal consequences result from the fully automated administrative act than from a manually and/or partially automated tax administrative act.[9] According to the corresponding explanatory notes of the Federal Government, taxpayers must be alerted to the fact that their tax returns may be processed fully automatically unless they make statements to the contrary in the qualified free-text field (see para 6).[10]

---

[5]BT-Drs. 18/7457, p. 82.
[6]BT-Drs. 18/7457, p. 83.
[7]BT-Drs. 18/7457, p. 79.
[8]BT-Drs. 18/8434, p. 122.
[9]BT-Drs. 18/7457, p. 83.
[10]BT-Drs. 18/7457, p. 79.

8　　　Further, the legal bases of fully automated tax assessment envisage no explicit freedom of choice. Taxpayers are unable to choose whether their tax returns are processed fully or partly automated. However, the qualified free-text field (Section 150(7) sentence 1 AO) which public officials need to consider (Section 155(4) sentence 3 AO) comes close to an option.

2.2 Risk Management Systems

9　　　Since January 1, 2017, Section 88(5) AO provides that German tax authorities may use RMS in order to filter out and manually check cases involving significant risk (sentence 1). Sentence 2 stipulates that due consideration must also be given to the principle of administrative efficiency. The law prescribes that these RMS determine a sufficient number of randomly selected cases for comprehensive examination by public officials (sentence 3 no. 1). This is intended to ensure an appropriate risk of detection and corresponding verification possibilities.[11] At the same time, random selection serves to control RMS modulation mechanisms (see paras 26–27; on 'experimental administration' see Hermstrüwer, paras 35 et seq.).[12]

10　　　In principle, RMS can be provided for all types of taxes to which the Tax Code applies (Section 1 AO).[13] For taxes administered by state financial authorities on behalf of the Federal Government[14] 'the supreme financial authorities are responsible for determining the details of risk management systems, in order to ensure the uniform enforcement of tax laws throughout the Federation in agreement with the Federal Ministry of Finance' (Section 88(5) sentence 5). Further, the law only provides for general minimum requirements: The RMS must enable officials both to inspect cases eliminated from fully automated processing and to select additional ones (sentence 3 nos. 2 and 3). In addition, the RMS must be subject to regular periodical reviews, in order to ensure its goal attainment (sentence 3 no. 4).

11　　　It is also envisaged that 'details of risk management systems' may not be published if this could impair the uniformity and legality of taxation (sentence 4). This requirement is based on the consideration that the uniformity and legality of taxation would be jeopardized if taxpayers were aware of RMS criteria or modes of functioning and could thus circumvent these filters.[15] At the same time, the regulation leaves unanswered the question which 'details' these are. Is it a question of RMS algorithms? Or does this refer to test parameters such as exceeding certain value limits, changes compared to the previous year, or logical contradictions evident in the tax return?[16]

---

[11]BT-Drs. 18/7457, p. 68.
[12]BT-Drs. 18/7457, p. 70.
[13]See also BT-Drs. 18/7457, p. 70.
[14]Cf. Article 108(3) *Grundgesetz*.
[15]Münch (2013), p. 2152.
[16]See, for instance, Ahrendt (2017), p. 540; Haunhorst (2010), pp. 2108–2109; Münch (2013), p. 213.

Or is it a question of personal data, based on which the risk of a taxpayer or a tax return is assessed?[17] In the end, all these aspects (algorithms, test parameters, personal data) fall under the secrecy requirement if the uniformity and legality of the taxation were thereby endangered.

2.3 Compatibility of Confidentiality Requirements with Basic Data Protection Regulations

Further legislation was needed to ensure that the confidentiality requirements concerning RMS (see Section 88(5) sentence 4 AO) were compatible with the General Data Protection Regulation (GDPR).[18] Since May 25, 2018, Articles 13 and 14 of the GDPR require tax authorities to inform taxpayers proactively if they intend to collect personal data about them or intend to process such data. Those concerned must in principle be informed when personal data are collected about them (Article 13(1) GDPR). Those concerned are also entitled to obtain confirmation from the responsible officials as to whether personal data pertaining to them are being processed (Article 15(1) GDPR).[19] In addition, the responsible official is required to provide the person concerned with further information needed 'to ensure fair and transparent processing' (Article 13(2) GDPR). No duty to provide information exists if the person concerned already possesses the information in question (Article 13(4) GDPR). This is the case, for example, with information obligations provided for by law or may result from the tax return.[20]

12

Based on the escape clause of Article 23(1) lit. e and lit. h GDPR, the German legislator enacted the necessary provisions for exceptions with regard to the use of RMS. Accordingly, there is no obligation to provide information if the provision of the information would jeopardize the proper performance of the duties and responsibilities falling within the jurisdiction of the tax authorities (Section 32a(1) no. 1 AO or Section 32b(1) no. 1 a AO). According to the legislator, this is the case, among others, if disclosing the information made it possible to draw 'conclusions about the arrangement of automation-supported risk management systems or planned control or examination measures and if the discovery of fiscally significant facts and circumstances were thus substantially impeded' (Section 32a(2) no. 2 AO and/or

13

---

[17]See Krumm (2017), p. 2191, who also sees profiling covered by Article 4 no. 4 GDPR and by Section 88(5) AO.

[18]Regulation (EU) 2016/679 of the European Parliament and Council of April 27, 2016 on the protection of individuals with regard to the processing of personal data, on the free movement of such data, and on repealing Directive 95/46/EG (General Data Protection Regulation), O.J. L 119 dated May 4, 2016, pp. 1–88.

[19]Investigations into RMS based on Article 15 GDPR are impeded by Section 32c(1) no. 1 AO. See Krumm (2017), p. 2194.

[20]Krumm (2017), p. 2192.

14 reference to Section 32a(2) in § 32b(1) sentence 2 AO). However, it remains unclear which personal data could reveal RMS functionality.

14 Exemption from the duty to provide information applies if the responsible officials intend to process the personal data collected from the person concerned for a purpose other than the original purpose of collection (Section 32a(1) AO in connection with Article 13(3) GDPR), or if personal data were obtained from third parties (Section 32b(1) AO in connection with Article 14(1), (2), and (4) GDPR). In other words, the duty to provide information on personal data that is processed for the original purpose of collection, remains.

15 Accordingly, with regard to RMS, the duty to provide information under Article 13(1) GDPR would only apply if the tax authorities collected personal data from the persons concerned for the direct purpose of using such data within the framework of RMS. So far, tax authorities did not collect data with the direct purpose of using such data for risk management purposes. What may be assumed instead is that the tax authorities will further process any data that they have collected from the persons concerned for a different purpose and, above all, any data that they have received from third parties (see Section 93c AO) within RMS. The restrictions of Sections 32a and 32b AO apply to this data. On balance, it can therefore be assumed that it will remain largely unknown which data will be processed within the framework of RMS.

3 The Use of AI Within RMS

16 It seems obvious to use AI in RMS given the large amounts of data[21] that an RMS is required to process and given the different cross-references (e.g., between different tax types) that can thereby be established.[22] An anomaly search based on machine learning is conceivable, for example. For reasons of efficiency, it seems plausible that an RMS is used to analyze the existing database based on a taxpayer's previous behavior and thus to forecast the taxpayer's future behavior.[23] It is therefore not surprising that the Federal Commissioner for Administrative Efficiency recommended the use of 'self-learning' RMS already in 2006, without adding further explanations, however.[24] Learning algorithms were also discussed during the hearing of experts in the legislative procedure for modernizing the taxation procedure.[25]

---

[21] The increasing importance of machine learning is related to the increasing availability of large amounts of data; see Goodfellow et al. (2016), pp. 18 et seq.

[22] The deliberations in this section are based on Braun Binder (2019).

[23] See, for instance, Krumm (2017), p. 2191.

[24] President of the Federal Audit Office in his function as Federal Commissioner for Administrative Efficiency (2006), p. 165. On the increasing importance of learning RMS in tax enforcement, see also Schmidt (2008), p. 50.

[25] Neumann (2016), pp. 5–6.

AI is a complex issue, as reflected by the wide variety of definitions. The term is used to describe systems that (should) possess human-like intelligence, are able to solve problems independently, and are constantly learning new things.[26] Among other things, this takes account of software agents, expert systems, robots, or neural networks. In the context of RMS, the principal criterion of AI is machine learning. There are various machine learning methods.[27] Currently, such AI applications are considered particularly interesting if they are based on machine learning procedures whose algorithms self-optimize their programming in the event of errors or false results and thus self-correct without human intervention.[28] Artificial neural networks, in particular 'deep neural networks', play an important role in unsupervised learning processes.[29]

However, it is unclear which types of machine learning procedures are (or could be) used within the framework of RMS. In view of the obligation to maintain secrecy,[30] it is difficult to obtain more detailed information about whether (and, if so, which form of) AI is actually used within the framework of RMS. Probably the only official reference to date can be found in a parliamentary paper published by the state of Baden-Württemberg,[31] according to which RMS based on artificial neural networks are used in some federal states, which analyze VAT advance returns for signs of so-called carousel (i.e., missing trader) fraud. The following thoughts, therefore, merely provide a general description of the requirements for the use of AI in RMS and a general assessment of whether these requirements can be met. This implies no claim to assess the fulfillment of these requirements in current practice.

3.1 Suitability of AI Within RMS

According to the wording of the law, RMS serves the purpose of 'assessing the need for further investigations and audits for uniform and lawful tax assessment' (Section 88(5) sentence 1 AO). The aim of RMS is therefore to identify and to signal potential tax reductions and deliberate fraud.[32] This is done by uncovering both implausible and risk-fraught cases.[33]

---

[26] Kaplan (2016), pp. 1 et seq.
[27] A distinction can be made, for example, between supervised and unsupervised learning; see Ertel (2016), pp. 191 et seq.
[28] Stiemerling (2015), p. 763.
[29] Kaplan (2016), pp. 28 et seq.
[30] See paras 9 et seq. and 12 et seq.
[31] See State Parliament of Baden-Württemberg, communication of the State Government dated December 14, 2011, Drs. 15/1047, pp. 12 and 19.
[32] BT-Drs. 18/7457, p. 69.
[33] See BT-Drs. 18/7457, p. 70, according to which RMS should conduct more than just plausibility checks. See also Seer (2017), § 88 AO, para 76.

20 It is debatable whether this goal can already be achieved today by means of AI. Examples from outside tax law show that fundamental errors may occur in AI-based risk assessments. In the USA, for example, an AI-based assessment software (COMPAS—Correctional Offender Management Profiling for Alternative Sanctions) was used in the judicial system; it systematically rated the risk of recidivism of colored offenders higher than that of white offenders.[34] This assessment was based on responses to a questionnaire that did not request respondents to disclose their skin color.[35] Nevertheless, the system reached mistaken conclusions.[36] It is questionable whether these false conclusions ought to be classified as 'bias' or system errors or rather as an inevitable consequence of the underlying data. The latter is explained, for example, by the fact that different race-oriented law enforcement or prosecution practices, which are reflected in the data of individual offenders, are also adopted by the algorithm.[37]

21 Similar problems arose in connection with AI-based risk analysis, which was used by Durham Constabulary in the UK to assess the risk of recidivism by offenders over a period of two years. The software used there (HART—Harm Assessment Risk Tool) had to be adapted to prevent people living in poorer neighborhoods from being systematically assessed worse than ones from more affluent neighborhoods.[38] In contrast to the COMPAS software, however, the HART questionnaire originally asked respondents to indicate their postal code. This information was later partially removed from the system.[39]

22 In Australia, AI was used by the government to automatically collect outstanding debts from citizens, for instance in the area of income taxes. It turned out that the algorithms misinterpreted the data. For example, the fact that two employers were registered for one person led to the conclusion that this person should be taxed twice. In fact, however, the person had changed the employer.[40] Other examples[41] support the impression that machine learning (still) has significant technical weaknesses.

---

[34]Cf. see Buchholtz, paras 11, 24, 30. Risk assessment software has been in use in the US judiciary for some time and in various areas. For an overview, see Kehl et al. (2017).

[35]A sample questionnaire, including 137 questions, is available online at https://www.documentcloud.org/documents/2702103-Sample-Risk-Assessment-COMPAS-CORE.html. Accessed 30 September 2018.

[36]See Angwin et al. (2016); Pasquale (2017). For a critical view of the study by Angwin et al. (2016), see Flores et al. (2016).

[37]See Stevenson (2017), p. 26. For a general view of the difficulty or impossibility of simultaneously satisfying different criteria of 'fairness' in algorithms, see Kleinberg et al. (2016).

[38]Burgess (2018).

[39]See Oswald et al. (2017); Urwin (2018); see, however, on the *dangers* associated with race-blind or—in this case—class-blind *creation* of AI-software see Tischbirek, paras 35 et seq., and see Rademacher, para 37.

[40]See Knaus (2017).

[41]In a joint study, MIT and Stanford University, for example, were able to demonstrate that three different commercially developed computer programs for image recognition, each based on neural networks, systematically determined the gender of light-skinned men more precisely than that of dark-skinned persons and/or women. See Buell (2018).

If these examples are transferred to taxation procedures, RMS could systematically lead to incorrect risk assessments despite correct initial data. This could result in implausible or risk-fraught cases *not* being excluded from fully automated processing. This would impair the principle of uniformity and legality of the taxation procedure. This threat can only be counteracted by effective controls.[42]

3.2 Controlling AI-based RMS

The statutory requirements on the control of RMS are extremely sparse. Section 88 (5) sentence 3 no. 4 AO merely prescribes a 'regular review of risk management systems to ensure that they fulfill their objectives.' The aim of RMS is to identify and signal potential tax evasion.[43] Regular checks must therefore be carried out to determine whether the RMS exclude risk-fraught cases and whether non-risk cases are processed fully automatically. Controls become difficult if RMS are AI-based. This applies in particular to cases of learning algorithms that can further develop their own programming. These programs are no longer predictable.[44] Besides, they may also deviate from the functionality originally intended by programming.[45]

With regard to the question of how this review should be carried out, the AO contains merely one clue: The RMS must determine a sufficient number of randomly selected cases for comprehensive review by public officials (Section 88(5) sentence 3 no. 1 AO). With regard to taxpayers, this random selection is intended to guarantee an appropriate risk of discovery and with regard to tax authorities, it is supposed to facilitate control. If random selection reveals risk-fraught cases that would otherwise not have been identified by the RMS, this provides an important indication that the RMS is not functioning optimally. In this respect, although random selection is an effective means of control, in practice it is unlikely to be sufficient because a large number of randomly selected cases may not be expected or, in the event of a large number of random cases, sufficient resources may not be available for a detailed personal examination of each case. Roman Seer assumes that a random selection of about two to three percent of cases is sufficient in order to guarantee an adequate risk of discovery.[46] In practice, however, this is not very realistic due to lacking human resources.[47] Furthermore, it is questionable whether an audit of two to three percent of cases would be sufficient for an effective control of machine learning procedures.

---

[42]Cf. also paras 24 et seq.
[43]Cf. paras 9 et seq.
[44]Tutt (2017), pp. 101 et seq.
[45]Kirn and Hengstenberg-Müller (2014), pp. 228 et seq.
[46]Seer (2017), para 77.
[47]Cf. Bundesrechnungshof (Federal Court of Auditors) (2012), pp. 25 et seq.

26   In order to ensure the uniformity and legality of the taxation procedure, it is necessary to provide for further control mechanisms in addition to random selection. In connection with learning algorithms, preventive control of the programs used will make little sense, since programs can change.[48] Therefore, only ex post controls seem feasible. For example, an algorithm-based mass data evaluation could take place, which would provide conclusions about erroneous criteria.[49] In other words: If, for example, AI-based RMS exclude significantly more people with foreign origins, this might indicate erroneous criteria.[50] However, it is questionable whether this is sufficient to ensure uniform and legal taxation when using AI-based RMS in fully automated taxation procedures.

4 Conclusion

27   It is unknown whether AI is already being used in RMS today. There are signs that suggest that this may be the case. If these are machine learning techniques without human intervention, this could lead to problems. The use of such machine learning methods by the judiciary and by public administration (still) reveals considerable weaknesses in practice. According to the current state of knowledge, these can only be countered by extensive controls. Saying that, the greatest challenge of using AI in RMS is control. Secrecy requirements make broad-based public control impossible. Establishing transparency could, however, contribute to enabling the professional community to address basic questions concerning the review of such systems.[51] This could provide valuable impulses for improving RMS.

References

Ahrendt C (2017) Alte Zöpfe neu geflochten – Das materielle Recht in der Hand von Programmierern. Neue Juristische Wochenschrift:537–540
Angwin J, Larson J, Mattu S, Kirchner L (2016) Machine bias – there's software used across the country to predict future criminals. And it's biased against blacks. https://www.propublica.org/article/machine-bias-risk-assessments-in-criminal-sentencing. Accessed 30 Sept 2018
Braun Binder N (2016) Ausschließlich automationsgestützt erlassene Steuerbescheide und Bekanntgabe durch Bereitstellung zum Datenabruf. DStZ:625–635

---

[48] Martini and Nink (2017), p. 12.
[49] Martini and Nink (2017), p. 12.
[50] Cf. Tischbirek, passim and esp. paras 31 et seq.
[51] Cf. Wischmeyer, paras 44 et seq. See also the activities of algorithmwatch, https://algorithmwatch.org/de. Accessed on 30 September 2018.

Braun Binder N (2019) Algorithmisch gesteuertes Risikomanagement in digitalisierten Besteuerungsverfahren. In: Unger S, von Ungern-Sternberg A (eds) Demokratie und Künstliche Intelligenz. Mohr Siebeck, Tübingen (in press). https://www.mohrsiebeck.com/buch/demokratie-und-kuenstliche-intelligenz-9783161581892

Buell S (2018) MIT researcher: artificial intelligence has a race problem, and we need to fix it. Boston Magazine, 23 February 2018. https://www.bostonmagazine.com/news/2018/02/23/artificial-intelligence-race-dark-skin-bias. Accessed 30 Sept 2018

Bundesrechnungshof (2012) Bericht nach § 99 BHO über den Vollzug der Steuergesetze, insbesondere im Arbeitnehmerbereich vom 17.1.2012

Burgess M (2018) UK police are using AI to inform custodial decisions – but it could be discriminating against the poor. WIRED, 1 March 2018. http://www.wired.co.uk/article/police-ai-uk-durham-hart-checkpoint-algorithm-edit. Accessed 30 Sept 2018

Ertel W (2016) Grundkurs Künstliche Intelligenz, 4th edn. Springer Vieweg, Wiesbaden

Flores AW, Bechtel K, Lowenkamp CF (2016) False positives, false negatives, and false analyses. http://www.uscourts.gov/federal-probation-journal/2016/09/false-positives-false-negatives-and-false-analyses-rejoinder. Accessed 30 Sept 2018

Goodfellow I, Bengio Y, Courville A (2016) Deep learning. The MIT Press, Cambridge

Haunhorst S (2010) Risikomanagement in der Finanzverwaltung – ein Fall für die Finanzgerichte? DStR:2105–2110

Kaplan J (2016) Artificial intelligence. What everyone needs to know. Oxford University Press, Oxford

Kehl D, Guo P, Kessler S (2017) Algorithms in the criminal justice system: assessing the use of risk assessments in sentencing. Responsive Communities. https://dash.harvard.edu/handle/1/33746041. Accessed 30 Sept 2018

Kirn S, Hengstenberg-Müller CD (2014) Intelligente (Software-)Agenten: Von der Automatisierung zur Autonomie? Verselbständigung technischer Systeme. MMR:225–232

Kleinberg J, Mullainathan S, Raghavan M (2016) Inherent trade-offs in the fair determination of risk scores. https://arxiv.org/abs/1609.05807. Accessed 30 Sept 2018

Knaus C (2017) Internal Centrelink records reveal flaws behind debt recovery system. The Guardian, 13 January 2017. https://www.theguardian.com/australia-news/2017/jan/13/internal-centrelink-records-reveal-flaws-behind-debt-recovery-system. Accessed 30 Sept 2018

Krumm M (2017) Grundfragen des steuerlichen Datenverarbeitungsrechts. DB:2182–2195

Martini M, Nink D (2017) Wenn Maschinen entscheiden... – vollautomatisierte Verwaltungsverfahren und der Persönlichkeitsschutz. NVwZ-extra 10:1–14. http://rsw.beck.de/rsw/upload/NVwZ/NVwZ-Extra_2017_10.pdf. Accessed 30 Sept 2018

Münch L (2013) Außergerichtlicher Rechtsschutz bei Korrekturen gemäß § 129 AO und § 173 AO nach faktischer Selbstveranlagung. DStR:2150–2156

Neumann L (2016) Stellungnahme des Chaos Computer Club. 13 April 2016. http://goo.gl/2Qm2uR. Accessed 30 Sept 2018

Oswald M, Grace J, Urwin S, Barnes G (2017) Algorithmic risk assessment policing models: lessons from the Durham HART Model and 'Experimental' Proportionality. https://papers.ssrn.com/sol3/papers.cfm?abstract_id=3029345. Accessed 30 Sept 2018

Pasquale F (2017) Secret algorithms threaten the rule of law. MIT Technology Review. https://www.technologyreview.com/s/608011/secret-algorithms-threaten-the-rule-of-law. Accessed 30 Sept 2018

Präsident des Bundesrechnungshofes in seiner Funktion als Bundesbeauftragter für Wirtschaftlichkeit in der Verwaltung (2006) Probleme beim Vollzug der Steuergesetze. https://goo.gl/92gu6r. Accessed 30 Sept 2018

Schmidt E (2008) Moderne Steuerungssysteme im Steuervollzug. DStJG 2008:37–57

Seer R (2017) § 88 AO. In: Tipke K, Kruse HW (eds) AO/FGO. Kommentar, 150th edn. Otto Schmidt, Köln

Stevenson (2017) Assessing risk assessment in action. George Mason University Legal Studies Research Paper Series, LS 17–25. https://papers.ssrn.com/sol3/papers.cfm?abstract_id=3016088. Accessed 30 Sept 2018

Stiemerling O (2015) "Künstliche Intelligenz" – Automatisierung geistiger Arbeit, Big Data und das Internet der Dinge. CR:762–765

Tutt A (2017) An FDA for algorithms. Adm Law Rev 69:83–123

Urwin S (2018) Durham Constabulary written evidence submitted to the Common Science &Technology Committee inquiry into algorithms in decision-making. 20 February 2018. http://data.parliament.uk/writtenevidence/committeeevidence.svc/evidencedocument/science-and-technology-committee/algorithms-in-decisionmaking/written/78290.pdf. Accessed 30 Sept 2018

Artificial Intelligence and Healthcare: Products and Procedures

Sarah Jabri

Contents

1. A Brief Case Study 308
2. Legal Framework: European Medical Devices Law in a Nutshell 310
3. Medical Device Term, Section 3 No. 1 MPG 311
   3.1 Physiological Component 312
   3.2 Mechanism of Action 313
   3.3 Intended Purpose 313
4. Market Access Regulation of Software As a Medical Device 314
   4.1 Categories of Medical Software 314
   4.2 Classification Rules 318
   4.3 Control-Related Process Modules 324
5. Post Market-Entry Surveillance of Software As a Medical Device 326
   5.1 Statutory Provisions of the MPG 327
   5.2 Challenging Information Issue 328
6. Outlook 332
References 332

Abstract This paper focuses on statutory regulation of learning machines that qualify as medical devices. After a brief case study, the article takes a procedural perspective and presents the main features of the European regulatory framework that applies to medical devices in order to identify the regulatory peculiarities in the use of machine learning. In this context, the Chapter will analyse the immanent risks of machine learning applications as medical devices as well as the role of machine learning in their regulation. The overall finding is that due to its lack of expertise and material equipment the state activates private companies for market access control, which are commissioned with the preventive inspection of medical devices. As a result, security measures adopted by the authority are in principle limited to the period after market-entry. This leads to a structural information deficit for the authority, which has no systematic information about the products on the market. The authority is limited to a challenging overall market observation. This raises the

S. Jabri (✉)
Department of Law, University of Constance, Constance, Germany
e-mail: sarah.jabri@uni-konstanz.de

© Springer Nature Switzerland AG 2020
T. Wischmeyer, T. Rademacher (eds.), *Regulating Artificial Intelligence*,
https://doi.org/10.1007/978-3-030-32361-5_14

question addressed in the fifth part of the paper: does the law guarantee sufficient instruments for the systematic transfer of knowledge from the risk actors to the authority about the potential risk of medical devices and does this in fact remedy the information deficit of the authority and ensure an effective post market-entry control of learning machines as medical devices?

1 A Brief Case Study

1   In a study, a team of researchers from the London-based company DeepMind developed a deep learning method using computer-assisted diagnostics (CAD) to triage patients according to treatment urgency in order to reduce the waiting time of critical patients by prioritizing them.[1] The deep learning method was used on optical coherence tomography (OCT), which scans the retina with coherent light and creates high-resolution images. In medical practice, there are few specialists who can evaluate OCTs, which regularly leads to a delay in treatment. In the worst case, this can lead to a blindness of patients. Countering this hazard, the researchers have developed an algorithm that examines OCTs for 53 diagnoses and categorizes the diagnoses according to the urgency of the treatment after training on only 14,884 retinal scans. Based on these scans, the algorithm learned which characteristics indicate which disease. Putting it to the test, the aim of the AI method was to achieve or exceed the performance of human experts as well as showing clinical applicability. The other side of the coin of the deep learning method, however, is that, similar to human decision making, it is difficult to see which features were decisive for the prioritization by the algorithm; an appearance of the black box phenomenon often identified in the context of artificial intelligence.[2] But transparency is indispensable in the medical field: physicians cannot (yet) simply rely on the decision of machines.[3] This concerns ethical issues as well as such of legal responsibility for wrong decisions.[4] The scenario is even more precarious when artificial intelligence is used not only to prioritize patients, but also to create tangible diagnoses. In cases where a physician supported by machine learning[5] reaches a conclusion that deviates from the automated diagnosis, the medical professional is always faced with the challenging task of weighing his possible behavioural options: is the physician able to rely on the automatically obtained result or isn't he? To enable the physician to understand the decision-making process, the study followed a two-phase approach:

---

[1]De Fauw et al. (2018), p. 1342 et seq.
[2]See Wischmeyer, paras 2 et seq.
[3]On the reliability of an output of a learning algorithm in the context of search algorithms, see European Court of Justice C-131/12 'Google Spain SL/AEPD' (13 May 2014) margin no. 61 et seq.
[4]See in detail Molnár-Gábor, paras 38 et seq.
[5]On the term of 'machine learning' see Hoffmann-Riem, para 3 and Hermstüwer, para 6.

in a first step, the algorithm segmented the OCT scan. On this basis, the algorithm examined the image for critical medical findings in a second step and highlighted them. Although this two-phase approach enables the physician to understand the individual case, such Explainable AI (XAI) is neither prescribed by law, nor does it represent the standard offer in the spectrum of medical devices offered on the market.

This scenario indicates: the increasing use of software[6] in modern medical procedures occurs in a multitude of sensible scopes[7] and may be determining the success of a therapy.[8] The growing importance of software in medical devices is linked to an increase in complexity. The development evolves from experience-based knowledge of the individual physician to evidence-based intervention using the best external scientific evidence currently available.[9] Therefore, the increasing use of software, especially artificial intelligence, leads to a heightened need for regulation: algorithms automatically support decisions that were previously reserved for humans and can significantly influence a self-determined human decision.[10] The increase in complexity often results from the lack of predictability of the output of learning algorithms. Learning algorithms are confronted with a wide variety of environmental stimuli and consequently change their decision basis and structure. This results in a continuous expansion of the analytical power and an ability of learning and thus complicates the effectiveness of preventive controls of learning algorithms. The comprehensive protection of citizens from risks and hazards that can arise from the use of medical technical products has always been a traditional task of the state,[11] which possesses also a constitutional dimension. Consequently, the state is now faced with the major issue of fulfilling its legal protection mandate despite the increasing complexity of the subject of regulation.

This paper is not intended to be a repeated description of the process of legal procedures for medical devices, but rather evaluates if the statutory regulations under EU law provide Member State administrations with effective regulatory tools to fulfil their legal mandate for market access control and post market-entry surveillance of medical devices. In particular, it will be analyzed whether the German Medical Devices Law, which inter alia transposes relevant procedural requirements of EU directives, takes account of the increased risks arising from the use of artificial intelligence in medical devices through special rules. For this purpose, after a brief introduction to the legal framework (see Sect. 2), the term of 'medical device' will be explained (see Sect. 3), as the so-called Conformity Assessment Procedure only applies if learning software qualifies as medical device in the sense of the legal definition. In a following step, software is to be differentiated according to its various appearances in medical devices

---

[6]Langkafel (2015), p. 27; Singh (2014), p. 157; Thuemmler (2017), p. 1.
[7]Cf. Hadank (2017), p. 811.
[8]Neubauer and Uilaky (2004), p. 151; Ostermayer and Kexel (2009), p. 106; Schmitt (2014), p. 26.
[9]Trute (2018), p. 1.
[10]Ernst (2017), p. 1026; Martini (2017a), p. 1017; Stiemerling (2015), p. 762.
[11]Jaumann (1980), p. 7; Kage (2005), pp. 19, 213 et seq.

in order to subsume the variants under the depicted medical device term (see Sect. 4.1). Subsequently, the risk dimension of learning machines as medical devices will be analyzed before the procedural steps will be described (see Sect. 4.2). To this end, it is appropriate to differentiate between two phases of control: market access control by notified bodies on the one hand (see Sect. 4) and post market-entry surveillance by the competent authorities on the other hand (see Sect. 5). Hereby, the information problem of the authorities resulting from this distribution of competences will be described in order to determine whether the recent change to the German Medical Devices Law provides the authorities with a cognitive instrument countering this problem and ensuring an effective post market-entry surveillance.

2 Legal Framework: European Medical Devices Law in a Nutshell

4 The regulation of medical devices in Germany is mainly influenced by EU law.[12] European Medical Devices Law is based on Article 114 AEUV[13] and the 'New Approach'[14] and pursues an amendment of the safety of medical devices as well as an enhancement of free movement of medical goods in the European Union. Basically, the legal framework for medical devices is conditioned by three Council Directives,[15] i.e. the Council Directive 90/385/EEC relating to active implantable medical devices (Active Implantable Medical Device Directive—AIMDD), the Council Directive 93/42/EEC concerning medical devices (Medical Device Directive—MDD) and the Council Directive 2007/47/EC amending the AIMDD and MDD as well as the Council Directive 98/8/EC. Through this set of regulation, the European legislator pursues a concept of device regulation aiming at legal provisions, which are vital for the compliance with essential safety requirements.[16] Part of the European rules and standards are so-called Conformity Assessment Procedures, making demands on manufacturers depending on the potential risk associated with the technical design and manufacture of the devices.[17] However, official approval, as in the case of medicinal products, is *not* a requirement for market access.[18] Rather, the regulations provide for an assessment procedure by private

---

[12]Igl (2018), p. 155; Jäkel (2016), p. 601.

[13]Cf. Council Directive 93/42/EEC, former Article 100a EEC.

[14]Council resolution of 7 May 1985 on a new approach to technical harmonization and standards (OJ EG No. C 136, p. 1); Braun and Püschel (2014), p. 136; Dieners and Vivekens (2017), p. 20; Tomasini (2015), p. 12 et seq.

[15]Part of the European Medical Devices Law is also the Council Directive 98/79/EC concerning in vitro diagnostic medical devices, which shouldn't be considered in this contribution.

[16]Cf. Recital 8 of the Council Directive 93/42/EEC.

[17]Cf. Recital 15 of the Council Directive 93/42/EEC.

[18]Braun and Püschel (2014), p. 136; a proposal for the establishment of an approval procedure at central level, at least for medical devices of the high-risk group, was made by Roth-Behrendt in the latest legislative reform of EU Medical Devices Law, cf. Heil (2014), p. 16.

companies, so-called 'notified bodies', and subsequent conformity marking by the manufacturers themselves[19] as a requirement for market access. The certification of medical devices by notified bodies thus has a substituting effect regarding official preventive control.[20] The role of the authorities in market access control is therefore basically limited to the monitoring of notified bodies.[21] The regulatory supervision of ensuring legal conformity of the certification objects hence mainly evolves within the framework of post market-entry control.

In Germany, it is essentially the *Medizinproduktegesetz* (MPG—Medical Devices Act)[22] which implements the requirements of the European Directives in national law.[23] Conceptually, the MPG is conceived as a framework law that is flanked by numerous implementation regulations under Medical Devices Law.[24] From a regulatory point of view, the national MPG is facing a system change with the enactment of the EU Medical Device Regulation (MDR)[25] in 2017—moving away from sectoral directives towards a regulation that is directly applicable in the Member States. The MDR is also influenced by the expectation of an increasing use of modern technology in medical devices[26] by, e.g., adapting the regulatory regime to innovative medical devices. However, the MDR will not enter into force in its entirety until 2020.[27]

5

3 Medical Device Term, Section 3 No. 1 MPG

Medical software appears in a multitude of different designs. Progressively the importance of software as a medical device was identified and incorporated into the European Medical Devices Law by dint of the clarifying amendments of Council

6

---

[19]For further details see below, paras 29 et seq., which describes the control-related process modules.

[20]Bieback (2008), p. 214.

[21]Cf. Article 16(3) of the Council Directive 93/42/EEC; implemented in detail in national law by Section 15 MPG.

[22]Gesetz über Medizinprodukte (Medizinproduktegesetz – MPG) in the version published on 07th August 2002 (BGBl. I p. 3146), last amended by Article 7 of the Act of the 18th July 2017 (BGBl. I p. 2757).

[23]For an overview of the historical development of national Medical Devices Law, in particular the implementation of the European directives by the MPG amendments, see Tomasini (2015), pp. 19 et seq.

[24]An overview is provided by Webel (2018), p. 852, margin no. 3.

[25]Regulation (EU) 2017/745 of the European Parliament and of the Council of 5th April 2017 on medical devices, amending Directive 2001/83/EC, Regulation (EC) No 178/2002 and Regulation (EC) No 1223/2009 and repealing Council Directives 90/385/EEC and 93/42/EEC, OJ EU 2017, No. L 117/1.

[26]Cf. Recitals 1, 13 and Annex IX section 4.5. of the MDR.

[27]Cf. Article 123(2) of the MDR.

Directive 2007/47/EC.[28] The classification of the software influences the content and scope of the Conformity Assessment Procedure and the subsequent CE-marking.[29] Thus the legal classification of medical software constitutes an essential factor in setting the course for the following considerations. Therefore, the requirements of the term of medical device according to the European Medical Devices Law and its implementation in national German law will be highlighted, due to the fact that the regulations of MDD and MPG as also their regulatory requirements only apply in the case of a medical device in this context.[30] Section 3 No. 1 MPG defines medical devices by dint of three attributes: a physiological component, the mechanism of action and the intended purpose. These attributes will be explained briefly to illustrate the meaning of the individual components for the categorization of learning machines as medical devices.

3.1 Physiological Component

7   The first attribute is the physiological component. It is described as any instrument, apparatus, appliance, software, material or other article.[31] This description appears rather extensive. It mentions software explicitly, so that software always corresponds to the first element of the term of medical device. It can be recognized that the attribute of the physiological component does not differentiate between static and learning software. However, the lack of distinction is not to be equated with a legislative assessment, to equate the specific risk construction of static and learning algorithms and consequently to make the same demands on the content and scope of the testing of the algorithms. The purpose of using the broad term of software is to open up a wide field of application for Medical Devices Law.[32] The legislator's assessments of the degree of risk associated with a software type are rather taken into account within the framework of classification into the relevant risk class by classification rules that determine the content and scope of control.[33]

---

[28]Tomasini (2015), p. 18.

[29]Irmer (2013), p. 145.

[30]The legal qualification of software in the medical scope was simplified by the 4th amendment of the MPG in 2010, cf. Gesetz zur Änderung medizinprodukterechtlicher Vorschriften vom 29. Juli 2009 (BGBl. I p. 2326); Irmer (2013), p. 145.

[31]Cf. Section 3 No. 1 MPG, adopted literally from Article 2 of the Council Directive 2007/47/EC; Tomasini (2015), p. 37.

[32]Cf. Bill of the Rederal Government, Parliamentary Printing Matter 16/12258, p. 26.

[33]See paras 22 et seq., in which the specific risk construction of learning machines is elaborated as a basis for their classification.

3.2 Mechanism of Action

The second component of the medical device term is related to the mechanism of action. Accordingly, the device should not achieve its principal intended action in or on the human body by pharmacological, immunological or metabolic means.[34] This attribute enables a dissociation from medicinal products,[35] which fall within the scope of the Council Directive 2001/83/EC and the *Arzneimittelgesetz* (AMG—German Pharmaceuticals Act).[36] Certainly it must be considered, that medical devices may indeed have these attributes, as long as they are merely a supporting factor in the mechanism of action of the medical device.[37] However, this attribute is not particularly relevant for software, because usually it has not the effects of a medicinal product. Therefore, the crucial factor deciding the qualification of learning software as a medical device remains the intended purpose.[38]

8

3.3 Intended Purpose

The core of the definition is the intended purpose of the device. Intended purpose means the 'use for which the device is intended according to the data supplied by the manufacturer on the labelling, in the instructions and/or in promotional materials.'[39] Section 3 No. 1 MPG requires that the device is intended by the manufacturer to be used for the purpose of diagnosis, prevention, monitoring, treatment or alleviation of human disease; for diagnosis, monitoring, treatment, alleviation of or compensation for an injury or handicap; for investigation, replacement or modification of the anatomy or of a physiological process; or for control of conception.[40] In short: Taking into account the intended purpose of a device, software meets the conceptual requirements namely if it assists in diagnosing issues or affects medical treatment.[41] As the manufacturer defines the intended purpose of a device, it is not based on

9

---

[34]Cf. Section 3 No. 1 MPG; Tomasini (2015), p. 37; Lücker (2014); pp. 1272 et seq., margin no. 7; Webel (2018), p. 863, margin no. 7 et seq.

[35]Kage (2005), p. 42; Lücker (2014); pp. 1272 et seq., margin no. 7; Webel (2018), p. 863, margin no. 7 et seq.

[36]Gesetz über den Verkehr mit Arzneimitteln (Arzneimittelgesetz—AMG) in the version published on 12th December 2005 (BGBl. I p. 3394), last amended by Article 1 of the Act of the 18th July 2017 (BGBl. I p. 2757).

[37]Lücker (2014), pp. 1272 et seq., margin no. 7.

[38]Czettritz and Strelow (2017), p. 434; Düwert and Klümper (2013), p. 23; Gassner (2017), p. 25; Hötzel (2018), p. 16; Kage (2005), p. 43; Oen (2009), p. 55; Pramann and Albrecht (2015), p. 132; Sachs (2013), p. 31; Tomasini (2015), p. 37.

[39]MEDDEV 2.1/6 (2016), Guidance document concerning the qualification and classification of stand-alone software, p. 4.

[40]Cf. Section 3 No. 1 MPG.

[41]Irmer (2013), p. 145.

objective criteria, as it is the case for medicinal products.[42] The intended use thus determines whether and with what content and scope market access control is carried out. In contrast, the degree of automation is not decisive. Hence, static and learning systems are categorized in the equal purposive manner. Learning machines can consequently be subject to the requirements of Medical Devices Law as far as the manufacturer assigns them a medical purpose.

4 Market Access Regulation of Software As a Medical Device

10   The term of medical device covers an exceedingly heterogeneous range of products whose hazard potential varies considerably.[43] Thus, it is necessary to classify medical software into different subordinate categories enabling an account that is detached from the individual case. Hereby it will be examined whether these categories can be subsumed under the delineated definition of a medical device with the consequence that the corresponding design of software is subject of the regulative market access requirements of the MDD and the MPG. Secondly, the legal classification rules will be described in order to identify the peculiarities of the classification of machine learning that qualifies as a medical device by describing its specific risk construction. On this basis, the main process modules will be examined.

4.1 Categories of Medical Software

11   Applications which meet the requirements of the medical device term and thus fall within the scope of the Medical Devices Law must comply with the legal requirements and must carry the CE-marking prior to its placing on the market.[44] As it turns out, the medical device term comprises a variety of products. Therefore, medical software will be divided into different superordinate categories: software incorporated in a device, stand-alone software, accessories on medical devices and software for general purposes. Hereinafter the necessary steps to qualify different types of software will be regarded distilling distinctions.

---

[42]Ibid.; Prinz (2017), p. 19.
[43]Merten (2004), p. 1212.
[44]MEDDEV 2.1/6 (2016), Guidance document concerning the qualification and classification of stand-alone software, p. 18.

Embedded Software

Software that is integrated as its finite component into a medical device and marketed together with it is called embedded software.[45] Embedded software is not standalone, it is supposed to control the entire product only technically, without having a medical purpose itself.[46] According to the above principles, embedded software is *not* a medical device. Instead, the medical device including the embedded software is to be regarded as a whole,[47] both with regard to the Conformity Assessment Procedure and with regard to the CE-marking.[48] In other words, embedded software itself is not subject to its own Conformity Assessment Procedure in accordance with Section 6(2) MPG, but is appropriately considered and tested as part of the Conformity Assessment Procedure for the main product.[49] Subsequently, only one CE mark is awarded, which covers the medical device as a whole.[50] Software which controls the power supply system of a medical device can be named as an example for embedded software.[51] As a rule, it cannot be distributed separately and displayed on any other medical device.[52]

Stand-Alone Software

In contrast to embedded software, stand-alone software is not incorporated in a medical device,[53] it can be used and distributed independently. For this reason, stand-alone software is mentioned separately in Section 3 MPG[54] The decisive factor for qualification as stand-alone is that the software is not incorporated in a medical device *at the time of its placing on the market* or its making available.[55] Certainly the software can also be used in combination with hardware by integration in a system. However, this does not alter the software's qualification.[56]

---

[45] Sachs (2013), p. 31.
[46] Klümper and Vollebregt (2009), p. 100; ensuing Tomasini (2015), p. 43.
[47] Courtin (1997), p. 64; Sachs (2013), p. 31; Tomasini (2015), p. 43.
[48] Oen (2009), p. 55.
[49] Graf (2017a), p. 59; Gassner (2016), p. 111; Hötzel (2018), p. 16; Oen (2009), p. 55; Tomasini (2015), p. 43.
[50] Klümper and Vollebregt (2009), p. 100; Tomasini (2015), pp. 43 et seq.
[51] Klümper and Vollebregt (2009), p. 100.
[52] Tomasini (2015), p. 44.
[53] MEDDEV 2.1/6 (2016), Guidance document concerning the qualification and classification of stand-alone software, p. 7; Tomasini (2015), p. 39.
[54] Cf. Gesetz zur Änderung medizinprodukterechtlicher Vorschriften vom 29. Juli 2009 (BGBl. I p. 2326).
[55] MEDDEV 2.1/6 (2016), Guidance document concerning the qualification and classification of stand-alone software, p. 7; Pramann and Albrecht (2015), p. 132.
[56] Tomasini (2015), p. 40; MEDDEV 2.1/6 (2016), Guidance document concerning the qualification and classification of stand-alone software, p. 8.

14   The categorization of stand-alone software as a medical device is determined by the manufacturers intended purpose, i.e. not all stand-alone software used within healthcare can be qualified as a medical device.[57] As opposed to embedded software, the intended purpose of the software itself is crucial for its classification, not the purpose of the hardware which the software is potentially integrated in.[58] This is an indication of the increasing importance of software in the field of medical devices.[59] While software used to be classified 'hardware-dependent' in former times, since software could be at most an accessory to a medical device in the sense of Medical Devices Law,[60] its self-contained operating mode is significant due to the increasing technical development. Thus, it is advisable to take a closer look at stand-alone software and the requirements for its distribution, as it is a reasonable approach for demonstrating the special regulatory features in the handling of medical software. Due to the diversity of conceivable learning systems as medical devices, the further provisions should particularly focus on learning algorithms that support diagnosis. An example of stand-alone software is the deep learning application for OCTs described at the beginning of this Chapter.

Accessories on Medical Devices

15   Software can also be an accessory on a medical device.[61] Under European Medical Devices Law, 'accessory' is understood to mean 'an article which whilst not being a device that is intended specifically by its manufacturer to be used together with a device to enable it to be used in accordance with the use of the device intended by the manufacturer of the device'.[62] This implies that the characteristic of an accessory is determined firstly by the manufacturers' intended purpose and secondly by the dependence of the medical device on the accessory for achieving its intended purpose.[63] However, not every support of the intended purpose of a medical device is sufficient for the characteristic of an accessory[64]; this would lead to an excessive scope of application.[65] Software as an accessory on medical devices therefore differs

---

[57]MEDDEV 2.1/6 (2016), Guidance document concerning the qualification and classification of stand-alone software, p. 8.

[58]Irmer (2013), p. 145.

[59]Cf. Recital 20 of the Council Directive 2007/47/EC.

[60]Cf. Bill of the Federal Government, Parliamentary Printing Matter 16/12258, p. 26.

[61]Other voices in the literature argue that software cannot be an accessory since the law on the amendment of medical device regulations (4th MPG amendment) came into force. This difference of views has been processed by Tomasini (2015), pp. 46 et seq.; also illustrated by Oen (2009), p. 56; Gassner (2016), p. 111.

[62]Cf. Article 1(2)(b) of the Council Directive 93/42/EEC; misleadingly implemented in Section 3 No. 9 MPG.

[63]Anhalt et al. (2017), p. 58.

[64]Ibid.; similarly Tomasini (2015), p. 45 with reference to Meyer (2011).

[65]To this see Tomasini (2015), p. 45.

from stand-alone software by the fact that software as an accessory does not serve its own medical purpose and thus does not fulfil the definition component of the medical indication, but is necessary in order to be able to use a medical device according to its intended purpose.[66]

Section 2(1) MPG clarifies in accordance with the MDD[67] that accessories to medical devices are to be treated as independent medical devices themselves.[68] Hence, software as an accessory to medical devices is provided with its own CE marking after conformity assessment and treated as an independent medical device.[69] One example of an accessory on a medical device is software that is used to control a medical device.[70]

Software for General Purposes

Software in the medical sphere that does not fall within the categories described is to be considered as software for general purposes. These do not fall within the scope of the MPG, as they do not fulfil the components of the medical device notion.[71] However, it must be taken into account that the use of stand-alone software in the sense described above can hardly be used without the simultaneous use of software for general purposes. Software can therefore consist of several modules, which do not all fall within the scope of Medical Devices Law and hence have to be classified and treated differently. The European Court of Justice has also recently confirmed this in a judgment issued in December 2017:

> In respect of medical software comprising both modules that meet the definition of the term 'medical device' and others that do not meet it and that are not accessories within the meaning of Article 1(2)(b) of Directive 93/42, only the former fall within the scope of the directive and must be marked CE.[72]

Software for general purposes must therefore not be regarded as a medical device.[73] This distinction of different components is an expression of the modular approach pursued by Medical Devices Law.[74] As an example of software for general

---

[66]MEDDEV 2.1/6 (2016), Guidance document concerning the qualification and classification of stand-alone software, p. 12; thereafter Tomasini (2015), p. 48.
[67]Cf. Article 1(1) of the Council Directive 93/42/EEC.
[68]Anhalt et al. (2017), p. 57.
[69]Cf. Article 1(1) of the Council Directive 93/42/EEC and the implementation in Section 2(1) MPG.
[70]Tomasini (2015), p. 49.
[71]Cf. Recital 19 of the Regulation (EU) 2017/745.
[72]European Court of Justice C-329/16 'Philips France/ Ministre des Affaires sociales et de la Santé' (7 December 2017), margin no. 36.
[73]Ibid.
[74]MEDDEV 2.1/6 (2016), Guidance document concerning the qualification and classification of stand-alone software, p. 17 et seq.

purposes, word processing programs can be mentioned which are required for creating the sort list in the scenario referred to at the introduction of this Chapter.

Subject of Monitoring Under Medical Devices Law

18   The execution of the categories of medical software has shown that a manufacturer must differentiate clearly in order to assign his product to the correct product class. Not all software used in the context of a medical devices is to be treated as such and is subject to the requirements of Medical Devices Law. Rather, only embedded software, stand-alone software and software as accessories on a medical device are subject to the Conformity Assessment Procedure required by European Medical Devices Law. Since embedded software is only included in the conformity assessment of the main product and the accessories for a medical device are also closely related to the main product, the category of stand-alone software seems to be of particular interest for further investigation. Classification rules, procedural requirements and control-related process modules will therefore be further specified on the basis of the category of stand-alone software.

4.2   Classification Rules

19   Before a medical device is placed on the market, its compliance with the Essential Requirements must be established in a formal Conformity Assessment Procedure.[75] The scope and intensity of the tests as part of the Conformity Assessment Procedure are determined by the classification of the medical device.[76] The classification is a risk-based system considering the potential risk associated with the devices.[77] Thus the allocation of the procedure to be applied basically requires the classification of the medical device into one of the following risk classes.

Risk Classes

20   Under current law, medical devices are divided into four product classes (Classes I, IIa, IIb and III).[78] The higher the risk class, the higher the requirements that a manufacturer must meet in order to demonstrate the conformity of his product

---

[75] Anhalt et al. (2017), p. 61.

[76] MEDDEV 2.4/1 Rev. 9 (2010), Guidance document concerning the classification of medical devices, p. 4; Braun and Püschel (2014), p. 136.

[77] Jäkel (2016), p. 602; MEDDEV 2.4/1 Rev. 9 (2010), Guidance document concerning the classification of medical devices, p. 4; Merten (2004), p. 1212.

[78] Cf. Article 3 of the Council Directive 93/42/EEC; Braun and Püschel (2014), p. 136.

with the basic requirements.[79] To facilitate classification and to create legal compliance, the relevant European directives contain implementing rules[80] to which the national Medical Devices Law refers.[81] Hence, the classification of a medical device is carried out by applying the 18 classification rules in accordance with the application rules specified therein.[82] These classification rules are based on various criteria such as invasivity[83] and the duration of contact with the patient.[84] While the existing rules may cover a majority of products, a small number of products are more demanding in their classification. These cases include in particular products that are borderline cases between several risk classes.[85] Countering such borderline cases, the MDD establishes a conflict rule. Therefore applies: if several rules apply to the same device, based on the performance specified for the device by the manufacturer,[86] the strictest rule resulting in the higher classification shall apply.[87] The characteristic features of the risk classes are the following:

Class I covers products with a low risk potential, which therefore require merely a minimum of control.[88] An exemplification are orthopaedic aids.[89] *Class IIa* includes products with medium risk potential, e.g. ultrasound equipment for diagnostics and hearing aids.[90] Products with increased risk potential are classified as *Class IIb*.[91] An instance for this are lung ventilators[92] and contraception products.[93] Lastly, products

---

[79]Tomasini (2015), p. 86; for further details on the basic requirements see para 30.

[80]Cf. Annex IX of the Council Directive 93/42/EEC.

[81]Section 13(1) MPG.

[82]Each medical device is classified separately, this also applies to accessories on medical devices, cf. Annex IX, section 2.2 of the Council Directive 93/42/EEC.

[83]Anhalt et al. (2017), p. 61.

[84]Cf. Annex IX of the Council Directive 93/42/EEC; MEDDEV 2.4/1 Rev. 9 (2010), Guidance document concerning the classification of medical devices, p. 7.

[85]MEDDEV 2.4/1 Rev. 9 (2010), Guidance document concerning the classification of medical devices, p. 4.

[86]If the manufacturer is unsure how to classify his product, he can consult a notified body. In case of a dispute between the manufacturer and the notified body resulting from the application of the classification rules, the matter shall be referred for decision to the relevant Competent Authority to which the notified body is subject, cf. Article 9(2) of the Council Directive 93/42/EEC.

[87]Cf. Annex IX, section 2.5 of the Council Directive 93/42/EEC; MEDDEV 2.4/1 Rev. 9 (2010), Guidance document concerning the classification of medical devices, p. 13.

[88]Anhalt et al. (2017), p. 61.

[89]MEDDEV 2.4/1 Rev. 9 (2010), Guidance document concerning the classification of medical devices, p. 37.

[90]Anhalt et al. (2017), p. 61; MEDDEV 2.4/1 Rev. 9 (2010), Guidance document concerning the classification of medical devices, p. 39.

[91]Anhalt et al. (2017), p. 61.

[92]Ibid.; MEDDEV 2.4/1 Rev. 9 (2010), Guidance document concerning the classification of medical devices, p. 40.

[93]Anhalt et al. (2017), p. 61; MEDDEV 2.4/1 Rev. 9 (2010), Guidance document concerning the classification of medical devices, p. 47.

with a particularly high risk potential are covered by *Class III*.[94] Products of this Class are inter alia prosthetic heart valves[95] and shoulder joint replacement systems.[96]

Risk Dimensions of Software As a Medical Device

22   Prior to examining the applicability of the individual classification rules to stand-alone software, the specific risk construction of static algorithms on the one hand and learning algorithms in medical devices on the other hand will be considered in order to identify particularities for the classification of machine learning applications that qualify as medical devices. The leading question in this context has to be whether learning systems as or in medical devices pose an increased risk potential that justifies higher requirements for their preventive control or post market-entry surveillance. The increased risk lies less in energy-related functional failures of systems, which are obviously noticeable for the user. Rather, the risks appear to be particularly sensitive when systems suggest to users that they are functioning in the correct way but conceal an inaccurate result. Detached from the type of a software error,[97] two dimensions of risk can be identified that are significant to the use of algorithms in medical devices.[98] Briefly spoken, the quality of the automatically acquired knowledge is at issue.[99]

23   One case of malfunction of software is a *false positive error*. A false positive error is characterized by the fact that the software in a medical device indicates the existence of a condition in its output data, such as a positive diagnosis, although such a condition does not exist.[100] The false positive result of the algorithm's decision program, if it is used for diagnosis, presents the treating physician in particular with the considerable challenge and responsibility of an intervention, especially if the physician comes to a different diagnosis after his personal decision (see Molnár-Gábor, paras 38 et seq.). However, it is not only physicians who can face challenges from false positive errors. The rights of patients must neither be disregarded. The supposed knowledge about a disease can lead patients into deep ethical abysses.[101] Patients therefore have an increased interest in *not* receiving certain information. This may be understood as a

---

[94]Anhalt et al. (2017), p. 61.

[95]MEDDEV 2.4/1 Rev 9 (2010), Guidance document concerning the classification of medical devices, p. 37.

[96]MEDDEV 2.4/1 Rev. 9 (2010), Guidance document concerning the classification of medical devices, p. 38.

[97]The BfArM has published a statistical evaluation of the risk reports on software errors in medical devices that were conclusively evaluated between 01st January 2005 and 31th December 2016. Available at: https://www.bfarm.de/SharedDocs/Downloads/DE/Service/Statistik/MP-Statistik/statist-Auswert_Fehlerart_Software.jpg?__blob=poster&v=6.

[98]For a description of instances for false negative and false positive errors see Hermstüwer, para 45.

[99]Trute (2018), p. 1.

[100]Colquhoun (2017), p. 2; van Cauter (1988), p. E786.

[101]See in detail Molnár-Gábor, paras 25–28.

right not to know, hence as a will-driven right to defend oneself against certain information contents.[102] Even only supposed knowledge, which is generated by false positive errors, can represent a risk sui generis.[103]

Another case of malfunction of software is a *false negative error*. A false negative error describes a binary output that pretends a condition does not exist although it does.[104] False negative errors in outputs of medical devices confront physicians and patients with challenges that are comparable to false positive errors in outputs. In particular, the physician's responsibility in dealing with automatically generated negative diagnostic results should be emphasized: To what extent can a physician rely on an automatically generated negative result and to what extent does he bear the responsibility for further monitoring of the patient despite the negative result? In qualitative respect, the risk dimensions described apply equally to static and learning algorithms in medical devices. Therefore, in a second step, it has to be questioned how the specific risk construction differs between static and learning algorithms in medical devices.

Algorithms perform actions because this function has been assigned to them by construction.[105] This applies without restriction to static algorithms, but merely in a certain way to learning algorithms, since these, too, can solely unfold within the scope of the autonomy granted by construction.[106] The regulative challenge associated with learning algorithms lies in the explanatory content of their output (see Wischmeyer, paras 3 et seq.).[107] Thereby, a distinction has to be drawn between the comprehensibility of the decision making in the individual case and the traceability of the capability development of the system, i.e. the adjustment of the premises and of the weighting of the variables on which the system is based. While the comprehensibility of the decision making of the learning system in the individual case can be made fairly simple for the end-user by using XAI-applications,[108] the traceability of the system's premises presents constructors and users of the algorithm with greater challenges. A diagnosis-supporting algorithm, for example, is able to learn independently through a type of in-built feedback loop, so that it can find its own identification signs for recognising diseases. These correlations can also be based on chance, depending on the selection and validity of the input data with which a learning algorithm is trained. Especially in cases in which medical research can refute a connection supposedly recognized by the algorithm, there is an increased need for the possibility of a corrective effect on the premises and the weighting of the variables. Such corrective intervention, however, presupposes that the application of the algorithm on the one hand reveals a comprehensible representation of the

24

25

---

[102]To the right not to know see Taupitz (1998), p. 591.
[103]To risk information in context of informed consent of patients see Molnár-Gábor, paras 34 et seq.
[104]Van Cauter (1988), p. E786.
[105]Herberger (2018), p. 2827.
[106]Ibid.
[107]Herberger (2018), pp. 2827 et seq.
[108]Everything else would be unsatisfactory in the medical field, so Herberger (2018), p. 2828. On Explainable AI see Rademacher, para 33, Wischmeyer paras 27 et seq.

development of the system premises and weighting of the variables to the user and on the other hand also permits intervention in the decision mechanism. Certainly, with the increasing expansion of the data basis, the complexity of the lines of development will reach an extent that even an above-average IT-trained user will not be able to comprehend the modifications (keyword Big Data). This is aggravated by the fact that the source code of the algorithms and thus the system's premises in particular are in most cases encrypted in the distributed hardware, which means that the algorithms cannot be immediately traced also for cryptographic reasons. This may mean that the perspective of generating knowledge about the functioning of learning medical devices has to change: Instead of recourse to the experience gained in the past, the generation of knowledge in the present through simulative black box testing is moving into the foreground.

In Particular: Classification of Stand-Alone Software

26   Based on this risk specification of learning software as a medical device,[109] particularities in the classification of these products will be identified. Classification is a risk-based system, therefore it is vital to relate to the described risk construction of learning algorithms. The risk-based system is due to the fact that in a liberal social order the state does not have to comprehensively control technological change as such, but has to concentrate the state's handling of innovations and risks on the production of safety.[110] In this context, there remains the question whether the current law classifies learning software as a medical device into a higher risk class than static software and whether such an upgrading is necessary in view of the increasing scope of requirements with increasing risk class in the market access procedure in order to counter the specific risk emanating from learning software.

27   Products that meet the requirements of the medical device definition are classified in accordance with Article 9(1) MDD according to Annex IX of the MDD.[111] In addition to definitions, Annex IX contains application and classification rules that are oriented towards the intended purpose of the products. Software is only mentioned two times in Annex IX, which prima facie contradicts a differentiated classification based on the specific risk construction of learning applications. According to this, software, which drives a device or influences the use of a device, falls automatically in the same class.[112] This may also apply to stand-alone software.[113] If, in contrast, it is independent of other products, it is classified on its

---

[109] For illustrative examples of qualification and classification of software used in the healthcare environment, see Annex 1 of MEDDEV 2.1/6 (2016), Guidance document concerning the Qualification and Classification of stand alone software, pp. 19 et seq.

[110] Scherzberg and Heym (2013), p. 176.

[111] Annex IX of the MDD is also referred to by national law in Section 13(1) sentence 2 MPG.

[112] Cf. Annex IX, section 2.3 of the Council Directive 93/42/EEC; also Annex VIII section 3.3 of the Regulation (EU) 2017/745; illustratively Tomasini (2015), p. 98.

[113] Frankenberger (2017), p. 127.

own.[114] In this case, stand-alone software is considered to be an active medical device,[115] meaning that according to the law hitherto in force the same classification rules apply as for those other products, which depend on a source of electrical energy or any source of power other than that directly generated by the human body or gravity and which acts by converting this energy.[116] It is striking that the European legislator subjected all energy-related products to one classification regime, which is broadly based on their intended use, e.g. therapeutic or diagnostic, but does not address specific risks. In this way, the legislator categorized and generalized the risks inherent in automated medical devices despite the specific risk construction of learning systems described above,[117] which goes beyond mere energy-related functional failures of systems. Consequently, the Directive and its subsequent implementation into national law do not differentiate between static and learning applications. As a result, this could ultimately even lead to a situation where a learning machine as a medical device, which serves neither therapeutic nor diagnostic purposes, is assigned to the *lowest* risk class I,[118] with the effect that a manufacturer can independently determine the conformity of the medical device with the Essential Requirements,[119] i.e. without the involvement of a notified body or government authority, and can place it on the market after the CE marking has been affixed by the manufacturer himself.[120] In principle, the new regulation does not alter this. Although software has now been given its own classification rule,[121] it does not sufficiently differentiate between the risks associated with static and learning systems.

It should certainly be noted that only few products are likely to fall within the scope of class I which is merely a catch-all rule.[122] The increased risks described above for the life and limb of patients are probably increasingly based on therapeutic and diagnostic learning products. This has already been demonstrated by the example presented above.[123] As active therapeutic or diagnostic medical devices, such applications are at least subject to Class IIa. Consequently, the participation of a notified body in the market access procedure is unavoidable. The specific risks of learning systems as medical devices – in comparison to static systems—is therefore not considered de lege lata in the classification of a medical device. The increased risk could, however, also be considered within the scope of the Conformity

28

---

[114]Cf. Annex VIII section 3.3 of the Regulation (EU) 2017/745; Graf (2017a), p. 59.

[115]Cf. Annex IX, section 1.4 of the Council Directive 93/42/EEC; also Article 2 of the Regulation (EU) 2017/745.

[116]Namely rules 9 to 12 of Annex IX, section 3 of the Council Directive 93/42/EEC.

[117]See paras 22 et seq.

[118]In accordance with rule 12.

[119]For further details on the Essential Requirements see para 30.

[120]Cf. Annex XIII of the Council Directive 93/42/EEC; Gassner points out the danger of overregulation, cf. Gassner (2016), p. 112.

[121]Cf. Rule 11 in Annex VIII section 6.3 of the Council Regulation (EU) 2017/745.

[122]The rule covers for instance hospital beds and patient lifts, cf. Frankenberger (2017), p. 139.

[123]See paras 1 et seq.

Assessment Procedure itself, in which the compliance with the Essential Requirements is verified by the notified bodies in accordance with Section 7 and Section 6 (2) sentence 1 MPG.[124] One of these product requirements is compliance with the 'generally acknowledged state of the art'—as a vague legal term *(unbestimmter Rechtsbegriff)* the gateway for harmonized technical standards.

4.3 Control-Related Process Modules

29 Notified bodies have a key function in implementing the requirements of European legislation on the safety of medical devices. In the context of increasing European harmonization, administrative preventive controls were replaced by market access controls carried out by private experts in the course of the New Approach, which largely removed the instrument of preventive controls from the hands of the Member State authorities.[125] Since then, the control has been structured as a two-stage supervision: Market access control by notified bodies with subsequent post market-entry surveillance by national authorities. Nevertheless, the shift of preventive control to private bodies does not lead to a general shift of responsibilities for health protection.[126]

30 Market access control by notified bodies is by no means an end in itself. Nowadays, national authorities are often unable to check compliance with technical regulations in considerable detail.[127] However, compliance with Essential Requirements[128] designed to ensure a high level of protection is compulsory, i.e. only products that meet these requirements may be placed on the market and put into service.[129] In contrast to traditional regulatory mechanisms of preventive control and monitoring, the certification model focuses on intra-organizational processes: it is about an access to the intra-organizational company knowledge by the notified bodies, linked with a self-observation of the medical device manufacturers.[130] The catalogue of applicable requirements is rather diverse and differentiates between general requirements and design or manufacturing requirements which are linked to specific product hazards.[131] Also, with regard to medical software, general safety and performance requirements are defined in Annex I of the new MDR, which a

---

[124]Section 7 MPG refers to Annex I of the MDD.

[125]For the basic principles of the New Approach, see Voßkuhle (2002), pp. 310 et seq.; Di Fabio (1996), pp. 1 et seq.; also Merten (2005), pp. 37 et seq., p. 108; similarly Pilniok (2017), p. 6.

[126]*Kage* (2005), p. 248.

[127]Cf. Pilniok (2017), p. 11, who describes accredited certification as a model for responding to an erosion of the classic forms of administrative knowledge generation; similarly Dieners and Vivekens (2017), p. 20.

[128]Further details on the basic requirements in this para.

[129]Di Fabio (1996), p. 69; Dieners and Vivekens (2017), p. 22.

[130]Pilniok (2017), p. 12.

[131]Ibid.

manufacturer must meet for his products.[132] Since the so-called 'global concept' of legal approximation follows a modular approach, the process and content of market access control are essentially determined by the process module chosen by the manufacturer.[133] A description of the different modules of the global concept would go beyond the scope of this paper. The intention is rather to identify overarching procedural steps which should enable the notified bodies to make an informed decision on the conformity of a medical device. Thereby it is suitable to differentiate between two process steps: the ascertainment and the assessment of risks.

Firstly, the notified bodies must collect the available data on which their subsequent assessment is based.[134] The relationship between manufacturers and notified bodies is usually based on private law contracts.[135] Ensuring the cooperation of the manufacturers beyond a mere contractual clause under private law, the legislator has legally standardized the obligation to cooperate.[136] In order to make all the data and records available to the notified bodies that are relevant for the conformity assessment of a medical device that is to be tested, manufacturers are obliged to cooperate and provide the data required for risk assessment; the risk producer himself must therefore compile the data as information.[137] This obligation also applies to a manufacturer even prior to the construction of his product in the design phase, in which the manufacturer must carry out a risk analysis and set out in writing which hazards result from the risk analysis and how these are to be assessed in relation to the medical benefit.[138] Particularly with regard to the technical requirements arising from European Medical Devices Law itself, but also from the concept of the state of the art shaped by harmonized standards, the special features of learning machines as medical devices can be considered. These are decisive for the content and scope of the manufacturers' technical documentation, which serves the notified bodies as the basis for conformity assessment.

31

Based on the information obtained, a risk assessment must subsequently be carried out by estimating the impact-related hazard potential for both users and patients in order to compare the hazard potential with the expected societal benefit.[139] The risk assessment certainly includes a socio-cultural and an ethical

32

---

[132]Cf. Annex I, section 17 of the Council Regulation (EU) 2017/745; categorized by Prinz (2017), p. 26.

[133]For an overview of the selectable modules depending on the risk class of the device, see Article 11 of the Council Directive 93/42/EEC with reference to the relevant Annexes to the Directive.

[134]Scherzberg and Heym (2013), p. 184.

[135]Voßkuhle (2002), p. 313; Röhl (2000), pp. 91 et seq.; also Pilniok (2017), p. 12; in contrast, the legal relationship between a notified body and the Accreditation Body is governed by public law, cf. Pilniok (2017), p. 15.

[136]Cf. Article 11(10) of the Council Directive 93/42/EEC; also Article 53(4) of the Council Regulation (EU) 2017/745.

[137]Voßkuhle (2002), pp. 340 et seq.; Scherzberg and Heym (2013), p. 184.

[138]Kage (2005), p. 246.

[139]Voßkuhle (2002), p. 331.

component[140] and cannot succeed without recourse to the resources of the manufacturer.[141] Therefore, the assessment is based on entrepreneurial data. In addition, risk characterization must probably consider the quality and reliability of the underlying data and information in order to determine, as far as possible, the extent of the risk.[142] Notified bodies must therefore not *exclusively* rely on the manufacturers' risk analyses. The certification system in Medical Devices Law is also characterized by a continuous risk ascertainment and assessment in the monitoring of certified quality management systems by notified bodies, which are systematically assigned to preventive control.[143] In particular with regard to learning applications, it is recommendable to confront the systems continuously with simulative test scenarios in order to observe the further development of their capabilities, comparable with a periodically recurring Algorithms-TÜV.[144]

5   Post Market-Entry Surveillance of Software As a Medical Device

33   After a medical device has been properly placed on the market, it is subject to market monitoring, which is essentially conducted by the competent national authorities, while the notified bodies are in principle not involved in law enforcement regarding the post market-entry period.[145] Market surveillance under Medical Devices Law on the basis of the new harmonization concept is not characterized by systematic official product control to avoid counteracting the presumption of conformity of CE-marked products.[146] To guarantee a high level of protection, Medical Devices Law rather contains accompanying mechanisms and instruments, the interaction of which is intended to enable effective control of the medical devices on the market in accordance with the protective purpose of the law, to ensure the safety of persons working with medical devices.[147] However, these control mechanisms can be implemented

---

[140] See Scherzberg and Heym (2013), p. 185.

[141] Scherzberg (2002), p. 136; also Stoll (2008); p. 42.

[142] Scherzberg and Heym (2013), p. 185.

[143] Merten (2005), p. 90.

[144] See Martini (2017b), p. 453. In Germany, 'TÜV' is the abbreviation for 'Technischer Überwachungsverein' and refers to associations that carry out safety checks as a technical testing organization. These are often safety inspections prescribed by law and carried out on a private basis as indirect state administration. The best-known of these is the main inspection for motor vehicles, which is also colloquially called 'TÜV'.

[145] Merten (2005), p. 109; see also Hoffmann-Riem, para 39, on the idea of a public body specifically tasked with monitoring AI applications.

[146] Merten (2005), p. 90.

[147] In this context, Voßkuhle refers to a process perpetuation, since the element of the final decision is a withdrawal in favour of a continuous control and monitoring obligation, cf. Voßkuhle (2002), p. 345; also Merten (2005), p. 109.

solely by collecting, recording and evaluating risk data as part of the market monitoring process,[148] since effective market surveillance requires an adequate information and knowledge base of the authorities.

5.1 Statutory Provisions of the MPG

For administrative post market-entry surveillance, the MPG contains a number of instruments and authorizations intended to gain data and information as a basis for a subsequent administrative decision and which apply both to the relationship between the authority and notified bodies,[149] which at least allows indirect access to the manufacturers' entrepreneurial data, information and knowledge, and to the relationship between the authority and the manufacturers themselves.[150] In this context, the instrument of random inspections will be particularly emphasised.

The instrument of random inspections of medical devices according to Section 26 (1) to (3) MPG[151] by the authorities of the Member States serves the purpose of obtaining and evaluating data and information. Consequently, it is not bound to a hazardous state.[152] Section 26(3) provides a comprehensive catalogue of measures for this purpose. This type of protection of legal interests, even below the threshold of a regulatory hazard, is an expression of the precautionary principle. In fulfilling its responsibilities in the context of post market-entry surveillance, the authority should particularly 'consider the possible risks' associated with a device.[153] This broad term of *possible* risks is not entirely uncontroversial in regard to its content, since contradiction prevention with European regulations requires a restrictive use of supervisory competences.[154] In particular, there is uncertainty whether the risk potential should be the connecting factor for the frequency of audits or for the audit intensity of individual controls.[155] As far as the random inspection of learning medical devices is concerned, the difficulties in an analysis that arise from the openness for developments of the system premises and the weighting of the variables in the future[156] and from the black box phenomenon have already been identified. For this reason, the instrument of random inspection of learning machines seems to be only suitable to a limited extent for the comprehensive monitoring of the

34

35

---

[148]Kage (2005), p. 248.
[149]Cf. exemplarily Section 15(2) sentence 4 and Section 18(3) No. 2 MPG.
[150]Cf. Section 25(1), Section 26(2) sentence 2 and 4 and Section 28(1) MPG.
[151]The European legislator maintains this instrument even when the new Regulation on Medical Devices is enacted, cf. Article 45 of the Council Regulation (EU) 2017/745.
[152]Merten (2005), p. 110.
[153]Cf. Section 26(2) sentence 2 MPG.
[154]Merten (2005), p. 111.
[155]Ibid.
[156]See also below, paras 37 et seq. for further remarks.

continuing development of learning systems. Random inspections can only meet these cognitive challenges if they are not based on error-prone, complex code analysis, but rather on black box testing through simulative testing. The monitoring of compliance with legal requirements for learning machines by national authorities does otherwise not seem to be consistently effective under the existing structures.

5.2 Challenging Information Issue

36 European harmonization at the level of law enforcement through the new approach has largely deprived the Member State authorities of the instrument of preventive control in product safety law.[157] The regulatory control of the risk actors themselves is therefore limited to the post market-entry phase, whereby systematic post market-entry surveillance of the products is not desirable in order not to counteract the presumption of conformity of the CE-marked products. Information and knowledge about potential hazards therefore mainly remain with the notified bodies.

Emergence of the Information Deficit

37 With the renunciation of the implementation of preventive approval procedures, the administration concerned with the enforcement of Medical Devices Law finds itself in a situation where it can no longer conduct its own risk assessments in advance.[158] The consequence is an information deficit for the Member State authorities, which initially have no systematic information on devices on the market. By its very nature, official observation of the overall market is much more difficult than systematic preventive market access control; the risks and hazards arising on the market must be identified and assessed on time in order to take appropriate defence measures.[159]

38 In addition, it is regularly impossible to determine the hazards of complicated products without examining the devices themselves. With the increasing influence of medical technology knowledge on the regulatory evaluation and decision-making process and the difficult assessment of complex risk issues with elusive cause-effect correlations,[160] the authority must first obtain the data and information that are necessary for its decision in order to be able to react effectively to risks and hazards arising on the market.[161] An information-generating investigation of learning applications through disassembly, however, is hardly practicable due to the black box phenomenon.[162] The verification of a correct functionality in an individual case can

---

[157]Merten (2004), p. 1211.
[158]Kage (2005), p. 248.
[159]Ibid.
[160]Laufs (2001), p. 3381; also Kage (2005), p. 248.
[161]Di Fabio (1994), p. 347; similarly Kage (2005), p. 248.
[162]For further details see Wischmeyer, paras 12 et seq.

indeed occur through the input of test data and the subsequent control of the correctness of the output, as long as an application does not already use an XAI.[163] The situation appears different for the control of the traceability of the system's premises, since, as considered, corrective interventions in the decision-making mechanism of a learning application may require a comprehensible representation of the development of the system's premises and the weighting of the variables for the user.

The MPG, in accordance with respective EU law, grants national authority the right of control and access to data and information as prerequisites for the generation of knowledge. On the one hand, the MPG authorises the authorities to access the data and information prepared by the notified bodies and thus also to indirectly access the data and information of the manufacturers themselves.[164] On the other hand, the MPG also explicitly grants the persons entrusted with monitoring the conformity of medical devices the right to directly obtain information by and access to the manufacturers in order to eliminate violations of the law, but also to prevent future violations.[165] These rights are concatenated with a passive duty of toleration and an active duty of supporting on the part of the manufacturers.[166] To avoid counteracting the presumption of conformity of CE-marked products, the national authorities must not control all medical devices systematically. Rather, the authorities check to an appropriate extent whether the requirements for placing on the market and using are fulfilled. To this end, however, the authorities need evidence that justifies the adoption of more detailed investigation measures relevant to fundamental rights. In order to deal with this conflict, instruments of systematic knowledge transfer on risk potentials between notified bodies and the Member State authorities are required, which provide the authorities with information and knowledge as a basis for further risk collection and assessment by the authorities through indirect access to the entrepreneurial data, information and knowledge of the risk actors.

The Amendments by the MDR As a Solution Approach?

The information deficit described certainly exists throughout Medical Devices Law by reason of the distribution of competences between notified bodies and national authorities. However, the administrative challenges of post market-entry surveillance are particularly significant in the monitoring of learning machines as medical devices. Due to the possible further development of the capabilities of learning systems, which is also desired by the manufacturer, a mere access to the

---

[163]See also above para 1.

[164]Cf. Section 15(2) sentence 4 MPG, which can be systematically assigned to the official monitoring of the activities of the notified bodies, but which, with regard to the range of tasks of the notified bodies, includes conformity assessment of medical devices in compliance with the law.

[165]Cf. Section 26(2) sentence 4, (3) MPG.

[166]Cf. Section 26(4) sentence 1 MPG.

documentation of the prepared information of the notified bodies can only report a status quo minus, which can represent the status quo of the system premises and the weighting of the variables at any later time of validation only to a limited extent. A transfer of data and information from notified bodies to supervising authorities can therefore at best be the starting point for a post market-entry surveillance in which the authorities themselves have to generate further information and knowledge.

41 In addition, in contrast to other medical devices, it cannot be assumed without further ado that from the legal development of one learning medical device from a design batch can be inferred the compliance of all other products from the same design batch. The open development can lead to the individuality of the different learning products, as long as they are not linked together in a network which ensures a synchronization of the system premises and weighting of the variables.[167]

42 To counter the systemic knowledge deficit of the supervising authorities, in the course of the legislative process of the MDR, a proposal was submitted for a 'Scrutiny Procedure', which was intended to serve as a knowledge generation instrument for the authorities for innovative high-risk products.[168] According to Dagmar Roth-Berendt, the conformity assessment model is not sufficient for innovative high-risk products; rather, these cases should be subject to a central approval procedure by a European approval authority.[169] In this way, the authorities would already have a systematic overview of the technically sensitive devices on the market through their involvement in the placing of an innovative medical device on the market. However, the Committee on Health of the European Parliament has distanced itself from this proposal, which is alien to the certification system, in favour of an 'Assessment Procedure in specific cases'.[170]

43 Certainly, of interest for the resolution of the information deficit of the authorities, thus for the improvement of the surveillance by the responsible authorities,[171] appears an effectively implemented modification of the Medical Devices Law by the MDR, which introduced a unique device identification system (UDI). The UDI Protection Identifier (UDI-PI) and the UDI Device Identifier (UDI-DI) enable the identification and traceability of products that are not custom-made and test products.[172] The UDI-DI is a unique numeric or alphabetic code that identifies the production unit of the product,

---

[167] If such a network of system premises exists, an efficient post market-entry control could be conceivable by a continuous, automatic data transfer of the changed premises to the supervising authority. A comparable situation is already known in the field of remote emission monitoring, cf. German (Federal) Constitutional Court 7 C 47/95 (13 February 1997). Solved from questions of the administrative burden and data protection concerns in the health-relevant field, however, considerable constitutional concerns would have to be included in the consideration of a transferability of the model, which would not only affect the manufacturer's right to exercise an occupation, but also the user's right to informational self-determination.

[168] Tomasini (2015), p. 145; Braun and Püschel (2014), p. 138.

[169] Explanation of the rapporteur's draft of 14th May 2013, 2012/0266(COD), PE510.741v03-00, p. 120; see also Hoffmann-Riem, para 14.

[170] Braun and Püschel (2014), p. 139.

[171] Cf. Recital 41 of the Council Regulation (EU) 2017/745; Graf (2017b), p. 318.

[172] Cf. Article 10(7), Article 27(1) of the Council Regulation (EU) 2017/745.

including software identification.[173] The Commission shall henceforth manage a UDI database (EUDAMED) in which the information set out in Annex VI of the MDR shall be validated, collated, processed and made available to the public.[174] To ensure incorporation of the information into the database, manufacturers are required to register each medical device in the UDI database prior to placing it on the market after allocation of the UDI-PI[175] and to maintain an updated list of all UDIs issued by a manufacturer as part of the technical documentation in accordance with Annex II.[176] This UDI database is also linked to the electronic vigilance system,[177] which is available to the authorities of the Member States to provide the national authorities with the information basis for effective product monitoring after marketing.[178] Article 93(1) MDR even explicitly encourages the national authorities to access the vigilance data as part of their monitoring activities. For learning machines as medical devices, this method of identification is of special interest, because on the one hand a systematic overview of the products on the market is guaranteed and on the other hand a change of a UDI software identification is necessary in all cases, where the algorithms are changed,[179] as far as the change is not only minor, as for example with error corrections.[180] In this way, the authority could not only monitor the learning systems available on the market, but also recognize changes in the system's premises and the weighting of the variables that a learning machine implements by changing the algorithms and thus initiates a change obligation of the UDI-DI by the manufacturer in the database. In order to ensure that this UDI-DI change obligation is also met if a product leaves the manufacturers' sphere towards an end-user, manufacturers remain responsible for updating the UDI database for changes within 30 days in addition to the initial transfer of the identification information to the UDI database.[181] Manufacturers must therefore program learning software in a manner that ensures compliance with this requirement. The legislator complements this canon of obligations with a corresponding authorization of the national authorities within the context of their market surveillance activities by ensuring that they are not only entitled to carry out unannounced inspections at the manufacturers' facilities,[182] but also, if necessary, at the facilities of professional users.[183] In this manner, the authorities are able to carry out precise random inspections on learning machines as medical devices, which have changed their decision-making mechanism and thus no longer solely possess the initial algorithm controlled by the

---

[173]Cf. Article 2 No. 15 and Annex VI Part C section 1 of the Council Regulation (EU) 2017/745.
[174]Cf. Article 28(1) of the Council Regulation (EU) 2017/745.
[175]Cf. Article 14(2), Article 29(1) of the Council Regulation (EU) 2017/745.
[176]Cf. Article 27(7) of the Council Regulation (EU) 2017/745.
[177]Cf. Article 92(1) of the Council Regulation (EU) 2017/745.
[178]Graf (2017b), p. 318.
[179]Cf. Annex VI Part C section 6.5.2 of the Council Regulation (EU) 2017/745.
[180]Cf. Annex VI Part C section 6.5.3 of the Council Regulation (EU) 2017/745.
[181]Cf. Annex VI Part. C section 5.2 and 5.8 of the Council Regulation (EU) 2017/745.
[182]For further details on the inspection competences see above para 35.
[183]Cf. Article 93(3)(b) of the Council Regulation (EU) 2017/745; Petersen (2018), p. 105.

notified bodies in the market access control. The ability to carry out precise random inspections may thus enable surveillance authorities to take a more targeted approach, since among the large number of (learning) products on the market, those which have changed their system premises and the weighting of their variables will be highlighted. However, this instrument represents only a first step in solving the information deficit of the authorities, and it still does not provide a solution to the questions of the traceability of the system's capability development, i.e. the adaptation of the premises and of the weighting of the variables on which the system is based, which is probably a prerequisite for a corrective impact on the algorithm. Recognising that the system premises or the weighting of variables have changed is not sufficient to assess the continued conformity with legal requirements. Rather, this assessment requires further testing of compliance with legal requirements.

6 Outlook

44   Medical Devices Law is in a state of flux, not least due to the increasing technical development. The European legislator seems to have recognized that software as a medical device is associated with new challenges in market access as well as in post market-entry surveillance. Compared to static systems, learning machines as medical devices in particular display a specific knowledge deficit which may have to be countered with specific regulatory instruments. So far, the legislator has not yet explicitly differentiated between static and learning software as a medical device; but it has introduced generally applicable new instruments for the gathering of information on medical devices, which might prove especially valuable when it comes to monitoring AI devices in practice. It still remains to inquire whether the introduction of the new UDI database will lead to an improved provision of information to national authorities in administrative practice. Certainly, it will not be sufficient to adequately monitor learning systems, therefore it may be necessary in a forward-looking perspective to make a legal distinction between static and learning systems in order to counter the specific risks of learning ability.

References

Anhalt E, Dieners P, Westphal V (2017) Einführung in die Grundlagen und die Systematik des deutschen Medizinprodukterechts. In: Anhalt E, Dieners P (eds) Medizinprodukterecht. Praxishandbuch, 2nd edn. C.H. Beck, München, pp 45–69

Bieback K (2008) Zertifizierung und Akkreditierung. Das Zusammenwirken staatlicher und nichtstaatlicher Akteure in gestuften Prüfsystemen. Nomos Verlagsgesellschaft, Baden-Baden

Braun J, Püschel C (2014) Medizinprodukterecht und Produktzulassung – Was bringt die Zukunft? In: Schwegel P, Da-Cruz P, Hemel U et al (eds) Medizinprodukte Management. P.C.O.-Verlag, Bayreuth, pp 136–147

Cauter E (1988) Estimating false-positive and false-negative errors in analyses of hormonal pulsatility. Am J Physiol 254:E786–E794

Colquhoun D (2017) The reproducibility of research and the misinterpretation of p-values. http://rsos.royalsocietypublishing.org/content/4/12/171085.full.pdf
Courtin E (1997) Software in Medizinprodukten. Medizinprodukte-Journal:62–68
Czettritz P, Strelow T (2017) 'Beam me up, Scotty' – die Klassifizierung von Medical Apps als Medizinprodukte. Pharmarecht:433–435
Di Fabio U (1994) Das Arzneimittelrecht als Repräsentant der Risikoverwaltung. Die Verwaltung 27:345–360
Di Fabio U (1996) Produktharmonisierung durch Normung und Selbstüberwachung. Carl Heymanns Verlag KG, Köln
Dieners P, Vivekens S (2017) Europarechtliche Rahmenbedingungen. In: Anhalt E, Dieners P (eds) Medizinprodukterecht. Praxishandbuch, 2nd edn. C.H. Beck, München, pp 1–43
Düwert H, Klümper M (2013) Gesundheits-Apps: Ein neuer Trend und seine rechtlichen Herausforderungen. Medizinprodukte-Journal:23–30
Ernst C (2017) Algorithmische Entscheidungsfindung und personenbezogene Daten. JuristenZeitung 2017:1026–1036
Fauw J, Ledsam J, Romera-Paredes B et al (2018) Clinically applicable deep learning for diagnosis and referral in retinal disease. Nat Med 24:1342–1350. https://doi.org/10.1038/s41591-018-0107-6
Frankenberger H (2017) Klassifizierung von Medizinprodukten. In: Anhalt E, Dieners P (eds) Medizinprodukterecht. Praxishandbuch, 2nd edn. C.H. Beck, München, pp 111–160
Gassner U (2016) Software als Medizinprodukt – zwischen Regulierung und Selbstregulierung. Medizin Produkte Recht 2016:109–115
Gassner U (2017) Die neue Medizinprodukteverordnung. Aktueller Text mit Einführung. Bundesanzeiger Verlag GmbH, Köln
Graf A (2017a) Revision des europäischen Rechtsrahmens für Medizinprodukte. Einfluss auf die Klassifizierung von Medizinprodukten. Pharmarecht:57–61
Graf A (2017b) Revision des europarechtlichen Rechtsrahmens für Medizinprodukte. Neue Vorgaben zu Vigilanz und Marktbeobachtung und die Eudamed-Datenbank als zentrales Regulierungsinstrument. Pharmarecht:317–322
Hadank B (2017) App statt Arzt? Entscheidungsfindung durch Algorithmen im Gesundheitswesen – Bericht zur Tagung 'Gesundheitsentscheidung durch Algorithmen - rechtliche Rahmenbedingungen der Digitalisierung des Gesundheitswesens', 6.9.2017 in Berlin. GesundheitsRecht:811–813
Heil M (2014) Zulassung für Medizinprodukte? Die ENVI-Änderungsvorschläge. In: Gassner U (ed) Reform des EU-Medizinprodukterechts – Stand und Perspektiven. Shaker Verlag, Aachen, pp 15–23
Herberger M (2018) 'Künstliche Intelligenz' und Recht. Ein Orientierungsversuch. Neue Juristische Wochenschrift 71:2825–2829
Hötzel G (2018) 'There is an app for that' – Aspekte des Rechts der Medizinprodukte und des ärztlichen Berufs- und Vergütungsrechts. Zeitschrift für das gesamte Medizin- und Gesundheitsrecht:16–20
Igl G (2018) § 27 Medizinprodukte (Überblick). In: Igl G, Welti F (eds) Gesundheitsrecht. Eine systematische Einführung, 3rd edn. Verlag Franz Vahlen, München, pp 155–156
Irmer F (2013) Medizinprodukterechtliche Einordnung von Software. Updates & Upgrades. Medizin Produkte Recht:145–148
Jäkel C (2016) Europarechtliche Aspekte der Zulassung von Medizinprodukten. Medizinrecht:601–602
Jaumann A (1980) Die Regelung technischer Sachverhalte. In: Lukes R (ed) Rechtliche Ordnung der Technik als Aufgabe der Industriegesellschaft. Heymann Verlag, Köln, pp 5–22
Kage U (2005) Das Medizinproduktegesetz. Staatliche Risikosteuerung unter dem Einfluss europäischer Harmonisierung. Springer-Verlag, Berlin

Klümper M, Vollebregt E (2009) Die Regulierung von Software bei Medizinprodukten. Die geänderten Anforderungen für die CE-Kennzeichnung und Konformitätsbewertung auf Grund der Richtlinie 2007/47/EG. Medizinprodukte-Journal 16:99–105

Langkafel P (2015) Auf dem Weg zum Dr. Algorithmus? Potenziale von Big Data in der Medizin. Aus Politik und Zeitgeschichte 65:27–32

Laufs A (2001) Arzneimittelprüfung. Neue Juristische Wochenschrift 54:3381–3382

Lücker V (2014) Kommentierung zum Gesetz über Medizinprodukte (Medizinproduktegesetz - MPG). In: Spickhoff A (ed) Beck'scher Kurzkommentar Medizinrecht, 2nd edn. C.H. Beck, München, pp 1260–1354

Martini M (2017a) Algorithmen als Herausforderung für die Rechtsordnung. JuristenZeitung 72:1017–1025

Martini M (2017b) Transformation der Verwaltung durch Digitalisierung. Die Öffentliche Verwaltung:443–455

Merten J (2004) Benannte Stellen: Private Vollzugsinstanzen eines Europäischen Verwaltungsrechts. Deutsches Verwaltungsblatt:1211–1216

Merten J (2005) Private Entscheidungsträger und Europäisierung der Verwaltungsrechtsdogmatik. Zur Einbindung benannter Stellen in den Vollzug des Medizinprodukterechts. Dunker & Humblot GmbH, Berlin

Meyer S (2011) Risikovorsorge als Eingriff in das Recht auf körperliche Unversehrtheit. Gesetzliche Erschwerung medizinischer Forschung aus Sicht des Patienten als Grundrechtsträger. Archiv des öffentlichen Rechts 136:428–478

Neubauer G, Uilaky R (2004) Bedeutung von Innovationen für die Medizinprodukteindustrie. In: Oberender P, Schommer R, Da-Cruz P (eds) Zukunftsorientiertes Management in der Medizinprodukteindustrie. P.C.O.-Verlag, Bayreuth, pp 149–161

Oen R (2009) Software als Medizinprodukt. Medizin Produkte Recht 2009:55–57

Ostermayer K, Kexel W (2009) Software – Ein Medizinprodukt mit hohem Risikopotenzial. Medizinprodukte-Journal:106–107

Petersen N (2018) Marktüberwachung bei Medizinprodukten. Was ändert sich für die nationalen Behörden nach der MDR? Medizinprodukte-Journal:102–107

Pilniok A (2017) Zertifizierung und Akkreditierung als Regulierungsstrategie im Wirtschaftsverwaltungsrecht. In: Krüper J (ed) Zertifizierung und Akkreditierung als Instrumente qualitativer Glücksspielregulierung. Mohr Siebeck, Tübingen, pp 1–33

Pramann O, Albrecht U (2015) Medizinische Software. Im regulatorischen Umfeld des Medizinprodukterechts am Beispiel von Medical Apps. Zeitschrift zum Innovations- und Technikrecht:132–137

Prinz T (2017) Entwicklung und Herstellung medizinischer Software. Normen in der Medizintechnik. VDE Verlag, Berlin

Röhl HC (2000) Akkreditierung und Zertifizierung im Produktsicherheitsrecht. Zur Entwicklung einer neuen Europäischen Verwaltungsstruktur. Springer, Berlin

Sachs G (2013) Software in Systemen und Problembehandlungseinheiten. In: Gassner U (ed) Software als Medizinprodukt – IT vs. Medizintechnik? Shaker Verlag, Aachen, pp 31–36

Scherzberg A (2002) Wissen, Nichtwissen und Ungewissheit im Recht. In: Engel C, Halfmann J, Schulte M (eds) Wissen – Nichtwissen – Unsicheres Wissen. Nomos, Baden-Baden, pp 113–144

Scherzberg A, Heym S (2013) Neue medizintechnische Möglichkeiten als Herausforderung an das Recht. In: Peter C, Funcke D (eds) Wissen an der Grenze. Zum Umgang mit Ungewissheit und Unsicherheit in der modernen Medizin. Campus, Frankfurt a. M., pp 161–207

Schmitt J (2014) Aktuelle und zukünftige Marktentwicklung im Bereich der Medizinprodukteindustrie. In: Schwegel P, Da-Cruz P, Hemel U et al (eds) Medizinprodukte Management. P.C.O.-Verlag, Bayreuth, pp 26–35

Singh M (2014) Produktemanagement in der Medizintechnik. In: Schwegel P, Da-Cruz P, Hemel U et al (eds) Medizinprodukte Management. P.C.O.-Verlag, Bayreuth, pp 148–161

Stiemerling O (2015) 'Künstliche Intelligenz'. Automatisierung geistiger Arbeit, Big Data und das Internet der Dinge. Computer und Recht:762–765

Stoll P (2008) Wissensarbeit als staatliche Aufgabe. Wissen als Leitbegriff für Reformüberlegungen. In: Döhmann I, Collin P (eds) Generierung und Transfer staatlichen Wissens im System des Verwaltungsrechts. Mohr Siebeck, Tübingen, pp 34–49

Taupitz J (1998) Das Recht auf Nichtwissen. In: Hanau P, Lorenz E, Matthes H (eds) Festschrift für Günther Wiese zum 70. Geburtstag. Luchterhand, Neuwied, pp 583–602

Thuemmler C (2017) The Case for Health 4.0. In: Thuemmler C, Bai C (eds) Health 4.0. How virtualization and big data are revolutionizing healthcare. Springer, Cham, pp 1–22

Tomasini R (2015) Standalone-Software als Medizinprodukt. Shaker Verlag, Aachen

Trute H (2018) Der Stellenwert von Real-World-Evidenz im deutschen Sozial- und Gesundheitsrecht. https://doi.org/10.1007/s00772-018-0471-z

Voßkuhle A (2002) Strukturen und Bauformen ausgewählter neuer Verfahren. In: Hoffmann-Riem W, Schmidt-Aßmann E (eds) Verwaltungsverfahren und Verwaltungsverfahrensgesetz. Nomos, Baden-Baden, pp 277–347

Webel D (2018) Kommentierung zum Gesetz über Medizinprodukte (Medizinproduktegesetz – MPG). In: Bergmann K, Pauge B, Steinmeyer H (eds) Nomoskommentar Gesamtes Medizinrecht, 3rd edn. Nomos, Baden-Baden

Artificial Intelligence in Healthcare: Doctors, Patients and Liabilities

Fruzsina Molnár-Gábor

Contents

1 Introduction: Artificial Intelligence in Medicine 338
    1.1 Applications of Artificial Intelligence in Medicine and Their Benefits and Limitations 338
    1.2 A Particular Definition for AI in Medicine: Evidence or Reason? 339
2 AI's Influence on the Status and Role of Physicians and Patients in Their Relation to Each Other in Medical Ethics 342
    2.1 The Physician-Patient Relationship in Medical Ethics 342
    2.2 Principles of Medical Ethics and Their Implementation in the Physician-Patient Relationship 343
    2.3 Challenges Presented by AI in Medical Ethics 344
3 AI's Influence on the Status and Role of Physicians and Patients in Their Relation to Each Other in Liability Law 347
    3.1 Issues of Medical Malpractice Law 348
    3.2 Issues of Product Liability Law 353
    3.3 Conclusions Based on Liability Law 354
4 The Status and Role of Physicians in Their Relation to Patients 355
References 358

Abstract AI is increasingly finding its way into medical research and everyday healthcare. However, the clear benefits offered to patients are accompanied not only by general limitations typical of the application of AI systems but also by challenges that specifically characterize the operationalization of the concepts of disease and health. Traditionally, these challenges have been dealt with in the physician-patient relationship in both medical ethics and civil law. The potential for incorrect decisions (and the question of who is responsible for such decisions) in cases where AI is used in a medical context calls for a differentiated implementation of medical ethical principles and a graduated model of liability law. Nevertheless, on closer examination of both fields covering relevant obligations towards patients and users against

F. Molnár-Gábor (✉)
Heidelberg Academy of Sciences and Humanities, BioQuant Center, Heidelberg, Germany
e-mail: fruzsina.molnar-gabor@adw.uni-heidelberg.de

the backdrop of current medical use cases of AI, it seems that despite a certain level of differentiation in the assignment of responsibilities through rules on liability, those affected, in the end, are generally left to deal with any AI-specific risks and damages on their own. The role played by the physician in all this remains unclear. Taking into account the physician-patient relationship as a contractual obligation in a broad sense can assist in clarifying physicians' roles and determining their duties in a sustainable and patient-friendly manner when applying AI-based medical systems. This can contribute to reinforcing their established ethical and legal status in the context of AI applications.

1 Introduction: Artificial Intelligence in Medicine

1.1 Applications of Artificial Intelligence in Medicine and Their Benefits and Limitations

Artificial intelligence (AI) is already used in many ways in medicine today, its scope of application covering various fields in both medical research and healthcare including drug discovery, screening, surgery, chronic disease management, and general healthcare organization.[1] Its currently most frequent and tested field of application, however, is at the core of curative healthcare: disease detection, particularly via medical imaging.[2] The evaluation of X-ray, CT, MRT or confocal laser scanning microscopy images created with the help of AI focuses on anomaly detection and segmentation via delimitation of biologically and medically distinguishable spatial areas (such as differentiation between diseased and healthy tissue) and subsequent classification by disease type. AI has already achieved considerable success in all of these work processes and often surpasses the quality of diagnostic findings by physicians and radiology personnel.[3]

Besides the explicit healthcare-related benefits for patients,[4] the further benefits of the current medical application of AI do not, at first glance, appear to differ from those in other fields. The main benefits include saved time (which, depending on the individual case, can nevertheless also promote healing success), cost reduction and increased availability of staff for activities that cannot be carried out by AI.[5] Its current main limitations are also well known in other application fields as they are

---

[1]Cf. only the Elsevier journal Artificial Intelligence in Medicine, https://www.journals.elsevier.com/artificial-intelligence-in-medicine.
[2]Cf. Ranschaert et al. (2019), which focuses on radiology but with universal findings related to general imaging.
[3]Haenssle et al. (2018).
[4]Albu and Stanciu (2015).
[5]The Economist (2018).

connected to, among others, limitations in computing power, analysis system interoperability, analysis standardization, result reliability or data quality, data protection (see Marsch) and data security and questions of transparency and justice in decision-making (see also, esp., Wischmeyer and Tischbirek, respectively).[6]

However, in the routinely life-or-death context of healthcare (and frequently also in medical research) the realization of benefits and overcoming of limitations is often further complicated by challenges that are related to the understanding of disease and health as core subjects in the application of any medical system, including those based on AI.

AI pursues the goal of systematizing human perceptual and mental performance and making them available through technical means. Because the concepts of disease and health combine both descriptive[7] and normative characteristics, they are not objective or entirely generalizable quantities or features but are instead based on value judgements that are linked to the respective personal context of the affected person and the socio-cultural context of medicine per se. Insofar as their concepts unite physical, psychological, social and cultural elements, their operationalization when applying AI presents specific challenges. Fundamentally, the consideration of the self-assessment of the person affected by illness as in need of help—now or in the future—based on an understanding of subjective well-being[8] is an important challenge in medicine. This challenge related to the operationalization of the concepts of disease and health of the affected person is aggravated by the fact that AI-based medical systems lack crucial formulae that are usually applied to overcome this challenge in traditional medical contexts, such as the ability to realize human characteristics like compassion and empathy or the adequate interpretation and employment of social 'knowledge' and communication based on multi-layered non-measurable information that then has to be creatively incorporated into medical care and related planning.[9] Furthermore, these formulae are also influenced by factors outside the narrow medical context such as political and social evaluations of the concepts of disease and health that blend into the respective cultural contexts so that their broad generalizability is exposed to limitations.

1.2 A Particular Definition for AI in Medicine: Evidence or Reason?

AI is often defined by its delivered result, according to which, in a medical context, AI-based systems should contribute to medical problem solving in a wide sense.

---

[6]Aftergood (2018).
[7]Cf. the definition of health in the WHO Constitution. See also Committee on Economic, Social and Cultural Rights, General Comment No.14 - The Right to the Highest Attainable Standard of Health (Article 12) [UN Doc E/C.12/2000/4, [2001] ESCOR Supp 2, 128], para 4.
[8]Lanzerath and Honnefelder (2000), pp. 51 et seq.; Eckart (2013), p. 300.
[9]Parks (2010), pp. 100–120; Loder and Nicholas (2018).

This is also communicated by the definition of AI as 'providing increased medical efficacy, patient comfort, and less waste'.[10] While this approach appears to be generally consistent with that of evidence-based medicine[11] in many ways, including its emphasis on the application's output (i.e. that the application of AI leads to certain results, which thus justify its application, e.g. the successful treatment and curing of diseases and disorders), it stands in contrast to the widespread expectation that characterizes the application of AI throughout various fields: that we can and should understand how AI actually works and thus why exactly it should be applied, following a reason-based approach (see Wischmeyer, esp. paras 25 et seq.).

With the help of algorithms, a network of interconnected artificial neurons is simulated, within which synaptic weights constantly change during the learning phase. The learning process also takes place through 'trial and error', according to which the inevitable occurrence of errors forms the basis of how the system will ultimately develop further. This means that the 'intuitive' behavior makes it very difficult or even impossible to predict beforehand how the learning system will behave in a particular situation.[12] Consequently, the AI's learning and what it has learned cannot be made visible by means of a logical sequence of comprehended individual development steps, but can only be represented indirectly and generally via the structure of the network.[13]

In both cases, however, the question arises as to how explicable we should expect an AI-based medical system to be, if it is capable of generating structured reports about findings. In principle, medical treatment must correspond to the current state of medical science at the time of treatment, i.e. the standard, which—to already anticipate its legal significance—represents the standard of care for the assessment of physicians' obligations and thus liability.[14]

The term 'medical standard' can be subdivided into the standard of the physician's conduct and the standard of care.[15] The latter concerns the politically-determined performance and quality assets of the healthcare system and primarily helps the economic assessment to control costs. The standard of the physician's conduct has not been conclusively defined. However, there is broad agreement that it is formed on three levels: scientific knowledge, medical experience and consensus within the medical profession. The standard is thus that which corresponds to the established state of medical science based on scientific findings and medical experience in the field in question and is recognized in medical practice for the treatment of the respective health disorder. This recognition is connected to the need to achieve the medical treatment objective and approval in trials.[16] The definition is

---

[10]Biegel and Kurose (2016).

[11]Sackett et al. (1996).

[12]Ebers (2017), p. 95.

[13]Ebers (2017), p. 107.

[14]Katzenmeier (2016), § 823, recital 366.

[15]For this general division and evaluation, also subsequently, cf. Schneider (2010), p. 11 (with further references).

[16]Steffen (1995), p. 190; Dressler (2010), p. 380.

nevertheless rather vague, because it does not clarify the relationship between the above three criteria and how they are to be weighted—this is particularly true for the required degree of scientific certainty, where AI might primarily play a role.[17] It is precisely this inaccuracy, however, that traditionally allows for the flexible use of the standard term, not only dependent on local conditions of healthcare and the respective state of knowledge in science (which must also lead to a continuous development of standards concurrent with medical progress),[18] but which—according to the term's normative content[19]—also acts as a dynamic gateway to the individual case and pushes towards sufficient consideration of the patient's right of self-determination. All the more so in fact, since it must always be taken into account that deviations from the standard are not treatment errors if required by the patient's disease situation. Here, the decisive factor is the medical plausibility of the reasons for the deviation.[20] Thus, altogether, it can be stated that the primary benchmark when applying a medical standard (or when in rare cases deviating from it) is set by the patient themselves.

Against the backdrop of this open definition of the medical standard applied to the work of physicians, one might nevertheless agree that nuanced questions related to, for instance, exactly which of an AI's internal processes formulated which particular medical results, and how, might not be justified. After all, physicians will, in the end, also only be able to refer to their medical training and experience when asked how a finding exactly came about, since access to their own 'inner processing' towards findings, must, in detail, remain denied.[21]

Additionally, while the many ways in which physicians can arrive at medical results and at which results they factually arrive is guided by using standards as an orientation aid, these methods are also strongly affected by the various formulae described above, that is, the ability to realize human characteristics used to overcome specific challenges in the operationalization of disease and health concepts in medicine dependent on the individual case.

These formulae have, until now, been mainly realized in the physician-patient relationship. It is thus crucial to further investigate this relationship and how it can serve as a platform to promote the subjective wellbeing of the patient against the backdrop of specific challenges AI might pose in this regard.

---

[17]Dressler (2010), p. 380.
[18]Laufs (1999), p. 626.
[19]Brüggemeier (1999), p. 63.
[20]Hart (1998), p. 13.
[21]Wischmeyer (2018), p. 1.

2 AI's Influence on the Status and Role of Physicians and Patients in Their Relation to Each Other in Medical Ethics

2.1 The Physician-Patient Relationship in Medical Ethics

12 Physicians and patients are in an asymmetrical relationship due to an imbalance of powers.[22] In a traditional medical context, this is due to the fact that the nature and level of their healthcare-related knowledge and their ability to judge this knowledge fundamentally differ. Due to training and practice, the physician can manage illnesses in a professional manner, whereas dealing with them is often a life-altering confrontation for the patient. The special trust they place in their attending physician shapes their relationship in a way that in many cases goes far beyond the interests between persons normally present in (legal) relationships.[23] It is thus of the utmost importance that medical ethics continue to work towards restoring the balance between these actors.[24]

13 The normative implications of the relationship between doctor and patient lead to different interpretation models.[25] Leaving the traditional paternalistic model[26] behind, the intermediate stages of the informative and interpretative or contractual model[27] have led to the establishment of today's status quo: the partnership model, also known as the participatory or shared decision-making[28] model.

14 In the partnership model, it is not only the task of the physician to provide the patient with information about consent, but also to help them to clarify their own goals and wishes, to evaluate them and to articulate them as actions allowing their

---

[22] Eckart (2013), p. 324.

[23] Janda (2013), p. 123; Kluth (2008), p. 39; Maclean (2009), p. 93.

[24] Jones (1999), p. 129. The Hippocratic Oath is the earliest expression of medical ethics and already emphasizes a crucial principle, that of non-maleficence, which has been preserved in theories of modern medical ethics (paras 17 and 24).

[25] Molnár-Gábor (2017), p. 111 et seq., with further references. Emanuel and Emanuel (2012), p. 107; Schöne-Seifert (2007), pp. 88 et seq.

[26] The paternalistic model is the original Hippocratic model, in which the physician's duty of care is largely decisive. The task of the physician to promote the well-being of the patient has priority over the will of the patient and also extends to future sensitivities. Boyd (2006), p. 31.

[27] On the contrary, the informative doctor-patient model states that the patient themselves decides on medical measures. The physician must convey the medical facts to the patient in an appropriate form to enable this, and the personal values or convictions of the physician may play no role. The contractual model, on the other hand, represents the interaction between physician and patient as a service in which the current will of the patient plays a leading role in the physician's actions. The will has priority over the patient's well-being even if the will is obviously not beneficial according to medical standards. The difference between the informative and contractual models is that in the former the doctor knows the personal values of the patient, while in the latter these are jointly determined. Emanuel and Emanuel (2012), p. 56.

[28] Maclean (2009), p. 129 et seq.; Elwyn et al. (2012), p. 1361.

implementation in the medical care plan. Thus the patient is regarded as a person in need of not only information but advice.[29] Consultation and providing information should, however, take place without any 'controlling influence'.[30] An important result of this model is that the patient more or less becomes an equal partner with the physician, bringing in particular knowledge into their relationship based on their human-personal biographical qualification that is crucial for opening up and evaluating medical-professional knowledge and making it useful in their individual case.[31] In order to enable this, and as means of realizing shared decision-making, the physician should rely on established principles of medical ethics.

2.2 Principles of Medical Ethics and Their Implementation in the Physician-Patient Relationship

The four-principle theory of Beauchamp and Childress[32] may be considered controversial by some,[33] but it enjoys the greatest level of acceptance in current medical ethics. It should therefore be the subject of analysis because, in comparison to other theories of medical ethics, it has increasingly proved to be an orientation aid re design of doctor-patient relationships regarding the operationalization of health and disease concepts.[34]

Beauchamp and Childress propose that physicians, in light of unresolved basic moral-philosophical controversies, orientate themselves in relation to their patients using principles that are compatible with various moral theories instead of a single supreme moral principle.[35] They reconstruct four non-hierarchical principles of medium scope, which are supposed to tie in with everyday moral convictions and thus embody consensus and can guide medical action[36]: respect for autonomy, non-maleficence, beneficence and justice (see para 21 et seq.)[37]

Both the strength and the weakness of this theory lie in the fact that it does not further prescribe a weighting of principles in the sense of a systematic relationship.[38] On the one hand, this factually allows a case-related interpretation and accessibility for different moral convictions. On the other hand, this flexibility goes hand in hand with a limited capacity to enable the finding of solutions; the lack of previous weighting of the principles leaves a much too wide margin for their appreciation

---

[29]Thiele (2013), pp. 560 et seq.
[30]Schöne-Seifert (2007), p. 44.
[31]Taupitz (2002), p. 132.
[32]Beauchamp and Childress (2013).
[33]Cf. Düwell (2008), p. 95.
[34]Spranger (2010), pp. 18 et seq.
[35]Marckmann et al. (2012), pp. 32 et seq.
[36]Marckmann et al. (2012), p. 33.
[37]Beauchamp and Childress (2013), pp. 101 et seq.
[38]Schöne-Seifert (2007), p. 32.

when solving concrete cases, meaning that in difficult moral conflict situations support via a more precise ethical orientation might be missing.[39] Despite their everyday plausibility, the principles need to be enriched with content and interpreted according to the particulars of each situation in order to guide a concrete decision, as there is no possibility for an intra-theoretical derivation of their exact relationship and weighing detached from the context of their concrete application that also determines situations where they might conflict.[40]

In response to this criticism, Beauchamp and Childress have developed their theory further and have tried to present it as an increasingly coherent normative framework.[41] They have elaborated on the consistent specification of their theory as a bridge between abstract principles and concrete problems and have developed an idea of common morality in this regard.[42] This idea is not about producing a unifying theory, but rather offering decision-making assistance in the form of the components of a moral code and thus advancing the concrete handling and solution of moral problems in medical contexts.[43]

What remains relevant for medical practice then is less the lack of a final justification of the principles, but rather the fact that they must still first be interpreted and applied on a case-by-case basis to directly initiate concrete actions for dealing with patients.[44] In order to be able to do this, the challenges presented for their implementation in the specific use case of AI systems should be considered in the next step.

2.3 *Challenges Presented by AI in Medical Ethics*

Issues that arise from the application of AI related to the implementation of the principles of medical ethics can be summarized as follows:

While AI can potentially empower patients, it can also have restrictive effects on their self-determination (and dignity).[45] The danger that AI might restrict choices based on calculations about risk or what is in the best interest of the user and in this way arguably manipulate them[46] must thus also be weighed against the principle of *autonomy* (see also Ernst, paras 11 et seq.). If AI systems are used to make a diagnosis or a treatment plan, but the physician is unable to explain how these were arrived at, this could be seen as restricting the patient's right to make free, informed decisions about their health.[47] Furthermore, with the increasingly 'strong'

---

[39]Marckmann et al. (2012), pp. 35 et seq.
[40]Wiesing (2005), pp. 77 et seq.
[41]Beauchamp and Childress (2013), p. 405.
[42]Beauchamp and Childress (2013), pp. 403 et seq.
[43]Clouser and Gert (1990), pp. 222 et seq.
[44]Wiesing (2005), p. 82.
[45]Cf. Nuffield Council on Bioethics (2018).
[46]Sharkey and Sharkey (2012), p. 5.
[47]Mittelstadt (2017).

application of AI in medicine, a danger of social isolation (e.g. in situations of care) might emerge where the patient will be unable to judge whether they are communicating with a real person or with technology.[48] This could also possibly lead to a perception of fraud.[49]

In assessing the impact of AI-based systems on patients, the implementation of the *principle of beneficence* means respect for the well-being of the patient must always come first. In this case, it is particularly important to discuss how the patient's subjective knowledge and life experience can be taken into account in decision-making, particularly in the evaluation of risk information, when defining which measures of explicability and communicability health-relevant decisions made by drawing on AI are subject to, and how to deal with false-positive and false-negative findings. 22

When implementing the *principle of non-maleficence*, issues surrounding reliability and safety become crucially important. If an error can be followed back to an AI system malfunction and said error is difficult to detect or has knock-on effects this could have serious implications.[50] AI could also be used for malicious purposes such as to covertly surveil or collect revealing information about a person's health without their knowledge based, for instance, on the analysis of motor behavior and mobility patterns detected by tracking devices.[51] 23

When applying AI in healthcare in a *just* manner, transparency and accountability can be seen as cornerstones to achieving such an application. As indicated above (see para. 6), it can be difficult or impossible to determine the underlying logic that generates the outputs produced by AI; either because is kept secret or because it is too complex for a human to understand, including their continuous tweaking of their own parameters and rules as they learn. This creates problems for validating the output of AI systems. Although AI applications have the potential to reduce human bias and error, they can also reproduce and reinforce biases in the data used to train them.[52] Concerns have been raised about the potential of AI to lead to discrimination in ways that may be hidden, as, for example, datasets used to train AI systems are often poorly representative of the wider population and, as a result, could make unfair decisions that reflect wider prejudices in society (cf. Rademacher, paras 35 et seq., Tischbirek, paras 5 et seq.).[53] Additionally, this might lead to the benefits of AI in healthcare not being evenly distributed. AI might work less well where data is scarce or more difficult to collect or render digitally, negatively affecting people with rare medical conditions, or who are underrepresented in clinical trials.[54] 24

Also, biases can be embedded in the algorithms themselves, reflecting the beliefs and prejudices of AI developers.[55] This ultimately means the relationship between 25

---

[48] Sharkey and Sharkey (2012).
[49] Wallach and Allen (2008).
[50] Wachter (2015), p. 4, cited in: Nuffield (2018), p. 4.
[51] Yuste et al. (2017), p. 6, cited in: Nuffield (2018), p. 6.
[52] Future Advocacy (2018), p. 30.
[53] Nuffield (2018), p. 5.
[54] Future advocacy (2018), p. 35.
[55] House of Lords (2018), pp. 41 et seq.; Future advocacy (2018), p. 39.

physician and patient (until now the space where the principles of medical ethics have been implemented according to the concrete use case) could also in itself be impaired. The conventional bilateral relationship between doctor and patient is dissolved, because new actors, programmers, product manufacturers and potentially AI applications themselves burst this bipolarity. This makes it difficult to implement the 'shared decision-making' model, which is intended to ensure a balanced, symmetrical relationship between both traditional actors. Upholding and implementing the established principles of medical ethics thus needs to take into account any shift in and influence on said bipolar relationship.

26   At the same time, this also influences the possible role of physicians in the application of AI, especially the practicable abilities they need to have to realize the autonomy and well-being of the patient and to avoid harm in a just manner in the course of medical care. This also affects practical aspects of their work such as their training, qualification requirements and any potential reservation of the application of AI for medical professionals only.[56] Also, keeping up their skills to be able to take over if AI systems fail might prove crucial.[57]

27   Ultimately, at a practical level, both physicians and patients need to be able to trust AI systems. In this regard, besides dealing with the challenges of realizing the principles of medical ethics in concrete cases, it is vital to guide the implementation of AI by also defining legal obligations towards patients, including clear norms on issues of liability, as they can guarantee fairness of compensation for damages.[58]

---

[56]Future advocacy (2018), p. 40; Nuffield (2018), pp. 5 et seq.; House of Lords (2018), p. 55, No. 164.

[57]Nuffield (2018), p. 6.

[58]Jansen (2003), p. 37. In Germany, the ethical and legal principles of the medical profession are defined in the (Model) Professional Code. It serves the medical associations as a model for their professional codes of conduct, in order that the development of professional law be as uniform as possible throughout Germany. The professional code of conduct of the respective medical association regulates the rights and duties applicable to individual physicians vis-à-vis patients, professional colleagues and their medical association. This code of conduct is a statutory law issued by the medical association on the basis of the Medical Profession and Chamber Act of the respective federal state. The medical associations are responsible for ensuring that doctors observe their professional duties, dealing with complaints about doctors and checking whether their conduct is in accordance with professional law. In the event of violations, they can appeal to the professional court. Cf. http://www.bundesaerztekammer.de/weitere-sprachen/english/german-medical-association/ (accessed 06 January 2019). Altogether, elaborating on the relationship between physicians' duties based on principles of general medical ethics, professional law and medical malpractice law would go beyond the scope of this chapter, and so we will simply cite Eberhard Schmidt [translation by the author]: 'Ethics of professional conduct are not isolated from the law, they have a constant, universal effect on the legal relationship between the physician and the patient. What professional ethics require from the physician, the law also largely assumes as a legal duty. Far more than in other social relations of human beings, the ethical and the legal merge in the medical profession." Schmidt (1957), p. 2; German Federal Constitutional Court 2 BvR 878/74 'medical liability' (25 July 1979) para 106 et seq. Regarding the relationship between medical standards, guidelines and directives, cf. Greiner (2018), § 839, recital 21.

3 AI's Influence on the Status and Role of Physicians and Patients in Their Relation to Each Other in Liability Law

The legal relationship between physician and patient is a treatment relationship. However, under the treatment contract, the doctor does not owe a certain success—the healing of the patient—but instead professional efforts with the aim of healing or alleviating patients' complaints.[59] Thus, according to the contractual obligations of the physician, at least under German law,[60] he owes compliance with the required duty of care during treatment. Where obligations in the treatment contract are violated, the civil law norm regulating compensation for the breach of obligations comes into effect.[61]

Medical liability also allows us to draw upon tort law, since the physician at the same time unjustifiably impairs health or violates physical integrity. Thus, in addition to contractual liability, tortious liability can also lead to liability for damages.[62]

There exists a differentiation between weak AI and strong AI. The former is characterized by algorithms written with medical expertise to, for example, calculate a score from several parameters and thus provide support for therapy planning and diagnostics. The latter describes a fairly independent neural network that learns to recognize medically relevant correlations and to assess plausibility from given connections therein.[63] However, even the former intelligent medical devices often already carry out treatment measures themselves within the framework of their functions and in this way at least partially replace the physician. As things stand at present, they supplement medical activity by providing the physician with the necessary information on the basis of which they can make their therapy decisions.

If AI is used for medical decision support or the final assessment of findings, but the decision of the physician re: the treatment according to medical standard remains

28

29

30

31

---

[59] It is generally accepted that the treatment contract is not classified as a contract for work ("Werkvertrag") but as a service contract ("Dienstvertrag") in accordance with § 611 BGB. This has not been affected by the special regulation of the treatment contract in the BGB since the Patient Rights Act came into force on 26 February 2013, and the subtitle 'Treatment Contract" has been included in the BGB, which deals with the medical treatment contract and the rights and obligations within the framework of treatment. Spickhoff (2018a, b), § 630a BGB, recital 5, § 630b BGB, recital 1.

[60] See §§ 280, 630a et seq. of the German Civil Code (BGB).

[61] § 280 para. 1 BGB states the following: If the obligor breaches a duty arising from the obligation, the obligee may demand damages for the damage caused thereby. This does not apply if the obligor is not responsible for the breach of duty.

[62] § 823 para. 1 BGB states: A person who unlawfully violates the life, body, health, etc. of another person is obliged to make compensation for the resulting damage. In German tort law, it is necessary to show a breach of one of the norms of the BGB and, contrary for instance to French civil law (Art. 1382 French Civil Code), it is not possible to bring a claim solely based on negligence. If there has been a breach of one of the norms, then there is unlawfulness prima facie, but this can be justified via a defense as in English law, van Dam (2014), p. 80.

[63] Dierks (2018).

decisive, then the case can be assessed according to the principles of medical malpractice (see paras 32 et seq.). Here, product liability law for the AI system should only be drawn on as an additional asset. We will first further consider the sufficiency of malpractice law in order to ascertain the current status of AI involvement in healthcare, and then consider rules on product liability including cases in which, for example, patients would be solely and directly treated by an AI system (see paras 47 et seq.). In addition to its aforementioned role, where it is to be consulted in addition to medical malpractice law, product liability law would become particularly relevant in the extreme case where, once it reaches a certain level of sophistication, AI diagnoses were to count as medical standards per se and accordingly essentially be given preference over potential differing human medical opinions. In this case, medical liability would in principle be ruled out and the manufacturer's liability alone would be decisive.

3.1 Issues of Medical Malpractice Law

32 In order for a medical action to be legitimate, it is essential that the medical measure, besides obviously not being contraindicated,[64] must be supported by the informed patient's consent and must be performed *lege artis*. When applying an AI system, liability for lack of information and for treatment errors appear to be the most relevant issues.

3.1.1 Informed Consent, Liability for Lack of Information

33 The goal of informed consent is that patients receive a general idea of the nature and severity of the disease, of the possible treatment, and of the burdens and risks associated with the planned medical measures or their omission.[65] Capturing the nature, significance and scope of the measures should enable them to make a competent decision about the treatment themselves.[66]

---

[64] Cf., however, regarding elective treatments Laufs (2015), Chapter I, recital 29. German Federal Court of Justice VI ZR 202/79 (10 March 1981); German Federal Court of Justice VI ZR 247/78 (18 March 1980).

[65] § 630 e and § 630 h BGB. Critically re: double regulation Spickhoff (2018a, b), § 630c BGB, recital 11.

[66] Laufs (2002), p. 121. In German law, this arises from the general right to personality as provided for in Art. 2 (1) and Art. 1 (1) of the German Basic Law. German Federal Constitutional Court 2 BvR 878/74 'medical liability' (25 July 1979) para 109 et seq.; German Federal Administrative Court 3 C 19.15 (2 March 2017). According to established case law, medically indicated treatment of diagnostic and therapeutic nature carried out to the standard of a specialist (*Facharztstandard*) also constitutes bodily harm (*Körperverletzung*) if the patient's consent has not been obtained. German Federal Court of Justice VI ZR 313/03 (15 March 2005); German Federal Court of Justice VI ZR 37/79 (22 April 1980).

A distinction is made between diagnostic, treatment, and risk information as well as information concerning the course of the treatment.[67] Treatment information mainly includes an explanation of the scope of the intervention.[68] If AI is used, this would, for example, include information about possible, unforeseeable, unintended or additional findings gathered within the framework of the treatment contract.

Risk information should include the potential side-effects of error-free medical treatment. Proper information about complications or harmful effects arising from *not* performing the treatment also helps to enable the patient to understand the pros and cons of the medical intervention in such a way that they are able to make an informed decision as to whether they wish to take the risk of the treatment and thus ultimately agree to the procedure, while preserving their freedom of choice.[69] In the context of informed consent, treatment risks do not have to be described to the patient in a medically precise manner, nor in all their conceivable manifestations.[70] It is sufficient to give the patient a general picture of the severity of the risk spectrum. The patient must generally know which disease is present, which intervention is planned, how urgent the intervention is, how it is carried out and what side effects and risks are associated with it.[71] The physician can usually leave it at that, and provide further details depending on the patient's questions.

Whether the application of AI definitively presents a circumstance in need of clarification depends on the degree of danger it poses to the patient's state of health and lifestyle should the worst happen. Whether the danger of the occurrence of malfunctions leads to the assumption of a duty of the physician to inform could depend on the extent to which risks could be countered, mitigated and excluded by technical and organizational measures (which should, in accordance with Nr. 17.2, Section I of the Medical Device Regulation (MDR),[72] already take place at the design level, (see also Jabri, para. 5). Although it could also be assumed that risks arising from the trial and error learning method of AI can always increase the danger posed to the patient, they do not need to be informed about general and purely theoretical complications, especially as they would unnecessarily confuse and disturb them.[73] Overall, depending on the performance of AI systems, it might therefore

---

[67]Gehrlein (2018), pp. 100 et seq.
[68]Quaas (2018), § 14, recital 1-135.
[69]German Federal Court of Justice VI ZR 131/02 (25 March 2003) para 18. Gehrlein (2018), pp. 101 et seq.
[70]German Federal Court of Justice VI ZR 65/88 (14 February 1989).
[71]German Federal Court of Justice VI ZR 232/90 (12 March 1991).
[72]Regulation (EU) 2017/745 of the European Parliament and of the Council of 5 April 2017 on medical devices, amending Directive 2001/83/EC, Regulation (EC) No 178/2002 and Regulation (EC) No 1223/2009 and repealing Council Directives 90/385/EEC and 93/42/EEC.
[73]German Federal Court of Justice VI ZR 83/89 (12 December 1989); German Federal Court of Justice VI ZR 323/04 (13 June 2006). In various areas there is disagreement in the literature about the physician's duty within the framework of informed consent to inform patients about established alternative treatment methods as well as those that are still being tested. Blechschmitt (2016), pp. 79 et seq.; in case of a new method: id., pp. 85 et seq.

be rather difficult to justify the doctor's duty to inform the patient about the risk of malfunctions caused by AI.[74]

3.1.2 Liability for Errors in Treatment and the Burden of Proof

37 Since the attending physician is not legally responsible for the success of their treatment,[75] a failed treatment *as such* does not justify any liability, at least not under German law.[76] That would require a medical error in the sense of a culpable violation of the physician's specific professional duties.[77] According to the standard of care, the attending physician owes the patient professional treatment as a service in accordance with the state of scientific knowledge.[78] The resulting contractual and tortious duties of care are identical.[79]

38 In this context of application, if the physician recognizes on the basis of their expertise that the information provided by the intelligent medical device is incorrect in the specific case, they must not make it the basis for their decision. It is part of their expertise that they evaluate information independently, and the more dangerous an error could prove, the more critically they must question the basis for their decision.[80]

39 Whether a doctor has culpably deviated from the medical standard in a specific case must be judged according to medical standards at the time of the medical treatment.[81] The influence of AI-based applications themselves on the medical standard and how the medical standard is to be determined at the relevant point in time under their influence is open to debate. The learning processes (and the speed such applications go through them) could, firstly, expose the state of knowledge to rapid changes, making the relevant point in time difficult to grasp. As the methods used by an AI system to arrive at a given suggestion are likely to be opaque, this could further complicate decisions re whether the physician has culpably deviated from the medical standard, particularly should their decision be different from one based on the application of the AI system. The physician is free to choose their means of diagnosis and therapy, but they are also responsible for their choice.[82] This includes responsibility for the selection and application of supporting systems.

---

[74] As is also derived by Droste (2018), p. 112.
[75] Hager (2017), § 823, recital 18.
[76] German Federal Court of Justice VI ZR 201/75 (15 March 1977) para 11 et seq.; German Federal Court of Justice VI ZR 213/76 (14 March 1978).
[77] Cf. § 630a BGB.
[78] BR-Drucks. 312/12, p. 26.
[79] Gehrlein (2018), p. 33, recital 1. Cf. footnotes 63 and 64.
[80] Taupitz (2011), p. 387.
[81] Gehrlein (2018), p. 34, recital 3.
[82] German Federal Court of Justice VI ZR 238/86 (22 September 1987) para 12 et seq.; German Federal Court of Justice VI ZR 132/88 (6 December 1988) para 6; German Federal Court of Justice VI ZR 323/04 (13 June 2006) para 6; German Federal Court of Justice VI ZR 35/06 (22 May 2007) para 12 et seq.

Depending on the concrete influence and role of AI systems in the medical decision making, the fact that AI system decisions are hard (if not impossible) to verify could lead to a divergence of action and liability, if the AI decides de facto and the physician remains de jure liable for the decision.[83] In this regard, it also becomes obvious that the distinction between the application of AI as supporting system and as a system making medical decisions that might qualify as medical standards per se might become increasingly challenging.

The medical duty of care in the use of medical devices is also concretized by § 4 (1) Medical Devices Act (MPG) (see Jabri, paras 6 et seq.).[84] According to this, medical devices may not be operated or used if there are reasonable grounds to suspect that they pose a direct or indirect risk to the safety and health of patients, users or third parties in case of improper use or maintenance, as well as in case of use for the purpose for which they are intended beyond a level that is justifiable in accordance with the findings of medical science. The problem here is also that the internal decision-making processes of the intelligent medical device might not be apparent to the physician (see paras 5 et seq.), which is why the hazard posed by the product will usually only become visible through a damaging event. In this case, the physician cannot be assigned any fault due to a lack of predictability.[85]

Nevertheless, as soon as the physician realizes that the use of a medical device involves unacceptable risks, they may not use the product until they have carried out the necessary repairs to which they are obliged under § 7 (1) Medical Devices Operator Ordinance (MPBetreibV).[86] Since the physician will normally not have the necessary technical knowledge to repair the medical device, the prevailing opinion is in favor of a decisive contribution to said repairs by the medical device manufacturer.[87]

The burden of proof is a procedural matter. The patient asserting a liability claim has to demonstrate that the treatment was wrong, that a right was violated, as well as the damage (i.e. the adverse effect on health) and the relevant chain of causality.[88]

The burden of proof can determine (legal) causation and therefore who wins the case. The determination of the causality of the treatment error for the infringement of a right very often presents itself in practice as a considerable problem. In many cases,

---

[83] Dierks (2018). It is necessary to distinguish between locked closed-loop AI applications and continuous learning closed-loop AI applications.

[84] The Act on Medical Devices of 2nd August 1994 (Federal Law Gazette I, p. 1963), in the version of 7th August 2002 (Federal Law Gazette I, p. 3146), last amended by Article 12 of the Act of 24th July 2010 (Federal Law Gazette I, p. 983). § 4 MPG is also a protective law within the meaning of § 823 Abs. 2 BGB, Edelhäuser (2014), § 6 MPG, recital 29a.

[85] Droste (2018), pp. 112–113.

[86] Medical Device Operator Ordinance, from the version published 21st August 2002 (BGBl. I p. 3396), last amended by Article 9 of the Ordinance of 29th November 2018 (BGBl. I p. 2034).

[87] One solution advocated to avoid liability risks is a contractual agreement between the physician and the manufacturer, whereby the manufacturer is obliged to maintain and repair the intelligent medical device. Wagner (2018), § 6, recital 7. Regarding further obligations of the manufacturer in this context cf. Droste (2018), p. 113.

[88] BR-Drucks. 312/12, pp. 40, 44.

despite the presence of one or more treatment errors, it is not always possible to exclude with the degree of certainty required by the rules of civil procedure[89] the possibility that the infringement would have occurred anyway, i.e. even without the treatment error. Therefore, the principle of the burden of proof and the possibilities of changing the burden of proof are of considerable importance.

44 Contrary to cases where there is an error due to the lack of information in the context of informed consent (see paras 33 et seq.), there are exceptions to the basic distribution of the burden of proof regarding treatment errors, for example according to § 630h (5) BGB, where the treatment error is so serious that it is to be classified as a gross treatment error, since such errors ought to be unthinkable for a physician.[90]

45 Furthermore, the legal concept of the so-called 'fully controllable risk' (or 'fully masterable risk') also provides for a less onerous burden of proof for patients. In such cases, the *physician* must explain why they are not at fault. According to § 630h (1) BGB, medical liability is presumed to be due to an error on the part of the treating physician if a general treatment risk has materialized which was fully controllable for the treating physician and which led to injury to the life, body or health of the patient. Basic controllability is not sufficient for the application of this burden of proof rule, the risk must be allocated to the practitioner's 'sphere of organization and control'.[91] Such risks are 'fully controllable' if they neither originate from the risk sphere of the patient's own human organism nor from the special features of medical intervention into said organism.[92] These conventionally include particular situations in which the patient has suffered injury due to faulty equipment or building fittings, or inadequate hygiene or organizational procedures.[93] In the case of medical equipment and materials for whose faultlessness, functionality and correct operation the physician is liable, the risk is fully controllable unless such equipment has a design error that cannot be detected, or it is scientifically impossible to explain how the damage occurred.[94]

46 Even if the processes of intelligent medical devices are indeterminate and difficult to comprehend, they could nevertheless be considered to be fully controllable through appropriate technical and organizational measures already, according to current technical possibilities. Consequently, the presumption provided for in § 630h (1) BGB is also applicable to such medical devices. For the presumption to be effective, however, the patient must provide full proof of the causal link between the fully controllable risk and the injury suffered.[95] Inspection of the treatment

---

[89]§ 286 Code of Civil Procedure as promulgated on 5 December 2005 (Bundesgesetzblatt (BGBl., Federal Law Gazette) I page 3202; 2006 I page 431; 2007 I page 1781), last amended by Article 1 of the Act dated 10 October 2013 (Federal Law Gazette I page 3786).

[90]Schreiber (2019), § 630h BGB, recitals 10 et seq. German Federal Court of Justice VI ZR 325/98 (8 February 2000); German Federal Court of Justice VI ZR 389/90 (26 November 1991); German Federal Court of Justice VI ZR 21/85 (24 June 1986).

[91]Gehrlein (2018), p. 88, recital 86.

[92]German Federal Court of Justice VI ZR 158/06 (20 March 2007).

[93]Gehrlein (2018), p. 42, recital 13.

[94]Gehrlein (2018), p. 91, Rn. 90.

[95]Droste (2018), p. 113.

documents can be an important measure for clarifying the facts of the case and, if necessary, for establishing liability on the part of the attending physicians.[96] Establishing liability in this context can nevertheless be made more difficult when applying AI should this influence treatment documentation, as liability for documentation obligations become relevant.[97]

3.2 Issues of Product Liability Law

Under German law, claims against the manufacturer of intelligent medical devices may be based on the principles of tortious producer liability or product liability law.[98] In order to avoid dangers that may emanate from their product, the manufacturer is subject to corresponding commercial obligations under tort producer liability. According to statutory regulation, the manufacturer's liability is linked to the concept of defect which, in German law, is based on the safety expectations of the product user.[99] These safety expectations are substantiated according to the same standards as the manufacturer's commercial obligations, so that the connecting factors for establishing liability are congruent.[100] According to producer liability in tort, a basic distinction can be made between design, manufacturing, instruction and product-monitoring obligations.[101] Here, in the case of AI, the design and manufacturing obligations are most decisive (the former not only—as already indicated—in interaction with medical malpractice law). However, in certain situations that are decisive for an AI-based product, the manufacturer's liability for design errors is excluded and the manufacturer thus has no duty of replacement.

47

In German law, this is the case if it can be assumed in the specific circumstances that the product did not have the defect that caused the damage when the manufacturer put it on the market.[102] Furthermore, the duty of replacement is excluded in the case of defects which, according to the state of the art in science and technology, could not be detected at the time the manufacturer placed the product on the market.[103] This means that subsequently occurring errors which are based on the learning ability of algorithms and which were not recognizable given the state of the

48

---

[96]Spindler (2018), § 823 BGB, recital 1018.

[97]According to § 630f BGB, and records need to be kept, not just as an aide-memoire, Scholz (2018), recital 1.

[98]Compare §§ 823 et seq. BGB for tortious liability and § 1 (1) sentence 1 Product Liability Act (ProdHaftG) for product liability law, Product Liability Act of 15 December 1989 (BGBl. I p. 2198), last amended by Article 5 of the Act of 17 July 2017 (BGBl. I p. 2421). Regarding this summary, compare Droste (2018), p. 110; Backmann (2012), p. 37, with further references.

[99]Foerste (2012), § 24 recital 4. § 3 ProdHaftG.

[100]Oechsler (2013), § 3, recital 13.

[101]Rolland (1990), part I, recital 39.

[102]Cf. § 1 (2) no. 2 ProdHaftG.

[103]Cf. § 1 (2) no. 5 ProdHaftG.

art of science and technology at the time the AI was placed on the market are not covered by the Product Liability Act's (ProdHaftG) strict liability. Liability under tort producer liability is also excluded for lack of fault if the existing fault could not be objectively detected, which will usually be the case due to the indeterminate behavior of intelligent products. If the use of an intelligent medical device results in damage based on such an exclusion of liability for a design error, the injured party remains without compensation.[104]

49 The Product Liability Act determines according to § 1 (4) ProdHaftG that the aggrieved party has to bear the burden of proof for the error, the damage and the causal connection between error and damage. Pursuant to § 1 (4) sentence 2 ProdHaftG, the manufacturer must prove the existence of the elements according to which his duty of replacement pursuant to the here relevant § 1 (2) is excluded. Even after the tortious producer liability, the burden of proof for the defectiveness of the product lies with the injured party. In case of opacity of the artificial decision-making processes of intelligent medical devices (see paras 6 et seq.), however, a retrospective examination of the machine's action based on a clear logic will not be possible, so that in this case the existence of a product defect is unlikely to be proven.

3.3 Conclusions Based on Liability Law

50 In summary, it can be stated that the establishment of liability based solely on malpractice law for both the lack of information on possible malfunctions of an AI system in the frame of informed consent and for errors in treatment is confronted with difficulties. Consequently, and as we move towards an increasing independence of AI systems, liabilities thus will tend to concentrate on the producer of the AI system.

51 However, challenges also surround the establishment of producer liability, and there are also question marks over the interplay of medical malpractice law and producers' liability. A misdiagnosis does not immediately imply an error in treatment: it must violate the relevant medical standard. If this is not the case, it might also be impossible to claim that there is a design fault which would give rise to manufacturer liability. If there *is* a violation of medical standards, this does not necessarily trigger the manufacturer's liability. While in the case of medical liability the physician is liable for his own treatment error causing the damage, the manufacturer is not liable for the treatment error committed by AI, but instead for his own behavior, i.e. the manufacture of a faulty product. Here, the reason and cause for the malfunction of the AI is necessarily decisive for establishing liability.[105]

52 Due to the network of human-machine relationships between manufacturers, programmers, physicians as operators and patients as users, in the vast majority of

---

[104]Droste (2018), p. 112.
[105]Heil and Sandrock (2017), § 23, recitals 30 et seq; Meyer (2018), p. 237.

cases the source of the error will not be clearly identifiable. Whether the damage results from a fully controllable risk or is ultimately due to an operating error by the physician or—in the case of a strong AI system—an application error by the patient themselves is thus unlikely to be clearly determinable according to the technological circumstances.

As a result, the injured party that has the burden of proof usually bears the risks of the usage of an intelligent medical device, since they cannot usually provide the necessary evidence to assert and enforce a claim for damages.

Altogether it appears obvious that it would be desirable to know and understand at least the main internal processes of medical AI products in order to be able to allocate risks, establish liabilities and to provide compensation for damages. As this is not yet the case (see paras 6 et seq.), various improvements for liability law have been proposed in the literature.[106] These proposals range from the design of AI as a separate legal entity with its own liability assets, to the insurance of innovation risks. In view of the AI as a 'black box', the demand for extended strict liability, which occurs independently of errors, seems to be the most-promoted solution. This also appears the most appropriate method to ensure that patients are not worse off than they would be in the case of treatment solely by a human physician. However, as noted above (see paras 45 et seq.), in contrast to such treatment, it might often not only be difficult but sometimes impossible to prove the cause of damage arising from a treatment error. Extended strict liability for intelligent medical devices should—according to these proposals—therefore provide for liability both for the manufacturer and for the patient, be limited to compensation for bodily harm and material damage, and provide for joint and several liability.[107] Depending on the degree to which AI is integrated into medical treatment, gross treatment errors could consequently be taken to indicate a serious design error (see para. 48).

Though dependent on the degree of integration of AI and its role in medical decision-making, against the backdrop of the liability of product manufacturer gaining increasing importance it must be asked which role physicians can still fulfill in order to help realize shared healthcare decision-making while relying on the application of an AI system.

4 The Status and Role of Physicians in Their Relation to Patients

The civil-law obligation between doctor and patient arises originally, under German law, upon conclusion of the treatment contract, whereby contractual consensus is proven via consent of the patient.[108]

---

[106]Cf. Spindler (2015), p. 776; Ortner and Daubenbüchel (2016), p. 2918; Keßler (2017), p. 589; Denga (2018), p. 69.
[107]Droste (2018), p. 114; Zech (2019), p. 214.
[108]Cf. § 311 (1) BGB.

57   The concept of a contractual obligation is to be understood simultaneously in the narrower and broader sense. While 'obligation' in the narrower sense refers to the right to performance, in the broader sense it encompasses the entire legal relationship between the physician and their patient from which the individual claims arise.[109] According to the principle of good faith (§ 242 BGB), the contracting parties are obligated to work towards the best possible execution of the contract. In addition to the main performance obligations, this results in obligations of conduct which can be divided into obligations to secure performance (secondary to the obligation to perform) and protective duties.[110] Secondary obligations to secure performance can have a preparatory and supporting effect.[111] Finally, protective duties can arise from the contractual obligation in accordance with § 241(2) BGB. Accordingly, each party is obliged to take into account the rights and legal interests of the other party.[112]

58   Furthermore, according to § 241(2) BGB, the scope of the protective duties is determined by the content of the contractual obligation, which must take into account the purpose of the contract, among other things. From the patient's point of view, the purpose of the contract is to promote their own health. The responsible physician's duties to advise, look after and care for the patient may then spring from the very same purpose (that is, to promote the patient's health), since the principle of loyalty to the contract requires the physician to work towards the best possible implementation of the contract.

59   As regards this interpretation of protective duties, the contractual obligation between physician and patient becomes the platform where an AI system is being applied, the gateway towards the dynamic obligation of jointly elaborating, determining and respecting patients' needs and well-being. Hindering disease and promoting health as crucial subjects of the contract particularly require respect for the understanding of health and disease as non-objective factors. This is also necessary for fulfilling contract obligations towards realizing its purpose, which further presupposes that the physician supporting the patient will consider any AI-based treatment suggestions and decisions according to the biographic assertiveness of the patient.

60   This may need to be accompanied by an 'extension' of the communication between physician and patient beyond the traditional informed consent process (as determined by both the therapeutic mandate and technical innovation) and reinforces relevant obligations of the physician including the general information obligations.[113]

61   Furthermore, this elevates those abilities and formulae in relation to the patient that AI cannot and only physicians can realize in order to operationalize the concepts of disease and health: the social and human components that must play a transformative role in the application of AI systems and in the interpretation of their

---

[109] Mansel (2011), § 241, recital 1.
[110] Mansel (2011), § 241, recitals 9, 10.
[111] Mansel (2011), § 241, recitals 9, 10.
[112] Grüneberg (2011), § 24, recital 6.
[113] According to § 630c BGB.

results.[114] These include planning of medical action according to the patient's expectations given their personal needs, which grant the physician-patient relationship a particular dynamism and spontaneity and thus a specifically-defined role throughout medical treatment and healthcare.

This is in line with interpreting the communication between physician and patient as a discourse process that always takes place only between concrete persons whose individuality is to be recognized in relational autonomy and that serves the goal of empowering and strengthening the patient while considering their vulnerability.[115] Only in this way can the shared decision-making model be realized in the sense that the self-determination of the patient is not understood as a contradiction to the medical treatment mandate, but as an appeal to the physician for a timely collaboration with the patient.[116] These obligations can then be used to realize patients' freedom by concretizing the principles of medical ethics, including within liability law, enabling factual personalization of healthcare and determining treatments based less on justifications by AI systems but more on their explicability in personal communication with patients (see Wischmeyer, paras 36 et seq.). At the same time, transparency of decision chains that are already baked into the AI system due to their being generalizable, or due to other reasons related to advantages of process, mean technologization remains crucial. Those baked-in processes can be enriched and further developed by feeding subjective patient needs into the decision-making process that emerge from dynamic discourse with the physician. This might hinder the possibly unethical depersonalization of healthcare and patient treatment and foster the realization of patient-friendly healthcare via technology, revaluating human factors that will, for the foreseeable future, remain indispensable in this context.

Thus, it might be concluded in the interim that the evaluation of an AI system's findings or treatment suggestions based on the patients' individual case must remain decisive. Accordingly, an only partially reason-based claim regarding the application of AI systems and the interpretation of their results, and an approach more influenced by patients' well-being appears vital. This should represent a first step towards clarifying what could count as a medical standard under the influence of AI, by concretizing the relationship between its established elements relying on this increased normativity.

Acknowledgement FMG acknowledges funding by the Volkswagen Foundation.

---

[114]Cf. also Buchholtz, paras 14 et seq., on the application of *law* as a necessarily social act.
[115]Rössler (2011), p. 226.
[116]Taupitz (2002), p. 132.

References

Aftergood S (2018) JASON: artificial intelligence for healthcare. Federation of American Scientists. Secrecy News of 1st February 2018. https://fas.org/blogs/secrecy/2018/02/ai-health-care/. Accessed 05 Jan 2018

Albu A, Stanciu LM (2015) Benefits of using artificial intelligence in medical predictions. Conference Paper. https://doi.org/10.1109/EHB.2015.7391610

Backmann B (2012) Produkthaftung bei Medizinprodukten. Medizin Produkte Recht:37

Beauchamp TL, Childress JF (2013) Principles of biomedical ethics, 7th edn. Oxford University Press, Oxford

Biegel B, Kurose JF (2016) The National artificial intelligence research and development strategic plan

Blechschmitt L (2016) Die straf- und zivilrechtliche Haftung des Arztes beim Einsatz roboterassistierter Chirurgie. Nomos, Baden-Baden

Boyd K (2006) Medical ethics: hippocratic and democratic ideals. In: McLean S (ed) First do not harm. Law, ethics and healthcare. Routledge, Hampshire, pp 29–38

Brüggemeier G (1999) Prinzipien des Haftungsrechts. Nomos, Baden Baden

Clouser D, Gert B (1990) A critique of principialism. J Med Philos 15:219–236

Denga M (2018) Deliktische Haftung für künstliche Intelligenz. Computer und Recht 34:69–77

Dierks C (2018) Wer haftet bei KI-Fehlern? Ärzte Zeitung online. Article of 19th December 2018. https://www.aerztezeitung.de/praxis_wirtschaft/w_specials/kuenstliche_intelligenz/article/978619/kuenstliche-intelligenz-haftet-ki-fehlern.html. Accessed 05 June 2019

Dressler WD (2010) Ärztliche Leitlinien und Arzthaftung. In: Bradner HE, Hagen H, Stürner R (eds) Festschrift für Karlsmann Geiß zum 65. Geburtstag, Köln/Berlin/Bonn/München, pp 379–388

Droste W (2018) Intelligente Medizinprodukte. Verantwortlichkeiten des Herstellers und ärztliche Sorgfaltspflichten. Medizin Produkte Recht:109–112

Düwell M (2008) Bioethik. Methoden, Theorien und Bereiche. Perlentaucher, Stuttgart/Weimar

Ebers M (2017) Autonomes Fahren: Produkt- und Produzentenhaftung. In: Oppermann H, Stender-Vorwachs J (eds) Autonomes Fahren. Rechtsfolgen, Rechtsprobleme, technische Grundlagen. C.H. Beck, München, pp 93–125

Eckart WU (2013) Geschichte, Theorie und Ethik der Medizin. Springer, Berlin

Edelhäuser R (2014) § 6 MPG. In: Prütting D (ed) Fachanwalts-Kommentar Medizinrecht, 4th edn. Luchterhand, München

Elwyn G, Frosch D, Thomson R et al (2012) Shared decision making: a model for clinical practice. J Gen Intern Med 27:1361–1367

Emanuel EJ, Emanuel LL (2012) Vier Modelle der Arzt-Patienten-Beziehung. In: Wiesing U (ed) Ethik in der Medizin, 4th edn. Reclam, Stuttgart, pp 107–110

Foerste U (2012) Verkehrspflichten im Bereich der Warensicherung. In: Foerste U, Graf von Westphalen F (eds) Produkthaftungshandbuch, 3rd edn. C.H. Beck, München

Future Advocacy (2018) Ethical, social and political challenges of Artificial Intelligence in health. A report with the Wellcome trust. https://wellcome.ac.uk/sites/default/files/ai-in-health-ethical-social-political-challenges.pdf. Accessed 06 Jan 2019

Gehrlein M (2018) Arzthaftungsrecht, 3rd edn. C.H. Beck, München

Greiner H-P (2018) § 839 BGB. In: Spickhoff A (ed) Kommentar zum Medizinrecht, 3rd edn. C.H. Beck, München

Grüneberg C (2011) § 241. In: Palandt O (ed) BGB, 70th edn. C.H. Beck, München

Haenssle HA, Fink C, Schneiderbauer R et al (2018) Man against machine: diagnostic performance of a deep learning convolutional neural network for dermoscopic melanoma recognition in comparison to 58 dermatologists. Ann Oncol. 29:1836–1842

Hager J (2017) § 823. In: Staudinger Kommentar zum Bürgerlichen Gesetzbuch. De Gruyter, Berlin

Hart D (1998) Ärztliche Leitlinien, Definitionen, Funktionen, rechtliche Bewertungen, MMR 8–16

Heil M, Sandrock A (2017) Produkthaftung für Medizinprodukte. In: Anhalt E, Dieners P (eds) Praxishandbuch Medizinprodukterecht, 2nd edn. C.H. Beck, München
House of Lords. Select Committee on Artificial Intelligence (2018) AI in the UK: ready, willing and able. HL Paper 100. https://publications.parliament.uk/pa/ld201719/ldselect/ldai/100/100.pdf. Accessed 06 Jan 2019
Janda C (2013) Medizinrecht, 2nd edn. C.H. Beck, München
Jansen N (2003) Die Struktur des Haftungsrechts. Mohr Siebeck, Tübingen
Jones MA (1999) Informed consent and other fairy stories. Med Law Rev 7:103–134
Katzenmeier C (2016) § 823. In: Dauner-Lieb B, Langen W (eds) Commentary BGB-Schuldrecht, 3rd edn. Nomos, Baden Baden
Keßler O (2017) Intelligente Roboter – neue Technologien im Einsatz. Multimedia und Recht 20:589–594
Kluth W (2008) Juristische Bewertung des Status quo: Stärkung der Autonomie oder Verlust der Freiberuflichkeit? In: Wienke A, Dierks C, Deutsche Gesellschaft für Medizin und Recht (eds) Zwischen Hippokrates und Staatsmedizin. Der Arzt am Beginn des 21. Jahrhunderts – 25 Jahre DGMR. Springer, Berlin
Lanzerath D, Honnefelder L (2000) Krankheitsbegriff und ärztliche Anwendung. In: Düwell M, Mieth D (eds) Ethik in der Humangenetik. Die neueren Entwicklungen der genetischen Frühdiagnostik aus ethischer Perspektive, 2nd edn. Francke, Tübingen, pp 51–77
Laufs A (1999) Zur Freiheit des Arztberufs. In: Ahrens H-J, von Bar C, Fischer G et al (eds) Festschrift für Erwin Deutsch. Carl Heymanns, Köln, pp 625–633
Laufs A (2002) Informed consent und ärztlicher Heilauftrag. In: Hillenkamp T (ed) Medizinrechtliche Probleme der Humangenetik. Springer, Berlin, pp 119–139
Laufs A (2015) Wesen und Inhalt des Arztrechts. In: Laufs A, Katzenmeier C, Lipp V (eds) Arztrecht, 7th edn. C.H. Beck, München, pp 3–28
Loder J, Nicholas L (2018) Confronting Dr. Robot. Creating a people-powered future for AI in health. Nesta Health Lab, May 2018. https://media.nesta.org.uk/documents/confronting_dr_robot.pdf. Accessed 05 Jan 2019
Maclean A (2009) Autonomy, informed consent and medical law. A relational challenge. Cambridge University Press, Cambridge
Mansel HP (2011) § 241. In: Jauernig O (ed) BGB. Kommentar, 14th edn. C.H. Beck, München
Marckmann G, Bormuth M, Wiesing U (2012) Allgemeine Einführung in die medizinische Ethik. In: Urban W (ed) Ethik in der Medizin, 4th edn. Reclam, Stuttgart, pp 23–37
Meyer S (2018) Künstliche Intelligenz und die Rolle des Rechts für Innovation. ZRP 51:233–238
Mittelstadt B (2017) The doctor will not see you now. In: Otto P, Gräf E (eds) 3TH1CS: a reinvention of ethics in the digital age? iRights Media, Berlin, pp 68–93
Molnár-Gábor F (2017) Die Regelung der Biotechnologie am Beispiel des Umgangs mit neuen genetischen Analysen. Duncker und Humblot, Berlin
Nuffield Council on Bioethics (2018) Artificial Intelligence (AI) in healthcare and research. Bioethics Briefing Note. May 2018. http://nuffieldbioethics.org/wp-content/uploads/Artificial-Intelligence-AI-in-healthcare-and-research.pdf. Accessed 06 Jan 2019
Oechsler J (2013) Produkthaftungsgesetz. In: Staudinger Kommentar zum Bürgerlichen Gesetzbuch. De Gruyter, Berlin
Ortner R, Daubenbüchel F (2016) Medizinprodukte 4.0 – Haftung, Datenschutz, IT-Sicherheit. Neue Juristische Wochenschrift 69:2918–2924
Parks A (2010) Lifting the Burden of Women's Care work: should robots replace the 'Human Touch'? Hypatia 25:100–120
Quaas M (2018) Die Rechtsbeziehungen zwischen Arzt (Krankenhaus) und Patient. In: Quaas M, Zuck R, Clemens T (eds) Medizinrecht, 4th edn. C.H. Beck, München, pp 240–293
Ranschaert E, Morozov S, Algra P et al (2019) Artificial intelligence in medical imaging. Opportunities, applications and risks. Springer, Berlin
Rössler D (2011) Vom Sinn der Krankheit. In: Voigt F (ed) Akzeptierte Abhängigkeit. Gesammelte Aufsätze zur Ethik, 211

Rolland W (1990) Produkthaftungsrecht. Rehm, München
Sackett DL, Rosenberg WM, Gray JA et al (1996) Evidence based medicine: what it is and what it isn't. Br Med J 312(7023):71–72
Schmidt E (1957) Der Arzt im Strafrecht. In: Ponsold A (ed) Lehrbuch der gerichtlichen Medizin, 2nd edn. Thieme Georg, Stuttgart, pp 1–65
Schneider L (2010) Neue Behandlungsmethoden im Arzthaftungsrecht. Behandlungsfehler – Aufklärungsfehler – Versicherung. Springer, Berlin
Scholz K (2018) § 10 MBÖ-Ä 1997. In: Spickhoff A (ed) Kommentar zum Medizinrecht, 3rd edn. C. H. Beck, München
Schöne-Seifert B (2007) Grundlagen der Medizinethik. Kröner, Stuttgart
Schreiber K (2019) § 630h BGB. In: Nomos Handkommentar zum BGB, 10th edn. Nomos, Baden Baden
Sharkey A, Sharkey N (2012) Granny and the robots: ethical issues in robot care for the elderly. Ethics Inf Technol 14:27–40
Spickhoff A (2018a) § 630a BGB. In: Spickhoff A (ed) Kommentar zum Medizinrecht, 3rd edn. C.H. Beck, München
Spickhoff A (2018b) § 630b BGB. In: Spickhoff A (ed) Kommentar zum Medizinrecht, 3rd edn. C.H. Beck, München
Spindler G (2015) Automation, künstliche Intelligenz, selbststeuernde Kfz – Braucht das Recht neue Haftungskategorien? Computer und Recht 20:767–776
Spindler G (2018) § 823 BGB. In: Beck Online Großkommentar. C.H. Beck, München
Spranger TM (2010) Recht und Bioethik. Mohr Siebeck, Tübingen
Steffen E (1995) Einfluss verminderter Ressourcen und von Finanzierungsgrenzen aus dem Gesundheitsstrukturgesetz auf die Arzthaftung. Medizinrecht 13:190–191
Taupitz J (2002) Grenzen der Patientenautonomie. In: Brugger W, Haverkate G (eds) Grenzen als Thema der Rechts- und Sozialphilosophie. ARSP-Beihefte 84. Franz Steiner, Stuttgart, pp 83–132
Taupitz J (2011) Medizinische Informationstechnologie, leitliniengerechte Medizin und Haftung des Arztes. Archiv für die civilistische Praxis 211:352–394
Thiele F (2013) Arzt-Patient Verhältnis und Menschenwürde. In: Joerden JC, Hilgendorf E, Thiele F (eds) Menschenwürde und Medizin. Ein interdisziplinäres Handbuch. Duncker und Humboldt, Berlin, pp 557–570
The Economist (2018) Artificial intelligence will improve medical treatments. 7 June 2018. https://www.economist.com/science-and-technology/2018/06/07/artificial-intelligence-will-improve-medical-treatments
Van Dam C (2014) European tort law, 2nd edn. Oxford University Press, Oxford
Wachter R (2015) The digital doctor: hope, hype and harm at the dawn of medicine's computer age. McGraw-Hill education, New York
Wagner SA (2018) § 6 MPG. In: Rehmann WA, Wagner SA (eds) Kommentar zum MPG, 3rd edn. C.H. Beck, München
Wallach W, Allen C (2008) Moral machines: teaching robots right from wrong. Oxford University Press, Oxford
Wiesing U (2005) Vom Nutzen und Nachteil der Prinzipienethik für die Medizin. In: Rauprich O, Steger F (eds) Prinzipienethik in der Biomedizin. Moralphilosophie und medizinische Praxis. Kultur der Medizin, vol 14. Campus Verlag, New York, pp 74–87
Wischmeyer T (2018) Regulierung intelligenter Systeme. Archiv des öffentlichen Rechts 143:1–66
Yuste R, Goering S, Arcas BAY (2017) Four ethical priorities for neurotechnologies and AI. Nature 551:159–163
Zech H (2019) Künstliche Intelligenz und Haftungsfragen. ZfPW:198–219

Artificial Intelligence and Competition Law

Moritz Hennemann

Contents

1 Introduction 362
2 Artificial Intelligence 363
   2.1 Definition(s) 364
   2.2 The Current Legal Framework 364
3 Artificial Intelligence and Its Challenges for Competition Law 365
   3.1 Market Definition 365
   3.2 Market Dominance 367
   3.3 Abuse of Market Power 371
   3.4 Prohibition of Cartels and Other Anti-Competitive Agreements 373
   3.5 Merger Control 375
   3.6 Liability 376
   3.7 Conclusions 378
References 383

Abstract Artificial Intelligence (AI) is 'in the air'. The disruptive technologies AI is based on (as well as respective applications) are likely to influence the competition on and for various markets in due course. The handling of opportunities and threats re AI are so far still an open question—and research on the competitive effects of AI has just commenced recently. Statements about AI and the corresponding effects are thereby necessarily only of a temporary nature. From a jurisprudential point of view, it is however important to underline (not only) the framework for AI provided by competition law. On the basis of the 9th amendment of the German Act Against Restraints of Competition (ARC) 2017, German competition law seems to be—to a large extent—adequately prepared for the phenomenon of AI. Nevertheless, considering the characteristics of AI described in this paper, at least the interpretation of German (and European) competition law rules requires an 'update'. In particular,

M. Hennemann (✉)
Institute for Media and Information Law, Department I: Private Law,
Albert-Ludwigs-Universität Freiburg, Freiburg, Germany
e-mail: moritz.hennemann@jura.uni-freiburg.de

tacit collusion as well as systematic predispositions of AI applications re market abuse and cartelization analyzed in this paper are to be pictured. Additionally, this paper stresses that further amendments to (European and German) competition law rules should be examined with respect to the liability for AI and law enforcement, whereby the respective effects on innovation and the market themselves will have to be considered carefully. Against this background, this paper argues that strict liability for AI might lead to negative effects on innovation and discusses a limited liability re public sanctions in analogy to intermediary liability concepts developed in tort law, unfair competition law and intellectual property law. Addressing the topic of a 'legal personality' for AI-based autonomous systems, this paper finally engages with the consequences of such a status for competition law liability.

1 Introduction

AI is facing—for good reason—increasing attention.[1] The debate on AI does not only raise technical questions, but has far-reaching political, ethical, economic, cultural, sociological, and military dimensions.[2] As it is an all-embracing technology, AI has the potential to affect all areas of life: By way of example, one might refer to robots used as 'robot caregiver', possible effects of social and political bots on media pluralism and diversity of opinions,[3] and autonomous weapon systems.[4]

From a competition perspective, it is likely that, in the not too distant future, AI and the related algorithm[5]-based applications will characterize both the competition *for* markets and competition *in* various markets.[6] Already today, there are various algorithm-based business models which attract interest (also) from a competition law perspective.[7] In this context, the current focus lies on the so-called *dynamic*

---

[1]For an introduction see Kaplan (2016) and Brockman (2017).
[2]See Hawking (2016); see also the comments by Elon Musk: Armbruster (2017) and by the Russian president Vladimir Putin: Holland (2017).
[3]See Hennemann (2017b), pp. 28 et seq.; Paal and Hennemann (2016, 2017a, b).
[4]See Federal Foreign Office (2017) as well as the expert commission on 'Lethal Autonomous Weapons Systems (LAWS)' (sic!) established in 2016 by the contracting states of the CCW.
[5]For definitions see OECD (2017), pp. 8 et seq. The OECD distinguishes *monitoring, parallel, signalling* and *self-learning algorithms* (pp. 24 et seq.). On algorithms from a legal perspective in general see Hoffmann-Riem (2017) and Martini (2017) as well as Pasquale (2015).
[6]See Ezrachi and Stucke (2015), pp. 3 et seq. as well as Ezrachi and Stucke (2017), pp. 24 et seq. specifying the various expectations regarding AI and competition law. On corporate management through algorithms and AI see Möslein (2018).
[7]See Ezrachi and Stucke (2016), Gal and Elkin-Koren (2017), Vestager (2017) and European Commission (2017a). See also ECJ C-74/14 'Eturas' (21 January 2016) as well as European Commission (2017b), para 602 et seq., 633 et seq. See to the contrary Schrepel (2017).

algorithmic pricing.[8,9] By way of example, reference can be made to the investigations by the German Federal Cartel Office against *Lufthansa*.[10] However, the identification and (legal) evaluation of the respective business models (and the algorithms used in this context) are still at the beginning.[11,12]

Against this backdrop, the following considerations will focus on the possibilities for approaching the topic of AI in competition law. To begin with, the legal evaluation requires an examination of the term AI. This subsequently enables the identification of the regulatory framework for AI *de lege lata* and *de lege ferenda*. Considering the great complexity of the phenomenon of AI, the main focus will lie on the structural challenges from the perspective of competition law and not on a detailed examination of individual issues or a general discussion on 'traditional' algorithms and competition law.[13]

2 Artificial Intelligence

The concept of AI has its roots in US-American debates of the 1950s[14] and encompasses a wide range of possible applications (Sect. 2.1). There is—*de lege lata*—no comprehensive or specific European or German legal framework regulating AI (Sect. 2.2).

---

[8] See Ebers (2016); Göhsl (2018); Käseberg and von Kalben (2018); Künstner and Franz (2017); Lindsay and McCarthy (2017); Mehra (2015), pp. 1334 et seq.; OECD (2017), p. 16; Roman (2018); Salaschek and Serafimova (2018); Ylinen (2018). For the US-American approach see' US v. Topkins' (2015) concerning the use of a pricing software (mutually agreed upon by the competitors) for the sale of posters, in this regard see also Mehra (2016); summarizing: Assistant Attorney General *Baer* (Department of Justice's Antitrust Division): 'We will not tolerate anticompetitive conduct, whether it occurs in a smoke-filled room or over the Internet using complex pricing algorithms.' (Department of Justice (2015)).

[9] Gal and Elkin-Koren (2017), p. 312 correctly point out that the focus often lies on the 'supply side', even though the use of algorithms (pars pro toto the use of Siri and Alexa) in the age of the 'Internet of Things' and the 'Industry 4.0' also influences the opposite market side (and its (purchase) decisions). See also Göhsl (2018), pp. 124 et seq.

[10] According to media reports, *Lufthansa* was defending itself against the accusation of a price-related abuse of market power (after the declaration of insolvency and the partial acquisition of *Air Berlin*) by stating that a (mere) software was responsible for determining the number of and prices for tickets per booking class—depending on offer and demand, see Spiegel Online (2017).

[11] See Ezrachi and Stucke (2015). See also (concerning specific aspects each) Heinemann and Gebicka (2016), pp. 440 et seq.; Käseberg and von Kalben (2018); Mehra (2015); Petit (2017); Salaschek and Serafimova (2018); Ezrachi and Stucke (2017); Surblytė (2017).

[12] See also OECD (2017), p. 49.

[13] See in that respect Paal (2011, 2012, 2015).

[14] For an introduction see Surblytė (2017), p. 121.

2.1 Definition(s)

4   At least in the public debate, the term 'Artificial Intelligence' is used heterogeneously.[15] Here the term is to be understood in the sense of a 'weak' AI. Such a weak AI—only—encompasses the (advanced) development of technical systems designed to support and facilitate human decision-making processes and actions.

5   Technical systems of weak AI function using mathematical and technological operations. The corresponding operations are no longer based on static and hierarchical if-then-patterns, but are instead characterized by an 'independent' or—rather—'self-learning' mechanisms (*machine learning*).[16] As of now, the highest level of efficiency of these mathematical and technological operations can be achieved by simulating the structure (*neural networks*) of the human brain (*deep learning*).[17] The concept of deep learning is characterized by the evaluation of data through different hierarchical layers. Characteristic features of such an evaluation are, for instance, the autonomous recognition of patterns, hierarchies, and correlations as well as the extraction of decision making parameters.[18] The algorithm underlying the *deep learning* procedure is, in principle,—and this is of crucial importance—adaptive and thus not aimed at being transparent or traceable.[19] Against this backdrop, AI based on *deep learning*, which this paper will further elaborate on, must be distinguished from the mechanisms based on 'traditional' if-then algorithms.

2.2 The Current Legal Framework

7   AI-based systems raise a number of questions from different fields of law.[20] There is, however, no *special* regulatory framework for AI technologies, the employment thereof or the business models based thereon. The reason for this lack of regulation is, aside from the dynamics of the development(s), the interdisciplinary nature of the matter.[21] Moreover, there currently exists no exclusive right to data ('data ownership')[22] which would otherwise (also) shape the competition *for* and *with*

---

[15] Cf. also Djeffal, para 3 et seq.
[16] OECD (2017), p. 9.
[17] See Kaplan (2016), pp. 28 et seq.; Surblytė (2017), pp. 121 et seq.
[18] Cf. Kaplan (2016), p. 34.
[19] OECD (2017), p. 11. Cf. Surblytė (2017), pp. 121 et seq. This is further underlined by reports stating that 'communicating' AI systems had developed their own 'language' (which—considering the mechanism behind AI—was not surprising but rather had to be anticipated), see Novet (2017).
[20] See the contributions in Gless and Seelmann (2016); (regarding the field of robotics) Leroux (2012) as well as, inter alia, see Ernst, paras 25 et seq.; Marsch, paras 1 et seq.; Tischbirek, paras 14 et seq.; Schemmel, paras 17 et seq.; Braun and Binder, paras 2 et seq.
[21] See also the initial considerations by the European Parliament (2017) and see in general: European Commission (2017d).
[22] Concerning the discussion see European Commission (2017c), p. 13 as well as Berberich and Golla (2016); Böhm (2016); Dorner (2014); Drexl (2017); Drexl et al. (2016); Ehlen and Brandt

AI.[23] In fact, the current legal and regulatory framework for technologies and business models based on AI is *de lege lata*—to a great extent—constituted and shaped by the general European (and the largely identical national) competition law(s).

3 Artificial Intelligence and Its Challenges for Competition Law

The competition law analysis of AI and big data mirrors the concept of the *more technological approach*.[24] For the purposes of this analysis, a fundamental distinction must therefore be made between the technologies of AI on one hand and the business models based on these technologies on the other. Both scenarios raise questions concerning the definition of the relevant market (Sect. 3.1), the determination of market power (Sect. 3.2), the abuse of market power (Sect. 3.3), the prohibition of cartels and anti-competitive agreements (Sect. 3.4), the regulation of mergers (Sect. 3.5) as well as the responsibility and liability under competition law (Sect. 3.6), all of which entail different implications for an adequate legal regulation *de lege ferenda* (Sect. 3.7). 8

3.1 Market Definition

First, the relevant markets for the competition *for* AI and the competition *with* AI have to be defined. 9

The Competition *for* AI

To begin with, there exists (and will continue to exist) competition *for* AI technologies. In this context, the definition of the relevant market (or relevant markets) raises various difficult questions as to its (or their) geographical and material delimitations. Regarding the geographical delimitation of markets, it is already questionable whether a distinction between different territories can or should (still) be made, since the markets in question may be of a global nature. However, with 10

(2016); Ensthaler (2016); Fezer (2017a, b); Grützmacher (2016); Härting (2016); Heymann (2016, 2015); Malgieri (2016); Paal and Hennemann (2017c), p. 1698; Schwartmann and Hentsch (2016); Specht (2016); Specht and Rohmer (2016); Zech (2015).

[23] See Surblytė (2017), pp. 124 et seq. for the negative consequences that such an exclusive right to AI-induced innovation may entail.

[24] Podszun (2015, 2014).

regard to other factors (such as language, culture, and technology as well as the respective legal framework) regional or national markets are also conceivable.

11 The relevant product market is determined in accordance with the well-established concept of demand-side substitution, i.e. according to the demands of the opposite market side.[25] Pursuant to this concept, the relevant product market consists of all those goods or services which the opposite market side compares and reasonably regards as interchangeable or substitutable for the fulfillment of a certain need.[26] In this context, certain technologies may (in the future) become the new (industrial) standards and thus shape their own product markets. An example for such a development could be a potential standard for AI-based technologies used for (traffic compatible) autonomous driving.

The Competition *with* AI

12 The relevant geographical and product market must also be defined for the competition *with* AI, i.e. the competition with AI-based applications. Depending on the specific technical application, a geographical distinction could be made between regional and global markets. In the sense of the demand market concept, a detailed analysis is required as to whether and to what extent 'conventional' goods or services can be functionally replaced by AI applications—or whether such applications, on the other hand, create independent 'new' markets. Regarding the product market and in line with the concept of demand-side substitution, it must be analyzed whether and to what extent 'traditional' goods or services can reasonably be regarded as interchangeable with applications of AI or whether these respective applications rather established independent and 'new' product markets. This may be exemplified when considering the aforementioned 'robot caregivers'.

13 In the innovative, dynamic, and disruptive field of AI, the consideration of potential markets is also of particular relevance.[27] It is already foreseeable that undertakings will (also) prepare themselves for future markets by collecting large amounts of data in order to secure a 'first mover advantage'.[28] In general, it is possible that—in the near future—this could (again) lead to an innovative competition *for* the respective market and not *on* the market.[29]

---

[25]Bechtold and Bosch (2015), Sec. 18 paras 5, 7.
[26]Bechtold and Bosch (2015), Sec. 18 para 7 with further references.
[27]Surblytė (2017), p. 121; cf. for a general overview Bechtold and Bosch (2015), Sec. 18 para 22.
[28]Surblytė (2017), p. 122; cf. also Grave (2017), Chapter 2 para 65.
[29]Surblytė (2017), p. 122.

3.2 Market Dominance

As a prerequisite for the prohibition of the abuse of market power, it must further be determined whether an undertaking holds a dominant position on the relevant market.[30]

The Ninth Amendment of the German ARC 2017

Pursuant to Sec. 18 (1) of the German ARC 2017, an undertaking is dominant where, as a supplier or purchaser of a certain type of good or commercial service on the relevant product and geographic market, it has no competitors (1), is not exposed to any substantial competition (2), or has a paramount market position in relation to its competitors (3). The following considerations will focus and elaborate on the criterion of the 'paramount market position' as stated in Sec. 18 (3) No. 3 ARC. In the course of the Ninth Amendment of the ARC in 2017, it was set out in the new Sec. 18 (3a) ARC that when assessing the market position of an undertaking, in particular in the case of multi-sided markets and networks, regard should be given to certain additional criteria. These criteria include direct and indirect network effects, the parallel use of services from different providers, and the switching costs for users, the undertaking's economies of scale arising in connection with network effects, the undertaking's access to data relevant for competition as well as the innovation-driven competitive pressure.[31] These newly codified criteria serve to clarify and specify the definition of market dominance. A closer examination reveals that the newly codified provision does not change competition law in substance.[32] At the same time, Sec. 18 (3a) ARC does, nevertheless, emphasize the necessity of a meticulous analysis of the particularities of digital, often multi-sided markets. Such multi-sided markets—and thus the criteria laid down in Sec. 18 (3a) ARC—will also play a decisive role when it comes to technologies of AI and the applications based thereon. Of the multitude of factors and different characteristics of innovation-driven markets, questions concerning data and 'data power' as well as the transparency of market-related information—which will be examined in more detail in the following—are likely to gain significance.

---

[30]The definition of market dominance is also of relevance to merger control (cf. Sect. 3.5), cf. only Grave (2017), Chapter 2 para 8.
[31]For further details see Grave (2017), Chapter 2 paras 1 et seq.; Paal and Hennemann (2018), pp. 68 et seq.
[32]Grave (2017), Chapter 2 para 10; Paal and Hennemann (2018), p. 68.

'Data Power'

16   In order to allow an adequate assessment of market dominance, the essential 'resource' and driving force behind the development of AI, i.e. data, must be examined. In this context, particular attention must be paid to the question whether and to what extent an undertaking's AI-related data(base) can lead to a dominant position on the market.[33] This mainly depends on the type of data and their specific use. Other decisive factors are also the personal or non-personal nature of the data in question, the quality of the data, the degree of exclusivity of the data and whether and to what extent third party rights of utilization and access exist. It should be noted that some access to data which could influence competition (cf. Sec. 18 (3a) No. 4 ARC) does not automatically lead to the assumption of a special market 'power'.[34] Instead, the focus must lie on a *special* access to data, which may enable the undertaking to escape competitive pressure.[35] Moreover, the degree of interoperability of the data formats used for AI—both between the competitors on a single market as well as between undertakings on different levels—will also play a key role in the assessment of an undertaking's market position.[36]

17   In view of the abovementioned findings, it should be noted that an undertaking which is in control over a certain 'data power' and/or sets standards for a certain AI-based technology cannot automatically be classified as holding a dominant position on the market. Instead, it should rather be taken into account, especially when referring to the innovative and dynamic field of AI, that a new development can quickly cause the markets to 'tip' despite the existence of an (absolute) market leader.[37] An undertaking could use its 'data power' to tip the market towards its own product (self-reinforcing effect).[38] Similarly, an undertaking which has set a standard for (certain) AI (and made this standard available as an open source) could rely on network- and corresponding lock-in-effects to achieve or secure the tipping of the market in its own favor.[39] However, the tendency of a market to tip generally depends on a number of other factors, such as the practice of *multihoming*, i.e. the parallel use of multiple services by

---

[33] Regarding the general discussion on data and data power in competition law see Autorité de la concurrence and Bundeskartellamt (2016), pp. 25 et seq.; Birnstiel and Eckel (2016); Grave (2017), Chapter 2 para 50 et seq.; Grave and Nyberg (2017); Holzweber (2016); Körber (2016); Paal und Hennemann (2018), pp. 49 et seq.; Tamke (2017); Nuys (2016); Telle (2017).

[34] See Körber (2016), pp. 305 et seq.

[35] Grave (2017), Chapter 2 para 51. See for further details Paal and Hennemann (2018), pp. 51 seq.

[36] Concerning the relevance of data for the assessment of an undertaking's market position see the elaborations of the president of the German Federal Cartel Office Andreas Mundt with regard to the proceedings against *Facebook*: '(...) *data, as in Facebook' case, are a crucial factor for the economic dominance of a company. On the one hand the social network offers a free service, on the other it offers attractive advertising space, which is so valuable because Facebook has huge amounts of personalized data at its disposal"*, Bundeskartellamt (2017b) (translated).

[37] In this context, the development of the market of mobile devices, which drastically changed with the introduction of modern smart phones (i.e. iPhone), may serve as a striking 'historic' example.

[38] See Grave (2017), Chapter 2 para 28; Paal and Hennemann (2018), pp. 51 et seq.

[39] In this context see Grave (2017), Chapter 2 para 29; Paal and Hennemann (2018), p. 52; Surblyté (2017), p. 123.

the opposite market side (cf. Sec. 18 (3a) No. 2 ARC).[40] In this context, the degree of interoperability of the data formats used is—again—of particular importance. Depending on the individual case, data and standards could create market entry barriers for AI and the applications based thereon.[41]

Lastly, with regard to personal data, related aspects of data protection law must also be taken into consideration. The 'value' of such data (also) depends on the legality of the processing of data granted under data protection law for the purposes of AI.[42] Particularly considering network- and lock-in-effects, Art. 20 of the General Data Protection Regulation (GDPR) introduces a right to data portability,[43] intended to facilitate switching to (or *multihoming* with) another provider. The effectiveness of this right—and thus its relevance for the determination of an undertaking's market position—ultimately depends on the interoperability between the respective market participants, even though this is not set out as a mandatory requirement under data protection law.

Transparency of Market-Related Information

When assessing market dominance, another essential factor that must be considered is the immediate (internet-based) availability of a large amount of market-related information. On one hand, this enables the access to information and the exchange thereof, which serves as an innovative driving source and regularly allows for a (desirable) transparency of the market. On the other hand, it must also be kept in mind that the ability to make use of this transparency largely depends on the efficient and rapid performance of the systems used. In the near future, market participants lacking such efficient systems may fall behind. The only undertakings that would remain capable of competition would be the ones equipped with the systems necessary for the exploitation of the abovementioned transparency. The availability of such systems would then constitute a market entry barrier, i.e. a factor that could hinder other market participants from entering a specific market (cf. Sec. 18 (3) No. 5 ARC).[44]

In addition, it should be noted that there exists a connection between market transparency, the use of algorithms, and *tacit collusion*. *Tacit collusion* is generally permissible and does not fall under the prohibition of cartels and anti-competitive agreements.[45] *Tacit collusion* may, however, be directly relevant to the determination of collective dominance on a relevant market and can lead to *supra competitive*

---

[40]Grave (2017), Chapter 2 para 33, 37 et seq.; Paal and Hennemann (2018), pp. 50 et seq.
[41]See also Käseberg and von Kalben (2018), p. 3.
[42]Cf. Grave (2017), Chapter 2 para 42, 52 et seq. For further detail with regard to data see also Paal and Hennemann (2018), pp. 36 et seq., 51.
[43]For further detail see Hennemann (2017a).
[44]Ezrachi and Stucke (2015), p. 24.
[45]See for instance—in the context of pricing algorithms—Käseberg and von Kalben (2018), p. 5; Salaschek and Serafimova (2018), p. 13; Ylinen (2018), pp. 21 et seq. For considerations regarding a revision of the requirements 'agreements' and 'concerted practices' see Mehra (2015), pp. 1359 et seq.; OECD (2017), pp. 36 et seq. and (to the contrary) Lindsay and McCarthy (2017). Regarding

pricing.[46] In their widely acclaimed work on *Virtual Competition*, *Ezrachi* and *Stucke*, in particular, make the assumption that there is an increase in *tacit collusion* when it comes to algorithm-based business models.[47] According to the authors, the decisive factor for this correlation is the high level of transparency of data and information as an integral part of these business models and thus the ability to react to other competitors' behavior in real time.[48] Furthermore, the use of algorithm-based systems would facilitate conscious parallel behavior especially on markets with a large number of competitors.[49]

21 However, it should also be kept in mind that the pricing strategies associated with the digital economy may not always be compatible with conscious parallel behavior.[50] Pricing strategies based on algorithms are generally intended to set personalized and dynamic prices and to adjust (and update) these prices automatically depending on contractual partners and interested parties. On this basis, algorithm-based pricing strategies which do not disclose relevant information—e.g. information on an individual user—to all market participants could be less prone to *tacit collusion(s)*. Similarly, it is argued that—at least—the use of heterogeneous algorithms could impede conscious parallel behavior between different market participants.[51]

22 Nevertheless, the outlined predispositions of *tacit collusion* are likely to intensify when it comes to the competition *with* AI, i.e. adaptive algorithms, if respective algorithms do use the same pool of data and rely on complete market transparency.[52] This is due to the mechanism behind the previously examined *deep learning*: The algorithms are designed to recognize and analyze patterns, hierarchies, and correlations by comparing data. The results of this analysis are then used to constantly adjust the decisive decision-making parameters and could eventually lead to the alignment of the different systems. Furthermore, it cannot be ruled out that even rather heterogeneous algorithms will be able to 'understand' each other, meaning that they will be capable of (preliminarily) assessing and (sufficiently) anticipating the functions of the other algorithm.

---

the existence of *plus factors* in connection with oligopolistic constellations see Gal and Elkin-Koren (2017), pp. 346 et seq.; cf. also Göhsl (2018), p. 123.

[46]See Ezrachi and Stucke (2017), pp. 26, 46 et seq.; see also (and for further references) Salaschek and Serafimova (2018), p. 10.

[47]Ezrachi and Stucke (2016), pp. 56 et seq.; Ezrachi and Stucke (2015), pp. 7, 23 et seq., 32; Ezrachi and Stucke (2017), pp. 3 et seq.; see also Gal and Elkin-Koren (2017), pp. 344 et seq.; Göhsl (2018), p. 121; Mehra (2015), pp. 1343 et seq. as well as OECD (2017), pp. 18 et seq.; to the contrary Petit (2017). See also European Commission (2017b), para 608. For an economic analysis (supporting a correlation between the use of pricing algorithms and tacit collusions) see Salcedo (2015). See also the analysis by Harrington (2017).

[48]Ezrachi and Stucke (2017), p. 4. See for instance also Göhsl (2018), p. 121 with further references.

[49]Ezrachi and Stucke (2017), p. 8. See also Ylinen (2018), p. 21.

[50]Petit (2017), p. 361; cf. also Ezrachi and Stucke (2017), p. 15.

[51]Petit (2017), pp. 361 et seq.

[52]See Ezrachi and Stucke (2016), pp. 71 et seq. ('Artificial Intelligence, God View, and the Digital Eye'). Cf. also Autorité de la concurrence and Bundeskartellamt (2016), p. 15: '[T]acit collusion could also be the result of sophisticated machine-learning.'

3.3 Abuse of Market Power

It is further necessary to analyze which specific questions may arise with regard to a potential abuse of a dominant position on the market (Sec. 18 et seq. ARC, Art. 102 TFEU) in connection with technologies and applications of AI. With regard to the large number of possible scenarios involving the abuse of market power, a restriction must be made in the context of AI. Therefore, this paper will refrain from elaborating on long established constellations and will focus on the ones of particular relevance in the context of adaptive algorithms. Pars pro toto, it should be noted that a 'classic' exploitive abuse involving unfair prices or conditions in connection with the trade of data can be considered, if certain (personal or non-personal) data of a (dominant) undertaking are essential for certain applications.[53] In constellations relating to intellectual property law, it must be asked whether protective rights for AI-based technologies constitute essential facilities (cf. Sec. 19 (2) No. 4 ARC).[54]   23

Standard-Essential Know-How

For the markets in question, a possible scenario for the abuse of market power could be the denial of access to standard-essential know-how concerning technologies or applications of AI. The ability to access certain information is of crucial importance for securing interoperability. The (first) legal standards for the competition law assessment of interoperability were set out 10 years ago in the EC-*Microsoft*-case. Back then, *Microsoft* dominated the market for (personal computer) operating systems and was *de facto* able to set a market standard. The company made the corresponding software interfaces freely available to others until it reached a 'critical mass' on the market. With regard to the information necessary for interoperability, *Microsoft* then relied on the protection of trade secrets. The subsequent competition law proceedings[55] raised general questions concerning the conflict between the abuse of power and the protection of innovation. The combination of data and AI will likely lead to comparable constellations in the near future. The current approach (co-)established by the *Microsoft* case[56] can (and should) be applied to the assessment of the abuse of market power in cases involving the setting of new standards and issues of innovation. Access claims and/or compulsory licenses serve as a balancing mechanism.[57] Furthermore, it is of particular importance to strike a   24

---

[53]Surblytė (2017), p. 124.
[54]For questions related to potential *reverse engineering* see Surblytė (2017), p. 126.
[55]See EC T-201/04 'Microsoft' (17. September 2007); relating thereto Huttenlauch and Lübbig (2016), para. 265 et seq.; Surblytė (2017), p. 123.
[56]In connection with Sec. 19 (2) No. 4 ARC see Loewenheim (2016), para. 82 et seq.; concerning essential facilities see also Kling and Thomas (2016), § 6 para 115 et seq., § 20 para 200 et seq.; Huttenlauch and Lübbig (2016), para 271 et seq.
[57]Cf. also Drexl (2017), pp. 418 et seq.

balance between the negative effects for individuals and the positive effects for the (entire) economic sector.[58] In this regard, special attention should be paid to the criterion of innovation, since a decrease in competition on concentrated markets will likely lead to negative innovation effects.

The Use of AI

25 Moreover, it is also difficult to determine the existence of an abuse of market power committed *by* an AI technology. By definition, a specific adaptive algorithm can only be influenced at the starting point of its 'creation'. Therefore, it is of great importance to analyze whether and to what extent AI technologies exhibit an inherent predisposition towards the abuse of market power.[59] One may presume that the 'perfect' AI system may possible also be the most anti-competitive. Especially, the most 'efficient' AI systems could regard an abusive competitive behavior as economically advantageous for the undertaking and apply it.[60] Such a conduct could be particularly relevant when it comes to the determination of (selling) prices and other conditions, (price) discrimination[61], and the transfer of market power to a different market.[62]

26 Other related aspects that should also be taken into consideration is the non-price-related competition with respect to privacy and behavioral discrimination.[63] AI systems could, for instance, evaluate and analyze user behavior and (potentially) discriminate in accordance with their findings. In addition, AI-based systems could be employed to customize or 'tailor' the utilized non-price related conditions such as general terms and conditions or data protection consent declarations.

27 If such a use of systems based on AI leads to violations of unfair terms law, data protection law and consumer law, then—under competition law—this could constitute an exploitive abuse by imposing unfair trading conditions. For instance, in connection with a specifically demanded declaration of consent,[64] a violation of data protection law or the law relating to unfair terms and conditions could be of relevance from a competition law perspective. In this respect, the current proceedings before the German Federal Cartel Office against *Facebook* may serve as an

---

[58] Cf. Surblytė (2017), p. 123 in connection with EC 'Microsoft' (cf. fn. 55).
[59] See Ezrachi and Stucke (2015), pp. 9, 22 et seq. To the contrary: Petit (2017), p. 361.
[60] See Ezrachi and Stucke (2017), pp. 38 et seq.
[61] See Ezrachi and Stucke (2017), p. 15.
[62] See Ezrachi and Stucke (2016), pp. 85 et seq.
[63] Petit (2017), p. 361; Ezrachi and Stucke (2015), pp. 7, 32; Ezrachi and Stucke (2017), pp. 15 et seq.; Ezrachi and Stucke (2016), pp. 101 et seq. See also Mehra (2015), pp. 1369 et seq. For questions relating to Sec. 21 ARC see Künstner and Franz (2017), p. 692.
[64] In regard to general terms and conditions of declarations of consent under data protection law see German Federal Court of Justice (BGH) III ZR 213/83 'Schufa-Klausel' (19 September 1985); BGH VIII ZR 348/06 'Payback' (16 July 2008) para 19 et seq.; BGH VIII ZR 12/08 'Happy Digits' (11 November 2009) para 7 et seq.; as well as (relating to the GDPR) Hennemann (2017c), pp. 548 et seq.

example.[65] The Federal Cartel office is investigating *Facebook* for the potential abuse of general terms and conditions which violate the data protection law.[66] The investigations are (also) based on the decision of the German Federal Court of Justice in the case *VBL-Gegenwert*.[67] According to this decision, the use of inadmissible standard terms constitutes an abuse of conditions, if the inadmissible clauses are an expression of the undertaking's market power.[68] Therefore, it must be decided whether the specific terms and conditions—which violate data protection law—deviate from those conditions that would likely have been applied in the case of an effective competition on the market and whether the respective undertaking's dominant market position was the cause for this deviation.[69] This case demonstrates that the examination of other areas of law can generally—and not only in connection with AI—play an important role in the field of (European and German) competition law.

3.4 Prohibition of Cartels and Other Anti-Competitive Agreements

Technologies based on AI and uses thereof also require special attention with regard to the ban on cartels according to Sec. 1 ARC, Art. 101 TFEU.[70] Anti-competitive agreements made in the 'real' world and only implemented by algorithms (the algorithm acting as a 'messenger')[71] as well as algorithms which were deliberately programmed to act in violation of competition law[72] shall not be discussed in the following. Instead, the focus will lie on exchange of information, *Hub-and-Spoke*-scenarios, and 'agreements' between AI systems.[73]

28

---

[65]Cf. the press release by the German Federal Cartel Office dated 2 March 2016, Bundeskartellamt (2016) and 19 December 2017, Bundeskartellamt (2017b) as well as Bundeskartellamt (2017a), p. 12. See also the press release by the German Federal Cartel Office relating to the launch of the sector inquiry into SmartTVs dated 13 December 2017, Bundeskartellamt (2017c).

[66]Regarding the proceedings and questions concerning competition law connected hereto see Franck (2016); Podszun and de Toma (2016), p. 2993; Wiemer (2018).

[67]See Bundeskartellamt (2017a), p. 12.

[68]See BGH KZR 58/11 'VBL-Gegenwert' (6 November 2011) para 65. Regarding general terms and conditions under competition law see Thomas (2017) as well as BGH KZR 47/14 'VBL-Gegenwert II' (24 Jan 2017). For the decision ECJ C-32/11 'Allianz Hungária' (14 March 2013) see Franck (2016), pp. 142 et seq.

[69]For a detailed assessment cf. Franck (2016), pp. 145 et seq., 151 et seq. with further references.

[70]For a classification of different scenarios regarding algorithms in general see Ezrachi and Stucke (2015), p. 10 et seq. as well as Salaschek and Serafimova (2018), pp. 10 et seq.

[71]See for example Ezrachi and Stucke (2016), pp. 39 et seq. as well as Salaschek and Serafimova (2018), p. 11; Ylinen (2018), p. 20.

[72]This was applied e.g. in the proceedings 'US v. Topkins' (2015) (cf. fn. 8) and ECJ 'Eturas' (cf. fn. 7). On these and other examples see Käseberg and von Kalben (2018), pp. 3 et seq. as well as Salaschek and Serafimova (2018), p. 16; Ylinen (2018), p. 20.

[73]On the use of a spied out (or otherwise illegally obtained) algorithm see Salaschek and Serafimova (2018), pp. 13 et seq.

Exchange of Information and *Hub-and-Spoke*-Scenarios

29 First, the availability of market-related information used by AI systems is to be considered. Whilst transparency of information is fundamentally pro-competitive, a possible *exchange* of information associated therewith may need to be reviewed from a competition law perspective,[74] as it reduces the strategic uncertainty on the relevant market.[75] In this context, it is therefore important to distinguish between conscious parallel behavior and behavior covered by the ban on cartels, e.g. concerted practice.[76] However, the borders blur, especially with regard to so-called *signalling*.[77] In this context, the ECJ observes in its *Eturas* decision: '[E]ach economic operator must determine independently the policy which it intends to adopt on the common market. Such a requirement of autonomy thus strictly precludes any direct or indirect contact between economic operators of such a kind as either to influence the conduct on the market of an actual or potential competitor or to reveal to such a competitor the conduct which an operator has decided to follow itself or contemplates adopting on the market, where the object or effect of those contacts is to give rise to conditions of competition which do not correspond to the normal conditions of the market in question (...)'.[78] Concerted practice may thus exist if the applied AI systems have an inherent predisposition to form cartels.[79] In the specific context of *dynamic pricing algorithms,* some authors have already pointed out that the use of standardized algorithms and data may lead to an anticompetitive exchange of information or so-called *Hub-and-Spoke*-scenarios.[80,81] This may be the case if the algorithm-based *pricing* is carried out by way of outsourcing, and several respective service providers access identical algorithms or (widely available) data.[82]

---

[74] See ECJ C-8/08 'T-Mobile Netherlands' (4 June 2009). It has been rightly pointed out that the combination of market transparency and the use of algorithms can foster the stabilization of cartels, as deviations from the agreed conditions by cartel members can be tracked in real-time, see for example Salaschek and Serafimova (2018), p. 10 as well as OECD (2017), pp. 26 et seq.

[75] Grave and Nyberg (2016), Art. 101 TFEU para 240 et seq.

[76] On the definition of concerted practice and on its distinction from conscious parallel behaviour see Kling and Thomas (2016), § 5 para 69 et seq., 83 et seq.

[77] See Ylinen (2018), p. 21.

[78] ECJ 'Eturas' (cf. fn. 7) para 27.

[79] See also Künstner and Franz (2017), p. 691.

[80] See on *Hub-and-Spoke*-scenarios Kling and Thomas (2016), § 19 para 123.

[81] Ezrachi and Stucke (2017), pp. 13 et seq.; Ezrachi and Stucke (2016), pp. 46 et seq. See also Käseberg and von Kalben (2018), p. 4; Salaschek and Serafimova (2018), p. 12.

[82] Ezrachi and Stucke (2017), pp. 13 et seq. See also Gal and Elkin-Koren (2017), p. 348. For a legal justification (pointing to a potentially more innovative form of competition) cf. Salaschek and Serafimova (2018), p. 12; cf. in this context also Göhsl (2018), p. 123.

'Agreements' Between AI Systems

Equally possible is a 'disruptive' scenario where different applications of AI—e.g. 'agents' used for trading—make (horizontal or vertical) anti-competitive agreements 'among themselves' or show concerted behavior.[83] In this context, it is presumed that the systems pursue the (defined) aim of maximizing the profits of the undertakings using them. In order to reach this objective, the systems will—in accordance with the basic mechanism of *deep learning*—aim to find the most favorable decision-making parameters by comparing and matching data as well as analysing patterns, hierarchies, and correlations.[84] As a (logical) result, the systems may conclude that it is most favorable to make an anticompetitive 'agreement' with the competitor's system.[85] The systems may thus 'want' to reach the aim of maximizing profit in a 'better' and more secure way by forming a cartel.[86] Even if one were to negate a concurrence of wills (in the sense of an agreement) of the undertakings behind the AI systems in this case, a concerted behavior may (in accordance with the case law of the ECJ based on its *Eturas*-decision) nevertheless come into question.[87] In that case, the undertakings applying such systems would potentially become cartel members[88] without having aimed to do so.[89] The decision-making process of the AI systems would by definition remain a *black box*.[90] Proving anti-competitive behavior would thus become much more difficult, even if the applied (and highly complex) adaptive algorithm were to be documented.[91]

30

3.5 Merger Control

In the context of merger control, the findings on AI could *de lege lata* already be taken into account more strongly.[92] This is especially true for the discussed effects of AI (and data as their 'resource') on the assessment of the undertakings' market

---

[83]Ezrachi and Stucke (2017), pp. 13, 39. See also Gal and Elkin-Koren (2017), pp. 344 et seq.; Käseberg and von Kalben (2018), pp. 4 et seq.; Mehra (2015), p. 1368; Salaschek and Serafimova (2018), p. 13 as well as OECD (2017), pp. 38 et seq.
[84]See also Salaschek and Serafimova (2018), p. 13.
[85]See Käseberg and von Kalben (2018), p. 3 with further references.
[86]Ezrachi and Stucke (2015), pp. 23 et seq.; Ezrachi and Stucke (2017), pp. 38 et seq.; OECD (2017), p. 31.
[87]Correctly Käseberg and von Kalben (2018), p. 5. See also Heinemann and Gebicka (2016), p. 440: '[T]he 'Cartel of the Machines' amounts to a cartel between undertakings. In these cases, traditional meetings or forms of communication are replaced by an algorithm which renders direct concertation superfluous.' Differing view Göhsl (2018), p. 122. See also Ebers (2016), p. 555.
[88]For questions of liability and responsibility cf. Sect. 3.6.
[89]OECD (2017), p. 31.
[90]OECD (2017), p. 33.
[91]Focusing on this aspect Lindsay and McCarthy (2017), p. 537.
[92]See Ezrachi and Stucke (2017), pp. 45 et seq.; OECD (2017), pp. 41 et seq.

position.[93] In the framework of future mergers, it will therefore be necessary to review which (conglomerate) effects the merger of (certain) data sets[94] and AI technologies could have on the affected markets. For instance, one will have to review if the combination of certain technologies (and potentially also of certain data) impairs fair competition *for* AI. As for the competition *with* AI, one will especially have to consider potential predispositions for conscious parallel behavior as discussed above and a possible collective market dominance associated therewith. This means that coordinated effects will have to be taken into focus even if there are various market players involved.[95]

3.6 Liability

31 In order to be responsible for the use of AI systems, the system's 'behavior' must be attributable to the respective undertaking. *Attribution* in this context refers to the objectively determinable misconduct.[96]

32 In this context and first, the parameters of attribution for the actions of an undertaking's employees are to be taken into account.[97] In general, undertakings are liable for wrongful behavior of their employees (*abstract responsibility*).[98] There is, however, no consensus on the question whether it makes a difference if an employee exceeds his or her internal or external power of representation or does not follow given instructions.[99] There are good reasons to argue that it is sufficient that the employee (who does not need to be identified individually[100]) was entrusted with the conclusion of agreements.[101] In that case, one can at least assume a respective power of representation of the employee.[102]

---

[93] Cf. Sect. 3.2. On the relevance of data in the process of merger controls see European Commission Decision COMP/M.4731—Google/DoubleClick (11 March 2008) para 364 and European Commission decision COMP/M.7217—Facebook/WhatsApp (3 October 2014).

[94] See Bundeskartellamt (2017a), pp. 9 et seq.

[95] Ezrachi and Stucke (2017), pp. 45 et seq.; OECD (2017), p. 41.

[96] On the difference between objectively determinable misconduct and fault (which is in some cases additionally required, e.g. for fines under Art. 23 (2) Reg. EU 1/2003) see Brömmelmeyer (2017), pp. 174 et seq.

[97] See *ECJ C-68/12* 'Protimonopolný' *(7 February 2013) para 22;* ECJ C-542/14 'SIA "VM Remonts"' (21 July 2016) para 20 et seq. with further references. For further details see Brömmelmeyer (2017), p. 175 et seq.

[98] Brömmelmeyer (2017), pp. 175 et seq. The ECJ ('SIA VM Remonts' cf. fn. 97 para 27) particularly affirmed an attribution in the case of 'a service provider which presents itself as independent is in fact acting under the direction or control of an undertaking ', citing its previous decisions in the case 'FNV Kunsten Informatie en Media'.

[99] For a discussion of the different opinions see Brömmelmeyer (2017), p. 176.

[100] ECJ C-338/00 'Volkswagen' (18 September 2003) para 98.

[101] See Roth and Ackermann (2017), Art. 81 para 1 EG Grundfragen para 212; Füller (2016), Art. 101 AEUV para 114 (highly debated).

[102] Brömmelmeyer (2017), p. 177.

The aforementioned principles should be applied *mutatis mutandis* to AI systems, especially when two (or more) systems make (anti-competitive) agreements on behalf of their respective undertakings.[103] The use of AI systems functionally replaces the respective (deliberately acting) employee and can be traced back to a specific human decision by an employee within the undertaking. The fact that the respective algorithms were programmed by a third party can thus not serve to exonerate the undertaking.[104] Rather, the decision to use a certain system generally determines a liability for the 'actions' of the system.[105,106] The attribution of certain behavior is thus linked to the respective competent decision maker.[107] When in breach of competition law, an AI system might 'act' in a way that is unintended by the undertaking, but still falls within the scope of its entrusted competences. Therefore, the competition law-violation comes 'from within the undertaking'.[108] It follows from the foregoing that undertakings are liable for all violations of competition law resulting from the use of AI.[109]

33

From a competition law perspective, the use of adaptive algorithms must thus be considered a potential 'hazard'[110] and is subject to a 'strict liability'.[111] The respective undertaking must bear the full operational risk inherent in adaptive algorithms. Such an extensive attribution is, however, not without doubt, as it might considerably inhibit innovation. Notwithstanding the necessary balance between disincentive effects on individuals and positive macroeconomic effects, the use of technologies based on AI bears substantial liability risks. A different appraisal would be appropriate if anti-competitive behavior of adaptive algorithms could be (largely) prevented using technical means.

34

---

[103]Dissenting opinion *(de lege lata)* Salaschek and Serafimova (2018), pp. 15 et seq. They cite the predictability as a decisive criterion, referring to the *Eturas* decision by the ECJ (cf. fn. 7). In that case, however, the position of an *independent* service provider was at issue (cf. Sect. Legal Personality of AI Systems).

[104]See Salaschek and Serafimova (2018), p. 15.

[105]See Vestager (2017): 'And businesses also need to know that when they decide to use an automated system, they will be held responsible for what it does.' Similarly Käseberg and von Kalben (2018), p. 7.

[106]See also BGH VI ZR 269/12 'Autocomplete' (14 May 2013) para 17.

[107]Dissenting opinion *(de lege lata)* Salaschek and Serafimova (2018), p. 14. They assume with regard to pricing algorithms that one would have to prove that the undertaking knew about the price coordination, and only consider a (rebuttable) presumption of the knowledge *de lege ferenda*.

[108]Brömmelmeyer (2017), p. 177.

[109]Dissenting opinion Salaschek and Serafimova (2018), p. 16. See also Ylinen (2018), p. 22.

[110]Similarly Salaschek and Serafimova (2018), p. 16.

[111]See Käseberg and von Kalben (2018), p. 7.

3.7 Conclusions

35 Effective legal compliance when using AI may *prima facie* seem like a theoretical desideratum—or, to put it in the words of the EU-Commissioner *Vestager*: '[They] need to be built in a way that doesn't allow them to collude.'[112] To reach this aim, all legal requirements would need to be implemented into the code of the systems, enabling an 'embedded compliance'.[113] Realistically, one will have to concede that an integration of all competition law requirements and other legal provisions into the code of an adaptive algorithm is an enormous challenge for programming, the accomplishment of which does not seem to be entirely possible (yet).[114] It is therefore necessary to discuss possible regulatory options. However, this discussion is still in its infancy.[115]

Public Enforcement and the Future Legal Framework

36 From the viewpoint of competition authorities, the question arises which (other) options to monitor and control AI systems and adaptive algorithms there are. *De lege ferenda*, different regulatory options (which do not necessarily have to be implemented cumulatively) are conceivable. When implementing any of these options, one will especially have to take into account that AI systems are not geared for transparency, making monitoring much more difficult.[116] In general, auditing an algorithm prior to its use or at regular intervals is therefore of limited use.[117] However, one should consider subjecting undertakings to certain compliance duties regarding the adaptive algorithms they use (*anti-trust compliance by design*).[118] Moreover, undertakings could be obligated to disclose the initial adaptive algorithms to the competent competition authorities (periodically). Competition authorities could further be empowered to audit the functioning and the effects of the applied adaptive algorithms without prior notification.[119] One could also consider obligating

---

[112] Vestager (2017) with regard to *pricing algorithms*. Cf. also Göhsl (2018), pp. 123 et seq.

[113] See Ezrachi and Stucke (2015), pp. 23, 30, 36 as well as Gal and Elkin-Koren (2017), p. 351.

[114] OECD (2017), p. 49. See also Göhsl (2018), p. 124.

[115] See only Ezrachi and Stucke (2016), pp. 203 et seq. as well as Harrington (2017), pp. 47 et seq.

[116] Ezrachi and Stucke (2017), pp. 34 et seq. The (assumed or actual) technical complexity must, however, not lead to the dismissal of any of the legislator's actions as pointless. In favor of this notion ibid. p. 26: 'The increased use of neural networks will indeed complicate enforcement efforts. But even then, one should not accept this black-box argument as a justification for apathy; the [anti-trust] agencies must critically review how these algorithms are affecting market dynamics.' See also Mehra (2015), p. 1327 fn. 26 as well as Göhsl (2018), p. 124; each one with further references.

[117] Ezrachi and Stucke (2017), pp. 34 et seq.; Ezrachi and Stucke (2016), pp. 230 et seq.; OECD (2017), p. 42.

[118] See Ezrachi and Stucke (2017), p. 35; Vestager (2017).

[119] Ezrachi and Stucke (2017), pp. 34 et seq.; regarding the proposal of an *Algorithmic Collusion Incubator* and other potential measures, including merger control, see ibid p. 42 et seq. See also Göhsl (2018), p. 124 with regard to *pricing algorithms*.

undertakings to store price data.[120] To this end—and to conduct sector inquiries—, competition authorities could themselves make use of AI technologies which calculate the likelihood of breaches of competition law provisions.[121] Furthermore, one should at least consider price regulation and other market controlling measures (e.g. measures preventing *tacit collusion*).[122]

Responsibility for Anti-Competitive Behavior

The use of adaptive algorithms and the inherent lack of transparency regarding the underlying decision-making parameters associated therewith *(black box)* give rise to fundamental questions with regard to creating a legal environment for AI that either fosters or hinders innovation.

In this context, the (future) assignment of responsibilities for AI is of crucial importance. Whilst in the following this paper only discusses competition law aspects of this topic, it should be recognized that this issue goes far beyond the scope of competition law. For competition law, a crucial question is whether the 'behavior' of AI systems should—*de lege lata* through a modified interpretation of the law or *de lege ferenda*—be attributed to the undertakings applying them. If so, the question arises to what extent undertakings can or should be held liable for the AI systems.[123] The concept of liability in this context is based on the assumption that AI systems act 'independently'. For lack of transparency and potential influence on the 'acts' of the system, one could propose that the 'chain of attribution' is interrupted. As a consequence, there would be no liable party for competition law infringements (for the issue of legal personality of AI systems see below). With regard to a claim for damages *(private enforcement)*, such a limited attribution would lead to an intolerable gap in the legal protection for claimants and must thus be rejected. Further, it seems appropriate to assume an attribution at least for the purposes of Art. 7 Reg. EU 1/2003 (court order to bar further infringement).[124]

---

[120]See Käseberg and von Kalben (2018), p. 6.
[121]See OECD (2017), pp. 13 et seq., 40 et seq. as well as the evolving 'Bid Rigging Indicator Analysis System (BRIAS)' (OECD (2016)). Concerning the proof of cartel infringement and the institutional challenges that national competition authorities face in this context see Käseberg and von Kalben (2018), pp. 6 et seq.
[122]For a comparison of advantages and disadvantages of such measures see Ezrachi and Stucke (2016), pp. 229 et seq.; OECD (2017), pp. 50 et seq. See also Gal and Elkin-Koren (2017), p. 347 and Käseberg and von Kalben (2018), pp. 5 et seq., which favor an expansion of the scope of Art. 101 (1) TFEU. See also Göhsl (2018), p. 122.
[123]See only OECD (2017), pp. 32, 39 et seq.
[124]A respective order does not require culpa, see in this context Käseberg and von Kalben (2018), p. 6.

'Duty to Maintain Safeguards' or *'Störerhaftung'* in Competition Law?

39   In the context of competition law sanctions (especially fines under Art. 23 (2) Reg. EU 1/2003), on the other hand, limiting undertakings' liability is debatable.[125] To this end, it should be considered to make use of the categorization of AI systems as a 'potential hazard' as discussed above.[126] Other areas of law can serve as examples for finding an adequate liability framework. Especially, the legal construct of (co-) liability for a wrongful conduct of a third party might be of assistance in this context. In the following, the focus shall therefore lie on the liability for indirect damages as used in tort law and the liability of intermediaries within unfair competition law and intellectual property law.

40   Transferring the principles of tort law regarding indirect damages to the present topic, this would mean that a liability for competition law sanctions requires not only that the risk materializes (*i.e.* that competition law is violated), but also that certain duties to maintain safety are infringed. To put it in the words of the German Federal Court of Justice, anyone 'who creates a hazardous situation of any form is, in principle, obligated to take the necessary and reasonable precautions to prevent a potential damage to others [...]. The legally required measures to maintain safeguards comprise those measures which a prudent, reasonable, and reasonably cautious person would consider necessary and sufficient to save others from damages.'[127] The court uses this principle within unfair competition law as well: 'A person who, through his actions in connection with business activities, causes the serious risk that third parties violate the unfair competition law-protected interests of market players is obligated to limit this risk as far as possible and reasonable as a duty of care. Whoever acts in breach of these unfair competition law duties commits an unfair business practice.'[128]

41   A different approach to a (competition law) concept of liability for the use of AI could be provided by the legal concept of *'Störerhaftung'*. Since the turn of the millennium, this concept has evolved to a mainstay for action against intermediaries (e.g. online platforms like *youtube.com*) within— inter alia—intellectual property law.[129] Under this concept, any person who—without being the main infringer—

---

[125]Käseberg and von Kalben (2018), p. 7 reckon that the employees should—at least—have to be aware of the possibility or the likelihood of the algorithm's illegal competitive behavior. See also Salaschek and Serafimova (2018), pp. 15 et seq.

[126]Assuming that the (original) algorithms were not purposely (or negligently) programmed to favor an anti-competitive behavior. In this regard, see also the Eturas-case decided by the ECJ (cf. fn. 7) as well as Drexl (2017), p. 416 fn. 4 and Heinemann and Gebicka (2016), pp. 440 et seq.

[127]BGH VI ZR 223/09 'Nachrüstungspflichten' (2 March 2010) para 5 (translated); for a more detailed examination of the topic see Wagner (2017), Sec. 823 para. 380 et seq.

[128]BGH I ZR 18/04 'Jugendgefährdende Medien bei eBay' (12 July 2007) (translated). See also BGH I ZR 114/06 'Halzband' (11 March 2009); Sosnitza (2016), Sec. 3 para. 62 et seq.; for a more detailed examination of the liability of intermediaries see Ohly (2017).

[129]Concerning the *'Störerhaftung'* and the liability of intermediaries see Leistner (2010) and Ohly (2015).

contributes to the creation or maintenance of an illegal damage and violates feasible and reasonable supervisory duties, is liable.[130]

The driving force of this development was the digitization and the (easy) possibility to infringe rights associated therewith. The lack of control of the intermediary regarding actions of third parties on or through the platform (in connection with economically rational interests) was balanced out by the imposition of duties regarding actions of third parties. In this context, the specific duties are often triggered when the intermediary is informed about an existing breach of the law on or through the platform.

In principle, these considerations can be transferred to competition law, supporting the assumption that 'duties to maintain safeguards' or a *'Störerhaftung'* regarding AI systems should be implemented in competition law. The AI systems would correspond to the main infringer. A liability for competition law sanctions would thus first presuppose that the respective undertaking either (in the sense of duties to maintain safeguards) creates the danger of competition law breaches or (in the sense of *'Störerhaftung'*) contributes to the creation or maintenance of an infringement. It could be reasonably assumed that both these cases are fulfilled in case the undertaking makes use of AI for competitive reasons. Moreover, the undertaking would have to have violated duties of care with regard to the use of AI. For instance, the undertaking could be found liable if it knew or should have known about possible infringements of competition law committed by the adaptive algorithm and tolerated them. The attribution to or liability of a undertaking (for sanctions) would thus depend on the time it receives knowledge about the competition law breach 'by' the algorithm.[131] Subsequent to diagnosing an infringement, a consistent transfer of the principles of *'Störerhaftung'*[132] and 'duties to maintain safeguards'[133] would mean that undertakings would actively have to prevent infringements (as far as technically possible) by intervening in the adaptive algorithm in order to avert liability.[134]

---

[130]See only BGH I ZR 304/01 'Internetversteigerung' (11 March 2004); BGH I ZR 139/08 'Kinderhochstühle im Internet' (2 July 2010) para 45 et seq.

[131]For a similar approach (relating to other undertakings) see ECJ 'SIA 'VM Remonts'' (cf. fn. 106, cf. Sect. Legal Personality of AI Systems for a more detailed examination of this decision) and ECJ Rs C-49/92 P 'Anic Partecipazioni' (08 July 1999) para 83 et seq.

[132]See BGH I ZR 174/14 'Goldesel' (26 November 2015) with regard to the *'Störerhaftung'* of an access provider.

[133]See also BGH 'Jugendgefährdende Medien bei eBay' (cf. fn. 128).

[134]Such a monitoring obligation is similar to the one which (*de facto*) results from the ECJ decision in the Eturas-case (cf. fn. 7) relating to communications which take place (or are received) on highly frequented platforms. See only Käseberg and von Kalben (2018), p. 4. Regarding the prevention of violations of personality rights see BGH 'Autocomplete' (cf. fn. 106).

Legal Personality of AI Systems

44 Furthermore, the fundamental discussion on whether autonomous systems should have a legal personality of some kind should be taken into consideration.[135] Such a status is linked to various questions regarding constitutional law, civil law, and criminal law, which cannot be covered here.[136] Assuming that autonomous systems were given a legal personality, however, competition law would be affected as well. For instance, the trading 'agents' used by undertakings would, in that case, have a legal personality.

45 In order to adequately cover this issue from a competition law perspective, one would have to distinguish the functions of the respective agents. If the agent functionally corresponds to an employee of the undertaking, the undertaking applying it (hereinafter: 'main undertaking') is liable for all competition law infringements committed by the agent according to the principles explained above.[137] The previously discussed issue that a liable party might be missing does not arise here. In this case, the agent, being equivalent to an employee, does not constitute an independent undertaking in the sense of competition law, as this would require the performance of an (independent) economic activity by the agent.[138]

46 However, if the agent acts independently on the market (and thus does not correspond to an employee), the question arises whether the main undertaking and the agent are to be considered *one* undertaking (in the sense of competition law) according to the principles of an economic unit. If so, the main undertaking would be liable (as well).[139] According to competition law principles, the main undertaking and the agent are to be considered as one undertaking if the agent does not constitute an independently acting entity and is not able to conduct business respectively.[140] This would, for instance, come into question if the agent were a dependent unit (in the sense of Sec. 17, 291 et. seq. of the German Stock Corporation Act (AktG)).[141] Despite of a potential 100%-shareholding, one could, however, doubt that such agents are 'dependent', as they are based on adaptive and non-transparent mechanism and do thus not follow traditional instructions or interferences as traditional dependent undertakings do.

---

[135] For the discussions on the legal subjectivity of robots see only Beck (2009); Beck (2013), pp. 254 et seq.; Kersten (2015); Schirmer (2016), pp. 663 et seq. For the perspective of an *ePerson* see also European Parliament (2017), Rec. AC, General Principles No. 1 ff., 59 lit. f. ('electronic person'). For a general examination of robots and law see Eidenmüller (2017).

[136] For a general analysis of AI and legal personality in this volume see Schirmer, para 1 et seq.

[137] Cf. Sect. 3.6.

[138] Grave and Nyberg (2016), Art. 101 TFEU para. 131 et seq. with further references.

[139] See ECJ C-170/83 'Hydrotherm Gerätebau' (12 July 1984) and ECJ C-97/08 P 'Akzo Nobel' (10 September 2009).

[140] See only ECJ 'Akzo Nobel' (cf. fn. 139).

[141] For the competition law principles on economic units see Grave and Nyberg (2016), Art. 101 TFEU para. 153 et seq.; Kling and Thomas (2016), Sec. 19 para 209 et seq.

However, an attribution to the main undertaking (in the sense of an economic unit) based on the case law of the ECJ emerging from the *SIA 'VM Remonts'* case could be considered. In its decision, the court affirmed the possibility to attribute the actions of a paid service provider to the principal in case the principal 'was aware of the anti-competitive objectives pursued by its competitors and the service provider and intended to contribute to them by its own conduct' or if the undertaking 'could reasonably have foreseen that the service provider retained by it would share its commercial information with its competitors and if it was prepared to accept the risk which that entailed (...)'.[142] That means that it suffices that the undertaking delegates certain tasks to the service provider. No further contribution is required for the actions to be attributed to the undertaking.[143]

If, in the light of the foregoing, agents were (nevertheless) to be classified as (independent) undertakings from a competition law perspective, the respective agents would also have to be considered independently as liable parties.[144] As a result, the issue of a lack of a liable party would, again, not arise. Instead, only general questions regarding legal personality of autonomous systems would arise, especially with regard to required assets and compulsory insurance of autonomous systems.[145]

Acknowledgements This contribution is a translation and slightly shortened version of my Article 'Künstliche Intelligenz und Wettbewerbsrecht' published (in German) in the Zeitschrift für Wettbewerbsrecht / Journal of Competition Law (2018), pp. 161–184. Parts of an earlier version of this article can also be found in GRUR Newsletter, no. 2 (2017), pp. 26–29. The manuscript was finished in April 2018. Laura Korn and Selma Nabulsi (Student Research Assistants at the Institute for Media and Information Law, Dept. I: Private Law, University of Freiburg) produced the translation and do deserve my greatest thanks for their tremendous assistance. I do also have to thank Isabel Kienzle (Student Research Assistant at the same institute) who—next to Selma Nabulsi—profoundly managed the formatting of this paper.

References

Armbruster A (2017) Elon Musk und Co. warnen vor Killer-Robotern. www.faz.net/aktuell/wirtschaft/kuenstliche-intelligenz-elon-musk-warnt-vor-killer-robotern-15161436.html. Accessed 28 Sept 2018
Autorité de la concurrence, Bundeskartellamt (2016) Competition law and data. www.bundeskartellamt.de/SharedDocs/Publikation/DE/Berichte/Big%20Data%20Papier.pdf?__blob=publicationFile&v=2. Accessed 28 Sept 2018
Bechtold R, Bosch W (2015) GWB, 8th edn. C.H. Beck, München
Beck S (2009) Grundlegende Fragen zum rechtlichen Umgang mit der Robotik. Juristische Rundschau:225–230

---

[142]ECJ 'SIA 'VM Remonts''(cf. fn. 97).
[143]Brömmelmeyer (2017), p. 179.
[144]For a competitive approach see Mehra (2015), pp. 1366 et seq.
[145]See the references in fn. 135 as well as see Schirmer, para 1 et seq.

Beck S (2013) Über Sinn und Unsinn von Statusfragen – zu Vor- und Nachteilen der Einführung einer elektronischen Person. In: Hilgendorf E, Günther J (eds) Robotik und Gesetzgebung. Nomos, Baden-Baden, pp 239–262

Berberich M, Golla S (2016) Zur Konstruktion eines 'Dateneigentums' – Herleitung, Schutzrichtung, Abgrenzung. Priv Germany 5:165–176

Birnstiel A, Eckel P (2016) Das Paper 'Competition Law and Data' des Bundeskartellamts und der Autorité de la concurrence – eine zusammenfassende Analyse. Wettbewerb in Recht und Praxis:1189–1195

Böhm F (2016) Herausforderungen von Cloud Computing-Verträgen: Vertragstypologische Einordnung, Haftung und Eigentum an Daten. Zeitschrift für Europäisches Privatrecht:358–387

Brockman J (ed) (2017) Was sollen wir von Künstlicher Intelligenz halten? 2nd edn. Fischer Taschenbuch, Frankfurt

Brömmelmeyer C (2017) Haftung und Zurechnung im Europäischen Kartellrecht – Für wen ist ein Unternehmen verantwortlich? Wirtschaft und Wettbewerb:174–182

Bundeskartellamt (2016) Press Release. www.bundeskartellamt.de/SharedDocs/Meldung/DE/Pressemitteilungen/2016/02_03_2016_Facebook.html. Accessed 28 Sept 2018

Bundeskartellamt (2017a) Big Data und Wettbewerb. www.bundeskartellamt.de/SharedDocs/Publikation/DE/Schriftenreihe_Digitales/Schriftenreihe_Digitales_1.pdf?__blob=publicationFile&v=3. Accessed 28 Sept 2018

Bundeskartellamt (2017b) Press Release. www.bundeskartellamt.de/SharedDocs/Meldung/DE/Pressemitteilungen/2017/19_12_2017_Facebook.html. Accessed 28 Sept 2018

Bundeskartellamt (2017c) Press Release. www.bundeskartellamt.de/SharedDocs/Meldung/DE/Pressemitteilungen/2017/13_12_2017_SU_SmartTV.html?nn=3591286. Accessed 28 Sept 2018

Department of Justice (2015) Press Release No 15-421. www.justice.gov/opa/pr/former-e-commerce-executive-charged-price-fixing-antitrust-divisions-first-online-marketplace. Accessed 28 Sept 2018

Dorner M (2014) Big Data und 'Dateneigentum', Grundfragen des modernen Daten- und Informationshandels. Computer & Recht:617–628

Drexl J (2017) Neue Regeln für die Europäische Datenwirtschaft? Neue Zeitschrift für Kartellrecht:339–344

Drexl J et al (2016) Ausschließlichkeits- und Zugangsrechte an Daten: Positionspapier des Max-Planck-Instituts für Innovation und Wettbewerb vom 16.8.2016 zur aktuellen europäischen Debatte. Gewerblicher Rechtsschutz und Urheberrecht International:914–918

Ebers M (2016) Dynamic Algorithmic Pricing: Abgestimmte Verhaltensweise oder rechtmäßiges Parallelverhalten? Neue Zeitschrift für Kartellrecht:554–555

Ehlen T, Brandt E (2016) Die Schutzfähigkeit von Daten – Herausforderungen und Chancen für Big Data Anwender. Computer & Recht:570–575

Eidenmüller H (2017) The rise of robots and the law of humans. Zeitschrift für Europäisches Privatrecht 25:765–777

Ensthaler J (2016) Industrie 4.0 und die Berechtigung an Daten. Neue Juristische Wochenschrift:3473–3478

European Commission (2017a) Antitrust: Commission fines Google €2.42 billion for abusing dominance as search engine by giving illegal advantage to own comparison shopping service – Factsheet

European Commission (2017b) Commission Staff Working Document accompanying the Commission Final report on the E-commerce Sector Inquiry:1–298

European Commission (2017c) Communication 'Building a European Data Economy'

European Commission (2017d) Proposal for a regulation of the European Parliament and of the Council on a framework for the free flow of non-personal data in the European Union

European Parliament (2017) Resolution of 16. February 2017 with recommendations to the Commission on Civil Law Rules on Robotics (2015/2103(INL))

Ezrachi A, Stucke M (2015) Artificial intelligence & collusion: when computers inhibit competition. University of Tennessee Legal Studies Research Paper 267:1–36
Ezrachi A, Stucke M (2016) Virtual competition. Harvard University Press, Cambridge
Ezrachi A, Stucke M (2017) Two artificial neural networks meet in an online hub and change the future (of Competition, market dynamics and society). University of Tennessee Legal Studies Research Paper 323:1–54
Federal Foreign Office (2017) www.auswaertiges-amt.de/blueprint/servlet/blob/204830/5f26c2e0826db0d000072441fdeaa8ba/abruestung-laws-data.pdf. Accessed 28 Sept 2018
Fezer K (2017a) Dateneigentum – Theorie des immaterialgüterrechtlichen Eigentums an verhaltensgenerierten Personendaten der Nutzer als Datenproduzenten. MultiMedia und Recht:3–5
Fezer K (2017b) Dateneigentum der Bürger – Ein originäres Immaterialgüterrecht sui generis an verhaltensgenerierten Informationsdaten der Bürger. Zeitschrift für Datenschutz:99–105
Franck J (2016) Eine Frage des Zusammenhangs: Marktbeherrschungsmissbrauch durch rechtswidrige Konditionen. Zeitschrift für Wettbewerbsrecht:137–164
Füller J (2016) Art. 101 AEUV. In: Busche J, Röhling A (eds) Kölner Kommentar zum Kartellrecht. Carl Heymanns, Köln
Gal M, Elkin-Koren S (2017) Algorithmic consumers. Harv J Law Technol 30:309–353
Gless S, Seelmann K (eds) (2016) Intelligente Agenten und das Recht. Nomos, Baden-Baden
Göhsl J (2018) Preissetzung durch Algorithmen und Art. 101 AEUV. Wirtschaft und Wettbewerb:121–125
Grave C (2017) Marktbeherrschung bei mehrseitigen Märkten und Netzwerken. In: Kersting C, Podszun R (eds) Die 9. GWB-Novelle. C.H. Beck, München, pp 17–44
Grave C, Nyberg J (2016) Art. 101 TFEU. In: Loewenheim U, Meessen K, Riesenkampff A, Kersting C, Meyer-Lindemann H (eds) Kartellrecht, 3rd edn. C.H. Beck, München
Grave C, Nyberg J (2017) Die Rolle von Big Data bei der Anwendung des Kartellrechts. Wirtschaft und Wettbewerb:363–368
Grützmacher M (2016) Dateneigentum – ein Flickenteppich. Computer & Recht:485–495
Harrington J (2017) Developing competition law for collusion by autonomous price-setting agents. papers.ssrn.com/sol3/papers.cfm?abstract_id=3037818. Accessed 28 Sept 2018
Härting N (2016) 'Dateneigentum' – Schutz durch Immaterialgüterrecht? Computer & Recht:646–649
Hawking S (2016) This is the most dangerous time for our planet. www.theguardian.com/commentisfree/2016/dec/01/stephen-hawking-dangerous-time-planet-inequality. Accessed 28 Sept 2018
Heinemann A, Gebicka A (2016) Can computers form cartels? About the need for European Institutions to revise the concentration doctrinein the information age. J Eur Compet Law Pract 7:431–441
Hennemann M (2017a) Datenportabilität. Priv Germany:5–8
Hennemann M (2017b) Künstliche Intelligenz – Algorithmen im Wettbewerb. Gewerblicher Rechtsschutz und Urheberrecht Newsletter:26–29
Hennemann M (2017c) Personalisierte Medienangebote im Datenschutz- und Vertragsrecht. Zeitschrift für Urheber- und Medienrecht:544–552
Heymann T (2015) Der Schutz von Daten bei der Cloud Verarbeitung. Computer & Recht:807–811
Heymann T (2016) Rechte an Daten. Computer & Recht:650–657
Hoffmann-Riem W (2017) Verhaltenssteuerung durch Algorithmen – Eine Herausforderung für das Recht. Archiv des öffentlichen Rechts 142:1–42
Holland M (2017) Putin: Wer bei KI in Führung geht, wird die Welt beherrschen. www.heise.de/newsticker/meldung/Putin-Wer-bei-KI-in-Fuehrung-geht-wird-die-Welt-beherrschen-3821332.html. Accessed 28 Sept 2018
Holzweber S (2016) Daten als Machtfaktor in der Fusionskontrolle. Neue Zeitschrift für Kartellrecht:104–112

Huttenlauch A, Lübbig T (2016) Art. 102 AEUV. In: Loewenheim U, Meessen K, Riesenkampff A, Kersting C, Meyer-Lindemann H (eds) Kartellrecht, 3rd edn. C.H. Beck, München

Kaplan J (2016) Artificial intelligence – what everyone needs to know. Oxford University Press, Oxford

Käseberg T, von Kalben J (2018) Herausforderungen der Künstlichen Intelligenz für die Wettbewerbspolitik. Wirtschaft und Wettbewerb:2–8

Kersten J (2015) Menschen und Maschinen. Rechtliche Konturen instrumenteller, symbiotischer und autonomer Konstellationen. JuristenZeitung:1–8

Kling M, Thomas S (2016) Kartellrecht, 2nd edn. Vahlen, München

Körber T (2016) 'Ist Wissen Marktmacht?' Überlegungen zum Verhältnis von Datenschutz, 'Datenmacht' und Kartellrecht. Neue Zeitschrift für Kartellrecht:303–310. 348–356

Künstner F, Franz B (2017) Preisalgorithmen und Dynamic Pricing: Eine neue Kategorie kartellrechtswidriger Abstimmungen? Kommunikation & Recht:688–693

Leistner M (2010) Störerhaftung und mittelbare Schutzrechtsverletzung. Gewerblicher Rechtsschutz und Urheberrecht Beilage:1–32

Leroux C (2012) A green paper on legal issues in robotics. www.researchgate.net/publication/310167745_A_green_paper_on_legal_issues_in_robotics. Accessed 28 Sept 2018

Lindsay A, McCarthy E (2017) Do we need to prevent pricing algorithms cooking up markets? Eur Compet Law Rev 38:533–537

Loewenheim U (2016) § 19 GWB. In: Loewenheim U, Meessen K, Riesenkampff A, Kersting C, Meyer-Lindemann H (eds) Kartellrecht, 3rd edn. C.H. Beck, München

Malgieri G (2016) Property and (Intellectual) ownership of consumers' information: a new taxonomy for personal data. Priv Germany:133–140

Martini M (2017) Algorithmen als Herausforderung für die Rechtsordnung. JuristenZeitung:1017–1025

Mehra S (2015) Antitrust and the robo-seller: competition in the time of algorithms. Minn Law Rev 100:1323–1375

Mehra S (2016) US v. Topkins: can price fixing be based on algorithms? J Eur Compet Law Pract 7:470–476

Möslein F (2018) Digitalisierung im Gesellschaftsrecht: Unternehmensleitung durch Algorithmen und künstliche Intelligenz? Zeitschrift für Wirtschaftsrecht:204–212

Novet J (2017) Facebook AI researcher slams 'irresponsible' reports about smart bot experiment. www.cnbc.com/2017/08/01/facebook-ai-experiment-did-not-end-because-bots-invented-own-language.html. Accessed 28 Sept 2018

Nuys M (2016) 'Big Data' – Die Bedeutung von Daten im Kartellrecht. Wirtschaft und Wettbewerb:512–520

OECD (2016) Country case: Korea's Bid Rigging Indicator Analysis System (BRIAS). www.oecd.org/governance/procurement/toolbox/search/korea-bid-rigging-indicator-analysis-system-brias.pdf. Accessed 28 Sept 2018

OECD (2017) Algorithms and collusion – competition policy in the digital age. www.oecd.org/daf/competition/Algorithms-and-colllusion-competition-policy-in-the-digital-age.pdf. Accessed 28 Sept 2018

Ohly A (2015) Die Verantwortlichkeit von Intermediären. Zeitschrift für Urheber- und Medienrecht:308–318

Ohly A (2017) Die Haftung von Internet-Dienstleistern für die Verletzung lauterkeitsrechtlicher Verkehrspflichten. Gewerblicher Rechtsschutz und Urheberrecht:441–451

Paal B (2011) Netz- und Suchmaschinenneutralität im Wettbewerbsrecht. Zeitschrift für Medien- und Kommunikationsrecht:521–532

Paal B (2012) Suchmaschinen, Marktmacht und Meinungsbildung. Nomos, Baden-Baden

Paal B (2015) Internet-Suchmaschinen im Kartellrecht. Gewerblicher Rechtsschutz und Urheberrecht International:997–1005

Paal B, Hennemann M (2016) Gefahr für die Vielfalt? www.faz.net/aktuell/politik/staat-und-recht/gastbeitrag-soziale-netzwerke-14250849.html. Accessed 28 Sept 2018

Paal B, Hennemann M (2017a) Meinungsbildung im digitalen Zeitalter – Regulierungsinstrumente für einen gefährdungsadäquaten Rechtsrahmen. JuristenZeitung:641–652

Paal B, Hennemann M (2017b) Meinungsvielfalt im Internet. Zeitschrift für Rechtspolitik:76–79

Paal B, Hennemann M (2017c) Big Data im Recht – Wettbewerbs- und daten(schutz)rechtliche Herausforderungen. Neue Juristische Wochenschrift:1697–1701

Paal B, Hennemann M (2018) Big Data as an Asset – Daten und Kartellrecht. www.abida.de/sites/default/files/Gutachten_ABIDA_Big_Data_as_an_Asset.pdf. Accessed 28 Sept 2018

Pasquale F (2015) The Black Box Society: the secret algorithms that control money and information. Harvard University Press, Cambridge

Petit N (2017) Antitrust and artificial intelligence: a research agenda. J Eur Compet Law Pract 8:361–362

Podszun R (2014) Kartellrecht in der Internet-Wirtschaft: Zeit für den more technological approach. Wirtschaft und Wettbewerb:249

Podszun R (2015) The more technological approach – competition law in the digital economy. In: Surblytė G (ed) Competition on the Internet. Springer, Heidelberg, pp 101–108

Podszun R, de Toma M (2016) Die Durchsetzung des Datenschutzes durch Verbraucherrecht, Lauterkeitsrecht und Kartellrecht. Neue Juristische Wochenschrift:2987–2994

Roman V (2018) Digital markets and pricing algorithms – a dynamic approach towards horizontal competition. Eur Compet Law Rev 39

Roth W, Ackermann T (2017) Art. 81 Abs. 1 EG Grundfragen. In: Jaeger W, Kokott J, Pohlmann P, Schroeder D, Kulka M (eds) Frankfurter Kommentar zum Kartellrecht, 9/2017. Dr. Otto Schmidt, Köln

Salaschek U, Serafimova M (2018) Preissetzungsalgorithmen im Lichte von Art. 101 AEUV. Wirtschaft und Wettbewerb:8–17

Salcedo B (2015) Pricing algorithms and tacit collusion. www.brunosalcedo.com/docs/collusion.pdf. Accessed 28 Sept 2018

Schirmer J (2016) Rechtsfähige Roboter? JuristenZeitung:660–666

Schrepel T (2017) Here's why algorithms are NOT (really) a thing. leconcurrentialiste.com/2017/05/15/algorithms-based-practices-antitrust/. Accessed 28 Sept 2018

Schwartmann R, Hentsch C (2016) Parallelen aus dem Urheberrecht für ein neues Datenverwertungsrecht. Priv Germany:117–126

Sosnitza O (2016) Sec. 3. In: Ohly A, Sosnitza O (eds) Gesetz gegen den unlauteren Wettbewerb, 7th edn. C.H. Beck, München

Specht L (2016) Ausschließlichkeitsrechte an Daten – Notwendigkeit, Schutzumfang, Alternativen. Computer & Recht:288–296

Specht L, Rohmer R (2016) Zur Rolle des informationellen Selbstbestimmungsrechts bei der Ausgestaltung eines möglichen Ausschließlichkeitsrechts an Daten. Priv Germany:127–132

Spiegel Online (2017) Kartellamtschef fertigt Lufthansa ab. www.spiegel.de/wirtschaft/unternehmen/lufthansa-kartellamt-kritisiert-begruendung-fuer-teure-tickets-a-1185247.html. Accessed 28 Sept 2018

Surblytė G (2017) Data-driven economy and artificial intelligence: emerging competition law issues? Wirtschaft und Wettbewerb 67:120–127

Tamke M (2017) Big data and competition law. Zeitschrift für Wettbewerbsrecht:358–385

Telle S (2017) Big Data und Kartellrecht. Zeitschrift zum Innovations- und Technikrecht:3–10

Thomas S (2017) Wettbewerb in der digital economy: Verbraucherschutz durch AGB-Kontrolle im Kartellrecht? Neue Zeitschrift für Kartellrecht:92–98

Vestager M (2017) Algorithms and competition. Rede auf der 18. Kartellrechtstagung des BKartA. ec.europa.eu/commission/commissioners/2014-2019/vestager/announcements/bundeskartellamt-18th-conference-competition-berlin-16-march-2017_en. Accessed 28 Sept 2018

Wagner G (2017) § 823 BGB. In: Habersack M (ed) Münchner Kommentar zum Bürgerlichen Gesetzbuch, 7th edn. C.H. Beck, München

Wiemer F (2018) Facebook: Kartellrechtlicher Datenschutz – das Ende der Gratiskultur im Internet? Wirtschaft und Wettbewerb 68:53–54

Ylinen J (2018) Digital Pricing und Kartellrecht. Neue Zeitschrift für Kartellrecht:19–22

Zech H (2015) 'Industrie 4.0' – Rechtsrahmen für eine Datenwirtschaft im digitalen Binnenmarkt. Gewerblicher Rechtsschutz und Urheberrecht 117:1151–1160

CPSIA information can be obtained
at www.ICGtesting.com
Printed in the USA
LVHW051927141220
674148LV00004B/197